W9-CBI-106

COMPUTERS

TOOLS
FOR AN
INFORMATION
AGE

SECOND EDITION

H. L. CAPRON

The Benjamin/Cummings Publishing Company, Inc.

Redwood City, California • Fort Collins, Colorado
Menlo Park, California • Reading, Massachusetts • New York
Don Mills, Ontario • Wokingham, U.K. • Amsterdam • Bonn
Sydney • Singapore • Tokyo • Madrid • San Juan

General Manager   **Sally D. Elliott**
Sponsoring Editor   **Michelle Miceli-Baxter**
Senior Developmental Editor   **Patricia S. Burner**
Editorial Assistant   **Devra Lerman**
Production Supervisor   **Bonnie B. Grover**
Production Assistant   **Daniel Heller**
Text and Cover Designer   **Christy Butterfield**
Cover Illustrator   **Michael Swaine**
Illustrator   **George Samuelson**
Art Coordinator   **Sharon Montooth**
Photo Editor   **Wendy Earl**
Photo Researcher   **Sarah Bendersky**
Copy Editor   **Toni Murray**
Composition and Film   **York Graphic Services**
Printing and Binding   **R. R. Donnelley & Sons Company**

Library of Congress Cataloging-in-Publication Data

Capron, H. L.
    Computers : tools for an information age / H.L. Capron. — 2nd ed.
       p.   cm.
    ISBN 0-8053-0040-6
    1. Computers. I. Title.
    QA76.C358   1990
    004—dc20   89-27455
                                                      CIP

ISBN 0-8053-0046-5

ABCDEFGHIJ-DO-8932109

The Benjamin/Cummings Publishing Company, Inc.
390 Bridge Parkway
Redwood City, California 94065

7 THE INSTRUCTOR'S EDITION OF
COMPUTERS:
TOOLS FOR AN INFORMATION AGE, SECOND EDITION, BY H. L. CAPRON

With the second edition of *Computers: Tools for an Information Age,* Benjamin/Cummings is offering this unique supplement to your course management package. This is the **Instructor's Edition**, an annotated version of the student textbook that puts complete course and lecture organization at your fingertips.

This **Instructor's Edition** references the other supplements, and provides lecture outlines, hints, and activities that will allow you to vary and expand your lectures on the spot. Throughout the margins you'll find eight different types of annotations in easily-read blue type:

- lecture outlines
- learning objectives
- lecture hints
- references to the testbank
- references to the transparency acetates
- discussion questions
- lecture activities
- student projects.

For further information about the **Instructor's Edition** or any other supplements to the second edition of *Computers: Tools for an Information Age,* contact your local Benjamin/Cummings representative or call, toll-free, 800/950-BOOK. We'll look forward to hearing from you.

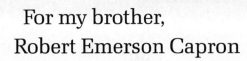

For my brother,
Robert Emerson Capron

The Capron Collection
A Complete Supplements Package

For further information, contact your Benjamin/Cummings sales representative or call toll-free (800) 950-BOOK.

Supplements to the Text

- **Instructor's Edition with Annotations** by J. Boettler (South Carolina State College) with H. L. Capron. Available for the instructor, this special edition contains annotations for lecture preparation and includes supplementary material not found in the Instructor's Guide. The annotations include lecture outlines, learning objectives, lecture hints, discussion questions, lecture activities, test bank references, transparency references, and student projects.

- **Instructor's Guide and Transparency Masters** by H. L. Capron (250 pages). Each chapter contains learning objectives, a chapter overview, a detailed lecture outline, and a list of key words. The Instructor's Guide also includes 26 transparency masters and the answers to the exercises in Appendix B.

- **Student Study Guide** by H. L. Capron (250 pages). For each chapter, the Study Guide provides objectives, an overview and outline, key words with blank space for definitions, study hints, self-tests with answers and motivational examples of real-life computer usage.

- **Test Bank** by F. Wondolowski (East Carolina University) (250 pages). The test bank contains 2500 items, with four types of questions: multiple choice, true/false, matching, and fill-in-the-blank. Each question is referenced to the text by page number. The test bank is available both as hard copy and in a computerized format for the IBM PC (and compatibles), PS/2, and Macintosh computers.

- **Color Transparency Acetates.** These full-color transparency acetates include artwork and diagrams taken directly from the text plus complementary outside sources.

Software

- **Instructor's Files Diskette.** For instructors, a data diskette is available that includes detailed lecture outlines, the initial documents for the examples and exercises in Appendix B, and the answers to the exercises in Appendix B.

- **University Gradebook** by D. Herrick (University of Oregon). This class record-keeping software is available for IBM PC and compatible computers.

Lab Support

- **Hands-On: MS-DOS, WordPerfect 5.0, Lotus 1-2-3 (2.01 and 2.2), dBASE III PLUS, Second Edition** by L. Metzelaar (Vincennes University) and M. Fox (Butler University) (288 pages). This text uses concepts and hands-on experience to teach the beginning user these popular software packages. Educational versions of WordPerfect 4.2 and dBASE III PLUS are available with this text. A conversion chart is provided for WordPerfect 4.2 users.

- **Microcomputer Exercises** by M. A. Webster, University of Florida at Gainesville (166 pages). This exercise manual offers advanced exercises and mini-cases on WordPerfect 4.2 and 5.0, Lotus 1-2-3, and dBASE III PLUS.

Of Related Interest

The Student Edition of Lotus 1-2-3, Second Edition (509 pages); **The Student Edition of dBASE IV** (704 pages); **The Student Edition of Framework II** (372 pages).

Brief Contents

Part 1

A First Look at Computers   1

Part 2

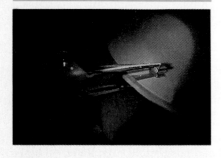

Hardware   51

Part 3

Understanding Software   187

Part 4

Using Microcomputers   321

Part 5

Computers in the Workplace   473

Detailed Contents

Preface xxvii

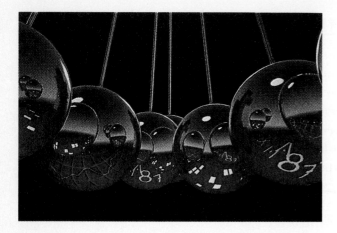

Part 1 A First Look at Computers 1

Gallery 2
Computers Around Us: The Many Uses of Computers
follows page 224

Part 3
Understanding Software 187

CHAPTER 7
Beginning Programming: A Structured Approach 189

Part 4
Using
Microcomputers 321

Buyer's Guide
How to Buy Your Own Personal Computer
follows page 320

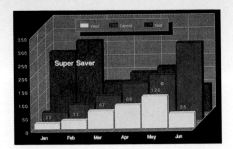

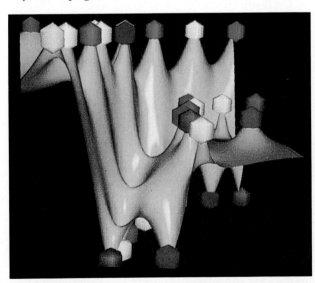

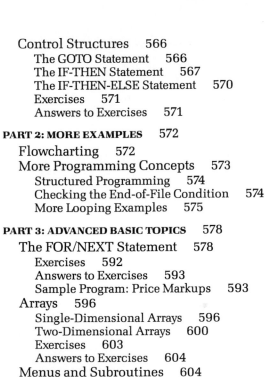

The Galleries and Buyer's Guide

The four full-color Galleries and the Buyer's Guide highlight topics in a photo-essay style, providing a look at some exciting uses of computers. The photos are accompanied by explanations of how computers are being used.

GALLERY 1

Making Microchips   Marvels of Miniaturization (*follows page 64*)

This gallery takes a look at how silicon chips are made. We follow the process from design to manufacturing to testing to packaging to the final product, a microcomputer.

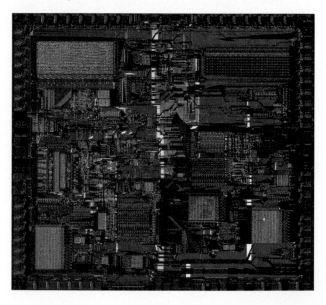

GALLERY 2
Computers Around Us   The Many Uses of Computers *(follows page 224)*

Gallery 2 examines some of the interesting uses of computers in our lives. We look at how computers are used in science, sports, entertainment, health and medicine, transportation, education, photography, and music.

BUYER'S GUIDE
How to Buy Your Own Personal Computer *(follows page 320)*

This special 16-page section presents issues and questions to consider before buying a personal computer and software. If you are thinking about buying a personal computer now or in the future, read this section carefully.

GALLERY 3
Computer Graphics   Color and Content *(follows page 416)*

Computer graphics offer variety, color, and drama. In this gallery we showcase computer graphics in the areas of geography, animation, architecture, design, realistic art, abstract art, fractal art, and fine art.

GALLERY 4
Computers in the Factory   Robots and Beyond *(follows page 512)*

The factory floor is now a hotbed of computer activity. In this gallery we explore the ways computers are being used to design, engineer, and manufacture products. The versatile robot is a featured player, and we end with a look at the ideal computer-integrated factory.

Preface

Just a few years have passed since the first edition of *Computers: Tools for an Information Age* was published. The world of computers, however, has continued to move forward, and we have moved with it. This new edition has been updated throughout, while retaining the appealing reading style. In addition, instructors will find in this text and its accompanying support package all the elements they need to teach the introductory computer course.

New in this Edition

- **WordPerfect 5.0, Lotus 1-2-3,** and **dBASE III PLUS,** the most popular software packages, are covered in our totally rewritten software applications chapters (Chapters 12–14). We use these packages to demonstrate the basic concepts of word processing, spreadsheets, business graphics, and database management systems.

- **Hands-on experience** with applications software has become an important component of many introductory courses. Appendix B provides (1) a list of keystrokes summarizing the examples in Chapters 12–14, (2) command reference guides, and (3) exercises. Appendix B can be used for introductory lab assignments in DOS, WordPerfect (versions 5.0 and 4.2), Lotus 1-2-3 (version 2.01), and dBASE III PLUS. A Files Diskette containing documents for the examples and exercises is available to instructors.

- **Desktop publishing** is covered in a new chapter. Chapter 15 examines the field from the vantage point of the beginning user, offering an overview of program features and basic design information.

- **"Computers on the Job"** (Chapter 16) is a new chapter that documents how computers change the way we work. Topics include the impact of personal computers in the workplace, the portable worker, and examples of how software helps people get the job done.

- **Issues and trends** are explored in the new Perspectives essay in each chapter. Controversies and new directions covered in these essays include information on electronic supervisors, computer use around the world, neural nets, and computer viruses.

- **The Macintosh computer** is introduced in several chapters through short discussions of the Macintosh operating environment, graphics, HyperCard, and PageMaker desktop publishing software.

7 Updated and Revised in this Edition

■ **Extensive microcomputer coverage.** Although we discuss all types of computers, we focus on microcomputers, reflecting their continuing prominence in business. We have incorporated a wide variety of new microcomputer examples throughout the text.

■ **Microcomputers in Action.** Each chapter includes a feature on microcomputers that demonstrates the range of tasks microcomputers fulfill. Most of these sections are new to this edition; they include topics such as the use of microcomputers in restaurants, on college campuses, and in hospital emergency rooms.

■ **Buyer's Guide.** Many students and their families are making important economic decisions about the purchase of a computer for the student's educational needs. This updated 16-page guide offers them the information they need to answer questions about hardware and software purchases.

■ **Mainframes in business settings.** Although microcomputers have become increasingly important in business, minicomputers and mainframes are still the core of the computer industry. In this second edition we continue to cover large computer systems, and we show how they are affected by microcomputers.

■ **Special topic galleries.** Four full-color photo essays vividly illustrate the world of computers, from walking the reader through the manufacture of silicon chips, to marveling at the many uses of computers, to displaying the sophistication of computer graphics, to showing how robots are used in factories.

■ **Margin notes.** To futher engage student attention, margin notes are carefully placed throughout the text. The margin notes extend the text material by providing additional information and interesting applications of computers.

■ **Extensive student learning aids.** The second edition features the following pedagogical support: a preview of each chapter, key terms boldfaced in the text, extensive summaries with boldfaced key terms, review questions, discussion questions, an extensive glossary, and an index.

■ **The BASIC Appendix** reflects Microsoft BASIC, stressing structured programming techniques. This revision is compatible with most popular versions of BASIC for microcomputers. The Appendix, which includes extensive examples and exercises, provides sufficient material for most introductory computer courses.

■ **The friendly writing style.** When students enjoy what they read, they remember it. The trademark of this textbook continues to be the friendly writing style that encourages the reluctant reader and increases the student's comprehension and confidence. For example, chapters involve the student right away with stories about computer users that will pique student interest and illustrate a key point from the chapter.

Organization of the Text

The text is divided into five parts. Part 1 offers an overview of computer systems and their uses in our society. Part 2 explores computer hardware. The communications chapter (Chapter 6) includes an expanded discussion of local area networks and the uses of communications technology such as electronic mail, voice mail, fax, and communications services.

Part 3 focuses on programming, operating systems, and systems analysis and design. The two chapters on beginning programming and structured design have been combined into a single chapter, and the chapter on programming languages has been condensed. Also, the operating systems chapter includes more information on MS-DOS in this edition.

Part 4 includes one chapter on microcomputers and four chapters on applications packages—word processing (WordPerfect 5.0), spreadsheets and business graphics (Lotus 1-2-3), database management systems (dBASE III PLUS), and desktop publishing. Part 5 looks at computers in the workplace, as well as security, privacy, and ethics.

Appendix A covers Microsoft BASIC programming. Appendix B offers a guide to using DOS, WordPerfect, Lotus 1-2-3, and dBASE III PLUS. Appendix C (formerly Chapter 3) describes the history of computing. These appendices provide flexibility to those who wish to teach these topics.

The Capron Collection: A Complete Supplements Package

- **Instructor's Edition with Annotations.** Written by J. Boettler of South Carolina State College with H. L. Capron, this special edition contains lecture outlines, learning objectives, lecture hints, discussion questions, lecture activities, test bank references, transparency references, and student projects.

- **Instructor's Guide and Transparency Masters.** Written by H. L. Capron, the Instructor's Guide provides learning objectives, a chapter overview, a detailed lecture outline, a list of key words, answers to the exercises in Appendix B, and 26 transparency masters.

- **Student Study Guide.** Also written by H. L. Capron, the Study Guide contains learning objectives, an overview of each chapter, a chapter outline, a list of key words with space for a student-supplied definition, study hints, self-tests (multiple choice, true/false, matching, and fill-in), answers to self-tests, additional margin notes, and "Close to home" sections that provide motivational examples of computer usage in everyday life.

- **Test Bank.** The test bank, containing 2500 items, has been prepared by F. Wondolowski of East Carolina University. There are four types of questions: multiple choice, true/false, matching, and fill-in-the-blank.

Each question is referenced to the text by page number. The test bank is available both as hard copy and in a computerized format for the IBM PC (and compatibles), PS/2, and Macintosh.

- **Transparencies.** 126 transparencies are available to adopters of this text (100 full-color acetates plus 26 transparency masters). These transparencies include artwork from this text and outside sources.

- **Instructor's Files Diskette.** For instructors, a data diskette is available that includes detailed lecture outlines, initial documents for the examples and exercises in Appendix B, and answers to the exercises in Appendix B. Available for the IBM PC (and compatibles), IBM PS/2, and Macintosh computers.

- **University Gradebook.** This complete class record-keeping software, developed by D. Herrick of the University of Oregon, is available for the IBM PC and compatible computers.

7 Lab Support

- **Hands-On: MS-DOS, WordPerfect 5.0, Lotus 1-2-3 (2.01 and 2.2), and dBASE III PLUS, Second Edition** by L. Metzelaar and M. Fox offers a lab supplement for courses requiring more extensive training on popular software packages. This text is available alone or with student edition software versions of WordPerfect 4.2 and dBASE III PLUS. (A conversion chart is provided for the benefit of WordPerfect 4.2 users.)

- **Microcomputer Exercises** by M. A. Webster extends the Appendix B exercises by providing additional practice in the form of more advanced exercises and mini-cases.

- If you want your students to get just a taste of the major applications packages, the basic skills developed by **Appendix B** may be appropriate for your course. To allow your students to spend more of their lab time on computer skills and less time on key entry, you may order the Instructor's Files Diskette, which includes the initial documents for the examples and exercises.

7 Special Note to the Student

We welcome your reactions to this book. It is written to open up the world of computing for you. Expanding your knowledge will increase your confidence and prepare you for a life that will be influenced by computers.

Your comments and questions are important to us. Write to the author in care of Computer Information Systems Editor, Benjamin/Cummings Publishing Company, 390 Bridge Parkway, Redwood City, California 94065. All letters with a return address will be answered by the author.

7 Acknowledgements

The success of this project is related to the contributions of many people. We would like to thank some of the key people now.

As before, Pat Burner was a major force in the preparation of this book, serving as the watchdog of quality. Bonnie Grover directed the efforts of many people to keep the book on its extraordinary schedule, permitting greater currency than would otherwise be possible. Wendy Earl played a significant and lively role in photo research, and Devra Lerman contributed quality research and supplementary materials in a timely manner. We appreciate the contributions of Nancy Dunn and Richard Rawles to the Macintosh essays.

Michelle Baxter provided coordination and inspiration for the second edition. The entire effort was managed by Sally Elliott, whose vision always keeps us one step ahead.

Reviewers and consultants from both industry and academia have provided valuable contributions that improved the quality of the book. Their names are listed in the following section, and we wish to express our sincere gratitude to them.

---

7 Reviewers

Second Edition

Roberta Baber
Fresno City College
Fresno, California

James Boettler
South Carolina State College
Orangeburg, South Carolina

John DaPonte
Southern Connecticut State University
Stratford, Connecticut

Ed Delaporte
Forest City Computer Services
Rockford, Illinois

Linda Denny
Sinclair Community College
Dayton, Ohio

Jeff Frates
Los Medanos Community College
Concord, California

Paul Higbee
University of North Florida
Jacksonville, Florida

Usha Jindall
Washtenaw Community College
Ann Arbor, Michigan

Rose Laird
Northern Virginia Community College
Annandale, Virginia

Joyce Little
Towson State University
Baltimore, Maryland

Michael Mehlman
Tennessee State University
Nashville, Tennessee

Patrick Ormond
Utah Valley Community College
Orem, Utah

Charles Prettyman
Mercer County Community College
Trenton, New Jersey

Richard St. Andre
Central Michigan University
Mt. Pleasant, Michigan

Bruce Sophie
North Harris County College
Houston, Texas

Frank R. Wondolowski
East Carolina University
Greenville, North Carolina

Reviewers

First Edition

Kay Arms
Tyler Junior College
Tyler, Texas

Mark Aulick
Louisiana State University
Shreveport, Louisiana

Gary Brown
Santa Rosa Junior College
Santa Rosa, California

Jane Burcham
University of Missouri
Columbia, Missouri

Patricia Clark
Management Information Systems
Seattle, Washington

Carole Colaneri
Mid-Florida Technical College
Orlando, Florida

James Cox
Lane Community College
Eugene, Oregon

Janet Daugherty
Seton Hall University
South Orange, New Jersey

Ralph Duffy
North Seattle Community College
Seattle, Washington

Neil Dunn
Massachusetts Bay Community
College
Wellesley, Massachusetts

John Hamburger
Advanced Micro Devices
Sunnyvale, California

Sharon Hill
Prince George's Community
College
Largo, Maryland

Cary Hughes
Middle Tennessee State University
Murfreesboro, Tennessee

Marcy Kittner
University of Tampa
Tampa, Florida

Mary Kohls
Austin Community College
Austin, Texas

Cliff Layton
Rogers State College
Claremore, Oklahoma

Vicki Marney-Petix
Marpet Technical Services
Fremont, California

Spencer Martin
North Shore Community College
Beverly, Massachusetts

Doug Meyers
Des Moines Area Community
College
Ankeny, Iowa

Jeff Mock
Diablo Valley Community College
Pleasant Hill, California

Charles Moulton
Beaver College
Glenside, Pennsylvania

Linda Moulton
Montgomery County Community
College
Blue Bell, Pennsylvania

Mike Nakoff
Cincinnati Technical College
Cincinnati, Ohio

Robert Oakman
Le Conte College, University of
South Carolina
Columbia, South Carolina

Dennis Olson
Pikes Peak Community College
Colorado Springs, Colorado

James Payne
Kellogg Community College
Battle Creek, Michigan

Gordon Robinson
Forest Park Community College
St. Louis, Missouri

Gerald Sampson
Brazosport College
Lake Jackson, Texas

Fred Scott
Broward Community College
Ft. Lauderdale, Florida

Lenny Siegel
Advanced Micro Devices
Sunnyvale, California

Debbie Smith-Hemphill
AT&T Information Systems
Honolulu, Hawaii

Bruce Sophie
North Harris County College
Houston, Texas

Rod Southworth
Laramie County Community
College
Cheyenne, Wyoming

Sandra Stalker
North Shore Community College
Beverly, Massachusetts

Dave Stamper
University of Northern Colorado
Greeley, Colorado

Sandy Stephenson
Southwest Virginia Community
College
Richlands, Virginia

Greg Swan
Mesa Community College
Mesa, Arizona

Earl Talbert
Central Piedmont Community
College
Charlotte, North Carolina

J. Langdon Taylor
Ohio University
Athens, Ohio

Tim Vanderwall
Joliet Junior College
Joliet, Illinois

Kenneth Walter
Weber State College
Ogden, Utah

William Wells
Sacramento City College
Sacramento, California

PART 1

A FIRST LOOK AT COMPUTERS

This book is about the future—your future. It is about your place in a technological revolution that will make—and is making—profound changes in your life. The instrument of this revolution is, of course, the computer. For many, the computer promises greater ease and an end to drudgery. For others, it is a source of dread and represents the ultimate takeover of a machine society. The key to survival in the computer age is literacy in computers—awareness, knowledge, and interaction.

You will travel a long way in just these two opening chapters. The first chapter should raise your awareness of computers to a higher level. The second chapter forms the foundation for the technical chapters that follow. It is easier than you think.

Chapter 1. The Unfinished Revolution: Your Place in the World of Computers

1

The Unfinished Revolution

Your Place in the World of Computers

The Computer Revolution may well be far more sweeping than the Industrial Revolution—and certainly far more sudden. The effects of the computer are now seen in spectacular ways in many areas of our lives: in government, robotics, transportation, commerce, agriculture, graphics, education, the sciences, and our personal lives. We cannot turn back the clock, nor would we want to. We must continue to march forward—with computers.

Come join the revolution—the Computer Revolution, that is. Join the people who have discovered that computers can make life easier and better. Despite some pockets of anxiety, people are generally optimistic about the information age. Although they might not put it this way, people have decided to join the Computer Revolution.

Don't Start the Revolution Without Me

The Industrial Revolution took place relatively rapidly. In less than 100 years, human society was changed on a massive scale. To live between 1890 and 1920, for instance, was to live with the dizzying introduction of electricity, telephones, radio, automobiles, and airplanes. Like the Industrial Revolution, the Computer Revolution is bringing dramatic shifts in the way we live, perhaps even in the way we think. This revolution, however, is happening a great deal more quickly than the Industrial Revolution.

The Computer Revolution is unfinished, and will probably roll on into the next century. Nevertheless, perhaps we can glimpse the future now. Let us see how far we have come, first in society and then on a more personal level.

Forging a New Society: The Information Age

Computers are not a fad, like miniskirts or crazy haircuts. Few fads result in hundreds of magazines and thousands of books. Only a major trend has the momentum to sustain these classic indicators of acceptance. But computers have gone beyond acceptance—they are shaping society in fundamental ways.

In traditional economics courses, we learned that the cornerstones of an economy are land, labor, and capital. That tradition now is being challenged, and we speak of *four* key economic elements: land, labor, capital, and information. We are converting from an industrial society to an information society. We are moving from physical labor to mental labor, trading muscle power for brain power. Just as people moved from the farms to the factories when the Industrial Revolution began, so we must adjust to the information age. You have already taken that first step, just by taking a computer class and reading this book. But should you go further and get your own computer? It certainly is a possibility. Let us consider why.

A Computer for You

Television ads have been enticing us with computer promises for some time. "A tool for modern times." "If you can point, you can use a computer." "A computer for the rest of us."

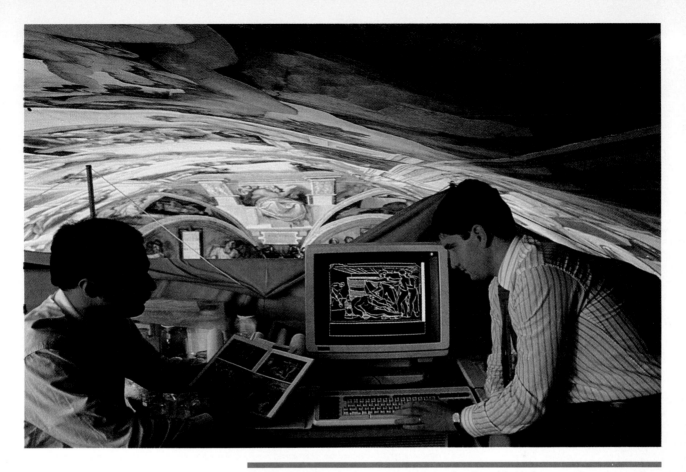

The Sistine Chapel. A computer system developed by Italian engineers maps the Sistine Chapel inch by inch as part of the restoration process.

Commercials featuring celebrities, families, or dogs—or all three— urge us to buy a personal computer. A personal computer, also called a microcomputer, is small enough to sit on a desk top. Personal computers have been hustled like encyclopedias: "For the price of a bicycle, you can help your child's future. . . ."

The marketing onslaught has had significant success, possibly in spite of the ads. Personal computers have moved into intimate corners of our lives. In the home, they are being used not only as playthings but also for keeping track of bank accounts, writing term papers and letters, learning a foreign language, designing artwork, turning on lawn sprinklers or morning coffee, monitoring temperature and humidity, teaching math and reading skills to children, and organizing Christmas card lists. Many people are also using computers on the job, whether they sit at a desk from 9 to 5 or run a farm. Personal computers are extremely useful for writing letters and reports; forecasting and updating budgets; creating and maintaining

Figure 1-1 Personal computer users. All these people—whether at home, at work, or at school—are making good use of the personal computer.

files; and producing charts, graphs, and newsletters. Almost any job you hope to get in the future will involve a computer in some way. Clearly, the computer user no longer has to be a Ph.D. in a laboratory somewhere. We are all computer users (Figure 1-1).

But just how happy are we with this new-found sophistication?

7 Worry About Computers? Me?

Terms such as **computer anxiety** and **computer phobia** have entered the language. People often fear the unknown and therefore practice avoidance. Even people in the business community who deal with computers on a daily basis may experience some form of **cyberphobia**—fear of computers. Some office workers are cyberphobes who, at the least, resent computers. In extreme cases, cyberphobia can be characterized by such symptoms as nausea, sweaty palms, and high blood pressure.

QUESTIONS YOU WERE AFRAID TO ASK

Q: Frankly, I'm not very interested in computers, but I don't want to be left behind. What should I do?

A: You're right—you may be left behind! Try to find out more about computers. You may become more interested as you learn more about them. This does not mean you have to become a computer expert. But you need to understand what computers can do and how they can impact your future, especially your future job.

Q: I'm a student studying in the field of *(fill in the blank)*. Are computers going to make my future career obsolete?

A: Probably not. It is factory workers who are in trouble. But the key is the computer: Can it enhance your work, as opposed to replacing it? In general, computers are changing the way jobs are performed, rather than eliminating the jobs.

Q: Will computers eventually become smarter than human beings and take over, as I have seen in some movies?

A: Who gets to pull the plug? Computers get only, and exactly, the control we humans decide to give them. The real question is *How might other humans use computers to control you?*

DISCUSSION QUESTION
Consider the following statement: "The computer is a great humanizing factor because it makes the individual more important. The more information we have on each individual, the more each individual counts." (Isaac Asimov, science fiction writer)

TEST BANK
Mult. Choice   7-8
T/F   13-15
Fill-in-the-Blank   7

What are people afraid of? Some people are nervous about the mathematical sound of the word *computer*. It seems to suggest that only a person with strong analytical and quantitative skills can use the machine. In fact, however, as we see all around us, computers are becoming more and more accessible to more and more people.

Some people are fearful of the whole environment of computing. The machinery looks intimidating to them. There is a notion that computers are temperamental gadgets, and that once a glitch gets into a computer system, it may wreak all kinds of havoc, from fouling up bank statements to launching nuclear missiles by mistake. Indeed, computer billing and banking errors are a problem. You should note, however, that errors usually result from mistakes made by the people who put the data into the computer system, not by the computer itself. Even so, correcting an error is often frustratingly slow.

People are also nervous that computers might be used to "get" them in some way—by the Internal Revenue Service, by credit bureaus, by privacy invaders of one sort or another. There are some things to worry about. Think of all the forms you have filled out for schools, jobs, medical matters, credit, taxes, and so on. There is scarcely any data related to your daily life that is not on a computer file somewhere. Might this information be obtained by unauthorized persons? The computer industry has been trying to deal with the privacy matter, but it is an expensive and difficult issue.

Many people are worried about computers in relation to their jobs. Some people doubt they have the skills to find jobs and keep them in the technological labor market of the future. A good many present-day executives whose companies are installing computer terminals in their offices worry about typing—either they do not know how or they are afraid they will lose status if they use a keyboard.

Interestingly, the fear related to computers cuts two ways. The more obvious fear is of the machine itself. The less obvious is the fear of being without computers. Some people fear they will be left out or left behind.

Eventually, the number of people suffering from computer anxiety will decline. The availability of cheaper, easier-to-use personal computers will reduce the intimidation factor. But probably more important, a new generation of children is growing up that is perfectly comfortable with the computer.

7 Computer Literacy for Everyone

Why are you reading this book? Why are you studying about computers? In addition to curiosity (and perhaps a course requirement!), you probably recognize that it will not be easy to get through the rest of your life if you do not know anything about computers.

CLIMB ABOARD

Is it really that important to be "computer literate"? Yes. You know it, schools know it, the general public knows it. But it was not always so. The average person worried about the disadvantages of computers but failed to recognize the advantages. The situation was similar to that in the early 1900s, when cars were first introduced. Historians tell us that the reaction to that newfangled contraption was much the same as people's reactions to computers. Today's traffic crush, however, is a good indication that attitudes changed somewhere along the way.

The analogy between computers and cars is a good one. In the very near future, people who refuse to have anything to do with computers may be as inconvenienced as people who refuse to learn to drive.

We offer a three-pronged definition of **computer literacy:**

- **Awareness.** As you study computers you will become aware of their importance, their versatility, their pervasiveness, and their potential for good and ill in our society.

- **Knowledge.** You will learn what computers are and how they work. This requires learning some technical jargon, but do not worry—no one expects you to become a computer expert.

- **Interaction.** Computer literacy also means learning to use a computer for some simple applications. By the end of this course, you should feel comfortable sitting down at a computer and using it for some suitable purpose.

Note that no part of this definition suggests that you must be able to form the instructions that tell a computer what to do. That would be akin to saying that everyone who plans to drive a car should become an auto mechanic. Someone else can write the instructions for the computer; the interaction part of the definition merely implies that you should be able to come along and make use of those instructions. For example, a bank teller can use a computer to see if a customer really has as much money as he or she wishes to withdraw. Computers can also be used by an accountant to prepare a report, a farmer to check on market prices, a store manager to analyze sales trends, or a teenager to play a video game. We cannot guarantee that these people are computer literate, but they have at least grasped the "hands-on" component of the definition—they can interact with computers.

Is it possible for everyone to be computer literate? That depends less on personal skills than on school budgets. Consider the debate about the "haves" and the "have-nots."

7 The Haves and the Have-Nots

Computer experts, social commentators, and even politicians see a future divided between the haves, who are information-rich, and the have-nots, who are information-poor. The source of that information, of course, is the computer. It has even been suggested that, in the near future, people who do not understand computers will have the same status as people today who cannot read. There is a growing chasm between the rich and the poor, because children who grow up with advantages have better access to computers. These children live in school districts that have the money to promote computers and computer literacy. In addition, the children may have access to computers at home. Children in poorer areas, however, may never have the opportunity to deal with computers as part of their education. And so another social gap is defined at an early age.

LEARN TO TYPE

There are some simple ways to communicate with a computer, including speaking and pointing, but for the moment the most important way is by typing. Teachers lament that students who want to learn about computers often have no typing skills at all. The self-taught two-finger method simply will not do.

The obvious way to take care of this problem is to take a typing class. Less obvious, and somewhat ironic, is that many people use the computer to learn to type. That is, typing lessons are one of the many applications of computers.

No need to linger on this point. Learn to type. Do it.

TEST BANK
Mult. Choice	9-21
T/F	16-37
Matching	5, 7-10
Fill-in-the-Blank	8-14

DISCUSSION QUESTION What aspects of computers make them desirable?

Some politicians have proposed to alter the social equation by providing federal funds for computers in schools. In fact, a bill called the Computer Education Assistance Act was introduced in the United States Senate, but it has yet to become law.

And Now That You Are Taking a Computer Class

Federal assistance or not, you are now taking your first computer class. Could you qualify as a computer user in a TV commercial? Is using a computer as easy as pointing? Most students don't think so. Students are usually surprised when they take their first computer course. In fact, some are not only surprised, they are confused and frustrated as well.

They are surprised by the subject matter, which was not what they thought it would be; they thought it would be fun, like video games. They are confused by the special language used in computer classes; some feel as if they have entered a foreign culture. They are frustrated by the hands-on experience, in which they have a one-to-one relationship with the computer. Their previous learning experiences, in contrast, have been shared and sheltered—they have been shared with peers in a classroom and were guided by some experienced person. Now it is just the student facing a machine, at least some of the time. So, this experience is different, and maybe slightly scary. But others have survived and even triumphed. You can too.

Since part of the challenge of computer literacy is awareness, let us now look at what makes computers so useful. We will then turn to the various ways computers can be used.

Everywhere You Turn

It seems that everywhere you turn these days, there is a computer—in stores, cars, homes, offices, hospitals, banks. What are some of the traits of computers that make them so useful?

The Nature of Computers

The computer is a workhorse. It is generally capable of laboring 24 hours a day, does not ask for raises or coffee breaks, and will do the ten-thousandth task exactly the same way it did the first one—and without complaining of boredom.

There are three key reasons why computers have become an indispensable part of our lives:

- **Speed.** By now it is human nature to be resentful if service is not fast. But it is "computer nature" that provides that fast service. Thus, unless we are prepared to do a lot more waiting—for pay-

Figure 1-2   Service means speed. The speed of a computer helps provide the fast service that customers expect.

checks, grades, telephone calls, travel reservations, bank balances, and many other things—we need the split-second processing of the computer (Figure 1-2). The speed of the computer also makes the machine ideal for processing large amounts of data, as in accounting systems and scientific applications.

- **Reliability.** Computers are extremely reliable. Of course, you might not think this from the way stories about "computer mistakes" are handled in the press. Unfortunately, what is almost never brought out in these stories is that the mistakes are not the fault of the computers themselves. True, there are sometimes equipment failures, but most errors supposedly made by computers are really human errors. Although one hears the phrase "computer error" quite frequently, the blame usually lies elsewhere.

- **Storage capability.** Computer systems are able to store tremendous amounts of data, which can then be retrieved quickly and efficiently. This storage capability is especially important in an information age.

These three—speed, reliability, and storage capacity—are fundamental characteristics of computers. But there are by-products of computers that are just as important. Consider these three:

- **Productivity.** Computers are able to perform dangerous, boring, or routine jobs, such as punching holes in metal or monitoring water levels. Granted, computers will eliminate some jobs, but computers free human beings for other work. We can also turn this idea around: If we were to abolish computers, we would have to hire millions of people to do what computers are now doing and ask them to perform some very tedious tasks. Most workers, however, will probably notice increased productivity in the office, where individuals are using computers to do their jobs better and faster.

- **Decision making.** Because of expanding technology, communications, and the interdependency of people, we suffer from an information deluge. Although this is in part brought on by the computer, it is also the computer that will help solve it. To make essential business and governmental decisions, managers need to take into account a variety of financial, geographical, logistical, and other factors. Using problem-solving techniques originally developed by humans, the computer helps decision makers sort the wheat from the chaff and make better choices.

- **Reduction in costs.** Finally, because it improves productivity and decision making, the computer helps reduce waste and hold costs down for labor, energy, and paperwork. Thus, computers help reduce the costs of goods and services.

With all these wonderful traits to its credit, it is no wonder that the computer has made its way into almost every facet of our lives. Let us look at some of the ways computers are being used to make our workdays more productive and our personal lives more rewarding.

(a)   (b)

Figure 1-3   Instant skyscraper. Architects can use computers to show how a proposed building will look in its surroundings. A photo of the existing skyline (a) is scanned by a laser beam and fed into the computer. A second photo of a *model* of the new building is also scanned and fed into the computer. Once the photos are in the computer, they can be combined. The resulting computer-generated photo (b) shows the proposed new skyscraper in the center of the picture.

7 The Uses of Computers

The jobs that computers do are as varied as we can imagine, but the following are some of the principal uses.

- **Graphics.** There is no better place to get a sense of the computer's impact than in the area of graphics. The computer as artist is evidenced in medicine, where brain scanners produce color-enhanced brain maps to help diagnose mental illness. Biochemists use computers to examine, in three dimensions, the structure of molecules. Architects use computer-animated graphics to give clients a visual walk-through of proposed buildings, to show possible exteriors, and to subject buildings to hypothetical earthquakes. Computers can even show how a skyscraper will look when added to the city's skyline (Figure 1-3).

  Business executives play artist, making bar graphs and pie charts out of tedious figures and using color to convey information with far more impact than numbers alone can do. Finally, a whole

Figure 1-4   Computer-generated art. Computers give artists a new creative tool.

new kind of artist has emerged who uses computers to create cartoon animation, landscapes, television logos, and still lifes (Figure 1-4).

- **Commerce.** Products from meats to magazines are now packaged with zebra-striped symbols that can be read by scanners at supermarket checkout stands to determine the price of the products. This Universal Product Code is one of the highly visible uses of computers in commerce; however, there are numerous others. Modern-day warehousing and inventory management could not exist without computers. Take your copy of this book, for instance. From printer to warehouse to bookstore, its movement was tracked with the help of computers.

- **Energy.** Energy companies use computers to locate oil, coal, natural gas, and uranium. Electric companies use computers to monitor their vast power networks. In addition, meter readers use handheld computers to record how much energy is used each month in homes and businesses.

MICROCOMPUTERS IN ACTION

Advertising Up Close and Personal

Studies show that supermarket customers often make their purchasing decisions right in the store. Advertisers would like to influence that decision, even as your hand reaches for the shelf. To get your undivided attention, the latest gimmick is a video screen right on your shopping cart, pitching products as you wheel down the aisle.

It is called VideOcart, and here is how it works. A commercial is beamed via satellite to the store's personal computer. Using radio waves, the ad is then transmitted from there to the carts in the store. As you walk down the canned vegetable aisle, a wall of look-alike cans confronts you. Which will you pick? But wait; the screen on your cart shows

Benton's Wax Beans and the flashing message "Buy me, buy me." Believe this, for it is true: The VideOcart knows exactly what aisle you are in at any given moment and sends the commercial message that matches the goods in that aisle.

There is more. The screens can provide maps to guide you around the store. They can also initiate games, with the customer participating to win prizes. And, finally, the screen can provide recipes.

Advertisers can, of course, measure the return on their investment by checking actual purchases at the checkout stand. The carts are in a testing phase at several supermarket sites. It remains to be seen whether customers

react favorably, by purchasing the products advertised on the carts, or whether they revolt against this gimmick by avoiding these products and—perhaps—the store that pushes them.

TALKING TO YOUR CAR

You have probably heard that some new car models come equipped with a computer. What you have probably not heard is that soon all cars will come with not one but as many as 14 computers. In fact, engineers are taking a new look at cars, trying to improve every function with on-board computers.

Some of these computers are out of sight and mind, busily regulating controls like the air/fuel mix fed to each cylinder. But the visible car computers promise to captivate us in new ways. Computer screens on the dashboard can give you maps for your destination, as shown above, or flash "oil change" if needed. But even that feature seems routine, compared with the car that listens to its master's voice.

Start by walking up to the car and saying something like "This is me." The car recognizes your voice. The door opens, the seat and steering wheel automatically adjust, and the radio tunes to your favorite station. Just how far out can we get, talking to our cars? Well, you could talk to the computer as you drive and have it flash stock-market quotes on the dashboard screen. Or most anything else. The key question is this one: Is it worth it?

- **Transportation.** Computers are used to help run rapid transit systems, load containerships, keep track of what railroad cars have been sent where (and send them rolling home again), fly and land airplanes and keep them from colliding, and schedule airline reservations. They are also used in cars and motorcycles to monitor fluid levels, temperatures, and electrical systems and to improve fuel mileage.

- **Paperwork.** There is no doubt that our society runs on paper. While in some ways the computer contributes to this problem—as in adding to the amount of junk mail you find in your mailbox—in many other ways it cuts down paper handling. The techniques of word processing, for example, allow letters and reports to be done in draft form and placed in storage that is accessible by computer. Corrections can be made to the draft and entered into the computer. The letter or report does not need to be completely retyped. Instead, the whole text regenerates automatically, with all errors eliminated. Even Supreme Court justices use word processing, storing their opinions in draft form for future reference. Computerized bookkeeping, record keeping, and document sending have also made paperwork more efficient.

- **Money.** Computers have revolutionized the way money is handled. Once upon a time it was possible to write a check for the rent on Tuesday and cover it with a deposit on Thursday, knowing it would take a few days for the bank to process the rent check and debit it against your account. With computers, however, the recording of deposits and withdrawals is done more quickly. Computers have also brought us the age of do-it-yourself banking, with automated teller machines (ATMs) available for simple transactions. Computers have helped fuel the cashless economy, enabling the widespread use of credit cards and instant credit checks by banks, department stores, and other retailers. Some oil companies are using credit-card activated, self-service gasoline pumps.

- **Agriculture.** Are we ready for high tech down on the farm? Absolutely. Farming is a business, after all, and a small computer—which can be a lot cheaper than a tractor—can help with billing, crop information, cost per acre, feed combinations, and so on. A Mississippi cotton grower, for example, boosted his annual profit 50% by using a computer to determine the best time to fertilize. Cattle breeders can also use computers for breeding and performance information about livestock. Furthermore, sheep can be sheared by a computer-run robotic shearing arm. The arm is guided by sensors and the dimensions of a typical sheep stored in the computer's memory. In addition to these specific uses, it is predicted that computers will give people the option of working at home instead of in city offices; thus, computers may end the isolation of country living and the movement of younger farm generations to the cities.

Figure 1-5   When will the storm get here? To improve the science of weather forecasting, researchers program various weather conditions into a computerized global weather model. They can then see what kind of weather develops from those conditions; this photo shows day 42 of a simulation sequence.

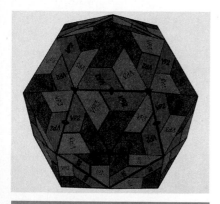

Figure 1-6   Cold virus. This computer-produced model of the cold virus culprit named HRV14 raises hopes that a cure for the common cold may be possible after all. With the aid of a computer, the final set of calculations for the model took one month to complete. Researchers estimate that without the computer the calculations might have required ten years of manual effort.

- **Government.** The federal government is the largest single user of computers. The Social Security Administration, for example, produces 36 million benefit checks a month with the help of computers. Computers are also used for forecasting weather (Figure 1-5), for servicing parks, for processing immigrants, for meting out justice, and—yes—for collecting taxes. The FBI keeps track of suspected criminals, compiling separate bits of information into elaborate dossiers that have already helped put several organized crime lords behind bars. A veteran can walk into a local Veterans Administration office and get a rundown of his or her benefits in moments. The Department of Agriculture keeps track of the amount of snow in the winter, then uses computers to predict how much water farmers will have in the summer. As one bureaucrat said, the only way you can survive in the government is to learn to use computers.

- **Education.** Computers have been used behind the scenes for years in colleges and school districts for record-keeping and accounting purposes. Now, of course, they are rapidly coming into the classroom—elementary, secondary, and college. Many parents and teachers feel that computer education is a necessity, not a novelty. Parents want to be sure that their children are not left behind in the computer age. The pressure is on school districts to acquire computers and train teachers and students in their use.

- **The home.** Are you willing to welcome the computer into your home? Many people already have, often by justifying it as an educational tool for their children. But that is only the beginning. Adults often keep records, write letters, prepare budgets, draw pictures, prepare newsletters, and connect with other computers— all with their own computers at home. The adventurous use computers to control heating and air conditioning, answer telephone calls, watch for burglars, and so on. The question about whether you *need* a home computer remains open to debate, but there is no question that it can make your life easier and more entertaining.

- **Health and medicine.** Computers have been used on the business side of medicine for some time; in addition, they are being used in the healing process itself. For instance, computers are used to produce cross-sectional views of the body, to provide ultrasound pictures, to help pharmacists test patients' medications for drug compatibility, and to help physicians make diagnoses. In fact, it is estimated that computers make a correct disease diagnosis with 85% accuracy. (The doctor, have no fear, makes the final diagnosis.) If you are one of the thousands who suffer one miserable cold after another, you will welcome the news that computers have been able to map, in exquisite atomic detail, the structure of the human cold virus; this is the first step to a cure for the common cold (Figure 1-6). Computers are also being used for health maintenance, in everything from weight-loss programs to recording heart rates.

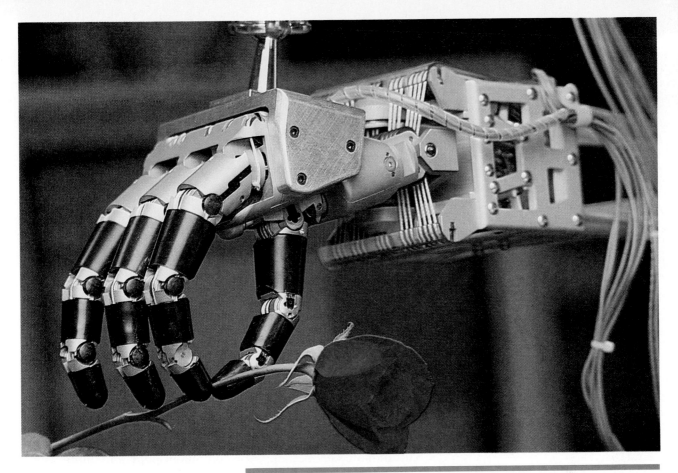

Figure 1-7   The robot hand. Robot chores do not usually require the delicate maneuvers required of this simulated hand, which can pick up a rose or an egg without crushing it.

DISCUSSION QUESTION
What is unrealistic about our portrayal of computers in movies and TV shows like Six Million Dollar Man? Movies and TV shows are aimed at being entertainment, not at being scientific. Only parts of Steve Austin are bionic: picking up a two-ton bolder would crush his back, which is not bionic. How can his non-bionic leg keep up with his bionic leg? The bionic and nonbionic must function as an integrated system.

- **Robotics.** With the age of the computer has arrived the age of the robot (Figure 1-7). These robots are information machines with the manual dexterity to perform tasks too unpleasant, too dangerous, or too critical to assign to human beings. Examples are pattern-cutting robots in garment businesses, which are able to get the most apparel out of bolts of cloth; robots used in defense to perform underwater military missions; robots used by fruit growers to pick fruit; and even robots that patrol jail corridors at night and report any persons encountered. Especially controversial are the robots that do tedious jobs better than human beings do—jobs such as welding or paint spraying in new-car plants. Clearly, these robots signal the end of jobs for many factory workers—a troublesome social problem. Robots are one more sign that we the people are moving away from industrial society and toward an information society.

Figure 1-8 Airplane design. Each new Boeing airplane is designed and tested by computers. This computer-generated graphic shows pressure contours for the Boeing 757.

■ **The sciences.** As you might imagine, computers are used extensively in the sciences, but note these examples involving scientific investigation. Consider first the beleaguered mouse, that mainstay of scientific research. Many mice will be spared exposure to suspected poisons, now that the Food and Drug Administration has a computer programmed to react the way a mouse's digestive system would react to such material. Computers are also used to generate models of DNA, the molecule that houses the genetic instructions that determine the specific characteristics of organisms. To test experimental airplanes, aerospace engineers use computers to simulate wind tunnel experiments (Figure 1-8). In England, researchers have used computers to invent a "bionic nose" that can distinguish subtle differences in fragrance—an invention that could have major benefits for the food, perfume, and distilling industries. On another front entirely, the National Aeronautics and Space Administration has developed a computerized system for use in Arecibo, Puerto Rico, to scan the heavens and listen in on eight million narrow-band radio frequencies in an attempt to find signs of communication from alien beings in outer space. (So far, no messages.)

■ **Training.** Computers are being used as training devices in industry and government. It is much cheaper, for instance, to teach aspiring pilots to fly in computerized "training cockpits," or simulators, than in real airplanes. Novice engineers can also be given the experience of running a train with the help of a computerized device.

■ **The human connection.** Are computers cold and impersonal? Look again. The disabled don't think so (Figure 1-9). Neither do other people who use computers in very personal ways. Computers can be used to assist humans in areas in which we are most human. Can the disabled walk again? Some can, with the help of computers. Can dancers and athletes improve their performance? Maybe they can, by using computers to monitor their movements. Can we learn more about our ethnic backgrounds and our cultural history with the aid of computers? Indeed we can.

We hope this discussion has stimulated your interest in computers. For more examples of how computers are used in our lives, see Galley 2, "Computers Around Us: The Many Uses of Computers."

7 Toward Computer Literacy

You know more than you think you do. Even though you may not know a lot about computers yet, you have been exposed to computer hype, computer advertisements and discussions, and magazine articles and newspaper headlines about computers. You have interacted with computers in the various compart-

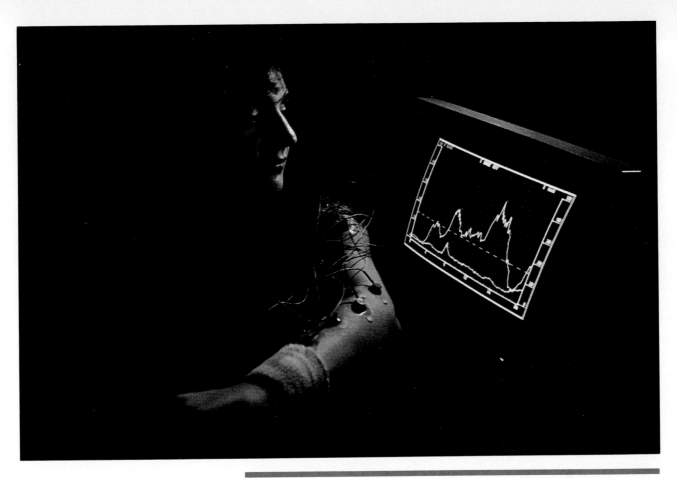

Figure 1-9   Computers assist the disabled. This biofeedback computer shows every flutter of a muscle. Such feedback helps this patient retrain her damaged nerves so that they will stimulate her arm muscles more effectively.

ments of your life—at the grocery store, your school, the library, and more. The beginnings of computer literacy are already apparent.

The Computer Revolution is an unfinished revolution, one that will continue throughout our lifetimes. But its seeds are already sown and growing. Throughout the rest of this book, we will describe the implications of the revolution for the tasks we must learn today.

We have written this book with two kinds of readers in mind. If you are contemplating a computer-related career, you will find a solid discussion of technology, computer applications, and various jobs associated with computers. Even if you are not interested in the technical side of computers, however, most careers involve computers in some way; this book will provide you with a foundation in computer literacy. For if the computer is to help us rather than confound us or threaten us, we must assume some responsibility for understanding it.

PERSPECTIVES

MOVING BOLDLY TOWARD THE YEAR 2000

Making predictions is a foolhardy business, but that has never stopped the experts—or us—from doing it. As we move toward the turn of the century, it seems like a good time for prognostications. However, there is a bit of a safety net: New technology usually takes about a decade from lab to practical product, and the items described here are already in the labs or just entering them. A sampler of predictions follows.

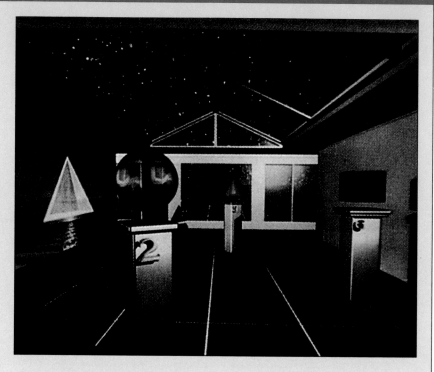

- Computers will lose their boxy shapes and, in fact, be all but unrecognizable, by today's standards. Some experts talk of wristwatch-size computers that understand human speech. Others suggest book-size computers that contain entire libraries of information in what appears to be a slim volume of poetry.

- Keyboards will be replaced by handwriting screens that look like flat blotters on desks. The computer will translate your handwriting into type. Those of us with wretched handwriting may have to mend our ways just a bit.

- Communications networks will explode—soon any computer will be able to communicate almost instantly with any other computer. Voice, data, and video will be transmitted with equal ease.

- Sensors will be placed on street corners to collect traffic data, which will then be routed to computers in nearby cars. The car computers will flash alternate routes on the computer screen to help motorists snake around traffic problems. (We have faith that the computer system will not send all of us on the same alternate route.)

- Your doctor will check your condition by having you walk through a computerized diagnostic machine that makes science-fiction writers want to take up another trade. Body-scanning technologies will open the interior of the body to a new view, so doctors will be able to diagnose problems in minutes instead of days and heart attacks in seconds instead of hours.

- Last, and perhaps best, will be the progress towards genuine ease of use. Using a computer will be like dialing a phone. Everyone will know how.

Technology has made astonishing leaps in just the last few years. The prevailing sentiment is "Why stop now?"

Summary and Key Terms

- Most people believe that computers make life easier and better, and are optimistic about computers.

- Like the Industrial Revolution, the Computer Revolution is making massive changes in society. However, it is happening more quickly than the Industrial Revolution.

- Land, labor, capital, and information are the cornerstones of our economy. We are changing from an industrial society to an information society.

- Personal computers can be used in the home and in business for a variety of purposes.

- Some people suffer from **computer anxiety, computer phobia,** or **cyberphobia**—fear of computers. Some people feel intimidated by computers; others fear computer errors, invasion of privacy, job loss or change, and depersonalization.

- **Computer literacy** includes (1) an awareness of computers, (2) knowledge about computers, and (3) interaction with computers. To use a computer, however, you do not need to be able to write the instructions that tell a computer what to do.

- Some experts believe that unless all students have equal access to computers, the gap between the "haves" and the "have-nots" will widen. Federal funding for computers in schools has been proposed.

- There are three key characteristics that make computers an indispensable part of our lives: speed, reliability, and storage capacity. By-products of these characteristics include productivity, decision making, and reduction in costs.

- Computers are used in many areas of our lives, including graphics, commerce, energy, transportation, paperwork, money, agriculture, government, education, the home, health and medicine, robotics, the sciences, training, and helping people lead more satisfying lives.

Review Questions

1. In what ways are the Industrial Revolution and the Computer Revolution similar? In what ways are they different?

2. What are the four cornerstones of today's economy?

3. List four uses of personal computers in the home.

4. List four uses of personal computers in business.

5. What are the fears people have about computers?

6. Name two reasons why computer anxiety will probably decline.

7. What are the three components of computer literacy?

8. List three characteristics that make computers indispensable.

9. Name one use of computers in each of the following areas: graphics, commerce, energy, transportation, paperwork, money, agriculture, government, education, the home, health and medicine, robotics, the sciences, training, and the human connection.

Discussion Questions

1. Do you believe that computers make life easier and better? Explain.

2. Do you feel any discomfort or anxiety about computers? Explain why or why not.

3. Why are you taking this class? What do you expect to learn from this class?

Chapter 2. Overview of a Computer System: Hardware, Software, and People

2

Overview of a Computer System

Hardware, Software, and People

The purpose of a computer system is to turn unprocessed data into usable information. This requires four main areas of data handling—input, processing, output, and storage. The equipment associated with a computer system is called hardware. A set of instructions to tell the hardware what to do is called software. People, however, are the most important component of a computer system.

LEARNING OBJECTIVES
- Familiarization with the basic components of a computer system: input, processing, output, and storage.
- Acquaintance with some common input, output, and storage media.
- Introduction to the various sizes of computers and to centralized versus decentralized computer systems.
- Introduction to software, including common applications software.
- Introduction to types of processing and common processing operations.
- Introduction to people who use and run a computer system.

TEST BANK

Mult. Choice	1-4
T/F	1-4
Matching A	1-2
Fill-in-the-Blank	1-4

Can you imagine a computer that is as easy to learn to use as a toaster? Computer manufacturers are very serious about making their computers easy to understand, and some of them refer to toasters only partly in jest. In just a few years computers *have* become easier to use, but they are still a long way from being like toasters. There is another comparison that is a better fit—learning to drive a car.

You do, of course, need some training in driving a car. You also need some training to use a computer. As in learning to drive, the experience is new and a little scary at first, but the average person can learn quite readily.

There is a major difference, though, between learning how to drive a car and learning how to use a computer: familiarity. Most of us have been around cars all our lives, so before we even started taking driver's training lessons, we already knew what a steering wheel was, what the ignition key was good for, and where to put the suitcases when we went on a long trip. Most of us, however, have *not* been around computers all our lives. Thus, we need to start on the road to computer literacy by learning some basics. That is the purpose of this chapter—to introduce you to the vocabulary and ideas that will lay the foundation for your computer education. Once you absorb some of the basics, you will be better prepared to sit down "behind the wheel" and learn how to use a computer. Even if you are already somewhat familiar with computers, you will probably pick up some new information as you read this chapter.

7 The Beginning of What You Need to Know

The computer and its associated equipment are called **hardware.** The instructions that tell a computer what you want it to do are called **software.** The term **packaged software,** also called commercial software, refers to software that is literally packaged in a container of some sort—usually a box or folder—and is sold in stores. Most packaged software is **applications software,** software that is *applied*—or put to use—to solve a particular problem. There is a great assortment of software to help us with a variety of tasks—writing papers, preparing budgets, drawing graphs, playing games, and so forth. The wonderful array of software available is what makes computers so useful.

Software is also referred to as programs. To be more specific, a **program** is a set of step-by-step instructions that directs the computer to do the tasks you want it to do and produce the results you want. A **computer programmer** is a person who writes programs. But most of us do not write programs—we *use* programs written by someone else. This means we are **users**—people who purchase and use computer software. In business, users are often called **end-users** because they are at the end of the "computer line," actually making

COMPUTERS VERSUS BARKING DOGS

If you decided to list every conceivable use of computers, you probably would not come up with this one: keeping barking—and possibly vicious—dogs at bay. Well, the computer itself does not intimidate the dogs, but it can provide assistance.

Confronting dogs has long been a problem for meter readers, who must enter yards protected by a variety of canines; Puget Sound Power and Light Company meter readers let their hand-held computers, used to record meter readings, tell them what to do about dogs. The computer must be given some dog information in advance. For each address on a meter reader's route, the dog's name and the command that the owner says the dog will obey are entered into the computer. Walking the route, the meter reader simply keys in the address, causing the dog's name and the appropriate command to appear on the tiny screen. The rest is up to the human.

use of the computer's information. We shall emphasize the connection between computers and computer users throughout this chapter and, indeed, throughout this book.

As we continue the chapter now, we will first examine hardware, followed by software, and then data. We will then consider how these components work together to produce information. Finally, we will devote a separate section to computers and people. As the title of this chapter indicates, what follows is an overview, a look at the "big picture" of a computer system. Thus, many of the terms introduced in this chapter are defined only briefly. In subsequent chapters we will discuss the various parts of a computer system in greater detail.

Hardware: Meeting the Machine

What is a computer, anyway? A six-year-old called a computer "radio, movies, and television combined!" A ten-year-old described a computer as "a television set you can talk to." That's getting closer, but still does not recognize the computer as a machine that has the power to make changes. A **computer** is a machine that can be programmed to accept data (input) and process it into useful information (output). The processing is directed by the software, but performed by the hardware, which we will examine in this section.

To function, a computer system requires four main areas of data handling—input, processing, output, and storage (Figure 2-1). The hardware responsible for these four areas operates as follows:

- **Input devices** accept data in a form that the computer can use and send the data to the processing unit.

- The **processor,** more formally known as the **central processing unit (CPU),** has the electronic circuitry that manipulates input data into the information wanted. The central processing unit actually executes computer instructions. **Memory** is associated with the central processing unit. Memory has the electronic circuitry that temporarily holds the data and instructions (programs) that the central processing unit needs.

- **Output devices** show people the processed data—information—in a form they can use easily.

- **Secondary storage devices** are units separate from the computer that can store additional data and programs. These devices supplement memory.

Now let us consider the equipment making up these four areas of data handling in terms of what you would find on a personal computer.

Figure 2-1   The four primary components of a computer system. To function, a computer system requires input, processing, output, and storage.

TRANSPARENCY ACETATE #2A
Figure #2-1

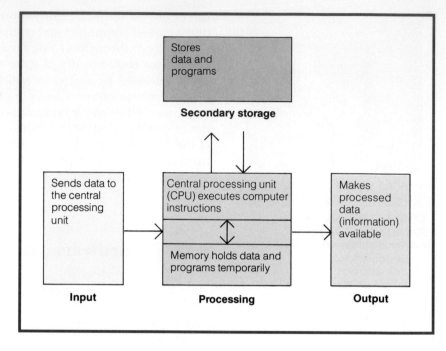

Stores data and programs

Secondary storage

Sends data to the central processing unit

Central processing unit (CPU) executes computer instructions

Memory holds data and programs temporarily

Makes processed data (information) available

Input   **Processing**   **Output**

DISCUSSION QUESTION
What kinds of input devices have you seen other than keyboards?

DISCUSSION QUESTION
Why must all computers, large and small, have a central processing unit?

7 Your Personal Computer Hardware

Suppose you want to do word processing on a personal computer, using the hardware shown in Figure 2-2. Word processing software allows you to input data such as an essay, save it, revise and resave it, and print it whenever you wish. The *input* device, in this case, is a keyboard, which you use to key in the original essay and any changes you want to make to it. All computers, large and small, must have a *central processing unit,* so yours does too—it is within the personal computer housing. The central processing unit uses the word processing software to accept the data you input through the keyboard. Processed data from your personal computer usually is *output* in two forms, on a screen and a printer. As you enter the essay on the keyboard, it appears on the screen in front of you. After you examine the essay on the screen, make changes, and determine that it is acceptable, you can print the essay on a printer. Your *secondary storage* device is a diskette, a magnetic medium that stores the essay until it is needed again.

Now we will take a general tour of the hardware needed for input, processing, output, and storage. These same components make up all computer systems, whether small, medium, or large. In this discussion we will try to emphasize the types of hardware you are likely to have seen in your own environment. These topics will be covered in more detail in Chapters 3, 4, and 5.

Secondary storage

Input

Processing

Output

Figure 2-2   A personal computer system. In this IBM PS/2 microcomputer system, the input device is a keyboard. The keyboard feeds data to the central processing unit, which is inside the computer housing. The central processing unit is an array of electronic circuitry on pieces of silicon. The two output devices in this example are the screen and the printer. The secondary storage device is a $3\frac{1}{2}$-inch disk. These four components of the system operate together to make the computer work for you.

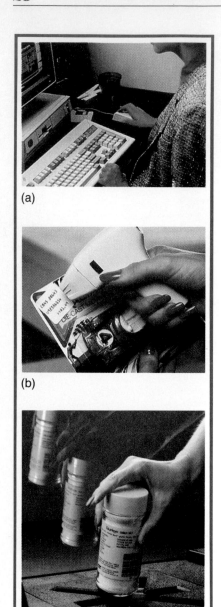

(a)

(b)

(c)

Figure 2-3   Input devices. (a) The most widely used input device is the keyboard. The mouse, however, is a common substitute for some keyboard functions. Movement of the mouse on a flat surface causes corresponding movement on the screen. (b) This wand reader scans special letters and numbers on price tags to input data. Wand readers are often found in department stores. (c) Bar code readers are used in supermarkets to input the bar codes found on product labels.

Input: What Goes In

Input is the data that is input—put in—to the computer system for processing. Some of the most common ways of feeding input data into the system are by:

- Typing on a **keyboard.** Computer keyboards operate in much the same way as electric typewriter keyboards, except that the computer responds to what you enter; that is, it "talks back" to you by displaying what you type on the screen in front of you (Figure 2-3a).

- Moving a **mouse** over a flat surface. As the ball on its underside rotates, the mouse movement causes corresponding movement on the computer screen. Buttons on the mouse let the user invoke commands (Figure 2-3a).

- Reading with a **wand reader,** which can be used to scan the special letters and numbers on price tags in retail stores (Figure 2-3b). Wand readers can read data directly from an original document. Thus, they significantly reduce the cost and potential error associated with manually entering data on a keyboard.

- Moving a product over a **bar code reader,** which scans **bar codes,** the zebra-stripe symbols now carried on nearly all products from meats to magazines (Figure 2-3c). Like wand readers, bar code readers collect data at the original source, reducing errors and costs.

An input device may be part of a **terminal** that is connected to a large computer. A terminal includes (1) an input device (a keyboard, wand reader, or bar code reader, for instance); (2) an output device (usually a television-like **screen**); and (3) a connection to the main computer. The screen displays the data that has been input, and after the computer processes this data, the screen displays the results of the processing—the information wanted. In a store, for instance, the terminal screen displays the individual prices (the data) and the total price (the desired information).

The Processor and Memory: Data Manipulation

The **processor** is the computer's center of activity. The processor, as we noted, is also called the **central processing unit,** or **CPU.** The central processing unit consists of electronic circuits that interpret and execute program instructions, as well as communicate with the input, output, and storage devices.

It is the central processing unit that actually transforms data into information. **Data** is the raw material to be processed by a computer. Such material can be letters, numbers, or facts—such as grades in a class, baseball batting averages, or light and dark areas in a photograph. Processed data becomes **information**—data that is organized,

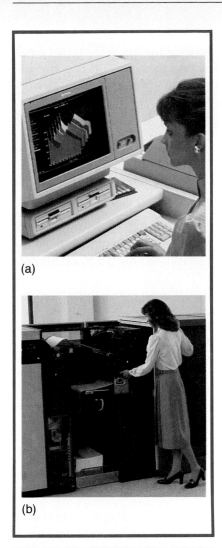

(a)

(b)

Figure 2-4   Output devices. Screens and printers are two types of output devices. (a) The graphics displayed on this screen are one form of output. (b) This high-speed printer is typically used in businesses that produce a high volume of printed materials.

meaningful, and useful. Data that is very uninteresting to one person may become very interesting information to another. The raw facts of births, eating habits, and growth rates of calves, for instance, may mean nothing to most people. But the computer-produced relationships among feed, growth, and beef quality are critical information to a cattle breeder.

The computer's **memory,** also known as **primary storage,** is closely associated with the central processing unit but separate from it. Memory holds the data after it is input to the system and before it is processed. It also holds the data after it has been processed but before it has been released to the output device. Memory also holds the programs (computer instructions) needed by the central processing unit. Memory consists of electronic circuits, just as the CPU does. Memory electronically stores letters, numbers, and special characters such as dollar signs and decimal points. Computer memory can even store images in digitized form.

The central processing unit and memory are usually contained in a cabinet or housing. In the past the cabinets of large computers also contained the computer **console**—a panel of switches and dials and colored buttons and winking lights that has inspired the control rooms of so many Hollywood-built spaceships. The console allowed the computer system to signal the operator when something needed to be done—for example, resupplying the printer with paper. Modern computers are less likely to have dials and lights; operators can communicate with the computer system by using a console terminal. For example, the operator can use the console terminal to determine which programs the system is executing.

7 Output: What Comes Out

The results produced by the central processing unit are, of course, a computer's whole reason for being; **output** is usable information. That is, raw input data has been processed by the computer into information. Some ingenious forms of output have been devised, such as music and synthetic speech, but the most common forms are words and numbers and graphics. Words, for example, may be the letters and memos prepared by office people using word processing software. Other workers may be more interested in numbers, such as those found in formulas, schedules, and budgets. As we shall see, numbers can often be understood more easily when output in the form of computer graphics.

Two common output devices are screens and printers. Screens are the same as those described under input. However, they can vary in their forms of display: Some may produce lines of written or numeric display; others may produce a display of color graphics (Figure 2-4a).

Printers are machines that produce printed reports at the instruction of a computer program (Figure 2-4b). Some printers form images on paper as typewriters do; they strike a character against a ribbon, which makes an image on the paper. Other printers form characters by using lasers, photography, or ink spray. In these types of printers there is no physical contact between the printer and the paper when the characters are being formed. Besides forming characters, some printers are able to produce graphic images.

7 Secondary Storage

Secondary storage is additional storage separate from the central processing unit and memory. For instance, it would be unwise for a college registrar to try to house the grades of all the students in the college in memory; if this were done, the computer probably would not have room to store anything else. Also, memory holds data and programs only temporarily—hence the need for secondary storage.

The two most common secondary storage media are magnetic disk and magnetic tape. A **magnetic disk** is a flat, oxide-coated disk on which data is recorded as magnetic spots. A disk can be a diskette or hard disk. A **diskette** looks something like a small stereo record. Diskettes that are $5\frac{1}{4}$ inches in diameter are called **floppy disks,** because they are somewhat flexible; however, the firm $3\frac{1}{2}$-inch diskettes are becoming the standard (Figure 2-5a). **Hard disks** hold more data and have faster access than diskettes. Hard disks are often contained in **disk packs.**

Disk data is read by **disk drives.** Personal computer disk drives read diskettes. Most personal computers also have hard disk drives. On some larger computer systems, the disk packs can be removed from the drives (Figure 2-5b). This permits the use of interchangeable packs, and the result is practically unlimited storage capacity.

Magnetic tape, which comes on a reel or cartridge, is similar to tape that is played on a tape recorder. Magnetic tape reels are mounted on **tape drives** when the data on them needs to be read by the computer system or when new data is to be written on the tape (Figure 2-5c). Magnetic tape is usually used for backup purposes—for "data insurance"—because tape is inexpensive.

The most recent storage technology, however, is **optical disk,** which uses a laser beam to store large volumes of data relatively inexpensively (Figure 2-5d).

7 The Complete Hardware System

The hardware devices attached to the computer are called **peripheral equipment.** Peripheral equipment includes all input, output, and secondary storage devices. In the case of microcomputers, some of the input, output, and storage devices are built into the same physical unit. In the personal computer we saw in Figure 2-2, for instance, the CPU and disk drive are all contained in the same housing; the keyboard and screen are separate.

DISCUSSION QUESTION
How do primary and secondary storage differ?

LECTURE ACTIVITY
Show class several sizes of disks and tapes. Identify the advantages and disadvantages of each.

DISCUSSION QUESTION
Why are the 3.5 inch disks more practical for transporting than the 5.25 inch disks?

DISCUSSION QUESTION
Why would a company want to copy information on a disk to a tape?

Figure 2-5   Secondary storage devices.
(a) A 3½-inch diskette is being inserted into a disk drive. (b) Hard disks are contained within the round disk pack shown on the top of the cabinets, which contain the disk drives. When it is to be used, a disk pack is lowered into the opened compartment. (c) Magnetic tape, shown here being mounted on a tape drive, travels off one reel and onto another. (d) Optical disk technology uses a laser beam to store large volumes of data.

LECTURE HINT
Disks have been shrinking in size and increasing in capacity for years. In successive generations the following disk sizes became popular: 14 inch (IBM), 8 inch (CPM), 5.25 inch (1980's), 3.5 inch (becoming standard now). Hewlett-Packard recently introduced a 2 inch disk for its laptop computer. Visionaries say that the main secondary storage device on microcomputers will some day be plastic cards the size of calling cards.

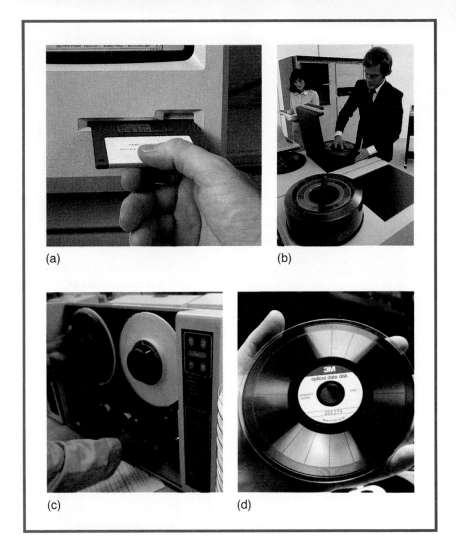

(a)   (b)

(c)   (d)

In larger computer systems, however, the input, processing, output, and storage functions may be in separate rooms, separate buildings, or even separate countries. For example, data may be input on terminals at a branch bank, then transmitted to the central processing unit at the bank's headquarters (Figure 2-6). The information produced by the central processing unit may then be transmitted to the bank's international offices, where it is printed out. Meanwhile, disks with stored data may be kept in the bank's headquarters, and duplicate data kept on disk or tape in a warehouse across town for safekeeping.

Although the equipment may vary widely, from the simplest computer to the most powerful, by and large the four elements of a computer system remain the same: input, processing, output, and storage. Now let us look at the various ways computers are classified.

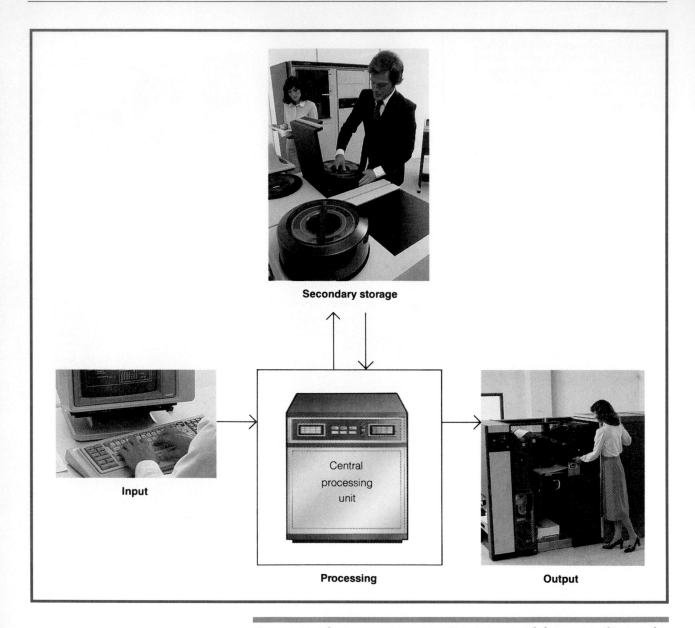

Secondary storage

Input

Central
processing
unit

Processing

Output

Figure 2-6   **A large computer system.** Data is input and then sent to the central processing unit, which may be at an entirely different location. Information can be output on a high-speed printer. Secondary storage may take the form of magnetic tape or, as shown here, magnetic disk.

Classifications: Computers Big and Small

Computers come in sizes from tiny to monstrous, in both appearance and power. The size of a computer that a person or an organization needs depends on the computing requirements. Clearly, the National Weather Service, keeping watch on the weather fronts of many continents, has requirements different from those of a car dealer's service department that is trying to keep track of its parts inventory. And the requirements of both of them are different from the needs of a salesperson using a small laptop computer to record client orders on a sales trip.

DISCUSSION QUESTION
How do the following differ: supercomputer, mainframe, minicomputer, supermicro, microcomputer?

Mainframes and Supercomputers

In the jargon of the computer trade, large computers are called **mainframes** (Figure 2-7a). Mainframes are capable of processing data at very fast speeds—millions of instructions per second—and have access to billions of characters of data. The price can vary from several hundred thousand to many millions of dollars. With

Figure 2-7   Computer classifications. (a) Despite the sterile look of this staged photo, it does show that a mainframe computer has many components. Shown here is the IBM mainframe called the Sierra, also known as the IBM 3090. (b) The Cray-2 supercomputer has been nicknamed Bubbles because of its bubbling, shimmering coolant liquids. You can own it for a mere $17.6 million. (c) The VAX, a popular minicomputer made by Digital Equipment Corporation (DEC). (d) This microcomputer is made by Hewlett-Packard.

(a)

(b)

(c)

(d)

LECTURE HINT
Until recently, supercomputers
were granted to a few elite users,
usually in the government. Now
they are becoming more
commonplace. Recent
applications include charting the
effects of pollution, fighting
diseases, and simulating anything
from a bulldozer to a factory.
Supercomputers are even finding
their way into business
institutions, helping make major
financial decisions.

LECTURE HINT
Companies which produce these
types of computers:
Supercomputer: Cray, Control
Data
Mainframe: IBM, DEC, Unisys
Minicomputer: IBM, DEC, NCR
Supermicros: Sun, Apollo, Next
Microcomputers: IBM, Apple,
Tandy

that kind of price tag, you will not buy a mainframe for just any purpose. Their principal use is for processing vast amounts of data quickly, so some of the obvious customers are banks, insurance companies, and manufacturers. But this list is not all-inclusive; other types of customers are large mail-order houses, airlines with sophisticated reservation systems, government accounting services, aerospace companies doing complex aircraft design, and the like.

The mightiest computers—and, of course, the most expensive—are known as **supercomputers** (Figure 2-7b). Supercomputers process *billions* of instructions per second, making them 40,000 to 50,000 times faster than a personal computer. Most people do not have a direct need for the speed and power of a supercomputer. In fact, supercomputer customers were an exclusive group for many years: agencies of the federal government. The federal government uses supercomputers for tasks that require mammoth data manipulation, such as worldwide weather forecasting, oil exploration, and weapons research.

But now supercomputers are moving toward the mainstream, for activities as varied as creating special effects for movies and analyzing muscle structures. The increasing application of supercomputers is reflected in impressive supercomputer sales: over 25% annual growth in the past ten years. Supercomputers can also produce super graphics (Figure 2-8).

Minicomputers

The next step down from mainframe computers are **minicomputers** (Figure 2-7c). Minicomputers are generally slower and have less storage capacity than mainframes, and are less costly. When minicomputers first appeared on the market, their lower price fell within the range of many small businesses, greatly expanding the potential computer market.

Minicomputers were originally intended to be small and serve some special purpose. However, in a fairly short time, they became more powerful and more versatile, and the line between minicomputer and mainframe has blurred. In fact, the appellation *mini* no longer seems to fit very well. The term **supermini** has been coined to describe minis at the top of the size/price scale. Minicomputers are widely used by retail businesses, colleges, and state and city agencies. However, the minicomputer market is diminishing somewhat as buyers choose a group of less expensive microcomputers.

Microcomputers

The smallest computers, such as desktop and personal or home computers, are called **microcomputers** (Figure 2-7d). For many years, the computer industry was on a quest for the next biggest computer. The search was always for more power and greater capacity. Prognosticators who timidly suggested a niche for a smaller computer were subject to ridicule by people who, as it turned out, could not have been more wrong. Now, for a few hundred dollars, anyone can have a small computer. (Most people, how-

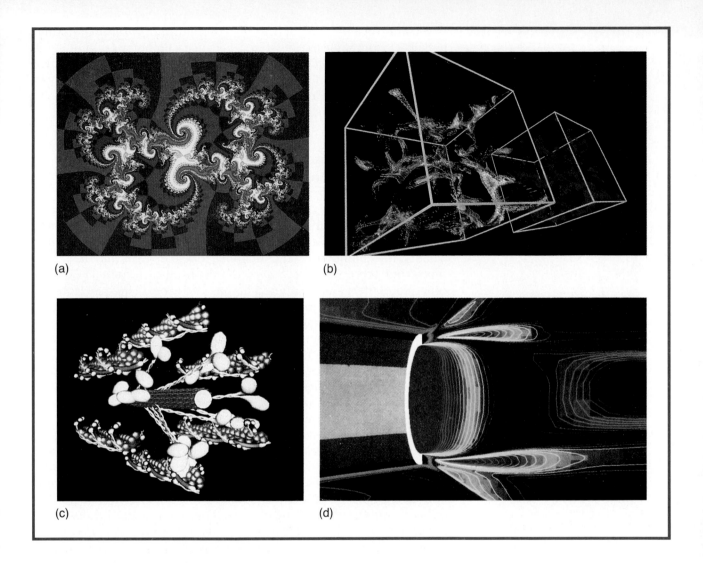

(a)   (b)   (c)   (d)

Figure 2-8   Super supercomputers.
These graphics represent (a) mathematical shapes, (b) a simulation of the evolution of the universe, (c) human muscle, and (d) density flow patterns of a jet engine.

ever, are more likely to choose a computer that costs a few *thousand* dollars.)

Just as the boom in minicomputers led to the development of superminis, the success of microcomputers paved the way for another classification of computers—**supermicros,** or **workstations.** These upper-end machines, used by workers such as engineers, scientists, and financial traders, are small enough to fit on a desktop but approach the power of a mainframe. As one computer company executive remarked, "What we've done is put the power and capability of an ocean liner into a speedboat."

The subject of microcomputers is so important that we will return to them again and again, in every chapter. In addition, we include an entire chapter on microcomputers (Chapter 11) and four chapters on microcomputer software (Chapters 12 through 15). You will probably also be interested in the Buyer's Guide, which describes how to buy a microcomputer.

Unfortunately, the definitions of *mainframe, minicomputer,* and *microcomputer* are not fixed because computer technology is changing so rapidly. One observer noted that looking at these three different types of computers is like trying to take a picture of three melting ice cubes. However, since these categories are still used throughout the industry, they are worth keeping in mind.

7 Data Communications: Processing Here or There

Originally, computer hardware was all kept in one place; that is, it was **centralized** in one room. Although this is still sometimes the case, more and more computer systems are **decentralized.** That is, the computer itself and some storage devices may be in one place, but the devices to access the computer—terminals or even other computers—are scattered among the users. These devices are usually connected to the computer by telephone lines. For instance, the computer and storage that has the information on your checking account may be located in the bank's headquarters, but the terminals are located in branch banks all over town so a teller anywhere can find out what your balance is. The subject of decentralization is intimately tied to **data communications,** the process of exchanging data over communications facilities. The topic of data communications is so important that we will study it in detail in Chapter 6.

Some systems decentralize processing as well, placing computers and storage devices in dispersed locations. This arrangement is known as **distributed data processing** because even the processing is distributed. There are several ways to configure the hardware; one common arrangement is to place small computers in local offices but still do some processing on a larger computer at the headquarters office. For example, an insurance company headquartered in Denver with branches throughout the country might process payments and claims through minicomputers in local offices. However, summary data could be sent regularly by each office for processing by the mainframe computer in Denver (Figure 2-9).

Many organizations find that their needs are best served by a **network** of microcomputers, that is, microcomputers that are hooked together so that users can communicate through them. Users can operate their microcomputers independently or in cooperation with other computers—micros, minis, or mainframes—to exchange data and share resources. The concept of connecting microcomputers and mainframe computers is referred to as the **micro-to-mainframe link.** This powerful idea is revolutionizing the way businesses operate. Users are able to obtain data directly from the mainframe computer and immediately analyze it on their own microcomputers. People have quick access to more information, which leads to better decision making. This important topic will be discussed further in Chapter 6.

DISCUSSION QUESTION
Why is it useful to decentralize a computer system?

LECTURE HINT
Some computer networks are world wide, and involve many mainframes. Suppose you are running a program requiring heavy computation with very little data, at noon in California. You find the local mainframe is slow because of so many users. You can transfer your program to a similar computer in France, where there are few users because of the time change. Your results will be obtained quickly.

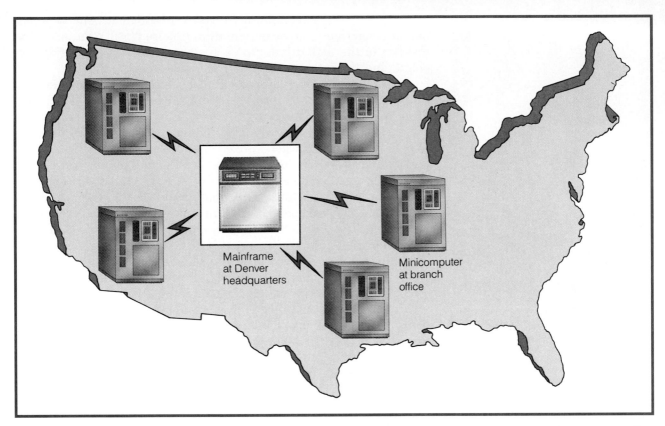

TRANSPARENCY ACETATE #2C
Figure #2-9

Figure 2-9   Distributed data processing system. Branch offices of an insurance company have their own computers for local processing, but can tie in to the mainframe computer in the headquarters office in Denver.

7 Software: Telling the Machine What to Do

In the past, when people thought about computers, they thought about machines. The tapping on the keyboard, the clacking of the printers, the rumble of whirling disk drives, the changing flashes of color on a computer screen—these are the attention getters. However, it is really the software—the planned, step-by-step instructions required to turn data into information—that makes a computer useful.

7 Software for Your Personal Computer

As we have already noted, you can buy packaged software that is ready for use. Packaged software for personal computers often comes in a box as colorful as a Monopoly game. Inside the box

Figure 2-10 Packaged software. The WordPerfect diskette, which will be inserted into the personal computer, has the software on it. Other diskettes contain related information, such as a spelling checker and a thesaurus. The instruction manual, or documentation, gives instructions for using the software.

you will find a diskette holding the software and an instruction manual, also referred to as **documentation** (Figure 2-10). You insert the diskette in the disk drive, type a specified instruction on the keyboard, and the software begins to run on the computer.

Most personal computer software is planned to be user friendly. The term **user friendly** has become a cliché, but it still conveys meaning; it usually means that the software is easy for a novice to use, or at least that it can be used with a minimum of training. Although software can be generalized enough to be mass marketed, it is possible to customize its use by personalizing the data you give it.

Let us consider an example. A software package called Personal Fitness is advertised thus: *"Talk about easy to use! Each day you'll spend less time at the keyboard than you do on a coffee break. With no computer jargon . . . just simple, sensible English."* Well. Sounds easy enough. When you insert the diskette and issue the startup command, questions appear on the screen. You type responses on the keyboard, and the responses also show on the screen, so that the dialogue between you and the computer appears in front of you.

If you indicate that this is the first time you have used the software, you will be asked initial questions about your age, height, weight, and so forth (Figure 2-11). The Personal Fitness program will analyze this data and then make recommendations for a "new and healthier lifestyle." As you continue to use the software over time, you will report (that is, key in) items such as caloric intake or pulse rate or miles walked. The software will produce charts and graphs showing weight loss, pulse pattern, and the like to help you monitor your progress. Note the input-process-output here. The *input data* to the program are your own habits (in number form) and continuing statistics. The *processing* is the analysis of that data by the software. The *output* is the set of recommendations and the charts and graphs.

It is a short step, conceptually, from packaged software for your personal use to packaged software for office use. For example, there are many software packages for accounts payable—software to help businesses pay their bills. The principles are the same. You provide input data such as invoice number, vendor name, and amount owed. The computer processes this data to produce output in the form of computer-generated checks and various reports to help you track expenses.

Let us consider some of the popular types of business software for microcomputers.

7 Some Problem-Solving Software

The collective set of business problems is limited, and the number of ways to solve these problems is limited too. Thus the problems and the software solutions fall, for the most part, into just a few categories. These categories can be found in most business environments. We begin with the categories often called, because of their widespread use, the Big Five: **word processing, spreadsheets, data-**

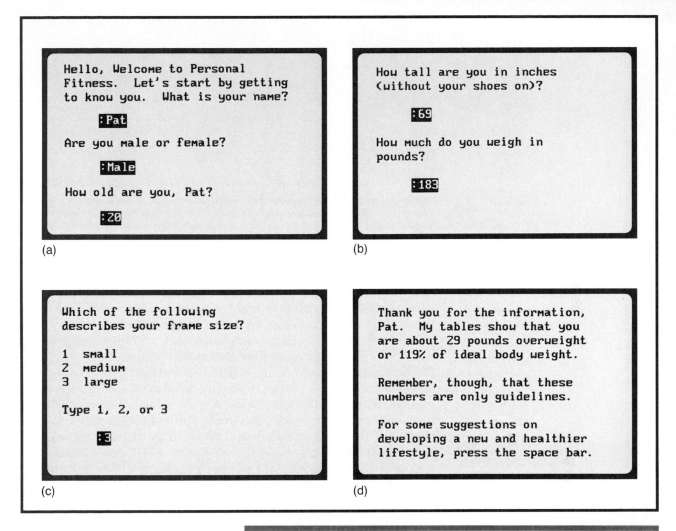

Figure 2-11 **Personal Fitness software screens.** These screens show the dialogue between computer and user.

base management, graphics, and communications. These are followed by **desktop publishing,** an important but somewhat less universal category. We shall present a brief description of each category.

Word Processing

The most widely used microcomputer software is **word processing** software. This software lets you create, edit, format, store, and print text. In this definition, the word that makes word processing different from plain typing is "store." Since you can store the memo or document you type on disk, you can retrieve it another time, change it, reprint it, or do whatever you like with it. The time-saving factor is that the unchanged parts of the saved document do not need to be retyped, and the whole thing can be reprinted as if new.

DISCUSSION QUESTION
Which type of business software package is the most widely used? What are its uses beyond the business environment?

EXPENSES	JAN. - MAR.	APR. - JUN.	JUL. - SEPT.	OCT. - DEC.	TOTAL
RENT	425.00	425.00	425.00	425.00	1700.00
PHONE	22.50	31.25	17.00	35.75	106.50
CLOTHES	110.00	135.00	156.00	91.00	492.00
FOOD	280.00	250.00	250.00	300.00	1080.00
HEAT	80.00	50.00	24.00	95.00	249.00
ELECTRICITY	35.75	40.50	45.00	36.50	157.75
WATER	10.00	11.00	11.00	10.50	42.50
CAR INSURANCE	75.00	75.00	75.00	75.00	300.00
ENTERTAINMENT	150.00	125.00	140.00	175.00	590.00
TOTAL	1188.25	1142.75	1143.00	1243.75	4717.75

Figure 2-12   A simple expense spreadsheet. This expense sheet is a typical spreadsheet of rows and columns. Note the calculations needed to generate the values in the rightmost column and the bottom row.

Spreadsheets

Used to organize business data, a **spreadsheet** is a worksheet divided into columns and rows. For example, the simple expense spreadsheet in Figure 2-12 shows time periods (quarters of the year) as columns and various categories (rent, phone, and so forth) as rows. Notice that figures in the rightmost column and in the last row are the result of calculations. Manual spreadsheets have been used as business tools for centuries. But a spreadsheet can be tedious to prepare, and when there are changes, a considerable amount of work may need to be redone. An **electronic spreadsheet** is still a spreadsheet, but the computer does the work. In particular, spreadsheet software automatically recalculates the results when a number is changed. This capability lets businesspeople try different combinations of numbers and obtain the results quickly. This ability to ask "What if . . . ?" helps businesspeople make better, faster decisions.

Database Management

Software used for **database management**—the management of a collection of interrelated files—handles data in several ways. The software can store data, update it, manipulate it, and report it in a variety of forms. By the time the data is in the reporting stage—given to a user in a useful form—it has become information. A concert promoter, for example, can store and change data about upcoming concert dates, seating, ticket prices, and sales. After this is done, the promoter can use the software to retrieve information such as the number of tickets sold in each price range or the percentage of tickets sold the day before the concert. Database software can be useful for anyone who must keep track of a large amount of information.

Graphics

It might seem wasteful to show businesspeople **graphics** when it would be less expensive to use the numbers in standard computer printouts. However, graphics, maps, and charts can help

THE COMPUTER AS A TOOL

When most people think of tools, they think of hand tools such as hammers and saws, or perhaps lug wrenches and screwdrivers. But think of a tool in a broader sense, as anything used to do a job. This expands the horizon to include stethoscopes, baseball bats, kettles, typewriters, and—yes—computers.

The computer is a sophisticated tool, but a tool nonetheless. But who would use such a tool? Carrying our analogy further, would you buy a stethoscope if you had no medical plans, or a baseball bat if you had no intention of hitting a ball? Probably not. You probably would not purchase a computer either, or learn how to use it, unless you had some use in mind. Businesspeople are not interested in buying useless tools. Instead, they have a plan in mind. Businesspeople purchase computers because they have a problem—or perhaps a set of problems—to solve.

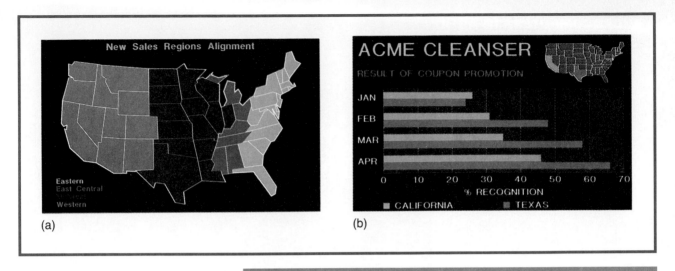

Figure 2-13 Business graphics. These colorful computer-generated graphics can help people compare data and spot trends.

people compare data and spot trends more easily, and make decisions more quickly (Figure 2-13). Three pages of confusion can be made into a chart that anyone can pick up and understand.

Communications

We have already described data communications in a general way. From the viewpoint of a worker with a personal computer, data communications mean—in simple terms—that he or she can hook a phone up to the computer and get at data stored in someone else's computer in another location.

Desktop Publishing

Since publishing in one form or another typically consumes up to 10% of a company's gross revenues, **desktop publishing** has been given a warm welcome by business. The two key elements of desktop publishing are desktop publishing software and high-quality printers. Desktop publishing packages let businesses use a computer to produce printed materials that combine graphics with text. The resulting professional-looking newsletters, reports, and brochures can improve communication and help organizations make a better impression on the outside world.

We have looked at packaged software here, but software can also be written for a specific client. In fact, not so long ago, most businesses had software written exclusively for them. That is still the case in many organizations, who employ their own staff of computer professionals for that purpose. Software, whether packaged or not, can be used by a person who has no training whatever in programming. But let us look a bit more closely at what programming entails.

LECTURE HINT
There are many other desirable software package types. Some are: drawing, drafting, circuit design, statistics, equation solvers, and computer-assisted instruction.

MICROCOMPUTERS IN ACTION

Teacher, Textbook, Computer

Although it seems silly today, in the 1950s some people worried that television sets would replace classroom teachers. Today the same thing is being said about computers. A computer is not a replacement for a teacher or even a textbook. However, a computer is a very effective supplement for lectures and textbooks. Consider some of the ways computers are being used in colleges today.

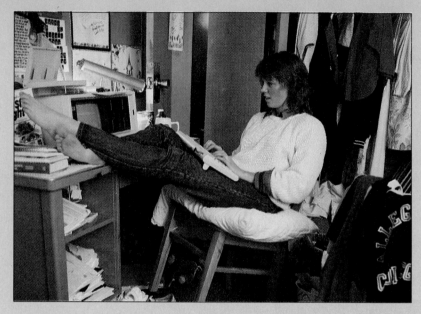

- At the University of Pennsylvania, students of German are studying a ''computer-video'' version of the Gunter Grass novel *The Tin Drum*. As students watch a dramatization of the book on the screen, they can switch to a computer file containing relevant information, such as a map of Germany.
- At Indiana University, physiology students experiment with computer software to learn how the power exerted by a muscle varies with the muscle's length and the weight of the load it must lift.
- Students of French history at Stanford use a faculty-written program, A Would-Be Gentleman, to study life in the time of Louis XIV. The software puts the student in seventeenth-

century France, in the role of a landowner trying to increase wealth and status by making the proper investments and currying favor with the proper people.
- At Drexel University, access to a Macintosh is a condition of enrollment. Ninety-eight percent of the students own Macs and the university provides Macs for those who do not. Drexel has thoroughly integrated computers into the cur-

riculum. For instance, chemistry students learn molecular structure by seeing different arrangements of atoms on the computer screen.

The integration of computers into college curriculums has had a positive effect on student morale. Studies indicate that as students become more adept at using computers, they tend to feel more optimistic about the future.

7 What Programmers Do

Programs—software—can be written in a variety of programming languages. Most programming languages in common use today are English-like in appearance, and there are very definite rules for using them. Some languages are used specifically for business or scientific applications. BASIC was designed for beginners but has become popular for use on mini- and microcomputers. (BASIC is described in some detail in Appendix A.) Some languages

SOME HELP WITH THE SAT

Each year thousands of students work up a full panic at the thought of taking that test of tests, the Scholastic Aptitude Test, not so fondly known as the SAT. The fortunes of many students, including the college of their choice, ride on the results of the SATs. Small wonder that students seek every mode of assistance. That help has traditionally been in the form of study aids such as special texts and classes.

Now, of course, all that has changed. The most sought-after aid is a computerized preparation course that offers at-home study on your own computer. The system includes diagnostic tests, instructions in the basics of the verbal and math SATs, and plenty of practice tests. Will these computer-tutors raise SAT scores? The jury is still out, but it looks promising.

DISCUSSION QUESTION
Compare the trends for hardware costs with trends for software costs; why are they different?

TEST BANK
Mult. Choice	42-44
T/F	66-68
Matching D	3-4
Fill-in-the-Blank	44-45

are relatively easy to learn and are even used by people whose primary occupation is not programming. We will discuss all the varieties of languages in Chapter 8.

Programmers must understand how to use a programming language so that they can convey the logic of a program to the computer in a form the computer understands. A program is keyed (typed) in line by line on a terminal or microcomputer. The program is then stored in some form of secondary storage, such as disk, from which it can be called into memory for testing and execution. Besides being able to use a programming language, programmers must also understand what the program is supposed to do and design it accordingly, test it to remove errors, and document—write about—what they did.

Because of miniaturization, standardization, and the growing popularity of computers, the cost of hardware is going down. The cost of software, however, depends on whether it is packaged or custom-made. Packaged software prices are going down, partly because of increased competition but mostly because the market is demanding lower prices. The price of custom software, on the other hand, is going up for a variety of reasons. Unlike hardware, the making of software depends chiefly on labor, and labor costs keep rising. In addition, as the Computer Revolution continues, computers are becoming easier, not harder, for people to use. That is, computers are becoming accessible to more people, and less training is required to use them. But it takes complicated software to give uncomplicated access to the computer—another reason why software costs are going up. For those interested in careers in the computer field, then, we suggest that the future lies in understanding software.

7 Processing Operations: College Bound

There are several operations common to the processing of data. With a computer you can:

- Input
- Inquire
- Store
- Sort
- Update
- Compute
- Output
- Classify
- Summarize
- Retrieve

The best way to explain these is to use an example. Figure 2-14 shows what happens when Karen Burner fills out two forms for college—the application form, which gets her name and personal data on file, and the registration form for classes for a particular semester. The following steps take place, corresponding to the processing operations we just listed.

① **Input.** Data is entered into the computer system for processing. In our example Karen's college application form is input by a clerk into the computer system.

② **Inquire.** A computer user usually inquires about data in a mainframe computer through a computer terminal. Here the

LECTURE ACTIVITY
Ask students to describe how
they registered for this course.

registration clerk makes an inquiry to find out if there is room in the classes Karen has said she wants to take, and the computer replies that there is. (And now more input takes place as Karen's registration data—the classes she signed up for—is entered into the system.)

③ **Store.** Data that has been processed is retained for future reference. Karen's application and registration data are stored in the student file on disk. Her registration data is also stored in the class file; these records are used by the instructors.

④ **Sort.** To sort means to arrange data into a particular sequence. For instance, student names are sorted by the computer into alphabetical order within a class. For CIS 110, "Computer Literacy," Burner, Karen, is second on the class roster.

⑤ **Update.** As new data is obtained, files must be brought up to date. For instance, the preceding steps took place at the start of the school semester. At the end of the semester, when Karen's instructor turns in a grade form, Karen's record is updated with new data: She received an "A" in CIS 110.

⑥ **Compute.** Addition, subtraction, multiplication, and division are arithmetic operations—computations that the computer can perform. In this example the computer uses these arithmetic operations to calculate Karen's grade-point average: 4.0.

⑦ **Output.** The computer produces the processing result in usable form. Karen's list of grades is printed out and mailed to her home.

⑧ **Classify.** To classify means to categorize data according to characteristics that make it useful. To help college administrators in their planning, the computer program classifies all students enrolled in the college according to age. Like the grade report, the age report and the others mentioned in Figure 2-14 constitute output.

⑨ **Summarize.** To summarize means to reduce data to a more concise, usable form. The computer summarizes the total number of students in the various schools and also gives an overall enrollment total—again, to help administrators in their planning.

⑩ **Retrieve.** Data stored in the system can be retrieved later for use. Here, when Karen decides she wants to transfer from this college to another, the computer is able to retrieve an official transcript showing all her grades and courses. Incidentally, it might seem that there is not much difference between inquiring and retrieving. Normally, however, making an inquiry involves asking (and the computer answering) a brief question on the screen, whereas retrieving usually produces a paper printout.

There are areas of overlap among many of these processing operations. The important point is to note the flow of data through the computer system.

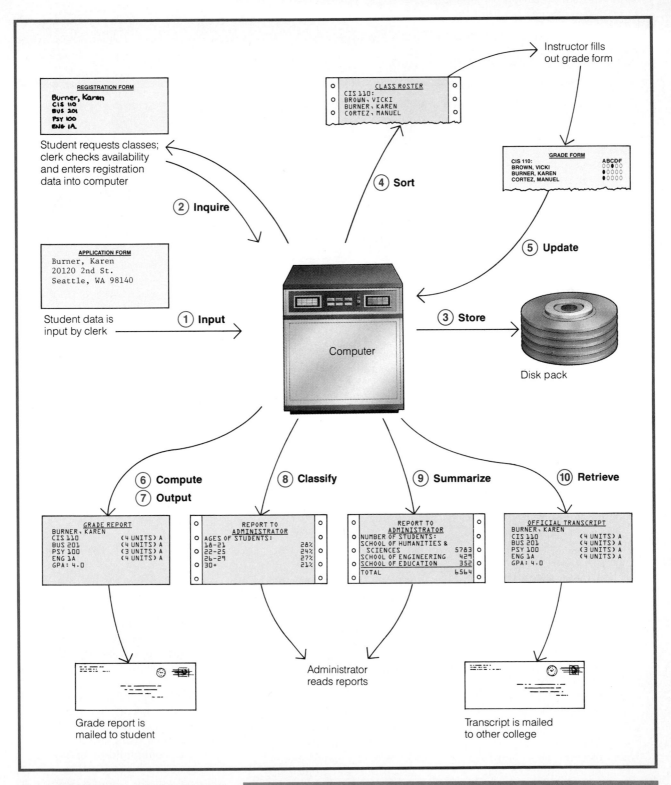

Figure 2-14   Karen Burner goes to college. The processing operations illustrated here are described in the text.

PERSPECTIVES

COMPUTERS AROUND THE WORLD

Computers, of course, are in use worldwide. However, we may lose track of that fact because there is little coverage in the national press. Let us consider some interesting computer applications in Australia, the USSR, France, China, and India.

- The oil spill in Valdez, Alaska, shook the world. Could it happen here? If "here" is Australia, there is at least some good news: The computer is in charge of the cleanup. That is, a computer has been programmed in advance to simulate what is likely to happen, taking into consideration the tides, current, wind speed, and kind and quantity of oil. Crews can telephone for these computer-generated models and use them to plan the cleanup.

- Hackers in the Soviet Union? Yes. Personal computers in the USSR are still rare—one for every several thousand citizens, compared to one for every eight Americans. Home computers are virtually unknown; personal computers are in factories, schools, and military bases. Most Soviet computers lack a disk drive, and diskettes are scarce. But hackers thrive on making do. Encouraged by some moderate commercial success and liberalized trade rules, the Russians are beginning to create software to sell in the Western market.

- In France, they are falling in love with their computers—and also through them. They use a computer terminal to send anonymous messages to some-

Minitel, the French computerized phone directory.

one they have never met. The matchmaking computer system, Minitel, started out as something quite different. Designed in 1978 as the world's first electronic phone directory, Minitel is distributed free to subscribers to provide consumer services 24 hours a day.

- "Made in China" will soon be stamped on computers that will compete in world markets. China may not be the first name to come to mind when discussing worldwide high tech, but consider its offerings thus far. The People's Republic of China has made its own supercomputer, a 100-million-instructions-per-second machine called the "Galaxy." It has its own microcomputers too—IBM compatibles called the "Great Wall" machines.

- When the bank unions in India signed an agreement that cleared the way for the use of computers in banking, it was considered a significant event. Perhaps even greater significance can be attached to the year: This event took place in 1986, approximately 35 years behind bank automation in most Western nations. But India is plunging headlong into the computer age, automating the airlines, the railways, and the steel industry. A major impediment to computer progress is the wretched state of communications systems in India. It is difficult to make even a telephone call, so the immediate prospects of using the phone lines to communicate among computers are not good.

People and Computers

We have talked about hardware, software, and data, but the most important element in a computer system is people. Anyone nervous about a takeover by computers will be relieved to know that computers will never amount to much without people— both the people who help make the system work and the people for whom the work is done.

Computers and You, the User

As we noted earlier, computer users have come to be called just *users,* a nickname that has persisted for years. Whereas once computer users were an elite breed—high-powered Ph.D.s, research-and-development engineers, government planners—today the population of users has broadened considerably. This expanded user base is due partly to user-friendly software for both work and personal use and partly to the availability of small, low-cost computers. There is a strong possibility that all of us will be computer users, but our levels of sophistication may vary.

A novice is a person with no computer training who is just beginning to learn about computers. This user may be a child playing computer games or a student experimenting with educational software. A more sophisticated user is one who uses a personal computer for home finances or as a hobby.

Above this level are those users who, to varying degrees, use the computer for business or professional reasons, although they are not computer professionals themselves. For instance, a person may be trained well enough to make the inquiries required in customer service, banking, or airline reservations. At a slightly higher level, a person may know what data is being entered into the computer and what information being produced would be useful in performing the job at hand.

A more sophisticated user is a person who has written some computer programs, understands computer jargon, and is well equipped to communicate with computer professionals.

Computer People

Another way to think about people and computers is within the context of an organization. Many organizations have a department called **Management Information Systems (MIS)** or **Computing Services** or **Information Services.** This department is made up of people responsible for the computer resources of an organization. Whether the department is within a university, a government bureau, or a corporation, this department may well be the institution's most important asset. Most of the institution's information is

United Way®

FOR THOSE IN NEED

Businesses use computers; everyone knows that. But stretch that point a little further: Everyone who has business applications can make good use of computers. The list of business applications users includes education, government, and—perhaps surprisingly—nonprofit agencies.

But think about it. Agencies certainly have to meet payrolls, keep accounting records, write letters, and so forth. What is more, they usually have smaller budgets than a private business of comparable size; this makes them obvious candidates for the cost savings a computer can provide.

Nonprofit agencies on New York's Long Island have taken this notion a step further. Led by the United Way agency, 60-plus agencies have banded together to form a computer user group. The group exchanges information and provides software training. Their efforts have been so successful that they have received a state grant for further growth and nationwide inquiries about how others can do the same thing.

contained in its computer files: research data, engineering drawings, marketing strategy, accounts receivable, accounts payable, sales information, manufacturing specifications, transportation plans, warehousing data—the list goes on and on. The guardians of this information are the same people who provide service to the users: the computer professionals. Let us touch on the essential personnel required to run computer systems.

Data entry operators prepare data for processing, usually by keying'it in a machine-readable format. **Computer operators** monitor the console, review procedures, and keep peripheral equipment running. **Librarians** catalog the processed disks and tapes and keep them secure.

Computer programmers, as we have noted, design, write, test, and implement the programs that process data on the computer system. **Systems analysts** are knowledgeable in the programming area but have broader responsibilities. They plan and design not just individual programs, but entire computer systems. Systems analysts maintain a working relationship with the users in the organization. Systems analysts work closely with users to plan new systems that will meet the users' needs. The department manager, often called the **chief information officer (CIO)** must understand more than just computer technology. This person must understand the goals and operations of the entire organization.

The End-User Revolution

In this section we have distinguished between "users" and "computer professionals." In the most general sense, the professionals provide the computer system and the users use it. But these two camps are not so distinct; in fact, there is common ground between them. In addition to buying and using packaged software, a growing number of users are becoming savvy about hardware—especially microcomputers—and many are even using user-oriented languages to write their own software. This phenomenon has been called the **end-user revolution.** The fact that many users are taking care of themselves is having a profound effect on the computer industry. We shall return to this theme again in the text as the story unfolds.

The End of the Beginning

In this chapter we have painted the computer industry with a broad brush, touching on hardware, software, data, and people. We now move on to the chapters that explain the information presented in this chapter in more detail, beginning with the central processing unit.

7 Summary and Key terms

- The machines in a computer system are called **hardware.** The **programs,** or step-by-step instructions that run the machines, are called **software.** Software sold in stores, and usually contained in a box or folder, is called **packaged software.** Most packaged software is **applications software,** software that is applied to solve a particular problem. **Computer programmers** write programs for **users** or **end-users,** people who purchase and use computer software.

- A **computer** is a machine that can be programmed to process data (input) into useful information (output). A computer system consists of three main areas of data handling—input, processing, and output—and is backed by a fourth, storage.

- **Input** is data put into the computer. Common **input devices** include a **keyboard;** a **mouse,** which translates movements on a flat surface to actions on the screen; a **wand reader,** which scans special letters and numbers such as those on specially printed price tags in retail stores; and a **bar code reader,** which scans the zebra-striped **bar codes** on store products. The wand reader and bar code reader read data directly from an original document, thus reducing the cost and human error associated with manual input.

- A **terminal** includes an input device, such as a keyboard or wand reader; an **output device,** usually a television-like **screen;** and a connection to the main computer. A screen displays both the input data and the processed information.

- The **processor,** or **central processing unit** (**CPU**), organizes raw **data** into meaningful, useful **information.** It interprets and executes program instructions and communicates with the input, output, and storage devices. **Memory,** or **primary storage,** is associated with the central processing unit but is separate from it. Memory holds the input data before processing and after processing, until the data is released to the output device. The operator can communicate with the computer system through the **console.**

- **Output,** raw data processed into usable information, is usually in the form of words, numbers, and graphics. Users can see output displayed on screens and use **printers** to display output on paper.

- The computer's memory is limited and temporary. Therefore, **secondary storage** is needed, most commonly in the form of magnetic disks and magnetic tape. **Magnetic disks** can be diskettes or hard disks. **Diskettes** may be $5\frac{1}{4}$ inches (**floppy disks**) or $3\frac{1}{2}$ inches in diameter. A **hard disk,** often contained in a **disk pack** holds more data and has faster access than a diskette. Disk data is read by **disk drives. Magnetic tape** comes on reels that are mounted on **tape drives** when the data is to be read by the computer. **Optical disk** technology uses a laser beam to store large volumes of data relatively inexpensively.

- **Peripheral equipment** includes all the input, output, and secondary storage devices attached to a computer. Peripheral equipment may be built into one physical unit, as in many microcomputers, or be contained in separate units, as in many larger computer systems.

- Computers can be loosely categorized according to their capacity for processing data. Large computers called **mainframes** are used by such customers as banks, airlines, and large manufacturers to process very large amounts of data quickly. The most powerful and expensive computers are called **supercomputers. Minicomputers,** which are widely used by colleges and retail businesses, were originally intended to be small but have become increasingly similar to mainframes in capacity. Therefore, the largest and most expensive minicomputers are now called **superminis.** The smallest computers, such as desktop office computers and home computers, are called **microcomputers. Supermicros,** or **workstations,** combine the compactness of a desktop computer with power that almost equals a mainframe's. As computer technology changes, distinctions between types of computers will also change.

- A **centralized** computer system does all processing in one location. In a **decentralized** system, the computer itself and some storage devices are in one place, but the devices to access the computer are somewhere else. Such a system requires **data communications**—the exchange of data over communications facilities. In a **distributed data processing** system, a local office usually uses its own small computer for processing local data but is connected to the larger organization's central computer for other purposes.

- Often organizations use a **network** of microcomputers, which allows users to operate their microcomputers independently or in cooperation with other computers to exchange data and share resources. Microcomputers connected to a mainframe computer form a **micro-to-mainframe link,** in which users can obtain data from the mainframe and analyze it on their own microcomputers. This leads to better decision making.

- Software is accompanied by an instruction manual, also called **documentation.** Software that is easy to use is considered **user friendly.** Software may be packaged for general use or specially written for a specific client.

- Software found in most business environments includes **word processing, electronic spreadsheets, database management, graphics, communications,** and **desktop publishing.**

- To create software, or programs, computer programmers use a variety of programming languages. Complicated programming is necessary to prepare easily usable software. Therefore, while miniaturization and standardization are reducing the cost of hardware, the increased labor necessary to produce user-friendly programs is raising the cost of software.

- The operations common to processing **input** (enter data), **inquire** (ask questions), **store** (retain processed data), **sort** (arrange in a particular sequence), **update** (bring files up to date), **compute** (perform arithmetic calculations), **output** (produce processing results in usable form), **classify** (categorize data), **summarize** (reduce data to concise form), and **retrieve** (request and receive paper printout).

- Computer users range from novices with no training to sophisticated users who can deal with computer professionals.

- People are vital to any computer system. An organization's computer resources department, often called **Management Information Services** (**MIS**) or **Computing Services** or **Information Services,** includes **data entry operators** (who prepare data for processing), **computer operators** (who monitor and run the equipment), **librarians** (who catalog disks and tapes), **computer programmers** (who design, write, test, and implement programs), **systems analysts** (who plan and design entire systems of programs), and a **chief information officer** (who coordinates the MIS department).

- In general, a distinction is made between computer professionals, who provide computer systems, and users, who use the systems. However, in a development called the **end-user revolution,** users have become increasingly knowledgeable about computers and less reliant on computer professionals.

7 Review Questions

1. Define *hardware* and *software.*

2. How do a wand reader and bar code reader differ from a keyboard as input devices?

3. Name two functions of the processor, or central processing unit (CPU).

4. Name three common forms of output and two common output devices.

5. Why is secondary storage necessary? Describe the most common forms of secondary storage.

6. Name and describe the three main types of computers.

7. What is distributed data processing?

8. What is documentation?

9. When people call software user friendly, what do they mean?

10. Name at least three things a computer programmer should be able to do.

11. Explain why the cost of custom software is going up.

12. What is the difference between data and information?

13. Name and define ten common processing operations.

14. State what each of the following computer people do:
    a. data entry operator
    b. computer operator
    c. systems analyst
    d. computer information officer

Discussion Questions

1. Of course, input, processing, output, and storage do not relate only to computers. Consider, for instance, the experience of writing a term paper that involves research. What would be the input? The processing? The output? The storage?

2. Why do you think many large companies prefer decentralized computer systems?

3. How do you think the end-user revolution will affect the computer industry?

PART 2

HARDWARE

You will probably come to see software as the main thrust of the computer industry, but first you must understand hardware, the physical equipment that makes up a computer system. We will begin with the most important part of a computer system—the central processing unit. As you will see, the miniaturized version of this key component—the microprocessor—is fundamental to widespread computer power. As recently as 20 years ago, experts had no idea that computers would be in the hands of everyday people.

In this part we will consider the hardware components of a computer system, a chapter at a time: the central processing unit, input and output devices, secondary storage devices, and data communications. In this part, in addition to taking a closer look at the hardware that goes into a computer system, we will try to suggest the directions hardware will take.

Chapter 3. The Central Processing Unit: Under the Hood

3

The Central Processing Unit

Under the Hood

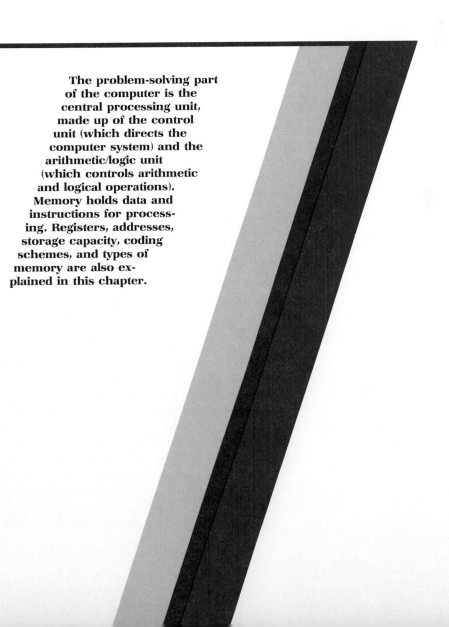

The problem-solving part of the computer is the central processing unit, made up of the control unit (which directs the computer system) and the arithmetic/logic unit (which controls arithmetic and logical operations). Memory holds data and instructions for processing. Registers, addresses, storage capacity, coding schemes, and types of memory are also explained in this chapter.

Have you ever wondered what is inside a computer? How does a computer work, anyway? In this chapter we will take a peek inside the computer to look at how it operates. You may be thinking that you do not really need to know how a computer works, but there are rewards for the computer user who chooses to dig a little deeper. For one thing, knowledge of how the computer works can enhance your use of the computer. For another, there is the satisfaction of knowing what is going on inside the "mysterious" machine you use. Finally, familiarity with the subject matter in this chapter could help you make more informed choices about selecting options for a new computer system.

Let us begin by seeing how the central processing unit works to change raw data into information. This is a complex process, which we have tried to simplify here. Even so, you will find this one of the more technical chapters, with a number of new terms. Once you get beyond this point, however, the going should be easier.

7 The Central Processing Unit

The central processing unit is the part of the computer whose operations we cannot see. The human connection is the data input and the information output, but the controlling center of the computer is in between. The **central processing unit** (**CPU**) is a highly complex, extensive set of electrical circuitry that executes stored program instructions. As Figure 3-1 shows, it consists of two parts:

■ The control unit

■ The arithmetic/logic unit

Before we discuss the control unit and the arithmetic/logic unit in detail, we need to briefly consider the kinds of data storage associated with the computer and explain their relationship to the CPU. Computers actually use two types of storage components: primary storage and secondary storage. The CPU interacts closely with **primary storage,** or **memory,** referring to it for both instructions and data. For this reason memory will be discussed with the CPU in this chapter. Technically, however, memory is not part of the CPU.

Memory holds data only temporarily, at the time the computer is executing your program. **Secondary storage** holds data that is permanent or semi-permanent on some external magnetic or optical medium. The diskettes that you have seen with personal computers are an example of secondary storage. Since the physical attributes of secondary storage devices are related to the way data is organized on them, we will discuss secondary storage and data organization together in Chapter 5.

Now, let us consider the components of the central processing unit.

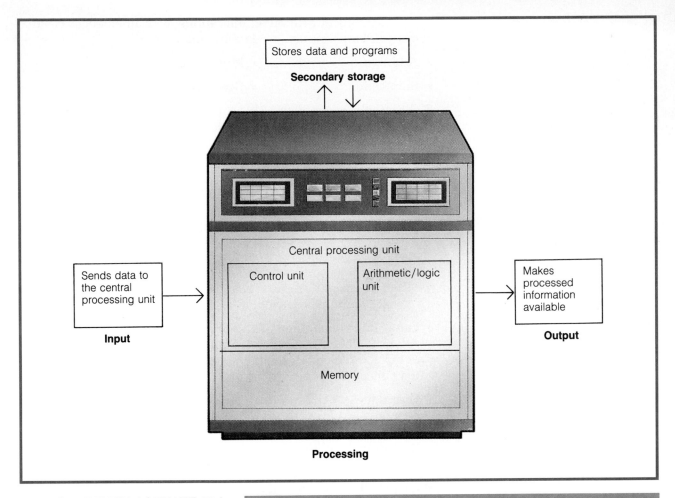

Stores data and programs

Secondary storage

Central processing unit

Sends data to the central processing unit

Input

Control unit

Arithmetic/logic unit

Makes processed information available

Output

Memory

Processing

TRANSPARENCY ACETATE #3A
Figure #3-1

Figure 3-1 The central processing unit. The two parts of the CPU are the control unit and the arithmetic/logic unit. Memory holds data and instructions temporarily at the time the program is being executed. The CPU interacts closely with memory, referring to it for both instructions and data.

The Control Unit

The **control unit** contains circuitry that, with electrical signals, directs and coordinates the entire computer system in carrying out, or executing, stored program instructions. Like an orchestra leader, the control unit does not execute the instructions itself; rather, it directs other parts of the system to do so. The control unit must communicate with both the arithmetic/logic unit and memory.

The Arithmetic/Logic Unit

The **arithmetic/logic unit** (ALU) contains the electronic circuitry that executes all arithmetic and logical operations.

Four kinds of **arithmetic operations,** or mathematical calculations, can be performed on data by this unit:

- Addition
- Subtraction
- Multiplication
- Division

To be strictly accurate, the ALU can only add and multiply; the subtraction and division operations are actually complements of addition and multiplication, respectively. However, for all practical purposes, we can think of the ALU as being capable of these four basic arithmetic operations.

Logical operations are usually comparing operations. The arithmetic/logic unit is able to compare numbers, letters, or special characters and take alternative courses of action. This is a very important capability. It is by comparing that a computer is able to tell, for instance, whether there are unfilled seats on airplanes, whether charge-card customers have exceeded their credit limits, and whether one candidate for Congress has more votes than another.

There are three basic comparing operations:

- **Equal to (=) condition.** The arithmetic/logic unit compares two values to determine if they are equal. For example: If the number of tickets sold *equals* the number of seats in the auditorium, then the concert is declared sold out.

- **Less than (<) condition.** In this logical operation the computer compares values to determine if one is less than another. For example: If the number of speeding tickets on a driver's record is *less than* three, then insurance rates are $425; otherwise, the rates are $500.

- **Greater than (>) condition.** A comparison that determines if one value is greater than another. For instance: If the hours a person worked this week are *greater than* 40, then multiply every extra hour by $1\frac{1}{2}$ times the usual hourly wage to compute overtime pay.

These three comparing operations may be combined to form a total of six commonly used operations: equal to, less than, greater than, less than or equal to, greater than or equal to, and less than or greater than. Note that less than or greater than is the same as not equal to.

7 Registers: Temporary Storage Areas

Registers are temporary storage areas for instructions or data. Registers are associated with the CPU, not memory. They are special additional storage locations whose advantage is speed. They can operate very rapidly in accepting, holding, and transferring instructions or data or in performing arithmetic or logical comparisons—all under the direction of the control unit of the CPU. In other words, they are temporary storage areas that assist transfers and arithmetic/logical operations.

LECTURE HINT
Many minicomputers before 1970 had only one arithmetic operation, namely addition; subtraction, multiplication and division were done by software. But virtually all 16-bit and 32-bit computers now have all four arithmetic operations, plus many logical operations. In addition to comparisons, the bigger computers also have instructions for zeroing; for converting data from one type to another; for bit manipulation to process AND, OR, NOT commands used in high level languages, plus many more instructions.

Many machines assign special roles to certain registers, including:

- An **accumulator,** which collects the results of computations.

- A **storage register,** which temporarily holds data taken from or about to be sent to memory.

- An **address register,** which tells where a given instruction or piece of data is stored in memory. Each storage location in memory is identified by an **address,** just as each apartment in an apartment building is identified by an address.

- A **general-purpose register,** which is used for several functions—arithmetic and addressing purposes, for example.

Consider registers in the context of the operation of the entire machine. Registers hold data *immediately* related to the operation being executed. Memory is used to store data that will be used in the *near future.* Secondary storage holds data that may be needed *later* in the same program execution or perhaps at some more remote time in the future. Let us look at a payroll program, for example, as the computer calculates the salary of an employee. As the multiplication of hours worked by rate of pay is about to take place, these two figures are ready in their respective registers. Other data related to the salary calculation—overtime hours, bonuses, deductions, and so forth—is waiting nearby in memory. The data for other employees is available on secondary storage. As the computer continues executing the payroll program, the data for the next employee is brought from secondary storage into memory and eventually into the registers as the calculations for that employee are ready to begin.

TEST BANK
Mult. Choice   9-10
T/F   15-18
Fill-in-the-Blank   10-12

LECTURE HINT
There are many kinds of memory. The earliest computers stored data on mechanical relays, capacitors or tiny iron magnetic rings called core. Most computers now use semiconductor memory.

7 Memory

Memory is also known as **primary storage, primary memory, main storage, internal storage,** and **main memory**—all these terms are used interchangeably by people in computer circles. Memory is the part of the computer that holds data and instructions for processing. Although closely associated with the central processing unit, technically, memory is separate from it. Memory is used only temporarily—it holds your program and data only as long as your program is in operation. For three reasons, it is not feasible to keep your program and data in memory when your program is not running:

- Most types of memory keep data only while the computer is turned on—data is destroyed when the machine is turned off.

- If your computer is a shared one, other people will be using the computer and will need the memory space.

- There may not be room in memory to hold your processed data.

Data and instructions from an input device are put into memory by the control unit. Data is then sent from memory to the arithmetic/logic unit, where an arithmetic operation or logical operation is performed. After being processed the information is sent to memory, where it is held until it is ready to be released to an output unit.

The chief characteristic of memory is that it allows very fast access to data and instructions in any location in it. We will discuss the physical components of memory—memory chips—in a later section.

7 How the CPU Executes Program Instructions

Let us examine the way the central processing unit, in association with memory, executes a computer program. We will be looking at how just one instruction in the program is executed. In fact, most computers today can execute only one instruction at a time. However, they execute that instruction very quickly. Even microcomputers can execute an instruction in one-thousandth of a second, whereas those speed demons known as supercomputers can execute an instruction in almost one-billionth of a second.

Figure 3-2 The machine cycle.
Program instructions and data are brought into memory from an external device, either an input device or secondary storage. The machine cycle executes instructions, one at a time, as described in the text.

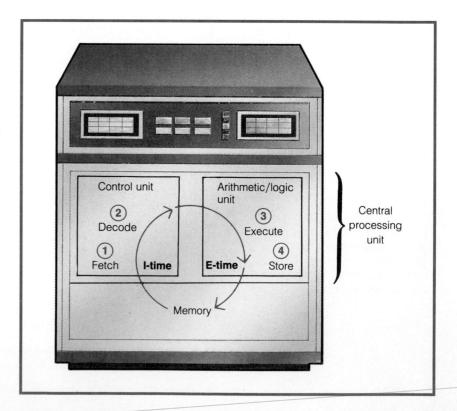

LECTURE HINT
One way to categorize computers is by the maximum number of data (addresses or registers) they can handle in one instruction. Suppose we want to add 5 and 7. In a one-address computer, we must first copy the 5 into the accumulator with one instruction, add the 7 using the next instruction, and then store the result using the third instruction. In a three-address computer, all of this can be done in one instruction.

A single machine instruction may consist of many sub-instructions (called microcodes), each taking a clock pulse to execute.

TRANSPARENCY ACETATE #3C
Figure #3-3

Figure 3-3   The machine cycle in action.   A set of program instructions has been planned to find the average of five test scores. To do this, the five scores must be totaled, then divided by 5. One way to proceed is to set the total to 0 to begin with and then add each of the five numbers, one at a time, to the total. Suppose the scores are 88, 76, 91, 83, and 87. In this figure we have already zeroed the total and added 88 to it. It is time to add the next number, 76, to the total. The instruction to do so would look something like this:

    ADD NEXT NUMBER TO TOTAL

Now follow the steps in the machine cycle. ① The control unit fetches the instruction from memory. ② The control unit decodes the instruction. It sees that addition must take place and gives instructions for the next number (76) to be placed in a storage register for this purpose. The total so far (88) is already in an accumulator register. ③ The ALU does the addition, increasing the total to 164. ④ In this case the new total is stored in the accumulator register instead of memory, since more numbers still need to be added to it. When the new total (164) is placed in the accumulator register, it erases the old total (88).

Before an instruction can be executed, program instructions and data must be placed into memory from an input device or a secondary storage device. As Figure 3-2 shows, the central processing unit then performs the following four steps for each instruction:

①   The control unit fetches (gets) the instruction from memory.

②   The control unit decodes the instruction (decides what it means) and gives instructions for necessary data to be moved from memory to the arithmetic/logic unit. These first two steps are called instruction time, or **I-time.**

③   The arithmetic/logic unit executes arithmetic and logic instructions. That is, the ALU is given control and performs the actual operation on the data.

④   The result of this operation is stored in memory or a register. Steps 3 and 4 are called execution time, or **E-time.**

After the appropriate instructions are executed, the control unit directs memory to release the results to an output device or a secondary storage device. The combination of I-time and E-time is called the **machine cycle.** Figure 3-3 shows an instruction going through the machine cycle.

Each CPU has an internal **clock,** which produces pulses at a fixed rate to synchronize all computer operations. A single machine-cycle instruction may be made up of a substantial number of subinstructions, each of which must take at least one clock cycle. These

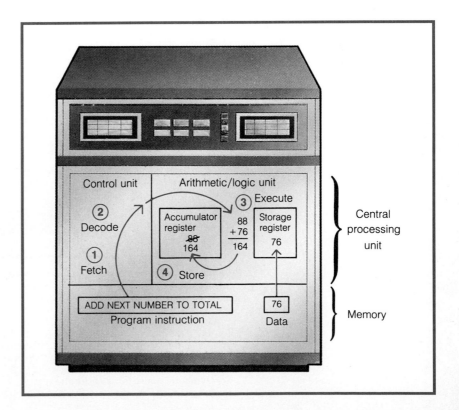

subinstructions are controlled by the **microcode.** Microcode instructions are executed directly by the computer's electronic circuits. The microcode instructions are permanently set inside the control unit; they cannot be altered. Programmers and users do not need to be concerned with microcode, even though the programmer's instructions actually invoke the microcode instructions. Neither the programmer nor user need be aware of them.

7 Storage Locations and Addresses: How the Control Unit Finds Instructions and Data

It is one thing to have instructions and data somewhere in memory and quite another for the control unit to be able to find them. How does it do this?

The location in memory for each instruction and each piece of data is identified by an **address.** That is, each location has an address number, like the mailboxes in front of an apartment house or numbers on bank safe-deposit boxes. And, like the mailbox numbers, the address numbers of the locations remain the same, but the contents (data and instructions) of the locations may change. That is, new data or new instructions may be placed in the locations when the old data or instructions no longer need to be stored in memory.

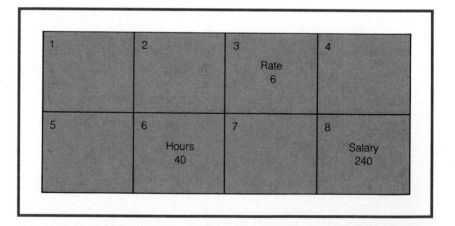

Figure 3-4   Addresses like mailboxes.   The addresses of memory locations are like the identifying numbers on apartment-house mailboxes. Suppose we want to compute someone's salary as the number of hours multiplied by rate of pay. Rate ($6) goes in memory location 3, hours (40) in location 6, and the computed salary ($6 × 40 hours, or $240) in location 8. Thus, *addresses* are 3, 6, and 8, but *contents* are $6, 40 hours, and $240. Note that the program *instructions* are to multiply the contents of location 3 by the contents of location 6 and move the result to location 8. (A computer language used by a programmer would use some kind of symbolic name for each location, such as R for Rate or Pay-Rate instead of the number 3.) The *data* are the actual contents—what is stored in each location.

Figure 3-4 shows how a program manipulates data in memory. When a payroll program is written, for example, it may give instructions to put the rate of pay in location 3 and the number of hours worked in location 6. To compute the employee's salary, then, instructions are given to multiply the data in location 3 by the data in location 6 and move the result to location 8. The choice of locations is arbitrary—any locations that are not already spoken for in the program can be used. Programmers using programming languages, however, do not have to worry about the actual address numbers—each data address is referred to by a name, called a symbolic address. In this example symbolic address names are *Rate* and *Hours*.

7 Data Representation: On/Off

We are accustomed to thinking of computers as complex mechanisms, but the fact is that these machines basically know only two things: on and off. This on/off, yes/no, two-state system is called a **binary system.** Using the two states—which can be represented by electricity turned on or off—the computer can construct sophisticated ways of representing data.

Let us look at one way the two states can be used to represent data. Whereas the decimal number system has a base of 10 (with the digits 0, 1, 2, 3, 4, 5, 6, 7, 8, and 9), the binary system has a base of 2. This means it contains only two digits, 0 and 1, which correspond to the two states off and on. Combinations of 0s and 1s are used to represent larger numbers.

7 Bits, Bytes, and Words

Each 0 or 1 in the binary system is called a **bit** (for *binary digit*). The bit is the basic unit for storing data in computer memory—0 means off, 1 means on.

Since single bits by themselves cannot store all the numbers, letters, and special characters (such as $ and ?) that must be processed by a computer, the bits are put together in a group called a **byte** (pronounced "bite"). There are usually 8 bits in a byte (Figure 3-5). Each byte usually represents one character of data—a letter, digit, or special character.

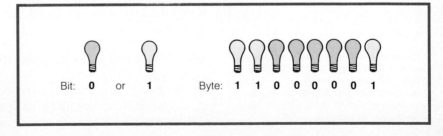

Bit: **0** or **1**   Byte: **1 1 0 0 0 0 0 1**

BINARY EQUIVALENT OF DECIMAL NUMBERS 0–15

Decimal	Binary
0	0000
1	0001
2	0010
3	0011
4	0100
5	0101
6	0110
7	0111
8	1000
9	1001
10	1010
11	1011
12	1100
13	1101
14	1110
15	1111

TRANSPARENCY ACETATE #3E
Binary number system

LECTURE ACTIVITY
Ask the class to add two positive binary numbers. Can they formulate rules for doing this?

Figure 3-5   Bit as light bulb. A light bulb operates as a binary digit (bit), with off representing 0 and on representing 1. Light bulbs, of course, are not used in computers, but vacuum tubes, transistors, silicon chips, or anything else that can conduct an electrical signal can be used. These eight on and off bulbs represent 1 byte.

TRANSPARENCY ACETATE #3D
Figure #3-5

Character	EBCDIC	ASCII
A	1100 0001	100 0001
B	1100 0010	100 0010
C	1100 0011	100 0011
D	1100 0100	100 0100
E	1100 0101	100 0101
F	1100 0110	100 0110
G	1100 0111	100 0111
H	1100 1000	100 1000
I	1100 1001	100 1001
J	1101 0001	100 1010
K	1101 0010	100 1011
L	1101 0011	100 1100
M	1101 0100	100 1101
N	1101 0101	100 1110
O	1101 0110	100 1111
P	1101 0111	101 0000
Q	1101 1000	101 0001
R	1101 1001	101 0010
S	1110 0010	101 0011
T	1110 0011	101 0100
U	1110 0100	101 0101
V	1110 0101	101 0110
W	1110 0110	101 0111
X	1110 0111	101 1000
Y	1110 1000	101 1001
Z	1110 1001	101 1010
0	1111 0000	011 0000
1	1111 0001	011 0001
2	1111 0010	011 0010
3	1111 0011	011 0011
4	1111 0100	011 0100
5	1111 0101	011 0101
6	1111 0110	011 0110
7	1111 0111	011 0111
8	1111 1000	011 1000
9	1111 1001	011 1001

Figure 3-6   The EBCDIC and ASCII codes. Shown are binary representations for letters and numbers. The binary representation is in two columns to improve readability.

Computer manufacturers express the capacity of memory in terms of the number of bytes it can hold. The number of bytes is expressed as **kilobytes.** *Kilo*, abbreviated as *K*, represents 2 to the tenth power (2^{10}), or 1024. (Sometimes K is used casually to mean 1000, as in "I earned $30K last year.") A kilobyte is K bytes—that is, 1024 bytes. Kilobyte is abbreviated **KB** or, simply, **K.** Thus, the memory of a 640K computer can store 640 × 1024, or 655,360 bytes. Memory capacity may also be expressed using *M*, which stands for *mega* (1024 × 1024). One **megabyte,** abbreviated **MB,** means, roughly, one million bytes. Recently, some large computers have expressed memory in terms of **gigabytes** (abbreviated **GB**)—billions of bytes.

Memory in a microcomputer usually holds a minimum of 256K (262,144) bytes on up to 16MB and even higher. At the other end of the spectrum, mainframe memories reach hundreds of megabytes.

A computer **word** is defined as the number of bits that constitute a common unit of data, as defined by the computer system. The length of a word varies by computer. Common word lengths are 8 bits (for some microcomputers), 16 bits (for traditional minicomputers and some microcomputers), 32 bits (for full-size mainframe computers, some minicomputers, and even some microcomputers), and 64 bits (for supercomputers).

A computer's word size is very important. In general, the larger the word size, the more powerful the computer. A larger word size means:

■ The computer can transfer more data at a time, making the computer faster.

■ The computer word has room to reference larger address numbers, thus allowing more memory.

■ The computer can support a greater number and variety of instructions.

The internal circuitry of a computer must reflect its word size. The parts of a computer are connected by collections of wires called **bus lines.** Each bus line has a certain number of data paths along which bits can travel from one part of the computer to another. Usually, the number of data paths in the bus line is equivalent to the number of bits in the computer's word size. For instance, a 32-bit central processing unit has a 32-bit bus, meaning that data can be sent over the bus lines in groups of 32 bits—that is, a word at a time. Obviously this is more efficient than sending data in groups of 16 bits, which is what an 16-bit central processing unit does.

Coding Schemes: EBCDIC and ASCII

As we said, a byte—a collection of bits—represents a character of data. But just what particular set of bits is equivalent to which character? In theory we could each make up our own definitions, declaring certain bit patterns to represent certain characters. But this would be about as practical as each of us speaking our own special language. Since we need to communicate with the computer and with each other, it is appropriate that we use a common scheme for data representation. That is, we must agree on which groups of bits represent which characters. There are two commonly used coding schemes for representing numbers, letters, and special characters: EBCDIC and ASCII.

EBCDIC (usually pronounced "EB-see-dick") stands for Extended Binary Coded Decimal Interchange Code. Established by IBM and used in IBM mainframe computers, it uses 8 bits to represent a single character. The letter *A*, for instance, is represented by 11000001.

LECTURE HINT
Most computers use binary arithmetic rather than decimal arithmetic. Note how the last five bits of the ASCII code change from one line to the next.

Another code, **ASCII** (pronounced "AS-key"), which stands for American Standard Code for Information Interchange, uses 7 bits for each character. For example, the letter *A* is represented by 1000001. The ASCII representation has been adopted as a standard by the U.S. government and is found in a variety of computers—particularly minicomputers and microcomputers. Figure 3-6 shows the EBCDIC and ASCII codes.

DISCUSSION QUESTION
What is the purpose of the parity bit?

TRANSPARENCY ACETATE #3F
Figure #3-7

	EBCDIC byte representation								Parity bit	Number of 1 Bits
S	1	1	1	0	0	0	1	0	1	5
U	1	1	1	0	0	1	0	0	1	5
S	0	1	1	0	0	0	1	0	1	4
A	1	1	0	0	0	0	0	1	0	3
N	1	1	0	1	0	1	0	1	0	5

Note error. First bit has been altered

Figure 3-7 Example of odd parity. A 0 or a 1 is added as a parity bit to the EBCDIC byte so that each byte always comes out with an odd number of 1 bits. Thus, with the second S here, the absence of the first 1 produces an even number of bits—which signals the computer that there is an error.

7 The Parity Bit: Checking for Errors

Suppose you just finished transmitting data over a telephone line or even within the computer system itself. How do you know it arrived safely—that is, that nothing was lost or garbled? Sometimes data is lost in transit, owing to timing problems, hardware failure, and the like.

To signal the computer that the bits in a byte have stayed the way they are supposed to, another 0 or 1 bit is added to the byte before transmission. This extra bit is called a **parity bit** or **check bit.** Thus, in an 8-bit EBCDIC byte, the parity bit is the ninth bit.

Here is how the system works: In an odd-parity system, a 0 or 1 is added to each EBCDIC byte before transmission so that the total number of 1 bits in each byte is an odd number (Figure 3-7). Then, if a 1 bit is lost in a particular byte during transmission, the total number of 1 bits in that byte is even, not odd. Thus, the computer system is alerted that something is wrong with that byte. Some computers use an odd-parity system and others use an even-parity system. The principle behind the two systems is the same, except that in an even-parity system the total number of 1 bits is even.

As you might suspect, a parity check is not infallible. For instance, for any of the letters in Figure 3-7, if two 1s were dropped, the number of 1 bits would still add up to an odd number—and the computer would not notice that the byte was erroneous. More advanced schemes have been developed to detect multibit errors.

The Intel Corporation has provided microcomputer makers with four—make that five—generations of microprocessor chips. The first was a standard-setter: the 8088 chip used by the first IBM PC (introduced in 1981) and its many imitators. The next member of the family, the 80186, fared less well; this transitional chip was used in just a few products before it was replaced by the 80286, which powered the IBM PC AT and, again, a slew of copycats.

Intel moved to increase power and flexibility with the introduction of the 80386 chip, first brought to the market in the Compaq 386. The 80386 chip lets users run several programs at once—a talent formerly reserved for minicomputers and mainframes. Software developers said this was the chip they had been waiting for. But close on its heels—on the market in 1989—was the 80486 (see Figure 3-8b), a chip whose speed and power make it a veritable mainframe on a chip. There seems to be no end in sight.

TEST BANK
Mult. Choice	24-26
T/F	42-44
Matching C	2
Fill-in-the-Blank	36-38

7 Inside Your Personal Computer

It is really pretty easy to have a look inside most personal computers; all you need is a screwdriver and sometimes not even that. (Caution: Some manufacturers are *not* interested in having you peer under the hood and doing so will void your warranty. Check your documentation—your instruction manual—first.) You will find an impressive array of electronic gear. Part of what you see before you is related to what we have talked about in this chapter: the central processing unit and memory.

Both the CPU and memory are on silicon chips, which are smaller than thumbtacks (Figure 3-8a). The word *chip* is bandied about a great deal, but it is not always understood. There are two basic kinds of chips; one kind corresponds to a central processing unit and another kind corresponds to memory. (Specific applications such as watches or microwave ovens may combine the CPU and memory on a single chip.) A miniaturized CPU can be etched on a chip, hence the term *computer on a chip*. A central processing unit, or processor, on a chip is a **microprocessor,** also called a **logic chip** (Figure 3-8b). Memory chips are different from microprocessors and come in a number of varieties.

We present the stories of microprocessors and memory chips in separate sections. Even though we discuss chips in the context of the personal computer, where they first came to prominence, most larger computers also use chips for the CPU and memory.

Gallery 1 shows how chips are designed and manufactured.

Figure 3-8   Microprocessor chips.   (a) Microprocessors are small enough to fit on the palm of a baby's hand—with room to spare. (b) This is Intel's 80486 microprocessor, which accommodates a 32-bit word. Although the circuitry is complex, the entire chip is smaller than your thumbnail.

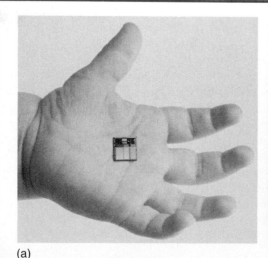
(a)

(b)

MAKING MICROCHIPS
Marvels of Miniaturization

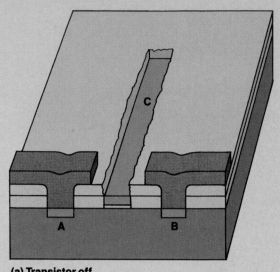

(a) Transistor off

KEY:

Positively doped silicon substrate

Silicon dioxide

Negatively doped silicon

Pathway C

Circuit pathway

Direction of electrical charge along pathway C

Direction of electrical charge along circuit pathway

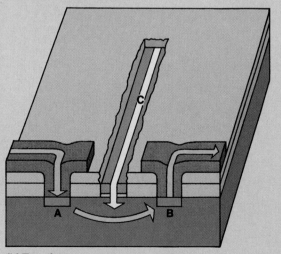

(b) Transistor on

Computer power in the hands of the people—we take it for granted now, but not so long ago computers existed only in enormous rooms behind locked doors. The revolution that changed all that was ignited by chips of silicon smaller than your fingernail. Silicon is one of the most common elements found on earth, but there is nothing commonplace about designing, manufacturing, testing, and packaging silicon chips. The collage shown on the opening page includes key elements of the process that we shall explore in this gallery.

The Idea Behind the Chip

Microchips form the lightning-quick "brain" of a computer. However, these complex devices ultimately work on a very simple principle: they "know" when the electric current is on and when it is off. They process information coded as a series of "on-off" electrical signals. Before the invention of microchips, these electrical signals were controlled by thousands of separate devices laboriously wired together to form an electronic circuit. Then came a revolutionary idea—the various components of a circuit could be created on a single silicon microchip, forming an integrated circuit.

Silicon is a semiconductor—it conducts electricity only "semi"-well. This does not sound like such an admirable trait, but the beauty of silicon is that it can be "doped" with different materials to make it either conduct electricity well or not at all. By doping various areas of a silicon chip differently, pathways can be set up for electricity to follow, surrounded by areas that do not conduct electricity. To create these pathways, layers are added to a silicon chip, grooves are etched in the layers, and the silicon substrate is doped.

(1) This simplified illustration shows the layers and grooves within a transistor, one of thousands of circuit components on a single chip. Pathway C controls the flow of electricity through the circuit. (a) When no electrical charge is added along pathway C, electricity cannot flow along the circuit pathway from area A to area B. Thus, the transistor is "off." (b) An added charge along pathway C temporarily allows electricity to travel from area A to area B. Now the transistor is "on" and electricity can continue to other components of the circuit. The control of electricity here and elsewhere in the chip makes it possible for the computer to process information coded as "on-off" electrical signals.

Preparing the Design

Try to imagine figuring out a way to place thousands of circuit components next to each other so that all the layers and grooves line up and electricity flows through the whole integrated circuit the way it is supposed to. That is the job of chip designers. Essentially, they are trying to put together a gigantic multi-layered jig-saw puzzle.

The circuit design of a typical chip requires over a year's work by a team of designers. Computers assist in the complex task of mapping out the most efficient electrical pathways for each circuit layer. (2) By drawing with an electronic pen on a digitizing tablet, a designer can arrange and modify circuit patterns and see them displayed on the screen. Superimposing the color-coded circuit layers allows the designer to evaluate the relationships between them. The computer allows the designer to electronically store and retrieve previously designed circuit patterns. (3) Here the designer has requested a close-up view of two small parts of one chip component, in this case the arithmetic/logic unit (abbreviated ALU on the screen display).

(4) The computer system can also provide a printed version of any or all parts of the design. This large-scale printout allows the design team to discuss and modify the entire chip design.

(5) The final design of each circuit layer must be reduced to the size of the chip. Several hundred replicas of the chip pattern are then etched on a chemically coated glass plate called a photomask. Thus, each photomask will be used to transfer the circuit layer pattern to hundreds of chips. One photomask is required for each layer of the chip. A typical chip design requires seven to 12 photomasks, but more complex chips may require as many as 20 different photomasks.

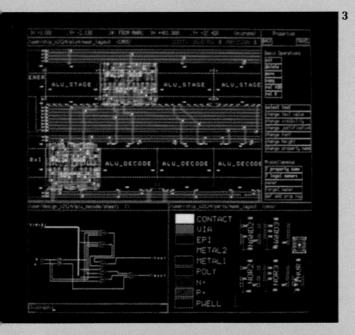

Manufacturing the Chip

The silicon used to make computer chips is extracted from common rocks and sand. It is melted down into a form that is 99.9% pure silicon and then doped with chemicals to make it either electrically positive or negative. **(6)** The molten silicon is then "grown" into cylindrical ingots in a process similar to candle-dipping. **(7)** A diamond saw slices each ingot into circular wafers 4 or 6 inches in diameter and $4/1000$ of an inch thick. The wafers are sterilized and polished to a mirror-like finish. Each wafer will eventually contain hundreds of identical chips. In the photo, an engineer is holding an experimental 8-inch wafer that can produce over 2,000 chips.

Since a single speck of dust can ruin a chip, they are manufactured in special air-filtered laboratories called clean rooms. Workers dress in "bunny suits," and their laboratory is 100 times cleaner than a hospital operating room.

(8) Chip manufacturing processes vary, but in one common technique, electrically positive silicon wafers are placed in an open glass tube and inserted in a 1200°C oxidation furnace. Oxygen reacts with the silicon, covering each wafer with a thin layer of silicon dioxide, which does not conduct electricity very well. Each wafer is then coated with a gelatin-like substance called photoresist, and the first photomask pattern is placed over it. Exposure to ultraviolet light hardens the photoresist, except in the areas concealed by the dark circuit pattern on the photomask.

6

7

8

(9) The wafer is then taken to a washing station in a specially-lit "yellow room" where it is washed in solvent to remove the soft photoresist. Next, the silicon dioxide that is revealed by the washing is etched away by hot gases. The silicon underneath, which forms the circuit pathway, is then doped to make it electrically negative. In this way the circuit pathway is distinguished electrically from the rest of the silicon. This process is repeated for each layer of the wafer, using a different photomask each time. In the final step, aluminum is deposited to connect the circuit components and form the bonding pads to which wires will later be connected.

(10) The result: a wafer with hundreds of chips. This photo shows the natural color of chips.
(11) Photographic lighting enhances this close-up view of a wafer with chips. **(12)** In this color-enhanced photo of a single chip on a wafer, the square and rectangular bonding pads are visible along the edges of the chip.

9

10

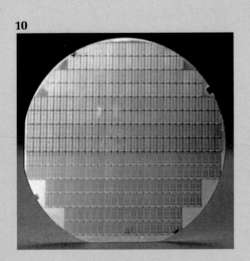

11

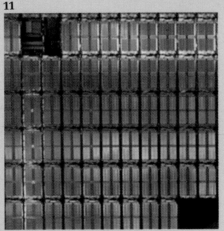

12

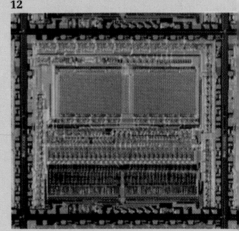

13

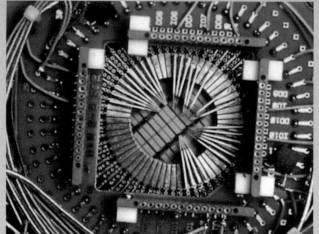

Testing the Chip

Although chips on a particular wafer may look identical, they do not perform identically. **(13)** A probe machine must perform millions of tests on each chip, its needle-like probes contacting the bonding pads, applying electricity, measuring the results, and marking ink spots on defective chips. The probe machine determines whether the chip conducts electricity in the precise way it was designed to. **(14)** Yield analyses determine the number of chips that can be expected from each wafer. **(15)** After the initial testing a diamond saw cuts each chip from the wafer, and defective chips are discarded.

14

IC WAFER
YIELD
ANALYSIS

RUN NUMBER: A-2357
NUMBER OF WAFERS: 18

MASK LIMITED
LOCATIONS: 239

ACTUAL GOOD
LOCATIONS: 239

GOOD CHIPS: 1280

NEXT   NO   RAW DATA   SMOOTHED   SMOOTHED   HISTO-   RETURN
            COLOR   (NUMBER)   (PERCENT) (COLOR)   GRAM

15

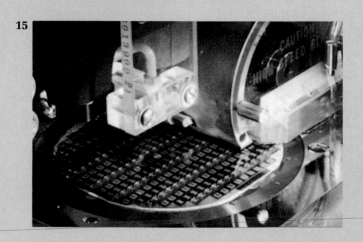

Packaging the Chip

Each acceptable chip is mounted on a protective package. **(16)** An automated wire-bonding device wires the bonding pads of the chip to the electrical leads on the package, using aluminum or gold wire thinner than a human hair.

A variety of packages are in use today. **(17)** Dual in-line packages have two rows of legs that are inserted into holes in a circuit board. In this photo, the protective cap has been cut away so that we can see the chip. **(18)** Square pin-grid array packages, which are used for chips requiring more electrical leads, look like a bed of nails. The pins are inserted into holes in a circuit board. Here again the protective cap has been removed, revealing the ultra-fine wires connecting the chip to the package. **(19)** This photo shows a dual in-line package (top) compared to two surface mount packages (bottom). Surface mount packages do not have to be inserted in circuit board holes. Instead, a machine drops the package in place on the board, where a laser or infrared beam bonds the package to the board. Another advantage of surface mount packages is that they are smaller than other packages, allowing more computing power in less space.

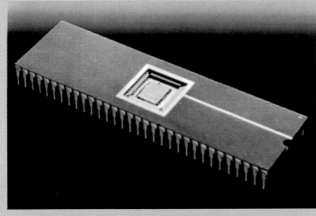

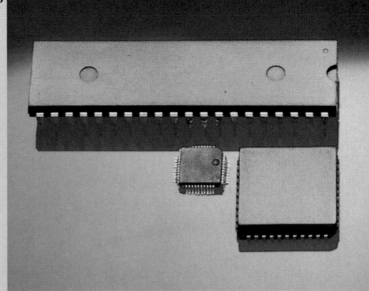

From Chip to Computer

(20) At the factory that manufactures the NeXT Computer, a robotic arm is inserting a pin-grid package into holes in a circuit board. Several surface mount packages have already been placed on the board. (21) Dual in-line packages of various sizes have been attached to this circuit board. (22) Metal lines on the board form electrical connections to the legs of the package, as shown in this color-enhanced close-up of some packages on a circuit board. (23) In the final step the board is inserted into one of the many personal computers that owe their existence to the chip. (24) This tiny device has truly brought computers into the hands of the people.

22

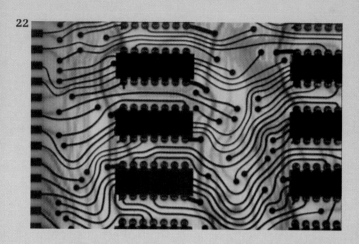

20

23

21

24

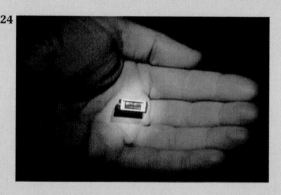

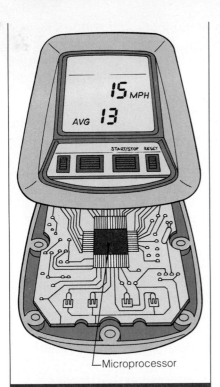

—Microprocessor

CHIPS INSIDE EVERYTHING

So popular is the tiny chip that people participate in the computer revolution every day by simple acts such as using a telephone, looking at a wristwatch, or going through a supermarket checkout line. Furthermore, chips are in cameras, blood pressure devices, microwave ovens, cars, and many other everyday devices. Homeowners can monitor heat, smoke, and security with strategically placed microprocessor chips.

Consider the bicycle odometer above. This little chip-driven device can pick up data from sensors placed on your bicycle wheels and pedals and produce the following information: current speed, average speed, maximum speed, distance, and cadence. If you were to pry the odometer open—not recommended—you would see the microprocessor revealed above.

LECTURE ACTIVITY
Display and identify various kinds of computer chips. A local computer store may be able to give you some no longer usable chips to show.

7 Microprocessor: Computer on a Chip

TEST BANK	
Mult. Choice	27-28
T/F	45-47
Fill-in-the-Blank	39

Over the years the architecture of microprocessors has become somewhat standardized. Microprocessors usually contain four key components: a control unit and an arithmetic/logic unit (the CPU), registers, buses, and a clock. (Clocks are often on a separate chip in personal computers.) These are exactly the items we have discussed in this chapter, all on one tiny chip. (Notably missing is memory, which comes on its own chip or chips.)

How much smaller? How much cheaper? How much faster? Two decades of extraordinary advances in technology have packed increasingly greater power onto increasingly smaller chips. Engineers can now imprint as much circuitry on a single chip as filled room-size computers in the early days of data processing. But are we approaching the limits of smallness? Current development efforts focus on a three-dimensional chip, built in layers. Chip capacities in the future do seem almost limitless.

There was a time when *Made in the USA* could be confidently stamped on most microprocessors. But the American stranglehold on microprocessors is being loosened by Japanese manufacturers. American companies, however, still produce most of the microprocessor designs in use worldwide. What is more, our lawmakers want to keep it that way. Congress passed a law in 1985 that states that an original chip design is the property of the chip designer, just as a book or a record is the property of the artist who created it. The law gave chip makers exclusive rights to make and sell their chip designs for 10 years.

7 Memory Components

TEST BANK	
Mult. Choice	29-38
T/F	48-58
Matching C	3-7
Fill-in-the-Blank	40-53

Earlier in the chapter we talked about memory and how it interfaces with the central processing unit. Now we will examine the memory components. Historically, memory components evolved from vacuum tubes to magnetic cores to semiconductors.

7 Semiconductor Storage: Let the Chips Fall Where They May

Most modern computers use semiconductor storage because it has several advantages: reliability, compactness (hence increased speed), low cost, and lower power usage. Since semiconductor memory can be mass-produced economically, the cost of memory has been considerably reduced. Chip prices have fallen and risen

BEE WEAR

We are not making this up. We will understand, however, if you find it hard to believe that bees will be buzzing around with chips glued to their backs. But we are not talking about just any old honeybees. Scientists are planning to attach chips to the aggressive "killer" bees that can damage livestock, crops, and humans.

The problem is so worrisome that scientists plan to track the movements of the killer bees—by monitoring bees equipped with solar-powered chips. The chip, which is being modeled here by a domestic European bee, transmits infrared signals to receivers up to a mile away.

LECTURE HINT
Another (less significant) disadvantage of semiconductors: they must be handled with care, especially in dry weather. A build-up of static electricity can destroy chips.

and fallen again, based on a variety of economic and political factors, but they continue to remain a bargain. Semiconductor storage has one major disadvantage: It is **volatile.** That is, semiconductor storage requires continuous electric current to represent data. If the current is interrupted, the data is lost.

Semiconductor storage is made up of thousands of very small circuits—pathways for electric currents—on a silicon chip. A chip is described as **monolithic** because the circuits on a single chip compose an inseparable unit of storage. Each circuit etched on a chip can be in one of two states: either conducting an electric current or not—on or off. The two states can be used to represent the binary digits 1 and 0. As we noted earlier, these digits can be combined to represent characters, thus making the memory chip a storage bin for data and instructions.

Memory chips that hold 256K bits of data are common and chips that hold 1 million data bits at any one time, or the equivalent of about 80 typed pages, are available. The current long-term goal is to create a superchip capable of storing more than 10 million bits (10 megabits) or more of data, the equivalent of 800 typed pages! Such a superchip would be miniaturized in the extreme, with circuits smaller than half a micron, or approximately seven-thousandths of the diameter of a human hair.

In current vernacular **large-scale integration** (**LSI**) means a chip has a large number of circuits, and the circuits are integrated—that is, they work together. More recently, the 1-megabit chips are described as **VLSI,** for **very large-scale integration.** In search of ever grander designations, the proposed 10-megabit chip is now referred to as **ULSI,** for **ultra large-scale integration.** Fortunately, no engineer has to speculate on a name to top that one—yet.

In the recent past foreign manufacturers have produced a large percentage of memory chips. The U.S. Department of Defense worries that computers, weapons, and telecommunications may grow dangerously dependent on foreign memory chips. In recent years the United States has made significant strides in memory chip production.

7 RAM and ROM

The two basic types of memory chips in every computer are popularly known as **random-access memory** (**RAM**) and **read-only memory** (**ROM**). These terms are actually a little misleading, since every chip, RAM or ROM, provides random-access storage. That is, the computer has access to all locations on each type of chip.

The real difference between RAM and ROM is that the data on ROM chips cannot easily be replaced with new data. ROM contains programs and data that are recorded into the memory at the factory. The contents of ROM can be read and used, but they cannot be changed by the user. ROMs are used to store programs, sometimes called **firmware,** that will not be altered. For example, a pocket calculator might have a program for calculating square roots in ROM; a

MICROCOMPUTERS IN ACTION

Design by Computer

A tedious manual task has little appeal, especially if the task must be repeated over and over. So it is with circuit design. After drawing a design by hand, engineers create a prototype of the circuit. This prototype, called a *breadboard,* is tested for defects. If the engineers find a flaw, they repeat the drawing, prototyping, and testing processes. Typically, engineers go through three or four breadboards before getting the perfect circuit.

An engineer at Eldec Corporation wanted to automate this process. He knew that computerizing the routine would reduce testing time significantly: Engineers could create and test circuits on the screen. Finding the right computer, however, was not so simple. He finally settled on the Compaq 386, which is based on the Intel 80386 chip. The Compaq 386 has enough speed—20 times faster than the original IBM PC—to handle the processor-intensive task of circuit design. Furthermore, the computer has the exceptional screen graphics needed to provide the sharp detail necessary for on-screen design. Engineers can now create and test circuits on the screen and get immediate results. If

changes are necessary, they can be made on-screen. This instant gratification is a significant time saving over the breadboarding days.

DISCUSSION QUESTION
How do RAM, ROM, and PROM differ?

LECTURE HINT
A PROM (a type of ROM) is designed so that data can be permanently burned in. An EPROM is an Erasable Programmable ROM. The data can be erased using strong ultraviolet light and high voltages. The chip can be programmed with a new set of data.

microcomputer might have a BASIC-interpreting program in ROM. ROM is nonvolatile—its contents do not disappear when the power is turned off.

With specialized tools called **ROM burners,** the instructions within some ROM chips can be changed. These chips are known as **PROM** chips, or **programmable read-only memory** chips. There are other variations on ROM chips, depending on the methods used to alter them. The business of programming and altering ROM chips is the province of the computer engineer. The rest of us are safe if we just leave ROM alone.

The memory designed for our use is RAM, the computer's temporary storage compartments. They hold the instructions and data for whatever programs we happen to be using. In fact, RAM has been described as the computer's scratch pad. RAM chips could accurately be described as read-write chips: A user can read the data stored there as well as write new data to replace what is there. The data can be accessed in an easy and speedy manner. RAM is usually volatile—that is, the data is lost once the power is shut off. This is one of the reasons, you recall, that we need secondary storage.

The more RAM in your computer, the more powerful the programs you can run. In recent years the amount of RAM storage in a personal computer has increased dramatically. An early personal computer, for example, was advertised as coming with "a full 4K RAM." By 1980, however, most personal computers came with a standard RAM of 64K. Now, since many personal computer users are in offices, 640K RAM is common, and 4M RAM—or more—is not unusual. More memory has become a necessity because sophisticated personal computer software requires significant amounts of memory. You can add to your personal computer's RAM by buying extra memory chips to add to your memory board or by buying an entire memory board full of chips. It is easier—but more expensive—to buy another board since it slips into place more readily than individual chips do.

TEST BANK
Mult. Choice   39-43
T/F   59-66
Matching C   8-10
Fill-in-the-Blank 54-61

LECTURE HINT
Radio Shack's PC-1 (hand-held) computer can perform ten square roots per second. The Apple IIe can perform more than 100 square roots per second. The VAX 780 can perform ten thousand square roots per second. A Cray-1 could do far more in 1 second.

7 Computer Processing Speeds

We have saved the discussion of speed until last. Although speed is basic to computer processing, speed is also an ever changing facet and a good jumping-off point to the future.

The characteristic of speed is universally associated with computers. Certainly all computers are fast, but there is a wide diversity of computer speeds. The execution of an instruction on a very slow computer may be measured in less than a **millisecond,** which is one-thousandth of a second (see Table 3-1). Most computers can execute an instruction measured in **microseconds,** one-millionth of a second. Some modern computers have reached the **nanosecond** range—one-billionth of a second. Still to be broken is the **picosecond** barrier—one-trillionth of a second.

7 More Speed? What's the Rush?

Computer speeds are beyond anything that we mortals can physically comprehend. The blink of an eye takes about half a second—500 times slower than a millisecond, the measuring stick of the *slow* computers. The fastest computers, it would seem, ought to be fast enough for even the most sophisticated computer users. But this is not so. This is not just a greed-for-speed scenario—some people really need still more computer speed.

Just who needs all that speed? A physicist at New York University, for one. He coaxed a big, powerful computer to simulate the behavior of helium atoms at −459° Fahrenheit—that is, near absolute zero. Each time he ran the program, it would grind away all weekend. It took two years to get the first satisfactory results. Scientists often work this way. A scientist has an idea of how something works—atoms or ocean currents or prime numbers—and can describe it in terms of numbers and equations. Then the scientist plays elaborate "What if . . . ?" games by changing the numbers and recalculating the equations. These new calculations, of course, are done on the computer. A lot of data means a lot of computer time—even on supercomputers.

The traditional approach to increased speed has been to decrease the distances that electronic signals must travel, because the

HOW FAST IS A NANOSECOND?

If one nano-second is . . .	Then one second is equivalent to . . .
one mile	2000 trips to the moon and back
one person	the population of China and the United States
one minute	1900 years
one square mile	17 times the land area of the entire world

Table 3-1   Units of Time: How Fast Is *Fast?*

Unit of Time	Fraction of a Second	Mathematical Notation
Millisecond	Thousandth: 1/1000	10^{-3}
Microsecond	Millionth: 1/1,000,000	10^{-6}
Nanosecond	Billionth: 1/1,000,000,000	10^{-9}
Picosecond	Trillionth: 1/1,000,000,000,000	10^{-12}

limiting factor is the speed electricity can travel. The circuits are packed closer together, making tighter and tighter squeezes into the same physical space. All these electronic devices humming together in such proximity produce an overheating problem, which must be attacked with elaborate cooling systems.

Another frequently mentioned approach has been the use of a material called **gallium arsenide** as a substitute for silicon in chip making. Currents can pass through gallium arsenide at a tremendous speed. The drawback of this substance, however, is that it is currently too expensive to be of practical use.

Modern approaches to increased computer speeds also include these two categories: RISC technology and parallel processing. These two topics are so important that they deserve sections of their own.

7 RISC Technology: Less Is More

It flies in the face of computer tradition: Instead of reaching for more variety, more power, more everything-for-everyone, proponents of **RISC—reduced instruction set computers—**suggest that we could get by with a little less. In fact, reduced instruction set computers offer only a small subset of instructions; the absence of bells and whistles increases speed. So we have a radical back-to-basics movement in computer design.

RISC supporters say that, on conventional computers, a hefty chunk of built-in instructions—the microcode—is rarely used. Those instructions, they note, are underused, inefficient, and impediments to performance. RISC computers, with their stripped-down instruction sets, zip through programs like racing cars—at speeds four to ten times those of today's most popular models. This is heady stuff for the merchants of speed who want to attract customers by offering more speed for the money.

The idea that less gives more is so compelling that a dozen or so companies are pressing forward with RISC technology. Startup firms offered the first RISC-based computers in 1983. IBM joined in with its PC RT, a RISC-based personal computer, in 1986. Now several major computing manufacturers are joining the adventure, aiming at the scientific market, where most of the speed demons lurk.

Meanwhile, some people are looking in a different direction altogether. They are actually changing computer architecture to achieve another solution: parallel processing.

MAKING CONNECTIONS AT DOW JONES

Dow Jones, a conservative financial organization, made a radical move: It bought not one, but two, Connection Machines—the most potent parallel processing computers ever made. A Connection Machine has 65,000 processors and costs over $2 million.

The Connection Machine is made by a tiny company called Thinking Machines in Cambridge, Massachusetts. A dozen or so machines have been sold to the military. The Dow Jones purchase is the first sale for commercial applications. Dow Jones uses computers to access databases, including financial data, newswire information, and corporate profiles.

TRANSPARENCY ACETATE #3G
Evolution of parallel processing

TEST BANK
T/F   67
Fill-in-the-Blank   62

7 Parallel Processing: The Ultimate Speed Solution

A wave of technological change is sweeping over the computer industry. Far-reaching claims such as this are not new in the computer business, so perhaps we could emphasize this point by saying that this change is akin to reinventing the computer. Consider the description of computer processing you have seen so far in this chapter: The processor gets an instruction from memory, acts on it, returns processed data to memory, then repeats the process. This is conventional **serial processing.**

The problem with the conventional computer is that the single electronic pathway, the bus line, acts like a bottleneck. The computer has a one-track mind because it is restricted to handling one piece of data at a time. For many applications, such as simulating the air flow around an entire airplane in flight, this is an exceedingly inefficient procedure. A better solution? Many processors, each with its own memory unit, working at the same time: **parallel processing.**

Some early computer inventors saw that parallel processors working in tandem were preferable, but the limited technology of the day made parallel processing out of the question. Inventors have been tinkering with parallel processors in the lab ever since. Now years of research are starting to pay off: A number of parallel processors are being built and sold commercially.

Let us return to the example of the airplane in flight. Using a single conventional processor, the computer could calculate flow between two points on the airplane's surface. Since there are millions of such pairs of points, this calculation method is not very efficient. A serial computer would waste most of its time repeatedly retrieving and storing vast amounts of data, with relatively little time devoted to actual computation. By contrast, a parallel processor could take several pieces of data and perform a series of operations on them in parallel.

The story of computer speeds has been with us since the first stirrings of electronic computers. There is every reason to believe that it will be a continuing story.

7 Next: Future Chip Talk

The future holds some exciting possibilities. New speed breakthroughs will always be a probability, but would you believe computers that are actually grown as biological cultures? So-called "biochips" may replace today's silicon chip. As far-fetched as this sounds, that is precisely the direction of some ongoing research.

BRAINPOWER: NEURAL NETS

A microprocessor chip is sometimes referred to as the "brain" of a computer. But, in truth, computers have not yet come close to the human brain, which has trillions of connections between billions of neurons. What is more, the most sophisticated conventional computer does not "learn" the same way the human brain learns. But let us consider an unconventional computer, one whose chips are actually designed to mimic the human brain. These computers are called neural networks, or, simply, neural nets.

If a computer is to function more like the human brain and less like an overgrown calculator, it must be able to experiment and to learn from its mistakes. Researchers are developing neurocomputers with a few thousand brain-like connections. Instead of following the usual chain-like series of instructions, neural net computers form a grid, much like a nerve cell in the brain. The grid is used to recognize patterns.

Consider a neural network with optical sensors, shown in the drawing, being "trained" to recognize the letter A. The computer begins by making random guesses. ① When the system makes an incorrect choice, the incorrect circuits are weakened. ② In contrast, when a correct choice, is made, those circuits are strengthened. ③ After several attempts with different forms of the letter A, in which the correct circuits are repeatedly strengthened, the neural net is able to identify the letter accurately.

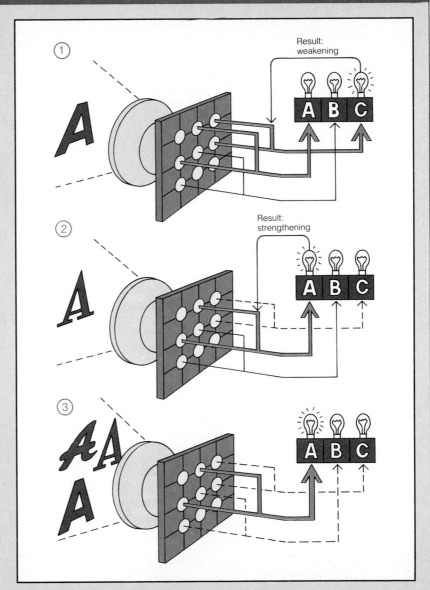

At best, today's neural networks consist of only a few thousand connections—still a far cry from the billions found in the human brain. Thus we, as a society, have a little more time to consider just how neural nets fit in. Even today, computer professionals sometimes must convince people that computers cannot "take over." Will intensified publicity about new brain-like computers revive these concerns? The answer remains the same: People are in charge of computers, not the other way around.

Summary and Key Terms

- The **central processing unit** (**CPU**) is an extensive, complex set of electrical circuitry that executes program instructions. It consists of two parts: a control unit and an arithmetic/logic unit.

- The CPU interacts closely with **primary storage,** or **memory.** Memory provides temporary storage of data while the computer is executing the program. **Secondary storage** holds the data that is permanent or semi-permanent.

- The **control unit** of the CPU coordinates the computer's execution of the program instructions by communicating with the arithmetic/logic unit and memory—the parts of the system that actually execute the program.

- The **arithmetic/logic unit** (**ALU**) contains circuitry that executes the arithmetic and logical operations. The unit can perform four **arithmetic operations:** addition, subtraction, multiplication, and division. Its **logical operations** are usually comparing operations, primarily the **equal to** (=) **condition,** the **less than** (<) **condition,** and the **greater than** (>) **condition.** These operations are commonly combined to form three other operations: less than or equal to, greater than or equal to, and less than or greater than.

- **Registers** are temporary storage areas associated with the CPU that quickly accept, hold, and transfer instructions or data. An **accumulator** is a register that collects the results of computations. A **storage register** temporarily holds data taken from memory or about to be sent to memory. An **address register** tells where instructions and data are stored in memory. Each storage location in memory is identified by an **address.** A **general-purpose register** can be used in several ways, such as arithmetic operations or addressing.

- Registers hold data that will be processed immediately, and memory stores the data that will soon be used in subsequent operations. Secondary storage holds data that may be needed for operations later.

- **Memory** is the part of the computer that temporarily holds data and instructions before and after they are processed by the arithmetic/logic unit. Memory is also known as **primary storage, primary memory, main storage, internal storage,** and **main memory.** Most types of memory keep data only when the computer is turned on.

- The CPU follows four main steps when executing an instruction: (1) getting the instruction from memory, (2) decoding the instruction and giving instructions for the transfer of appropriate data from memory to the ALU, (3) directing the ALU to perform the actual operation on the data, and (4) directing the result of the operation to be stored in memory or a register. The first two steps are called **I-time** (instruction time), and the last two steps are called **E-time** (execution time).

- A **machine cycle** is the combination of I-time and E-time. The internal **clock** of the CPU produces pulses at a fixed rate to synchronize computer operations. A machine-cycle instruction may include many subinstructions, each of which must take at least one clock cycle period. These subinstructions are controlled by **microcode** instructions permanently set inside the control unit.

- Each location in primary storage is identified by an **address.** Address numbers remain the same, but the contents of the locations may change.

- Since a computer can recognize only whether electricity is on or off, data is represented by an on/off **binary system.** Two digits, 0 and 1, correspond to off and on. Combinations of 0s and 1s can represent numbers, letters, or special characters.

- Each 0 or 1 in the binary system is called a **bit** (*binary digit*). A group of bits (usually 8 bits) is called a **byte.** Each byte usually represents one character of data, such as a letter, digit, or special character. Memory capacity is expressed in **kilobytes** (**KB** or **K**), which are equal to 1024 bytes; **megabytes** (**MB**), which are millions of bytes; and **gigabytes** (**GB**), which are billions of bytes.

- A computer **word** is the number of bits that make up a unit of data, as defined by the computer system. Common word lengths vary from 8 bits to 64 bits. In general, a larger word length means a more powerful computer—the computer can transfer more information at a time, can have a larger memory, and can support a greater number and variety of instructions.

- Word length usually determines the capacity of the computer's **bus lines.** These collections of wires provide data paths for transferring bits from one part of the computer to another.

- Commonly used coding schemes for representing characters are **EBCDIC** (Extended Binary Coded Decimal Interchange Code), which uses 8-bit characters, and **ASCII** (American Standard Code for

Information Interchange), which uses 7-bit characters.

- A **parity bit,** or **check bit,** is an extra bit added to each byte; it alerts the computer if a bit is wrong.

- A CPU on a chip is called a **microprocessor,** or **logic chip.** Microprocessors usually contain a control unit and an ALU, registers, bus lines, and a clock. For memory, most modern computers use **semiconductor storage,** thousands of circuits on a silicon chip. The memory chip is **monolithic** because these circuits form an inseparable storage unit. Semiconductor storage is compact and economical, but it is also **volatile**—if the computer's power is shut off the data is lost.

- **Large-scale integration** (**LSI**) means that a chip has a large number of circuits that work together. A 1-megabit chip is described as having **very large-scale integration** (**VLSI**), and the proposed 10-megabit chip is said to have **ultra large-scale integration** (**ULSI**).

- There are two basic types of memory chips, **random-access memory** (**RAM**) and **read-only memory** (**ROM**). RAM provides volatile temporary storage for data and instructions and can be increased by adding extra memory chips. Data in RAM must be saved in secondary storage before the computer is turned off. ROM is nonvolatile— ROM programs (or **firmware**), which are recorded into the memory at the factory, remain after the computer is turned off. The data and instructions on **programmable read-only memory** (**PROM**) chips can be changed with **ROM burners.**

- Computer speed can be measured in **milliseconds** (one-thousandth of a second), **microseconds** (one-millionth of a second), and even **nanoseconds** (one-billionth of a second). The **picosecond** barrier (one-trillionth of a second) is yet to be broken.

- Research is continuing on various ways to increase computer speed: (1) Decrease the distance electronic signals must travel by packing circuits closer together. (2) Make chips out of **gallium arsenide,** a substance that conducts electricity faster than silicon. (3) **Reduced instruction set computers** (**RISC**) increase processing speed by reducing the microcode. (4) **Parallel processing** uses many processors working at the same time—a method that could replace the traditional **serial processing.** Unlike serial processing, parallel processing allows the computer to handle more than one piece of data at a time.

/ Review Questions

1. Name and describe the functions of the two parts of the central processing unit.

2. How does memory differ from secondary storage?

3. Name and describe the functions of the four types of registers.

4. What is the function of the computer's memory?

5. Describe the steps in the execution of a program instruction.

6. How does the control unit find instructions and data?

7. Explain why the binary system is used to represent data to the computer.

8. Define the following: bit, byte, kilobyte, megabyte, gigabyte, and word.

9. Why is a computer's word size important?

10. What is a bus line?

11. Name and describe the two main coding schemes.

12. Explain how a parity bit identifies errors.

13. What are the advantages of semiconductor storage?

14. Define the following: RAM, ROM, and PROM.

15. Define the following: millisecond, microsecond, nanosecond, and picosecond.

16. Describe ways of increasing computer speed.

/ Discussion Questions

1. Give an example of a practical application of each of the three basic logical operations.

2. Why is writing instructions for a computer more difficult than writing instructions for a person?

3. Do you think there is a continuing need to increase computer speed? Explain your answer.

Chapter 4. Input and Output: Data Given, Information Received

4

Input and Output

Data Given, Information Received

Input is the bridge between data and processing. Input devices include the commonly used keyboard and devices that collect data at its source. Some devices, such as screens, are involved in both input and output. Output is the human connection with computing. Output devices include printers, computer output microfilm, and voice output. Specialized input and output devices produce computer-generated graphics.

Just how are input and output related to a computer system? How do you "get in" to a computer system? Or, more formally, how do you provide your own input in a way that the computer can accept? And, if you can figure that much out, how do you get something back from the computer? And what might the output from the computer be, considering what you gave it as input? There are many possible answers to these questions, but Paul Yen's experience is fairly typical.

Paul did not have computers in mind as he thumbed through the catalog from Lands' End, a mail-order firm in Wisconsin that offers quality preppy and sports clothing. Paul decided to order a knit shirt and a leather belt, and he wrote these items on the order form. Paul's action, whether he knew it or not, started the computer action rolling.

The items on the order form became the input data to the computer system. In this example, input is the data related to the customer order—customer name, address, and (possibly) charge-card number—and, for each item, catalog number, quantity, description, and price. If this input data is handwritten on an order form, it is keyed into the system as soon as it arrives in the mail; if the order is received on their toll-free phone line, the Lands' End operator keys the data as the customer speaks the order. This data is placed on customer and order files to be used with files containing inventory data and other related data.

The computer can process this data into a variety of outputs, as shown in Figure 4-1. Some outputs are for individual customers, and some show information combined from several orders: warehouse orders, shipping labels (to send the shirt and belt), backorder notices, inventory reports, supply re-order reports, charge-card reports, demographic reports (showing which merchandise sells best where), and so forth. And—to keep the whole process going—Lands' End also computer-prints Paul's name and address on the next catalog.

7 Input and Output: The People Connection

We have already alluded to the fact that the central processing unit is the unseen part of a computer system. But users are very much aware—and in control—of the input data given to the computer. They submit data to the computer to get processed information, the output. Output is what makes the computer useful to human beings.

Sometimes the output is an instant reaction to the input. Consider these examples:

- Zebra-stripe bar codes on supermarket items provide input that permits instant retrieval of outputs such as price and item name right at the checkout counter.

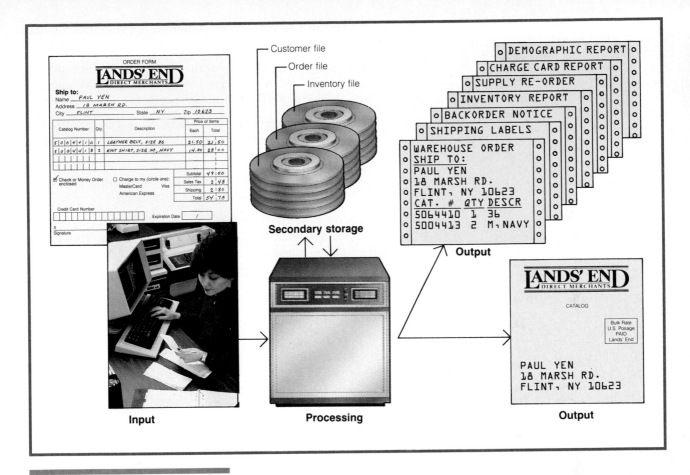

Figure 4-1 Lands' End. At this mail-order house customer order data is input, processed, and used to produce a variety of outputs.

TRANSPARENCY ACETATE #4A
Figure #4-1

- You use a joy stick—a kind of hand-controlled lever—to input data to guide the little pac-man or rabbit—or whatever—character on the screen. The output is the movement of the character according to your wishes.

- A bank teller queries the computer through the small terminal at the window by giving a customer's account number as input and immediately receiving the customer's account balance as output on that same screen.

- A forklift operator speaks to a computer directly through a microphone. Words like *left*, *right*, and *lift* are the actual input data. The output is the computer's instant response, which causes the forklift to operate as requested.

- In an innovative restaurant input is your finger touching the listing of the item of your choice on a computer screen. The output is the order that appears immediately on the kitchen screen, where employees get to work on your Chili Hamburger Deluxe.

Some of these input/output examples may seem a bit frivolous, but all are possible and the concepts underlying them have practical applications.

LECTURE HINT
Here is another example of input
and output that is separated by
time: Traffic jams at bridge toll
booths may be eased by an
experimental billing system. As a
car equipped with a special
identification code passes by a
sensor at the toll booth, the car's
code is read. At the end of the
month a bill for bridge tolls is
mailed to the owner of the car.

TEST BANK
Mult. Choice   3-24
T/F   4-29
Matching A   1-10
Matching B   1-5
Fill-in-the-Blank   1-18

Input and output are sometimes separated by time and/or distance. Some examples:

- Factory workers input data by punching in on a time clock as they go from task to task. The outputs are their paychecks and management reports that summarize hours per project.

- A college student writes checks whose data is used as input to the computer and eventually processed to prepare a bank statement once a month.

- Charge-card transactions in a retail store provide input data that is processed at month's end to produce customer bills.

- Water-sample data is determined at lake and river sites, keyed in at the environmental agency office, and used to produce reports that show patterns of water quality.

The examples in this section show the diversity of computer applications, but, in all cases, the litany is the same: input-processing-output. We have already had an introduction to processing. Now, in this chapter, we will examine input and output methods in detail. We begin with a description of types of input, then consider computer screens (used for both input and output), and then examine devices that are used for output only. We will conclude with a look at computer graphics.

Types of Input

Some input data can go directly to the computer for processing, as with bar codes or speaking or pointing. Some input data, however, goes through a good deal of intermediate handling, such as when it is copied from a **source document** (jargon for the original written data) and translated to a medium that a machine can read, such as magnetic disk. In either case the task is to gather data to be processed by the computer—sometimes called *raw data*—and convert it into some form the computer can understand. The evolution of input devices is toward equipment that is easy to use, fast, and accurate.

Keyboard Entry

The most popular input device is the keyboard. A keyboard, which usually is similar to a typewriter, may be part of a personal computer or part of a terminal that is connected to a computer somewhere else (Figure 4-2a). Not all keyboards are traditional, however. A fast-food franchise like McDonald's, for example, uses keyboards whose keys each represent an item, such as large fries or a Big Mac (Figure 4-2b). Even less traditional is the keyboard shown in Figure 4-2c, which is used to enter Chinese characters.

Figure 4-2   Keyboards. (a) A traditional computer keyboard. (b) Workers at McDonald's press a key for each item ordered. The amount of the order is totaled by the computer system, then displayed on a small screen so the customer can see the amount owed. (c) Chinese characters are significantly more complicated than the letters and digits found on a standard keyboard. To enter Chinese characters into the computer system, a person uses a stylus on this special keyboard to select the character wanted. A graphics interpretation of the character is then displayed on the computer screen.

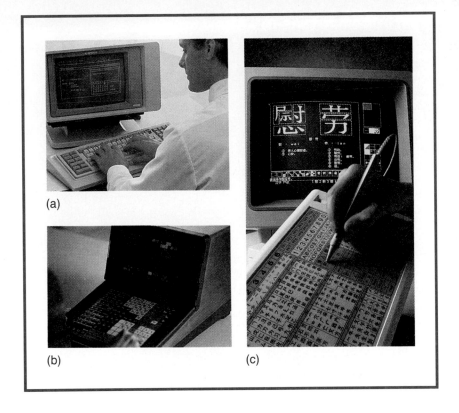

(a)

(b)   (c)

Keyboards and Personal Computer Users

Users of personal computers find that familiarity with a keyboard breeds productivity. Consider the traditional flow of paperwork in an office: A manager writes a memo by hand or dictates it, then a secretary types it. The manager checks the typed memo; if there are changes to be made, the secretary must retype the memo. With a personal computer on the manager's desk, however, the manager can enter the memo through the keyboard, read it on the screen, and make any necessary changes before it is printed. This greatly reduces the lag time between writing a memo and getting it in the mail.

Keyboards and Data Entry Operators

Entering large amounts of data via keyboard calls for the services of data entry operators. **Data entry operators** use computer terminals or perhaps personal computers to enter data from some nonautomated form, usually handwriting on paper (see photo in Figure 4-1). Such a system is often used to process large quantities of data that can be handled in groups, or batches, such as engineering drawing data, customer payments, or bank transactions received in the mail.

The data that operators enter into the system is stored on either magnetic tape or magnetic disk. The tapes or disks are then sent to the main computer for processing.

MICROCOMPUTERS IN ACTION

Finding Your Way Around a Keyboard

Most microcomputer keyboards have three main parts: function keys, the main keyboard in the center, and numeric keys to the right. Extended keyboards, such as the IBM PS/2 keyboard shown here, have additional keys between the main keyboard and the numeric keys and status lights in the upper right-hand corner.

Function Keys

The function keys (highlighted in green on the diagram) are an easy way to give certain commands to the computer. What each function key does is defined by the particular software you are using. For instance, using WordPerfect, a popular word processing program, you press function key F4 to indent and F8 to underline text. Function keys can be lo-

cated across the top of the keyboard, as shown here, or on the left side of the keyboard.

Main Keyboard

The main keyboard includes the familiar keys found on a typewriter keyboard (dark blue), as well as some special command keys (light blue). The command keys can have different uses depending on the software being used. Some of the most common uses are listed here.

 The Escape key, Esc, is used in different ways by different programs; often it allows you to "escape" to the previous screen of the program.

 The Tab key allows you to tab across the screen and set tab stops as you would on a typewriter.

 When the Caps Lock key is depressed, uppercase letters are produced. Numbers and symbols are not affected—the number or symbol shown on the bottom of the key is still produced. When the Caps Lock key is depressed, the status light under "Caps Lock" lights up.

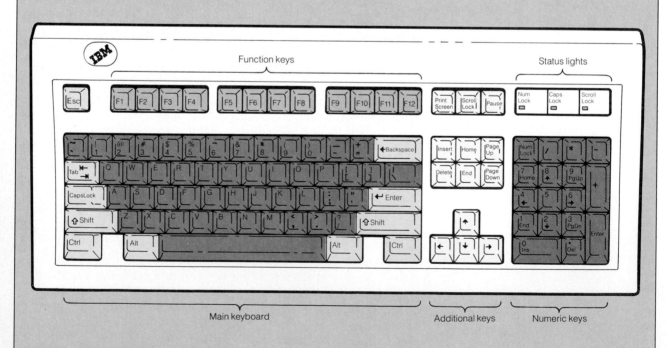

DISCUSSION QUESTION　　Find the non-typewriter keys on a typical IBM-compatible keyboard, and describe their function. Which keys are never used by themselves?

The Shift key allows you to produce uppercase letters and the upper symbols shown on the keys.

 The Control key, Ctrl, is pressed in combination with other keys to initiate commands as specified by the software.

 The Alternate key, Alt, is also used with other keys to initiate commands.

 The Backspace key is most often used to delete a character to the left of the cursor, moving the cursor back one position. (The cursor is the flashing indicator on the screen that shows where the next character will be inserted.)

 The Enter key moves the cursor to the beginning of the next line. It is used at the end of a paragraph, for instance.

Numeric Keys

The numeric keys (purple) serve one of two purposes, depending on the status of the Num Lock key. When the computer is in the Num Lock mode, these keys can be used to enter numeric data and mathematical symbols (/ for "divided by", * for "multiplied by", −, and +). In the Num Lock mode, the status light under "Num Lock" lights up. When the computer is not in the Num Lock mode, the numeric keys can be used to move the cursor and perform other functions, as described below.

 The End key moves the cursor to the bottom left-hand corner of the screen.

 This key moves the cursor down.

 The Page Down key, PgDn, advances one full screen while the cursor remains in the same position.

 This key moves the cursor to the left.

 This key moves the cursor to the right.

 The Home key moves the cursor to the top left-hand corner of the screen.

 This key moves the cursor up.

 The Page Up key, PgUp, backs up to the previous screen while the cursor remains in the same position.

 The Insert key, Ins, can be used to insert additional characters within a line.

 The Delete key, Del, deletes a character or space.

Additional Keys

Extended keyboards include additional keys (yellow) that duplicate the cursor movement functions of the numeric keys. Users who enter a lot of numeric data can leave their computers in the Num Lock mode and use these additional keys to control the cursor.

At the top of the keyboard, to the right of the function keys, are keys that perform additional tasks, as described below.

 The Print Screen key, when pressed with the Shift key, causes the current screen display to be printed.

 The Scroll Lock key causes lines of text—not the cursor—to move when cursor keys are used. When the computer is in the Scroll Lock mode, the status light under "Scroll Lock" lights up.

 The Pause key causes the screen to pause when information is appearing too fast to read.

TRANSPARENCY ACETATE #4C
IBM PC keyboard

LECTURE HINT   The description of the keys given here is for IBM-compatible computers only.

7 The Mouse

The **mouse,** popularized by the Macintosh computer, is a computer input device that actually looks a little bit like a mouse (Figure 4-3a). The mouse, which has a ball on its underside, is rolled on a flat surface, usually the desk on which your computer sits. The rolling movement that results when you push the mouse causes the related output, a corresponding movement on the screen. Moving the mouse allows you to reposition the **pointer,** or **cursor,** an indicator on the screen that shows where your next interaction with the computer will take place. The cursor can also be moved by various keyboard keys. You can communicate with the computer by pressing a button on top of the mouse.

Some people who write software for personal computers have made the mouse an important part of using the software. For example, some software displays pictorial symbols called **icons** (Figure 4-3b). One icon might be a picture of a sheet of paper, used to represent a memo you have stored. If you want to retrieve the memo, roll the mouse on the desk surface until the pointer is over the picture of the paper. Then signal the computer that you wish to open the file by rapidly pressing the mouse button twice. These actions replace typing commands on the keyboard.

Some people facetiously suggest that they cannot even keep track of their usual desk tools, much less a rodent. But most users are easy converts, and they often turn to the mouse as a quick substitute

(a)

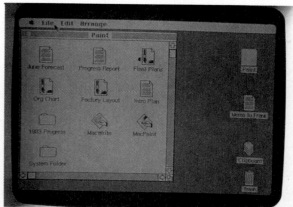

(b)

Figure 4-3   Macintosh mouse. (a) Commands can be given to the computer via the mouse instead of the keyboard. (b) Moving the mouse causes the pointer (arrow) on the screen to move. This Macintosh software uses pictures, or icons, to represent different files. To open a file, you move the mouse until the arrow is on the file's icon, then press the mouse's button twice.

for the keyboard. Mice are a hot item for personal computers. Recent mouse models have appeared with rubber-coated control balls for smoother, near-silent operation on all surfaces.

Source Data Automation: Collecting Data Where It Starts

The challenge to productive data entry is clear: Cut down the number of intermediate steps required between data and processing so data processing becomes more efficient. This is best accomplished by **source data automation**—the use of special equipment to collect data at the source and send it directly to the computer. Source data automation is an enticing alternative to keying input, because it eliminates the intermediate keying function and, therefore, reduces both costs and opportunities for human-introduced mistakes. Since data about a transaction is collected when and where the transaction takes place, source data automation also improves the speed of the input operation.

One characteristic of source data automation is that the data entry equipment needs to be fairly easy to use, reliable, and maintenance-free. The people who use it are often data entry personnel who do not receive much computer training—meter readers, shop clerks, and grocery clerks, for example.

For convenience we will divide this discussion into four areas related to source data automation: magnetic-ink character recognition, optical recognition, data collection devices, and voice input. Let us consider each of these in turn.

Magnetic-Ink Character Recognition

Abbreviated **MICR,** pronounced "miker," **magnetic-ink character recognition** is a method of machine-reading characters made of magnetized particles. The most common example of magnetic characters is the array of futuristic-looking numbers on the bottom of your personal check. Figure 4-4 shows what some of these numbers and attached symbols represent.

The MICR process is, in fact, used mainly by banks for processing checks. Checks are read by a machine called a **MICR reader/ sorter,** which sorts the checks into different compartments and sends electronic signals—read from the magnetic ink on the check— to the computer.

Most magnetic-ink characters are preprinted on your check. If you compare a check you wrote that has been cashed and cleared by the bank with those that are still unused in your checkbook, you will note that the amount of the cashed check has been reproduced in magnetic characters in the lower right-hand corner. These characters were added by a person at the bank by using a **MICR inscriber.** (If you find a discrepancy between the amount you wrote on your check and the amount given on your bank statement, look at this lower right-hand number. Maybe someone had trouble reading your handwriting.)

Figure 4-4   The symbols on your check.   Magnetic-ink numbers and symbols run along the bottom of a check. The symbols on the left are pre-printed; the MICR characters in the lower right-hand corner of a cashed check are entered by the bank that receives it. Note that the numbers should correspond to the amount of the check.

TRANSPARENCY ACETATE #4E
Figure #4-4

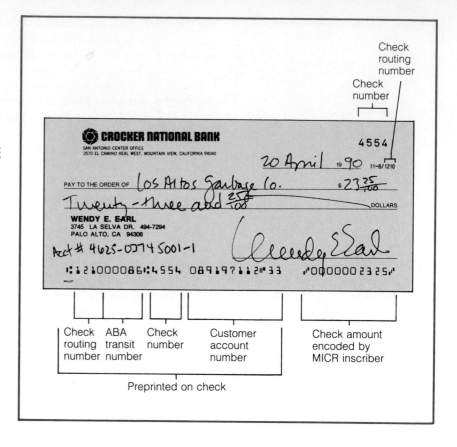

When your check is run through the reader/sorter, it is sorted by account number so that it can be stored along with all of your other checks and returned to you with your statement at the end of the month. (Some banks, however, keep the checks themselves in the interest of saving handling and postage.) Torn and otherwise mutilated checks that cannot be read by the machine are sent to a separate compartment of the machine. The banking transaction is later recorded by a person who handles the check manually.

Optical Recognition

Optical recognition systems read numbers, letters, special characters, and marks. An electronic scanning device converts the data into electrical signals and sends the signals to the computer for processing. Various optical recognition devices can read these types of input:

- Optical marks
- Optical characters
- Handwritten characters
- Bar codes

Optical Mark Recognition

Abbreviated **OMR, optical mark recognition** is sometimes called mark sensing because a machine senses marks on a piece of paper. As a student, you may immediately recognize this

```
ABCDEFG
HIJKLMN
OPQRSTU
VWXYZ,.
$/*-123
4567890
```

Figure 4-5   OCR-A typeface.   This is a common standard font for optical character recognition.

DISCUSSION QUESTION
How do MICR and OCR differ?

TRANSPARENCY ACETATE #4F
Figure #4-6

Figure 4-6   Wand reader.   The photo shows a clerk using a wand reader to scan a price tag printed with OCR-A characters. The price and merchandise number are entered into the computer through the point-of-sale (POS) terminal. The computer retrieves a description of the merchandise from secondary storage and calculates the total price of the purchase. A printer in the POS terminal produces a receipt for the customer. Later, computer reports can be generated for store personnel to use.

approach as the technique used to score certain tests. Using a pencil, you make a mark in a specified box or space that corresponds to what you think is the answer. The answer sheet is then graded by a device that uses a light beam to recognize the marks and convert them to electrical signals, which are sent to the computer for processing.

Optical Character Recognition

Abbreviated **OCR, optical character recognition** devices also use a light source to read special characters and convert them into electrical signals to be sent to the CPU. The characters—letters, numbers, and special symbols—can be read by both humans and machines. They are often found on sales tags in department stores or imprinted on credit-card slips in gas stations after the sale has been written up. A standard typeface for optical characters, called **OCR-A,** has been established by the American National Standards Institute (Figure 4-5).

The hand-held **wand reader** is a popular input device for reading OCR-A. There is an increasing use of wands in libraries, hospitals, and factories, as well as in retail stores. In retail stores the wand reader is connected to a **point-of-sale** (**POS**) **terminal** (Figure 4-6). This terminal is like a cash register in many ways, but it performs many more functions. When a clerk passes the wand reader over the price tag, both the price and the merchandise number are entered into the computer system. Given the merchandise number, the computer can retrieve a description of the item from a file. This description is displayed on the screen of the POS terminal along with the price. (Some systems, by the way, input only the merchandise number and retrieve both price and description.) A small printer produces a customer receipt that also shows both the item description and the price. The computer calculates the subtotal, the sales tax (if any), and the total. This information is displayed on the screen and printed on the receipt.

The raw purchase data becomes valuable information when it is summarized by the computer system. This information can be used

LECTURE HINT
Some computer magazines supply computer programs in BASIC. But copying these programs into a computer by hand is a tedious error-prone job taking several hours. The Cauzin Company, which designed a scanner device called a Soft-strip recorder, printed the programs in a set of strips in the magazines. Readers who owned a Soft-strip recorder could use it to copy the programs into their computer in seconds. However, the recorder cost so much ($200) that few readers bought one. An easier alternative is to buy disks with the programs already on them.

by the accounting department to keep track of how much money is taken in each day, by buyers to determine what merchandise should be reordered, and by the marketing department to analyze the effectiveness of their ad campaigns. Thus, capturing data at the time of the sale provides many benefits beyond giving the customer a fancy computerized receipt.

Some OCR readers are less finicky than others. The Postal Service uses scanners that can handle 30,000 letters an hour. The human eye can barely follow individual envelopes as they are sucked out of a feeder, run through the OCR scanner, and dispatched to one of several slots. Eleven people using conventional equipment and their own eyes cannot sort as fast as one machine. However, not all the letters mailed end up on the scanner. Most handwritten zip codes are sent to human sorters.

Handwritten Characters

Machines that can read handwritten characters are yet another means of reducing the number of intermediate steps between capturing data and processing it. There are many instances where it is preferable to write the data and immediately have it usable for processing rather than having data entry operators key it in later. However, not just any kind of handwritten scrawl will do; the rules as to the size, completeness, and legibility of the handwriting are fairly rigid (Figure 4-7). The Internal Revenue Service uses optical scanners to read handwritten numbers on some income tax forms. Taxpayers must follow the directions for forming numbers, however.

Bar Codes

Each product on the store shelf has its own unique number, which is part of the **Universal Product Code** (**UPC**). This code number is represented on the product's label by a pattern of vertical marks, or bars, called **bar codes.** You need only look as far as the back cover of this book to see an example of a bar code. These zebra

TRANSPARENCY ACETATE #4F
Figure #4-7

	Good	Bad
1. Make your letters big	TAPLEY	TAPLEY
2. Use simple shapes	25370	25370
3. Use block printing	STAN	STAN
4. Connect lines	B5T	135T
5. Close loops	9068	9068
6. Do not link characters	LOOP	LOOP

Figure 4-7 Handwritten characters. Legibility is important in making handwritten characters readable by optical recognition.

LECTURE HINT
The post office has joined the bar code act. For example, envelopes sent to potential magazine subscribers for use in returning their checks are bar-coded to represent the destination address. However, not every post office is equipped to process the bar codes.

DISCUSSION QUESTION
What are the advantages for stores that use the UPC system?

stripes can be sensed and read by a **bar code reader,** a photoelectric scanner that reads the code by means of reflected light. As with the wand reader in a retail store, the bar code reader in a bookstore or grocery store is part of a point-of-sale terminal. When you buy a container of, say, chocolate milk mix in a supermarket, the checker moves it past the scanner that reads the bar code (Figure 4-8a). The bar code merely identifies the product to the store's computer; the code does not contain the price, which may vary. The price is stored in a file that can be accessed by the computer. (Obviously, it is easier to change the price once in the computer than to have to repeatedly restamp the price on each container of chocolate milk mix.) The computer automatically tells the point-of-sale terminal what the price is; a printer prints the item description and price on a paper tape for the customer.

There are a great many benefits of using the UPC system—benefits that help slow the rise of grocery prices:

- Prices determined at the POS terminal by scanning are more accurate than those rung up by human checkers.

- Checkout is faster.

- Checkout training is easier, since the machine does most of the work previously done by people punching keys.

- Cash register tapes are more complete, since they identify not only prices but also their corresponding purchases by name.

Figure 4-8 Bar codes. (a) This photoelectric bar code scanner, often seen at supermarket checkout counters, reads the product's zebra-stripe bar code. The bar code identifies the product to the store's computer, which retrieves price information. The price is then automatically rung up on the point-of-sale terminal. (b) The Australian Red Cross combines personal computers and hand-held bar code readers to verify blood type labels.

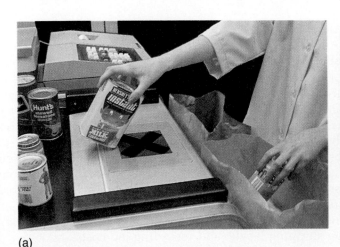

(a)

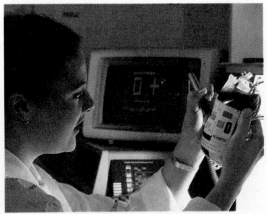

(b)

- Labor costs are reduced.

- Inventory control is easier. Marketing personnel receive instant data on what shoppers are buying. As goods are moved through the checkout stand, the computer can keep a tally of what is left on the shelves and signal the store manager when restocking and re-ordering are necessary.

Although bar codes were once found primarily in the supermarket, there are a variety of other interesting applications. Bar coding has been described as an inexpensive and remarkably reliable way to get data into a computer. It is no wonder that virtually every industry has found a niche for bar codes. In Brisbane, Australia, bar codes help the Red Cross manage their blood bank inventory (Figure 4-8b). Also consider the case of Federal Express, a $1 billion corporation. Their management attributes a large part of their success to the bar-coding system they use to track packages. A ten-digit bar code uniquely identifies each package. As each package wends its way through the transportation system, the bar code is read at each point, and the bar-code number is fed to the computer. An employee can use a computer terminal to query the location of a given shipment at any time; the sender can request a status report on a package and receive a response within 30 minutes. The figures are impressive: The company has an accuracy rate in controlling packages of better than 99%.

One of the original uses of bar codes was as identifiers on railroad cars; the scanned data helped the computer system keep track of wayward cars. More recently, the codes have been useful in libraries, keeping track of books checked in and out. Bar codes have also been officially embraced by the promoters of the Boston Marathon: As each runner completes the 26-mile course, he or she hands in a bar-coded tab that helps officials tabulate the final results swiftly. It seems likely that new applications for bar codes will continue to be developed.

Data Collection Devices

Another direct source of data entry is made through direct **data collection devices,** which may be located in the warehouse or factory or wherever the activity that is generating the data is located (Figure 4-9). This process eliminates intermediate steps and ensures that the data will be more accurate. As we noted earlier in the chapter, factory employees can use a plastic card to punch job data directly into a time clock.

Such devices must be sturdy, trouble-free, and easy to use, since they are often located in dusty, humid, and hot or cold locations. They are used by people such as warehouse workers, packers, forklift operators, and others whose primary work is not clerical. Examples of remote data collection devices are machines for taking inventory, reading shipping labels, and recording job costs.

Figure 4-9   Data collection device.
Such devices are designed for use in
demanding factory environments for
collection of data at the source.

Voice Input

Have you talked to your computer recently? Has it talked
to you? Both feats are possible with current technology, even though
there are some limitations. In this chapter we will examine both
"speakers," you and the computer. Since we are presenting input
here, we will begin with you, as you talk to your computer. What
could be more direct than speaking to a computer? Talk about going
straight to the source!

Voice input is more formally known as **speech recognition,** the
process of presenting input data to the computer through the spoken
word (Figure 4-10). Voice input is about twice as fast as keyboard
input by a skilled typist. **Speech recognition devices** accept the spoken word through a microphone and convert it into binary code that
can be understood by the computer (0s and 1s). There are a great
many uses for this process, quite apart from being an aid to status-
conscious executives who hate to type. In fact, voice input is creating new uses for computers. Typical users are those with "busy
hands" or hands that are too dirty for the keyboard or hands that
must remain cleaner than using a keyboard would permit. Among
current uses are:

- Controlling inventory in an auto junkyard

- Reporting analysis of pathology slides under a microscope

- Making phone calls from a car

- Calculating a correct anesthetic dosage for a patient in surgery

- Changing radio frequencies in airplane cockpits

- Asking for stock-market quotations over the phone

- Sorting packages

- Inspecting items coming along an assembly line

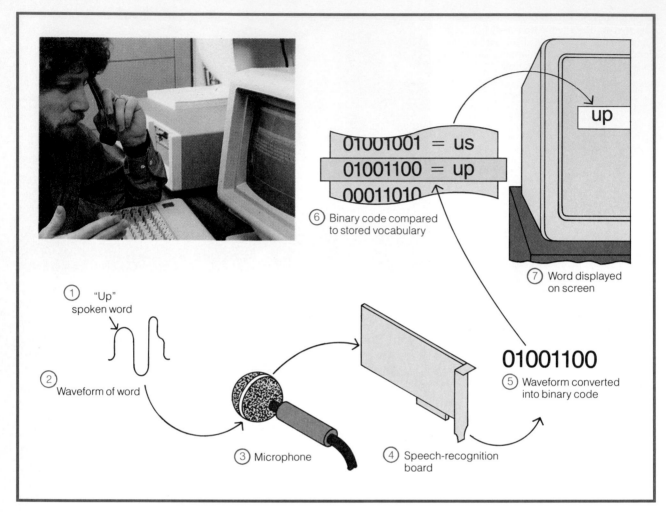

TRANSPARENCY ACETATE #4G
Figure #4-10

Figure 4-10   How voice input works.   The user speaks into a microphone or telephone. A chip on a board inside the computer analyzes the word's waveform and changes it to binary numbers the computer can understand. These digits are compared with the numbers in the stored vocabulary list; if a match is found, the corresponding word is displayed on the screen.

- Allowing physically disabled users to enter commands

- Starting the motor, locking the doors, or turning on the windshield wipers of a car

In each of these cases, the speech recognition system "learns" the voice of the user, who speaks isolated words repeatedly. The voiced words the system "knows" are then recognizable in the future. The package sorter, for instance, speaks digits representing zip codes. The factory inspector voices the simple words *good* or *bad*, or *yes* or *no*. A biologist tells a microscope to scan "Up," "Down," "Right," and "Left." Today voice input is even available on personal computers. Video games that anyone can talk to will be here soon,

LECTURE HINT
Some anesthesiologists are now using voice-activated computers in the operating room. Talking to the computer frees their hands to deal with the human in front of them. For example, saying the word *drips* asks the computer to calculate the correct dosage for an anesthetic for a patient.

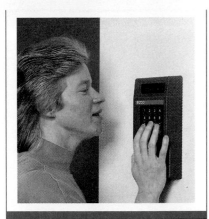

OPEN SESAME

You forgot your door key and there is no one home. But it *is* your house. Does technology exist to let you speak a code word to automatically unlock the door for you? Of course.

A little preplanning is required. Begin by purchasing a computer-based device and installing it in your door. Next, follow instructions to store in electronic memory a secret identification number and matching spoken code word for each member of the household.

When you want to open the door, simply punch your personal identification number into the keypad of the device. The system then knows which of the voices in its memory to expect. Now speak the one-word command into the transmitter and the door unlocks. The device, from Ecco Industries in Danvers, Massachusetts, costs about $1200.

TEST BANK
Mult. Choice   25-36
T/F   30-46
Matching B   6-10
Matching C   1-5
Fill-in-the-Blank   19-35

accepting verbal commands like "Bombs away!," "Dive! Dive! Dive!," and other important instructions.

What are the problems of voice recognition? First of all, speech communication is a very subtle process. Computers are not yet discerning enough to cope with all the ambiguities of spoken language. For example, will the computer know the difference between a *pair* of shoes and a *pear* on a plate? (Some systems are indeed this sophisticated, recognizing the true word from its context.) Second, most speech recognition systems are speaker dependent—that is, they must be separately trained for each individual user. Speech technologists are still wrestling with the wide range of accents and tonal qualities, although a system developed at Carnegie-Mellon can recognize about 1000 English words spoken by anyone. Third, there is the problem of distinguishing voice from background noise and other interfering sounds. Finally, voice input systems usually have a relatively small vocabulary.

Many speech recognition systems, called **discrete word systems,** are limited to isolated words, and speakers must pause between words. Now some systems support sustained speech, so users can speak normally. This type of system is called a **continuous word system,** which can be used, for instance, in the automatic transcription of spoken English into typed text. We can assume that this will eventually lead to word processors that take dictation.

Experts have tagged speech recognition as one of the most difficult things for a computer to do. Some of the world's largest companies—AT&T, IBM, Exxon—have been developing speech technology for years without the hoped-for degree of success. But someday machines that recognize speech will be commonplace. People will routinely talk to their computers, toys, TV sets, refrigerators, ovens, automobiles, and door locks. And no one will stare at them when they do. The research goes on.

7   Computer Screens: Input/Output Devices

The relationship between input and output is an important one. Although some people naively think that the computer wields magical power, the truth is that the output produced is directly related to the input given. Programmers have a slang phrase for this fact: garbage in, garbage out—abbreviated **GIGO.** That is, the quality of the information the computer produces can be no better than the quality and accuracy of the data given to it in the first place. That fact is most obvious when input and output devices are closely related. For instance, computer screens are involved in both input and output: When data is entered, it appears on the screen; the computer response to that data—the output—also appears on the screen. Thus, if a mistake is made in entering data or there is a problem with the computer program, the mistake shows up right away on the screen.

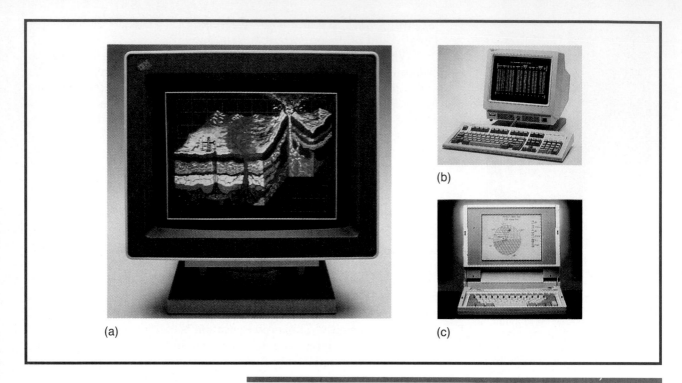

(a)

(b)

(c)

Figure 4-11   A variety of screens. (a) This high-resolution brilliance is available only on a color graphics display. (b) Studies show that amber screens reduce eyestrain. (c) Laptop computers use liquid crystal display (LCD) technology for their small, lightweight screens.

Figure 4-12   An automated teller machine. By inserting a plastic card and punching in a secret code, a user can perform many banking functions, including deposits, cash withdrawals, and funds transfers.

Computer screens come in many different shapes, sizes, and colors. The most common type of screen is the **cathode ray tube,** or **CRT.** Color monitors are available for displaying color graphics (Figure 4-11a). Some screens are **monochrome**—characters and graphics appear in only one color. The most common monochrome screen displays green letters and numbers on a dark background, but amber characters are also available and are thought to be easier on the eyes (Figure 4-11b). Another type of screen is the **liquid crystal display** (**LCD**), a flat display screen found on laptop computers (Figure 4-11c). These screens are much smaller and lighter than CRTs, but the quality suffers. The screens on point-of-sale terminals are even smaller—just large enough to display the item name and price.

A screen you can see any time is part of the **automated teller machine** (**ATM**), found at your bank (Figure 4-12). You can insert your plastic card and key in a personal identification number, then give the machine your instructions, such as telling it to make a cash withdrawal. A small computer screen both gives instructions on the machine's operation and responds to your requests. When you make such a routine transaction, you probably do not pause to ponder the amazing fact that this machine can accept your input and, almost instantly, produce an output response and follow your instructions.

LECTURE HINT
ATMs have sometimes been easy targets for crooks. There is little to prevent an insider from making up phony automatic teller machine cards and heisting cash from the machines. Some culprits have been caught by tips; others remain at large. Banks are considering switching to voice identification systems.

LECTURE ACTIVITY
Several vendors have very impressive graphics displays to demonstrate their computers that can be demonstrated to students. One example is a model jet shown rotating on the screen of a Commodore Amiga computer. Another is a varying music score on an Apple IIGS computer, with corresponding stereo sound coming out of Bose speakers. Inquire at your local computer store for further suggestions.

LECTURE HINT
To the user, a computer terminal looks like one device. But to a computer, the keyboard is an input device, and the screen is an output device.

DISCUSSION QUESTION
How do dumb, smart, and intelligent terminals differ?

CRT Screen Technology

Most CRT screens use a technology called **raster-scan technology.** The image to be displayed on the screen is sent electronically from the computer to the cathode ray tube, which directs a beam of electrons to the screen. The beam causes the phosphor-coated screen to emit a light, which causes an image on the screen. But the light does not stay lit very long, so the image must be **refreshed** often. If the screen is not refreshed often enough, the fading screen image appears to flicker. A **scan rate**—the number of times the screen is refreshed—of 60 times per second is usually adequate to retain a clear screen image.

A computer display screen that can be used for graphics is divided into dots that are called "addressable" because they can be *addressed* individually by the graphics software. These displays are called **dot-addressable displays** or **bit-mapped displays.** Each dot can be illuminated individually on the screen. Each dot is potentially a *picture element*, or **pixel.** The **resolution** of the screen—its clarity—is directly related to the number of pixels on the screen: The more pixels, the higher the resolution. Some computers, by the way, come with built-in graphics capability. Others need an extra device, called a **graphics card** or **graphics adapter board.** To display graphics, you need both a color monitor and color graphics circuitry, either built-in or on a board.

Terminals

A screen may be the monitor of a self-contained personal computer or it may be part of a terminal that is one of many terminals attached to a larger computer. A **terminal** consists of an input device, an output device, and a communications link to the main computer. Most commonly, a terminal has a keyboard for an input device and a screen for an output device, although there are many variations on this theme. A terminal with a screen is called a **video display terminal (VDT).**

There are three kinds of terminals: dumb, smart, and intelligent. A **dumb terminal** does not process data; it is merely a means of entering data into a computer and receiving output from it. Far more common is the **smart terminal,** which can do some processing, usually to edit data it receives. In contrast an **intelligent terminal** can be programmed to perform a variety of processing. Most supermarket point-of-sale terminals are smart. They have CPUs in them that can edit data right at the checkout stand.

The keyboard is an important component of a terminal. To communicate with the main computer through a terminal keyboard, you make what is called an **inquiry.** An inquiry is a request for information. The result is usually displayed on the CRT screen very quickly. Sometimes the computer, in turn, will request data or a command of you, the user of the computer. This is known as a **prompt.** Suppose

PERSPECTIVES

TO YOUR HEALTH

Can all this "computering" be good for you? Are there any unhealthy side effects? The computer seems harmless enough. How bad can it be, sitting in a padded chair in a climate-controlled office?

How Bad Is It?

Health questions have been raised by the people who sit all day in front of a computer screen. Are they getting bad radiation? What about eye strain? And what about the age-old back problem, updated with new concerns about workers who hold their hands over a keyboard? Despite extensive studies over several years, the answer seems to be, "We are not quite sure." Even so, unions and legislators are taking steps to limit exposure to video screens.

Ergonomics

Meanwhile, there are a number of things workers can do to take care of themselves. A good place to begin is with an ergonomically-designed work station. *Ergonomics* is the study of human factors related to computers. A properly designed work station takes a variety of factors into account, such as the distance from the eyes to the screen and the angle of the arms and wrists.

Workers in the *Los Angeles Times* newsroom work in a proper ergonomic environment. Each employee has an adjustable chair and a screen that swivels. Indirect lighting and anti-glare screens help reduce eyestrain.

How We Cope

Experts recommend these steps as coping mechanisms:

- Turn the screen away from the window to reduce glare and cover your screen with a glare deflector (see photo). Turn off overhead lights; illuminate your work area with a lamp.
- Put your monitor on a tilt-and-swivel base.

- Get a pneumatically adjustable chair. Position the seat back so your lower back is supported.
- Place the keyboard low enough to avoid arm fatigue. Do not bend your wrists when you type. Do not rest your wrists on a sharp edge.
- Sit with your feet firmly on the floor.
- Exercise at your desk. Better yet, get up and walk around.

you work in police communications and receive a report that a police officer has sighted a suspicious-looking car with a license plate beginning with *AXR*. You make an inquiry of the computer and ask it to display a list of all stolen cars in your state with licenses beginning *AXR*. The computer does this, then provides a prompt:

```
DO YOU WISH DETAILS FOR A SPECIFIC NUMBER FROM
THIS LIST?
YES (Y) OR NO (N)
```

You type Y, and the computer provides another prompt:

TYPE SPECIFIC LICENSE NUMBER

You do so, and you receive details about the make and the year of the car, its owner, address, and so on.

So far, we have looked at types of input and at screens, which are input/output devices. Now it is time to examine output devices.

7 Types of Output

Output can take many forms, such as screen output, paper printouts, overhead transparencies, and 35mm slides. Other forms of output include microfilm and voice. Even within the same organization there can be different kinds of output. You can see this the next time you go to a travel agency that uses a computer system. If you ask for airline flights to Toronto, Calgary, and Vancouver, say, the travel agent will probably make a few queries to the system and receive output on a screen indicating availability on the various flights. After the reservations have been confirmed, the agent can ask for printed output of three kinds: the tickets, the traveler's itinerary, and the invoice. The agency may also keep records of your travel plans, which may be output on microfilm. In addition, agency management may periodically receive printed reports and charts, such as monthly summaries of sales figures or pie charts of regional costs.

As you might already suspect, the printer is one of the principal devices used to produce computer output.

7 Printers: The Image Makers

A **printer** is a device that produces printed paper output—known in the trade as **hard copy** because it is tangible and permanent (unlike soft copy, which is displayed on a screen). Some printers produce only letters and numbers, whereas others are also able to produce graphics.

Letters and numbers are formed by a printer either as solid characters or as dot-matrix characters. **Dot-matrix printers** create characters in the same way that individual lights in a pattern spell out words on a basketball scoreboard. Dot-matrix printers construct a character by activating a matrix of pins that produces the shape of the character. Figure 4-13 shows how this works. A typical matrix is 5×7—that is, five dots wide and seven dots high. These printers are sometimes called 9-pin printers, because they have two extra vertical dots for creating the parts of lowercase letters g, j, p, and y that go below the text line. The 24-pin dot-matrix printer uses a series of overlapping dots—the more dots, the better the quality of the letter produced. This printer is becoming the dominant dot-matrix printer. Some dot-matrix printers can produce color images.

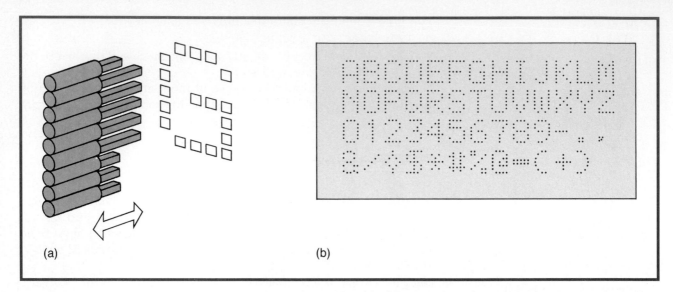

(a)   (b)

TRANSPARENCY ACETATE #4H
Figure #4-13

Figure 4-13   Forming dot-matrix characters.   (a) This art shows the letter G
being printed as a 5 × 7 dot-matrix character. The moving matrix head has nine
vertical pins, which move back and forth as necessary to form each letter. (b) This
art shows letters, numbers, and special characters formed as 5 × 7 dot-matrix
characters. Although not shown in this figure, dot-matrix printers can print lowercase letters too. The two lower pins are used for the parts of lowercase letters g, j,
p, and y that go below the line.

Distinguishing printers according to whether they produce dot-
matrix or solid characters is one way to distinguish printers. But the
two principal ways of classifying printers are:

- According to the means of making an image on the paper

- According to the amount of information they print at a time

There are two ways of making an image on paper: the impact method
and the nonimpact method. An **impact printer** is much like a typewriter. It forms characters by physically striking paper, ribbon, and
print hammer together. A **nonimpact printer** forms characters by
using a noncontact process—that is, there is never physical contact
between the printer and the paper.

Let us take a closer look at these differences.

Impact Printers

The term *impact* refers to the fact that impact printers use
some sort of physical contact with the paper to produce an image.
The impact may be produced by a character-shaped print hammer
striking a ribbon against the paper or by a print hammer hitting
paper and ribbon against a character. Impact printers are of two
kinds: character and line.

Character printers are like typewriters. They print character by
character across the page from one margin to the other. A typical
character printer is the **daisy wheel.** Noted for high-quality printing,

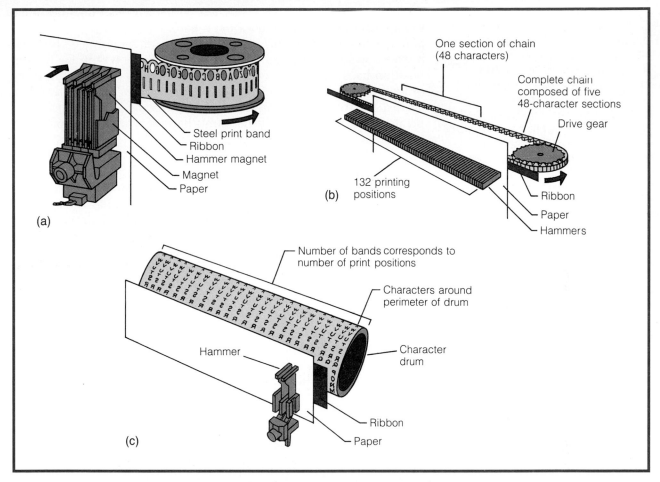

(a)

Steel print band
Ribbon
Hammer magnet
Magnet
Paper

One section of chain
(48 characters)

Complete chain
composed of five
48-character sections

Drive gear

132 printing
positions

(b)

Ribbon
Paper
Hammers

Number of bands corresponds to
number of print positions

Characters around
perimeter of drum

Character
drum

Hammer

Ribbon

Paper

(c)

TRANSPARENCY ACETATE #4I
Figure #4-14

Figure 4-14   Three kinds of impact line-printer mechanisms.   (a) Band printer mechanism. The band or belt can be easily changed to print different styles of type. Some band printers can print up to 600 lines per minute. (b) Chain printer mechanism. Some print up to 3000 lines per minute. (c) Drum printer mechanism. Some of these also print up to 3000 lines per minute.

LECTURE HINT
Diablo popularized the daisy wheel print head. IBM used a thimble, which is also removable. Other vendors use a rounded cylinder.

this kind of printer is useful for word processing and professional correspondence. The daisy wheel consists of a removable wheel with a set of spokes, each containing a raised character. The entire wheel rotates to line up the appropriate character, which is then struck by a hammer. The user can change type styles (fonts) by changing wheels. Most new electronic typewriters use the daisy-wheel technique.

    Line printers assemble all characters on a line at one time and print them out practically simultaneously. There are several types of impact line printers. The **band printer,** the most popular type of impact printer, uses a horizontally rotating band that contains characters, as shown in Figure 4-14a. The characters on the band are struck by hammers through paper and ribbon. The **chain printer** consists of characters on a chain that rotate past all print positions

(Figure 4-14b). Hammers are aligned with each position, and when the appropriate character goes by, a hammer strikes paper and ribbon against it. The **drum printer** consists of a cylinder with embossed rows of characters on its surface (Figure 4-14c). Each print position has a complete set of characters around the circumference of the drum. As the drum turns, a hammer strikes paper and ribbon against the drum. A drum printer is considered a dinosaur among printers, but many can still be found hard at work in computer installations.

Nonimpact Printers

There are many advantages to nonimpact printers, but there are two main reasons for their growing popularity: They are faster and quieter. Speed derives from the fact that nonimpact printers have fewer moving parts; they have no type elements or hammers that move around. The lowering of the noise level results from the absence of the impact—the striking of print hammers against ribbon and paper.

Other advantages of nonimpact printers over conventional mechanical printers are their ability to change typefaces automatically and their graphics capability.

The major technologies competing in the nonimpact market are ink jet and laser. They use the dot-matrix concept to form characters. Let us briefly consider each of these.

Ink-Jet Printers

Spraying ink from jet nozzles, **ink-jet printers** are up to ten times faster than impact printers. The ink, which is charged, passes through an electric field, which deflects it to produce a dot-

Figure 4-15   Ink-jet printer. Ink-jet printers are noted for high-quality graphics output.

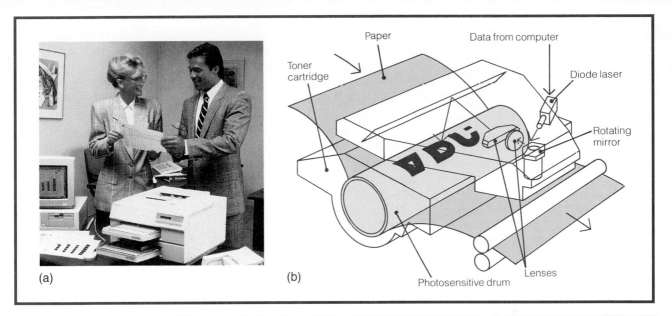

Paper   Data from computer

Toner cartridge   Diode laser

Rotating mirror

(a)   (b)

Lenses

Photosensitive drum

TRANSPARENCY ACETATE #4J
Figure #4-16

Figure 4-16   Laser printers.   (a) Even though they are at the high end of the price scale, the high-quality print and durability of the Hewlett-Packard LaserJet II printers make them best-sellers. (b) A laser printer works in a fashion similar to a photocopy machine. Using patterns of small dots, a laser beam conveys information from the computer to a positively-charged drum inside the laser printer. Wherever an image is to be printed, the laser beam is turned on, causing the drum to become neutralized. As the drum passes by a toner cartridge, toner sticks to the neutral spots on the drum. The toner is then transferred from the drum to a piece of paper. In the final step, heat and pressure fuse the toner to the paper. The drum is then cleaned for the next pass.

matrix character. Ink-jet printers, by using multiple nozzles, can print in several different colors of ink. Color ink-jet printers, as shown in Figure 4-15, produce excellent graphics. However, these printers often produce poor-quality text and at relatively slow speeds.

Laser Printers

A generation of children has watched movies in which space travelers use a laser, a powerful beam of bright light, to cut a hole through a wall or zap a flying target. Lasers have a true home, however, with computers, where **laser printers** use a light beam to help transfer images to paper (Figure 4-16). A laser beam "writes" an image onto the surface of a rotating metal drum. Then ink-like toner is deposited on the drum; it adheres where the image was "written." The toner is then transferred to paper. The result is an extremely high-quality image. A laser printer can print a page at a time at record-breaking speeds.

Laser printers have been around for a number of years, but their initial high cost—hundreds of thousands of dollars—limited their use to companies whose need for speed made them cost-effective. Technological advancements, however, have now significantly reduced costs so that low-end laser printers can be purchased for a few thousand dollars or even less. The Oregon legislature has taken advantage of the new affordability by placing laser printers in key administrative areas. Legislators who used to wait hours for drafts of new legislation to be delivered by courier now have easy access to draft bills from a nearby printer. "It's as quiet as the copy machine," marveled one politician. "All you can hear is the paper moving."

The price of a good laser printer is now low enough to tempt people who care about first-rate printing. The rush to laser printers has been influenced by the trend toward desktop publishing—using a personal computer, a laser printer, and special software to make professional-looking publications. We will examine desktop publishing in detail in Chapter 15.

Which Type of Printer?

A lot has been said about nonimpact printers. The trade press and industry consultants have embraced nonimpact technology, and market acceptance increases with every price decrease. But impact printers will not necessarily be swept aside by the onrushing wave of nonimpact machines. A key reason is the seeming invincibility of impact printers: They chatter away day after day, year after year, without missing a beat—and rarely need repair. Another reason is pragmatic: multiple-part forms. Companies that print W-2 forms, stock certificates, mass-mailing cards, legal documents—anything requiring copies—will continue to use impact printers.

Choosing a printer does not get any easier for personal computers, as you can see in Table 4-1. Printers made especially for personal computers come in just about all the varieties we have already discussed. People are often surprised to discover that it is as difficult to choose a printer as it is to choose the computer itself. Some people are also startled to find that the printer they want may cost twice as much as the computer. Printers for microcomputers will be examined in Chapter 11.

PRINTER SPEEDS

This list of printers is not all inclusive, but these speeds are typical. Characters per second is represented by *cps*, lines per minute by *lpm*.

Daisy wheel—50 to 80 cps

Dot-matrix character—50 to 500 cps

Dot-matrix line—300 to 900 lpm

Band—400 to 3600 lpm

Ink jet—110 to 400 cps

Laser—10,000 to 20,000 lpm

Table 4-1   Personal computer printer comparison chart. Suit your convenience and your pocketbook when you choose a printer.

	Daisy wheel	Dot-matrix 9-pin	Dot-matrix 24-pin	Ink-jet	Laser
Speed	Slow	Medium	Fast	Medium	Very fast
Versatility	Low	Medium	Medium	Medium	High
Quality	Good	Fair	Good	Good	Excellent
Cost	Medium	Low	Medium	High	High
Graphics	No	Yes	Yes	Yes	Yes
Color	No	No	Some	Yes	No
Noise	Loud	Loud	Loud	Quiet	Quiet

Figure 4-17   Continuous form paper. Some printout paper is continuous form, as shown here. Other printers use single sheets of paper.

LECTURE HINT
NCR is also the standard abbreviation for the National Cash Register Company, which is very active in the computer industry. These two are sometimes confused.

Figure 4-18   Computer output microfilm. One 4- by 6-inch microfiche sheet can hold the equivalent of over 200 pages.

Paper

Now that you know something about printers, you can appreciate the fact that they use a variety of papers. Some printers use ordinary paper; others require special paper.

Computer output may be produced on a variety of different kinds of paper—cheap newsprint, lined-stock tabulating paper (called **stock tab**), shaded-band paper (called **green-bar paper**), or even fancy preprinted forms with institutional logo and address.

Paper may come in a letter-size sheet; this size is becoming more common as the use of laser printers increases. But more likely it comes in a roll or in one continuous folded form called **continuous form** (Figure 4-17). Continuous form paper has sprocket holes along the sides, which help feed the paper rapidly through the printer without slippage. A computer operator puts a box of continuous paper under the printer, feeds the paper through the printer, and allows the printer output to accumulate—folded—in another box. The continuous paper must then be separated, a process called **bursting.**

If multiple copies are required, carbon paper for computer printers is available. The process of removing the carbon paper from between the layered copies is called **decollating.** A special paper called **NCR paper** (NCR stands for *no carbon required*) allows several copies to be made without the need for carbon paper. NCR paper is more convenient but more expensive than carbon paper.

Although the intent of computer processing is to increase productivity, its misuse has contributed to a scourge of the modern world—paper pollution. The computer may enhance the productivity of direct-mail advertisers, but it may inhibit your own productivity if you find your mailbox clogged with computer-produced junk mail.

7 Computer Output Microfilm

How many warehouses would it take to store all the census data for this country? How many rooms in an insurance company would be required to hold all the printed customer records? To save space, **computer output microfilm** (generally referred to by its abbreviation, **COM**) was developed (Figure 4-18). Computer output is produced as very small images on sheets or rolls of film. A microfilm record can be preserved on a roll of film (usually 35mm) or on 4- by 6-inch sheets of film called **microfiche;** users often call them just fiche.

COM has many advantages, not the least of which is space savings. At 200 pages per microfiche, this book, for instance, could be stored on four 4- by 6-inch microfiche. The major disadvantage of COM is that it cannot be read without the assistance of a microfilm reader. COM may soon disappear, however, in favor of storage on disk—when everyone has a computer to access the disk.

Numbers and pictures are—by far—the most common output forms, but voice output is also a possibility.

7 Voice Output: Your Master's (Digital) Voice

We have already examined voice input in some detail. As you will see in this section, however, computers are frequently like people in the sense that they find it easier to talk than to listen. **Speech synthesis**—the process of enabling machines to talk to people—is much easier than speech recognition.

"The door is ajar," your car says to you in a male voice. Why male? Because male voices have a narrower range than female voices and thus—an interesting, nonsexist reason—require less capacity in the memory of the microprocessor from which the voices originate! These are not, after all, real human voices. They are the product of **voice synthesizers** (also called **voice-output devices** or **audio-response units**), which convert data in main storage to vocalized sounds understandable to humans.

There are two basic approaches to getting a computer to talk. The first is **synthesis by analysis,** in which the device analyzes the input of an actual human voice speaking words, stores and processes the spoken sounds, and reproduces them as needed. The process of storing words is similar to the digitizing process we discussed earlier when considering voice input. In essence, synthesis by analysis uses the computer as a digital tape recorder.

The second approach to synthesizing speech is **synthesis by rule,** in which the device applies a complex set of linguistic rules to create an artificial spoken language. Synthesis based on the human voice has the advantage of sounding more natural, but it is limited to the number of words stored in the computer. Synthesis by rule has no vocabulary restriction, but the spoken product is often mechanical and sounds like no voice from this planet.

Voice synthesizers can be relatively inexpensive ($200 or so) and connect to almost any computer. Most synthesizers plug into the computer where the printer does and, rather than print the output, they speak it. Speed and pitch can usually be adjusted.

Eager candidates for voice synthesizers are often those who have speech impairments. Several software packages exist that let people communicate on the phone by typing their messages, which are then converted to synthetic speech. For example: "Hello. I am not able to speak, but I am able to hear you, and my computer is doing the talking for me. Would you please tell me if you have tickets for the Beethoven concert on Friday, the 18th?" This message can be keyed before the phone call. After the call is dialed and someone answers, the user pushes the Speak button, and the message goes out over the phone.

In addition, a reading machine has been devised that is of considerable help to the blind. Scanning a page, it recognizes letters and words, applies phonetic rules, and produces spoken sentences. The machine can even put in stresses and accents.

Voice output has become common in such places as airline and bus terminals, banks, and brokerage houses. It is typically used when an inquiry is followed by a short reply (such as a bank balance or flight time). Many businesses have found other creative uses for voice output as it applies to the telephone. Automatic telephone voices ("Hello, this is a computer speaking . . .") take surveys, inform customers that catalog orders are ready to pick up, and remind consumers that they have not paid their bills. (By using voice output one utility company saved the cost of hiring people to call the thousands of customers who do not pay on time.)

One more note. Perhaps it has occurred to you that voice input and voice output systems can go together. This is true. Today's technology permits combined voice input and output—consider the car system that you can talk to and get responses from. But that technology, by today's standards, is really very limited, and applications are few indeed.

Now it is time to return to computer screens and consider everyone's favorite, computer graphics.

7 Computer Graphics

Computer output in the form of graphics has come into its own in a major—and sometimes spectacular—way. What reader of this book could possibly be unaware of the form of graphics known as video games? Who has not seen TV commercials or movies that use computer-produced animated graphics? Computer graphics can also be found in education, computer art, science, sports, and more (see Figure 4-19 and Gallery 3). But perhaps the most prevalent use of graphics today is in business.

TEST BANK
Mult. Choice   53-58
T/F   57-65
Matching D   7-10
Fill-in-the-Blank   50-54

Figure 4-19   Computer graphics. Both the world of science and the world of art benefit from the power of computer graphics.

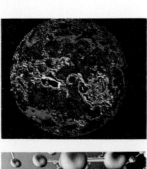
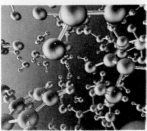

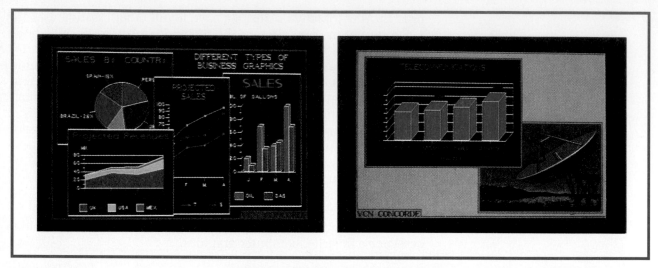

TRANSPARENCY ACETATE #4K
Figure #4-20

Figure 4-20 Business graphics.   Colorful pie charts, line graphs, and bar charts help businesspeople understand information quickly.

7 Business Graphics: Pie Chart Picassos

It might seem wasteful to display in color graphics what could more inexpensively be shown to managers as numbers in standard computer printouts. However, colorful graphics, maps, and charts can help managers compare data more easily, spot trends, and make decisions more quickly. The use of color also has an impact that helps people get the picture—literally. Finally, although color graphs and charts have been used in business for years—usually to make presentations to higher management or outside clients—the computer allows them to be rendered quickly, before information becomes outdated.

The headlines all say about the same thing: THE BOOM IN BUSINESS GRAPHICS or THE BUSINESS GRAPHICS EXPLOSION. The boom is here all right, but the real story is the staggering number of business graphics software packages. Graphics software can be used to prepare the traditional line graphs, bar charts, and pie charts used to illuminate and analyze data (Figure 4-20). For example, a stockbroker can view stock-market price and volume charts of data from the day's sales transactions. One user refers to business graphics as "computer-assisted insight." The entire spectrum of business graphics is presented in Chapter 13.

7 Video Graphics

Unbound by the fetters of reality, video graphics can be as creative as an animated cartoon (Figure 4-21). Although **video graphics** operate on the same principle as a moving picture or car-

Figure 4-21 And the Oscar goes to . . . This toddler, programmed to gurgle, sneeze, and cry, is featured in an animated film called *Tin Toy,* which won the first Academy Award ever given for a completely computer-generated film.

toon—one frame at a time in quick succession—they are produced by computers. Video graphics have made their biggest splash on television, but many people do not realize they are watching the computer at work. The next time you watch television, skip the sandwich and pay special attention to the commercials. Unless there is a live human in the advertisement, there is a good chance that the moving objects you see, such as floating cars and bobbing electric razors, are computer output. Another fertile ground for video graphics is the network's logo and theme. Accompanied by music and swooshing sounds, the network symbol spins and cavorts and turns itself inside out, all with the finesse that only a computer could supply.

Video graphics do not have to be commercial in nature, of course. Some video artists produce beauty for its own sake. An important scientific use of video graphics is to construct moving models such as a model of DNA molecules whose atoms, represented by gleaming spheres, twist and fold.

Computer-Aided Design/Computer-Aided Manufacturing

For more than a decade, computer graphics have also been part and parcel of a field known by the abbreviation **CAD/CAM**—short for **computer-aided design/computer-aided manufacturing.** In this area computers are used to create two- and three-dimensional pictures of everything from hand tools to tractors. CAD/CAM provides a bridge between design and manufacturing. As a manager at Chrysler said, "Many companies have design data and manufacturing data and the two are never the same. At Chrysler, we have only one set of data that everyone dips into." For the results of their efforts, see Figure 4-22.

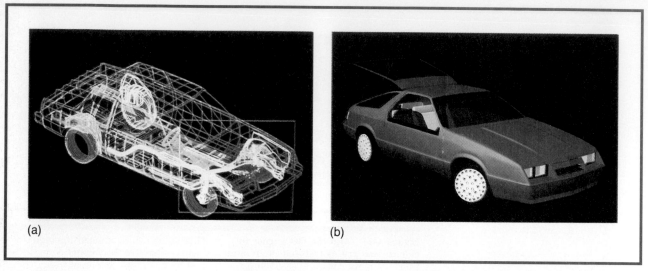

(a)   (b)

TRANSPARENCY ACETATE #4K
Figure #4-22a

Figure 4-22   CAD/CAM. With computer-aided design and computer-aided manufacturing (CAD/CAM), the computer can keep track of all details, maintain designs
of parts in memory, and combine parts electronically as required. (a) A computer-
aided design wireframe used to study design possibilities. (b) A polygonal, shaded
image used to evaluate the appearance—is it pleasing or not?—of a car's body
design.

We will examine CAD/CAM in more detail in Gallery 4, which
describes manufacturing systems. In Chapter 13 we will be looking
at the software used to create graphics. For now let us look at the
input and output devices that make computer graphics possible.

7 Graphics Input Devices

There are many ways to produce and interact with screen
graphics. The following are some of the most common. Some of
these devices can also be used for input other than graphics.

Light Pen

For direct interaction with your computer screen, few
things beat a light pen. It is versatile enough to modify screen graphics or make a menu selection—that is, to choose from a list of activity choices on the screen. A **light pen** (Figure 4-23) has a light-sensitive cell at the end. When the light pen is placed against the screen, it
closes a photoelectric circuit that pinpoints the place where pictures
or data on the screen are entered or modified.

Digitizer

An image—whether a drawing or a photo—can be
scanned by a device called a **digitizer** (Figure 4-24a), which converts
the image into digital data that the computer can accept and represent on the screen. However, a **digitizing tablet** (Figure 4-24b) lets

Figure 4-23   Light pen. When a pen
with a light-sensitive cell at the end is
placed against the screen of this graphics display terminal, it closes a photoelectric circuit, enabling the terminal to
identify the point on the screen. This
engineer is using a computer with a
light pen to test a jet aircraft system.

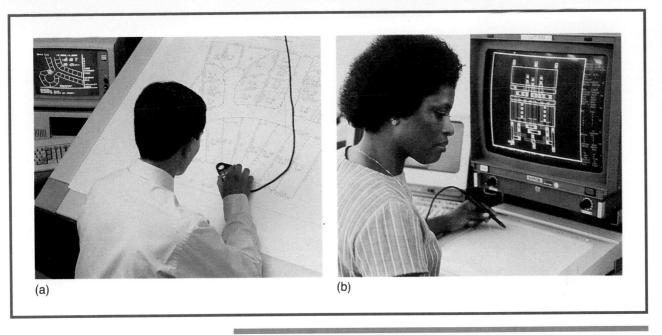

(a)   (b)

Figure 4-24   Digitizers.   (a) This land developer is using a digitizer to input a map of a housing tract in Hayward, California. (b) This engineer is using a digitizing tablet and color monitor to verify the design of an integrated circuit.

you create your own images. This device has a special stylus that can be used to draw or trace images, which are then converted to digital data that can be processed by the computer.

Joy Stick

Another well-known graphics display device, the **joy stick,** is that gadget dear to the hearts of—indeed, we might say the joy of—video game addicts. It is, of course, a gizmo that allows fingertip control of figures on a CRT screen (Figure 4-25).

Figure 4-25   A joy stick. Musicians can use computers and software to compose music. In this example, the process is controlled by (a) a joy stick. (b) As you can see on the bottom of the screen pictured here, a composer has a choice of notes, sharps, clef signs, and other music symbols, which can be selected and "picked up" by the joy stick and placed on the staff above. Also, the composer can have the computer play the notes so the user can hear how they sound.

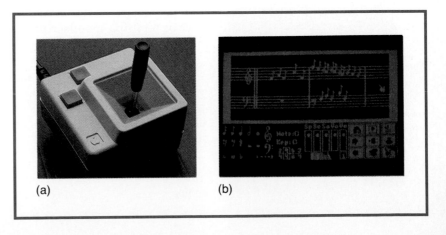

(a)   (b)

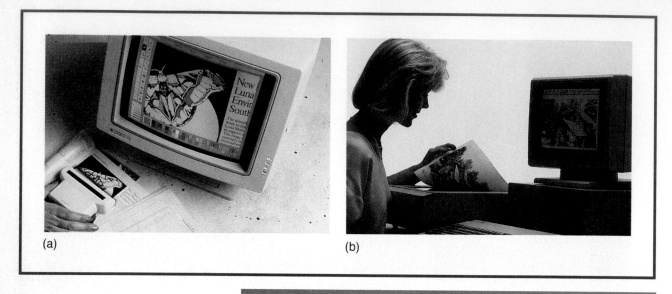

(a)   (b)

Figure 4-26   Scanners.   (a) As this hand-held scanner is moved over a picture, the image appears on the computer screen. (b) With a desktop scanner, the picture is laid face down on the scanner, which looks somewhat like a small copy machine. Once an image is scanned, it can be altered and it can be combined with text to produce a document complete with illustrations.

Scanner

"You are about to witness something amazing." The word *amazing* is actually part of an advertisement for a hand-held scanner. A demonstration *is* rather amazing. As you watch a **scanner** being moved over written text and pictures, the same text and picture images appear on the screen of the attached computer—and can be stored on a disk file. Scanners come in both hand-held and desktop models (Figure 4-26). Although all scanners can scan images, they vary in their ability to scan text. Files created by scanning can be used like any other files: They can be edited, printed, and so forth, making the scanner a very useful device.

Who would use such a device? Anyone who prefers scanning to typing. For example, teachers can scan text in books for use in classroom exercises. Lawyers can scan contracts. Publishers can save the cost of retyping manuscripts.

Touch Screen

If you disdain pens and sticks and mice, perhaps you would prefer the direct human touch, your finger. **Touch screens** accept input data by letting you point at the screen to select your choice (Figure 4-27). Sensors on the edges of the screen pinpoint the touched location and cause a corresponding action on the screen.

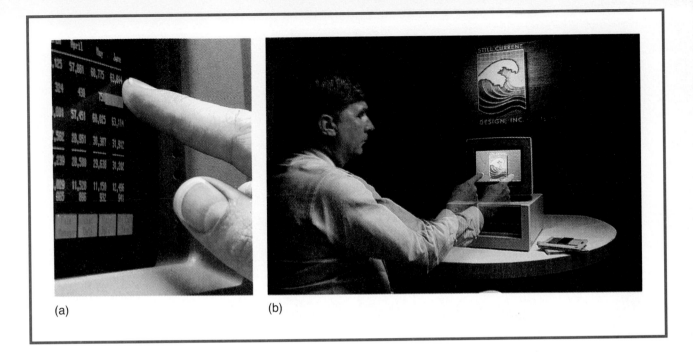

(a)   (b)

Figure 4-27   Touch screen.   (a) Light beams from the screen edge detect a pointing finger and note the location of the beams intersecting at the touched point. (b) Touchscreen technology combined with pictures stored on disk provides a new twist to visual aids. With a touch of the finger, viewers can focus on topics of interest, skipping quickly from one topic to another without having to flip through numerous slides or rewind a VCR.

7 Graphics Output Devices

Just as there are many different ways to input graphics to the computer, there are many different ways to output graphics. Essentially, graphics can be output on a screen, paper, an overhead transparency, or a 35mm slide. We have already discussed screens, so now we will look at other graphics output devices.

Plotters

Plotters draw hard-copy graphics output in the form of maps, bar charts, engineering drawings, and even two- or three-dimensional illustrations. Plotters often come with a set of four pens in four different colors. Most plotters also offer shading features. Plotters are of two types: flatbed and drum.

A **flatbed plotter** looks like a drafting table with a sheet of paper on it and a mechanical pen suspended over it (Figure 4-28a). The pen is at an angle to the table and moves around on the paper under the control of a computer program. The flatbed is commonly used for engineering drawings. Small flatbed plotters are also available for personal computers.

The paper for a **drum plotter** is rolled on a drum instead of being flat on a table (Figure 4-28b). A pen is poised over the drum. If the pen is placed on the paper while the drum unrolls the paper (to be taken up temporarily on another drum), a straight line is drawn along its length. On the other hand, if the pen is moved across the paper while the paper remains in place, a line is drawn across the

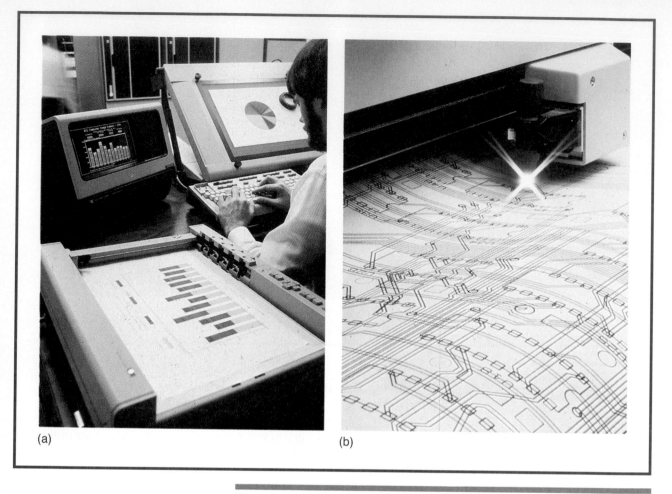

(a)

(b)

Figure 4-28   Plotters. Designers of circuit boards, street maps, schematic diagrams, and similar applications can work in fine detail on a computer screen, then print the results on a plotter. (a) Flatbed plotter. (b) Drum plotter.

paper. You can visualize the various diagonal lines and curves that may be drawn with combinations of drum and pen movement. One advantage of a drum plotter is that the sheet of paper can be quite long, which is necessary in certain scientific work.

Printers

As we noted earlier, some printers are capable of producing graphics. Although graphics are most dramatic on a screen or on a slide produced from a screen, many users need to include graphics in reports, so printers that can produce graphics play an important role.

Overhead Transparency Makers

When making a presentation to a group, fancy graphics are not much help when they appear only on your computer screen or on paper. Transparencies used on an overhead projector are one way to present information to a group. Some plotters and printers are capable of producing overhead transparencies—just use a sheet of acetate instead of paper. Machines that produce only transparencies are also available.

35mm Slide Makers

Various devices are available that produce 35mm slides of computer graphics. The camera of such a device has a cone whose narrow end fits over the camera while the wide rectangular end fits exactly over your screen. Click, and you have captured your computer graphic on film. Of course, the film must now be developed. The Polaroid Palette, however, produces instant slides. Also, this system does not photograph your screen; it uses your graphics data to produce an image. You can even create color slides from a black-and-white CRT.

7 Yet to Come

Almost weekly, new forms of computer input and output are announced, with an array of benefits for human use. As we will see in the chapters on personal computers and data communications, they promise to have an enormous impact on our lives. Their effectiveness, however, depends on two components that we have not yet discussed: storage and software. We will study the first of these in the next chapter.

STUDENT PROJECT
Contact local companies to find out how they have implemented ergonomic principles. Present your findings to the class.

7 Summary and Key Terms

- Inputting is the procedure of providing data to the computer for processing.

- The keyboard is a common input device used by owners of personal computers, as well as by **data entry operators,** who use computer terminals to enter large amounts of data from **source documents.** The data that operators enter is stored on magnetic tape or magnetic disk before being sent to a main computer for processing.

- A **pointer,** or **cursor,** is a flashing indicator on a screen that shows where the next user–computer interaction will take place. The cursor can be moved by pressing certain keys on the keyboard or by rolling a **mouse** on a flat surface. A mouse also has a button which can be pressed to give certain commands to the computer.

- An **icon** is a pictorial symbol on a screen. A computer user can interact with an icon by using a mouse.

- **Source data automation,** the use of special equipment to collect data and send it directly to the computer, is a more efficient method of data entry than keyboarding. Four means of source data automation are magnetic-ink character recognition, optical recognition, data collection devices, and voice input.

- **Magnetic-ink character recognition (MICR)** readers read characters made of magnetized particles, such as the preprinted characters on a personal check. The characters are put on documents by **MICR inscribers** and are read by **MICR reader/sorters.**

- **Optical recognition systems** convert optical marks, optical characters, handwritten characters, and bar codes into electrical signals to be sent to the computer. **Optical mark-recognition (OMR)** devices use a light beam to recognize marks on paper. **Optical character-recognition (OCR)** devices use a light beam to read special characters, such as those on price tags. These characters are often in a standard typeface called **OCR-A.** A commonly used OCR device is the hand-held **wand reader,** which is often connected to a **point-of-sale (POS) terminal** in a retail store. Some optical scanners can read precise handwritten characters. A **bar code reader** is a stationary photoelectric scanner used to input a **bar code,** the pattern of vertical marks that represents the **Universal Product Code (UPC)** that identifies a product.

- **Data collection devices** allow direct, accurate data entry in places such as factories and warehouses.

- **Voice input,** or **speech recognition,** is the process of presenting input data to the computer through the spoken word. **Speech recognition devices** convert spoken words into a digital code that a computer can understand. The two main types of devices are **discrete word systems,** which require speakers to pause between words, and **continuous word systems,** which allow a normal rate of speaking.

- **GIGO** stands for *garbage in, garbage out,* which means that the quality of the output depends on the quality of the input.

- Some computer screens are **monochrome**—the characters appear in one color on a black background. Color screens are also available to display color graphics. The most common type of screen is the **cathode ray tube (CRT).** Another type is the **liquid crystal display (LCD),** a flat screen found on laptop computers.

- When bank customers use an **automated teller machine (ATM),** they are using a complex set of input/output devices connected to a computer; input and output both appear on a screen.

- CRT images are usually created through **raster-scan technology,** in which electron beams cause the screen to emit light, and the result is the screen image. The screen image is **refreshed,** or kept lit, at a particular **scan rate.**

- **Dot-addressable displays,** or **bit-mapped displays,** are graphics display screens that are divided into dots, each of which can be illuminated as a *picture element,* or **pixel.** The greater the number of pixels, the greater the **resolution,** or clarity, of the image.

- To display graphics, you need both a color monitor and color graphics circuitry, either built-in or on a **graphics card** or **graphics adapter board.**

- A screen may be the monitor of a self-contained personal computer, or it may be part of a **terminal,** an input-output device linked to a main computer. A terminal with a screen is called a **video display terminal (VDT).**

- A **dumb terminal** does not process data; it only enters data and receives output. A **smart terminal** can do some processing (usually data editing), but it cannot be programmed by the user. An **intelligent terminal** can be programmed to perform a variety of processing tasks.

- An **inquiry** is a user's request for information from the computer. A **prompt** is a computer request for data or a command from the user.

- **Printers** produce **hard copy,** or printed paper output. Some printers produce solid characters; others, **dot-matrix printers,** construct characters by producing closely spaced dots.

- Printers can also be classified as being either **impact printers,** which form characters by physically striking the paper, or **nonimpact printers,** which use a noncontact printing method.

- Impact printers include **character printers** (such as the **daisy-wheel**) and **line printers.** (Line printers can be **band, chain,** or **drum printers.**)

- Nonimpact printers, which include **ink-jet** and **laser printers,** are faster and quieter than impact printers.

- The main types of computer paper are lined-stock tabulating paper (**stock tab**) and shaded-band paper (**green-bar paper**). Computer paper is usually **continuous form** paper with sprocket holes along the sides. **Bursting** is the process of separating the folded paper after printing. **Decollating** is the process of removing the carbon paper from layered copies. **NCR paper** (*no carbon required*) is a more convenient but more expensive alternative to carbon paper.

- With **computer output microfilm (COM),** output is stored on 35mm film or 4- by 6-inch sheets called **microfiche.**

- Computer **speech synthesis** has been accomplished through **voice synthesizers** (also called **voice-output devices** or **audio-response units**). One approach to speech synthesis is **synthesis by analy-**

sis, in which the computer analyzes stored tapes of spoken words. In the other approach, called **synthesis by rule,** the computer applies linguistic rules to create artificial speech.

- Computer graphics are used in many areas—such as video games, movies, commercials, art, and education—but are perhaps most common in business.

- **Video graphics** are computer-produced animated pictures.

- In **computer-aided design/computer-aided manufacturing (CAD/CAM),** computers are used to create two- and three-dimensional pictures of manufactured products such as hand tools and vehicles.

- Common graphics input devices include **light pens, digitizers, digitizing tablets, joy sticks, scanners,** and **touch screens.**

- Graphics output devices include screens, plotters, printers, overhead transparency makers, and 35mm slide makers.

- Plotters draw graphics output on paper. **Flatbed plotters** look like drafting tables, but on **drum plotters** the paper is rolled on a drum instead of being flat on a table.

Review Questions

1. Explain what magnetic-ink character recognition is and how it is used by banks to process checks.

2. Name the types of optical character-recognition devices and explain how each one works.

3. Describe the two types of speech recognition systems and discuss the problems involved in speech recognition.

4. What is the difference between an inquiry and a prompt?

5. What is hard copy?

6. How does a dot-matrix printer differ from a solid-character printer?

7. How do character printers differ from line printers?

8. What are the advantages of nonimpact printers? What are the advantages of impact printers?

9. Explain what COM is and why it was developed.

10. Name the two basic approaches to computer speech synthesis and explain how they differ.

11. Name five graphics input devices and explain how each one works.

12. Name and describe two types of plotters.

Discussion Questions

1. Do you think that continued research into voice input is worthwhile? In your answer discuss the practicality of current and potential uses.

2. What should a buyer consider when comparing different models of printers?

3. Some people predict that offices of the future will rely on soft copy output rather than hard copy. Explain why you agree or disagree with this prediction.

5

Storage Devices and File Processing

Facts on File

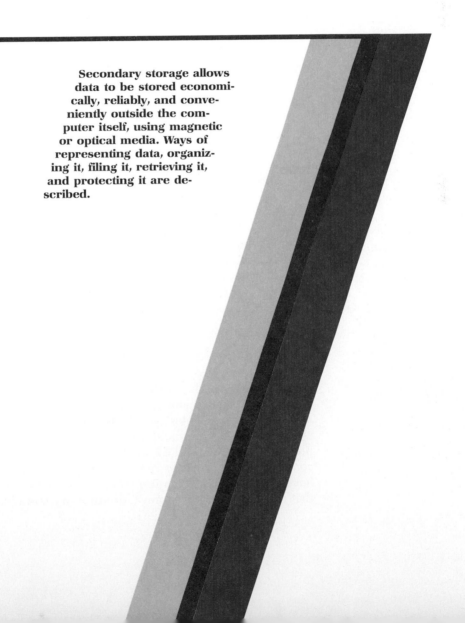

Secondary storage allows data to be stored economically, reliably, and conveniently outside the computer itself, using magnetic or optical media. Ways of representing data, organizing it, filing it, retrieving it, and protecting it are described.

LEARNING OBJECTIVES
- Understanding the need for secondary storage.
- Understanding how data is organized and processed.
- Understanding the principal types of secondary storage—magnetic tape and magnetic disk—and their advantages and disadvantages.
- Understanding three methods of file organization: sequential, direct, and indexed sequential.
- Understanding the storage media available for personal computers.
- Appreciating new approaches to storage media, particularly optical technology.

TEST BANK
Mult. Choice	1-2
T/F	1-2
Matching A	1
Fill-in-the-Blank	1-3

LECTURE ACTIVITY
Display various kinds of disks and magnetic tapes usable on computers, some of historical interest.

Consider the following disks: IBM Winchester disk packs, 14 inch cartridges, CPM 8 inch floppies, standard 5.25 inch floppies, the new standard 3.5 inch diskettes, I omega Bernoulli disks. Show external disk drives for various disks.

Consider the following tapes: 2400 feet magnetic tape reel, computer–certified audio cassette tape, 3M tape cartridges, DEC or LINC tapes.

When Pete James, an airline executive, first considered getting a personal computer, it was with some reluctance. Several of his colleagues seemed to be computer hotshots, and Pete was, frankly, a little concerned about stepping onto the bottom rung. But he knew that he could not hold the position that computing was good for everyone in the company except him.

Pete took a little time to investigate personal computers. He wanted a machine that had growth potential. Working with a professional from the Management Information Systems department of his company, Pete decided on a mid-priced model, a 32-bit machine with 1 megabyte RAM, and a color monitor. Anticipating the need to produce professional correspondence, Pete selected a laser printer.

Pete hesitated about the storage, however. The MIS advisor convinced him that he would really be glad he had both a diskette drive and a hard drive. As we will see, this arrangement is timesaving and convenient. But Pete had some misgivings about the capacity of the hard disk. Could he ever really use the 60MB disk the advisor recommended? How could he possibly come up with 60 *million* characters of data? Pete chose a 30MB disk, which seemed more than adequate.

The choices for storage, whether for a large or small computer, are complicated. Pete did not do too badly. We will check back with him later in the chapter to see how his choices worked out. We switch now from personal computer storage to the broader needs of a large corporation or government agency.

7 Why Secondary Storage?

Picture, if you can, how many filing-cabinet drawers would be required to hold the millions of files of, say, criminal records held by the U.S. Justice Department or employee records kept by General Motors. The rooms would have to be enormous. Computer storage—the ability to store many records in extremely compressed form and to have quick access to them—is unquestionably one of the computer's most valuable assets.

The Benefits of Secondary Storage

Secondary storage, you will recall, is necessary because memory, or primary storage, can be used only temporarily: if you are sharing your computer, you must yield memory to someone else after your program runs; if you are not sharing your computer, your programs and data will disappear from memory when you turn most computers off. However, you probably want to store the data you have used or the information you have derived from processing, and that is why secondary storage, or **auxiliary storage,** is needed. Also,

TEST BANK
Mult. Choice   3-11
Matching A   2-4
Matching B   1-2
Fill-in-the-Blank 4-7

memory is limited in size, whereas secondary storage media can store as much information as necessary.

The benefits of secondary storage are

- **Economy.** It is less expensive to store data on magnetic tape or disk, the principal means of secondary storage, than in filing cabinets. This is primarily because of the cost savings in storage space and the increased accuracy in filing and retrieving data.

- **Reliability.** Data in secondary storage is basically safe, since the medium is physically reliable and the data is stored in such a way that it is difficult for unauthorized people to tamper with it.

- **Convenience.** Authorized people can locate and access the data quickly with the help of a computer.

These benefits reach across the various secondary storage devices, but—as you will see—some devices are better than others.

What Are the Choices and Which Is Best?

We will spend most of the chapter answering these questions. We can take an advance look, however. Magnetic tape is a storage medium that has its place, but almost everyone—small-time and big-time—wants disk because it offers singular advantages: speed and immediate access to a particular record.

There are other choices too. Will we stick with traditional magnetic media or consider, instead, the new optical storage technology? As usual, there are advantages and disadvantages both ways.

What about the personal computer user? We have already hinted that storage decisions in that arena require some thoughtful planning. We will examine all the possibilities. And, of course, we will return to Pete James, to see if he is happy with his disk decision.

First, though, we will consider how data is organized and how it is processed. These topics are intimately related to our choice of a storage medium.

Data: Getting Organized

Data cannot be dumped helter-skelter into a computer. The computer is not a magic box that can bring order out of chaos. In fact, submitting data to a computer cannot be chaotic in the least—it must be carefully planned.

To be processed by the computer, raw data is organized into characters, fields, records, files, and databases. We will start with the smallest element, the character.

DISCUSSION QUESTION
How is data sub-divided and
organized for storage on disks and
tapes?

■ A **character** is a letter, number, or special character (such as $, ?, or *). One or more related characters constitute a field.

■ A **field** contains a set of related characters. For example, suppose a health club is making address labels for a mailing. For each person it might have a member-number field, a name field, a street-address field, a city field, a state field, a zip-code field, and a phone-number field (Figure 5-1).

■ A **record** is a collection of related fields. Thus, on the health club list, one person's member number, name, address, city, state, zip code, and phone number constitute a record.

■ A **file** is a collection of related records. All the member records for the health club compose a file.

■ A **database** is a collection of interrelated files stored together with minimum redundancy. Specific data items can be retrieved for various applications. For instance, if the health club is opening a new outlet, it can pull out the names and addresses of all the people with specific zip codes that are near the new club. The club can then send a special announcement about opening day to those people. The concept of a database is complicated; we will return to it in more detail in Chapter 14.

7 Processing Data into Information

There are several methods of processing data in a computer system. The two main methods are batch processing (processing data transactions in groups) and transaction processing (processing the transactions one at a time as they occur). A combination of these two techniques may also be used. We will now look at these methods and give examples of their use.

7 Batch Processing

Batch processing is a technique in which transactions are collected into groups, or batches, to be processed. Let us suppose that we are going to update the health club address-label file. The **master file,** a semi-permanent set of records, is, in this case, the list of all members of the health club and their addresses. The **transaction file** contains all changes to be made to the master file: additions (transactions to create new master records for new names added), deletions (transactions with instructions to delete master records of people who have resigned from the health club), and changes or revisions (transactions to change fields such as street addresses or phone numbers on the master records). Each month the master file is

DISCUSSION QUESTION
How do master and transaction
files differ? How are they used?

DISCUSSION QUESTION
What are three kinds of changes in
a master file which a transaction file
can cause?

Figure 5-1   How data is organized.
Data is organized into characters,
fields, records, and files. A file is a collection of related records.

TRANSPARENCY ACETATE #5A
Figure #5-1

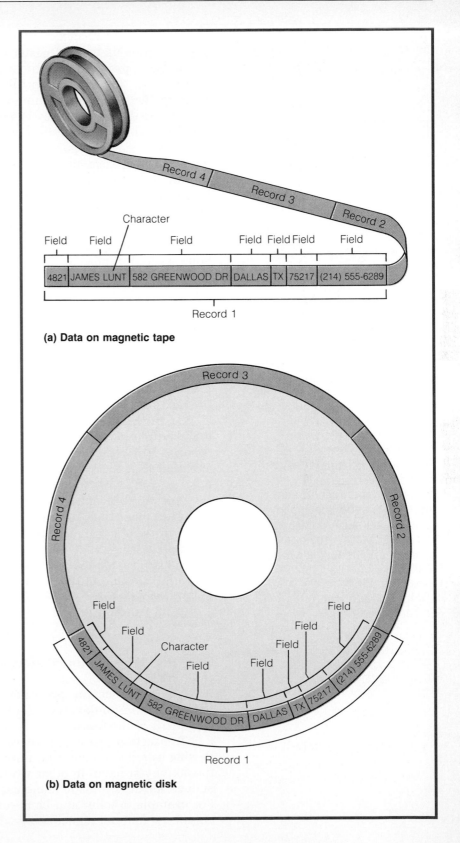

(a) Data on magnetic tape

(b) Data on magnetic disk

updated with the changes called for on the transaction file. The result is a new, up-to-date master file (Figure 5-2).

In batch processing, before a transaction file is matched against a master file, the transaction file must be **sorted** (usually by computer) so that all the transactions are in sequential order according to a field called a key. The **key** is a unique identifier for a record. It is usually a number; since two or more people may have the same name, names are not good keys. Social Security numbers are commonly used as keys. In updating the health club address-label file, the key is the member number assigned by the health club. The records on the master file are already in order by key. Once the changes on the transaction file are sorted by key, the two files can be matched and the master file updated. Note that keys are also used to locate specific records within a file; that is why you always need to provide your account number when paying a bill or inquiring about a bill. Your record is located by number, not your name.

During processing the computer reads from the master and transaction files and takes action on whichever of the two key numbers is lower. If the keys are the same, the record in the master file should be revised or deleted as specified by the transaction file. If the master file key is higher, the transaction should be added to the master file (if it is not an addition, it is some sort of error); if the master file key is lower, there is no change of any sort to that master file record.

As the processing takes place, a new master file is produced; this new file incorporates all the changes from the transaction file. Also, an error report will be printed. The error report calls the user's attention to requests for deletions and revisions of records that do not exist and requests for additions that have been added previously.

An advantage of batch processing is that it is usually less expensive than other types of processing because it is more efficient: A group of records is processed at the same time. A disadvantage of batch processing is that you have to wait. It does not matter that you want to know what the gasoline bill for your car is now; you have to wait until the end of the month when all your credit-card gas purchases are added up. Batch processing cannot give you a quick response to your question.

7 Transaction Processing

Transaction processing is a technique of processing transactions in random order—that is, in any order they occur. No presorting of the transactions is required.

Transaction processing is real-time processing. **Real-time processing** can obtain data from the computer system in time to affect the activity at hand. In other words, a transaction is processed fast enough for the results to come back and be acted upon right away. For example, a teller at a bank (or you at an automatic teller machine) can find out immediately what your bank balance is. You can

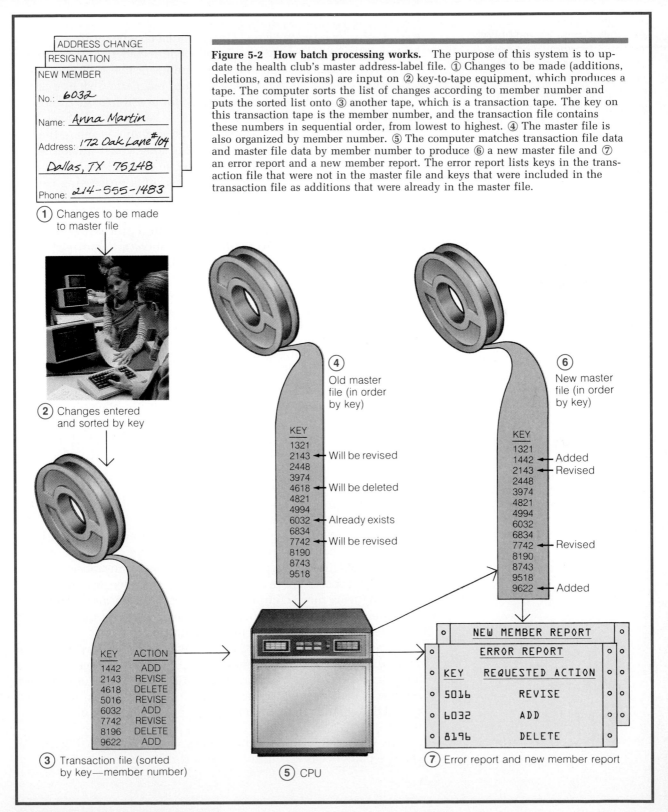

Figure 5-2   How batch processing works.   The purpose of this system is to update the health club's master address-label file. ① Changes to be made (additions, deletions, and revisions) are input on ② key-to-tape equipment, which produces a tape. The computer sorts the list of changes according to member number and puts the sorted list onto ③ another tape, which is a transaction tape. The key on this transaction tape is the member number, and the transaction file contains these numbers in sequential order, from lowest to highest. ④ The master file is also organized by member number. ⑤ The computer matches transaction file data and master file data by member number to produce ⑥ a new master file and ⑦ an error report and a new member report. The error report lists keys in the transaction file that were not in the master file and keys that were included in the transaction file as additions that were already in the master file.

ADDRESS CHANGE
RESIGNATION
NEW MEMBER

No.: 6032

Name: Anna Martin

Address: 172 Oak Lane #104

Dallas, TX 75248

Phone: 214-555-1483

① Changes to be made to master file

② Changes entered and sorted by key

KEY	ACTION
1442	ADD
2143	REVISE
4618	DELETE
5016	REVISE
6032	ADD
7742	REVISE
8196	DELETE
9622	ADD

③ Transaction file (sorted by key—member number)

④ Old master file (in order by key)

KEY
1321
2143 ← Will be revised
2448
3974
4618 ← Will be deleted
4821
4994
6032 ← Already exists
6834
7742 ← Will be revised
8190
8743
9518

⑥ New master file (in order by key)

KEY
1321
1442 ← Added
2143 ← Revised
2448
3974
4821
4994
6032
6834
7742 ← Revised
8190
8743
9518
9622 ← Added

⑤ CPU

NEW MEMBER REPORT

ERROR REPORT

KEY	REQUESTED ACTION
5016	REVISE
6032	ADD
8196	DELETE

⑦ Error report and new member report

TRANSPARENCY ACETATE #5B
Figure #5-2

Magnetic tapes are essentially sequential media. They are usually read or written only in the forward direction. They are not direct access media. If you are seeking a particular record on tape, you have to read each record in succession until it is found. Suppose the record you want is the first one on the tape and you have just read the last record on the tape; the tape must be completely rewound to the beginning, which could take five to ten minutes. Thus, magnetic tape is not practical as a direct access device.

The density of data on magnetic tapes is measured in bytes per inch (bpi); 800, 1600, and 6250 bpi are common densities. The tapes are typically 2400 feet long; but 300, 600, and 1200 feet tapes are also available. Current tapes have nine channels, one for each bit of a byte, plus parity (some old tapes have only seven channels).

then decide right away how much money you can afford to withdraw. For processing to be real-time, it must also be **on-line**—that is, the user's terminals must be directly connected to the computer.

The great leap forward in the technology of real-time processing was made possible by the development of magnetic disk as a means of storing data. With magnetic tape it is not possible to go directly to the particular record you are looking for—the tape might have to be advanced several feet first. However, just as you can move the arm on your stereo directly to the particular song you want on an LP record, with disk you can go directly to one particular piece of data. The invention of magnetic disk meant that data processing is more likely to be **interactive**—the user can communicate directly with the computer, maintaining a dialogue, or conversation back and forth.

There are several advantages to transaction processing. The first is that you do not need to wait. For instance, a department store salesclerk using a point-of-sale terminal can key in a customer's charge-card number and a code that asks the computer the question, "Is this charge card acceptable?" With transaction processing, the clerk gets an immediate reply. Immediacy is a distinct plus, since everyone expects fast service these days. Second, transaction processing permits continual updating of a customer's record. Thus, the salesclerk can not only verify your credit, but also record the sale in the computer; you will eventually be billed through the computerized billing process.

Transaction processing systems are usually time-sharing systems. **Time-sharing** is a system in which two or more users can, through individual terminals, share the use (the time) of a central computer and, because of the computer's speed, receive practically simultaneous responses. Thus, an airline can have reservations clerks in far-flung cities interact with the same computer at the same time to keep informed on what flights are scheduled and how many seats are available on each.

Transaction processing does have some drawbacks. One is expense. Unlike batch processing, which uses the computer only for the amount of time needed to get the job done, transaction processing gives you access to the computer at all times. Because transaction processing uses more computer resources, it costs more. However, when weighed against the alternative, such as lack of quick service, the added expense may be a minor matter.

A more serious drawback is the security risk. If many users have access to the same data, it is more difficult to protect that data from theft, tampering, destruction by disgruntled employees, or unauthorized use. It has become necessary, therefore, for the computer industry to take greater precautions to protect the security of computer files.

An example of transaction processing is given in Figure 5-3, where a patient has submitted a prescription for processing.

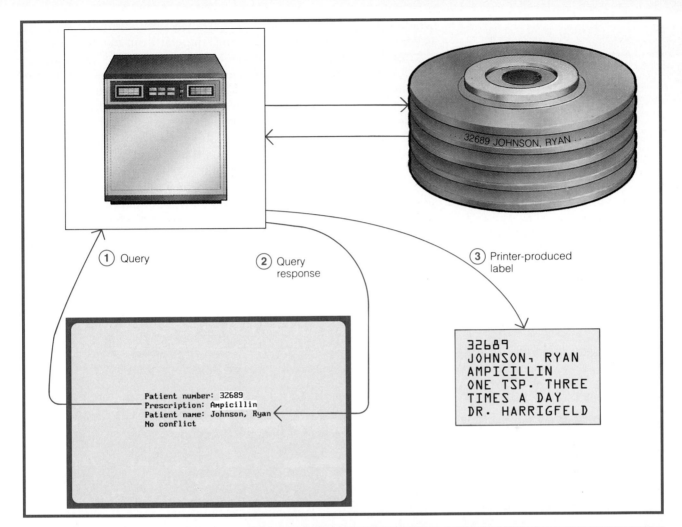

Patient number: 32689
Prescription: Ampicillin
Patient name: Johnson, Ryan
No conflict

(1) Query

(2) Query
response

(3) Printer-produced
label

32689
JOHNSON, RYAN
AMPICILLIN
ONE TSP. THREE
TIMES A DAY
DR. HARRIGFELD

TRANSPARENCY ACETATE #5C
Figure #5-3

Figure 5-3 How transaction processing works.   The purposes of this pharmacy system are to verify that a patient's prescription is safe, produce a prescription label for the medication bottle, and update the patient's medical records. Because of the possibility of patients having the same name, the file is organized by patient number rather than by name. Here Ryan Johnson, patient number 32689, brings his prescription to the pharmacist. (1) Through the terminal the pharmacist asks the computer system whether the ampicillin prescribed is apt to conflict with other medication the patient is taking. (2) The computer screen shows that 32689 is Ryan Johnson and displays the message "No conflict." The computer then updates Johnson's file so other physicians can see later that ampicillin was prescribed for him. (3) A printer attached to the computer system prints a prescription label that the pharmacist can place on the ampicillin bottle. All this is done while the patient is waiting.

7 Batch and Transaction Processing: The Best of Both Worlds

Numerous computer systems combine the best features of both of these methods of processing. A bank, for instance, may record your withdrawal transaction during the day at the teller window whenever you demand your cash. However, the deposit that you leave in an envelope in an "instant" deposit drop may be recorded during the night by means of batch processing. Many oil company credit-card systems also combine both methods: A gas station employee can instantaneously check the status of your credit by keying your card number on a computer terminal, but for billing purposes all your gasoline purchases may be batched and totaled at one time.

Police license-plate checks for stolen cars work the same way. As cars are sold throughout the state, the license numbers, owners' names, and so on, are updated on the motor vehicle department's master file, usually via batch processing on a nightly basis. But when police officers see a car they suspect may be stolen, they can radio headquarters, where an operator with a terminal checks the master file immediately to see if the car was reported missing.

Both batch and transaction processing can also be used in a store. Using point-of-sale terminals, inventory data is captured as sales are made; this data is processed later in batches to produce inventory reports.

As we have mentioned, two primary media for storing data are magnetic tape and magnetic disk. Since these media have been the staples of the computer industry for three decades, we will begin with them.

TEST BANK

Mult. Choice	26-38
T/F	26-37
Matching B	5-8,10
Matching C	1-4,6
Matching E	4-5
Fill-in-the-Blank	15-31

Figure 5-4 Magnetic tape. Magnetic tape on 10½-inch-diameter reels has been the workhorse of data processing for years. However, a smaller tape cartridge has been introduced that can hold 20% more data in 75% less space.

7 Magnetic Tape Storage

Magnetic tape looks like the tape used in home tape recorders—plastic Mylar tape, usually ½ inch wide and wound on a 10½-inch-diameter reel (Figure 5-4). The tape has an iron-oxide coating that can be magnetized. Data is stored as extremely small magnetized spots, which can then be read by a tape unit into the computer's main storage. Some tapes (so-called "minitapes") are only 600 feet in length, but the most common length is 2400 feet.

The amount of data on a tape is expressed in terms of **density**, which is the number of **characters per inch** (**cpi**) or **bytes per inch** (**bpi**) that can be stored on the tape. (A byte is essentially the same as a character.) Although some tapes can store as many as 6250 bpi, a common density is 1600 bpi.

7 Data Representation on Tape

How is data represented on a tape? As Figure 5-5 shows, one character is represented by a cross section of a tape. As the figure also shows, the tape contains **tracks**, or **channels**, that run the length of the entire tape. On most modern computer tapes, one cross section

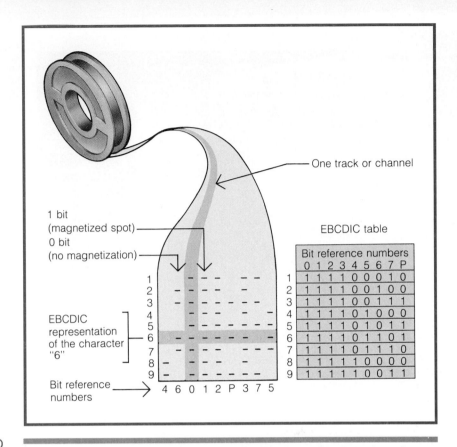

TRANSPARENCY ACETATE #5D
Figure #5-5

Figure 5-5   How data is represented on magnetic tape. This shows how the numbers 1 through 9 are represented on tape in EBCDIC code, using combinations of 1 bits and 0 bits. For each character there are 8 bits. The ninth bit is a parity bit represented by the letter P. In the odd-parity system illustrated here, each byte is always made up of an odd number of 1 bits. In an odd-parity system, an even number of 1 bits suggests that something is wrong with the data. Note that the parity-bit track appears close to the middle of the tape. The bits are out of order on the tape because the most commonly used bit locations are placed toward the center of the track, as far from dirt and grime as possible.

of the tape, representing one character, contains 9 bits, one on each of the tracks. There are nine locations. Each location has either a magnetized spot, which represents the 1 bit, or no magnetization, which represents the 0 bit. A common data representation code is EBCDIC (Extended Binary Coded Decimal Interchange Code), which we discussed in Chapter 3. Eight of the nine bit locations are used to represent a character in EBCDIC; the ninth bit is a parity bit, which we explained in Chapter 3.

Figure 5-5 describes how the tracks are used. In addition you should note that the tracks that have the most magnetized spots are clustered toward the middle of the tape. This is to protect the data from dirt and damage, which are more apt to affect the edges of the tape.

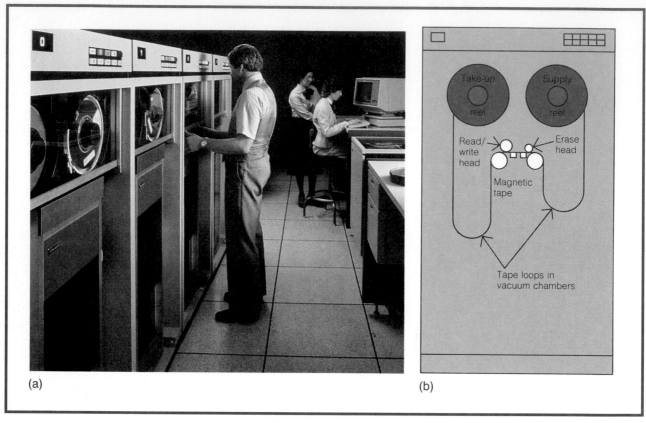

(a)   (b)

Figure 5-6   Magnetic tape units.   Tapes are always protected by glass from out-side dust and dirt. (a) Magnetic tape on reels is run on these tape drives. (b) This diagram highlights the read/write head and the erase head found in magnetic tape units.

7 The Magnetic Tape Unit

As Figure 5-6a shows, a **magnetic tape unit** is about the size and shape of a refrigerator and indeed may even have a door that opens in the front. The purpose of the unit is to write and to read—that is, to record data on and retrieve data from—magnetic tape. This is done by a **read/write head** (Figure 5-6b), an electromagnet that reads the magnetized areas on the tape and converts them into electrical impulses, which are sent to the processor. The reverse procedure is called writing. When the machine is writing on the tape, the **erase head** first erases any data previously recorded on the tape.

Two reels are used, a **supply reel** and a **take-up reel.** The supply reel, which has the tape with data on it or on which data will be recorded, is the reel that is changed. The take-up reel always stays with the magnetic tape unit. As Figure 5-6b illustrates, the tape is allowed to drop down into vacuum chambers, airless chambers that lessen drag on the tape and prevent it from breaking if there is a sudden burst of speed. When operations are complete, the tape is rewound onto the supply reel.

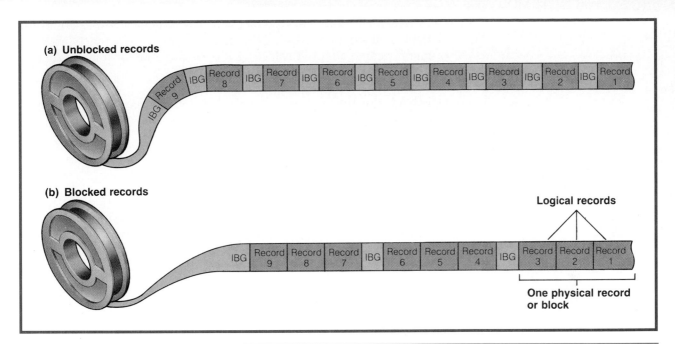

Figure 5-7   **Blocking.**   (a) In the unblocked records each record is a physical record and also a logical record. Each physical record (block) is separated from the next by an interblock gap (IBG). (b) In the blocked records, three logical records are grouped into one physical record. This saves space, because there are fewer interblock gaps (IBGs), and it increases processing speed.

7 Blocking

Speed of access to records is important; therefore, magnetic tape units are designed to provide fast access to records processed one after another on tape. However, just as you cannot stop a car on a dime, you cannot stop a tape instantly. Thus, it is necessary to have some room between records for stopping space. This space is called an **interrecord gap** (**IRG**) or **interblock gap** (**IBG**). Typically, it is blank space on the tape $\frac{3}{5}$ inch long.

However, having many IRGs on a tape wastes space and adds to processing time. To avoid this, records are grouped together, using a process called blocking. Figure 5-7 shows how this works. **Blocking** consists of putting together logical records into one physical record, or block, followed by an interblock gap. By **logical record** here we mean the record written by an applications program; it is called logical because it is related to the logic of the program. A **physical record,** otherwise known as a **block,** is the collection of logical records grouped together on a tape. Programmers use the term **blocking factor** to refer to the number of logical records in one physical record. That is, for the tape shown in Figure 5-7b they would say the blocking factor is 3—there are three logical records in a physical record. The number of records blocked together—that is, the blocking factor—depends on the amount of memory available to the program and the size of each logical record. Files on disk can be blocked too, in which case the blocking factor is also affected by the size of the track on the disk containing the file. With some experience programmers become adept at selecting the blocking factor for a particular file.

Although blocking saves time and space, there are costs involved: the time spent to block and deblock as well as the extra memory needed to hold the larger records.

7 Magnetic Disk Storage

Magnetic disk storage is another common form of secondary storage. A **hard magnetic disk,** or **hard disk,** is a metal platter coated with magnetic oxide that looks something like a stereo

Figure 5-8   Magnetic disks.   (a) Hard magnetic disks come in a variety of sizes, as shown by these three individual disks. Also, disk packs can vary in the number of disks they contain, as illustrated by the two disk packs shown here. (b) This 5¼-inch diskette is in a square protective paper jacket. (c) This 3½-inch diskette is protected by a firm plastic exterior cover.

(a)

(b)

(c)

record but does not act like one. Hard disks come in a variety of sizes; 14, 5¼, and 3½ inches are typical diameters. Several disks are assembled together in a **disk pack** (Figure 5-8a). A disk pack looks like a stack of stereo records, except that daylight can be seen between the disks. There are different types of disk packs, with the number of platters varying by model. Each disk has a top and bottom surface on which to record data. Many disk devices, however, do not record data on the top of the top platter or on the bottom of the bottom platter.

Another form of magnetic disk storage is the **diskette,** which is a round piece of plastic coated with magnetic oxide (Figure 5-8b,c). Diskettes and small hard disks are used with personal computers. We will discuss secondary storage for personal computers later in this chapter, but keep in mind that the principles of disk storage discussed here also apply to disk storage for personal computers.

TRANSPARENCY ACETATE #5G
Figure #5-9

Figure 5-9 Surface of a disk. Note that each track is a closed circle, unlike the tracks on a phonograph record. This drawing is only to illustrate the location of the tracks; you cannot actually see the tracks on the disk surface.

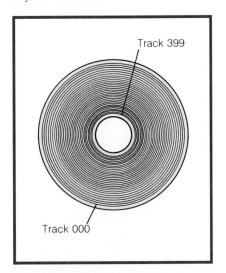

Track 399

Track 000

DISCUSSION QUESTION
In what ways does a magnetic computer disk differ from a phonograph record?

LECTURE HINT
Another way LPs and magnetic disks differ: LPs do not use magnetic surfaces.

7 How Data Is Stored on a Disk

As Figure 5-9 shows, the surface of each disk has tracks on it. Data is recorded as magnetic spots on the tracks. The number of tracks per surface varies with the particular type of disk.

But note how a disk differs from a stereo record: The track on a long-playing record allows the arm of the stereo to move gradually from the outside toward the center; a track on a disk is a closed circle—when the arm is on a particular track, it always stays the same distance from the center. All tracks on one disk are concentric; that is, they are circles with the same center.

The same amount of data is stored on every track, from outermost (track 000) to innermost (track 399 of a 400-track disk), and it takes the same amount of time to read the data on the outer track as on the inner, even though the outer track moves faster. (The disk can be compared to a chain of ice skaters playing crack the whip: The outside skater is racing, but the inside skater is only inching around—but both take the same amount of time to circle.) Disks rotate at a constant speed.

A magnetic disk is a **direct-access storage device (DASD)**. With such a device you can go directly to the record you want. With tape storage, on the other hand, you must read all preceding records on the file until you come to the record you want. Data can be stored either sequentially or randomly on a direct-access storage device.

7 The Disk Drive

A **disk drive** is a machine that allows data to be read from a disk or written on a disk. A diskette is inserted into a disk drive that is part of a personal computer. A disk pack, however, is mounted on a disk drive that is a separate unit connected to the main

Figure 5-10 Disk drive units.
Looking like cake covers, these disk-pack containers are sitting atop disk drive units. The disk packs themselves sit beneath the top-loading glass doors when the machine is running.

computer (Figure 5-10). Some disks are permanently mounted inside a disk drive. Generally, these are used in personal computers or in cases where several users are sharing data. A typical example is a disk with files containing flight information that is used by several airline reservations agents.

In the disk drive a diskette rotates at speeds of 300 to 400 revolutions per minute. Typically, hard disks rotate 3600 revolutions per minute. In a disk pack all disks rotate at the same time, although only one disk is being read or written on at any one time.

The mechanism for reading or writing data on a disk is an **access arm;** it moves a read/write head into position over a particular track (Figure 5-11a). The access arm acts somewhat like the arm on a stereo, although it does not actually touch the surface. A disk pack has a series of access arms, which slip in between the disks in the pack (Figure 5-11c). Two read/write heads are on each arm, one facing up for the surface above it, one facing down for the surface below it. However, only one read/write head can operate at any one time.

Winchester Disks

In some disk drives the access arms can be retracted; then the disk pack can be removed from the drive. In other cases, however, the disks, access arms, and read/write heads are combined in a **sealed module** called a **Winchester disk,** or a **Winnie.** (These devices were named by IBM after the Winchester rifle because the company planned to produce a dual-disk system with 30 megabytes storage each. IBM later abandoned the dual-disk idea, but the name *Winchester* remained.) Winchester disk assemblies are put together in clean rooms so even microscopic dust particles do not get on the disk surface. Many Winchester disks are built-in, but some are removable in the sense that the entire module can be lifted from the

DISCUSSION QUESTION
What common contaminants can destroy a hard disk? (Smoke, hairspray, dust).

LECTURE HINT
One company kept losing its disks due to disk "crashes". A chemist examined the bad disks and found a thin layer of hair spray on them, which caused the disk heads to scrape against it, rubbing off magnetic material, and destroying information on the disk. The company forbade women working to use hair sprays until the computer center obtained its own separate air conditioner.

Computer centers now routinely have their own air conditioning system to prevent contaminants from other places in the building from seeping in. Another reason for the special air conditioning is that some computers work best at temperatures lower than humans care to work in.

LECTURE HINT
The top and bottom surfaces of a multi-platter disk are more likely to be corrupted by dust and other contaminants than other surfaces, and are not used often.

TRANSPARENCY ACETATE #5G
Figure #5-11b

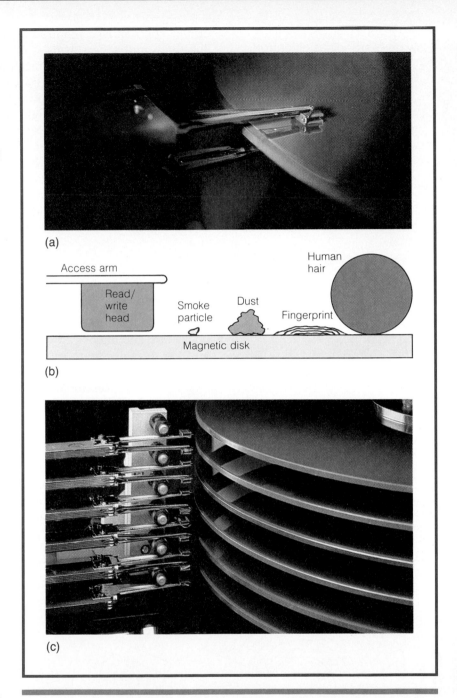

Figure 5-11 **Read/write heads and access arms.** (a) This photo shows a read/write head on the end of an access arm poised over a hard disk. (b) When in operation, the read/write head comes very close to the surface of the disk. In fact, particles as small as smoke, dust, fingerprints, and a hair loom large when they are on a disk. If the read/write head crashes into such a particle, data is destroyed and the disk damaged. You can see why it is important to keep disks and disk drives clean. (c) Note that there are two read/write heads on each access arm. Each arm slips between two disks in the pack. The access arms move simultaneously, but only one read/write head operates at any one time.

drive. The removed module, however, remains sealed and contains the disks and access arms.

Winchester disks were originally 14 inches in diameter, but now smaller versions are made. Hard disks on microcomputers—$5\frac{1}{4}$- and $3\frac{1}{2}$-inch disks—always employ Winchester technology. Until 1980 the most common type of high-speed storage consisted of removable disk packs. Since then that technology has been supplanted by Winchester disks; around 85% of all disk storage units sold are of the fixed, Winchester variety. The principal reasons for their popularity are that Winchester disks cost about half as much but go twice as long between failures as removable disk packs. This increased reliability is because operators do not handle the Winchester disk at all and because the sealed module keeps the disks free from contamination.

7   How Data Is Organized on a Disk

There is more than one way of physically organizing data on a disk. The methods we will consider here are the sector method and the cylinder method.

The Sector Method

In the **sector method,** each track is divided into sectors that hold a specific number of characters (Figure 5-12a). Data on the track is accessed by referring to the surface number, track number, and sector number where the data is stored. The sector method is used for diskettes as well as disk packs.

Most personal computers use **soft-sectored diskettes,** meaning that the sectors are determined by the software. A soft-sectored diskette has a small hole to mark the beginning of the track (Figure 5-12b).

Figure 5-12   Sector data organization. (a) When data is organized by sector, the address is the surface, track, and sector where the data is stored. (b) The small hole in a soft-sectored diskette marks the beginning of the track; the number of sectors is determined by the software.

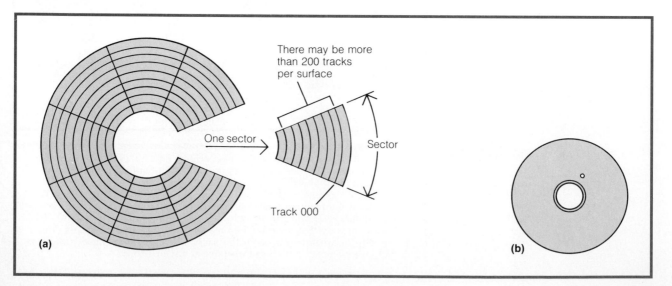

There may be more than 200 tracks per surface

One sector

Sector

Track 000

(a)   (b)

DISCUSSION QUESTION
How do sectors, tracks, and
cylinders differ?

The Cylinder Method

Another way to organize data on a disk is the **cylinder method,** shown in Figure 5-13. Most hard disks use the cylinder method. The organization in this case is vertical. The purpose is to minimize seek time, the movement of the access arms. It is clear that once the access arms are in position, they are in the same vertical position on all disk surfaces.

To appreciate this, suppose you had an empty disk pack on which you wished to record data. You might be tempted to record the data horizontally: start with the first surface, fill track 000, then track 001, track 002, and so on, then move to the second surface and again fill tracks 000, 001, 002, and so forth. Each new track and new surface, however, would require movement of the access arms, a relatively slow mechanical process. Recording the data vertically, on the other hand, substantially reduces access arm movement: The data is recorded on the tracks that can be accessed by one positioning of the access arms, that is, on one **cylinder.** By using cylinder organization, it is as though you dropped a cylinder (like a tin can) straight down through all disks in the disk pack: The access arms mechanism has equal access to track 000 of all surfaces, and so on. The cylinder method, then, means all tracks of a certain cylinder on a disk pack are lined up one beneath the other, and all the vertical tracks of one cylinder are accessible by the read/write heads with one positioning of the access arms mechanism. Tracks within a cylinder are numbered according to this vertical perspective: A 20-surface disk pack contains cylinder tracks numbered 0 through 19, top to bottom.

TRANSPARENCY ACETATE #5I
Figure #5-13

Figure 5-13   Cylinder data organization.   To visualize the cylinder form of organization, imagine that a cylinder such as a tin can were dropped straight down through all the disks in the disk pack. Within cylinder 150 the track surfaces are numbered (except for the top and bottom surfaces) as shown. This is a vertical system of track numbering.

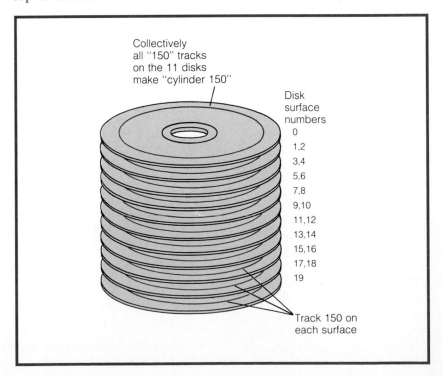

Collectively all "150" tracks on the 11 disks make "cylinder 150"

Disk surface numbers
0
1,2
3,4
5,6
7,8
9,10
11,12
13,14
15,16
17,18
19

Track 150 on each surface

Now that we have seen how data can be written vertically on disk with the cylinder method, we can also see how to establish a disk address for a particular record. The disk address is the cylinder number, surface number, and record number, in that order. For example, the disk address of a record might be cylinder 150, surface 16, record 4. Now consider access to data on disk.

7 Disk Access to Data

Four primary factors determine the time needed to access data:

- **Seek time.** This is the time it takes the access arm to get into position over a particular track. (On an IBM 3350 disk drive, for instance, seek time averages about 25 milliseconds.) Keep in mind that all the access arms move as a unit, so actually, they are simultaneously in position over a series of tracks.

- **Head switching.** The access arms on the access mechanism do not move separately; they move together, all at the same time. However, only one read/write head can operate at any one time. Head switching is the activation of a particular read/write head over a particular track on a particular surface. Since head switching takes place at the speed of electricity, the time it takes is negligible.

- **Rotational delay.** With the access arm and read/write head in position, ready to read or write data, the read/write head waits in position for a short period until the record on the track moves under it. (On the IBM 3350 average rotational delay is about 8.4 milliseconds.)

- **Data transfer.** This activity is the transfer of data between memory and the place on the disk track—to the track, if you are writing, from the track to memory if you are reading. (The data transfer rate for the IBM 3350 is 1,198,000 bytes per second.)

With these four motions users can quickly get at any particular record any place on a disk, provided they have a method of finding where it is.

7 File Organization: Three Methods

There are three major methods of storing files of data in secondary storage:

- **Sequential file organization** simply means records are organized in sequential order by key.

- **Direct file organization** means records are organized randomly, not in any special order.

- **Indexed file organization** is a combination of the above two: Records are organized sequentially, but, in addition, indexes are built into the file so that a record can be accessed either sequentially or directly.

We will study each of these in turn.

7 Sequential File Processing

In **sequential file processing,** records are usually in order according to a key field. If it is an inventory file, the key might be the part number. A file describing people might use a Social Security number or credit-card number as the key. We have already seen an example of sequential file processing in our discussion of batch processing (see Figure 5-2).

7 Direct File Processing

Direct file processing, or **direct access,** allows you to go directly to the record you want by using a record key; the computer does not have to read all preceding records in the file as it does if the records are arranged sequentially. (Direct access is sometimes called **random access** because the records can be in random order.) It is this ability to access any given record instantly that has made computer systems so convenient for people in service industries—for travel agents checking a flight for available seats, for example, and bank tellers determining individual bank balances.

Obviously, if we have a completely blank area on the disk and can put records anywhere—in other words, place them randomly—then there must be some predictable system for placing a record at a disk address and for retrieving the record at a subsequent time. In other words, once the record has been placed on a disk, it must be possible to find it again. This is done by choosing a certain formula to use on the record key, thereby deriving a number to use as the disk address. **Hashing,** or **randomizing,** is the name given to the process of applying a formula to a key to yield a number that represents the address.

There are various formulas, but a simple one is to divide the key by a prime number and use the remainder from the division operation as an address. A prime number is any number that can be divided evenly only by itself or 1; it cannot be divided by any other number. Examples of prime numbers are 7, 11, 13, and 17. Figure 5-14 shows how dividing a key by a prime number produces a remainder that, in this case, indicates the track location. Now the record can be written on the first available location on that track, or, if reading, that track can be read until the desired record is found.

The reason for using remainders is that they produce disk addresses of manageable size. Some keys, such as Social Security numbers, are quite long; indeed, keys may run 20 digits or more. The

Figure 5-14   A simple hashing scheme.   Dividing the key number 1269 by the prime number 17 yields remainder 11, which can be used to indicate track location on a disk.

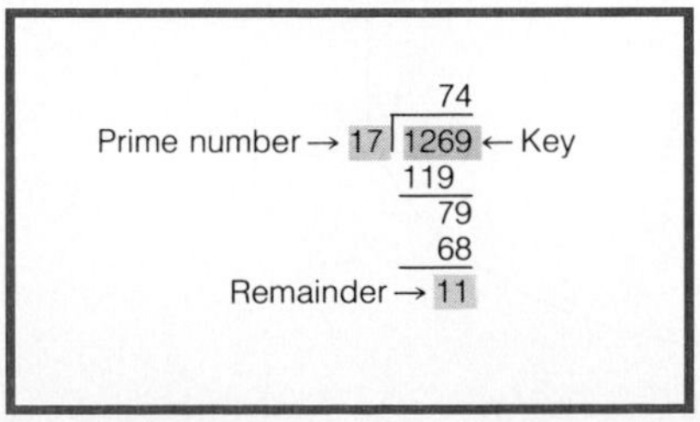

```
                         74
 Prime number → 17 | 1269 ← Key
                    119
                     79
                     68
      Remainder →    11
```

main reason for using a key is that it is predictable: By applying the same hashing formula to the same key, you can obtain the exact same address; therefore, you can always find that record again. For instance, if our hashing formula is to divide the key by prime number 13 and use the remainder as the addresses, then key 54 yields address 2 (54 divided by 13 yields remainder 2). The record for key 54 is then placed on the disk in location 2. (The example is intentionally simple to illustrate this point.) At some later time, this record can be found by applying the same formula to key 54 again; the remainder is still 2, and so we have rediscovered the address.

What happens, you might ask, if two keys divided by the same prime yield the same remainder so that you have duplicate addresses? (For instance, 7 divided by 3 produces remainder 1, but so does 10 divided by 3.) Records with duplicate addresses are called **synonyms,** and are said to cause **collisions.** One approach is to put each synonym in the closest available location—the next address, or, if that one is full, the address after that, and so on.

Figure 5-15 gives a very simplified example of how direct processing works.

Figure 5-15   An example of direct processing.   Assume there are 13 addresses (0 through 12) available on the file. Dividing the key number 661, C. Kear's employee number, by the prime number 13 yields remainder 11. Thus, 11 is the address for key 661. However, for the key 618, dividing by the prime 13 yields remainder 7—and this address has already been used (by the key 137). Hence, the address becomes the next location, that is, 8. Note, incidentally, that keys (and therefore records) need not appear in any particular order. (The 13 record locations available are, of course, too few to hold a normal file; a small number was used to keep the example simple.)

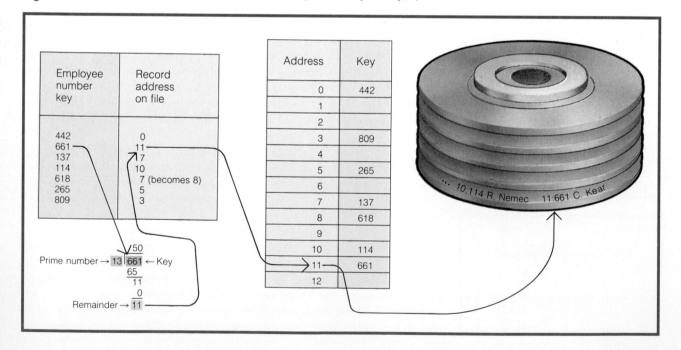

7 Indexed File Processing

Indexed file processing, or **indexed processing,** is the third method of file organization, and it represents a compromise between sequential and direct methods. It is useful in cases where files need to be in sequential order but where, in addition, you need to be able to go directly to specific records.

An indexed file works as follows: Records are stored in the file in sequential order, but the file also contains an index. The index contains entries consisting of the key to each record stored on the file and the corresponding disk address for that record. The index is like a directory, with the keys to all records listed in order. To access a record directly, the record key must be located in the index; the address associated with the key is then used to locate the record on the disk. Figure 5-16 illustrates how this works.

Figure 5-16   An example of indexed processing. In a credit department a terminal operator can make an inquiry about a customer's account by typing in the customer number on the terminal. The index then directs the computer to the particular disk address, which indicates the customer information.

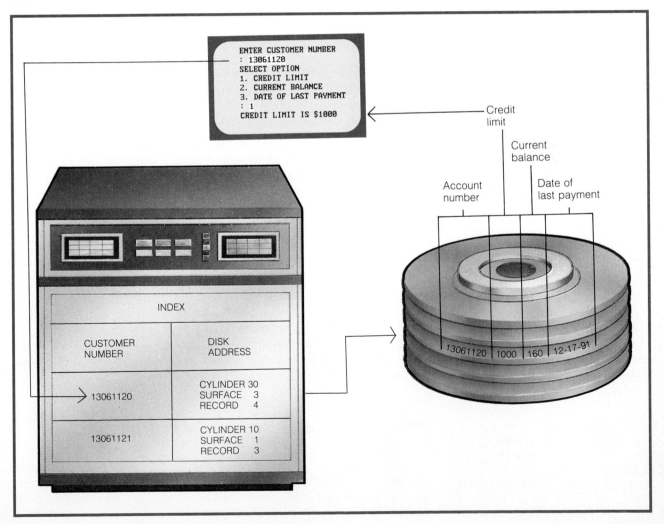

CAMERAS GET IN THE ACT

Things have changed a lot since you bought your first camera. Internal computer chips control camera settings for distance and lens opening. But the latest gimmick is a hybrid camera that combines still photography with video—made possible by still another chip and a petite diskette.

The camera does its work electronically. Film processing has been eliminated because there is no film. Instead, light is gathered by a chip. The chip's tiny photoreceptors capture the scene being photographed; the image is converted by the chip to electrical impulses that are transferred to the diskette. The diskette can be inserted in viewing equipment for shot selection. Commercial photographers, particularly news reporters, can transmit the diskette data by phone lines to their newspaper for immediate use.

TEST BANK
Mult. Choice   63-64
T/F   60-62

DISCUSSION QUESTION
What are the main advantages of using magnetic disk as secondary storage?

TEST BANK
Mult. Choice   65-68
T/F   63-68
Matching E   8-9
Fill-in-the-Blank   52-55

A record can also be accessed sequentially in two different ways. To retrieve an entire file of records, begin with the first record and proceed through the rest of the records. A second method for sequential retrieval is to begin with the retrieval of a record with a certain key—that is, to begin somewhere in the middle of the file— and then proceed through the file as before.

A disadvantage of indexed processing is that the process of looking up the key in the index adds one more operation to retrieval. It is therefore not as fast as direct file processing.

7 The Case for Disk Storage

Subtitle: And a few words for tape, too. As we have seen, disk has many advantages over tape. There are those in the industry who wonder why tape is still around at all. Disk does indeed seem the very model of a good storage medium:

- Disk has high data-volume capacity and allows very fast access.

- Data on disk is very reliable.

- Disk files may be organized directly, which allows immediate access and updating of any given record. This is the biggest advantage and is basic to real-time systems that facilitate instant credit checks and airline reservations.

- Using direct access, information may be updated easily. In contrast to a sequentially processed record, a single direct-access record may be read, updated, and returned to the disk, without the necessity of rewriting the entire file (this is called being updated in place.)

And tape? We have seen that records cannot be processed directly on tape. Even so, tape has certain advantages that make it a viable storage medium. It is portable—a reel of tape can be carried or mailed. It is relatively inexpensive: A reel of 2400-foot tape costs less than $15. (A full-size disk pack costs $300 and up.)

The chief uses of magnetic tape today are in standard sequential processing (for example, payroll) and as a convenient backup medium for disk files. Backup copies of disk files are made regularly on tape as insurance against disk failure. Future use of tape will probably be exclusively as a backup medium.

7 Personal Computer Storage

The market for data storage devices is being profoundly affected by the surge in popularity of personal computers. Storage media are available in two basic forms: diskettes and hard disk. Let us consider each of these.

7 Diskettes

Diskettes are popular among microcomputer users. The $5\frac{1}{4}$-inch diskette is well entrenched; it can hold from 360K to 1MB or 2MB of data. The newer $3\frac{1}{2}$-inch diskette is also very popular and can hold even more data (Figure 5-17).

Apple Computer set the $3\frac{1}{2}$-inch standard for diskettes with its popular Macintosh computer. The $3\frac{1}{2}$-inch diskette comes in a hard plastic housing. The $5\frac{1}{4}$-inch diskette is being phased out. The future belongs to smaller diskettes, which offer some nice advantages. First, the small diskette is sturdier and easier to store—it fits into a shirt

Figure 5-17   Diskettes.   (a) Cutaway view of a $5\frac{1}{4}$-inch diskette. (b) Cutaway view of a $3\frac{1}{2}$-inch diskette.

TRANSPARENCY ACETATE #5L
Figure #5-17

LECTURE HINT
In the mid-1970's, the only inexpensive device available for storing data for microcomputers was audio cassette tape. The right volume record level had to be set on the cassette recorder or the tape would not record properly. This caused hours of anguish among users. However, in the late 1970's, floppy disks became available for microcomputers. Soon cassettes were used only in exchanging programs and files among users. Audio cassettes are hardly ever used now, as they are too unreliable. Some companies are developing cassette tape drives that are reliable, for use as backup on microcomputers.

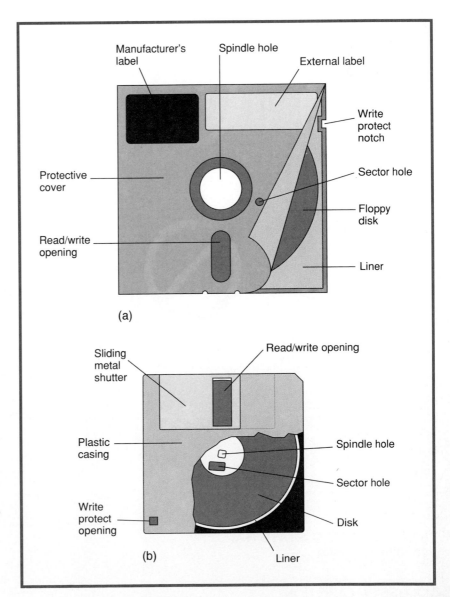

MICROCOMPUTERS IN ACTION

How to Handle Diskettes

Do not lock your diskette in the trunk of the car on a hot day, or leave it on the dashboard in the sun, or pin it to the door of your refrigerator with a magnet. Avoid smoking cigarettes around your computer, since particles deposited on the diskette will cause the head to scratch the diskette surface. Keep diskettes away from subways and telephones, which have magnetic coils.

These are only a few of the rules for taking care of diskettes. The main forces hostile to diskettes are dust, magnetic fields, liquids, vapors, and temperature extremes. Although $3\frac{1}{2}$-inch diskettes have plastic jackets and are thus less fragile than $5\frac{1}{4}$-inch diskettes, all require care in handling.

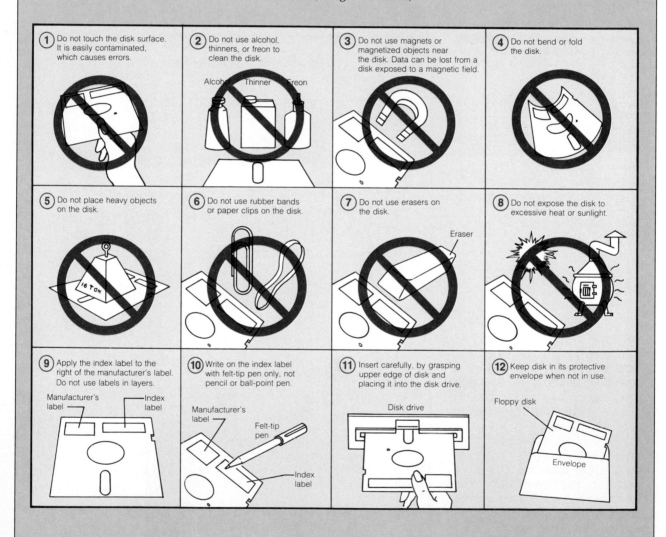

1. Do not touch the disk surface. It is easily contaminated, which causes errors.

2. Do not use alcohol, thinners, or freon to clean the disk.
   Alcohol Thinner Freon

3. Do not use magnets or magnetized objects near the disk. Data can be lost from a disk exposed to a magnetic field.

4. Do not bend or fold the disk.

5. Do not place heavy objects on the disk.
   16 TON

6. Do not use rubber bands or paper clips on the disk.

7. Do not use erasers on the disk.
   Eraser

8. Do not expose the disk to excessive heat or sunlight.

9. Apply the index label to the right of the manufacturer's label. Do not use labels in layers.
   Manufacturer's label — Index label

10. Write on the index label with felt-tip pen only, not pencil or ball-point pen.
    Manufacturer's label Felt-tip pen Index label

11. Insert carefully, by grasping upper edge of disk and placing it into the disk drive.
    Disk drive

12. Keep disk in its protective envelope when not in use.
    Floppy disk Envelope

TRANSPARENCY ACETATE #5M
How to handle disks

DISCUSSION QUESTION
Why are precautions necessary in handling diskettes?

LECTURE HINT
Some specialists say not to write on a floppy disk cover at all. Write on your label first, and then transfer the label to your floppy disk cover. Otherwise, you may dent the diskette inside.

LECTURE HINT
Diskettes have become a new medium of presenting products to upscale customers. As an example, a printed advertisement for General Motors Corporation offered a Buick commercial ("infomercial") on disk, promising an animated sequence of the engine revving up, competitive statistics such as miles per gallon and a chart for computing monthly payments. General Motors Corporation anticipated 20,000 requests but received 67,000 requests.

pocket or purse. It weighs less and consumes less power. Its higher capacity allows companies to offer several applications programs on a single diskette, so users do not have to shuffle so many diskettes around. One long-range advantage of the 3½-inch diskette is that manufacturers can make their computers smaller, so they take up less desk space.

7 Hard Disks

Hard disks are 5¼-inch or 3½-inch Winchester disks in sealed modules (Figure 5-18). The cost has come down substantially: A hard disk with a capacity of 30 megabytes of storage now costs about $300, down from several thousand just a few years ago. Hard disks are extremely reliable, since they are sealed against contamination by outside air or human hands.

Hard disks can save you time as well as space. You do not even have to need all the storage hard disk provides; just the way the hard disk speeds up your computing can make buying one worthwhile. Accessing files on a hard disk is significantly faster than on diskettes—up to about 20 times faster. The convenience of a hard disk is a factor too, saving time for the user. As one convert noted, "Diskettes are a pain. The idea of a computer in the first place was to get

Figure 5-18   Hard disks.   (a) A bank of hard disks. The police in Sauk County, Wisconsin, use a battery of computers and hard disks to keep track of traffic offenders who cross the county line. (b) Innards of a hard disk. This drive stores about 20 million characters on a pair of 3½-inch disks.

(a)

(b)

Figure 5-19   A removable hard disk. This drive can be removed for safe-keeping or to transport it to another computer.

work done faster, and it seems like juggling diskettes is a step backward." The promise of speedier processing did far more to win him over than the promise of more disk storage space.

Unlike a diskette, however, most hard disk units cannot be transported from one computer to another. For that reason most hard-disk systems include at least one diskette drive to provide users with software and data portability. However, removable hard disk units are available for those who are especially concerned about security or need to transport the hard disk elsewhere (Figure 5-19).

7 Hardcards

Most people, especially in business, are surprised at how fast a hard disk fills with data. Imagine your own personal computer with a hard disk built-in. Now where do you turn? You could buy another hard-disk drive and attach it to your machine. A more attractive option, however, is the **hardcard** (Figure 5-20), which has a 20–40MB hard disk on a circuit board that fits in a slot inside your computer. The primary advantage of a hardcard is that it is out of sight and not cluttering up your desk.

7 RAM Disks: Turning Your Micro into a Hot Rod

DISCUSSION QUESTION
In what ways is a RAM disk a disk?
In what ways is it not a disk?

It is called a **RAM disk,** or an **electronic disk,** or a **phantom disk,** but it is not really a disk at all. A RAM disk is a chip that fools your computer into regarding part of its memory as another disk drive that can be used to store programs and data. The advantage of a RAM disk is that it works much faster than a standard disk drive.

A RAM disk is particularly helpful if a user is sending data from one computer to another. Instead of delays waiting for the diskette or hard disk to send data, the data can be sent directly from the RAM disk. Another ingenious use of RAM is memory-resident programs. For example, as a personal computer is turned on, an "office manager" is called in from the hard disk to reside temporarily in an unused corner of RAM. Whenever you wish to use this program to make a few notes, or use a calculator, or telephone another computer (yes, there are programs that do all these tasks), the instructions are available speedily. If, instead, you had to take the time to slip in a diskette, you might as well use a real notepad or calculator or phone directory.

So why not put all files on RAM disk and enjoy the pure speed? RAM disk, alas, is volatile. Its contents are lost if the computer is turned off or there is a power failure. It is acceptable to lose program files in such a way if they are stored permanently on the original disk files. Data files, which are always changing, must be saved on disk before you turn off your computer. In fact, it is a good idea to save

Figure 5-20   Hardcard. (a) This disk drive on a card—a hardcard—is being inserted into a slot inside a microcomputer. (b) Interior of a hardcard, showing the disk.

(a)

(b)

your files periodically as you are working on them, to avoid data loss due to power surges or power failures. So, in summary, you can load your programs onto RAM disk for the day, but you must save new data on disk files.

Backup Systems

Although a hard disk is an extremely reliable device, the drive is subject to electromechanical failure. With any method of data storage, a **backup system**—a way of storing data in more than one place to protect it from damage and loss—is vital. There are inexpensive solutions that can store data on diskettes, and this is appropriate for small hard drives—of, say, 10 to 20MB. But such a system is too slow and cumbersome for larger systems. Personal

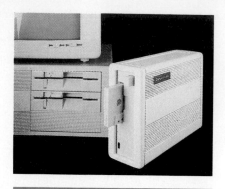

Figure 5-21   Tape backup system.
This tape backup unit permits backup of part or all of a hard disk for security purposes.

computer users often use **tape backup systems** to copy the data from their disks onto cassettes or cartridges (Figure 5-21). A single cassette or cartridge can hold 20MB, 30MB, or more megabytes of data. Data thus saved can be restored to the hard disk later if needed. A key advantage of a tape backup system is that it can copy the entire hard disk in minutes, saving you the trouble of swapping diskettes in and out of the machine. Such systems are sometimes called streaming tape backup systems because the tape does not stop and start, but moves in a continuous stream.

Checking an Earlier Decision

We left Pete James with his personal computer equipped with a 30MB hard drive. It worked just fine for its original purposes—notes, letters, outlines, speeches, and position papers. But he soon began branching out in other directions, using various types of software. He tracked names and phone numbers, analyzed financial data, and even produced some business graphics. He used the computer as a system for filing ideas that he could access instantaneously. All these activities used data files, and Pete eventually found that his hard drive was getting crowded.

A common theme among computer professionals is to estimate your disk needs generously and then double that amount. But estimating future needs is rarely easy. Many users, therefore, make later adjustments. Pete chose a hardcard to accommodate his expanded storage needs. To quote Pete, "Before, I just couldn't envision how computers could be used. Now I think of my computer as an extension of my brain."

TEST BANK
Mult. Choice   69-70
T/F   69-73
Matching E   10
Fill-in-the-Blank 56

Optical Storage: Superdisk Takes Off

Now that you have a thorough grounding in traditional magnetic media, you can appreciate the technology that is now upon us in the form of **optical disk.** The explosive growth in storage needs drives the computer industry to provide storage devices that are higher in capacity, cheaper, more compact, and more versatile. This demanding shopping list is a description of the optical disk.

How Optical Disks Work

The technology works like this. A laser hits a layer of metallic material spread over the surface of the disk. When data is being entered, heat from the laser produces tiny spots on the disk's surface. To read the data, the laser scans the disk, and a lens picks up different light reflections from the various spots.

PERSPECTIVES

THE WHOLE WORLD ON OPTICAL DISK

Why is optical disk embraced as "superdisk"? It is certainly super in capacity, as attested by the government agencies, insurance firms, and banks that are transferring their microfilm data to optical disk. Consider more specific examples:

- To hold the content of the *Encyclopaedia Britannica*, whose 450 million characters reside in 30 volumes, would require 1250 standard diskettes. But the entire set of volumes can fit quite nicely on a single 540 MB optical disk with room to spare.

- A CD-ROM software offering from Microsoft called Bookshelf includes the *American Heritage Dictionary, Roget's Thesaurus, Bartlett's Familiar Quotations, The World Almanac, A Manual of Style, Business Information Sources,* and a zip code directory.

- Grolier Electronic Publishing is putting an entire 20-volume encyclopedia onto a single optical disk. It will include words, audio pronunciations, photographs, games, and videos. Users can select items from a series of menus. Choosing "rhinoceros," for example, produces text, photographs, maps, and a rhino braying sound.

- "A catalog you can listen to," boasts the makers of *The Electronic Whole Earth Catalog,* on optical disk. The catalog, developed for the Macintosh computer, holds over 400 MB of text, graphics, and sound—about the equivalent of 500 diskettes.

LECTURE HINT
Though optical disks can store hundreds of megabytes of information, they are slow compared to magnetic hard disks, needing ninety milliseconds to access data rather than sixteen milliseconds.

THE LATEST AND GREATEST

The NeXT Computer System (*top photo*), developed by Steve Jobs, offers a combination of high-performance components at a price below some less-advanced microcomputer systems. In particular, it offers 256MB *erasable* optical disk storage (*bottom photo*), enough to store approximately 128,000 pages of data.

At the introduction ceremony, Jobs put the computer, housed in a fetching matte black magnesium case, through its paces in a stunning debut performance that had the media audience gasping for adjectives. Among other feats, Jobs demonstrated how the machine can run four stopwatches at once; simulate an oscilloscope; recite Martin Luther King, Jr.'s "I Have a Dream" speech; and play the "flute." Jobs also emphasized the power of the machine by demonstrating a database of all articles from the Wall Street Journal for a given year.

DISCUSSION QUESTION
What are the advantages and disadvantages of optical disks over magnetic disks?

Optical storage technology is categorized according to its read/write capability. **Read-only** media are recorded on by the manufacturer and can be read from but not written to by the user. This technology is sometimes referred to as **OROM,** for **optical read-only memory.** Such a disk could not, obviously, be used for your files, but manufacturers could use it to supply software. Current multiple-application packages—word processing, spreadsheets, graphics, database—sometimes take as many as six diskettes; all these could fit on one OROM disk.

Write-once, read-many media, also called **WORM media,** may be written to once. Once filled, a WORM disk becomes read-only media. A WORM disk is nonerasable. For applications demanding secure storage of original versions of valuable documents or data, the primary advantage of nonerasability is clear: Once they are recorded, no one can erase or modify them. Write-once optical media can provide a secure comparison base for auditing changes to original data—an invaluable function to, say, geophysical applications where a difference of a few bits can signal the presence of oil. Optical disk has opened up a wide range of new capabilities and novel applications.

A variation on the optical technology is the **CD-ROM,** for **compact disk read-only memory.** CD-ROM has a major advantage over other optical disk designs: The disk format is identical to *audio* compact disks, so the same dust-free manufacturing plants that are now stamping out digital versions of Bach or Springsteen can easily convert to producing anything from software to the *Encyclopaedia Britannica*. Since producing CD-ROM is simply a matter of pressing out copies from a master disk, it is much more economical than traditional magnetic storage, which makes copies byte by byte.

7 The Future Approaches

Early optical disks could not be written on, but now that has changed. **Erasable optical disks** can indeed be written on, and their future seems limitless. There is good storage technology on the market; you do not have to wait for optical disk. But when it is available for your computer, your storage needs may have grown to the point where you will need it.

7 Onward

What is the future of storage? Whatever the technology, it seems likely that we will be seeing greater storage capabilities in the future. Such capabilities have awesome implications; think of the huge data files for law, medicine, science, education, government, and ultimately . . . you.

To have access to all that data from any location, we need data communications. To which we now turn in the next chapter.

7 Summary and Key Terms

- **Secondary storage,** or **auxiliary storage,** is necessary because memory, or primary storage, can only be used temporarily. The benefits of secondary storage are economy, reliability, and convenience. Two common means of secondary storage are magnetic tape and magnetic disk; optical storage is a newer technology.

- To be processed by a computer, raw data is organized into characters, fields, files, and databases. A **character** is a letter, number, or special character (such as $). A **field** is a set of related characters, a **record** is a collection of related fields, a **file** is a collection of related records, and a **database** is a collection of interrelated files.

- The two main methods of data processing are **batch processing** (processing data transactions in groups) and **transaction processing** (processing data transactions one at a time). Many computer systems combine features of both types of processing.

- Batch processing involves a **master file,** which contains semi-permanent data, and a **transaction file,** which contains additions, deletions, and changes to be made to **update** the master file. These new transactions are **sorted** sequentially by a **key,** or a field that identifies records. The master file, which is already in order, is then updated by being compared against the transaction file.

- An advantage of batch processing is the cost saving resulting from processing records in groups. Disadvantages include both the delay in receiving the initial output and the additional time needed later to locate a particular record in a group.

- In **transaction processing** the transactions are processed in the order they occur, without any presorting. This is **real-time processing** because the results of the transaction are available quickly enough to affect the activity at hand. Real-time processing requires the user's terminals to be **on-line** (directly connected to the computer). The development of magnetic disk made processing faster and more **interactive** (involving a "dialogue" between user and computer) by providing users with easier access to data.

- Transaction processing systems are usually **time-sharing** systems, in which users share access to a central computer that can process their transactions almost at the same time.

- Advantages of transaction processing include quick results of transactions and continual updating. Disadvantages include the expense of continual access to the computer and the difficulty of protecting the security of computer files.

- The amount of data on a **magnetic tape** is expressed in terms of **density,** as the number of **characters per inch** (**cpi**) or **bytes per inch** (**bpi**) that can be stored on a tape.

- **Tracks,** or **channels,** run the length of the magnetic tape. On most tapes a cross section representing one character contains 9 bits, one for each track. A magnetized spot represents a 1 bit; a location with no magnetization represents a 0 bit.

- A **magnetic tape unit** records and retrieves data by using a **read/write head,** an electromagnet that can convert magnetized areas into electrical impulses (to read) or reverse the process (to write). When the machine is writing, the **erase head** erases any previously recorded data.

- The magnetic tape is inserted into the unit on a **supply reel,** passed through the read/write head, and attached to the **take-up reel.** During processing the tape moves back and forth between the two reels, then is rewound onto the supply reel when the processing is complete.

- Since the fast-moving magnetic tape cannot stop instantly, some blank stopping space is necessary between records. This space is called an **interrecord gap** (**IRG**), or **interblock gap** (**IBG**). To avoid wasting space on a tape, **blocking** is used. That is, **logical records,** the records written by the applications program, are blocked, or put together, into **physical records,** or **blocks.** The term **blocking factor** refers to the number of logical records in one physical record.

- A **hard magnetic disk,** or **hard disk,** consists of a metal platter coated with magnetic oxide. When more than one hard disk is assembled as a unit, the group is called a **disk pack.** A **diskette** is a round piece of plastic coated with magnetic oxide.

- The surface of a magnetic disk has tracks on which data is recorded as magnetic spots. All the tracks are closed circles having the same center, and the same amount of data is stored on each track.

- A disk or diskette storage device is a **direct-access storage device** (**DASD**) because it locates a record directly (unlike magnetic tape, which requires the read/write head to read all the preceding records on the file). With a DASD data can be stored either sequentially or randomly.

- A **disk drive** rapidly rotates a disk, diskette, or disk pack as an **access arm** moves a read/write head that detects the magnetized data.

- A **Winchester disk,** also called a **Winnie,** combines disks, access arms, and read/write heads in a **sealed module.** Some disk modules are built in to the drive; others are removable.

- The two main methods of writing data on a disk or diskette are the **sector method** and the **cylinder method.**

- In the sector method each track is divided into sectors, with data identified by surface, track, and sector numbers. Most personal computers use **soft-sectored diskettes,** in which sectors are determined by the software.

- The cylinder method accesses a set of tracks lined up one under the other, one from each surface. Such a set of vertically aligned tracks is called a **cylinder.** The cylinder method means fewer movements of the access arms mechanism and faster processing.

- The time needed to access data is determined by four factors: (1) **seek time,** the time it takes the access arm to get into position over the track; (2) **head switching,** the small amount of time needed to activate the appropriate read/write head; (3) **rotational delay,** the time necessary for the appropriate record to get into position under the head; and (4) **data transfer,** the time required for data to be transferred between memory and the disk track.

- The three main methods of storing files of data in secondary storage are **sequential file organization, direct file organization,** and **indexed file organization.**

- In **sequential file processing,** records are usually in order according to a key field.

- **Direct file processing** (also called **direct access** or **random access**) allows direct access to a record by using a record key; the user does not have to wait for the computer to read preceding records in the file. **Hashing,** or **randomizing,** is the process of applying a formula to a key to yield a number that represents the address. Records with duplicate addresses are called **synonyms,** and are said to cause **collisions.**

- In **indexed file processing,** or **indexed processing,** records are stored in sequential order, but the file also contains an index of record keys so an individual record can be located.

- Disk storage provides high-volume data capacity and allows direct file processing, which enables the user to immediately find and update records. Tape storage does not allow direct file processing, but it is portable and less expensive than disk storage.

- Common storage media for personal computers are diskettes and hard disks. **Diskettes** include $5\frac{1}{4}$-inch and $3\frac{1}{2}$-inch sizes. A **hard disk** is more expensive than a diskette and cannot be moved from computer to computer, but it does provide more storage and faster processing.

- The storage capacity of a personal computer with a built-in hard disk can be increased through the addition of either another hard disk drive or a **hardcard.**

- Despite the reliability of data storage devices, a **backup system**—a way of protecting data by copying it and storing it in more than one place—is vital. Hard disk can be backed up efficiently with a **tape backup system,** which can hold many megabytes of data. Such backup units can copy an entire hard disk in minutes, and—if needed—restore it just as quickly.

- A **RAM disk,** (also called an **electronic disk** or **phantom disk**) is a RAM chip that fools the computer into regarding part of its memory as another disk drive for storing programs and data. A RAM disk works much faster than a standard disk drive and is useful for sending data from computer to computer, but its disadvantage is that it is volatile.

- In **optical disk** technology, a laser beam records data by producing tiny spots on the optical disk's metallic surface. Data is read by having the laser scan the disk surface while a lens picks up different light reflections from the spots.

- Optical storage technology is categorized according to its read/write capability. **Read-only media** are recorded on by the manufacturer through a technology sometimes called **optical read-only memory (OROM). Write-once, read-many media (WORM)** can be written to once; then it becomes read-only media.

- A variation on the optical technology is the **CD-ROM,** which stands for **compact disk read-only memory.** CD-ROM has the same format as audio compact disks.

- An **erasable optical disk** has been developed that allows data to be stored, moved, changed, and erased—just as on magnetic media.

Review Questions

1. Describe the benefits of secondary storage.

2. Define the following: character, field, record, file, and database.

3. Explain how batch processing differs from transaction processing.

4. Discuss the advantages and disadvantages of batch processing.

5. Discuss the advantages and disadvantages of transaction processing.

6. Explain how batch and transaction processing may be combined.

7. Explain how data is represented on magnetic tape.

8. Explain the function of blocking.

9. Describe how a disk drive works.

10. Explain how the sector method differs from the cylinder method.

11. Describe the three major methods of file organization.

12. How do hard disks differ from diskettes?

13. Describe how optical disks work.

Discussion Questions

1. Provide your own example to illustrate how characters of data are organized into fields, records, files, and databases. If you wish, you may choose one of the following examples: department-store data, airline data, or Internal Revenue Service data.

2. Give your own examples to illustrate the use of each of the following types of processing: batch processing, transaction processing, and a combination of batch processing and transaction processing.

3. Imagine that you are buying a personal computer. What would you choose for secondary storage and why?

Chapter 6. Communications: Reaching Out to Touch a Computer

6

Communications

Reaching Out to
Touch a Computer

The world of communications takes on new meaning when we combine communications technology with computer technology. This chapter describes how data is transmitted and examines the various kinds of communications networks and their uses.

LEARNING OBJECTIVES

- Introduction to the evolution of data communications systems, from centralized data processing systems, to teleprocessing systems, to distributed data processing, to local area networks.
- Knowledge of data transmissions methods, including types of signals, modulation, and choices among transmission modes.
- Differentiating the different kinds of communication links.
- Understanding network configurations.
- Acquaintance with examples of networking such as electronic mail, voice mail, teleconferencing, facsimile technology, electronic fund transfers, bulletin boards, shopping, and computer commuting.

TEST BANK

Mult. Choice	1-5
T/F	1-6
Matching A	1-2
Matching B	1
Matching C	1
Matching D	1
Fill-in-the-Blank	1-4

LECTURE ACTIVITY

With a modem attached to a microcomputer, access a nearby bulletin board or possibly an information utility such as CompuServe. If this is not convenient, consider the school library, which usually has a hookup to information databases.

Let us pause to consider some recent—and rather frightening—history. Three West German men broke into key military and research computers in the United States. What is more, they sold purloined codes and data to the Soviets. How could this happen? Did they climb a fence, pick a lock, compromise an insider? Not at all. They obtained everything they wanted by using their own computers—from *inside* West Germany. It would be nice to wrap up this story with a tale of FBI derring-do, but the fact is that the interlopers were discovered accidentally by an astronomer in California who was tracking a 75-cent error in his computer accounting system. He devoted two years to entrapping the thieves.

This gives you a broad view of the possibilities for linking computers together—the subject of this chapter. In fact, potentially, any two computers in the world can be linked together using communications equipment. Although there are some things to be wary of, the merger of communications and computers—**telecommunications**—is an exceptional benefit, helping people get full value from each technology. Telecommunications gives people access to on-line information, puts services like banking and shopping into the home, and links professionals together in complex computer networks. People who use telecommunications technology are just as casual about linking up with a computer in another state or country as they are about using the telephone. These topics and the technology that makes them possible are highlighted in this chapter. We will begin with a look at the past.

7 Data Communications: How It All Began

Mail, telephone, TV and radio, books, and periodicals—these are the principal ways we send and receive information, and they have not changed appreciably in a generation. However, **data communications systems**—computer systems that transmit data over communications lines such as public telephone lines or private network cables—have been gradually evolving since the mid 1960s. Let us take a look at how they came about.

In the early days large computers were often found in several departments of large companies. There could be, for example, different computers to support engineering, accounting, and manufacturing. However, because department managers generally did not know enough about computers to use them efficiently, expenditures for computers were often wasteful. The response to this problem was to centralize computer operations.

Centralization provided better control, and the consolidation of equipment led to economies of scale; that is, hardware and supplies could be purchased in bulk at cheaper cost. **Centralized data processing** placed everything—all processing, hardware, software, and storage—in one central location. Computer manufacturers re-

WHO NEEDS PAPER?

Predictions of the "paperless office" have been made since the dawn of the computer age. The idea was that businesses would convert all those file drawers full of paper to disk and then update and access the files by using data communications systems. The automated office was supposed to hurry the process along.

It has not quite worked out that way. In fact, the opposite is true. Everyone wants paper. People still want printed reports, and they cannot scribble notes on a disk.

A recent report shows that the fastest growing category of computer-related supplies is not disks or printer ribbons, but ordinary paper. The primary reason for the growth in paper demand seems to be the increased use of computers coupled with attractive output produced by laser printers. Also, it is so easy to make changes on the computer that a report can be amended and printed out over and over. The paperless office is nowhere in sight.

DISCUSSION QUESTION
What were the steps involved in decentralizing the main computer?

LECTURE HINT
Some other advantages of distributed data processing: (1) reduced phone costs in accessing main computer, (2) less susceptible to down-time of main computer, (3) better security, (4) less delay in completing jobs that can be done locally.

DISCUSSION QUESTION
How does a micro-to-mainframe link differ from a network?

sponded to this trend by building even larger, general-purpose computers so that all departments within an organization could be serviced efficiently.

Eventually, however, total centralization proved inconvenient. All input data had to be physically transported to the computer, and all processed material had to be picked up and delivered to the users. Insisting on centralized data processing was like insisting that all conversations between people be face-to-face in one designated room. The next logical step was to connect users via telephone lines and terminals to the central computer. Thus, in the 1960s, the centralized system was made more flexible by the introduction of time-sharing through **teleprocessing systems**—terminals connected to the central computer via communications lines. Teleprocessing systems permitted users to have remote access to the central computer from their terminals in other buildings and even other cities. However, even though access to the computer system was decentralized, all processing was still centralized—that is, performed by one central computer.

In the 1970s businesses began to use minicomputers, which were often at a distance from the central computer. These were clearly decentralized systems because the smaller computers could do some processing on their own, yet some also had access to the central computer. This new setup was labeled **distributed data processing (DDP)**. It is similar to teleprocessing, except that it accommodates not only remote *access* but also remote *processing*. Processing is no longer done exclusively by the central computer. Rather, the processing and files are dispersed among several remote locations and can be handled by computers—usually mini- or microcomputers—all hooked up to the central host computer, and sometimes to each other as well. A typical application of a distributed data processing system is a business or organization with many locations, branch offices, or retail outlets. DDP communications systems are more complex and usually more expensive than exclusively centralized computer systems, but they provide many more benefits to users.

The whole picture of distributed data processing has changed dramatically with the advent of networks of personal computers. By **network,** we mean a computer system that uses communications equipment to connect two or more computers and their resources. DDP systems are networks. Of particular interest in today's business world are **local area networks (LANs),** which are designed to share data and resources among several individual computers (Figure 6-1). We will examine networking in more detail in later sections of the chapter.

Another type of connection is the **micro-to-mainframe link.** Although users have a variety of business software available for their personal computer, they often want to use that software to process corporate data that resides in the mainframe files. Giving users access to that data is a hot issue. The connection itself is a problem because the two computers—mainframe and personal—may not be

Figure 6-1 Local area network. This photo montage suggests the sharing of resources possible with a hard-wired local area network.

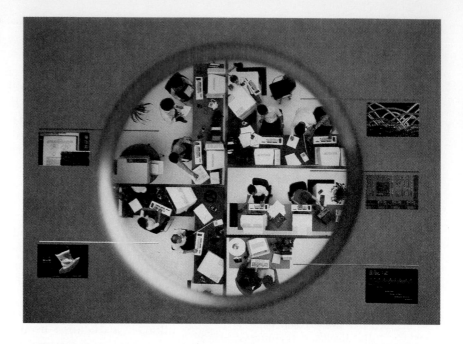

compatible. But a more serious problem is the security and integrity of the data after it has been unleashed.

In the next section we will preview the components of a communications system to give you an overview of how these components work together.

7 The Complete Communications System—And How It All Fits Together

The components are few. The complications are many. The basic configuration—how the components are put together—is pretty straightforward, but the choices for each component are open-ended and the technology ever changing. Assume that you have some data—a message—to transmit from one place to another. The basic components of a data communications system to transmit that message are (1) the sending device, (2) a communications link, and (3) the receiving device. Suppose, for example, that you work at a sports store. You might want to send a message to the warehouse to inquire about a Wilson tennis racquet, an item you need for a customer. In this case the sending device is your terminal at the store, the communications channel is the phone line, and the receiving machine is the central computer at the warehouse. As you will see, however, there are many other possibilities.

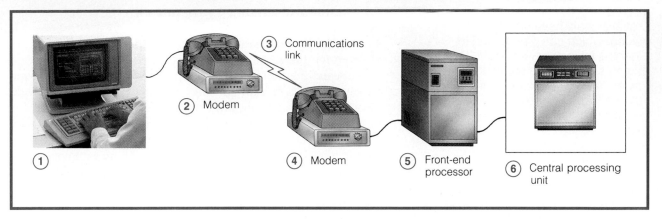

Figure 6-2   Communications system components.   Data originated from (1) a sending device is (2) converted by a modem to data that can be carried over (3) a link and (4) reconverted by a modem at the receiving end before (5) being processed by a front-end processor and (6) sent to the computer.

There is another often needed component that must be mentioned in this basic configuration, as you can see in Figure 6-2. This component is a modem, which is sometimes needed to convert computer data to signals that can be carried by the communications channel and vice versa.

Large computer systems may have additional components. At the computer end, data may travel through a communications control unit called a **front-end processor,** which is actually a computer itself. Its purpose is to relieve the central computer of some of the communications tasks and so free it for processing applications programs. In addition, a front-end processor usually performs error detection and recovery functions. Small computers, we should note, usually perform communications functions by using a special logic board in the computer itself.

Let us see how these components work together, beginning with how data is transmitted.

7 Data Transmission

A terminal or computer produces digital signals, which are simply the presence or absence of an electric pulse. The state of being on or off represents the binary number 1 or 0. Some communications lines accept digital transmission directly, and the trend in the communications industry is toward digital signals. However, most telephone lines through which these digital signals are sent were originally built for voice transmission, and voice transmission requires analog signals. We will look at these two types of transmissions and then study modems, which translate between them.

7 Digital and Analog Transmission

Digital transmission sends data as distinct pulses, either on or off, in much the same way that data travels through the computer. This means that computer-generated data can be transmitted directly over digital communications media. However, most communications media are not digital. Communications devices such as telephone lines, coaxial cables, and microwave circuits are already in place for voice transmission. The path of least resistance for most users is to piggyback on one of these. These most common communications devices have a common characteristic: They all use analog transmission.

Analog transmission uses a continuous electric signal in the form of a wave. The wave form has three characteristics, as shown in Figure 6-3.

- **Amplitude** is the height of the wave, which indicates the strength of the signal.

- **Phase** is the relative position in time of one complete cycle of the wave.

- **Frequency** is the number of times the wave repeats during a specific time interval.

We have already noted that computers produce digital signals but that most communications equipment transmits analog signals. A digital signal, therefore, must be converted to analog before it can be sent over analog lines. It is converted by altering an analog signal, which is called a **carrier wave.** These alterations can be to the amplitude or the phase or the frequency of the wave, as you can see in Figure 6-3.

The height—amplitude—can be changed, for example, to represent a 1 bit, whereas leaving the height alone can represent the 0 bit. This type of change is called **amplitude modulation.** Another alternative is to tamper with the frequency. When the frequency changes, a change can be made from a 1 bit to a 0 bit or vice versa. These types of changes are called **frequency modulation.** You probably know amplitude and frequency modulation by their abbreviations, AM and FM, the methods used for radio transmission.

Conversion from digital to analog signals is called **modulation** and the reverse process—reconstructing the original digital message at the other end of the transmission—is called **demodulation.** So we see that the marriage of computers to communications is not a perfect one. Instead of just "joining hands," a third party may be needed in between. This extra device is called a modem.

7 Modems

A **modem** is a device that converts a digital signal to an analog signal and vice versa (Figure 6-4a). *Modem* is short for *modulate/demodulate.*

TRANSPARENCY ACETATE #6B
Figure #6-3

DISCUSSION QUESTION
What are three types of carrier
waves for transmitting audio
signals? What are their
characteristics?

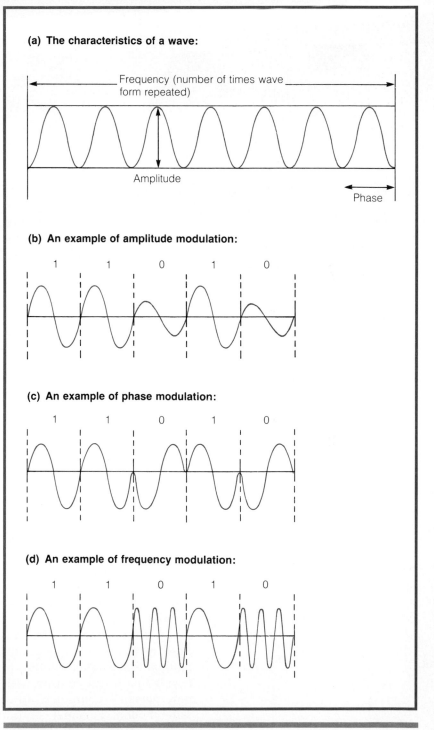

(a) The characteristics of a wave:

(b) An example of amplitude modulation:

(c) An example of phase modulation:

(d) An example of frequency modulation:

Figure 6-3   Analog signals.   (a) In this figure a wave is labeled with its characteristics: amplitude, phase, and frequency. The lower figures show how a wave
can be changed to accept a message, either through (b) amplitude modulation (in
this case, a change to smaller wave height), (c) phase modulation (in this case,
waves reverse direction), or (d) frequency modulation (in this case, wave signals
are more frequent).

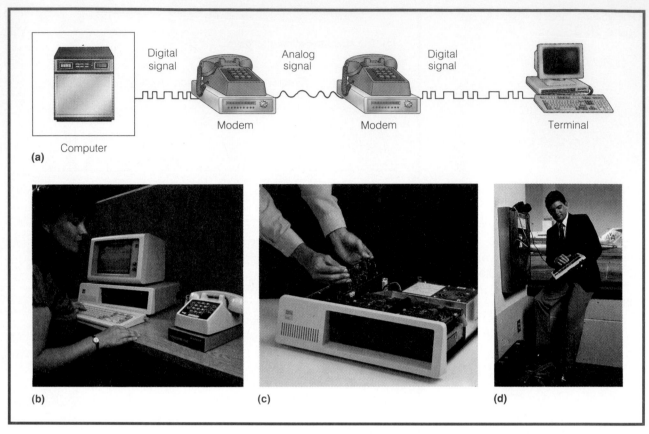

(a) Computer — Digital signal — Modem — Analog signal — Modem — Digital signal — Terminal

(b)   (c)   (d)

Figure 6-4   Modems.   (a) Modems convert—modulate—digital data signals to analog signals for traveling over the communications links, then reverse the process—demodulate—at the other end. (b) This external modem rests under the telephone that hooks the computer to the outside world. (c) This internal modem slips into an expansion slot inside the computer. The phone cord plugs into a jack, accessible through the back of the computer. (d) The phone can be cradled by this acoustic coupler, which is also a modem.

DISCUSSION QUESTION
How do direct-connect and acoustic modems differ? Which one is more reliable?

Types of Modems

Modems vary in the way they connect to the telephone line. There are two main types: direct-connect modems and acoustic coupler modems.

A **direct-connect modem** is directly connected to the telephone line by means of a telephone jack. An **external direct-connect modem** is separate from the computer (Figure 6-4b). Its main advantage is that it can be used with a variety of computers. If you buy a new personal computer, for example, you can probably keep the same modem. Personal computer users who regard a modem as one more item taking up desk space can buy a modem that is out of sight—literally. All major microcomputer manufacturers now offer **internal modem boards** that can be inserted by users (Figure 6-4c). Some new microcomputers even have an internal modem built-in as part of the standard equipment.

An **acoustic coupler modem** is connected to a telephone receiver rather than directly to a telephone line (Figure 6-4d). Some acoustic couplers are connected to the computer by a cable, but others are built-in. The advantage of acoustic couplers is that they can be connected to any phone, but the quality suffers since they are not connected directly to the telephone line.

Modem Features

Modems now come with features that make communication as automatic and natural as possible. For example, most modems include **auto-answer,** whereby the modem answers all incoming calls. With **auto-disconnect** a modem disconnects a call automatically whenever the other party hangs up or a disconnect message is received. The **auto-dial** feature allows you to call another computer with a minimum of action on your part. The **automatic redial** feature allows a modem to redial a call that resulted in a busy signal. Finally, a **time delay** allows your computer to call another computer and transfer a file at a future time of your choosing—presumably at night, when rates are lower. Just a few years ago, when most modems did not have these features, users performed dial and answer functions manually.

Modem Data Speeds

In addition to new features, modems are moving into the fast lane. In general, modem users use normal telephone lines to connect their computers and pay telephone charges based on the time they are connected. Thus, there is a strong incentive to transmit as quickly as possible. For years 300 bps (bits per second) was the slow speed and 1200 bps was the high speed for both home and business transmission. Now most manufacturers offer a modem that transmits at 2400 bps, and even higher speeds are offered for use with some business systems. That is good news for users ever in search of speed and for everyone who wants to save money transmitting data. Note the transmission time comparisons in Figure 6-5.

7 Asynchronous and Synchronous Transmission

Sending data off to a far destination works only if the receiving device is ready to accept it. By "ready" we mean more than just available; the receiving device must be able to keep in step with the sending device. Two techniques commonly used to keep the sending and receiving units dancing to the same tune are asynchronous and synchronous transmission.

When **asynchronous transmission** (also called the **start/stop method**) is used, a special start signal is transmitted at the beginning of each group of message bits—a group is usually a character. Likewise, a stop signal is sent at the end of the group of message bits (Figure 6-6a). When the receiving device gets the start signal, it sets up a timing mechanism to accept the group of message bits.

DISCUSSION QUESTION
What are some of the automatic features now available on modems?

TRANSPARENCY ACETATE #6C
Figure #6-5

Figure 6-5   Data transfer rates compared.

DISCUSSION QUESTION
How do asynchronous and synchronous transmission differ?

Data transfer rate (bps)	Time to transmit a 20-page single-spaced report
300	40 min
1200	10 min
2400	5 min
4800	2.5 min
9600	1.25 min

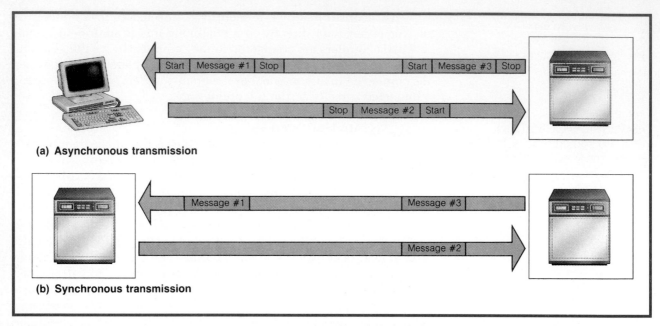

(a) Asynchronous transmission

(b) Synchronous transmission

Figure 6-6   Asynchronous and synchronous transmission.   (a) Asynchronous transmission uses start/stop signals surrounding each character. (b) Synchronous transmission uses a continuous stream of characters.

Synchronous transmission is a little trickier because characters are transmitted together in a continuous stream (Figure 6-6b). There are no call-to-action signals for each character. Instead, the sending and receiving devices are synchronized by having their internal clocks put in time with each other by a bit pattern transmitted at the beginning of the message.

Synchronous transmission equipment is more complex and more expensive than the equipment required for start/stop transmission. The payoff, however, is speedier transmission that is free from the bonds of the start/stop signals.

Simplex, Half-Duplex, and Full-Duplex Transmission

As Figure 6-7 shows, data transmission can be characterized as simplex, half-duplex, or full-duplex, depending on permissible directions of traffic flow. **Simplex transmission** sends data in one direction only; everyday examples are television broadcasting and arrival/departure screens at airports. A simplex terminal can send or receive data, but it cannot do both. It would seem that data collection—say, sending data from a deposit slip to a bank's computer storage—is a good application for simplex transmission. But the operator would want some sort of response, at least a confirmation that the data was received and, probably, error indications as well.

Figure 6-7   Transmission directions. (a) The seldom used simplex transmission sends data in one direction only. (b) Half-duplex transmission can send data in either direction, but only one way at a time. (c) Full-duplex transmission can send data in both directions at once.

TRANSPARENCY ACETATE #6E
Figure #6-7

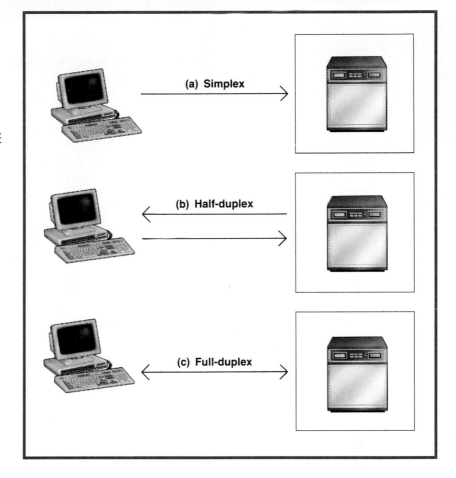

Simplex transmission will not handle even this limited type of situation.

   Half-duplex transmission allows transmission in either direction, but only one way at a time. An analogy is talk on a CB radio. Using half-duplex transmission, the operator in the bank deposit example can send the data and, after it is received, the program in the computer can send a confirmation reply. **Full-duplex transmission** allows transmission in both directions at once. An analogy is a telephone conversation in which, good manners aside, both parties can talk at the same time.

   We have discussed data transmission at some length. Now it is time to turn to the actual media that transmits the data.

7 Communications Links

As we have seen, computers are no longer islands unto themselves. The cost for linking widely scattered machines can be substantial (as much as one-third of the data processing budget), so it is worthwhile to examine the communications options. Telephone lines are the most convenient communication channel because an extensive system is already in place, but there are many other options. A communications **link** is the physical medium used for transmission.

7 Types of Communications Links

There are several kinds of communications links. Some may be familiar to you already.

Wire Pairs

One of the most common communications media is the **wire pair,** also known as the **twisted pair.** Wire pairs are wires twisted together to form a cable, which is then insulated (Figure 6-8a). Wire pairs are inexpensive and frequently used to transmit information over short distances. However, they are sometimes susceptible to electrical interference, or noise. **Noise** is anything that causes distortion in the signal when it is received.

Coaxial Cables

Known for contributing to high-quality transmission, **coaxial cables** are bundles of insulated wires within a shielded enclosure (Figure 6-8b) that can be laid underground or undersea. These cables can transmit data much faster than wire pairs. Coaxial cables are used in local area networks, where their high-volume capacity can be put to good use in an office environment.

Fiber Optics

Traditionally, most phone lines transmitted data electrically over wires made of metal, usually copper. These wires, being metal, must be protected from water and other corrosive substances. **Fiber optics** technology was developed by Bell Laboratories to solve these problems (Figure 6-8c). Instead of using electricity to send

Figure 6-8 Communications links. (a) Wire pairs are pairs of wires twisted together to form a cable, which is then insulated. (b) A coaxial cable. (c) Fiber optics consists of hair-like glass fibers that carry voice, television, and data signals.

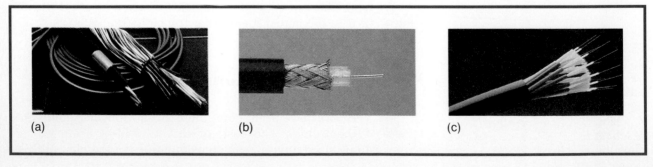

(a) (b) (c)

USA TODAY: NEWSPAPER IN SPACE

"Without our satellite system, it would be impossible to produce the newspaper." The speaker is William Hider, who ought to know. He is in charge of telecommunications for *USA Today,* the "nation's newspaper." And around the nation it is, first thing every morning at homes, bus stops, and eateries from Maine to Oregon. This is obviously not a paper delivered in an ordinary way.

USA Today is faxed via satellite. Four-color graphics for the newspaper are sent in all directions by the world's largest and most sophisticated satellite network. The heart of the system is a dish antenna atop the passageway between two high-rise office buildings at the newspaper's headquarters near Washington, D.C. The dish sends newspaper data to its orbiting satellite which, in turn, relays the data to 31 printing plants scattered across the United States, each equipped with its own receiving dish.

data, fiber optics uses light. The cables are made of glass fibers, thinner than a human hair, that can guide light beams for miles. Fiber optics transmits data faster than some technologies, yet the materials are lighter and less expensive than wire cables.

Microwave Transmission

Another popular medium is **microwave transmission** (see Figure 6-9), which uses what is called line-of-sight transmission of data signals through the atmosphere. Since these signals cannot bend around the curvature of the earth, relay stations—usually, antennas in high places such as the tops of mountains, towers, and buildings—are positioned at points approximately 30 miles apart to continue the transmission. Microwave transmission offers speed, cost-effectiveness, and ease of implementation. Unfortunately, there are some real problems with interference in microwave transmission. In major metropolitan areas, for instance, intervening tall buildings can sometimes jam signals.

Satellite Transmission

Communications satellites are suspended in space 22,300 miles above the earth. The basic components of **satellite transmission** are earth stations, which send and receive signals, and a satellite component called a transponder. The **transponder** receives the

Figure 6-9   Microwave transmission.   To relay microwave signals, dish-shaped antennas such as these are often located atop buildings, towers, and mountains. Microwave signals can follow only a line-of-sight path, so stations must relay this signal at regular intervals to avoid interference from the earth's curvature.

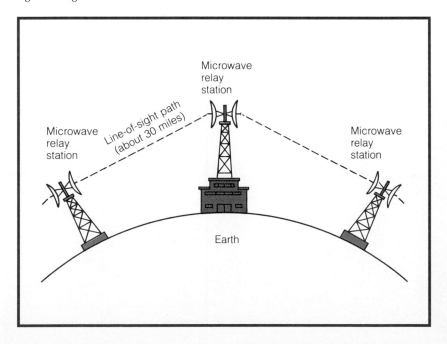

transmission from an earth station, amplifies the signal, changes the frequency, and retransmits the data to a receiving earth station (Figure 6-10). (The frequency is changed so that the weaker incoming signals will not be impaired by the stronger outgoing signals.) This entire process takes a matter of a few seconds.

7 Protocols

Can we talk? A line **protocol** is a set of rules for the exchange of data between a terminal and a computer or between two computers.

Protocol Communications

Two devices must be able to ask each other questions (Are you ready? Did you get my last message? Is there trouble at your end?) and to keep each other informed (I am sending data now). In addition, the two devices must agree on how data is to be transferred, including data transmission speed and duplex setting. But this must be done in a formal way. When communication is desired among machines from different vendors (or even different models from the same vendor), the software development can be a nightmare because different vendors use different protocols. Standards would help.

Figure 6-10   Satellite transmission.   This satellite acts as a relay station and can transmit data signals from one earth station to another. A signal is sent from an earth station to the relay satellite in the sky, which changes the signal frequency before transmitting it to the next earth station.

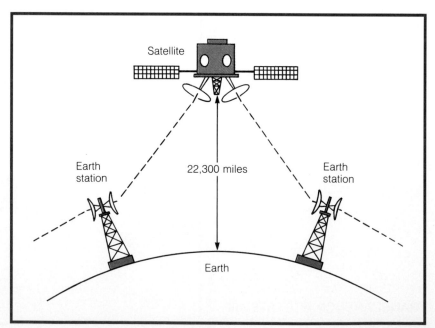

Setting Standards

Standards are important in the computer industry; it saves money if we can all coordinate effectively. Nowhere is this more obvious than in data communications systems, where many components must "come together." But it is hard to get people to agree to a standard.

Communications standards are, however, on the way. They provide a framework for how data is transmitted. The International Standards Organization (ISO) has defined a set of communication protocols called the **Open Systems Interconnection (OSI) model.** (Yes, that's ISO giving us OSI.) The first commercially available product, however, was IBM's **Systems Network Architecture (SNA),** which differs from the OSI model and has become well entrenched in the United States. (IBM usually sets its own de facto standard.) But wait. There is another player in this cast of characters, a player whose name we would not bother to trip over if it were not so important: the **Consultative Committee on International Telegraphy and Telephony. CCITT,** as it is known, is an agency of the United Nations and has tremendous worldwide clout. In 1984 CCITT endorsed the OSI model. What could IBM do but go along? IBM has made changes to allow SNA networks to communicate with OSI networks.

7 Line Configurations

There are two principal line configurations, or ways of connecting terminals with the computer: point-to-point and multipoint.

The **point-to-point line** is simply a direct connection between each terminal and the computer, as Figure 6-11 shows, or computer to computer. The **multipoint line** contains several terminals connected on the same line to the computer. In many cases a point-to-point line is sufficient; in other cases it is not efficient, convenient, or cost-effective. For instance, if the computer is at the head office in Dallas, but there are several branch offices with terminals in Houston, it does not make sense to connect each terminal individually to the computer in Dallas. It is usually better to run one line between the two cities and hook all the terminals on it in a multipoint arrangement. On a multipoint line only one terminal can transmit at any one time, although more than one terminal can receive messages from the computer simultaneously.

7 Carriers and Regulation

A company wishing to transmit messages can consider various communications facilities. In the United States the facilities are regulated by an agency of the federal government,

Figure 6-11   Point-to-point and multi-point lines.   (a) In point-to-point lines, each terminal is connected directly to the central computer. (b) In multipoint lines, several terminals share a single line, although only one terminal can transmit at a time.

TRANSPARENCY ACETATE #6G
Figure #6-11

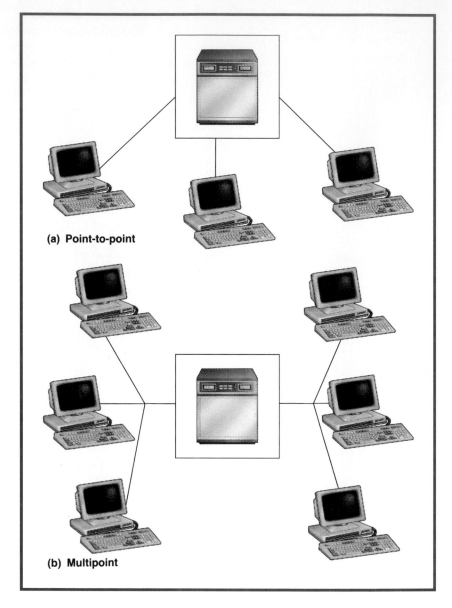

(a) Point-to-point

(b) Multipoint

the **Federal Communications Commission** (**FCC**), and by state regulatory agencies. Any organization wishing to offer communications services must submit a tariff to the FCC. A **tariff** is a list of services and the rates to be charged for those services. The FCC commissioners' view of the public good determines whether the FCC grants a license to the organization.

An organization that has been approved to offer communications services to the public is called a **common carrier.** The two largest common carriers are American Telephone & Telegraph (AT&T) and Western Union.

DISCUSSION QUESTION
How do switched and leased
phone lines differ?

7 Carrier Lines

Common carriers offer two types of lines: switched and private. **Switched lines,** like those used with your phone service, connect through switching centers to a variety of destinations. You as the user pay only for the services used, but, as with ordinary phone use, you may find the line busy or the connection poor. **Private** (or **leased**) **lines** offer communication to fixed destinations. A private line is dedicated to one customer. The key advantage of this service is that the line is always available. Another important advantage is security—that is, the private line is indeed private, unshared by others and thus less subject to snooping. Private lines may be conditioned (improved) by the carrier to reduce noise and can accommodate very high transmission rates.

7 Ma Bell Changes Everything

In 1968 the FCC handed down the landmark **Carterfone decision,** the first in a series of decisions that have permitted competitors—many from the data processing industry—to enter the formerly regulated domain of AT&T. The gist of the decision is that other companies can interface independent equipment with the public telephone network. These decisions spurred all kinds of independent activity in the communications industry. In 1972 communications companies were even permitted to launch their own satellites.

An outgrowth of this trend is the **value-added network** (**VAN**). In this type of system, a value-added carrier leases communications lines from a common carrier. These lines are then enhanced by adding improvements such as error detection and faster response time.

For many years AT&T and the U.S. government locked horns in an antitrust suit. Finally, in January 1982, the government agreed to drop its charges if the corporation would divest itself of the 22 local operating companies that then made up the Bell System. AT&T got to keep Bell Laboratories, its research arm; Western Electric, which makes equipment; and the long-distance telephone service. Most important, it was allowed to enter areas from which it was formerly barred by federal regulations—namely, data processing, computer communications, and the manufacture of computer equipment.

LECTURE HINT
Bell Telephone Laboratories has been active in the computer field for many years, designing and making their own computers, terminals, and software. But, because of the anti-trust suit, they could not sell these to the public. So these computer items were used internally. But 1982 changed all of that. AT&T is attempting to make a commercial profit from its computer work.

TEST BANK
Mult. Choice   48
Matching A   3
Fill-in-the-Blank 34

7 Overview of Networks

Computers that are connected so that they can communicate among themselves are said to form a **network.** Wide area networks send data over long distances by using the telephone system. Local area networks send data among computers linked together in one building or in buildings that are close together. Let us consider each of these types of networks.

7 Wide Area Networks

A **wide area network** (WAN) is a network of geographically distant computers and terminals. In business, a personal computer sending data any significant distance is probably sending it to a minicomputer or mainframe computer. Since these larger computers are designed to be accessed by terminals, a personal computer can communicate with a minicomputer or mainframe only if the personal computer emulates, or imitates, a terminal. This is accomplished by using **terminal emulation software** on the personal computer. The larger computer then considers the personal computer as just another user input/output communications device—a terminal. However, if a personal computer presents itself as a terminal, it is then subject to the limitations of a terminal.

The larger computer to which the terminal is attached is called the **host computer.** A user can use the terminal to type keystrokes to the host computer, and the host computer can display output on the terminal screen. Terminals usually do not have their own disk drives or central processing units, so programs and data files are stored on the host computer's disk drives. Since terminals cannot store files, files cannot be sent from the terminal to the host. For the same reason, the terminal can display a file sent to it by the host but it cannot store the file. When using a personal computer as a terminal, these limitations can be overcome by **file transfer software.** With file transfer programs you can **download** files—retrieve files from another computer and store them in your computer memory—or **upload** files—send files from your computer to another computer.

An alternative network is a local area network, which can communicate information much faster than most wide area networks.

7 Local Area Networks

A **local area network** (LAN) is a collection of computers, usually microcomputers, that share hardware, software, and information. In simple terms, LANs hook personal computers together through communications media so that each personal computer can share the resources of the others. All the devices—personal computers and other hardware—attached to the LAN are called **nodes** on the LAN. As the name implies, LANs cover short distances, usually one office or building or a group of buildings that are close together.

Here are some typical tasks for which LANs are especially suited:

- A personal computer can read data from a hard disk belonging to another personal computer as if it were its own. This allows users who are working on the same projects to share word processing, spreadsheet, and database data.

DISCUSSION QUESTION
What kind of networks might be
appropriate in these situations?
(1) A small architectural firm wants
each user to have a personal
computer, but wants project
records stored on shared hard
disk and some output printed on a
shared expensive plotter. (LAN)
(2) An insurance firm with
geographically distant offices
keeps key computer files at the
headquarters office. They want
regional offices to be able to
access data from their own
terminals. (WAN)

- A personal computer may print one of its files on the printer of another personal computer. (Since few people need a laser printer all the time, this more expensive type of printer can be hooked to only a few computers.)

- One copy of an applications program, when purchased with the proper license from the vendor of the program, can be used by all the personal computers on the LAN. This is less expensive than purchasing a copy of the program for each user.

As any or all of these activities are going on, the personal computer whose resource is being accessed by another can continue doing its own work.

These advantages go beyond simple convenience; some applications require that the same data be shared by coworkers. Consider, for example, a company that sends catalogs to customers, who can then place orders over the telephone. Waiting at the other end of the phone line are customer service representatives, who key the order data into the computer system as they are talking to the customer.

Each representative has a personal computer on which to enter orders, but all representatives share common computer files that provide information on product availability and pricing. It is not practical to provide a separate set of files for each representative because then one representative would not know what the others had sold. That is, an individual representative's file would reflect only the sales made by that particular representative. One representative, for example, could accept an order for 20 flannel shirts when there are only 5 shirts in stock because other representatives already accepted orders for that product.

In this kind of application, workers must have access to one central master file that will reflect the activities of other workers. Then, when a representative checks the file to see whether there is enough of a product available to accept an order, the representative can be confident that the quantity on hand has been updated and is correct.

7 Local Area Network Components

Not all networks of computers in an office or building are LANs. LANs do not use the telephone network. Networks that are LANs are made up of a standard set of components.

- All networks need some kind of cabling system. On some LANs, the nodes are connected by a shared **network cable.** Low-cost LANs are connected with twisted wire pairs like those used to connect the telephones in a building. However, many LANs use coaxial cable or fiber optic cable; these are more expensive but allow faster transmission.

- LANs use a hardware device called a **cable interface unit,** a set of electronic components in a box outside the computer, to send and receive signals on the network cable.

- A **network interface card,** inserted into a slot inside the personal computer, contains the electronic components needed to send and receive messages on the LAN. A short cable connects the network interface card to the cable interface unit.

- A **gateway** is a hardware device—sometimes even a separate computer—that connects two dissimilar networks. A gateway, for example, can connect a wide area network to a local area network. Users on both networks can share devices and exchange information.

- A **bridge,** sometimes called a **router,** connects two LANs of the same type so that messages can be sent from a node on one LAN to a node on a different LAN.

LECTURE HINT
Another type of local area network configuration is a direct connection between computers, similar to a ring except that the first and last computers are not connected together. This system makes it easy to attach another computer to the end of the line. However, if a computer is inserted somewhere other than the end, all computers beyond it cannot access the server until the computer is completely installed. If a line fails at one point, all computers beyond the failure can no longer access the main computer or server.

Local Area Network Topology

The physical layout of a local area network is called a **topology.** Local area networks come in three basic topologies: star, ring, and bus networks. A **star network** has a central computer that is responsible for managing the LAN. It is to this central computer—sometimes called a **server**—that the shared disks and printers are usually attached (Figure 6-12a). All messages are routed through the server. A **ring network** links all nodes together in a circular manner, without benefit of a server (Figure 6-12b). In ring networks, if one computer goes down, the entire network goes down. Disks and printers are scattered throughout the system. A **bus network** assigns a portion of network management to each computer but preserves the system if one component fails (Figure 6-12c). The majority of LANs are bus-structured.

Types of Local Area Networks

The two most common types of local area networks are popularly known as Ethernet and IBM's Token Ring Network.

Ethernet is the most popular type of local area network. Ethernet uses a high-speed network cable. Since all the nodes in a LAN use the same cable to transmit and receive data, they must follow a set of rules; otherwise, two or more nodes could transmit at the same time, causing garbled or lost messages. Before a node can transmit data, it must check the cable to see whether or not it is being used. If the cable is in use, the node must wait. When the cable is free from other transmissions, the node can begin transmitting immediately.

IBM's **Token Ring Network** connects nodes in a ring topology by using a network cable of twisted wire pairs. The protocol for controlling access to the shared network cable is called **token passing.** The idea is similar to the New York City subway: If you want to ride—transmit data—you must have a token. The token is a special signal that circulates from node to node along the ring-shaped LAN.

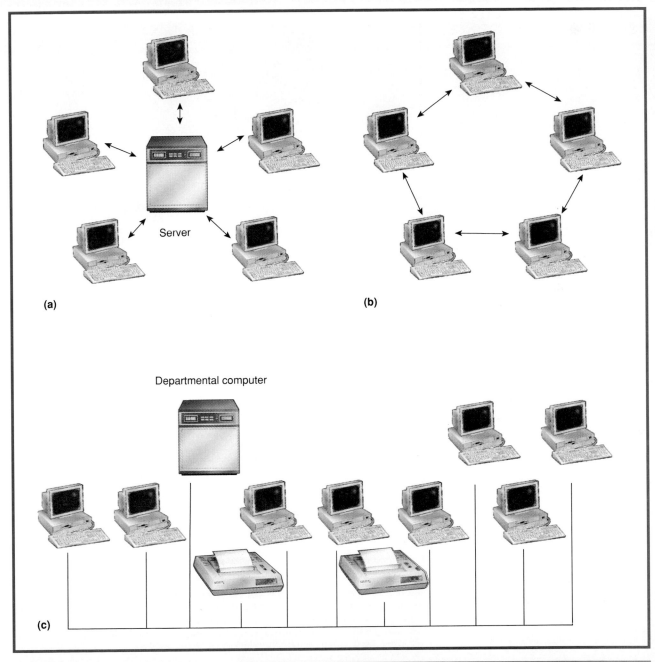

(a)

(b)

Server

Departmental computer

(c)

Figure 6-12   LAN topologies.   (a) The star topology has a central host computer that runs the LAN. (b) The ring topology connects computers in a circular fashion. (c) The bus topology assigns a portion of network management to each computer but preserves the system if one computer fails.

TRANSPARENCY ACETATE #6J
Figure #6-13

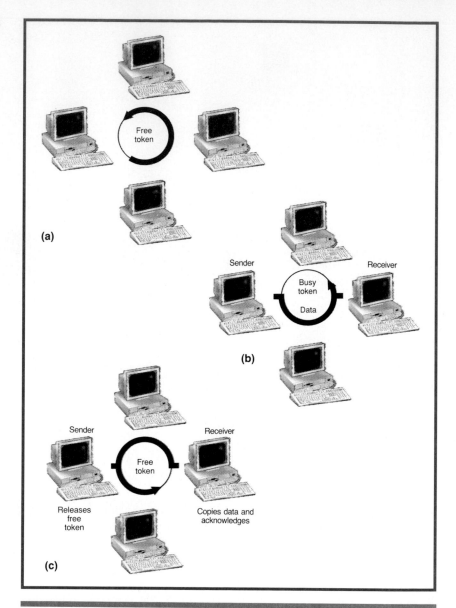

Figure 6-13   IBM Token Ring Network. This type of network connects nodes in a ring. An electronic signal, or token, circles the ring. (a) The sender waits for the token to pass by and then (b) captures the token to transmit data. (c) The receiver retrieves the data and sends the token back to the sender.

Only one token is available on the network. When a node on the network wishes to transmit, it first captures the token; then it can transmit data. When the node has sent its message, it releases the token back to the network (Figure 6-13). Since only one token is circulating around the network, only one device is able to access the network at a time and problems are avoided.

MICROCOMPUTERS IN ACTION

Computers at the Store

Computers are not limited to stores that sell computers. Computers are hidden—or not so hidden—in most retail stores. The most obvious sign of a computer presence is at the cash register, where scanning systems tote up the cost of your purchases. But there are many other computer activities in the store, some of which relate directly to the customer. Some examples:

- Giggling children gather around the computer games in the children's department at the Dayton-Hudson store in Burnsville, Minnesota. As they are being entertained, they are also receiving a sales pitch for Levi clothing via the animated screen—an activity Levi calls "visual merchandising."
- The average shopper may not notice, but customer traffic flows smoothly down the aisles in the Nordstrom store in Seattle. What is more, products have been placed within easy reach of the customer. These features were planned using a computerized floor plan layout system.
- Customers in the Florsheim Shoe Store in San Francisco can let their fingers do the shopping, using an in-store computer to order shoes electronically. Customers can view the shoe on the screen and, if it is not in stock, order it to be delivered to a home address.
- Toys R Us uses a distributed network to connect its 300 stores nationwide. The network is the key to managing inventory. If a doll is back ordered in one store, for example, excess dolls in another store can be sent to the undersupplied store.
- The computer-customer relationship does not end as the customer exits the store. Stores want to gather information to draw the customer back to the store. In fact, the amount of information stores accumulate is rather astonishing: how often the customer shops at the store, how often he or she uses checks or credit cards, and what types of items he or she likes to buy. Sears, Roebuck, and Co. is developing a single database containing such customer profiles.

TEST BANK
Mult. Choice   64-68
T/F   54-62
Fill-in-the-Blank   51-59

7 The Work of Networking

Think of it: There are more than 500 million telephones installed throughout the world and, theoretically, you can call any one of them. Further, every one of these phones has the potential to be part of a networking system. Although we have discussed other communications media, it is still the telephone that is the basis for action for the user at home or in the office. Revolutionary changes are in full swing in both places, but particularly in the office.

The use of automation in the office is as variable as the offices themselves. As a general definition, however, **office automation** is the use of technology to help achieve the goals of the office. Much automated office innovation is based on communications technology. We begin this section with several important office technology topics—electronic mail, voice mail, teleconferencing, and facsimile.

LECTURE HINT
E-mail has brought cultural changes to some organizations. In particular, e-mail flattens the organizational structure by letting the lowest-ranking members of the organization communicate directly with the higher echelons.

Electronic Mail

You know all about telephone-tag. From your office you call Ms. Jones. She is not in, so you leave a message. You leave your office for a meeting, and when you return you find a message from Ms. Jones; she returned your call while you were out . . . and so it goes. Few of us, it seems, are sitting around waiting for the phone to ring. It is not unusual to make dozens of calls—or attempts at calls—to set up a meeting among just a few people. **Electronic mail** is the process of sending messages directly from one terminal or computer to another. Electronic mail releases workers from the tyranny of the telephone.

Perhaps a company has employees who find communication difficult because they are geographically dispersed or are too active to be reached easily. Yet these may be people who need to work together frequently, whose communication is valuable and important. These people are ideal candidates for electronic mail.

A user can send messages to a colleague downstairs; a query across town to that person who is never available for phone calls; even memos simultaneously to regional sales managers in Chicago, Raleigh, and San Antonio (Figure 6-14). The beauty of electronic mail, or **e-mail,** as it is also called, is that a user can send a message to someone and know that the person will receive it.

Electronic mail works, of course, only if the intended receiver has the electronic mail facility to which the sender is connected. There are several electronic mail options. A user can enlist a third-party service bureau that provides electronic mail service for its customers. Another popular option is to use a public data network such as CompuServe. Or a user may purchase an electronic mail software package for a microcomputer or large computer system.

The service bureau creates as many electronic "mailboxes"— space allotments on its computer's disk storage—as needed for each user company. Users get their mail by giving proper identification from their own computers.

Public data services offer their own version of electronic mail. CompuServe users can send e-mail messages to any other Com-

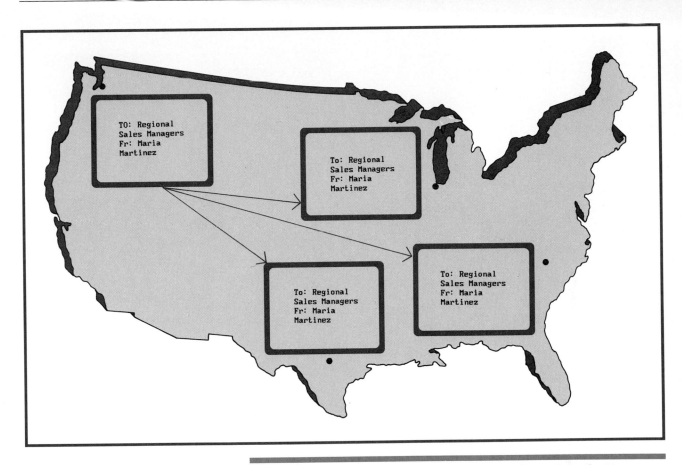

Figure 6-14 Simultaneous memo transmission with electronic mail.   From company headquarters in Seattle, Maria Martinez is able to send a memo simultaneously to sales managers in Chicago, Raleigh, and San Antonio. This is made possible by an electronic mail system linking the computers in the home office and the regional offices.

puServe subscriber. Users get flashing messages when they turn on their machines if mail awaits them.

Finally, you could consider putting your own custom electronic mail software in place. Major hardware manufacturers are becoming more communications-oriented and are offering software or office systems packages that support e-mail. A key advantage of such packages is that they may be paid for just once; third-party services must be paid for on a continual basis.

Electronic mail users shower it with praise. It crosses time zones, can reach many people with the same message, reduces the paper flood, and does not interrupt meetings the way a ringing phone does. It has its limitations, however. The current problem is similar to the problem faced by telephone users a hundred years ago: It is not of much use if you have the only one. As usage of electronic mail escalates, so will its usefulness.

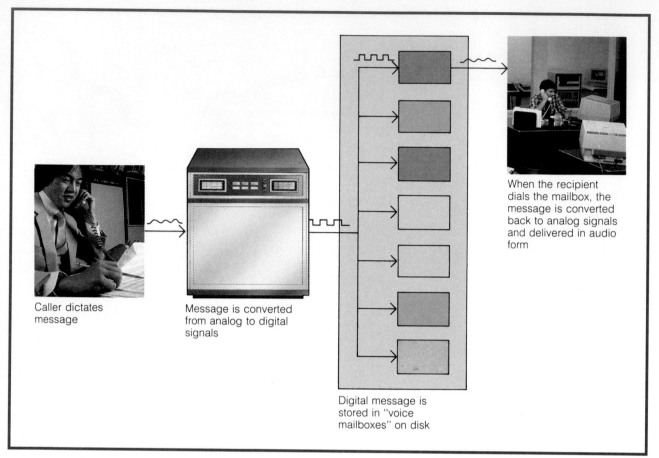

Caller dictates
message

Message is converted
from analog to digital
signals

Digital message is
stored in "voice
mailboxes" on disk

When the recipient
dials the mailbox, the
message is converted
back to analog signals
and delivered in audio
form

TRANSPARENCY ACETATE #6K
Figure #6-15

Figure 6-15   A voice mail system.   The caller's message is stored in the recipient's voice mailbox on disk. Later, the recipient can check his mailbox to get the message.

Voice Mail

Here is how **voice mail** typically works. A user dials a special number to get on the voice mail system, then tries to complete a call by dialing the desired number in the normal way. If the recipient does not answer, the caller can then dictate his or her message into the system. The voice mail computer system translates the words into digital impulses and stores them in the recipient's "voice mailbox." Later, when the recipient dials his or her mailbox, the system delivers the message in audio form (Figure 6-15).

This may sound like a spoken version of electronic mail. There is one big difference between electronic mail and voice mail, however. To use electronic mail you and the mail recipient must have compatible devices with a keyboard and be able to use them. In contrast, telephones are everywhere and everyone knows how to use them.

Senders can instruct some voice mail systems to redial specific numbers at regular intervals to deliver urgent messages or simply set

COMMUNICATING BY COMPUTER

Some people keep in touch the easy way, using a combination of the phone system and computers. Some examples:

- **Electronic house calls.** Patients with high blood pressure, each equipped with a home blood pressure kit, call their doctor's talking computer. Patients respond to the computer's questions by pressing keys on their Touch Tone phones. The computer system replies with an appropriate comment, such as this gentle scolding to a patient who admitted not taking her medication: "Your blood pressure is not so good today. If you took your medication it might be lower."

- **Applications by computer.** Applying to a college by computer is pretty simple: From a local personal computer, you dial into the school's network and fill out an application "form" right on the computer screen. The application is then submitted directly to the school's computerized admissions files. The whole process takes about ten minutes. The Georgia Institute of Technology was the first, but other schools are rapidly following its lead.

- **One-room schools.** Montana has a far-flung school system of more than 100 rural one-room schools. Teachers have begun an educational network system that can be useful in developing rural teaching programs. The system contains a software library and lessons for students and teachers. Furthermore, teachers discuss education matters on-line with students, parents, and other educators through a bulletin board system.

- **Gadgets and gizmos on-line.** Do you have questions about VCRs, stereo systems, phone products, computers, satellite gear? Would you like to swap information, or even equipment? All this, and more, is available through the electronics forum, one of several hobbyist support groups sponsored by CompuServe.

one delivery time and date. Another useful feature allows users to circulate messages among associates for comment. This method is far more efficient than circulating the traditional paper intraoffice memo.

There are some problems, however—not with the technology, but with user acceptance of the technology. Some people do not like talking to a machine. Others will not tell a machine anything important. A more serious problem is the lack of editing capability—most users simply cannot organize their thoughts as well when they speak as they do when they write.

But electronic "meetings" are more spontaneous and less demanding of writing perfection. That brings us to teleconferencing.

7 Teleconferencing

An office automation development with great promise is **teleconferencing,** a method of using technology to bring people and ideas "together" despite geographic barriers. The technology has been available for years, but the acceptance of it is quite recent. The purpose of teleconferencing is to let people conduct meetings with others in different geographic locations.

There are several varieties of teleconferencing. The simplest, computer conferencing, is a method of sending, receiving, and storing typed messages within a network of users. Computer conferences can be used to coordinate complex projects over great distances and for extended periods of time. Participants can communicate at the same time or in different time frames, at the users' convenience. Conferences can be set up for a limited period of time to discuss a particular problem, as in a traditional office gathering. Or they can be ongoing networks for weeks or months or even years.

A **computer conferencing system** is a single software package designed to organize communication. The conferencing software runs on a network's host, either a mini- or mainframe computer. In addition to the host computer and the conferencing software, each participant needs a personal computer or word processor, a telephone, a modem, and data communications network software.

Computer conferencing is a many-to-many arrangement; everyone is able to "talk" to anyone else. Messages may be sent to a specified individual or set of individuals or "broadcast" to all receivers. Recipients are automatically notified of incoming messages.

Would you like your picture broadcast live across the miles for meetings? Add cameras to computer conferencing, and you have another form of teleconferencing called **videoconferencing** (Figure 6-16). The technology varies, but the pieces normally put in place are a large screen (possibly wall size), cameras that can send "three-dimensional" pictures, and an on-line computer system to record communication among participants.

Although this setup is expensive to rent and even more expensive to own, the costs seem trivial when compared to travel expenses

Figure 6-16   A videoconferencing system.   Geographically distant groups can hold a meeting with the help of videoconferencing. Note the camera in the upper right-hand corner; it films the local participants for the benefit of distant viewers.

for in-person meetings. Airfare, lodging, and meals for a group of employees are very costly.

But there are drawbacks to videoconferencing. Consider that picture of you. Most people do not like the way they look on camera. We tend to be uncomfortable about our appearance, and balk when we envision slouching posture, crooked tie, or fidgeting fingers. There is also fear that the loss of personal contact will detract from some business functions, especially those related to sales.

But employees are overcoming their reluctance. Videoconferencing may be an idea whose time has come.

7 Facsimile Technology

One alternative to meetings is to use computers and data communications technology to transmit drawings and documents from one location to another. **Facsimile technology,** operating something like a copy machine connected to a telephone, uses computer technology to send quality graphics, charts, text, and even signatures almost anywhere in the world. The drawing—or whatever—is placed in the facsimile machine at one end, as shown in Figure 6-17, where it is digitized. Those digits are transmitted across the miles and then reassembled at the other end into the original picture. All this takes only minutes—or less. Facsimile is not only faster than overnight delivery services, it is less expensive. Facsimile is abbreviated **fax,** as in "I faxed the report to the Chicago office." Fax has become the norm in many offices.

A variation on the fax machine is the **fax board,** which fits inside a personal computer. A user can send computer-generated text and graphics without interrupting other applications programs in use. When a fax comes in, it can be reviewed on the screen and printed out. The only missing ingredient in this scheme is paper; if

Figure 6-17   Faxing it.   This facsimile machine can send drawings and graphs long distance.

the document to be sent is on paper, it must be scanned into the computer first.

7 Electronic Fund Transfers: Instant Banking

You may already be handling some financial transactions electronically instead of using checks. In **electronic fund transfers (EFTs)**, people pay for goods and services by having funds transferred from various accounts electronically, using computer technology. One of the most visible manifestations of EFT is the ATM—the automated teller machine that we described in Chapter 4.

Incidentally, over 650 million Social Security checks have been disbursed by the government directly into the recipients' checking accounts via EFT rather than by mail. Unlike those sent via U.S. mail, no such payment has ever been lost. Moreover, such payments are traceable—again, unlike the mail.

7 Bulletin Boards

Person-to-person data communication is one of the more exhilarating ways of using your personal computer, and its popularity is increasing at breakneck speed. A **bulletin board system (BBS)** uses data communications systems to link personal computers to provide public-access message systems.

Electronic bulletin boards are similar to the bulletin boards you see in Laundromats or student lounges. Somebody leaves a message, but the person who picks it up does not have to know the person who left it. To get access to someone else's computer, all you really have to know is that computer's bulletin board phone number. You can use any kind of computer, but you need a modem so you can communicate over the phone lines. Anyone who has a personal computer can set up a bulletin board: It takes a computer, a phone line, a couple of disk drives, and some software that costs around $50. You just tell a few people about your board, and you are in business.

Bulletin boards perform a real service. For example, a message can give advice about a particular vendor's product, post a notice to buy or sell a computer, or even announce a new business venture.

7 Data Communications Shopping

In recent years there has been a trend toward nonstore retailing in such forms as telephone- and mail-generated orders to department stores, offerings of records and tapes of popular music through television commercials ("Not available in any store!"), and airline in-flight shopping catalogs. One of the newest forms of retailing is interactive two-way cable **videotex**—data communications merchandising.

MY TWO OFFICES

No, these offices are not at the opposite ends of your far-flung east-west empire, nor even your official and hideaway offices in the workplace. Your two offices are in the two places you spend the most time: your employer's office and your home.

The proliferation of such dual offices, connected by communications systems, is upon us. If you think about it, it had to come—not just for telecommuters, but for people whose job is 100% at the office. First of all, many workers take work home; it makes sense that they can continue their computer work at home too.

Today's key players, however, are part of single-parent families or two-parent working families. These parents cannot linger at the office; they must pick up their children at day care. So they pop a few diskettes and supporting paperwork into their briefcases and head home, to work in their home offices later. Another scenario familiar to working parents is leaving work midday to care for a sick child. The doctor can fix the child and the home computer can take care of the interrupted work activity, perhaps with the parent sending messages to the office from home via computer.

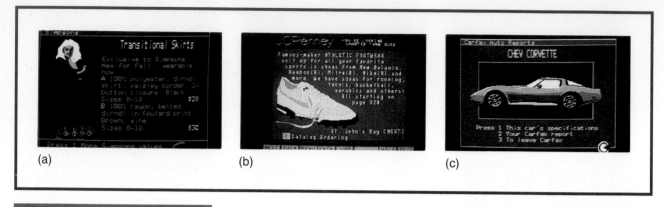

(a)   (b)   (c)

Figure 6-18 Catalog shopping.
Computer users can "window shop" from the comfort of their homes. Typical products are the (a) skirts and (b) shoes shown here. Viewers also can solicit product information, as indicated by (c), the Corvette screen.

Consumers with accounts with the videotex merchandiser shop at home for a variety of products and services. Using an in-home video display catalog, they can get information about a product or order products from a participating retailer (Figure 6-18). When an order is received in the computer, this retailer assembles the goods from a fully automated warehouse. Simultaneously, funds are transferred from the customer's to the retailer's bank account. Customers choose between picking up the order at a nearby distribution point or having it delivered to their door.

LECTURE HINT
CompuServe is the biggest information utility, with about 300,000 members and 400 databases to serve them.

7 Commercial Communications Services

We have talked about specific services, but some companies offer a wide range of services. Users can connect their personal computers to commercial consumer-oriented communications systems via telephone lines. These services—known as **information utilities**—are widely used by both home and business customers. Two major information utilities are The Source and CompuServe Information Service.

The Source offers a broad range of services, including the United Press International newswire, extracts from the New York Times Consumer Data Base, and a Wall Street stock index, as well as electronic games. The Source heavily advertises electronic mail and computer conferencing.

LECTURE HINT
You can check airline flights yourself on your own computer, make your own reservation, and choose your seat on the plane, too. The reservation service is offered through various communications services and also by The Source and CompuServe. The average cost of an inquiry is about three dollars, but this can be offset by the money saved on fares, which are listed in order from the least to the most expensive.

CompuServe, far the larger of the two on the basis of subscriptions, offers program packages, text editors, encyclopedia reference, games, a software exchange, and a number of programming languages. CompuServe services include travel reservations, home shopping, banking, weather reports, and even medical and legal advice. Of particular interest to business users are investment information, world news, and professional forums—enough to keep any communications junkie busy. Finally, if you really have nothing to do tonight, you can participate in an on-line auction, interacting with auctioneers electronically.

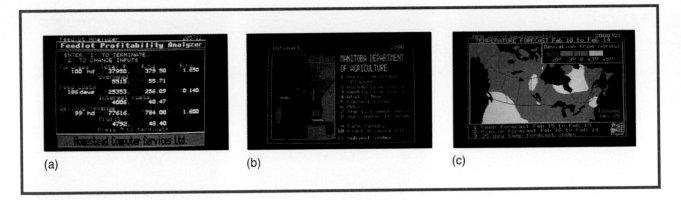

(a)   (b)   (c)

Figure 6-19   Commercial services.
Canadian farmers use their own computers to access the Grassroots Service to (a) analyze feedlots, (b) plan herbicide usage, and (c) check weather conditions.

Other commercial communications facilities offer specialized services: Knowledge Index (general-interest information), NewsNet (news), Official Airline Guide (travel), and Grassroots (agriculture) (Figure 6-19).

These commercial services usually charge an initiation fee and a monthly fee, neither of which is insignificant. The charges on your phone bill are additional. Some communities, however, have local-line access to information utilities like The Source and CompuServe, so users do not have to pay for long-distance charges.

7 Computer Commuting

A logical outcome of computer networks is **telecommuting,** the substitution of telecommunications and computers for the commute to work. Many in the work force are information workers; if they do not need face-to-face contact in their work, they are candidates for using telecommuting to work at home.

Although the original idea was that people would work at home all the time, telecommuting has evolved into a mixed activity. That is, most telecommuters stay home two or three days a week and come into the office the other days. Time in the office permits the needed personal communication with fellow workers and also provides a sense of participation and continuity.

Potential benefits of telecommuting include savings in fuel costs and commuting time, an opportunity to work at your own pace, increased productivity, and an opportunity for workers to work in an undisturbed environment.

There are, of course, problems also. One problem associated with telecommuting is the strain on families as a result of a family member working in the home. A more common complaint is that at-home employees miss the interaction with coworkers at the office. At the head of the list, however, is this, from the telecommuters themselves: They work too much!

PERSPECTIVES

SOME THORNS AMONG THE ROSES

A system as powerful as a computer network is also subject to significant abuse. Here are a few samples.

- **Junk fax.** The fax is in the mail. But—guess what—you did not order it. In fact, it is an advertisement sent to your fax machine from another computer. It is bad enough that this ties up your fax machine; to add insult to injury, you have to pay for the paper to print it. This kind of abuse is already being outlawed in some states.

- **Bulletin boards under attack.** Bulletin boards provide an opportunity for users to share a variety of information. But there is one bit of sharing that authorities think goes beyond mischief: sharing the phone numbers and passwords—that is, access—to computer systems. Some bulletin boards carry such information as casually as they post the time of the next club meeting. Information that is supposed to be a closely guarded secret is on view for the bulletin board public. One government official noted that you might as well have a billboard on the street that says "Here is the combination to the bank vault in case you want to use it." In some states legislation has been introduced to curb such practices.

- **Not-so-funny joke file.** Stanford University officials deleted a file of 1000 jokes that circulate around the country electronically. Citing ethnic, racial, and sexist content, the university found the content offensive and of no educational purpose.

- **Black Monday.** In October 1987 the stock market took a frightening dive, leaving many investors significantly poorer on paper. Although some experts predicted the coming market weakness, few were prepared for the orgy of selling—driven by computer networks. Brokers placed orders to be executed automatically, under certain conditions, by the computer. In this case, orders to sell at certain lower prices set off a chain reaction among computers.

- **E-mail attractions.** Users are attracted to electronic mail by its speed, relatively low cost, and even its high-tech status. However, managers are less than pleased to discover some employees using e-mail for personal purposes. It began with users exchanging personal messages via e-mail. Soon after, users began sending amusing computer graphics cartoons via e-mail. More than one employee has sent out holiday greetings through the system. Perhaps the most offensive use, from management's point of view, was an e-mail chain letter, which was (among other things) illegal.

7 Networks and Security

Networks mean that access to information is dispersed. Valuable files are in many locations, data is transmitted over different kinds of communications lines, and many people have access to information. Clearly, the question of security arises: If it is so easy for authorized people to get information, what is to stop unauthorized people from tapping it? The safety of data is of paramount importance and deserves a chapter by itself. We will address this question in Chapter 18.

7 Our Crystal Ball

The near future in data communications is not difficult to see. The demand for services is just beginning to swell. Electronic mail already pervades the office, the campus, and the home. Expect instant access to all manner of databases from a variety of convenient locations. Prepare to be blasé about automated services available in your own home and everywhere you go.

What are we waiting for? For easier access. For public education and acceptance. And for the price to come down.

STUDENT PROJECT
Access a local bulletin board and report on the kind of information found on it, describing the discussions found on the bulletin board.

7 Summary and Key Terms

- **Telecommunications** is the merger of communications and computers.

- **Data communications systems** are computer systems that transmit data over communications lines such as public telephone lines or private network cables.

- **Centralized data processing** places all processing, hardware, software, and storage in one central location.

- In **teleprocessing** systems, terminals at various locations are connected by communications lines to the central computer that does the processing.

- Businesses with many locations or offices often use **distributed data processing** (DDP), which allows both remote access and remote processing. Processing can be done by the central computer and the other computers that are hooked up to it.

- In a network called a **micro-to-mainframe link,** microcomputer users can process data from the files of a mainframe computer.

- The basic components of a data communications system are a sending device, a communications link, and a receiving device. Some large systems also have a **front-end processor,** a computer that functions as a communications control unit, which frees the central computer for processing applications programs.

- **Digital transmission** sends data as distinct on or off pulses. **Analog transmission** uses a continuous electronic signal in a wave form having a particular **amplitude, phase,** and **frequency.** Radio transmissions are made by altering amplitude or frequency—that is, by **amplitude modulation** or **frequency modulation.**

- Computers produce digital signals, but most types of communications equipment use analog signals. Therefore, transmission of computer data involves altering the analog signal, or **carrier wave.** Digital signals are converted to analog signals by **modulation** (change) of the amplitude, frequency, or phase of the carrier wave. **Demodulation** is the reverse process; both processes are performed by a device called a **modem.**

- A **direct-connect modem** is connected directly to the telephone line by means of a telephone jack.

An **external direct-connect modem** is not built in to the computer and can therefore be used with a variety of computers. An **internal modem** is on a board that fits inside a microcomputer. An **acoustic coupler modem** allows a standard telephone receiver to be coupled to a computer terminal.

- Most modems include **auto-answer, auto-disconnect, auto-dial, automatic redial,** and **time-delay** features.

- Two common methods of coordinating the sending and receiving units are **asynchronous transmission** and **synchronous transmission.** The asynchronous, or **start/stop,** method keeps the units in step by including special signals at the beginning and end of each group of message bits—a group is usually a character. In synchronous transmission, the internal clocks of the units are put in time with each other at the beginning of the transmission, and the characters are transmitted in a continuous stream.

- **Simplex transmission** allows data to move in only one direction (either sending or receiving). **Half-duplex transmission** allows data to move in either direction but only one way at a time. With **full-duplex transmission,** data can be sent and received at the same time.

- A communications **link** is the physical medium used for transmission. Common communications links include **wire pairs** (**twisted pairs**), **coaxial cables, microwave transmission, satellite transmission,** and **fiber optics.** In satellite transmission a **transponder** ensures that the stronger outgoing signals do not interfere with the weaker incoming ones. **Noise** is anything that causes distortion in the received signal.

- A line **protocol** is a set of rules for exchanging information between a terminal and a computer or between two computers. Two standard sets of protocols are the **Open Systems Interconnection** model (**OSI**), developed by the International Standards Organization, and **Systems Network Architecture** (**SNA**), developed by IBM. Since the **Consultative Committee on International Telegraphy and Telephony** (**CCITT**) endorsed the OSI model, IBM has ensured that SNA networks can communicate with OSI networks.

- A **point-to-point line** is a direct connection between a terminal and a computer or between two computers. In a **multipoint line** several terminals are connected on the same line to a computer.

- Any organization wishing to become a **common carrier,** or supplier of communications services to the public, must apply to the **Federal Communications Commission** (**FCC**) by submitting a **tariff,** or list of services and rates. Common carriers can provide both **switched lines,** which are connected through switching centers, and **private** (or **leased**) **lines,** which are used exclusively by one customer for communication to a fixed destination.

- The 1968 **Carterfone decision** opened the door for other communications companies to use the public telephone network. This development led to the **value-added network** (**VAN**), in which a communications company leases communication lines from a common carrier and adds improvements.

- Computers that are connected so that they can communicate among themselves are said to form a **network.** A **Wide Area Network** is a network of geographically distant computers and terminals. The computer to which the terminal is attached is called the **host computer.** In a situation in which a personal computer is being used as a network terminal, **file transfer software** enables the personal computer to store files. With this software the user can **upload** files (retrieve them from another computer and store them) and **download** files (send files to another computer). To communicate with a microcomputer or mainframe, the personal computer must employ **terminal emulation software.**

- A **local area network** (**LAN**) is a collection of personal computers that share hardware, software, and information. All the devices—personal computers and other hardware—attached to the LAN are called **nodes** on the LAN. The nodes on some LANs are connected using a shared **network cable.** LANs use a hardware device called a **cable interface unit,** a set of electronic components in a box outside the computer, to send and receive signals on the network cable. A **gateway** is a hardware device—sometimes even a separate computer—that connects two dissimilar networks.

- A **bridge,** sometimes called a **router,** connects two LANs of the same type so that messages can be sent from a node on one LAN to a node on a different LAN.

- The physical layout of a local area network is called a **topology.** A **star network** has a central computer that is responsible for managing the LAN; it is to this central computer—sometimes called a **server**—that the shared disks and printers are usually attached. A **ring network** links all nodes together in a circular manner without benefit of a server. A **bus network** assigns a portion of network management to each computer but preserves the system if one component fails.

- **Ethernet** is the most popular type of local area network; this system accesses the network by listening for a free carrier signal. IBM's **Token Ring Network** controls access to the shared network cable by using **token passing.**

- **Office automation** is the use of technology to help achieve the goals of the office. **Electronic mail (e-mail)** and **voice mail** allow workers to transmit messages to the computer files of other workers. **Teleconferencing** includes **computer conferencing**—in which typed messages are sent, received, and stored—and **videoconferencing**—computer conferencing combined with cameras and large screens. **Facsimile technology (fax)** can transmit graphics, charts, and signatures. **Fax boards** can be inserted inside computers. In **electronic fund transfers (EFTs)**, people pay for goods and services by having funds transferred from various checking and savings accounts electronically, using computer technology. **Bulletin board systems** use data communications to link personal computers into public-access message systems. People can shop at home by using **videotex,** a video-display catalog.

- **The Source** and **CompuServe** are two major commercial communications services, or **information utilities.**

- **Telecommuting** is the substitution of telecommunications and computers for the commute to work.

- A problem with dispersed information is securing the information against unauthorized persons.

Review Questions

1. What is telecommunications?

2. Discuss the advantages and disadvantages of centralized data processing.

3. Explain how distributed data processing and teleprocessing differ.

4. What are the functions of a front-end processor?

5. Explain what modems are used for.

6. Why is a high modem speed important?

7. Why is synchronous transmission faster than asynchronous transmission?

8. Differentiate the following types of transmission: simplex, half duplex, and full duplex.

9. Describe the advantages of each of the following: wire pairs, coaxial cables, microwave transmission, satellite transmission, and fiber optics.

10. What is a protocol, and why are protocol standards important?

11. How do wide area networks and local area networks differ?

12. How does a star network differ from a ring network?

13. Describe electronic mail, voice mail, teleconferencing, and facsimile.

14. What is a bulletin board system, and how is it useful?

15. Describe how networking systems can be used for banking and shopping.

16. Define telecommuting and discuss its advantages and disadvantages.

Discussion Questions

1. Describe two situations, one in which a point-to-point line is preferable and one in which a multipoint line is preferable.

2. Discuss the advantages and disadvantages of teleconferencing versus face-to-face business meetings.

3. Discuss your opinion of telecommuting. Do you think you would like to telecommute? Why or why not?

PART 3

UNDERSTANDING SOFTWARE

Hardware has grown in spectacular technological leaps, as we have seen. But hardware can be no better than the software run on it. In this section we will consider what is necessary to produce good software.

There are four chapters in this section: beginning programming, programming languages, operating systems, and systems analysis and design.

If you are considering a computer career, this section gives you an overview of the software aspect of the industry. If you want to be a programmer, the first chapter in this section gives you an idea of what programmers do and whether you would like doing it. The chapters on languages and operating systems tell you more about programming tools and how to use them. Finally, the chapter on systems analysis and design shows you how software fits into the larger context of the computer system.

Chapter 7. Beginning Programming: Getting Started

7

Beginning Programming

A Structured Approach

In this chapter we describe how programmers work: They define the problem; plan the solution; and code, test, and document the program. Some basic planning techniques—flowcharting and pseudocode—are also shown. These techniques can be used to represent the first draft of the program solution. The control structures of structured programming are introduced. A problem solution expressed in both a flowchart and pseudocode is developed into a program. Finally, we examine the concepts of structured programming.

This classic story takes place several years ago, when teachers were first showing students the ways of computer programming. A student sat, brow furrowed, chewing her pencil as she examined her latest flawed program printout. Suddenly she turned to her instructor, the gleam of discovery on her face, and announced, "I've figured these computers out. They do what you *tell* them to do, not what you *want* them to do!"

Perhaps the essentials of computer wisdom are contained in that one sentence. Nothing has changed in all these years. You still have to make sure that what you tell the computer to do is really what you want it to do. Although program solutions are based on just a few concepts, programs can quickly become complex. It is not a simple task to make sure the program does exactly what you *want* it to do. In this chapter, we will make a start.

7 Why Programming?

You may already have used software to solve problems. But perhaps now you are ready to learn how to write some software, too. As we noted earlier, a **program** is a set of step-by-step instructions that directs the computer to do the tasks you want it to do and produce the results you want. This chapter introduces you to the programming process. When used in conjunction with a guide to a specific language (such as BASIC, which is described in Appendix A), this chapter should help you use the computer for a variety of activities.

There are at least two good reasons for learning programming at this point:

■ Programming helps you understand computers. The computer is simply a tool. Learning to write simple programs as you master the machine increases your confidence level.

■ Learning programming lets you find out quickly whether you like programming and whether you have the analytical turn of mind programmers need. Even if you decide that programming is not for you, trying your hand at it will certainly increase your computer literacy and give you an appreciation of what programmers do.

An important point before we proceed, however: You will not be a programmer when you finish reading this chapter or even when you finish reading the final chapter. Programming proficiency takes practice and training beyond the scope of this book. But you will have written programs if you put into practice what we are about to describe, and you will have a good idea of what programmers do.

A PREDICTION THAT DID NOT COME TRUE

"It may be supposed that, as happened with television and then color television, the enthusiasts and the well-to-do will be the first to install computer consoles in their homes. Eventually, however, everyone will consider them to be essential household equipment. People will soon become discontented with the "canned" programs available; they will want to write their own. The ability to write a computer program will become as widespread as driving a car."

These immortal words were written by a fellow named John McCarthy and printed in a magazine called *Information* in 1966. That's over 20 years ago, time enough for his prediction to come true. Of course, in 1966, the personal computer was not even invented; Mr. McCarthy thought we would all have individual consoles, a kind of terminal. He did not say so, but he must have imagined all of us hooked up to central computers. Still, his prediction was very bold.

Mr. McCarthy thought programming was pretty easy stuff. He went on to say that programming was not as difficult as learning a foreign language or algebra. He would probably get an argument on that today. At the least, we can say that we have not turned into a nation of programmers. Although making predictions is a risky business, we think we can say with some confidence that this will continue to be the case.

Try your hand at a few programs and see what you think.

TEST BANK
Mult. Choice   4-19
T/F   3-17
Matching A   2-10
Matching B   1-2
Matching C   1-7
Fill-in-the-blank   2-13

7 What Programmers Do

TEST BANK
Mult. Choice   3
T/F   2
Fill-in-the-Blank   1

In general, the programmer's job is to convert problem solutions into instructions for the computer. That is, the programmer prepares the instructions of a computer program and runs, tests, and corrects the program. The programmer also writes a report on the program. These activities are all done for the purpose of helping a user fill a need—to pay employees, bill customers, admit students to college, and so forth. Programmers help the user develop new programs to solve problems, weed out errors in existing programs, or perform changes on programs as a result of new requirements (such as a change in the payroll program to make automatic union dues deductions).

The activities just described could be done, perhaps, as solo activities. But a programmer typically interacts with a variety of people. For example, if a program is part of a system of several programs, the programmer coordinates with other programmers to make sure that the programs fit together well. If you were a programmer, you might also have coordination meetings with users, managers, and with peers who evaluate your work—just as you evaluate theirs.

Let us turn now from programmers to programming.

7 The Programming Process

Developing a program requires five steps:

1. Defining the problem
2. Planning the solution
3. Coding the program
4. Testing the program
5. Documenting the program

Let us discuss each of these in turn.

7 1. Defining the Problem

Suppose that, as a programmer, you are contacted because your services are needed. You meet with users from the client organization to analyze the problem or you meet with a systems analyst who outlines the project. Eventually, you produce a written agreement that, among other things, specifies the kind of input, processing, and output required. This is not a simple process. It is closely related to the process of systems analysis, which is discussed in Chapter 10.

PERSPECTIVES

YOUR CAREER: IS THE COMPUTER FIELD FOR YOU?

There is a shortage of qualified personnel in the computer field but, paradoxically, there are many people at the front end trying to get entry-level jobs. Before you join their ranks, consider the advantages of the computer field and what it takes to succeed in it.

The Joys of the Field

Although many people make career changes into the computer field, few choose to leave it. In fact, surveys of computer professionals consistently report a high level of job satisfaction. There are several reasons for this contentment. One is the challenge—most jobs in the computer industry are not routine. Another is security, since established computer professionals can usually find work. And that work pays well—you will probably not be rich, but you should be comfortable. The computer industry has historically been a rewarding place for women and minorities. And, finally, the industry holds endless

fascination since it is always changing.

What It Takes

You need, of course, some credentials, most often a two- or four-year degree in computer information systems or computer science. The requirements and salaries vary by the organization and the region, so we will not dwell on these here. Beyond that, the person most likely to land a job and move up the career ladder is the one with excellent communication skills, both oral and written. These are also the qualities that can be observed by potential employers in an interview.

Open Doors

The outlook for the computer field is promising. Using the Bureau of Labor Statistics as its source, the *Wall Street Journal* reports that in the 1990s the need for programmers will increase 72% and the need for systems analysts by 69%. These two professions are predicted to be the number two and number three high-growth jobs. (In case you are curious, the number one high-growth job area is predicted to be the paralegal profession.) The reasons for continued job increase in the computer field are more computers, more applications of computers, and more computer users.

Career Directions

Traditional career progression in the computer field was a path

7. 2. Planning the Solution

Two common ways of planning the solution to a problem are to draw a flowchart and/or write pseudocode. Essentially, a **flowchart** is a symbolic pictorial representation of an orderly step-by-step solution to a problem. It is a map of what your program is going to do and how it is going to do it. **Pseudocode** is an English-like language that you can use to state your solution with more precision than you can in plain English but with less precision than is required when using a formal programming language. We will discuss flowcharts and pseudocode in greater detail later in this chapter.

from programmer to systems ana-lyst to project manager. This is still a popular direction, but it is complicated by the large number of options open to computer pro-fessionals. Computer profession-als sometimes specialize in some aspect of the industry such as data communications, database management, personal computers, graphics, or equipment. Others may specialize in the computer-related aspects of a particular industry such as banking or in-surance. Still others strike out on their own, becoming consultants or entrepreneurs.

Keeping Up

Your formal education is merely the beginning. In the ever-chang-ing computer field, you must take responsibility for your ongoing education. There are a variety of formal and informal ways of keeping up: college or on-the-job classes, workshops, seminars, conventions, exhibitions, trade magazines, books, and profes-sional organizations. Organiza-

tions are particularly important; by attending a monthly meeting you can exchange ideas with other professionals, make new contacts, and hear a speaker ad-dress some current topic. Some of the principal professional soci-eties are:

- **AFIPS.** The American Federa-tion of Information Processing Societies is an umbrella federa-tion of organizations relating to information processing.
- **ACM.** The Association for Computing Machinery is a worldwide society devoted to developing information process-ing as a discipline.
- **ASM.** The Association for Sys-tems Management keeps mem-bers current on developments in systems management and information processing.
- **AWC.** The Association of Women in Computing is open to professionals interested in promoting the advancement of women in the computer indus-try.

- **DPMA.** The Data Processing Management Association, one of the largest of the professional societies in the computer field, is open to all levels of informa-tion management personnel. The group seeks to encourage high standards and a profes-sional attitude toward data pro-cessing.

You should also consider be-coming a Certified Data Processor (CDP), which is granted on com-pletion of a five-part examination that covers: (1) computer hard-ware (2) computer programming and software, (3) principles of management, (4) methods (ac-counting, mathematics, statistics) and applications, and (5) systems. There are other certificates avail-able for computer professionals, including the ACP (Associate Computer Professional) to mea-sure entry-level programmers. For information, write to ICCP (Insti-tute for Certification of Computer Professionals), Suite 268, 2200 East Devon Avenue, Des Plaines, Illinois 60018-4503.

3. Coding the Program

As the programmer, your next step is to code the pro-gram—that is, to express your solution in a programming language. You will translate the logic from the flowchart or pseudocode—or some other tool—to a programming language. There are many pro-gramming languages: BASIC, COBOL, Pascal, FORTRAN, and C are common examples. You may find yourself working with one or more of these. These languages operate grammatically, somewhat like the English language, but they are much more precise. To get your pro-gram to work, you have to follow the rules—the **syntax**—exactly of the language you are using. Of course, using the language correctly is no guarantee that your program will work, any more than speaking grammatically correct English means you know what you are talking about. The point is that correct use of the language is the required first step. Then your coded program must be keyed, often at a terminal, in a form the computer can understand.

One more note here. An experienced programmer can often write code for simple programs directly at a terminal or microcomputer, skipping the coding-on-paper step. However, we do not recommend that beginners skip any steps. And even experienced programmers can get into trouble and waste a lot of time when they do not define the problem and plan the solution carefully before beginning to code.

7 4. Testing the Program

Some experts forcefully support the notion that a well-designed program can be written correctly the first time. In fact, they assert that there are mathematical ways to prove that a program is correct. However, the imperfections of the world are still with us, so most programmers get used to the idea that there are a few errors in their programs. This is a bit discouraging at first, since programmers tend to be precise, careful, detail-oriented people who take pride in their work. Still, there are many opportunities to introduce mistakes into programs, and you, like those who have gone before you, will probably find several of them.

So, after coding and keying the program, you test it to find the mistakes. This step involves these phases:

- **Desk-checking.** This phase, similar to proofreading, is sometimes avoided as a shortcut by the programmer who is eager to run the program on the computer, now that it is written. However, with careful desk-checking you may discover several errors and possibly save yourself several computer runs. In **desk-checking,** you simply sit down and mentally trace, or check, the logic of the program to ensure that it is error-free and workable.

- **Translating.** A **translator** is a program that translates your program into language the computer can understand. A by-product of the process is that the translator tells you if you have improperly used the programming language in some way. These types of mistakes are called **syntax errors.** The translator produces descriptive error messages. For instance, if in FORTRAN you mistakenly write $N = 2*(I + J))$—which has two closing parentheses instead of one—you will get a message that says, "UNMATCHED PARENTHESES." (Different translators may provide different wording for error messages.) Programs are most commonly translated by a compiler or an interpreter. A **compiler** translates your entire program at one time, giving you all the syntax error messages—called

TELL US ABOUT THE BUGS

Computer literacy books are bursting with bits and bytes and disks and chips and lessons on writing programs in BASIC. All this is to provide quick enlightenment for the computer illiterate. But the average newly literate person has not been told about the bugs.

It is a bit of a surprise, then, to find that the software you are using does not always work quite right. Or, perhaps the programmer who is doing some work for you cannot seem to get the program to work correctly. Both problems are "bugs," errors that were introduced unintentionally into a program when it was written. The term *bug* comes from an experience in the early days of computing. One summer day in 1945, the Mark I computer came to a halt. Working to find the problem, computer personnel actually found a moth inside the computer (see photo above). They removed the offending bug, and the computer was fine. From that day forward, any mysterious problem was said to be a bug.

LECTURE HINT
The story on bugs originated with Grace Hopper, the inventor of the first assembly language and of COBOL.

TEST BANK
Mult. Choice	20-42
T/F	18-49
Matching B	3-10
Matching C	8-10
Matching D	1-6
Matching E	1-2
Fill-in-the-Blank	14-35

diagnostics—at once. An **interpreter,** often used for the BASIC language, translates your program one line at a time. Some BASIC interpreters signal syntax errors as each line is keyed in. The translation process is described in more detail in Chapter 9.

- **Debugging.** A term used extensively in programming, **debugging** means detecting, locating, and correcting "bugs" (mistakes) by running the program. These bugs are **logic errors** such as telling a computer to repeat an operation but not telling it how to stop repeating. In this phase you run the program against test data, which you devise. You must plan the test data carefully to make sure you test every part of the program.

5. Documenting the Program

Documenting is an ongoing, necessary process—although, like many programmers, you may be eager to pursue more exciting computer-related activities. **Documentation** is a written detailed description of the programming cycle and specific facts about the program. Typical program documentation materials include the origin and nature of the problem, a brief narrative description of the program, logic tools such as flowcharts and pseudocode, data-record descriptions, program listings, and testing results. Comments in the program itself are also considered an essential part of documentation. Many programmers document as they code. In a broader sense, program documentation can be part of the documentation for an entire system, as described in Chapter 10 on systems analysis and design.

The wise programmer continues to document the program throughout its design, development, and testing. Documentation is needed to supplement human memory and to help organize program planning. Also, documentation is critical to communicate with others who have an interest in the program, especially other programmers who may be part of a programming team. And, since turnover is high in the computer industry, written documentation is needed so that those who come after you can make any necessary modifications in the program or track down any errors that you missed.

Planning the Solution: A Closer Look at Flowcharts and Pseudocode

We have described the five steps of the programming process in a general way. We noted that the first step, defining the problem, is related to the larger arena of systems analysis and design, a subject we will examine more closely in Chapter 10. (In fact, in some companies, only a person with the title *programmer/*

analyst may participate in the problem-definition phase.) The last three steps of coding, testing, and documenting the program are done in the context of a particular programming language. We offer the BASIC language in Appendix A for this purpose.

We will study the second step, planning the solution, in this chapter. This discussion will help you understand how to develop program logic. The following sections in this chapter offer an introduction to flowcharting and pseudocode, followed by examples showing both approaches to the same problem. Note that, normally, only one or the other would be used for a given solution; both are presented here so you can compare the two methods.

Flowcharts were the primary planning device for many years. They were favored because it is easier to follow logic in a picture than in words. But flowcharts have some drawbacks: They are not easy to change and they tend to be too detailed. The idea is that a programmer draws a flowchart, then writes a program based on that flowchart; both the flowchart and the program listing are part of the program documentation. As the program changes—and it will—corresponding changes should be made on the flowchart. And therein is the problem: Most programmers simply do not keep flowcharts up-to-date. However, there is a new wrinkle that makes flowcharts more palatable: They can be drawn and revised using software.

Pseudocode is easier to maintain. Since pseudocode is just words, it can be kept on a computer file and changed easily, using text editing or word processing. Although pseudocode is not a visual tool, it is nevertheless a good vehicle for stating and following program logic. For these reasons, flowcharts have fallen out of favor and pseudocode has become popular. But flowcharts are often used as a teaching device, so we include them here.

Another important topic is introduced in these sections: structured programming, an accepted standard of programming that minimizes logic complexity. Let us begin with the pictures—flowcharts.

7 Flowcharts

As we stated, a flowchart is essentially a picture. The flowchart consists of arrows that represent the direction the program takes and of boxes and other symbols that represent actions. Note that in this discussion we are talking about a **logic flowchart,** a flowchart that represents the flow of logic in a program. A logic flowchart is different from a **systems flowchart,** which shows the flow of data through an entire computer system. We will examine systems flowcharts in Chapter 10.

Some standard flowchart symbols have been established and are accepted by most programmers. These symbols, shown in Figure 7-1,

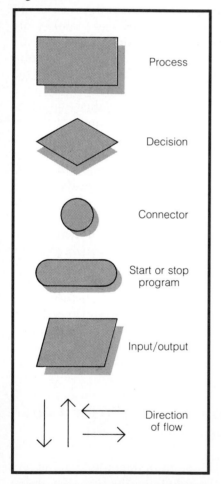

Process

Decision

Connector

Start or stop program

Input/output

Direction of flow

Figure 7-1   ANSI flowchart symbols.

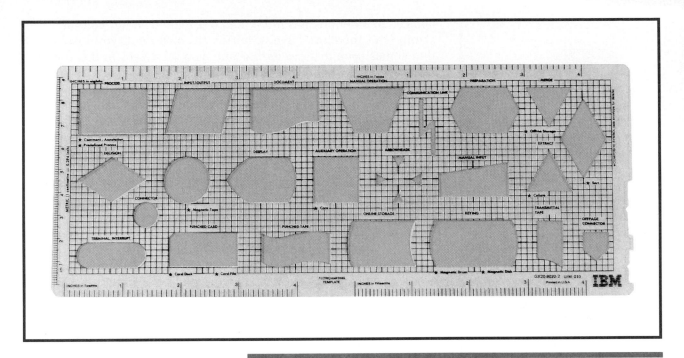

Figure 7-2   A template containing standard ANSI flowchart symbols.   Templates like this one are used as drawing aids.

are called ANSI symbols. (**ANSI** stands for American National Standards Institute.) Templates of ANSI symbols (Figure 7-2) are available in many office-supply stores and college bookstores and are helpful in drawing neat flowcharts. The most common symbols you will use represent process, decision, connector, start/stop, input/output, and direction of flow. Let us now look at two examples.

An Example: Preparing a Letter

Figure 7-3 shows you how you might diagram the steps of preparing a letter for mailing. There is usually more than one correct way to design a flowchart; this becomes obvious with more complicated examples.

The rectangular **process boxes** indicate actions to be taken—"Address envelope," "Fold letter," "Place letter in envelope." Sometimes the order in which actions appear is important, sometimes not. In this case the letter must be folded before it can be placed in the envelope.

The diamond-shaped box ("Have stamp?") is a **decision box.** The decision box asks a question that requires a yes-or-no answer. It has two **paths,** or **branches**—one path represents the response *yes,* the other, *no.* Note that the decision box is the only box that allows a

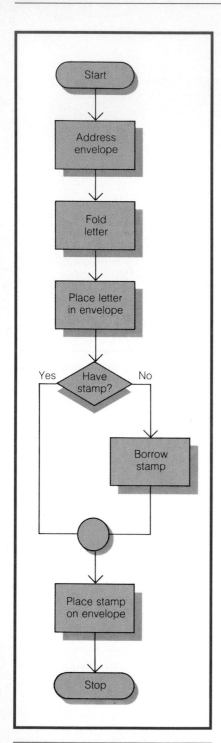

Figure 7-3   A simple flowchart. This flowchart shows how to prepare a letter for mailing.

choice; no other box has more than one exit. Whether you do need a stamp (and therefore have to borrow it) or do not, you take a path that comes back to a circle that puts you on a path to the end. The circle is called a **connector** because it connects the paths. (This symbol can also be used as an on-page connector when transferring to another location on the same sheet of paper.) Notice that the flowchart begins and ends with the oval **start/stop symbol.**

This example of preparing a letter suggests how you can take almost any activity and diagram it in flowchart form—assuming, that is, that you can always express your decisions as choices between yes and no, or something equally specific, such as true or false. Now let us use flowcharting to show just what programming is all about.

An Example: Summing Numbers from 1 through 100

Figure 7-4 shows how you might flowchart a program to find the sum of all numbers between 1 and 100. There are a number of things to observe about this flowchart.

First, the program uses two places in the computer's memory as storage locations, or places to keep intermediate results. In one location is a counter, which might be like a car odometer: Every time a mile passes, the counter counts it as a 1. In the other location is a sum—that is, a running total of the numbers counted. The sum location will eventually contain the sum of all numbers from 1 through 100: $1 + 2 + 3 + 4 + 5 + \cdots + 100$.

Second, as we start the program, we must initialize the counter and the sum. When you **initialize,** you set the starting values of certain storage locations, usually as the program execution begins. We will initialize the sum to 0 and the counter to 1.

Third, note the looping. You add the counter to the sum and a 1 to the counter, then come to the decision diamond, which asks if the counter is greater than 100. If the answer is "No," the computer loops back around and repeats the process. The decision box contains a **compare operation;** the computer compares two numbers and performs alternative operations based on the comparison. If the result of the comparison is "Yes," the computer produces the sum as output, as indicated by the print instruction. Notice that the parallelogram-shaped symbol is used for printing the sum because printing is an output process.

A **loop**—also called an **iteration**—is the heart of computer programming. The beauty of the loop, which may be defined as the repetition of instructions under certain conditions, is that you, as the programmer, have to describe certain instructions only once rather than describing them repeatedly. Once you have established the

TRANSPARENCY MASTER #1
Figure #7-3

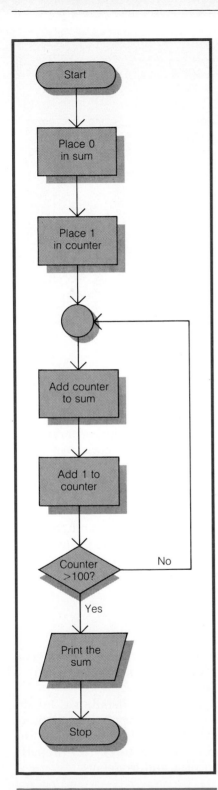

Figure 7-4 A loop example. This flowchart uses a loop to find the sum of numbers from 1 through 100.

loop pattern and the conditions for concluding (exiting from) the loop, the computer continues looping and exits as it has been instructed to do. The loop is considered a powerful programming tool because the code is reusable; once written, it can be called upon many times. Notice also that the flowchart can be modified easily to sum the numbers from 1 through 1000 or 500 through 700 or some other variation.

7 Pseudocode

As you have learned, pseudocode is an English-like way of representing the solution to a problem. It is considered a "first draft" because the pseudocode eventually has to be translated into a programming language. Although pseudocode is English-like and has some precision to it, it does not have the very definite precision of a programming language. Pseudocode cannot be executed by a computer. When using pseudocode to plan a program, you can concentrate on the logic and not worry about the rules of a specific language. It is also easy to change pseudocode if you discover a flaw in your logic, whereas most people find that it is more difficult to change logic once it is coded in a programming language. Pseudocode can be translated into a variety of programming languages, such as Pascal or COBOL.

. Now let us consider how flowcharts and pseudocode can be used in structured programming.

7 Structured Programming Using Flowcharting or Pseudocode

Structured programming is a technique that emphasizes breaking a program into logical sections by using certain universal programming standards. Structured programming makes programs easier to write, check, read, and maintain. The computer industry widely accepts structured programming as the most productive way of programming. We will examine the rationale and concepts of structured programming more thoroughly later in this chapter. For now we just introduce some basic concepts of structure in this discussion of flowcharts and pseudocode. Note, however, that a programmer would use flowcharting or pseudocode (or possibly some other method) to plan a solution. We present them together here so you can see how both methods can be used to solve the same problem.

In a program, **control structures** control how the program executes. Structured programming uses a limited number of control

MICROCOMPUTERS IN ACTION

Home Sweet Home

Maybe programmers should work at home. The idea is not new, but new factors are affecting the decision to work at home or in the office. The first is the freedom derived from the personal computer and the second is the newfound influence of environment on productivity.

First the personal computer. Many programmers still work on terminals that interact with a large mainframe computer. The response time from the mainframe is either uniformly awful or so unpredictable that it becomes difficult to plan work effectively. In contrast, a single-user personal computer provides relatively instant and uniform response times for any programming task.

Now, what about the environ-ment? Recent studies have shown that a programmer's physical work environment influences software productivity more profoundly than managers had suspected. Although programming productivity has long been known to vary dramatically from one individual to another, these variances have usually been attributed to differences in experience and ability. But Tom De-Marco of Atlantic Systems Guild reports that his studies suggest something quite different. When he compared groups of people in different environments, he found that productivity is linked to such environmental factors as desk size, noise levels, and privacy.

The direction seems clear. Get a personal computer for home

use, place it on a large desk in a quiet room, and lock yourself in. Your productivity should soar. Well, it is hardly that simple, but the findings are worthy of consideration by both programmers and managers.

structures to minimize the complexity of programs and thus cut down on errors. There are three basic control structures in structured programming:

- Sequence

- Selection

- Iteration

These three are considered the basic building blocks of all program construction. You will see that we have used some of these structures already, in Figures 7-3 and 7-4.

Before we discuss each control structure in detail, it is important to note that each structure has only one **entry point** (the point where control is transferred to the structure) and one **exit point** (the point where control is transferred from the structure). This property makes structured programs easier to read and to debug.

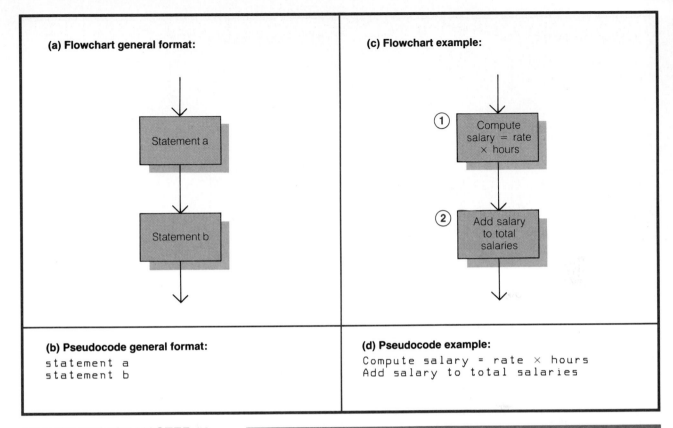

(a) Flowchart general format:

(b) Pseudocode general format:
```
statement a
statement b
```

(c) Flowchart example:

(d) Pseudocode example:
```
Compute salary = rate × hours
Add salary to total salaries
```

TRANSPARENCY MASTER #3
Figure #7-5c-d

Figure 7-5   Sequence. (a and b) General format of the sequence control structure. (c and d) Example of sequence control structure. To compute the total of movie extras' wages, ① determine one extra's salary for that week's shooting by multiplying the hourly rate times the number of hours worked on the picture that week. ② Add that extra's salary to those of other extras to find the total.

(continued from p. 200) (3) All lines start and end on boxes; none should remain suspended, going nowhere. (4) Decisions should be labeled, so that the true and the false exits are clear. (5) The only time there is more than one line entering a box is when it unites portions of an earlier decision, or if the box is the start of a loop. (6) Loops have only one entrance, namely at the beginning. (7) A subprogram has only one entrance (at the beginning) and only one exit (at the end). (8) All lines are directed (have implied or explicit arrows). If arrows are missing, we assume that the lines point to the right or down.

Sequence

The **sequence control structure** is the most straightforward: One statement simply follows another in sequence. The left side of Figure 7-5 shows the general format of a sequence control structure as it is used in flowcharting or in pseudocode. The right side of Figure 7-5 shows an example of a sequence control structure: the two steps follow in sequence.

Selection

The **selection control structure** is used to make logical decisions. This control structure has two forms: IF-THEN-ELSE and IF-THEN. The IF-THEN-ELSE control structure works as follows: "IF (a condition is true), THEN (do something), ELSE (do something different)." For instance, "IF the alarm clock goes off and it is a weekend morning, THEN just turn it off and go back to sleep, ELSE get up and go to work." Or, to use a more specific example, "IF a student is

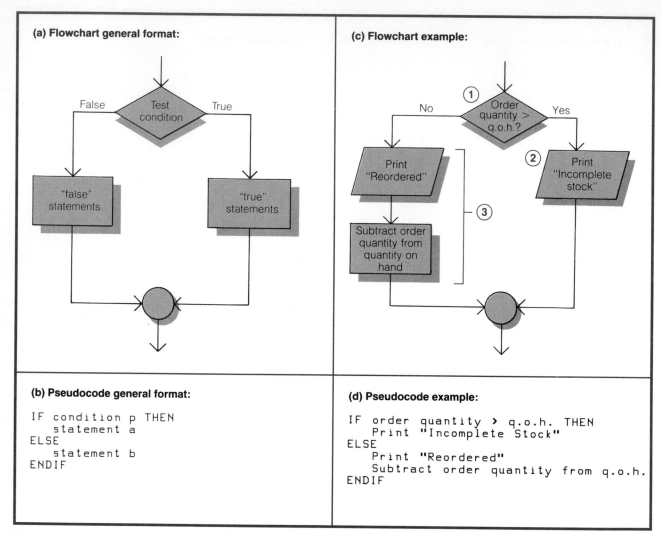

(a) Flowchart general format:

(b) Pseudocode general format:

```
IF condition p THEN
    statement a
ELSE
    statement b
ENDIF
```

(c) Flowchart example:

(d) Pseudocode example:

```
IF order quantity > q.o.h. THEN
    Print "Incomplete Stock"
ELSE
    Print "Reordered"
    Subtract order quantity from q.o.h.
ENDIF
```

TRANSPARENCY MASTER #4
Figure #7-6c-d

Figure 7-6   IF-THEN-ELSE.   (a and b) General format of the IF-THEN-ELSE control structure. There can be one or more statements for each of the two paths, "True" or "False." (c and d) Example of an IF-THEN-ELSE control structure. A trucker orders tires at a truck-tire warehouse. IF ① the quantity of tires ordered is greater than the quantity on hand (q.o.h.), THEN ② the computer prints "Incomplete stock," ELSE ③ it prints "Reordered" and subtracts the quantity ordered from the quantity on hand.

LECTURE HINT
The selection control structure has a third form, the CASE statement, found in Pascal and other modern computer languages. The CASE statement allows multiple branches, with only one of them being executed. But the CASE statement can be simulated using nested IF statements.

a resident, THEN the fee equals credits times $95, ELSE fee is credits times $125." Figure 7-6 shows the general format and an example of IF-THEN-ELSE in both a flowchart and in pseudocode.

IF-THEN is a special case of IF-THEN-ELSE. The IF-THEN selection is less complicated: "IF the condition is true, THEN do something—but if it is not true, then do not do it." For example, "IF the shift worked is shift 3, THEN add bonus of $50." Note that there will always be some resulting action using IF-THEN-ELSE; in contrast, the IF-THEN may or may not produce action, depending on the condition. The IF-THEN variation is shown in Figure 7-7.

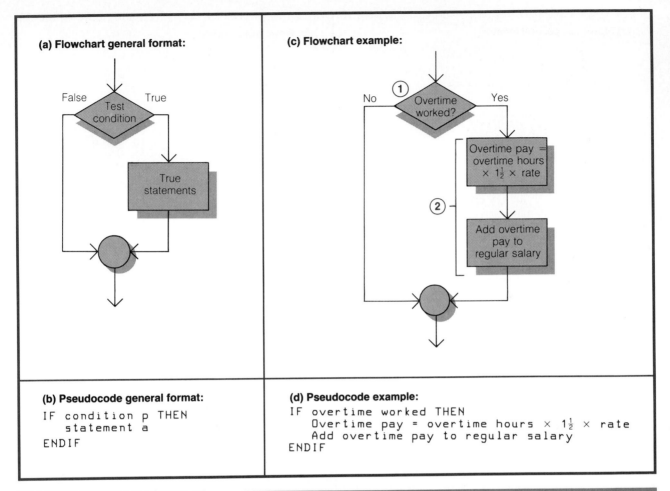

(a) Flowchart general format:

False   Test condition   True

True statements

(c) Flowchart example:

① No   Overtime worked?   Yes

Overtime pay = overtime hours × 1½ × rate

② Add overtime pay to regular salary

(b) Pseudocode general format:

```
IF condition p THEN
    statement a
ENDIF
```

(d) Pseudocode example:

```
IF overtime worked THEN
    Overtime pay = overtime hours × 1½ × rate
    Add overtime pay to regular salary
ENDIF
```

TRANSPARENCY MASTER #5
Figure #7-7c-d

Figure 7-7 IF-THEN. (a and b) General format of the IF-THEN control structure. (c and d) Example of an IF-THEN control structure. IF ① a department store employee worked overtime, THEN ② the program computes overtime pay by multiplying the overtime hours by 1½ times the hourly rate; the total is added to the employee's regular salary.

LECTURE HINT
There is another loop structure; the FOR loop in BASIC and Pascal, or the DO loop in FORTRAN and PL/I. It is actually a special form of the DOWHILE loop which applies if one variable varies, and controls the completion of the loop.

Iteration

The **iteration control structure** is a looping mechanism. The only necessary iteration structure is the DOWHILE structure ("do . . . while"), as shown in Figure 7-8. An additional form of iteration is called DOUNTIL; DOUNTIL is really just a combination of sequence and DOWHILE. Although DOUNTIL is not one of the three basic control structures, it is convenient to introduce the DOUNTIL structure ("do . . . until") now, as shown in Figure 7-9.

When looping, you must give an instruction to stop the repetition at some point, otherwise, you could—theoretically—go on looping forever and never get to the end of the program. There is a basic rule of iteration, which is related to structured programming: *If you have several statements that need to be repeated, a decision about when to stop repeating has to be placed either at the beginning of all the loop statements or at the end of all the loop statements.*

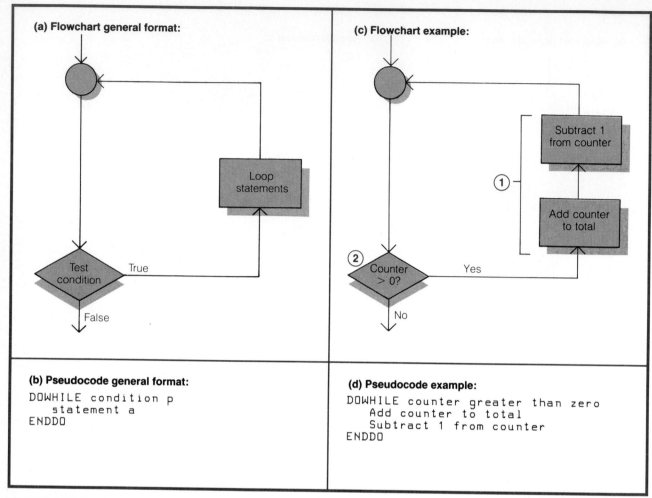

(a) Flowchart general format:

Loop statements

Test condition — True

False

(b) Pseudocode general format:

```
DOWHILE condition p
    statement a
ENDDO
```

(c) Flowchart example:

Subtract 1 from counter

Add counter to total

①

② Counter > 0? — Yes

No

(d) Pseudocode example:

```
DOWHILE counter greater than zero
    Add counter to total
    Subtract 1 from counter
ENDDO
```

TRANSPARENCY MASTER #6
Figure #7-8c-d

Figure 7-8   DOWHILE.   (a and b) General format of the DOWHILE control structure. (c and d) Example of a DOWHILE control structure. DO ① add counter to total and subtract 1 from counter WHILE ② counter is greater than 0.

Whether you put the loop-ending decision at the beginning—a **leading decision**—or at the end—a **trailing decision**—constitutes the basic difference between DOWHILE and DOUNTIL. As Figure 7-8 shows, DOWHILE tests at the beginning of the loop—the diamond-shaped decision box is the first action of the loop process. The DOUNTIL loop tests at the end, as you can see in Figure 7-9. The DOUNTIL loop, by the way, guarantees that the loop statements are executed at least once because the loop statements are executed before you make any test about whether to get out. This guarantee is not necessarily desirable, depending on your program logic. Also note that the test condition of DOUNTIL must be False to continue the loop—this is an important difference from the DOWHILE loop.

These basic control structures may seem a bit complex in the beginning, but in the long run they are the most efficient technique for programming, and it is worth taking your time to learn them.

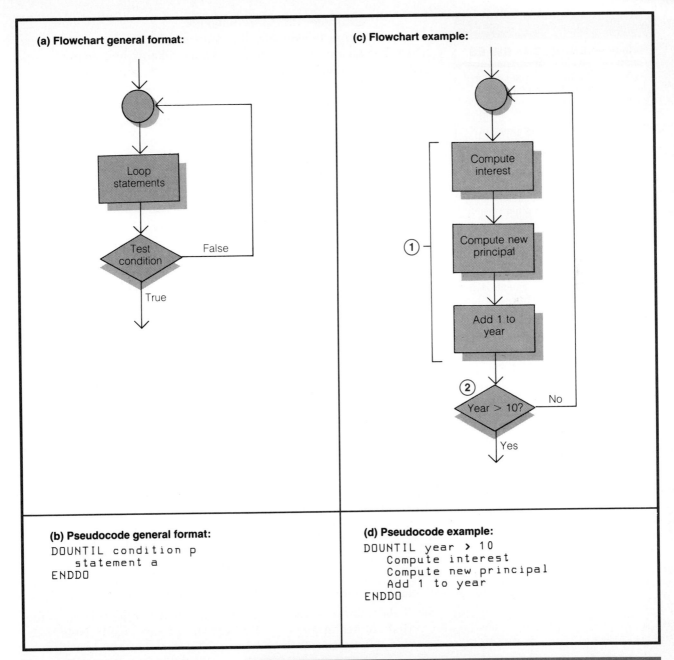

(a) Flowchart general format:

(c) Flowchart example:

(b) Pseudocode general format:

```
DOUNTIL condition p
    statement a
ENDDO
```

(d) Pseudocode example:

```
DOUNTIL year > 10
    Compute interest
    Compute new principal
    Add 1 to year
ENDDO
```

TRANSPARENCY MASTER #7
Figure #7-9a-b

TRANSPARENCY MASTER #8
Figure #7-9c-d

Figure 7-9   DOUNTIL.   (a and b) General format of the DOUNTIL control structure. (c and d) Example of a DOUNTIL control structure. DO ① compute interest, compute principal, and add the number 1 to the total years UNTIL ② the number of years is greater than 10.

7 Examples Using Flowcharts or Pseudocode

Let us now consider four extended examples. In each example, solutions are shown in both flowchart and pseudocode form. Keep in mind that only one approach or the other would be used.

SOME PSEUDOCODE RULES

Although pseudocode is not as formal as a programming language, many programmers follow rules like these:

- Begin each program or program section with "Start" and finish with "End".
- Capitalize control words such as IF and THEN.
- Write sequence statements in order, one under the other.
- Use IF-THEN-ELSE for decisions. Begin the decision with IF and end with ENDIF. THEN goes at the end of the IF line. If an ELSE is needed, align it with the IF and ENDIF. Indent the statements that go under THEN or ELSE.
- Use DOWHILE or DOUNTIL for iteration (looping). Indent the statements after the DO statement. End each DO with ENDDO, in the same margin as the DO.

Example: Counting Salaries

Suppose you are the manager of a personnel agency, which has 50 employees, and you want to know how many people make over $20,000 a year, $10,000 to $20,000, and under $10,000.

Figure 7-10 shows a solution to your problem. Let us go through the flowchart. The circled numbers below correspond to the circled numbers in the illustration. Use the pseudocode for comparison. We observe the following:

1. We initialize four counters to 0. The employee counter will keep track of the total number of employees in the company; the others—the high-salary counter, the medium-salary counter, and the low-salary counter—will count the numbers of employees in the salary categories.

2. In the parallelogram-shaped input box, we indicate that the computer reads the salary at this point. **Read** may be defined as bringing something that is outside the computer into memory; to *read*, in other words, means to *get*. The read instruction causes the computer to get one employee's yearly salary; since the instruction is in a loop, the computer will eventually get all salaries.

3. The first of the diamond-shaped decision boxes is a test condition that can go either of two ways—"Yes" or "No." Note that if the answer to the question "Salary > $20,000?" is "Yes," then the computer will process this answer by adding 1 to the high-salary count. If the answer is "No," the computer will ask, "Salary < $10,000?"—and so on.

4. For every decision box, no matter what decision is made, you should come back to a connector. And, as the flowchart shows, each decision box has its own connector. Note that, in this case, each connector is directly below the decision box to which it relates.

5. Whatever the kind of salary, the machine adds 1 (for the employee) to the employee counter, and a decision box then asks, "Employee counter = 50?" (the total number of employees in the company).

6. If the answer is "No," the computer makes a loop back to the first connector and goes through the process again. Note that this is a DOUNTIL loop because the decision box is at the end rather than at the beginning of the computing process ("DO keep processing UNTIL employee counter equals 50").

7. When the answer is finally "Yes," the computer then goes to an output operation (a parallelogram) and prints the salary count for each of the three categories. The computing process then stops.

Review the flowchart and observe that every action is one of the three control structures we have been talking about: sequence, selection, or iteration.

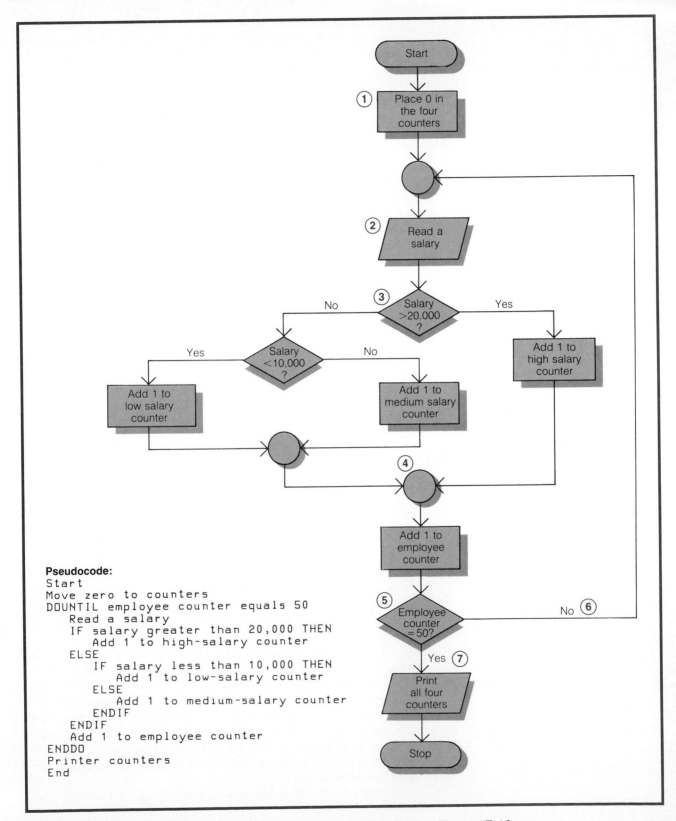

Pseudocode:
```
Start
Move zero to counters
DOUNTIL employee counter equals 50
    Read a salary
    IF salary greater than 20,000 THEN
        Add 1 to high-salary counter
    ELSE
        IF salary less than 10,000 THEN
            Add 1 to low-salary counter
        ELSE
            Add 1 to medium-salary counter
        ENDIF
    ENDIF
    Add 1 to employee counter
ENDDO
Printer counters
End
```

TRANSPARENCY MASTER #9   Figure #7-10

Figure 7-10   Counting salaries.

Example: Customer Credit Balances

In this example, illustrated in Figure 7-11, let us consider how to flowchart the process of checking a retail customer's credit balance. The accompanying pseudocode provides another solution. The file of customer records is kept on some computer-accessible medium, probably disk. This is a more true-to-life example than the previous salary example because, rather than a file with exactly 50 records, the file here has an unknown number of records. The program has to work correctly no matter how many customers there are.

As store manager, you need to check the customer file and print out the record of any customer whose current balance exceeds the credit limit, so salesclerks will not ring up charge purchases for customers who have gone over their credit limits. (Recall that a record is a collection of related data items; a customer record would likely contain customer name, address, account number, and—as indicated—current balance and credit limit.) The interesting thing about this flowchart is that it contains the same input operation, "Read customer record," twice (see the parallelograms). We will see why this is necessary. Let us proceed through the flowchart:

① After reading the first customer record and proceeding through the connector, you have a decision box that asks, "Record received?" This is a test to see if you have run out of all customer records (which you probably would not have the first time through).

② If the answer is "No," you have reached an **end of file**—there are no more records in the file—and the process stops.

③ If the answer is "Yes," the program proceeds to another decision box, which asks a question about the customer whose record you have just received: "Balance > limit?" This is an IF-THEN type of decision. If the answer is "Yes," then the customer is over the limit and, as planned, the computer prints the customer's record and moves on to the connector. If the answer is "No," then the computer moves directly to the connector.

④ Now we come to the second Read statement, "Read customer record." Why are two such statements needed? Couldn't we just forget the second one and loop back to the first Read statement again?

The answer lies in the rules of structure. As we stated, a loop requires a decision either at the beginning or at the end. If we omitted the second Read statement and looped back to the first Read statement, then the decision box to get us out of the loop ("Record received?") would be in the middle, not the beginning or the end, of the loop. Why not put "Record received?" at the end? You cannot because then you would have done the processing before you were sure you even had a record to process.

In summary: The decision box cannot go at the end, and the rules say it cannot be in the middle; therefore, the deci-

Figure 7-11 Checking a credit balance.

TRANSPARENCY MASTER #10
Figure #7-11

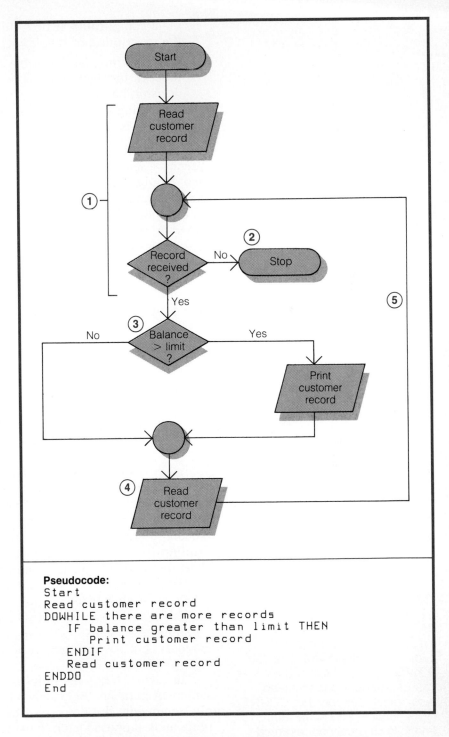

Pseudocode:
```
Start
Read customer record
DOWHILE there are more records
    IF balance greater than limit THEN
        Print customer record
    ENDIF
    Read customer record
ENDDO
End
```

sion must go at the beginning of the processing. Thus, the only way to read a second customer record after the computer has read the first one is to have the second Read statement where you see it. The first Read statement is sometimes called the **priming read.** This concept of the double read may

DISCUSSION QUESTION
Why is a priming read necessary in this example?

seem complicated at first, but it is very important. Rereading the description of this flowchart may help.

⑤ Next, the program loops back to the connector and repeats the process. Incidentally, this is a DOWHILE loop because the decision box is at the beginning rather than at the end of the computing process ("DO keep processing WHILE records continue to be received").

Note that, as before, each action in the program is either a sequence, a selection, or an iteration. In fact, since you have now seen two totally different examples—counting salaries and checking credit balances—you can begin to see how the control structures can be used for different applications. That is, the subject matter of the program may change, but the structured programming principles remain the same.

Example: Shift Bonus

Here is a description of the problem whose solution is represented in Figure 7-12. The problem concerns awarding employees bonuses based on the shift worked. The example is a little more elaborate because it involves moving data—employee number, name, and bonus—to a report line to set it up before printing. As Figure 7-12 shows, a first-shift employee gets a bonus of 5% of regular pay, but employees who work the second or third shift get a 10% bonus. Also, a count is needed of employees on the second or third shifts—that is, one count for both shifts. If the shift is not 1, 2, or 3, then an error message is printed.

Example: Student Grades

Now let us translate a flowchart or pseudocode into a program. You could type this program in on a computer terminal connected to a mainframe computer or key it directly into your microcomputer. It would deliver back to you, on a terminal screen or in printout form, the answers you seek. Figure 7-13 shows the flowchart, pseudocode, program, and output.

The program is written in the programming language called BASIC (described in more detail in Appendix A). BASIC is similar to English in many ways, so you can understand the program even with no knowledge of BASIC. There are several "dialects" of the BASIC language, but we have chosen to use simple generic BASIC in this example. Generic BASIC runs on any BASIC version you may have.

In Figure 7-13c, the numbers in the far left column are called statement numbers. *REM* stands for a remark statement, which simply documents the program. The REMs briefly describe what the program is supposed to do or list variable names. Variable names are symbolic names of locations in main storage. The PRINT statement tells the computer what message or data to print out, the READ statement reads the data to be processed, the GOTO (go to) statement tells which statement the computer is to go to, and DATA statements list the data to be read by the computer.

Pseudocode:
```
Start
Move zero to counter
Read employee record
DOWHILE there are more records
    Move employee number and name to report line
    If first shift THEN
        bonus = regular pay × .05
        move bonus to report line
    ELSE
        IF second shift or third shift THEN
            bonus = regular pay × .10
            move bonus to report line
            add 1 to counter
        ELSE
            move error message to report line
        ENDIF
    ENDIF
    Print report line
    Read employee record
ENDDO
Print counter
End
```

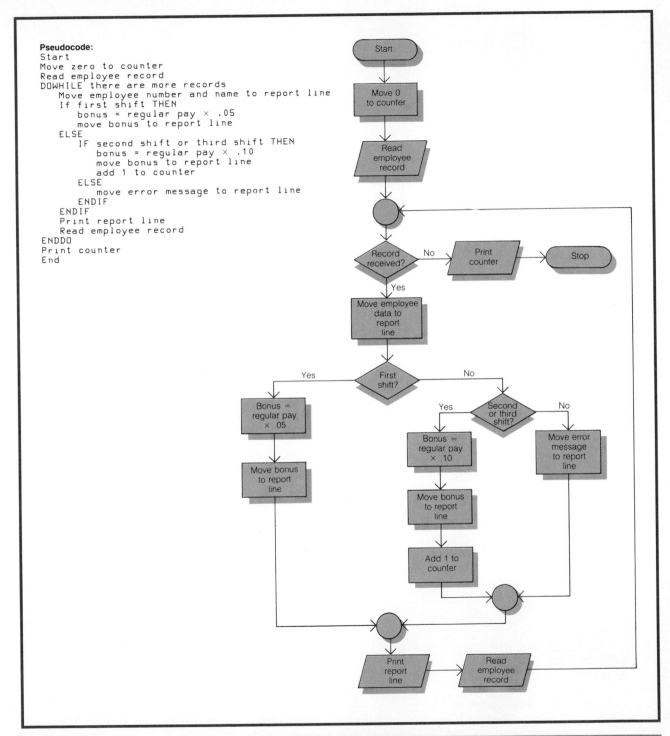

Figure 7-12 Shift bonus. This example describes the logic for awarding employee bonuses. The pseudocode reflects the flowchart and vice versa.

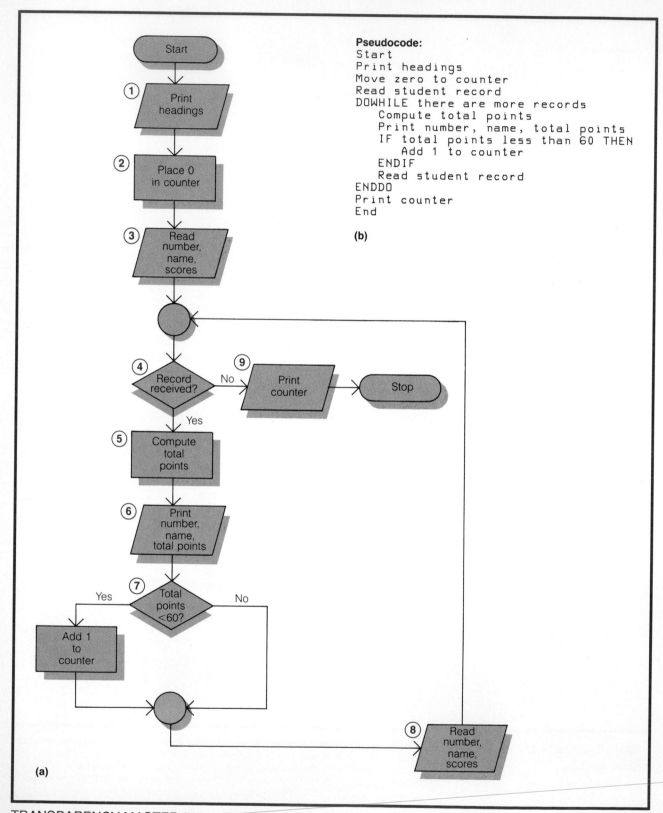

Pseudocode:
```
Start
Print headings
Move zero to counter
Read student record
DOWHILE there are more records
    Compute total points
    Print number, name, total points
    IF total points less than 60 THEN
        Add 1 to counter
    ENDIF
    Read student record
ENDDO
Print counter
End
```

(b)

(a)

TRANSPARENCY MASTER #12   Figure #7-13a-b

```
10   REM PROGRAM TO COMPUTE STUDENT POINTS
20   REM
30   REM THIS PROGRAM READS, FOR EACH STUDENT,
40   REM   STUDENT NUMBER, STUDENT NAME, AND
50   REM   4 TEST SCORES. THE SCORES ARE TO
60   REM   BE WEIGHTED AS FOLLOWS:
70   REM
80   REM      TEST 1: 20 PERCENT
90   REM      TEST 2: 20 PERCENT
100  REM      MIDTERM: 25 PERCENT
110  REM      FINAL: 35 PERCENT
120  REM
130  REM VARIABLE NAMES USED:
140  REM
150  REM   COUNT   COUNT OF STUDENTS SCORING LESS THAN 60
160  REM   NUM     STUDENT NUMBER
170  REM   NAM$    STUDENT NAME
180  REM   S1      SCORE FOR TEST 1
190  REM   S2      SCORE FOR TEST 2
200  REM   S3      SCORE FOR MIDTERM
210  REM   S4      SCORE FOR FINAL
220  REM   TOTAL   TOTAL STUDENT POINTS
230  REM
240  PRINT
250  PRINT "    STUDENT GRADE REPORT"
260  PRINT
270  PRINT "STUDENT","STUDENT","TOTAL"
280  PRINT "NUMBER","NAME","POINTS"
290  PRINT
300  PRINT
310  LET COUNT = 0
320  READ NUM,NAM$,S1,S2,S3,S4
330  IF NUM = -9999 THEN 390
340  LET TOTAL = .20*S1+.20*S2+.25*S3+.35*S4
350  PRINT NUM,NAM$,TOTAL
360  IF TOTAL < 60 THEN COUNT = COUNT+1
370  READ NUM,NAM$,S1,S2,S3,S4
380  GOTO 330
390  PRINT
400  PRINT "NUMBER OF STUDENTS WITH POINTS < 60:";COUNT
410  STOP
420  DATA 2164,ALLEN SCHAAB,60,64,73,78
430  DATA 2644,MARTIN CHAN,80,78,85,90
440  DATA 3171,CHRISTY BURNER,91,95,90,88
450  DATA 5725,CRAIG BARNES,61,41,70,53
460  DATA 6994,RAOUL GARCIA,95,96,90,92
470  DATA 7001,KAY MITCHELL,55,60,58,55
480  DATA -9999,XXX,0,0,0,0
490  END
```

(c)

```
STUDENT GRADE REPORT

STUDENT      STUDENT               TOTAL
NUMBER       NAME                  POINTS


2164         ALLEN SCHAAB          70.4
2644         MARTIN CHAN           84.4
3171         CHRISTY BURNER        90.5
5725         CRAIG BARNES          56.5
6994         RAOUL GARCIA          92.9
7001         KAY MITCHELL          56.8

NUMBER OF STUDENTS WITH POINTS < 60: 2
```

(d)

Figure 7-13 Student grades. The (a) flowchart and (b) pseudocode for (c) the program that produces (d) a student grade report.

Our problem is, first, to compute the student grades (ranging from 0 through 100) for six students, and, second, to count the number of students who have scored less than 60 points. The grade points are based on student performance on two tests, a midterm exam, and a final exam, the scores of which have been weighted in a certain way.

Let us conceive of the problem in terms of input, processing, and output.

Input

The circled numbers in the text correspond to the circled numbers in the flowchart, but you may follow the pseudocode if you prefer. Corresponding statement numbers from the program follow in parentheses.

① **"Print headings"** (lines 240 through 300). This statement refers to the headings on the report (skip ahead to Figure 7-13d to see what they will look like). The first is the overall heading, "STUDENT GRADE REPORT." Lines that contain only the word PRINT, as line 240 does, cause blank lines to print on the output; this provides better spacing. Next the coding instructs the printer to print the three column headings.

② **"Place 0 in counter"** (line 310). This is not a form of input data; it is an initialization process required here, at the outset. This counter will count the number of students who score less than 60 points, as we will see later.

③ **"Read number, name, scores"** (line 320). The input data is given in lines 420 through 480.

Processing

④ **"Record received?"** (line 330). Note that this is a DOWHILE loop because the decision box is at the beginning of the process. In generic BASIC, DOWHILE is implemented with IF-THEN-ELSE. The decision box asks if the particular student number, name, and scores read are the last ones in the file. How will the computer know this? Because the digits −9999 will tell it "end of file." You will note that the student numbers are four digits other than −9999 (see lines 420 through 470). The −9999 decision instructs the computer to advance to statement 390 when the end of the file is reached.

⑤ **"Compute total points"** (line 340). The scores are weighted 20% for the first test, 20% for the second test, 25% for the midterm, and 35% for the final exam. The total of these weighted scores gives the course grade. In the program these percentages are documented in remark statements (lines 80 through 110). The formula that totals the scores and incorporates the weightings is stated in line 340. Here the expression ".20*S1" means 20% times the first test score. (In BASIC * is used as the multiplication symbol.)

⑥ **"Print number, name, total points"** (line 350). Printing is really an output operation; we include it here for convenience because it is part of the loop.

⑦ **"Total points < 60?"** (line 360). This decision box is given as an IF-THEN statement. If a student's points are less than 60, 1 is added to COUNT.

⑧ **"Read number, name, scores"** (line 370). As in our last example, we have here an instance of a repeated Read statement. A GOTO statement is used to close the loop. That is, we repeat the input instruction given in step 3.

We now make the loop back to the first connector and continue to DO this processing WHILE the answer to the question "Record received?" is "Yes."

Output

⑨ **"Print counter"** (line 400). When we reach the end of the file, we print the total number of students with points less than 60. At this point, then, you should have the printout of results shown in Figure 7-13d.

All this is probably a bit confusing if you are a beginner. Practice helps. Appendix A offers several flowchart-to-program translations for your perusal.

7 Structured Programming Concepts

In the 1950s the programmer was hardly noticed, wrote the well-known software expert Edsger Dijkstra (pronounced "DIKE-stra"). For one thing, the computers themselves were so large and so cantankerous to maintain that they attracted most of the attention. For another, Dijkstra said, "The programmer's somewhat invisible work was without any glamour: you could show the machine to visitors and that was several orders of magnitude more spectacular than some sheets of coding." Programmers flourished, nevertheless, as the demand for software grew.

In the 1960s hardware overreached software. The development of hardware and storage capabilities proceeded apace, but software development could not keep up. Projects ran over budget, schedules slipped, and when projects were finally completed they often did not meet the users' needs.

In the 1970s some determined attempts were made to make software development more manageable. Hardware costs had already decreased dramatically while software costs continued to rise; it was apparent that, if money was to be saved, there would have to be considerable improvements in software. No longer would programmers be allowed to produce programs that were casually tested or that were readable only to them. The use of obscure coding in an attempt to shave a microsecond of computer time was discouraged.

CONSCIENCE OF THE COMMUNITY

The computer community, that is. He has been hovering over the computer world since the early 1960s. Few people have made such an impact or had such a lasting effect. On the other hand, few have so polarized the industry; no one is neutral about Edsger Dijkstra.

For his outspoken views, Dijkstra has been praised as a visionary by some. Others see him as a dreamer or—worse—a troublemaker. Dijkstra ignores both camps, blissfully going his own way. A prolific writer, Dijkstra turns out articles, essays, and even satires that remind the industry of its faults. In one address, for example, he denounced some programming languages in typically colorful terms: "The sooner we can forget that FORTRAN ever existed, the better. It wastes our brainpower, and it is too risky and therefore too expensive to use." He did not have kind words for PL/I either, a language he compared to "a plane with 7000 buttons and switches in the cockpit." He continued, "I absolutely fail to see how we can keep our growing programs firmly within our intellectual grip when by its sheer baroqueness the programming language—our basic tool, mind you!—already escapes our intellectual control."

It became clear that, first, problem complexity had to be accepted as fact and that, second, tools had to be devised to handle it. The programmer's job was no longer "invisible work."

7 The Move to Structured Programming

How did people go about programming in the early '60s? One computer scientist wrote: "Computer programming was so badly understood that hardly anyone even thought about proving programs correct; we just fiddled with a program until we 'knew' it worked." Dijkstra, in fact, has nagged and cajoled programmers to think in advance instead of using a rear-guard action for finding errors *after* the program is written.

Finding program errors after the fact was—and still is, in some quarters—an accepted way of programming. That is, a programmer wrote a program that seemed to solve the problem, then the program was put to the test. As soon as an error turned up, that one was fixed. This would continue until, eventually, the programmer got the program working well enough to use. To Dijkstra, this seemed a shoddy way of doing things. "Program testing," he said, "is a very convincing way of demonstrating program errors but never their absence."

A Profound Proposal

Enter structured programming. In 1966 C. Bohm and G. Jacopini published a paper in *Communications of the ACM* (the journal of the Association for Computing Machinery), a paper they had previously published in Italy. In this paper they proved mathematically that any problem solution could be constructed using only three basic control structures—the three structures that we have been calling *sequence*, *selection* (IF-THEN-ELSE), and *iteration*. It is interesting to note that the concept of structured programming has remained unchanged since it was proposed two decades ago.

These three control structures—sequence, selection, and iteration—were, of course, used before 1966. But other control structures were also used, notably the transfer, also known as the GOTO. Since the need for only the three basic control structures was now proven, the time had come to cut down on the number of GOTO statements.

The idea of structured programming was given a boost in March 1968, when Dijkstra published a now famous letter in *Communications of the ACM*. Under the heading "Go To Statements Considered Harmful," Dijkstra contended that the GOTO statement was an invitation to making a mess of one's program and that reducing the number of GOTOs reduced the number of programming errors. GOTOs, he said, could be compared to a bowl of spaghetti: If a person took a program and drew a line from each GOTO statement to the statement to which it transferred, the result would be a picture that looked like a bowl of spaghetti. Since then, people have referred to excessive GOTOs in a program as "spaghetti code." Note the comparison of programs with and without GOTOs in Figure 7-14.

LECTURE HINT
Notice the software maintenance in Figure 7-14. It is not easy to untangle spaghetti code. Sometimes it is easier to experiment to see what the program does, and then to reprogram it than to revise a bad program. There are standard techniques for revising such programs.

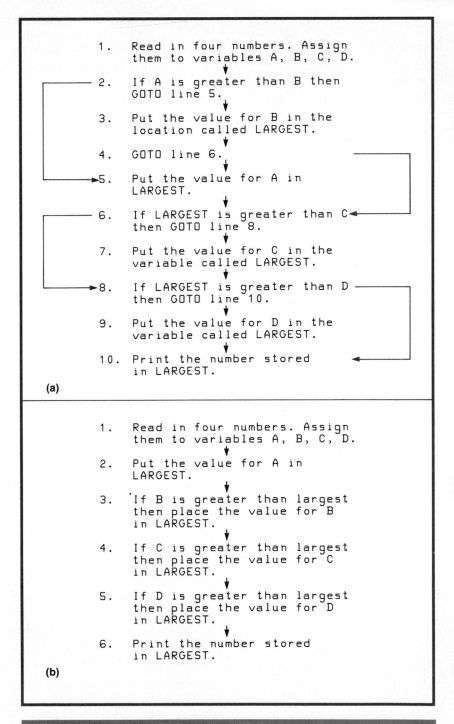

(a)

1. Read in four numbers. Assign them to variables A, B, C, D.
2. If A is greater than B then GOTO line 5.
3. Put the value for B in the location called LARGEST.
4. GOTO line 6.
5. Put the value for A in LARGEST.
6. If LARGEST is greater than C then GOTO line 8.
7. Put the value for C in the variable called LARGEST.
8. If LARGEST is greater than D then GOTO line 10.
9. Put the value for D in the variable called LARGEST.
10. Print the number stored in LARGEST.

(b)

1. Read in four numbers. Assign them to variables A, B, C, D.
2. Put the value for A in LARGEST.
3. If B is greater than largest then place the value for B in LARGEST.
4. If C is greater than largest then place the value for C in LARGEST.
5. If D is greater than largest then place the value for D in LARGEST.
6. Print the number stored in LARGEST.

Figure 7-14 With and without GOTO statements. These two programs, written here in plain English, do the same thing: Each finds the largest of four numbers. Such a task could be used, for example, to locate the salesperson with the largest sales for the month. (a) An illustration of GOTO programming. Even this small example demonstrates how confusing GOTO programming can be. (b) A solution for the same problem in GOTOless programming; it does the job in a tidy, sequential manner.

Structured Programming Takes Off

The first major project using structured programming was developed for the *New York Times*. The results were published in 1972. In this large undertaking the newspaper's clipping file was automated in such a way that, using a list of index terms, users could browse through abstracts (summaries) of all the paper's articles, automatically retrieve the text of an article, and display it on a terminal. The project involved 83,000 lines of source code and took 22 calendar months and 11 person-years to produce, yet it was delivered under budget and ahead of schedule. Equally important, there was an amazingly low error rate: Only 21 errors were found during the five weeks of acceptance testing, and only 25 additional errors appeared during the first year of the system's operation.

In December 1973 *Datamation*, one of the principal trade journals of the computer industry, devoted an entire issue to structured programming. This issue brought the subject to the attention of many programmers in the United States. One article hailed structured programming as a programming revolution.

And a revolution it has been. The theory—if not total practice—has been universally accepted in the computer industry. One obvious proof of this acceptance is the number of programming language textbooks on the market with the word *structure* in the title. No one would even consider publishing a text for unstructured COBOL (COBOL is a popular programming language for business). So the trainees coming into the industry have "structure" fresh in their heads, and what do they find? For some, the purest of structured shops. Many, however, are shocked to find existing programs—fat, messy, programs—dripping with GOTOs. Why is this? These programs were written in the '60s and even the '70s, before structured programming had taken hold. Managers would love to have them redone in structured code, but there often seem to be more pressing priorities or budget constraints. Occasionally, a trainee is welcomed with open arms as the savior who is going to convert some of the dinosaurs to structured code. This may be the ultimate challenge—structuring a 5000-line program that has been massaged by perhaps 50 different programmers over the last 15 years. The biggest problem may be that no one really understands how the program works anymore!

Managers have estimated that structured techniques increase programming productivity by approximately 25%. Here are some of the reasons why this is so. Structured programming:

- Increases the clarity and readability of programs (partly because you can read the program sequentially instead of hopping all over with GOTOs)

- Reduces the time required to test programs

- Decreases the time required to maintain programs (because increased clarity means less time spent in trying to read and understand programs)

So far, we have discussed the historical significance and rationale for structured programming and tied it to the three fundamental structures: sequence, selection, and iteration. But the issue of structure cuts deeper.

DISCUSSION QUESTION
Are programs without any GOTOs automatically structured programs?

7 Expanding the Structured Programming Concept

When the concept of program structure was first introduced, some people thought their programs would be structured if they simply got rid of GOTOs. There is more to it than that. Structured programming is a method of designing computer system components and their relationships to minimize complexity. So, in addition to limited control structures (again: sequence, selection, and iteration), two important aspects of structured programming are (1) top-down programming design and (2) module independence through coupling and cohesion. Before we describe these concepts, let us pause for an expanded formal definition: **Structured programming** is a set of programming techniques that include a limited number of control structures, top-down design, and module independence.

When a programmer uses **top-down design,** one of the first steps in writing is to identify basic program functions. These functions are further divided into smaller and smaller subfunctions of more manageable size. These subfunctions are called modules. Top-down design is demonstrated most easily by using structure charts.

Structure Charts

A **structure chart** graphically illustrates the structure of a program by showing hierarchical, independent modules. This high-level picture identifies major functions that are the initial component parts of the structure chart. Each major component is then broken down into subcomponents, which are, in turn, broken down still further until sufficiently detailed components are shown. As we noted, this is considered a top-down approach to program design. Since the components are pictured in hierarchical form, a drawing of this kind is also known as a **hierarchy chart.** A structure chart is easy to draw and easy to change, and it is often used as a supplement to or even a replacement for a logic flowchart.

Consider an example, Figure 7-15. As the illustration shows, the top level of the structure chart gives the name of the program, "Payroll process." The next level breaks the program down into its major functions—in Figure 7-15, these are "Read inputs," "Compute pay," and "Write outputs." Each of these major modules is then subdivided further into smaller modules. (We could break them down even further, but space does not permit it.)

Note the relationship of the structure chart in Figure 7-15 to top-down design. The major functions are repeatedly subdivided into smaller modules of manageable size. Each of the modules is

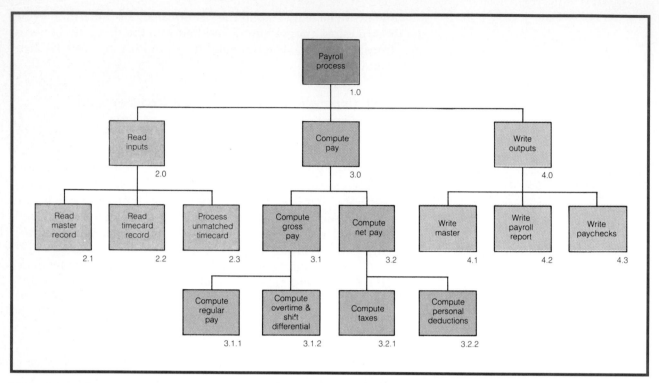

Figure 7-15   A structure chart. The numbers outside the boxes refer to more detailed diagrams of these functions.

THE SOFTWARE IS A MESS

The good news is that the new space telescope is ready to fly. The software that will run the telescope in space will be used by astronomers to plan and perform their operations. The bad news is that it is years—yes, *years*—behind schedule. The delays have caused major embarrassment for NASA and major dollars for the taxpayers.

What went wrong? One programmer described the software in simple terms: "It's a mess." Although some problems go back to mistaken concepts of what the computer can do, people close to the project identify the major problem as lack of modern programming techniques—specifically, a lack of structured programming. For example, structured programming calls for programs to be put together in modular form, so that changes to one part do not impact other parts. But changes to this software have been known to bring down the entire system, sometimes, as one participant put it, "for days."

also, according to plan, as independent of the others as possible. For example, module 4.1, "Write master," will be executed independently of any activity in module 4.3, "Write paychecks."

Now let us look more closely at the way modules are planned.

Modularity

Computer professionals recognize that the way to efficient development and maintenance is to break the programs in a system into manageable pieces—modules. The way that a system is divided into various pieces has a significant effect on the structure of the system. We have already noted in our structure chart discussion that structured design involves organizing the pieces of a system in a hierarchical way. High-level components of the structure chart are programs; lower-level components are called modules. Once converted to programmed form, a **module** is a set of logically related statements that performs a specific function.

One relationship between modules is called **coupling**. It is the measure of the strength of the relationship between two modules. Ideally, that relationship should be weak so that the modules are independent; then, if a change is made in one module, it will not affect other modules. Another relationship is called **cohesion,** the measure of the inner strength of an individual module. The best

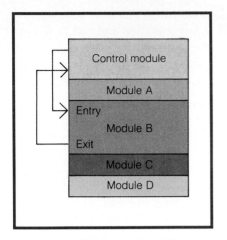

Figure 7-16   Single entry, single exit.
The program control module executes
module B by transferring to its entry
point. After the instructions in module
B are executed, the module is exited
via its exit point. Program control returns, in this case, to the point of departure, the control module.

relationship here is a strong one; a module should have a single
function, although that is not always possible. An example of a single function is the computation of withholding tax. This function
would not be included with other functions, such as computing insurance deductions. Strong cohesion encourages module independence, which—in turn—makes future changes easier.

In addition, a module should have a **single entry** and a **single
exit.** *Single entry* means that the execution of a program module
must begin at the same place, usually at the beginning; the module
can be entered at only a single point. Similarly, the module may be
exited from only one place, as shown in Figure 7-16. It is easier for us
to keep track of what is going on in the program if there is only one
way to get in and one way to get out of each module in the program.

A module should also be of manageable size. A single page of
coded program instructions is often considered an ideal size.

7 Structure Forever? A Surprising Answer

We have focused on structure and its acceptance in the
computer community. We have industrywide agreement on this
important issue and can consider it settled, right? No, not quite.

Structured programming makes sense if you are using what is
called a **procedural language**—that is, a language that presents a
step-by-step process for solving a problem. It is the steps—program
statements—of the procedure that need structuring. Most languages
in use today, including the popular COBOL mentioned earlier, are
procedural languages.

But nothing stays the same for long in the computer industry.
New, easy-to-use languages are being used with increasing frequency. The ease of their use stems from the fact that they do not
have procedures. In fact, they are called **nonprocedural languages.**
Instead of stating *how* to accomplish a task—the step-by-step way—
you just say *what* you want to accomplish. We will study this development in more detail as we study languages in Chapter 8. For now,
just be aware that structured programming may not always be an
issue.

DISCUSSION QUESTION
How are nonprocedural languages
different from what we have
studied in this chapter?

STUDENT PROJECT
Select a daily activity of your
choice, and describe the steps
needed to perform this activity.
Make sure routine is
unambiguous, complete, and
covers all likely problems that
might arise.

7 Is Programming for You?

In this chapter we have glimpsed the habits of mind and
carefulness required to write programs. What we have
seen is just an overview. The is-this-for-me question can really be
answered only after you have given programming a try. The exact
process of producing a program is given in Appendix A.

7 Summary and Key Terms

- A programmer converts solutions to the user's problems into instructions for the computer. This process involves defining the problem, planning the solution, coding the program, testing the program, and documenting the program.

- Defining the problem means discussing it with the users or a systems analyst to determine the necessary input, processing, and output.

- Planning can be done by using a **flowchart,** which is a pictorial representation of the step-by-step solution, and by using **pseudocode,** which is an English-like outline of the solution.

- Coding the program means expressing the solution in a programming language.

- Testing the program consists of desk-checking, translating, and debugging. The rules of a programming language are referred to as its **syntax. Desk-checking** is a mental checking or proofreading of the program before it is run. In translating, a **translator** program converts the program into language the computer can understand and in the process detects programming language errors, which are called **syntax errors.** Two types of translators are **compilers,** which translate the entire program at one time and give all the error messages (**diagnostics**) at once, and **interpreters,** which translate the program one line at a time. **Debugging** is running the program to detect, locate, and correct mistakes—**logic errors.**

- Typical **documentation** contains a detailed written description of the programming cycle and the program along with the test results and a printout of the program.

- A flowchart consists of arrows representing the direction the program takes and boxes and other symbols representing actions. A **logic flowchart** represents the flow of logic in a program, and a **systems flowchart** represents the flow of data through an entire computer system.

- The standard symbols used in flowcharting are called **ANSI** (American National Standards Institute) symbols. The most common symbols are process, decision, connector, start/stop, input/output, and direction of flow. The rectangular **process box** shows an action to be taken. The diamond-shaped **decision box** (with two **paths,** or **branches**) is the only symbol that allows a choice. The **connector** is

a circle that connects paths. The oval **start/stop symbol** is used at the beginning and end of a flowchart.

- To **initialize** is to set the starting values of certain storage locations before running a program.

- A **loop,** or **iteration,** is the repetition of instructions under certain conditions. The computer can recognize these conditions by performing a **compare operation.**

- Pseudocode must be translated into a programming language before the program can be run. Pseudocode allows a programmer to plan a program without being concerned about the rules of a specific programming language.

- Structured programming uses three basic **control structures:** sequence, selection, and iteration.

- The **entry point** is the point where control is transferred to a program structure. The **exit point** is the point where control is transferred from the structure. Each structure must have only one entry point and only one exit point.

- In **sequence control structure,** one statement follows another. **Selection control structure** involves test conditions and has two variations: IF-THEN and IF-THEN-ELSE. The basic **iteration control structure** is DOWHILE, which is used in looping. The three basic control structures are supplemented by a fourth structure, DOUNTIL, which is another form of looping. The basic rule of iteration: If you have several statements that need to be repeated, a decision about when to stop repeating has to be placed either at the beginning of all the loop statements or at the end of all the loop statements.

- In a DOWHILE loop the loop-ending decision is at the beginning and is called a **leading decision.** The decision in a DOUNTIL loop occurs at the end and is called a **trailing decision.**

- In program instructions to **read** means to bring something into memory.

- **End of file** means that there are no more records in the file.

- When a Read statement is repeated, the first Read statement is sometimes called the **priming read.**

- During the 1960s, development of new hardware outpaced the development of new software, creating the need for more efficient methods of creating software.

- In 1966 C. Bohm and G. Jacopini published a paper on structured programming in which they proved that any problem solution could be constructed using the three basic control structures: sequence, selection, and iteration. The structured programming concept was further supported by Edsger Dijkstra, who emphasized that programs are less complex if the use of other control structures—especially the GOTO statement—is reduced.

- **Structured programming** is a set of programming techniques that includes a limited number of control structures, top-down design, and module independence. Structured programming increases programming productivity by increasing the clarity and readability of programs, reducing test time, and decreasing the time required to maintain programs.

- **Top-down design** identifies basic program functions before dividing them into subfunctions called modules.

- A **structure chart,** or **hierarchy chart,** illustrates the top-down design of a program and is often used to either supplement or replace a logic flowchart.

- When converted to program form, a **module** is a set of logically related statements that performs a specific function.

- **Coupling** is the measure of the strength of the relationship between two modules. Weak coupling is ideal because a change in one module does not affect other modules. **Cohesion** is the measure of the inner strength of a module. Strong cohesion makes modules more independent, a characteristic that facilitates future changes. A module should also have a **single entry** and a **single exit** so that it is easier to keep track of the flow of logic in the program.

- A **procedural language,** such as COBOL, is a language that presents a step-by-step process for solving a problem. **Nonprocedural languages** simply state what task is to be accomplished but do not state the steps that accomplish it.

7 Review Questions

1. Name the five steps in the programming process.

2. Describe the two common ways of planning a program, and discuss their advantages and disadvantages.

3. Describe the phases in testing a program.

4. Why is documentation important?

5. Explain what ANSI symbols are used for and name the common ones.

6. Describe the three main control structures in structured programming. Name and describe the specific types of statements.

7. Explain how the three control structures are evident in the flowchart for counting salaries (Figure 7-10) and in the flowchart for checking credit balances (Figure 7-11).

8. Write the pseudocode for this problem: Read a file of records and, if the account type is business, check further. (Hint: There is an IF statement within an IF statement, as you have seen in Figure 7-10.) If the order amount is greater than 1000, then set the discount rate to the maximum; otherwise, set the discount rate to the minimum. But if the account type is other than business—an ELSE situation—then set the discount rate to 0. After making these checks, compute the discount, compute the amount due, and write the record and the amount due. Note also that, as in Figure 7-11, you need a priming read. And remember to start and end the program.

9. Explain the contributions that Edsger Dijkstra and the team of C. Bohm and G. Jacopini made to structured programming.

10. How did structured programming differ from the way programming had been done previously?

11. State the benefits of structured programming.

12. Explain how maintaining a limited number of control structures helps to make programming less complex.

13. Describe top-down design.

14. Explain the concept of modularity.

7 Discussion Questions

1. Should students taking a computer literacy course be required to learn some programming? Why?

2. Do you think you might like to become a computer programmer or other computer professional?

3. In your opinion what kind of person makes a good programmer? Discuss specific characteristics and explain why they are important.

Chapter 8. Languages: A Survey

COMPUTERS AROUND US
The Many Uses of Computers

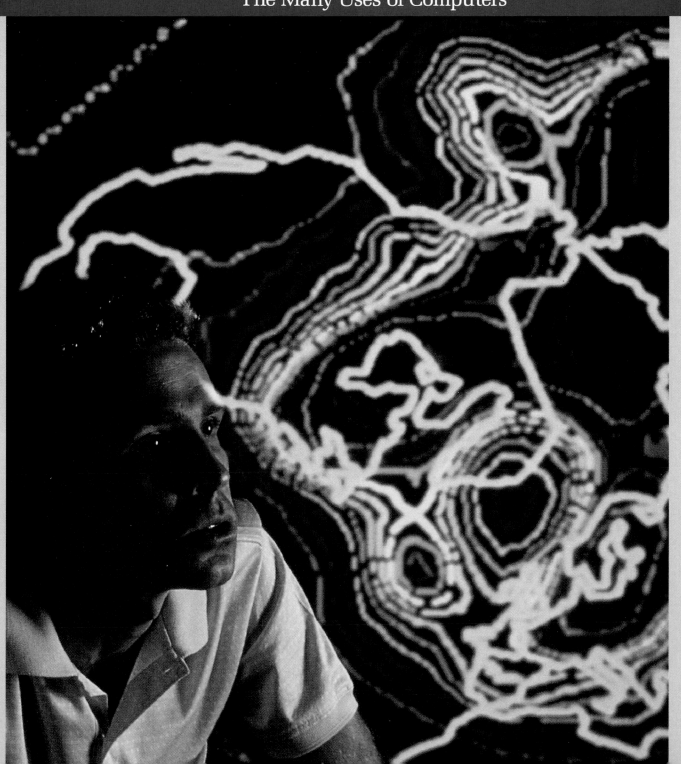

1

2

In this gallery we will look at how computers are used in science, sports, entertainment, health and medicine, transportation, education, photography, and music. In the photo on the opening page, a researcher at the European Center for Scientific and Engineering Computing in Rome, Italy, studies world weather patterns using computer-generated maps.

Science

(1) This researcher is using a laser to analyze the composition of a gas.

(2) Genetic researchers use the computer to analyze tissue cultures.

(3) This computer graphic map is used by Texaco to aid in oil exploration.

(4) At the Center for Astrophysics in Cambridge, MA, a researcher studies a map of a galaxy to learn about the "dark matter" around it.

(5–6) Both of the computer-generated images in this pair show a double helix DNA molecule; **(5)** shows a side view of the molecule and **(6)** gives us a church-windowlike end view.

(7) Researchers use supercomputer graphics to simulate the formation and evolution of a galaxy over the galaxy's lifetime. This "landscape" plots the density of the interstellar matter.

3

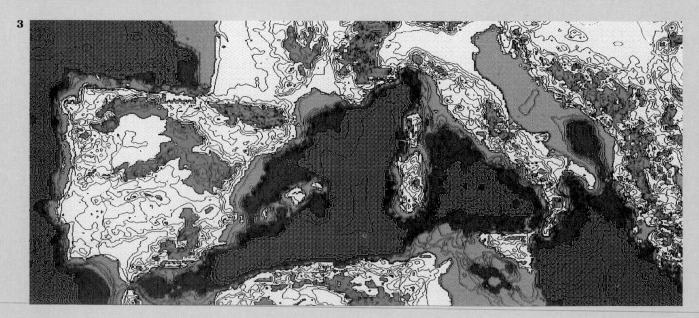

4

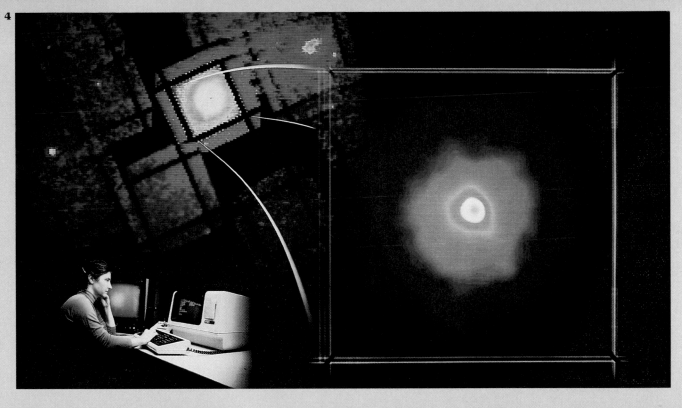

5

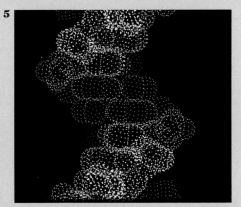

6

7

Sports

(8) This Hewlett-Packard computer system provides information for sports editors who cover the European tennis tour.

(9) Footage of actual golf courses lends realism to this home computer golf game.

(10) The computer embedded in this Adidas running shoe keeps track of the time spent running, the distance that was run, the rate per mile, and the miles run per month. The computer helps the runner assess progress on personal goals.

(11) Sophisticated software and hardware is used to design sports equipment. Images on screen can be rotated and viewed from any angle, and designs can be altered instantaneously.

(12) A member of the United States Olympic cross-country skiing team wears a computerized device that records data from the soles of her feet. **(13)** Computerized graphics help analyze cross-country skiing performance.

8

9

10

11

12

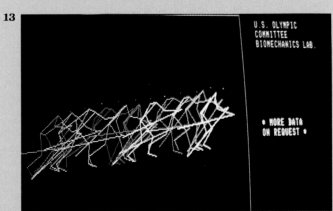

13

U.S. OLYMPIC
COMMITTEE
BIOMECHANICS LAB.

* MORE DATA
ON REQUEST *

Entertainment

(14) Rick Lazzarini used a personal computer to create the 20-foot queen for the movie *Aliens*.

(15–17) Board games get automated: Realistic in appearance, these classic board games— Monopoly, Clue, and Scrabble—can be played against the computer or against human opponents.

(18) Computer sports games of all kinds are popular. This basketball simulation, featuring superstar Magic Johnson, is fairly typical. It includes animated players and officials, complete statistics, and a training sequence to teach you to "make shots."

(19) This three-dimensional computer-generated graphics logo for the ABC Network swoops and swirls on the screen to get our attention.

15

14

16

17
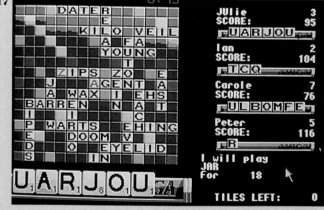

20

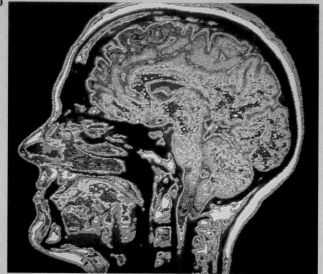

Health and Medicine

(20–22) Modern medicine has many diagnostic tools at its disposal. Head, heart, knee—any ailment can be examined more closely with computer-enhanced pictures. The head and heart shown here are healthy, but the knee shows an area of cancer just behind the kneecap.

(23) This computer-enhanced image of an ultrasound test shows the baby quite clearly. Ultrasound, unlike radiation, has no adverse effect on living tissues.

(24) This infant's vision is being tested by measuring brain wave response to visual stimuli.

(25) Orthopedic implants can be designed with a computer. The screen here shows designs for a hip joint implant. Some actual joint prostheses are on the table, along with the bones that they connect.

(26) This computer-generated model of the virus that causes the human cold helps researchers come closer to a cure. **(27)** This computer-produced image shows how a human antibody (red) attaches to a common cold virus (blue).

21

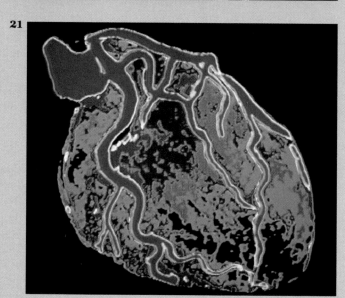

23

22

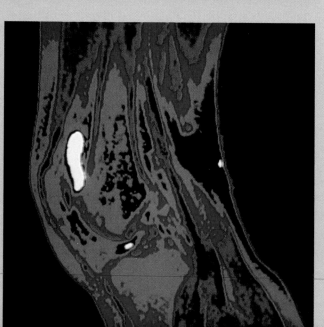

24

25

26

27

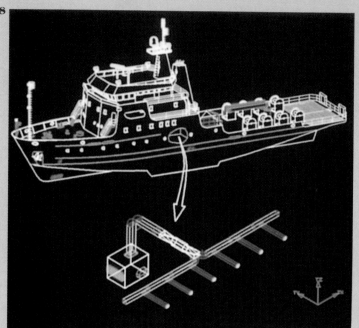

28

Transportation

(28) When designing shipping routes, a graphics display such as this can be used. Engineers and customers can manipulate the image in a "What if . . ." manner to arrive at a final solution.

(29) It might be a photo but, no, a closer look reveals a detailed computer graphics image. This flight simulator is part of a flight training program for pilots.

(30–31) This computerized traffic control system is in place in Los Angeles. Major thoroughfares around the city are linked to city hall by fiber optics. The controller can monitor traffic patterns and manipulate signals or even re-route traffic in case of an accident or emergency.

Auto repair is not quite the mystery it once was. Mechanics can get expert advice from the computer, both **(32)** on the job and **(33)** in computer-based classes where students can interact with lessons at their own pace.

29

30

31

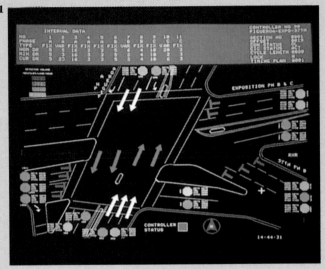

32

33

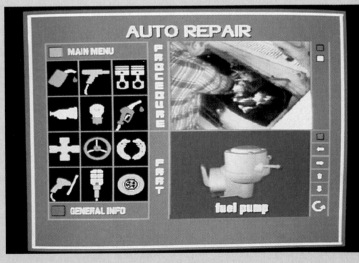

Education

(34) In the language lab at Brown University, students sit in front of dual screens. The computer, on the left, provides lessons, references, and corrections. The laser disk player provides motion video clips for lesson presentation and review.

(35) Students at Apple's Vivarium Open School in Los Angeles consider the computer an everyday learning tool.

(36) This world map screen is produced by software that lets students work interactively with the computer to learn geography.

(37) Students training to be veterinarians need tools beyond the classroom, in this case a horse and a computer to record and access pertinent data.

(38) This child takes special delight in her computer reading lessons, featuring Zug the Megasaurus. **(39)** Zug talks, wears amazing costumes, and loves to play games and tell stories. Zug is a feature player in the Dinosaur Discovery Kit, a package which includes software and coloring books.

(40) The Electric Cadaver, developed at Stanford University, provides computerized anatomy lessons for medical students. The system includes a laser disk of images connected to a Macintosh computer. Using the mouse attached to the computer, a student can point to a part of the body, press the mouse button, and obtain more detailed information about that part.

34

35

36

37

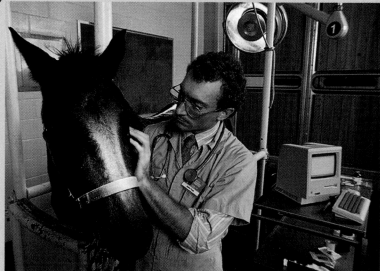

38

39

40

Photography

(41) This worker uses the computer to retouch and alter photographs. She first uses a digitizer to convert the photo to a computer-usable form. The photo then can be displayed on the screen, and she can change it in any way that suits her. The phrase "the camera never lies" should fall into disuse.

(42) This Renault was photographed, then stretched by computer for Grey Advertising.

(43) Headline: SAN FRANCISCO BAY FREEZES OVER! Well, not really . . . Two separate photos, the top and bottom of this picture, were digitized and combined by computer.

(44) Assorted buildings on an ordinary street in Charlotte, North Carolina were photographed, digitized into computer-usable form, and transformed by a computer into images of **(45)** the proposed Gateway Center, a classy new building complex.

41

42

43

46

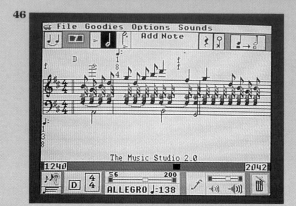

Music

With sophisticated software and a personal computer equipped with a special sound microchip, composers can have all the benefits of a music studio. The sound chip in the computer can simulate 15 different instruments, which can all play at once, allowing songs to be played with the sound of a symphony orchestra or a rock band. **(46)** On the screen, notes played by different instruments are represented by different colors. **(47)** Composers now keep their computers as close as their keyboards.

(48) Dartmouth music students use personal computers to study notation in an electronic music studio. All Dartmouth students take a "computer survival skills" course when they first arrive on campus.

47

48

8

Languages

A Survey

Five levels of program-
ming language—machine,
assembly, high-level, very
high-level, and natural—
are discussed in their historical context. Six widely
used languages are sur-
veyed: FORTRAN, COBOL,
BASIC, Pascal, Ada, and C.
Important features are
pointed out, and samples
of the languages them-
selves are presented. In
addition, other important
languages are described
briefly.

LEARNING OBJECTIVES

- Introduction to the levels of programming languages—machine, assembly, high level, very high level, and natural.
- Introduction to some important languages—FORTRAN, COBAL, BASIC, Pascal, Ada, and C.
- Brief introduction to other major languages: LISP, PROLOG, ALGOL, PL/I, APL, LOGO, PILOT, Smalltalk, FORTH, Modula-2, and RPG.

DISCUSSION QUESTION

What are some examples of the ambiguity of the English Language? (Present, lie, stew, fan, belt).

DISCUSSION QUESTION

Why do programming languages have a limited vocabulary?

TEST BANK

Mult. Choice   1-3
T/F   1
Matching A   1
Fill-in-the-Blank   1

LECTURE ACTIVITY

Play a recording of Abbott and Costello's *Who's On First*, to illustrate ambiguity of English. Draw baseball field on board and add names of players in respective positions as mentioned in recording. [This dialogue is included in many comedian treasury collections on LPs.]

Suppose that you manage an urban entertainment complex that features both domestic and foreign variety acts. You need to plan a year in advance, considering the availability of performers, the time of year, and a balanced selection. Several factors vary with the type of act and must be considered in the early planning stages, including local props, special lighting effects, union extras, work permits, and so forth. The set of tasks is complex and difficult to coordinate. You need to communicate with the computer because you have work that requires computer power.

The easiest way to communicate is to use an existing commercial software package. Using existing software is also the fastest and least expensive way if the software fits your needs. Commercial scheduling software may work for part of the problem. But, after consulting with a computer professional, it seems clear that most of the problems are too complicated and too company-specific for commercial software. You need a custom program and someone to write it: a programmer.

But your decisions are not over yet. What language will the programmer use to communicate with the computer? Surely not the English language, which—like any human language—is loosely configured, ambiguous, full of colloquialisms, slang, variations, and complexities. And, of course, the English language is constantly changing. A programming language is needed. A **programming language**—a set of rules that provides a way of instructing the computer what operations to perform—is anything but loose and ambiguous.

A programming language, the key to communicating with the computer, has certain definite characteristics. It has a limited vocabulary. Each "word" in it has precise meaning. Even though a programming language has limitations, it can still be used in a step-by-step fashion to solve complex problems. There is not, however, just one programming language; there are many.

7 Programming Languages

At present, there are over 200 programming languages—and these are the ones that are still being used. We are not counting the hundreds of languages that for one reason or another have fallen by the wayside over the years. Some of the languages have rather colorful names: INTELLECT, DOCTOR, UFO. Where did all these languages come from? Do we really need to complicate the world further by adding programming languages to the Tower of Babel of human languages?

Initially, programming languages were created by people in universities or in government and were devised for special functions. Some languages have endured because they serve special purposes

LECTURE HINT
Computer languages have
ambiguities also. Without warning
a compiler will take one possible
meaning, ignoring the rest. The
programmer must be aware of how
the compiler translates code. The
expression 2*3+4*5 equals 26 in
BASIC (multiplication before
addition); 46 in APL (right to left);
50 in VAX assembly (left to right);
and 70 in a language that does
addition before multiplication.

Even in one computer
language, different dialects may
treat the same expression
differently: right$(A$, 5) has one
meaning in VAX BASIC, and a
different meaning in Microsoft
BASIC.

In studying a language, it is
important to stick with one
implementation.

TEST BANK
Mult. Choice   4-20
T/F   2-30
Matching A   2-10
Matching B   1-3
Matching C   1
Matching D   10
Fill-in-the-Blank   2-16

in science, engineering, and the like. However, it soon became clear that some standardization was needed. It made sense for those working on similar tasks to use the same language.

There are several languages in common use today, and we will discuss the most popular ones later in the chapter. Before we turn to the hit parade of languages, however, we need to discuss levels of language.

7 Levels of Language

Programming languages are said to be "lower" or "higher," depending on how close they are to the language the computer itself uses (0s and 1s—low) or to the language people use (more English-like—high). We will consider five levels of language. They are numbered 1 through 5 to correspond to level, or generation. In terms of ease of use and capabilities, each generation is an improvement over its predecessors. The five generations of languages are:

1. Machine language
2. Assembly languages
3. High-level languages
4. Very high-level languages
5. Natural languages

Note the time line for the language generations in Figure 8-1. Let us look at each of these categories.

Figure 8-1 Language generations on a time line.   The darker shading indicates the period of greater use by applications programmers; the lighter shading indicates the time during which a generation faded from popular use or is expected to fade.

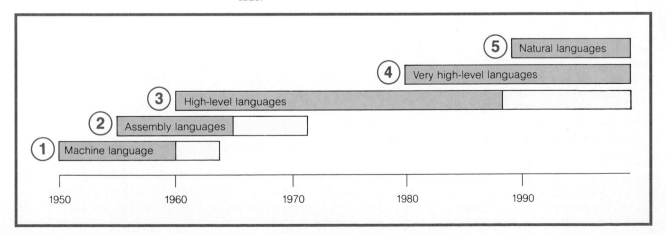

```
FD   71   431F   4153
F3   63   4267   4321
96   F0   426D
F9   10   41F3   438A
47   40   40DA
47   F0   4050
```

Figure 8-2   Machine language. True machine language is all binary—only 0s and 1s—but since an example would take too much space here, we are showing an example of machine language in the hexadecimal (base 16) numbering system. (The letters A through F in hexadecimal represent the numbers 10 through 15 in the decimal system.) The computer commands shown, taken from machine language for the IBM 360/370 series computers, are operation codes instructing the computer to divide two numbers, compare the quotient, move the result into the output area of the system, and set the result up so that it can be printed.

Machine Language

Humans do not like to deal in numbers alone—they prefer letters and words. But, strictly speaking, numbers are what machine language is. This lowest level of language, **machine language,** represents information as 1s and 0s—binary digits corresponding to the "on" and "off" electrical states in the computer.

An example of machine language is shown in Figure 8-2. This is a language taken from a mainframe computer. In the early days of computing, each computer had its own machine language, and programmers had rudimentary systems for combining numbers to represent instructions such as add and compare. Primitive by today's standards, the programs were not convenient for people to read and use. The computer industry moved to develop assembly languages.

Assembly Languages

Today, **assembly languages** are considered very low-level—that is, they are not as convenient for people to use as more recent languages. At the time they were developed, however, they were considered a great leap forward. Rather than using simply 1s and 0s, assembly language uses abbreviations or mnemonic codes to replace the numbers: A for Add, C for Compare, MP for Multiply, and so on. Although these codes were not English words, they were still—from the standpoint of human convenience—preferable to numbers alone.

The programmer who uses an assembly language requires a translator to convert his or her assembly language program into machine language. A translator is needed because machine language is the only language the computer can actually execute. The translator is an **assembler program,** also referred to as an assembler. It takes the programs written in assembly language and turns them into machine language. A programmer need not worry about the translating aspect; he or she need only write programs in assembly language. The translation is taken care of by the assembler.

Although assembly languages represent a step forward, they still have many disadvantages. A key disadvantage is that assembly language is detailed in the extreme, making assembly programming repetitive, tedious, and error prone. This drawback is apparent from Figure 8-3. Assembly language may be easier to read than machine language, but it is by no means crystal clear.

High-Level Languages

The first widespread use of **high-level languages** in the early 1960s transformed programming into something quite different from what it had been. The harried programmer working on the nitty-gritty details of coding and machines became a programmer

```
            PRINT NOGEN
PROG8       START 0
CARDFIL     DTFCD DEVADDR=SYSRDR,RECFORM=FIXUNB,IOAREA1=CARDREC,C
                  TYPEFLE=INPUT,BLKSIZE=80,EOFADDR=FINISH
REPTFIL     DTFPR DEVADDR=SYSLST,IOAREA1=PRNTREC,BLKSIZE=132
BEGIN       BALR  3,0                REGISTER 3 IS BASE REGISTER
            USING *,3
            OPEN  CARDFIL,REPTFIL  OPEN FILES
            MVC   PRNTREC,SPACES   MOVE SPACES TO OUTPUT RECORD
READLOOP    GET   CARDFIL          READ A RECORD
            MVC   OFIRST,IFIRST    MOVE ALL INPUT FIELDS
            MVC   OLAST,ILAST       TO OUTPUT RECORD FIELDS
            MVC   OADDR,IADDR
            MVC   OCITY,ICITY
            MVC   OSTATE,ISTATE
            MVC   OZIP,IZIP
            PUT   REPTFIL          WRITE THE RECORD
            B     READLOOP         BRANCH TO READ AGAIN
FINISH      CLOSE CARDFIL,REPTFIL  CLOSE FILES
            EOJ                    END OF JOB
CARDREC     DS    0CL80            DESCRIPTION OF INPUT RECORD
IFIRST      DS    CL10
ILAST       DS    CL10
IADDR       DS    CL30
ICITY       DS    CL20
ISTATE      DS    CL2
IZIP        DS    CL5
            DS    CL3
PRNTREC     DS    0CL132           DESCRIPTION OF OUTPUT RECORD
            DS    CL10
OLAST       DS    CL10
            DS    CL5
OFIRST      DS    CL10
            DS    CL15
OADDR       DS    CL30
            DS    CL15
OCITY       DS    CL20
            DS    CL5
OSTATE      DS    CL2
            DS    CL5
OZIP        DS    CL5
SPACES      DC    CL132''
            END   BEGIN
```

TRANSPARENCY MASTER #16
Figure #8-3

DISCUSSION QUESTION
What information is being
processed in Figure 8-3? Hint:
the I in IFIRST stands for input and
the FIRST is a person's first name.
CL10 indicates a character field of
10 characters in length. (IFIRST is
the first 10 characters of a
person's first name.)

Figure 8-3   Assembly language.   This example shows the IBM assembly language BAL used in a program for reading a record and writing it out again. The left column contains symbolic addresses of various instructions or data. The second column contains the actual operation codes to describe the kind of activity needed; for instance, MVC stands for "Move characters." The third column describes the data on which the instructions are to act. The far right column contains English-like comments related to the line or lines opposite. This entire page of instructions could be compressed to a few lines in a high-level language.

who could pay more attention to solving the client's problems. The programs could solve much more complex problems. At the same time they were written in an English-like manner, thus making them more convenient to use. As a result of these changes, the programmer could accomplish more with less effort.

Third-generation languages spurred the great increase in data processing that characterized the '60s and '70s. During that time the number of mainframes in use increased from hundreds to tens of thousands. The impact of third-generation languages on our society has been enormous.

Of course, a translator is needed to translate the symbolic statements of a high-level language into computer-executable machine language; this translator is usually a **compiler.** There are many compilers for each language and one for each type of computer. Since the machine language generated by one computer's COBOL compiler, for instance, is not the machine language of some other computer, it is necessary to have a COBOL compiler for each type of computer on which COBOL programs are to be run.

Some languages are created to serve a specific purpose, such as controlling industrial robots or creating graphics. Many languages, however, are extraordinarily flexible and are considered to be general-purpose. In the past, the majority of programming applications were written in BASIC, FORTRAN, or COBOL—all general-purpose languages. In addition to these three, other popular high-level languages today are Pascal, Ada, and C.

We noted that high-level languages relieve the programmer of burdensome hardware details. However, with this convenience comes an inevitable loss of flexibility. A few high-level languages such as C and FORTH offer some of the flexibility of assembly language together with the power of high-level languages, but these languages are not well suited to the beginning programmer.

We will discuss and demonstrate several high-level languages later in the chapter.

7 Very High-Level Languages

Languages called **very high-level languages,** are often known by their generation number. That is, they are called **fourth-generation languages,** or—more simply—**4GLs.** But if understanding the name is easy, the definition is not.

Definition
Will the real fourth-generation languages please stand up? There is no consensus about what constitutes a fourth-generation language. 4GLs are essentially shorthand programming languages. An operation that requires hundreds of lines in a third-generation language such as COBOL typically requires only five to ten lines in a 4GL. However, beyond the basic criterion of conciseness, 4GLs are difficult to describe.

Characteristics
Fourth-generation languages share some characteristics. The first is that they make a true break with the prior generation. Also, they are basically nonprocedural. A **procedural language** tells

IF IT'S TOO EASY, IT CAN'T BE PROGRAMMING

You have learned to do a job and do it well. You got the training, put in the time, and now you are a respected professional with a salary to match. You are a programmer. But now your hard-earned skills are being eroded in the marketplace: There are new languages that anyone can use. A quiet panic sweeps over you.

This little scene is common across the land. Programmers sometimes resist the new tools. Managers complain about underutilization of fourth-generation languages by professional programmers. There is another reason besides the fear of obsolescence: Old habits die hard. When someone has worked in a traditional language for many years, it is hard to make a switch to something new. There is the element of culture shock, and what is more, programmers sometimes think that if a language is easy to use, it must be for someone else. "Real" programmers have to use a language that is difficult.

the computer *how* a task is done: Add this, compare that, do this if something is true, and so forth—a very specific step-by-step process. The first three generations of languages are all procedural. In a **nonprocedural language,** the concept changes. Here, users define only *what* they want the computer to do; the user does not provide the details of just how it is to be done. Obviously, it is a lot easier and faster to just say what you want rather than how to get it. This leads us to the issue of productivity, a key characteristic of fourth-generation languages.

Productivity

Folklore has it that fourth-generation languages can improve productivity by a factor of 5 to 50. The folklore is true. Most experts say the average improvement factor is about 10—that is, you can be ten times more productive in a fourth-generation language than in a third-generation language. Consider this request: Produce a report showing the total units sold for each product, by customer, in each month and year, and with a subtotal for each customer. In addition, each new customer must start on a new page. A 4GL request looks something like this:

```
TABLE FILE SALES
SUM UNITS BY MONTH BY CUSTOMER BY PRODUCT
ON CUSTOMER SUBTOTAL PAGE BREAK
END
```

Even though some training is required to do even this much, you can see that it is pretty simple. The third-generation language COBOL, however, typically requires over 500 statements to fulfill the same request. If we define productivity as producing equivalent results in less time, then fourth-generation languages clearly increase productivity.

The Downside of 4GLs

Fourth-generation languages are not all peaches and cream and productivity. Fourth-generation languages are still evolving, and that which is still evolving cannot be fully defined or standardized. What is more, since many 4GLs are easy to use, they attract a large number of new users, who may then overcrowd the computer system. A common perception of 4GLs is that they do not make efficient use of machine resources; however, the benefits of getting an application finished more quickly can far outweigh the extra costs of running it.

4GL Benefits

Fourth-generation languages are beneficial because:

- They are results-oriented; they emphasize *what* instead of *how*.

- They improve productivity because programs are easy to write and change.

- They can be used with a minimum of training by both programmers and nonprogrammers.

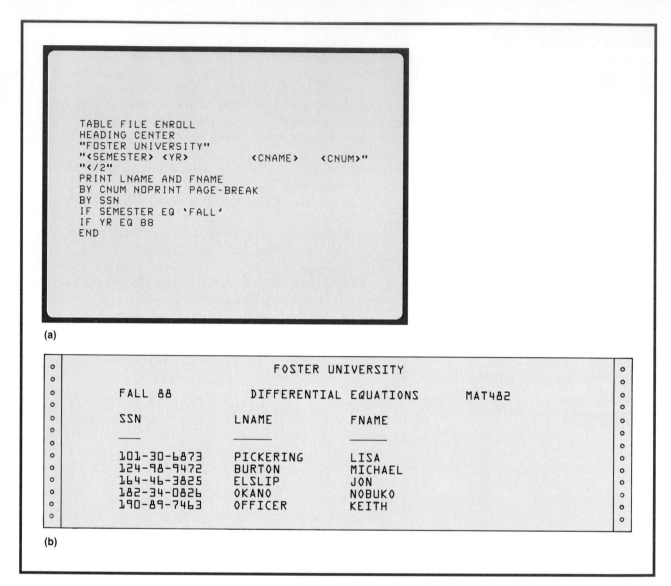

```
TABLE FILE ENROLL
HEADING CENTER
"FOSTER UNIVERSITY"
"<SEMESTER> <YR>          <CNAME>    <CNUM>"
"</2"
PRINT LNAME AND FNAME
BY CNUM NOPRINT PAGE-BREAK
BY SSN
IF SEMESTER EQ 'FALL'
IF YR EQ 88
END
```

(a)

```
                    FOSTER UNIVERSITY

    FALL 88          DIFFERENTIAL EQUATIONS        MAT482

    SSN              LNAME            FNAME
    ___

    101-30-6873      PICKERING        LISA
    124-98-9472      BURTON           MICHAEL
    164-46-3825      ELSLIP           JON
    182-34-0826      OKANO            NOBUKO
    190-89-7463      OFFICER          KEITH
```

(b)

TRANSPARENCY MASTER #17
Figure #8-4

Figure 8-4   An example of Focus.   (a) The code here produces (b) the Foster University roster for a differential equations class. To print field names in the heading, you must use angle brackets (<>) as delimiters. The sequence "</2" tells Focus to skip two lines after the heading. The program begins a new page every time the course number (CNUM) changes. The IF clauses prints records only if they pertain to the fall semester of 1988.

- They shield users from needing an awareness of hardware and program logic.

As recently as the late 1970s, few people believed that 4GLs would ever be able to replace third-generation languages by the 1980s. Now the transformation is well under way. Figure 8-4 illustrates a 4GL called Focus.

MINING BY COMPUTER

PROSPECTOR is an expert system developed by SRI International that predicts the potential for finding mineral deposits in a certain area. PROSPECTOR was developed by interviewing expert prospectors—geologists who are experts in locating underground mineral deposits. In the photo, geologist Dennis Cox (*left*), an authority on copper deposits, is being interviewed by an SRI knowledge engineer, who will convert Cox's knowledge about geology into thousands of rules a computer can use. By formalizing the rules that expert geologists follow and putting them into a computer system, the expert's knowledge is available for more people to use.

7 Natural Languages

The word *natural* has become almost as popular in computing circles as it is in the supermarket. But fifth-generation languages are, as you may guess, even more ill-defined than fourth-generation languages. They are most often called **natural languages** because of their resemblance to the "natural" spoken English language. And, to the computerphobic managers to whom these languages are now aimed, *natural* means human-like. Instead of being forced to key correct commands and data names in correct order, a manager tells the computer what to do by keying in his or her own words.

A manager can say the same thing any number of ways. For example, "Get me tennis racket sales for January" works just as well as "I want January tennis racket revenues." Such a request may contain misspelled words, lack articles and verbs, and even use slang. The natural language translates human instructions—bad grammar, slang, and all—into code the computer understands. If it is not sure what the user has in mind, it politely asks for further explanation.

Natural languages are sometimes referred to as knowledge-based languages because natural languages are used to interact with a base of knowledge on some subject. The use of a natural language to access a knowledge base is called a **knowledge-based system.** A species of knowledge-based systems is the expert system, although the terms for each type are often used interchangeably. An **expert system** offers the computer as an expert on some topic. The system's expertise is usually equivalent to that of a human expert and can be queried—asked questions—in a similar way. We will examine expert systems for business in Chapter 17.

The use of natural language to access a knowledge base is the foundation of **artificial intelligence.** Bill Gates, founder of the Microsoft Corporation, can be credited with a common-sense definition of artificial intelligence: "anything that makes software softer." In other words, the goal is to let the user focus on the task rather than the computer.

Consider this request that could be given in the 4GL Focus: "SUM ORDERS BY DATE BY REGION." If we alter the request and, still in Focus, say something like "Give me the dates and the regions after you've added up the orders," the computer will spit back the user-friendly version of "You've got to be kidding" and give up. But some natural languages can handle such a request. Users can relax the structure of their requests and increase the freedom of their interaction with the data.

Here is a typical natural language request:

```
REPORT THE BASE SALARY, COMMISSIONS AND YEARS OF SERVICE
BROKEN DOWN BY STATE AND CITY FOR SALESCLERKS IN NEW
JERSEY AND MASSACHUSETTS.
```

It seems that you cannot get much closer to conversational English than that.

LANGUAGES AND ARTIFICIAL INTELLIGENCE

Natural languages are associated with artificial intelligence (AI), a field of study that explores how computers can be used for tasks that require the human characteristics of intelligence, imagination, and intuition.

But how can a computer understand natural language when there is nothing very predictable about it? For example, consider these phrases: Alan sold Judy a book for five dollars. Judy bought a book for five dollars from Alan. Judy gave Alan five dollars in exchange for a book. The book that Judy bought from Alan cost five dollars. It takes a very sophisticated program (not to mention enormous memory) to unravel all these statements and see them as equivalent. Languages today are not up to the task. Progress is being made, but commercial systems available today are not this far along.

But we have made a start, using natural language to ask the computer questions on a variety of subjects—in other words, by using natural languages with expert systems. Expert systems promise to be invaluable productivity tools in manufacturing, education, the law, medicine, finance—almost every field requiring human expertise. But expert systems, by definition, are limited to a field of expertise. To imitate the functioning of the human mind, the machine with

artificial intelligence would have to be able to examine a variety of facts, not be limited to a single subject, and devise a solution to a problem by comparing those new facts to its vast storehouse of data from many fields. So far, artificial intelligence systems do not do original thinking. Nor can they match the performance of a truly superior intellect, a person who solves problems through original thought instead of using familiar patterns as a guide.

There are many arguments for and against crediting computers with the ability to think. Some say, for example, that computers cannot be considered intelligent because they do not compose like Beethoven or write like Shakespeare; the rejoinder is that most of us do not compose like Beethoven or write like Shakespeare—you do not have to be superhuman to be intelligent.

Look at it another way. Suppose you beat your brains out on a problem and then—Aha!—the solution comes to you as a jolt. Now, how did you do that? You do not know, and nobody else knows either. A big part of human problem solving seems to be that jolt of recognition, that ability to suddenly see things as a whole. Further experiments have shown that people rarely solve problems using step-by-step logic, the very thing that computers do best. Most modern com-

puters still chug through problems one step at a time. The brain beats computers at "Aha!" problem solving because it has millions of neurons working simultaneously.

So, can a computer think or not? Listen to Alan Turing. Several years ago, this English mathematician proposed a test of thinking machines. In the Turing Test, a human being is seated before two terminals that are connected to hidden devices. One terminal is connected to a different terminal run by another person, and the second terminal is connected to a computer. The individual is asked to guess, by carrying out conversations through the terminals, which is the person and which is the computer. If the human judge cannot tell the difference, the computer is said to have passed and is considered, for all practical purposes, a thinking machine.

But perhaps we are asking the wrong question: Will a computer ever *really* think? One possible answer: Who cares? If a machine can perform a task really well, does it matter if it *really* thinks? Still another answer is: Yes, machines will really think, but not as humans do. They lack the sensitivity, appreciation, and passion that mark some of our great human thinkers.

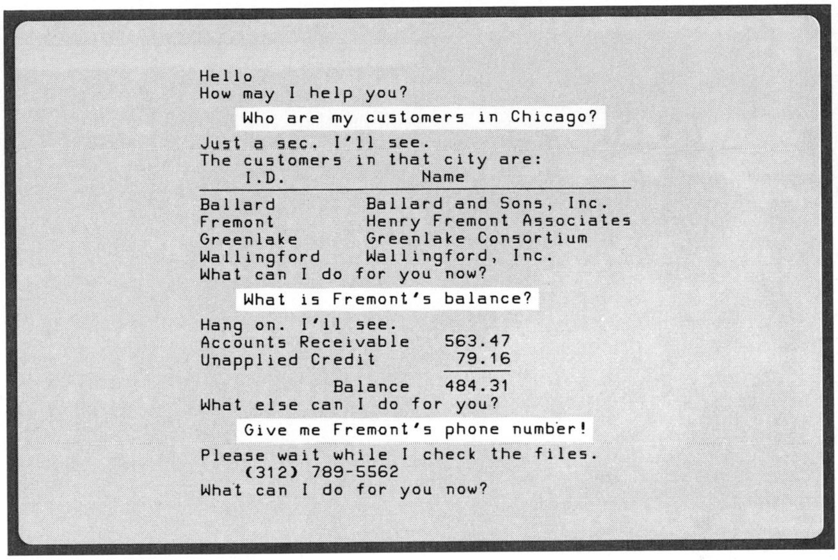

Figure 8-5 A natural language. This package, called Cash Management System, uses a language that is so "natural" that some might think it a little too cute, as in "Just a sec."

TRANSPARENCY MASTER #18
Figure #8-5

```
Hello
How may I help you?
    Who are my customers in Chicago?
Just a sec. I'll see.
The customers in that city are:
    I.D.            Name
Ballard         Ballard and Sons, Inc.
Fremont         Henry Fremont Associates
Greenlake       Greenlake Consortium
Wallingford     Wallingford, Inc.
What can I do for you now?
    What is Fremont's balance?
Hang on. I'll see.
Accounts Receivable    563.47
Unapplied Credit        79.16
            Balance    484.31
What else can I do for you?
    Give me Fremont's phone number!
Please wait while I check the files.
    (312) 789-5562
What can I do for you now?
```

An example of a natural language is shown in Figure 8-5. Natural languages excel at easy data access. Indeed, the most common application for natural languages is interacting with databases. So if we limit our needs to data queries, computer access for the masses seems to be at hand. However, fifth-generation languages are not yet ready to handle complicated logic, so they are not likely to be vehicles for professional programmers in the immediate future.

7 Choosing a Language

How do you choose the language in which to write your program? Perhaps you will use a particular language because it is the only one available at your installation. Perhaps your manager has decreed that everyone on your project will use a certain language. Perhaps you know only one language!

A sensible approach is to pick the language that is most suitable for your particular program application. The following sections on individual languages will give you an overview of the languages in common use. We describe these languages: FORTRAN, COBOL, BASIC, Pascal, Ada, and C—all third-generation languages in common use today. Special features of each language are noted, including the types of applications for which they are often used. Table 8-1 summarizes the applications for which these languages are usually used.

To accompany our discussion of FORTRAN, COBOL, BASIC, Pascal, Ada, and C, we will show a program and its output to give you a sense of what each language looks like. All these programs are designed to average numbers; in our sample output, we find the average of three numbers. Since we are performing the same task with

Table 8-1   Applications of some important programming languages

Language	Application
FORTRAN—FORmula TRANslator (1954)	Scientific
COBOL—COmmon Business-Oriented Language (1959)	Business
BASIC—Beginner's All-purpose Symbolic Instruction Code (1965)	Education, Business
Pascal—named after French inventor Blaise Pascal (1971)	Education, systems programming, scientific
Ada—named after Ada, the Countess of Lovelace (1980)	Military, general
C—evolved from the language B at Bell Labs (1972)	Systems programming, general

DISCUSSION QUESTION
Are all computer language names acronyms?

DISCUSSION QUESTION
Why are BASIC and COBOL still used when there are newer and more sophisticated languages?

LECTURE HINT
Research in FORTRAN was started in 1954. The first FORTRAN compiler was made available to the public in 1957.

all six programs, you will see some of the differences and similarities between the languages. We do not expect you to understand each line of these programs; they are here merely to let you see what each language looks like in a program. Figure 8-6 provides a flowchart and pseudocode for the task of averaging numbers. As we discuss each language, we will provide a program for averaging numbers that follows the logic shown.

7 FORTRAN: The First High-Level Language

Developed by IBM and introduced in 1954, **FORTRAN**—for FORmula TRANslator—was the first high-level language. FORTRAN is a scientifically oriented language—in the early days use of the computer was primarily associated with engineering, mathematical, and scientific research tasks. FORTRAN is still the most widely used language in the scientific community.

FORTRAN is noted for its brevity, and this characteristic is part of the reason why it remains popular. This language is very good at serving its primary purpose, which is execution of complex formulas such as those used in economic analysis and engineering. It is not, however, particularly useful for file processing or data processing; its control structures are quite limited, as are its means of describing data. Consequently, it is not very suitable for business applications. Moreover, there is no requirement to define data elements before they are used. This lack contributes to the language's simplicity and brevity but also makes FORTRAN susceptible to error.

Not all programs are organized in the same way. They vary depending on the language used. In many languages (such as COBOL) programs are divided into a series of parts. FORTRAN programs are

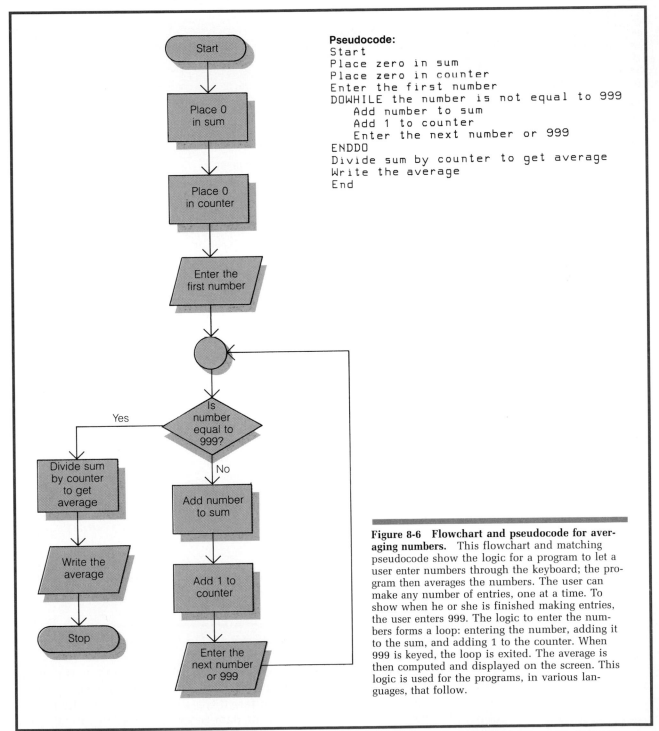

Pseudocode:
```
Start
Place zero in sum
Place zero in counter
Enter the first number
DOWHILE the number is not equal to 999
    Add number to sum
    Add 1 to counter
    Enter the next number or 999
ENDDO
Divide sum by counter to get average
Write the average
End
```

Figure 8-6   Flowchart and pseudocode for averaging numbers. This flowchart and matching pseudocode show the logic for a program to let a user enter numbers through the keyboard; the program then averages the numbers. The user can make any number of entries, one at a time. To show when he or she is finished making entries, the user enters 999. The logic to enter the numbers forms a loop: entering the number, adding it to the sum, and adding 1 to the counter. When 999 is keyed, the loop is exited. The average is then computed and displayed on the screen. This logic is used for the programs, in various languages, that follow.

DISCUSSION QUESTION
In Figure 8-6, is 999 part of the data to be averaged in this program?

Figure 8-7　A FORTRAN program and sample output. This program is interactive, prompting the user to supply data. (a) The first two lines are comments, as they are in the rest of the programs in this chapter. The WRITE statements send output to the screen in the format called for by the second numeral in the parentheses. The READ statements accept data from the user and place it in location NUMBER, where it can be added to the accumulated SUM. The IF statement checks for 999 and, when it is received, diverts the program logic to statement 2, where the average is computed. The average is then displayed. (b) This screen display shows the interaction between program and user.

TRANSPARENCY MASTER #21
Figure #8-7

```
C          FORTRAN PROGRAM
C          AVERAGING INTEGERS ENTERED THROUGH THE KEYBOARD
           WRITE (6,10)
           SUM = 0
           COUNTER = 0
           WRITE (6,60)
           READ (5,40) NUMBER
    1      IF (NUMBER .EQ. 999) GOTO 2
           SUM = SUM + NUMBER
           COUNTER = COUNTER + 1
           WRITE (6,70)
           READ (5,40) NUMBER
           GO TO 1
    2      AVERAGE = SUM / COUNTER
           WRITE (6,80) AVERAGE
   10      FORMAT (1X, 'THIS PROGRAM WILL FIND THE AVERAGE OF ',
         * 'INTEGERS YOU ENTER ',/1X, 'THROUGH THE ',
         * 'KEYBOARD. TYPE 999 TO INDICATE END OF DATA.',/)
   40      FORMAT (I3)
   60      FORMAT (1X, 'PLEASE ENTER A NUMBER   ')
   70      FORMAT (1X, 'PLEASE ENTER THE NEXT NUMBER   ')
   80      FORMAT (1X, 'THE AVERAGE OF THE NUMBERS IS ',F6.2)
           STOP
           END
```

(a)

```
THIS PROGRAM WILL FIND THE AVERAGE OF INTEGERS YOU ENTER
THROUGH THE KEYBOARD. TYPE 999 TO INDICATE END OF DATA.
PLEASE ENTER A NUMBER   6
PLEASE ENTER THE NEXT NUMBER   4
PLEASE ENTER THE NEXT NUMBER   11
PLEASE ENTER THE NEXT NUMBER   999
THE AVERAGE OF THE NUMBERS IS   7.00
```

(b)

not composed of different parts (although it is possible to link FORTRAN programs together); a FORTRAN program consists of statements one after the other. Different types of data are identified as the data is used. Descriptions for data records appear in format statements that accompany the READ and WRITE statements. Figure 8-7 shows a FORTRAN program and a sample output from the program.

GRACE M. HOPPER: "GRANDMA COBOL"

Rear Admiral Hopper (U.S. Navy, Retired), a Phi Beta Kappa graduate of Vassar College with an M.A. and Ph.D. from Yale University, joined the U.S. Naval Reserve in 1943. She was assigned to the Bureau of Ordinance Computation Project at Harvard, where she learned to program the first large-scale digital computer, the Mark I.

In 1948 she joined the Eckert–Mauchly Computer Corporation as senior mathematician. She later became senior programmer for the UNIVAC I, the first commercial large-scale electronic computer. There she pioneered in the development of the COBOL compiler and later became one of the prime movers in the development of the COBOL programming language in the 1950s.

Hopper has always delighted in confounding interviewers. Witness this exchange:

Interviewer: What do you think of the personal computer?

Hopper: It's a little bit ahead of the Mark I.

Interviewer: Well, what do you see as the next generation of personal computers?

Hopper: I don't know. It hasn't happened yet.

7 COBOL: The Language of Business

In the 1950s FORTRAN had been developed, but there was still no accepted high-level programming language appropriate for business. The U.S. Department of Defense in particular was interested in creating such a standardized language, and so it called together representatives from government and various industries, including the computer industry. These representatives formed **CODASYL**—COnference of DAta SYstem Languages. In 1959 CODASYL introduced **COBOL**—for COmmon Business-Oriented Language. The U.S. government offered encouragement by insisting that anyone attempting to win government contracts for computer-related projects had to use COBOL. The American National Standards Institute (ANSI) first standardized COBOL in 1968 and in 1974 issued standards for another version known as **ANS-COBOL.** And, after more than seven controversial years of industry debate, the standard known as **COBOL 85** was approved, making COBOL a more usable modern-day software tool. The principal benefit of standardization is that COBOL is relatively machine-independent—that is, a program written for one type of computer can be run with only slight modifications on another for which a COBOL compiler has been developed.

The principal feature of COBOL is that it is English-like—far more so than FORTRAN or BASIC. The variable names are set up in such a way that even if you know nothing about programming you can still understand the general purpose of a program. For example:

```
IF SALES-AMOUNT IS GREATER THAN SALES-QUOTA
    COMPUTE COMMISSION = MAX-RATE * SALES-AMOUNT
ELSE
    COMPUTE COMMISSION = MIN-RATE * SALES-AMOUNT.
```

Once you understand programming principles, it is not too difficult to add COBOL to your repertoire. COBOL can be used for just about any task related to business programming; indeed, it is especially suited to processing alphanumeric data such as street addresses, purchased items, and dollar amounts—the data of business. However, the feature that makes COBOL so useful—its English-like appearance and easy readability—is also a weakness because a COBOL program can be incredibly verbose. It is not usual for a programmer to sit down and bat out a quick COBOL program. In fact, there is hardly such a thing as a quick COBOL program; there are just too many program lines to write, even to accomplish a simple task. For speed and simplicity, BASIC, FORTRAN, and Pascal are probably better bets.

As you can see in Figure 8-8, a COBOL program is divided into four parts called divisions. The *identification division* identifies the program by name and often contains helpful comments as well. The *environment division* describes the computer on which the program

TEST BANK

Mult. Choice	26-32
T/F	37-45
Matching B	6-8
Matching D	9
Fill-in-the-Blank	20-27

Figure 8-8 A COBOL program and sample output. The purpose of the program and its results are the same as those of the FORTRAN program, but (a) the look of the COBOL program is very different. Note the four divisions. In particular, note that the logic in the procedure division uses a series of PERFORM statements, diverting logic flow to other places in the program. After a section has been performed logic flow returns to the statement after the one that called the PERFORM. DISPLAY writes to the screen and ACCEPT takes the user input. (b) This screen display shows the interaction between program and user.

TRANSPARENCY MASTER #22
Figure #8-8

```
****************************************************************
 IDENTIFICATION DIVISION.
****************************************************************
 PROGRAM-ID.   AVERAGE.
* COBOL PROGRAM
* AVERAGING INTEGERS ENTERED THROUGH THE KEYBOARD.
****************************************************************
 ENVIRONMENT DIVISION.
****************************************************************
 CONFIGURATION SECTION.
 SOURCE-COMPUTER.          H-P 3000.
 OBJECT-COMPUTER.          H-P 3000.
****************************************************************
 DATA DIVISION.
****************************************************************
 FILE SECTION.
 WORKING-STORAGE SECTION.
 01 AVERAGE        PIC ---9.99.
 01 COUNTER        PIC 9(02)        VALUE ZERO.
 01 NUMBER-ITEM    PIC S9(03).
 01 SUM-ITEM       PIC S9(06)       VALUE ZERO.
 01 BLANK-LINE     PIC X(80)        VALUE SPACES.
****************************************************************
 PROCEDURE DIVISION.
****************************************************************
 100-CONTROL-ROUTINE.
     PERFORM 200-DISPLAY-INSTRUCTIONS.
     PERFORM 300-INITIALIZATION-ROUTINE.
     PERFORM 400-ENTER-AND-ADD
             UNTIL NUMBER-ITEM = 999.
     PERFORM 500-CALCULATE-AVERAGE.
     PERFORM 600-DISPLAY-RESULTS.
     STOP RUN.
 200-DISPLAY-INSTRUCTIONS.
     DISPLAY
         "THIS PROGRAM WILL FIND THE AVERAGE OF INTEGERS YOU ENTER".
     DISPLAY
         "THROUGH THE KEYBOARD. TYPE 999 TO INDICATE END OF DATA.".
     DISPLAY BLANK-LINE.
 300-INITIALIZATION-ROUTINE.
     DISPLAY "PLEASE ENTER A NUMBER".
     ACCEPT NUMBER-ITEM.
 400-ENTER-AND-ADD.
     ADD NUMBER-ITEM TO SUM-ITEM.
     ADD 1 TO COUNTER.
     DISPLAY "PLEASE ENTER THE NEXT NUMBER".
     ACCEPT NUMBER-ITEM.
 500-CALCULATE-AVERAGE.
     DIVIDE SUM-ITEM BY COUNTER GIVING AVERAGE.
 600-DISPLAY-RESULTS.
     DISPLAY "THE AVERAGE OF THE NUMBERS IS ",AVERAGE.
```

(a)

```
THIS PROGRAM WILL FIND THE AVERAGE OF INTEGERS YOU ENTER
THROUGH THE KEYBOARD. TYPE 999 TO INDICATE END OF DATA.
PLEASE ENTER A NUMBER
 6
PLEASE ENTER THE NEXT NUMBER
 4
PLEASE ENTER THE NEXT NUMBER
 11
PLEASE ENTER THE NEXT NUMBER
999
THE AVERAGE OF THE NUMBERS IS    7.00
```

(b)

will be compiled and executed. It also relates each file of the program to the specific physical device, such as tape drive or printer, that will read or write the file. The *data division* contains the detailed information about data processed by the program, such as type of characters (whether numeric or alphanumeric), number of characters, and placement of decimal points. The *procedure division* contains the statements that give the computer specific instructions to carry out the logic of the program.

It has been fashionable for some time to criticize COBOL: It is old-fashioned, cumbersome, and inelegant. But this golden oldie is still with us. And all the criticism does not alter the fact that if you are interested in making money as a business programmer, COBOL is still your best bet.

TEST BANK
Mult. Choice   33-34, 37
T/F   46
Matching C   2
Matching D   1
Fill-in-the-Blank   28-29

BASIC: For Beginners and Others

We have already touched on **BASIC**—Beginners' All-purpose Symbolic Instruction Code—in Chapter 7 (and we go into it in some detail in Appendix A); here we will present a quick overview. BASIC is a common language that is easy to learn. Developed at Dartmouth College, BASIC was introduced by John Kemeny and Thomas Kurtz in 1965 and was originally intended for use by students in an academic environment. In the late 1960s it became widely used in interactive time-sharing environments in universities and colleges. The use of BASIC has extended to business and personal mini- and microcomputer systems.

The primary feature of BASIC is one that may be of interest to many readers of this book: BASIC is easy to learn, even for a person who has never programmed before. Thus, the language is used often in training students in the classroom. BASIC is also used by nonprogramming people, such as engineers, who find it useful in problem solving. However, BASIC does have limitations; it is not a language suitable for complex programs. An example of a BASIC program and its output is shown in Figure 8-9.

TEST BANK
Mult. Choice   35-36
T/F   47
Matching C   3
Matching D   2
Fill-in-the-Blank   30

LECTURE HINT
Why is the language that Niklaus Wirth (pronounced Veert) introduced in Europe in 1971 popular?

Pascal: The Language of Simplicity

Named for Blaise Pascal, the seventeenth-century French mathematician, **Pascal** was developed as a teaching language by a Swiss computer scientist, Niklaus Wirth, and first became available in 1971. Since that time it has become quite popular, first in Europe and now in the United States, particularly in universities and colleges offering computer science programs.

The foremost feature of Pascal is that it is simpler than other languages—it has fewer features and is less wordy than most. Pascal

```
 10 REM   BASIC PROGRAM
 20 REM   AVERAGING INTEGERS ENTERED THROUGH THE KEYBOARD.
 30 PRINT "THIS PROGRAM WILL FIND THE AVERAGE OF INTEGERS YOU ENTER"
 40 PRINT "THROUGH THE KEYBOARD. TYPE 999 TO INDICATE END OF DATA."
 50 PRINT
 60 SUM=0
 70 COUNTER=0
 80 PRINT "PLEASE ENTER A NUMBER"
 90 INPUT NUMBER
100 IF NUMBER=999 THEN 160
110 SUM=SUM+NUMBER
120 COUNTER=COUNTER+1
130 PRINT "PLEASE ENTER THE NEXT NUMBER"
140 INPUT NUMBER
150 GOTO 100
160 AVERAGE=SUM/COUNTER
170 PRINT "THE AVERAGE OF THE NUMBER IS ";AVERAGE
180 END
```

(a)

```
THIS PROGRAM WILL FIND THE AVERAGE OF INTEGERS YOU ENTER
THROUGH THE KEYBOARD. TYPE 999 TO INDICATE END OF DATA.
PLEASE ENTER A NUMBER
?6
PLEASE ENTER THE NEXT NUMBER
?4
PLEASE ENTER THE NEXT NUMBER
?11
PLEASE ENTER THE NEXT NUMBER
?999
THE AVERAGE OF THE NUMBERS IS     7
```

(b)

Figure 8-9   A BASIC program.   (a) A BASIC program looks very much like a FORTRAN program. The main difference is in the input and output statements. Here, PRINT displays data right in the statement on the screen. INPUT accepts data from the user. (b) This screen display shows the interaction between program and user.

has become very popular in college computer science departments. Because of its limited input/output capabilities, it is unlikely, in its present form, to have a serious impact on the business community. But Pascal is making large strides in the microcomputer market as a simple yet sophisticated alternative to BASIC. An example of a Pascal program and a sample output is shown in Figure 8-10.

```
PROGRAM AVERAGE (INPUT, OUTPUT);
(* PASCAL PROGRAM *)
(* AVERAGING INTEGERS ENTERED THROUGH THE KEYBOARD *)
VAR
   COUNTER, NUMBER, SUM : INTEGER;
   AVERAGE : REAL;
BEGIN
WRITELN ('THIS PROGRAM WILL FIND THE AVERAGE OF INTEGERS YOU ENTER');
WRITELN ('THROUGH THE KEYBOARD. TYPE 999 TO INDICATE END OF DATA.');
WRITELN;
SUM := 0;
COUNTER := 0;
WRITELN ('PLEASE ENTER A NUMBER');
READ (NUMBER);
WHILE NUMBER <> 999 DO
   BEGIN
   SUM := SUM + NUMBER;
   COUNTER := COUNTER + 1;
   WRITELN ('PLEASE ENTER THE NEXT NUMBER');
   READ (NUMBER);
   END;
AVERAGE := SUM / COUNTER;
WRITELN ('THE AVERAGE OF THE NUMBERS IS',AVERAGE :6:2);
END.
```

(a)

```
THIS PROGRAM WILL FIND THE AVERAGE OF INTEGERS YOU ENTER
THROUGH THE KEYBOARD. TYPE 999 TO INDICATE END OF DATA.
PLEASE ENTER A NUMBER
6
PLEASE ENTER THE NEXT NUMBER
4
PLEASE ENTER THE NEXT NUMBER
11
PLEASE ENTER THE NEXT NUMBER
999
THE AVERAGE OF THE NUMBERS IS  7.00
```

(b)

TRANSPARENCY MASTER #24
Figure #8-10

Figure 8-10 A Pascal program and sample output. (a) Comments are from (* to *). Each variable name must be declared. The symbol := assigns a value to the variable on the left; the symbol <> means not equal to. WRITELN by itself puts a blank line on the screen. (b) This screen display shows the interaction between program and user.

7 Ada: The Language of Standardization?

Is any software worth over $25 billion? Not any more, according to Defense Department experts. In 1974 the U.S. Department of Defense had spent that amount on all kinds of software for a hodgepodge of languages for its needs. The answer to this problem turned out to be a new language called **Ada**—named for Countess Ada Lovelace, "the first programmer" (see Appendix C). Sponsored by the Pentagon, Ada was originally intended to be a standard language for weapons systems, but it has also been used for successful commercial applications. Introduced in 1980, Ada has the support not only of the defense establishment but also of such industry heavyweights as IBM and Intel, and Ada is even available for some microcomputers. Although some industry experts have said Ada is too complex (futurist Charles Lecht describes it as a klutz), others say that it is easy to learn and that it will increase productivity. Indeed, some experts believe that it is by far a superior commercial language to such standbys as COBOL and FORTRAN. An example of an Ada program and a sample output is shown in Figure 8-11.

Widespread adoption of Ada is likely to take years, as even its most optimistic advocates admit. Although there are many reasons for this (the military services, for instance, have different levels of enthusiasm for it), probably its size—which may hinder its use on microcomputers—and complexity are the greatest barriers.

7 C: A Sophisticated Language

A language that lends itself to systems programming (operating systems and the like) as well as to more mundane programming tasks, C was invented by Dennis Ritchie at Bell Labs in 1972. Its unromantic name evolved from earlier versions called A and B. C produces code that approaches assembly language in efficiency while still offering high-level language features such as structured programming. C contains some of the best features from other languages, including PL/I and Pascal. C compilers are simple and compact. Because C is independent of any particular machine's architecture, it is suitable for writing "portable" programs—that is, programs that can be run on more than one type of computer.

Although C is simple and elegant, it is not simple to learn. It was developed for gifted programmers, and the learning curve is steep indeed. Straightforward tasks may be solved easily in C, but complex problems require mastery of the language.

```
--   ADA PROGRAM
--   AVERAGING INTEGERS ENTERED THROUGH THE KEYBOARD.
with TEXT_IO; use TEXT_IO;
procedure AVERAGE is
    package INT_IO is new INTEGER_IO(INTEGER);
    AVERAGE:                    FLOAT                           ;
    COUNTER:                    INTEGER            := 0;
    NUMBER:                     INTEGER                         ;
    SUM:                        INTEGER            := 0;
begin
    PUT_LINE("THIS PROGRAM WILL FIND THE AVERAGE OF INTEGERS YOU ENTER");
    PUT_LINE("THROUGH THE KEYBOARD. TYPE 999 TO INDICATE END OF DATA.");
    NEW_LINE;
    PUT("PLEASE ENTER A NUMBER");
    INT_IO.GET(NUMBER);
    while NUMBER /= 999 loop
        SUM := SUM + NUMBER;
        COUNTER := COUNTER + 1;
        PUT("PLEASE ENTER THE NEXT NUMBER");
        INT_IO.GET(NUMBER);
    end loop;
    AVERAGE := SUM/COUNTER;
    PUT("THE AVERAGE OF THE NUMBERS IS");
    FLO_IO.PUT(AVERAGE);
end AVERAGE;
```

(a)

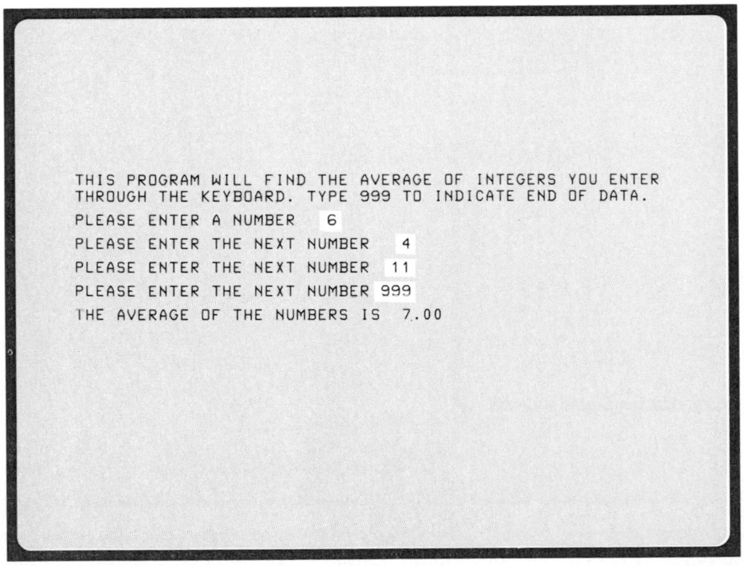

```
THIS PROGRAM WILL FIND THE AVERAGE OF INTEGERS YOU ENTER
THROUGH THE KEYBOARD. TYPE 999 TO INDICATE END OF DATA.
PLEASE ENTER A NUMBER   6
PLEASE ENTER THE NEXT NUMBER   4
PLEASE ENTER THE NEXT NUMBER  11
PLEASE ENTER THE NEXT NUMBER 999
THE AVERAGE OF THE NUMBERS IS  7.00
```

(b)

TRANSPARENCY MASTER #25
Figure #8-11

Figure 8-11 An Ada program and sample output.   (a) Comments begin with a double hyphen. Ada requires that each variable be declared before the logic begins. NEW_LINE displays a blank line, and PUT_LINE displays data on the screen. The symbol /= means is not equal to. (b) This screen display shows the interaction between program and user.

```
/* C PROGRAM */
/* AVERAGING INTEGERS ENTERED THROUGH THE KEYBOARD */
main()
{ float average;
  int counter = 0; number; sum = 0;
  printf("THIS PROGRAM WILL FIND THE AVERAGE OF INTEGERS YOU ENTER\n");
  printf("THROUGH THE KEYBOARD. TYPE 999 TO INDICATE END OF DATA.\n\n");
  printf("PLEASE ENTER A NUMBER");
  scanf("%d",&number);
  while (number != 999)
    {
        sum = sum + number;
        counter ++ ;
        printf("PLEASE ENTER THE NEXT NUMBER");
        scanf("%d",&number);
    }
  average = sum / counter;
  printf("THE AVERAGE OF THE NUMBERS IS %F ",AVERAGE);
}
```
(a)

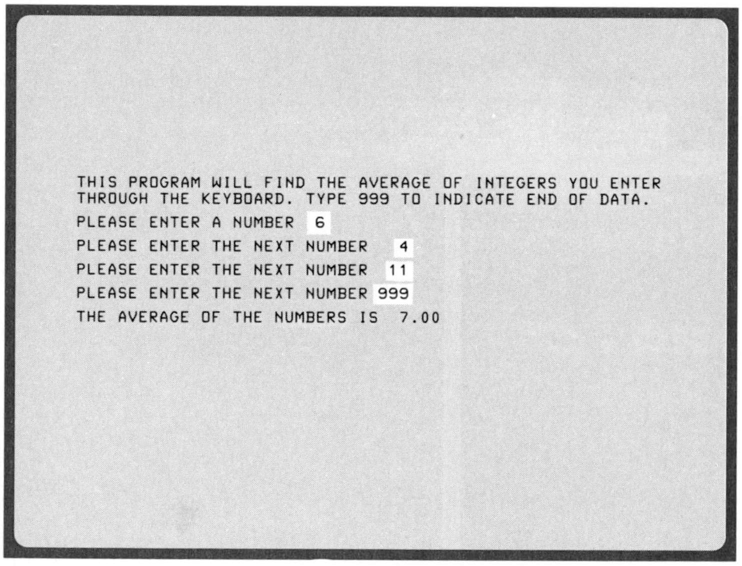

```
THIS PROGRAM WILL FIND THE AVERAGE OF INTEGERS YOU ENTER
THROUGH THE KEYBOARD. TYPE 999 TO INDICATE END OF DATA.
PLEASE ENTER A NUMBER  6
PLEASE ENTER THE NEXT NUMBER   4
PLEASE ENTER THE NEXT NUMBER  11
PLEASE ENTER THE NEXT NUMBER 999
THE AVERAGE OF THE NUMBERS IS  7.00
```
(b)

TRANSPARENCY MASTER #26
Figure #8-12

Figure 8-12   A C program and sample output.   (a) Comments are between /* and */. All variable names, such as number, must be declared. The command printf sends output to the screen and scanf takes data from the user. (b) This screen display shows the interaction between program and user.

An interesting sidenote is that the availability of C on personal computers has greatly enhanced the value of personal computers for budding entrepreneurs. That is, a software cottage industry can use the same basic tool—the language C—used by established software companies like Microsoft. An example of a C program and a sample output is shown in Figure 8-12.

TEST BANK
Mult. Choice   42-52
T/F   52-63
Matching B   9
Matching C   4-10
Matching D   5-8
Fill-in-the-Blank   31-38

LECTURE HINT
Other computer languages, by
category:

Statistics:
SPS--Statistical Package for Social
Science
SA--Statistical Analysis System
Pennsylvania State's Mini-Tab
package
Simulation:
GPSS--General Purpose
Simulation System:
Simscript, Simula, Dynamo
**From Bell Telephone
Laboratories:**
Lex--to write to compilers
YACC--to write compilers.
Miscellaneous:
CORAL--multiple processors
Mathematica--symbolic math
Maxzyma--symbolic math
SQ--data base inquiry language
COGO--for civil engineering.

7 Some Other Languages

The languages just described are probably the major ones used today. Many of them occupy their privileged positions for no reason other than they got there first or they were backed by powerful organizations. But other languages, though not as popular as the most common ones, have still managed to flourish. You are apt to see these mentioned, and it is important to know about them. Notice that many of them are special-purpose languages, a fact that helps to account for their more limited use. Here, in no particular order, are some other noteworthy languages.

ALGOL
Standing for ALGOrithmic Language, **ALGOL** was introduced in 1960. Though popular in Europe, it has never really caught on in the United States. ALGOL was developed primarily for scientific programming and is considered the forerunner of PL/I and Pascal.

LISP
Developed in 1958 at the Massachusetts Institute of Technology by John McCarthy, **LISP**—short for list processing—is designed to process nonnumeric data—that is, symbols, such as characters or words. LISP can be used interactively at a terminal. It is a popular language for writing programs dealing with artificial intelligence.

PROLOG
A relatively recent addition to the short list of artificial-intelligence programming languages, **PROLOG** (PROgramming in LOGic) is receiving increasing attention as a tool for natural language programming. It was invented in 1972 by Alan Colmerauer at the University of Marseilles, but it only attracted widespread attention in 1979, when a more efficient version was introduced. PROLOG was selected by the Japanese as the official language of their fifth-generation computer project, and it has become popular with many artificial-intelligence professionals.

PL/I
Introduced in 1964, **PL/I**—for Programming Language One—was sponsored by IBM. It was designed as a compromise for both scientific and business use. PL/I is quite flexible; in fact, it is easy to learn the rudiments by studying examples. However, being all things to all people, some critics claim, makes the language so loaded down with options that it loses some of its usefulness.

APL
Short for A Programming Language, **APL** was conceived by Kenneth Iverson and was introduced by IBM in 1968. APL is

powerful, interactive, and particularly suited to table handling—that is, to processing groups of related numbers in a table. APL has a score of funny symbols, and that is one reason you would have trouble running the language on your home computer—it uses many symbols that are not part of the familiar ASCII character set. Some of these symbols represent very powerful operations. Having a large number of operators means that the APL compiler must be rather large, so it is apt to be available only on systems with large memories.

LOGO

If you overhear a couple of programmers (or even school-teachers) using the word *turtle* in conversation, it is a fair guess they are talking about **LOGO.** A dialect of LISP developed at the Massachusetts Institute of Technology by Seymour Papert, it is known at this time as a language that children can use. The "turtle" is actually a triangular pointer on the screen that responds to a few simple commands such as FORWARD and LEFT. The language is interactive, which means that a person can learn to use LOGO through dialogue sessions with the computer. Figure 8-13 gives an example of LOGO program design.

PILOT

Invented in 1973, **PILOT** was originally designed to introduce children to computers. PILOT is now most often used to write computer-aided instruction in all subjects. It is especially suited for such instructional tasks as drills and tests. PILOT is not a good choice for complex computational problems.

Smalltalk

Most interaction with a computer consists of "remembering and typing." With the **Smalltalk** language, however, you "see and print" instead. Here is the way it works: The keyboard is used to enter text into the computer, but all other tasks are accomplished with the use of a mouse. You move the mouse around to direct the movement of a pointer on the screen. You press a button on the mouse to select a command. Invented by Alan Kay at the Palo Alto (California) Research Center and developed by Xerox Corporation, Smalltalk constitutes a dramatic departure from traditional computer science because it supports an especially visual computer system. The basis of Smalltalk is that it is an object-oriented language rather than a procedure-oriented language: The interaction is between people and things or classes of objects.

FORTH

Released by Charles Moore in 1975, **FORTH** was designed for real-time control tasks (such as guiding astronomical telescopes) as well as assorted business and graphics programs. But it

LECTURE HINT
Smalltalk was the first object-oriented language. Apple used it in writing the Macintosh operating system.

Objects may be defined. Other objects can inherit characteristics from them. For example, say a vehicle is defined as an object with certain characteristics. Sub-objects could be a car, truck, bike, train. Sub-objects of a truck could be an 18-wheeler or pick-up. The vehicle characteristics of a pick-up do not have to be specified again, as it inherits those characteristics.

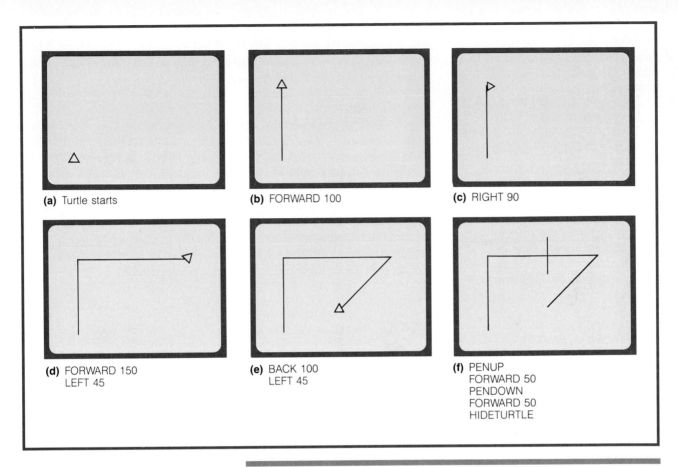

(a) Turtle starts

(b) FORWARD 100

(c) RIGHT 90

(d) FORWARD 150
LEFT 45

(e) BACK 100
LEFT 45

(f) PENUP
FORWARD 50
PENDOWN
FORWARD 50
HIDETURTLE

Figure 8-13   LOGO logic.   The "turtle," or triangular pointer, can be moved with a simple sequence of LOGO commands. FORWARD moves the turtle in the direction the apex is facing; BACK moves the turtle backward. The number following one of these commands indicates the length of the line to be drawn. RIGHT and LEFT followed by a number indicates the direction the turtle is to be rotated and the number of degrees it is to be rotated. PENUP and PENDOWN raise and lower the "pen"—the turtle leaves a trace when it moves with the pen down. HIDETURTLE causes the turtle to disappear from the screen.

was also designed to make the best possible use of a computer's memory and speed. Thus, FORTH is an excellent language for microcomputers; a typical FORTH program runs much faster and uses much less memory than an equivalent BASIC program. Today, FORTH is available on almost every kind of computer, from micros to mainframes. FORTH requires little computer memory, but only skilled programmers can use it properly.

Modula-2

Pascal programmers have no trouble recognizing **Modula-2** because the two languages look almost identical. Perhaps this

LECTURE ACTIVITY

For a rapidfire question and answer session, ask the class to match the language with the description.

- Developed at Bell Labs? (C)
- Developed at MIT? (LISP)
- Developed at Xerox? (Smalltalk)
- Developed by a Frenchman? (Pascal)
- Developed for the Department of Defense? (Ada)
- Developed to replace FORTRAN, ALGOL, and COBOL? (PL/I)
- Developed while teaching computer science? (Pascal)
- Developed while teaching grade-school students? (Logo or Pilot)
- Developed for artificial intelligence? (Prolog)
- Developed to simplify the writing of reports? (RPG)
- The first scientific language developed in Europe, with profound influence on later languages? (ALGOL)
- Developed by a committee? (COBOL)
- Higher level language closest to English? (COBOL)
- First scientific higher level language still in common use? (FORTRAN)
- Two languages based on Pascal? (C, Modula-2)
- Easiest common language to learn programming? (BASIC)
- Commonly used to implement commercial software packages? (C)
- Language resulting in fastest compact machine code? (Assembly)

STUDENT PROJECT

The English language contains many ambiguities, making it unsuitable for computer programming. Prepare a simple computer program that contains words with multiple meanings. Students can identify the ambiguities and correct the program.

should not be surprising, since both languages were invented by Niklaus Wirth. Pascal was intended to be a teaching language, a task it performs very well. But Modula-2 shines where Pascal does not—it is specifically designed to write systems software.

RPG

The problem-oriented language **RPG**—for Report Program Generator—was designed to solve the particular problem of producing business reports. It is also capable of doing some file updating. Developed at IBM, RPG was introduced in 1964 and was intended primarily for small computer systems. An updated version called RPG II was introduced in 1970 and extended the language's original capabilities. A still more recent version, RPG III, is an interactive language that uses menus to give the programmer easy choices to plan programs. RPG is so easy to learn that businesspeople believe they get the maximum return on their investment.

7 Some Advice

TEST BANK
Mult. Choice   53

If you are planning to be an applications programmer, there is a good chance that you will take your first steps in BASIC or Pascal, then receive more formal training in a business-oriented language—probably COBOL. Perhaps you will be able to add another language like FORTRAN or C. Many new programmers go into the job world with these language tools. But notice something: All these are third-generation languages.

This chapter has addressed the direction of language use. It seems clear that fourth-generation languages are not just the wave of the future, they are here now. But they are offered at only a few schools. Why is this? There are several reasons. No 4GL has emerged as number one, the way COBOL did for business. Could a school dare to turn out 4GL programmers without a clear signal from the community of local employers? (The schools that have replaced their COBOL courses with a 4GL are almost all in large urban environments where, presumably, some of everything is needed.) Other obstacles—lack of a 4GL compiler or the money for one, a need for teacher training, and the difficulty of fitting a 4GL into the existing curriculum—can be overcome once the big question is answered: which 4GL?

Meanwhile, where does this leave you? Your training in third-generation languages is valuable because it teaches you to think analytically and gives you skills in languages that are still in demand. But you must be alert for opportunities on the job to learn a 4GL. Most people who program in 4GLs learned to do so from employer-sponsored classes. Be ready to take the opportunity when it comes your way.

MICROCOMPUTERS IN ACTION

Computing Power at Stanford University

Clearly, a major university teaches a variety of computer languages to students who would be programmers. But a campus computer system often goes significantly beyond teaching programming languages. At Stanford University (Palo Alto, California) distributed computing—using personal computers—provides many services and dominates the campus.

Campus computing falls into four major areas. The university's data center features mainframe computers and databases that administrators can access via terminals or their own personal computers. Students use academic computing services for programming or computer applications. Students can use a computer system to search for books in the campus library by title, author, subject, or keyword. And, finally, computers join telephone, television, and data communications networks as part of a campuswide strategy for communications of all types.

It was not always this way. Stanford's computer decisions were dictated by the prevailing technology, which changed over time from a centralized mainframe to distributed minicomputers to vast numbers of personal computers disbursed in all directions. Personal computers gave power—rather suddenly—to indi-

viduals, who could cook up their own files and pursue their own computing interests.

It is possible to graduate from Stanford without touching a computer, but it is increasingly unlikely. Many professors have gotten into the act, relating computers directly to their classes. Physics professors, for example, wrote programs to illustrate ballistic equations. An English professor wrote a program to help student directors convert Shakespeare to the stage. A history professor constructed a game

that lets students learn how to survive, and perhaps prosper, in seventeenth-century France.

Stanford students have taken to personal computers with a vengeance. Many of them have their own personal computers, which manufacturers make available at a significant discount. Between the students on campus and the hundreds who call in from their computers at home, Stanford is about as microcomputer-saturated as it can be.

Summary and Key Terms

- A **programming language** is a set of rules for instructing the computer what operations to perform. A programming language has a limited vocabulary, has a precise meaning for each word, and can be used to solve complex problems in a step-by-step manner.

- Programming languages are described as being "lower" or "higher," depending on how close they are to the language the computer itself uses (0s and 1s—low) or to the language people use (more English-like—high). There are five main levels, or generations, of languages: (1) machine language, (2) assembly language, (3) high-level language, (4) very high-level language, and (5) natural language.

- **Machine language,** the lowest level, represents information as 1s and 0s—binary digits corresponding to the "on" and "off" electrical states in the computer.

- **Assembly languages** use letters as abbreviations or mnemonic codes to replace the 0s and 1s of machine language. An **assembler program** is used to translate the assembly language into machine language. Although assembly languages provide great flexibility in tapping a computer's capabilities, they also have disadvantages. For instance, assembly languages vary according to the type of computer and are extremely detailed.

- **High-level languages** are written in an English-like manner. Each high-level language requires a different **compiler,** or translator program, for each type of computer on which it is run.

- **Very high-level languages,** also called **fourth-generation languages** or **4GLs,** are basically nonprocedural. A **nonprocedural language** defines only *what* the computer should do, without detailing the procedure. A **procedural language** tells the computer specifically *how* to do the task.

- Although fourth-generation languages still require further standardization, they have a number of clear benefits, including primary emphasis on results (*what*) rather than procedure (*how*), improved productivity, and less required training for both programmers and users.

- Fifth-generation languages are often called **natural languages** because they resemble "natural" human language.

- The use of a natural language to access a knowledge base is called a **knowledge-based system.** One type of knowledge-based system, the **expert system,** offers the computer as an expert on some topic.

- Knowledge-based systems are closely related to **artificial intelligence,** with its emphasis on easier interaction between users and computers. However, natural languages are not yet able to handle complicated logic.

- The first high-level language, **FORTRAN** (FORmula TRANslator), is a scientifically oriented language that was introduced by IBM in 1954. Its brevity makes it suitable for executing complex formulas.

- **COBOL** (COmmon Business-Oriented Language) was introduced in 1959 by **CODASYL** (COnference of DAta SYstem Languages) as a standard programming language for business. The American National Standards Institute (ANSI) standardized COBOL in 1968, again in 1974 (in a version called **ANS-COBOL**), and more recently in a version known as **COBOL 85.** Since COBOL is English-like, it is useful for processing business data such as street addresses and purchased items, but the wordiness of COBOL programs means a sacrifice of speed and simplicity.

- A COBOL program has four divisions: identification, environment, data, and procedure.

- When **BASIC** (Beginners' All-purpose Symbolic Instruction Code) was developed at Dartmouth and introduced in 1965, it was intended for instruction. Now its uses include business and personal computer applications.

- **Pascal,** named for the French mathematician Blaise Pascal, first became available in 1971. It is popular in college computer courses.

- **Ada,** named for Countess Ada Lovelace, was introduced in 1980 as a standard language for weapons systems. Although it also has commercial uses, experts disagree regarding how easy it is to learn.

- Invented by Bell Labs in 1974, **C** offers high-level language features such as structured programming while producing code that is almost as efficient as assembly language. C is suitable for writing "portable" programs that can be run on more than one type of computer.

- Other important languages include: **ALGOL,** popular in Europe for scientific programming; **LISP,** used for nonnumeric data processing and artificial intelligence programs; **PROLOG,** popular for natural language programming; **PL/I,** designed for scientific and business uses; **APL,** used for processing related numbers in tables; **LOGO,** designed as an interactive language that children can use; **PILOT,** used for computer-aided instruction; **Smalltalk,** designed as an object-oriented language; **FORTH,** known for its very efficient use of a computer's memory and speed; **Modula-2,** a Pascal look-alike designed for writing systems software; and **RPG** (for Report Program Generator), a problem-oriented language for producing business reports.

Review Questions

1. In general, how do programming languages differ from human language?

2. What do *high* and *low* mean in reference to programming languages?

3. Explain how the following types of languages differ: machine language, assembly language, and high-level language.

4. Explain why fourth-generation languages represent increased productivity when compared to third-generation languages.

5. Discuss the advantages and limitations of natural languages.

6. How does COBOL differ from FORTRAN and BASIC?

7. How are BASIC and Pascal similar? How do they differ?

8. Discuss the appropriate and inappropriate uses of each of the following languages: FORTRAN, COBOL, and Pascal.

9. Discuss the advantages of the C language.

10. Briefly identify the uses of each of the following languages: ALGOL, LISP, PROLOG, PL/I, APL, LOGO, PILOT, Smalltalk, FORTH, Modula-2, and RPG.

Discussion Questions

1. Discuss the advantages of standardizing a programming language.

2. Discuss why a particular language stays in use or goes out of use.

3. Do you think there will be less demand for programmers as languages become easier to use? Explain.

4. Consider the six program examples (Figures 8-7 through 8-12) that find the average of three integers. How would you change the programs to find the sum of only two integers?

Chapter 9. Operating Systems: The Hidden Software

9

Operating Systems

The Hidden Software

In this chapter we describe an operating system, the set of programs that allows the computer to control resources, execute programs, and manage data. We also consider the special problems related to sharing resources through multiprogramming or time-sharing. After a brief look at translators and service programs, we consider generic operating systems and then give special attention to operating systems for personal computers.

LEARNING OBJECTIVES
- Appreciating the need for operating systems.
- Understanding the benefits of multiprogramming and time-sharing.
- Understanding the special problems related to sharing resources.
- Knowledge of translators and service programs.
- Introduction to generic operating systems.
- Introduction to operating systems for personal computers.

LECTURE HINT
An Apple II user will be unaware that an operating system is loading an application into memory after the computer is turned on. To use many applications on the IBM PC, the user must interact with the operating system.

TEST BANK
Mult. Choice	1-5
T/F	1-7
Matching A	1-2
Fill-in-the-Blank	1-3

LECTURE ACTIVITY
Demonstrate several games on an Apple (or similar) computer, to show the minimal interaction with the operating system. Contrast this by demonstrating the interaction with the operating system of the IBM PC and popular applications.

Some commercial software packages, especially games for personal computers, hide the operating system from the user. Just about anyone can quickly learn to use packaged software that handles the operating system in a way that is transparent—that is, not noticeable—to the user. But many software packages for personal computers do not make the operating system transparent. Before you can use the software, you must load an operating system into the computer. An **operating system** is a set of programs that allows the computer to control resources, execute programs, and manage data.

The work of operating systems is hidden from view, performing many necessary tasks behind the scenes. Once you have some understanding of those chores, you will be glad that you do not have to be bothered with them. You must, however, be able to interact with an operating system at some rudimentary level.

To use the power of the computer, you need some training. No book can tell you about all the operating systems that exist and how to use them. However, we can examine the basic functions of operating systems. In this chapter we will present the rationale for operating systems and give some idea of how they work. Many operating systems concepts apply only to large, multiuser computers, and we will begin there. But we will finish with a more detailed discussion of operating systems for personal computers.

7 Operating Systems: Powerful Software in the Background

An operating system allows the computer system to manage its own resources. Those resources include the central processing unit, memory, secondary storage devices, and various input/output devices like printers. In a broader sense resources also include data, programs, and people. Figure 9-1 gives a conceptual picture of operating system software as a cushion between the hardware and applications programs such as a word processing program on a personal computer or a payroll program on a mainframe. In other words, whether or not you are aware of it, using any software application requires that you invoke—call into action—the operating system as well. Whether you are a user of software or a programmer, you will come to appreciate the fact that the operating system takes care of many chores automatically.

Let us pause briefly to trace the beginnings of operating systems and imagine what computer use was like without them. Consider the early days of computing, when the primary goal was to get a computer that was bigger and faster. In those days a computer system executed only one program at a time. (This may not seem peculiar in the context of a personal computer, but remember that we are now talking about big, expensive computers.) This meant that all the system's resources—the central processing unit, all the memory and

Figure 9-1   A conceptual diagram of an operating system.   Closest to the user are applications programs—software that helps a user compute a payroll or play a game or calculate the trajectory of a rocket. The operating system is the set of programs between the applications programs and the hardware.

TRANSPARENCY ACETATE #9A
Figure #9-1

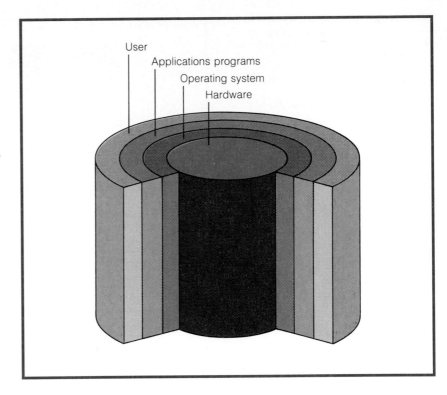

User
Applications programs
Operating system
Hardware

DISCUSSION QUESTION
What was inefficient about the use of early big computers?

secondary storage at hand, and all peripheral devices such as printers—were available on demand for that one program. However, it also meant that these components were idle most of the time; while a record was being read from tape, for instance, the CPU and printer were inactive.

Time was also wasted while the system waited for the computer operator to finish tasks: to set up tapes, push buttons on the console, and so on. A program came to the end of its run, and the entire system was idle while the operator got the next job ready to run.

All this was inefficient use of an expensive machine. To improve the efficiency of computer operations, operating systems were introduced in the 1960s. An operating system, as we have said, is a set of programs. It handles many chores implicitly, without being told to do so by each individual programmer. An operating system has three main functions:

■ to control computer system resources

■ to execute computer programs

■ to manage data

The control programs, one part of the operating system, minimize operator intervention so that the computer operations flow smoothly and without interruption. The most important program in the system is the **supervisor program,** most of which remains in memory. It controls the entire operating system and calls in other

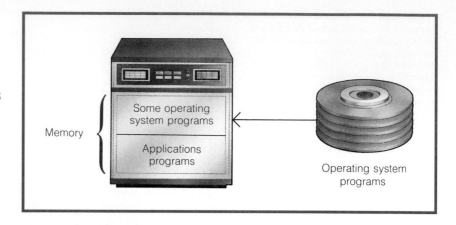

operating system programs from disk storage as needed (Figure 9-2). These operating system programs stay in memory while they are executing. But they do not remain in memory all the time; that would be an inefficient use of space. To free up space in memory, the supervisor program returns other operating system programs to disk storage when they are not in use.

The operating system improves efficiency in two ways: (1) It is the medium for cooperation among users, helping them make the best use of computer system resources (memory, the central processing unit, peripheral devices, and so on) so that everyone benefits. (2) It invokes translators and other programs to take care of certain common tasks. This helps free applications programmers from repetitive, machine-oriented details so that they can concentrate on solving problems for clients.

The operating system, in summary, is not hocus-pocus, not a collection of tricks done with mirrors. It is just a set of programs that performs useful functions. Let us now examine some of the various ways operating systems help in sharing resources.

7 Sharing Resources

We have noted the inefficiency of running just one program at a time on a big computer and indicated that all that has changed. Indeed it has. Such a computer can now handle many programs at the same time—although we are not saying that the programs necessarily run simultaneously. Before we explain that, let us acknowledge some related questions that often come up when computer users first realize that their applications program is "in there" with all those other programs.

Question: If there are several other programs in memory at the same time as my program, what keeps the programs from getting mixed up with one another?

Answer: The operating system.

Question: And if my program and another program both want to use the CPU at the same time, what decides which program gets it?

Answer: The operating system.

Question: But what if one of the other programs gets in an endless loop and won't give up the CPU? Who is going to step in and set things right?

Answer: The operating system.

Question: Well, the printer must be a problem. If we all need it, what prevents our output files from coming out in one big jumble?

Answer: The operating system!

This litany may be tedious, but it does make a point: The operating system programs anticipate all these problems so that you, as a user or programmer, can share the computer's resources with minimum concern about the details of how it is done.

We begin with the basic process of sharing resources, called multiprogramming, then move to a variation called time-sharing.

TRANSPARENCY ACETATE #9C
Multiprogramming

7 Multiprogramming

Multiprogramming means that two or more programs are being executed concurrently on a computer and are sharing the computer's resources. What this really means is that the programs are taking turns; one program runs for a while, then another one. The key word here is *concurrently* as opposed to *simultaneously*. If there is only one central processing unit, for example (the usual case), it is not physically possible that more than one program use it at the same time—that is, simultaneously. But one program could be using the CPU while another does something else such as writing a record to the printer. Concurrent processing means that two or more programs are using the central processing unit in the same time frame—during the same hour, for instance—but not at the exact same time. *Concurrent*, in other words, means that one program uses one resource while another program uses another resource. This gives the illusion of simultaneous processing. As a result, there is less idle time for the computer system's resources.

Concurrent processing is effective because CPU speeds are so much faster than input/output speeds. During the time it takes to execute a read instruction for one program, for example, the CPU can execute several calculation instructions for another program. If the first program is in memory by itself, however, the CPU is idle during the read time.

We emphasize concurrent processing here because, except for personal computers, most computers today use concurrent process-

DISCUSSION QUESTION
How is an interrupt handled by an operating system?

LECTURE HINT
When an interruption occurs, the operating system saves information on the current job. When the user returns, the operating system identifies at which step the interruption occurred and can continue.

Watching a movie on a VCR when the phone rings, the "user" puts the VCR on pause. When the "user" returns, the VCR resumes playing the movie.

LECTURE HINT
Multiple interruptions can occur. Operating systems classify interrupts on a priority bases. The highest-priority interrupts are processed first. If the U.S. president, the college president, the dean of the school and the department chairperson place phonecalls to the same individual, they would be answered in the same way the computer processes highest priority interrupts.

DISCUSSION QUESTION
How do event- and time-driven systems differ?

ing. That is because these computers each have only a single CPU. Recall the discussion of parallel processing in Chapter 3 on the central processing unit. **Parallel processing** uses multiple CPUs, a feature that permits *simultaneous* processing.

Multiprogramming is **event-driven.** This means that programs share resources based on events that take place in the programs. Normally, a program is allowed to complete a certain activity (event), such as a calculation, before relinquishing the resource (the central processing unit, in this example) to another program that is waiting for it.

The operating system implements multiprogramming through a system of interrupts. An **interrupt** is a condition that causes normal program processing to be suspended temporarily. If, for example, a program instructs the computer to read a record, the program is interrupted and the operating system takes over to pursue this activity. Meanwhile, the program waiting for the record relinquishes control of the central processing unit to another program; the computer may then proceed to execute calculations in this second program. When the record for the first program has been read, the interrupt is over; that program may then continue to execute, subject to the availability of the CPU. Thus, although to the programmer it seems as if the program is executing continuously from start to finish, in fact it is being constantly interrupted as the operating system allocates the computer system resources among different programs.

Programs that run in an event-driven multiprogramming environment are usually batch programs. Typical examples are programs for payroll, accounts receivable, sales and marketing analysis, financial planning, quality control, and stock reporting.

7 Time-Sharing

The concurrent use of one machine by several people is called **time-sharing.** Time-sharing, a special case of multiprogramming, is usually **time-driven** rather than event-driven. A common approach is to give each user a **time slice**—typically, a few milliseconds or even microseconds—during which the computer works on that user's tasks. However, the operating system does not wait for completion of the event; at the end of the time slice, the resources are taken away from the user and given to someone else. This is hardly noticeable to the user: When you are sitting before a terminal in a time-sharing system, the computer's response time will be quite short—fractions of a second—and it will seem as if you have the computer to yourself. **Response time** is the time between your typed computer request and the computer's reply. Even if you are working on a calculation and the operating system interrupts it, sending you to the end of the line until other users have had their turns, you may not notice that you have been deprived of service. Not all computer systems give ideal service all the time, however; if a computer system is trying to serve too many users at the same time, response time may deteriorate.

DISCUSSION QUESTION
How do round-robin and high-priority systems differ?

Notice that, generally speaking, you as the user do not have control over the computer system. In a time-sharing environment the operating system has actual control because it controls the users by allocating time slices. Giving the users the processor in turns is called **round-robin scheduling;** Figure 9-3 shows this type of operation. However, sometimes a particular user will, for some reason, be entitled to a higher priority than other users. Higher priority translates to faster and better service. A common method of acknowledging higher priority is for the operating system to give that user more turns. Suppose, for example, that there are five users who would normally be given time slices in order: A-B-C-D-E. If user B is assigned a higher priority, the order could be changed to A-B-C-B-D-B-E-B, giving B every other turn.

Typical time-sharing applications are credit checking, point-of-sale systems, engineering design, airline reservations, and hospital information systems. Each of these systems has several users who need to share the system resources.

TRANSPARENCY ACETATE #9D
Figure #9-3

Figure 9-3   Round-robin scheduling.   The computer gives each user a turn in circular fashion.

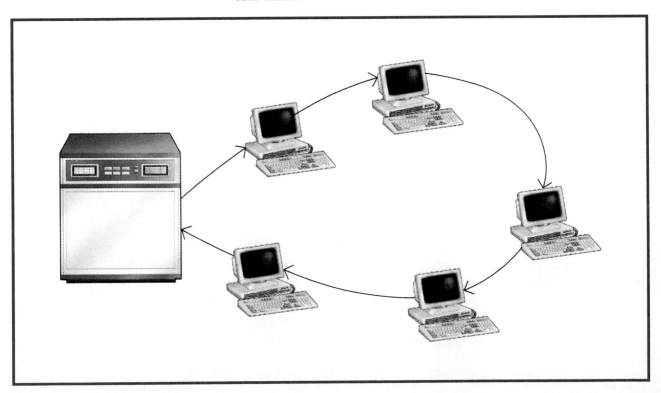

DISCUSSION QUESTION
On a highly secure system, can one program interfere with another program of the same or higher priority? Explain.

LECTURE HINT
A deadlock is similar to an 18-wheeler blocking an intersection. Cars approaching in all four directions can move neither forward nor backward.

    Some deadlocks have solutions. In the above example, a policeman orders a car into the left lane. Cars in back move forward enough to allow the 18-wheeler in back to no longer block the intersection. Then the cars blocked by that 18-wheeler can move (the police will not let them continue around the block, lest a new deadlock occur). Finally, the car in the left lane moves back in line.

    Sometimes there is no solution to the deadlock other than to shut down the system and cancel all jobs. This is drastic. Most systems can sense when a deadlock might occur, and take measures to prevent it.

7 Managing Shared Resources: The Traffic Cop

When several programs share the same computer resources, special problems of control must be considered. Just as a traffic cop controls the flow of vehicles, someone or something must determine which program will be executed next. For example, a given program must be able to access needed devices. Memory space must be available to the program, and that program must be protected from inadvertent interference from other programs. We will now consider how the operating system handles some of these types of problems.

7 Resource Allocation

How does the operating system actually fairly allocate various resources of the computer system—such as the central processing unit, memory, secondary storage and input/output devices— to the various programs as they are needed? **Resource allocation** is the process of assigning resources to certain programs for their use. Those same resources are deallocated—removed—when the program using them is finished, then reallocated elsewhere.

A program waiting to be run by the computer is placed on disk, with other waiting programs. A scheduling program, part of the operating system, selects the next job from the input queue. This decision is based on such factors as memory requirements, priority, and devices needed. In other words, the selection is based to some extent on whether available resources can satisfy the needs of the waiting program.

In the course of the resource allocation, the operating system must consider the input/output devices available and their use. For example, at any given moment, the operating system knows which program is using which particular tape drive and knows which devices are free and can be allocated to a program waiting in the input queue. The scheduling program would not allow a job to begin, for example, if it needed three tape drives and only two were currently available.

It is theoretically possible for two programs to need resources during processing that are unavailable to them; each may want a resource held captive by the other. What is more, neither may be willing to give up the resource it is holding until it gets the one the other is holding, a condition known as a **deadlock.** Note the example in Figure 9-4. Most operating systems are able to anticipate and thus prevent deadlocks; others force one of the contenders to back off after the fact.

Memory also needs to be allocated, but this special resource merits its own section.

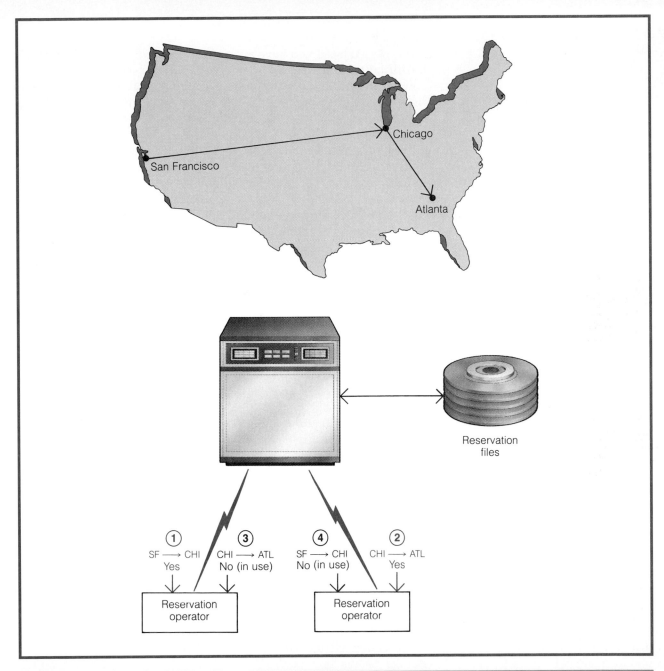

TRANSPARENCY ACETATE #9E
Figure #9-4

Figure 9-4   A deadlock. Each reservation operator, it just so happens, has a customer who wants to fly from San Francisco to Chicago to Atlanta. When an operator wants to make a reservation for a customer, the flight record must be made temporarily unavailable to other operators, lest one operator wipe out another's updates. In this case, let us suppose that ① one operator takes the record for the San Francisco to Chicago flight, while ② the other operator begins with the Chicago to Atlanta flight. ③ When the first operator tries to get the Chicago–Atlanta segment, it is unavailable because the other operator is using it. If the first operator holds on to the San Francisco–Chicago record while waiting for Chicago–Atlanta, ④ he or she might wait forever because the other operator might not give up Chicago–Atlanta until he or she gets San Francisco–Chicago.

7 Memory Management

What if you have a very large program, for which it might be difficult to find space in memory? Or what if several programs are competing for space in memory? These questions are related to memory management. **Memory management** is the process of allocating memory to programs and of keeping the programs in memory separate from each other.

There are many methods of memory management. Some systems simply divide memory into separate areas, each of which can hold a program. The problem is how to know how big the areas, sometimes called partitions or regions, should be; at least one of them should be large enough to hold the largest program. Some systems use memory areas that are not of a fixed size—that is, the sizes can change to meet the needs of the current assortment of programs. In either case—whether the areas are of a fixed or variable size—there is a problem with slivers of memory between programs. When these are too small to be used, space is wasted.

Foreground and Background

DISCUSSION QUESTION
How do foreground and background differ? Which has higher priority?

Large all-purpose computers often divide their memory into foreground and background areas. The **foreground** is for programs that have higher priority. A typical foreground program is in a time-sharing environment, with the user at a terminal awaiting response. The **background,** as the name implies, is for programs with less pressing schedules and, thus, lower priorities. Typical background programs are batch programs in a multiprogramming environment. Foreground programs are given privileged status—more turns for the central processing unit and other resources—and background programs take whatever they need that is not currently in use by another program. Programs waiting to run are kept on the disk in **queues** suitable to their job class, as you can see in Figure 9-5.

This discussion has been purposely general, but the principles do apply to many large computers. Another technique, is virtual storage, which—as you will see—expands the memory management possibilities.

Virtual Storage

Many computer systems manage memory by using a technique called **virtual storage** (also called **virtual memory**). Virtual storage means that part of the program is stored on disk and is brought into memory for execution only as needed. (Again, the delay in time may not be noticeable.) The user appears to be using more memory space than is actually the case. Since only part of the program is in memory at any given time, the amount of memory needed for a program is minimized. Memory, in this case, is considered **real storage,** while the secondary storage holding the rest of the program is considered virtual storage.

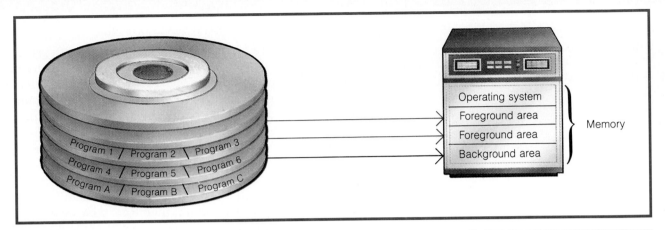

TRANSPARENCY ACETATE #9F
Figure #9-5

Figure 9-5 Programs waiting in queues. These programs are waiting on disk in queues organized by program class. That is, time-sharing programs (1 through 6) wait in their own queue for a foreground area to open up, and batch programs (A through C) wait in a queue for a background area to be free.

LECTURE HINT
Some operating systems use segmentation instead of paging. A program/data segment is a logical unit that works together. It may vary in length. Though segmentation may result in fewer swaps between main memory and secondary memory, main memory may be fragmented--left with unusable fragments of memory. If main memory is wasted, fewer programs will run simultaneously.

Virtual storage can be implemented in a variety of ways. Consider the paging method, for example. Again, suppose you have a very large program, which means there will be difficulty finding space for it in the computer's memory. Remember that memory is shared among several programs. If your program is divided into smaller pieces, it will be easier to find places to put those pieces. This is essentially what paging does. **Paging** is the process of dividing a program into equal-size pieces called **pages** and storing them in equal-size memory spaces called **page frames.** All pages and page frames are the same fixed size—typically, 2K or 4K bytes. The pages are stored in memory in *noncontiguous* locations—that is, locations not necessarily next to each other.

Even though the pages are not right next to each other in memory, the operating system is able to keep track of them. It does this through a page table, which lists the number of pages that are part of the program and the beginning addresses of areas in memory where they are placed.

Memory Protection

In a multiprogramming environment it is theoretically possible for the computer, while executing one program, to destroy or modify another program by transferring it to the wrong memory locations. That is, without protection, one program might accidentally hop into the middle of another, causing destruction of data and general chaos. To avoid this problem, the operating system confines each program to certain defined limits in memory. If a program inadvertently transfers to some memory area outside those limits, the operating system terminates the execution of that program. This process of keeping your program from straying into others' programs and their programs from yours is called **memory protection.**

7 Spooling

Suppose you have a half dozen programs active at a given moment, but your system has only one printer. If all programs took turns printing out their output a line or two at a time, interspersed with the output of other programs, the resulting printed report would be worthless. To get around this problem, a process called **spooling** is used: Each program writes onto a disk each file that is to be printed. When the entire program is on the disk, spooling is complete, and the disk files are printed intact (Figure 9-6).

Spooling also addresses another problem—relatively slow printer speeds. Writing a record on disk is much faster than writing that same record on a printer. A program, therefore, completes execution more quickly if records to be printed are written temporarily on disk instead. The actual printing can be done at some later time when it will not slow the program execution. Some installations use a separate (usually smaller) computer dedicated exclusively to the printing of spooled files.

7 Translators and Service Programs

Most of the tasks just described in the section on sharing resources are done by the operating system without applications programmer involvement. Although, as a programmer you may need to make requests for input and output devices, generally speaking, you do not need to give specific instructions on the use of these operating system features. Activities such as paging and spool-

Figure 9-6 Spooling. Program output that is destined for the printer is written first to a disk—spooled—and later transferred to a printer.

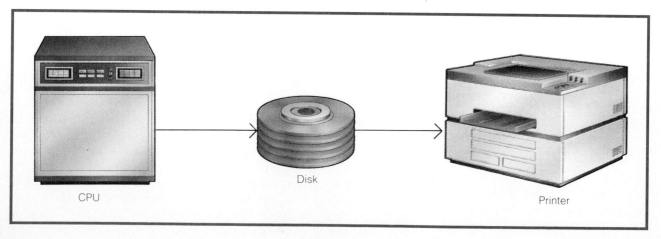

CPU   Disk   Printer

ing go on without your explicit commands. In the following discussion, however, we will describe situations that do require specific instructions to the operating system. Since the commands vary from computer to computer, we will make no attempt to include them here. The discussion is general and is applicable to most computer systems.

One more point: Strictly speaking, translators and service programs are not part of the operating system. These programs are invoked by the operating system. We include them in this chapter because, like operating systems, they perform standard services and are not directly related to specific applications programs.

7   Translators and the Link/Loader

When you write a program in BASIC, COBOL, or a similar high-level language, you need a **translator,** a program that translates your language into machine language that the computer can understand. There are three types of translators. If you are using a high-level language, the translator program is usually a **compiler,** which translates your program all at once before the program is executed. Sometimes, high-level languages are translated using an **interpreter,** which translates and executes your program one instruction at a time. If you are using an assembly language, you would use a translator called an **assembler.** Compilers, interpreters, and assemblers are programs that use your programs as input data, and in this case your program is called the **source module** (also called a source program or source code).

Compilers and assemblers produce three possible outputs: (1) an object module, (2) diagnostic messages, and (3) a source program listing. The **object module** is a version of your program that is now in machine language. **Diagnostic messages** inform you of **syntax errors.** Syntax errors are not errors in logic but errors in use of the language—errors that could be caused by mistakes in typing or because you did not understand how to use the language. If you have diagnostic messages, your program probably did not compile. (Sometimes, however, the messages are warning messages, which tell you of minor errors that do not prevent compilation.) The **source program listing** is a list of your program as you wrote it. In most cases you will refer to the listing right on the screen, but it is also useful to print the listing at regular intervals. You can use the source program listing to find any corrections necessary to your program.

There are many potential compilers—one for every language and every type of computer on which the language can be used. Thus, for any particular machine, you will have to use a COBOL compiler if you are running a program in COBOL and a C compiler if you are running a program in C.

LECTURE HINT
Some computers have several different compilers for the same language. A student and a research scientist would both use FORTRAN. Each would have individual requirements for diagnostic hints and execution. Two different FORTRAN compilers would optimize the specific needs of each user.

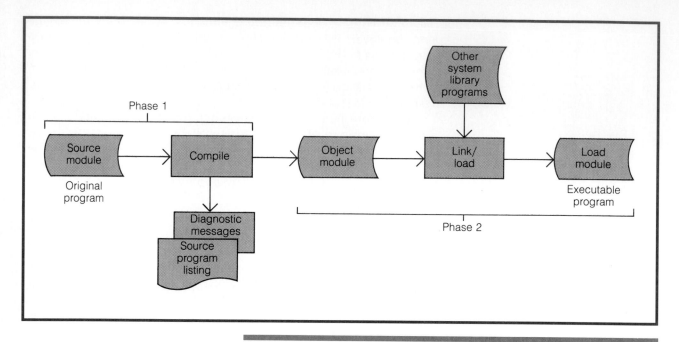

Phase 1

Source module — Compile — Object module — Link/load — Load module

Original program

Other system library programs

Executable program

Diagnostic messages

Source program listing

Phase 2

Figure 9-7   Preparing your program for execution.   Your original program, the source module, is compiled into an object module, which represents the program in machine language. The compiler may produce diagnostic messages, indicating syntax errors. A listing of the source program may also be output from the compiler. After the program successfully compiles, the object module is linked with system library programs, as needed, and the result is an executable load module.

DISCUSSION QUESTION
What is the purpose of the linker?

Figure 9-7 shows what generally happens during the process of writing and correcting a program. The object module produced is often considered temporary because if you are in the testing phase of program development, you will be correcting errors. Since the program is going to be changed, it will be recompiled. Notice in the figure that after the object module is ready there is a **link/load phase.** The object module of your program may be linked with prewritten, standard programs before it is run on the computer. The link/load program (also called the linkage editor) is used to add such prewritten programs to your program. These other programs are usually stored on disk in a system library. An example of a standard program is one that computes a square root. By calling in the standard program and adding it to your own, you are spared the tedious process of writing out all the steps of computing the square root. The output from the link/load step is called the **load module.** Stored on disk, the load module is now ready to be read into memory and executed.

Because an interpreter translates and executes your program directly, one instruction at a time, neither an object module nor prior diagnostics are generated. Thus, a disadvantage of using an interpreter is that syntax errors may not be discovered until the program is executed. Interpreters are used, for the most part, with BASIC on microcomputers.

7 Utility Service Programs

Why reinvent the wheel? Duplication of effort is what **utility programs** are supposed to avoid. Many repetitive file-handling tasks can be handled easily by prewritten standard programs, once certain information (such as record length) has been specified. Utility programs perform file conversions and sort/merge operations.

DISCUSSION QUESTION
What utility programs are typically available on computer systems?

File-handling utility programs convert files from one form to another (disk to tape, disk to disk, tape to printer, and so on) and handle the general logic of reading a file from one place and writing it to another. In the course of using these utility programs, you can usually specify certain options. For instance, if the utility program is concerned with printer output, you can elect to do a number of things that will improve the report appearance, such as put in headings, add page numbers, and double space the lines.

To use a sort/merge utility, the programmer specifies the input file name and the file output, then indicates which fields are to be sorted and where they are located in the records. The utility program then performs these operations. For instance, if you wish to sort a file by Social Security number, you indicate in which column the number starts and the length of the field (in this case nine characters) and whether you wish to have records sorted in ascending or descending order. A merging operation combines two sequenced files into one file. For example, two files, each arranged by Social Security number, could be merged into a single file containing all the records from both files in order by Social Security number.

Thus far in this chapter, we have examined general properties and services of operating systems. Now we turn to some specific trends in operating systems, especially those related to personal computers.

TEST BANK
Mult. Choice   45-46
T/F   57-63
Matching C   10
Matching D   5

7 The UNIX Phenomenon

Once upon a time when you bought a computer, the operating system came with the hardware. First it was free, later not free, but in the large mainframe world, operating systems still are usually defined by the vendor, with the user silently acquiescing.

But some changes have occurred in recent years. There is a trend toward buying what is known as a **generic operating system**—that is, an operating system with a more general nature that works with more than one manufacturer's computer system. Generic operating systems are frequently created by software companies. There are several generic operating systems, but we will discuss the one that is particularly influential: UNIX.

LECTURE HINT
Thompson and Ritchie were originally working on a huge Multics operating system for a large GE computer. But Bell Labs withdrew from that costly project, leaving Thompson and Ritchie without a project. They developed their own operating system on an idle PDP-7 (later on an idle PDP-11), using almost the opposite philosophy of Multics.

LECTURE HINT
Bell Labs charged very little for UNIX because, in an anti-trust suit, the federal government restricted Bell Labs profits to the phone business. Neither the UNIX operating system nor the hardware could be sold at a profit without breaking government rules. Most of the computer equipment they built was used inside the company, and not sold to the public.

DISCUSSION QUESTION
Why does UNIX have disadvantages in certain environments?

TEST BANK
Mult. Choice   47
T/F   64-65
Matching D   6

7 Emerging UNIX

UNIX was developed in 1971 by Ken Thompson and Denis Ritchie at AT&T's Bell Laboratories for use on Bell's DEC minicomputers. The designers were surprised to see UNIX become the dominant operating system of the computer industry during the late 1970s and early 1980s. How did this come about?

Part of the reason may involve a social factor, not the software itself—namely, the "UNIX graduate" phenomenon. In the late 1970s Bell gave away UNIX to many colleges and universities, and students became accustomed to using it. Consequently, when many of these schools' graduates entered the work force, they began agitating for the acceptance of UNIX in industry. Another reason is that in 1981 Bell Labs reduced the price of executable versions of UNIX to as little as $40 a copy, which set in motion a new wave of interest in the operating system.

Though not everyone agrees, some consider UNIX a computer professional's dream. A multi-user, time-sharing operating system, it was originally implemented for a minicomputer but now also runs on mainframes and even on some microcomputers. However, it is a very sophisticated operating system.

7 The Drive for a UNIX Standard

Is UNIX a standard? It is struggling mightily to be one. An outgrowth of the UNIX graduate phenomenon is that UNIX is the only operating system that has become user-driven. That is, key UNIX supporters—the scientific community, the federal government, the aerospace industry—often name UNIX in their bid specifications to computer manufacturers. In other words, "If you want our business, you better offer a system that includes UNIX." Vendors, therefore, that cannot offer UNIX-supported hardware are effectively cut out of the bidding process. This is a powerful incentive to offer UNIX with a hardware system. Today UNIX runs on everything from the massive Cray-2 to personal computers.

But UNIX has some drawbacks. It has never been considered very user friendly. Critics point, for example, to capricious use of abbreviations and inadequate documentation. However, the unfriendliness has now been successfully replaced by the now traditional menus that look much like those of other systems. Also, UNIX lacks sophisticated security features. Still, UNIX supporters take on a fervor that has been described as cult-like. Said one adherent, "Sure it's got problems—but show me something better." Today nearly all other operating systems are measured against the standard of UNIX.

GARY WASN'T HOME, BUT BILL WAS

The first person to have some success promoting an operating system standard for personal computers was Gary Kildall, who wrote and marketed CP/M through his company, Digital Research. He was the fellow IBM turned to to write an operating system for their own personal computer, and IBM representatives set up an appointment with him. On the fateful day, the IBM contingent showed up, only to learn that Kildall was out.

Kildall's lawyer was on the premises, the story goes, and was reluctant to sign IBM's standard pretalk nondisclosure agreement. Later, Kildall got involved in the process and telephoned IBM. But two weeks later Kildall's IBM contact was off the project, and Kildall could not reach the new project leaders.

He never did, because they were in contact with Bill Gates (shown above), the young president of Microsoft. Gates delivered MS-DOS (which IBM calls PC-DOS—the two programs are almost identical) for the IBM PC and the rest is history. Microsoft has diversified to applications software and is now one of the leading independent software houses.

Operating Systems for Personal Computers

We have already indicated that some software packages hide the operating system interface, but others want you to use your own copy of the operating system, probably the one that came with the machine. This is called **booting** the system—that is, loading the operating system into memory. The word *booting* is used because the operating system seemingly pulls itself up by its bootstraps. A small program (in ROM—read-only memory) "bootstraps" the basic components of the operating system in from a diskette or hard disk.

If you are using the popular operating system called MS-DOS (for Microsoft Disk Operating System), the net observable result of booting MS-DOS is an A> on the screen. (See a detailed description of booting in the box "How to Use MS-DOS on p. 272.") The A refers to the disk drive; the > is a **prompt,** a signal that the system is *prompting* you to do something. (Note: The notation is C> if you are using the hard disk drive.) The prompt indicates that the operating system is waiting for a command from the user. At this point you must give some instruction to the computer. Perhaps all you need to do is insert a commercial software disk, then type certain characters to make the applications software take the lead. But it could be more complicated than that because A> is actually the signal for direct communication between the user and the operating system.

Using MS-DOS

TEST BANK
Mult.Choice	48-57
T/F	66-83
Matching D	7-9
Fill-in-the-Blank	39-45

To use the computer to run applications programs, you need to understand some basics about your operating system. You will use the operating system whenever you use your computer. Here we consider MS-DOS, still the most entrenched operating system for personal computers, in more detail. We refer to MS-DOS by its abbreviated name, DOS, which rhymes with *boss*.

DOS programs are stored on one or more diskettes, which were probably purchased with the computer. These programs are executed by issuing a **command,** a name that invokes the correct program. Whole books have been written about DOS commands, but we will consider only the commands you need to use an applications program. These commands let you:

- Access DOS files by using DOS commands
- Prepare (format) new diskettes for use
- List the names of the files you have on your disk
- Name new files on disk and change the names of old files
- Copy files from one disk to another

    Erase files from a disk.

MICROCOMPUTERS IN ACTION

How to Use MS-DOS

When you learn how to use a computer, you sometimes hear a little voice within you that plants a seed of doubt ("Are you *sure* you want to press *that* key?") and hints that the computer will self-destruct if you make a mistake. Some software saves you from this uncertainty. You simply insert the applications program, turn on the computer, and follow the step-by-step instructions on the screen. However, there are times when the computer waits for you to give the instructions. For instance, some tasks require knowing how to use an operating system disk, which prepares the computer for particular applications programs. Below are the directions for loading MS-DOS, followed by directions for two common tasks requiring MS-DOS. The first task is formatting a blank disk, which means preparing it for holding data files and a file directory. The second task is copying files from one disk to another.

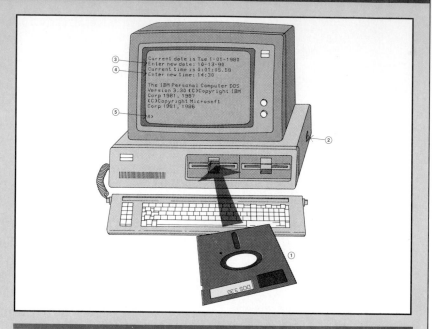

Booting the system using MS-DOS. See the section called Loading MS-DOS.

Loading MS-DOS

As you read these steps, follow along on the drawing.

1. Insert the MS-DOS disk in the left-hand disk drive (drive A) and shut the disk-drive door.
2. Turn the computer on. The red light in drive A goes on, and the drive whirs for a few seconds. Then the red light goes off.
3. When the screen requests the date, you can either enter the new date (month-day-year; for example, 10-13-90) and press Enter or simply press Enter without entering the new date.
4. When the screen requests the

time, you can either enter the new time (military time; for example, 14:30) and press Enter or simply press Enter without entering the new time.
5. When the A> appears on the screen, MS-DOS is loaded in drive A. (If you are going to insert an applications program in drive A, you may now remove the MS-DOS disk.)

Formatting a Blank Disk

1. Load MS-DOS as previously described.
2. Insert the blank disk in drive B.
3. After A> type:
   FORMAT B:
4. Press Enter.
5. Press any key.
6. When the red light in drive B goes off, the disk has been formatted and is ready to use.

Copying Files

1. Load MS-DOS as previously described. Remove disk.
2. Insert the original disk (the one to be copied) in drive A.
3. Insert the formatted disk (the one to be copied to) in drive B.
4. a. To copy a specific file on the disk in drive A to the disk in drive B, after A> type:

   COPY A:file name B:

   For example, if the file name is PAYROLL, the screen should read:

   A>COPY A:PAYROLL B:

   b. To copy *all* the files on the disk in drive A to the disk in drive B, after A> type:

   COPY A:*.* B:
5. Press Enter.
6. When the light in drive B goes off, the computer has completed the copying.

LECTURE HINT
The military time for afternoon hours is found by adding twelve to the clock time.

7 Internal DOS Commands

Although you may not use all DOS commands, certain programs invoked by DOS commands must be in your computer's memory before you can use DOS or an applications program such as Lotus 1-2-3. These essential DOS programs are accessed using commands referred to as the **internal DOS commands.** The internal DOS programs must be loaded—placed—into your computer's memory when you turn on your computer. Once the internal DOS programs are in memory, you can remove the DOS disk but still use the internal DOS programs. However, internal DOS sometimes must be reloaded when you stop using one applications program and wish to use a different applications program. And, of course, since the computer loses whatever is in its memory when you turn off the machine, you must reload internal DOS into memory whenever you turn the computer on to use an applications program.

DISCUSSION QUESTION
What other functions does MS-DOS fulfill in addition to running application programs?

When you want to use an internal DOS program, tell DOS to execute the program by typing in the appropriate command. Internal DOS commands execute immediately because the internal DOS programs are loaded into the computer when it is booted. (In contrast, *external DOS programs*, which we will discuss shortly, reside on disk as program files and must be read from disk before they can be executed.) Two important internal DOS commands are the *COPY command*, which lets you make copies of files, and the *DIR command*, which lets you list the names of files stored on a disk.

DISCUSSION QUESTION
How do internal and external commands in MS-DOS differ?

7 External DOS Commands

Most applications programs require a lot of the computer's memory to run. Therefore, only internal DOS programs, which are necessary to support the work of applications programs, are loaded into memory when the computer is booted. The other DOS programs, which reside in files on the DOS disk, are accessed using commands referred to as the **external DOS commands.** One of the most important external commands is the *FORMAT command*, which prepares a disk so that it is capable of storing files.

The point of this discussion is that you must have access to the external DOS programs before you can use them. Therefore, you must have the DOS disk in the proper disk drive before you can use the external commands. Usually, however, all you will need are the internal DOS commands.

Now let us consider the hardware you will need to run DOS.

7 A Brief Hardware Discussion

As you know from your earlier reading, a computer has several distinct pieces of hardware. The *central processing unit* executes the instructions in a computer program. The computer's memory contains program instructions and data. Internal DOS programs

---

PERSPECTIVES

THE QUEST FOR STANDARDS

What if you know all about MS-DOS but want to use a different computer? Is your knowledge about MS-DOS transferable? Maybe, but maybe not. That brings us to the issue of standards. That is, can we not do things the same way?

Like their forebearers, early microcomputer manufacturers took the path already traveled and produced their own unique operating systems. What this means is that the terrific software you see somewhere may not work on another manufacturer's microcomputer. The reason: Your computer does not have the same operating system. Video game addicts who covet a friend's new acquisition on a different home computer may find this lack of standardization particularly distressing.

The popularity of the personal computer opened the way for software entrepreneurs, who wanted to write programs that would be purchased by the vast personal computer audience. The potential for sales was enormous. Eager as the entrepreneurs were, though, they hung back, waiting for a standard operating system to emerge. Since software written to run on one operating system generally will not run on another operating system, nobody wanted to spend a lot of development time on a product only to find that they had guessed wrong about which operating system would become dominant.

For a while CP/M (Control Program for Microcomputers) looked promising because it was an operating system used by a number of manufacturers—but none of them was big enough to gamble on. Then IBM chose MS-DOS from Microsoft. Everybody breathed a sigh of relief that a standard had at last been established. Since that watershed period, IBM has captured a significant market share, and others are fighting for a grip on IBM's coattails.

Why IBM? Is it because IBM's operating system has been proven to be the finest or the most efficient? Not necessarily. Quite simply, everyone knew that IBM would sell a lot of personal computers. And where IBM sells hardware, software is sure to follow. Software was written for IBM's operating system because that is the truest path to the greatest software sales. There have been strong counter-currents—such as the Apple Macintosh—since the IBM wave began to roll, but IBM's influence on the market has been enormous.

Many other personal computers now use MS-DOS, so software written for IBM machines can be run on their machines. Some vendors approach the standardization problem from another viewpoint, offering software "connections" so that software can be transported seamlessly among different operating systems.

DISCUSSION QUESTION
What factors have resulted in MS-DOS dominance of the market?

LECTURE HINT
When IBM contacted Microsoft, it was a company that developed computer languages. Microsoft had very little experience in writing operating systems. Nearby Seattle Computer Company had written an operating system. To save time, Microsoft bought the rights from Seattle Computer Company. Microsoft cleaned up the code, removed the bugs, and sold it as MS-DOS.

are loaded into memory. Secondary storage is needed, usually one or more disk drives. Since many DOS commands involve files on disk, we are particularly concerned about disk drives in this chapter.

Disk Drive Configuration

There are two kinds of disk drives: diskette drives and hard disk drives, or hard drives. If you have two diskette drives, they are called drives A and B. A hard drive is called drive C. (Occasionally, there is a second hard drive, called drive D.) Configurations vary, but the three most common are shown in Figure 9-8. The first has diskette drive A on the left and diskette drive B on the right. The second has diskette drive A on the left and hard-drive C on the right. The third has diskette drives A and B stacked on the left (A on top, B on the bottom) and hard-drive C on the right.

From now on, to make your reading a little easier, we will use the word *disk* to refer to both diskettes and hard disks. When it is necessary to distinguish between these two storage devices, we will use the terms *diskette* and *hard disk*.

The Default Drive

Since some DOS commands refer to disk files, which store programs and data, we need to pause for a moment to consider where those files are. For example, the DIR command displays a list of files—but how does DOS know which drive contains the disk that the files are stored on? Although DOS commands let you specify a particular drive, it is easier to omit a drive specification, thus permitting DOS to use the default drive.

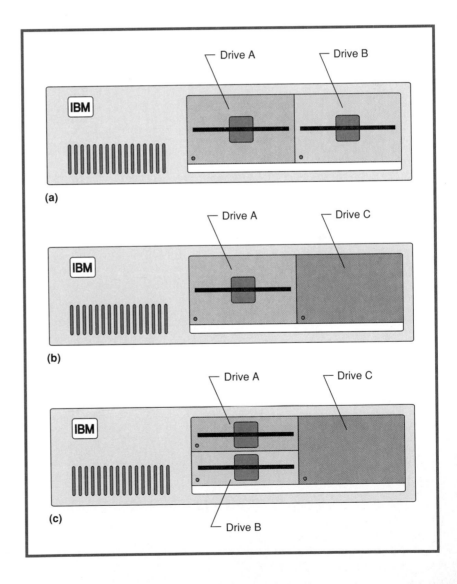

Figure 9-8 Disk Drive Configurations. As you use different computers, you may see several different types of disk drive combinations. The following are common: (a) Diskette drive A on the left, diskette drive B on the right. (b) Diskette drive A on the left, hard-drive C on the right. (c) Diskette drives A and B stacked on the left, hard-drive C on the right.

DISCUSSION QUESTION
How do you specify the default disk
drive in MS-DOS?

The **default drive,** also called the **current drive,** is the drive that the computer is currently using. If your computer does not have a hard disk, DOS will always start with drive A as the default drive. If you do have a hard disk, drive C is usually the default drive. DOS will always remind you which drive is currently the default drive by means of the prompt. If you see A>, then the default drive is A. Similarly, B> means the default drive is B, and C> means the default drive is C.

You can change to another default drive if you wish: Type the letter of the desired drive, followed by a colon, and then press Enter. Suppose, for example, that the default drive is currently drive A, but you want to access files on the disk that you have in drive B. To change the default drive to B, type:

    B:

and then press Enter. (You can, by the way, type an upper- or lower-case B. DOS recognizes either.) Now the screen shows a B>.

Only one disk drive at a time can be the default drive. If you ask DOS to retrieve a file for you and DOS replies that it cannot find the file, perhaps the file is not on the disk in the default drive. You may need to change the default drive or place another disk in the current default drive.

Types of Disks

The three types of disks you will use are (1) DOS disks, (2) applications software disks, and (3) data disks. What do these three have in common? All contain files. DOS disk files contain the operating system programs. Applications software disks contain the applications software, such as a word processing program. Data disk files contain the data that is related to applications software.

When are these three types of disks used? The DOS disk is used to start the computer system and, as you proceed, to provide services and control of software and files. Applications software disks are used after the internal DOS programs are loaded into memory. (Sometimes internal DOS and applications software are on the same disk.) Data disks are used concurrently with applications software, either to supply input data or, more likely, to store the files you create.

Data disks are different from DOS and applications software disks. To begin with, the DOS and applications software may belong to your school or company, and they may be used by several people. Data disks, however, are usually purchased by you, belong to you, are used only by you, and contain data created by you. When you first purchase a data disk, it contains no files; that is, the disk is empty. To prepare a disk to receive the files you will create, you must use the FORMAT command. (In contrast, DOS and applications software disks, which already have files on them, have been formatted and should not be formatted again.)

Table 9-1 Some MS-DOS commands. Here are some simple MS-DOS operating system commands (when you see the A> prompt) and a general description of what they do. Although they are specifically part of MS-DOS, they represent the kinds of things you can do on most personal computers.

Command	Use
CHKDSK	Check disk. Display information about the status of a disk, including number of files, number of bytes used in files, and number of bytes available for use.
CLS	Clear the screen.
COMP	Compare two files to see if they are identical.
COPY	Make another copy of a file.
DATE	Enter the current date.
DEL or ERASE	Delete a file.
DIR	Directory. List all files on a disk.
DISKCOPY	Copy all files on a disk to another disk.
FORMAT	Prepare a disk for use.
RENAME	Give a file a new name.
TIME	Enter the current time.
TYPE	Display a file on the screen.

When you create files for your data disk, you choose a name for the file. When there are several files on the disk, you may want to see a list of all the files. You may want to copy files from one data disk to another so you can have a backup copy. You may want to erase files you no longer need. To do these things, you need to know how to use the appropriate DOS commands. Table 9-1 is a sampler of operating system commands and what they do. Although the details of these commands are mostly beyond the scope of this book, you can see how the commands are used by reading the box "How to Use MS-DOS." In addition, several DOS commands are described in more detail in Appendix B.

Figure 9-9 Operating environments. This illustration is identical to Figure 9-1, except that an environment layer has been added to shield the user from having to know commands of the operating system.

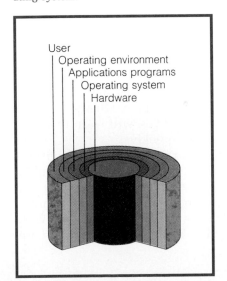

User
 Operating environment
  Applications programs
   Operating system
    Hardware

7 Operating Environments: The Shell Game

Figure 9-9 tells the story at a glance: Compare Figure 9-9 to Figure 9-1, and you will see that another layer has been added between the operating system and the user. This layer is often called a **shell** because it forms a "coating" around the operating system. More formally, this layer is called an **operating environment** because it "moves" the user to a new environment—one more palatable to many users than A>.

Figure 9-10   Microsoft Windows.
This operating environment can run several programs concurrently and let users follow their progress on a screen divided into windows. Windows offers easy-to-use menu systems, the ability to transfer data among different types of files as well as user-friendly access to the operating system. Windows uses an approach called tilting, which arranges windows to fit the screen completely to make the best use of the screen display area.

TRANSPARENCY ACETATE #9H
Figure #9-10

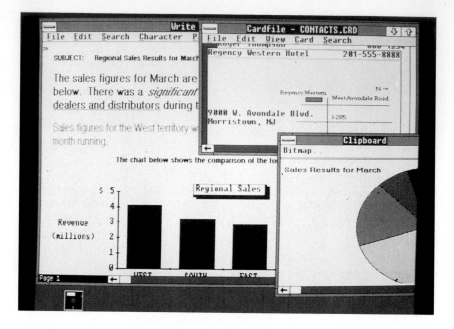

When using an operating environment, you see pictures and/or simply worded choices instead of the A> or some other prompt. Instead of having to *know* some command to type, you have only to make a selection from the choices available on the screen. Apple's Macintosh paved the way for simple interfaces between users and the operating system, but various products are battling over future operating environment standards. A key product is Microsoft Windows, a colorful graphics interface that eases access to the operating system (Figure 9-10). IBM's newest personal computer operating system, called OS/2, also uses a simplified interface.

7 Do I Really Need to Know All This?

The answer to that question depends on how you expect to use a computer. If your primary use of a computer is as a tool to enhance your other work, then you may have minimum interaction with an operating system. In that case, whether you are using a personal computer or a mainframe, you will learn to access the applications software of choice very quickly.

But there are other options. In fact, there are far more options than we are able to present in this introductory chapter. As a sophisticated user, you can learn your way around the operating system of any computer you might be using. If you plan to be a programmer, then there is no question about whether you need to know everything in this chapter; you will need to know this and much more.

Macintosh®

The Mouse That Roared: The Macintosh Operating Environment

A simple idea lies behind the operating environment of the Apple Macintosh computer: People should not have to think like a machine in order to use a personal computer.

With this goal in mind, the Mac designers created the Macintosh desktop, a computer screen that resembles the top of your desk—you can even rearrange it if it gets messy. As shown in screen (a) below, the desktop appears when you start up the Macintosh—you see symbols and words instead of the A prompt (A>). These symbols, called icons, represent disks, application programs, and data files. The words at the top of the screen indicate menus—lists of commands—that are hidden from view. When you want to use a command, you can view the entire menu, as shown in screen (b). The Mac menus are called pull-down menus because you pull them down to use them, just as you pull down a window shade.

Icons and pull-down menus can be manipulated with a mouse, a small device attached to the computer. The mouse lets you easily *select*—choose—icons or commands. The mouse plays a primary role in getting things done on the Mac.

Computing on the Mac can be boiled down to a single instruction—select something and then do something to it. For example, to copy a file or program, you first select its icon and then choose the Duplicate command from the File menu. All Mac application programs follow this select-and-do approach. Indeed, virtually all Mac applications have the same look as the operating environment. The resulting consistency makes it easy for people to get acquainted with new programs—opening, closing, saving, copying, deleting, and printing a file work the same way in nearly all programs.

When the Mac first appeared, some skeptics referred to the desktop as the Caveman Interface, designed for the computer illiterate. Despite the jeers, the Mac's easy-to-use operating environment laid the foundation for the machine's success. Now other companies are following in the mouse's footsteps.

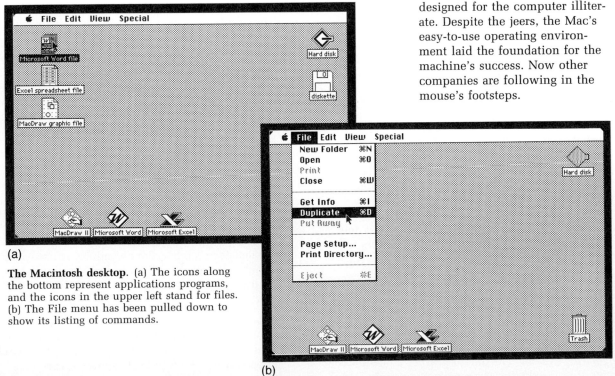

(a)

The Macintosh desktop. (a) The icons along the bottom represent applications programs, and the icons in the upper left stand for files. (b) The File menu has been pulled down to show its listing of commands.

(b)

TRANSPARENCY ACETATE #9I Macintosh Box

Summary and Key Terms

- An **operating system** is a set of programs through which the computer manages its own resources (the central processing unit, memory, secondary storage devices, and input/output devices, and so on). Thus, applications programs do not have to provide all the instructions that the computer requires. This allows programmers to focus on solving problems for clients.

- An operating system has three main functions: (1) to control computer system resources, (2) to execute computer programs, and (3) to manage data.

- The **supervisor program** controls the entire operating system, ensuring that other programs in the system are called into memory as needed and that memory space is used efficiently.

- The operating system improves efficiency in two ways: (1) by helping users get maximum benefit from computer system resources and (2) by invoking translator programs and other programs that take care of certain common tasks.

- **Multiprogramming** is running two or more programs concurrently on the same computer and sharing the computer's various resources. Multiprogramming is **event-driven,** meaning that one program is allowed to use a particular resource (such as the central processing unit) to complete a certain activity (event) before relinquishing the resource to another program. In multiprogramming, the operating system uses **interrupts,** which are conditions that temporarily suspend the execution of individual programs.

- **Time-sharing** is a special case of multiprogramming in which several people use one machine at the same time. Time-sharing is **time-driven**—each user is given a **time slice** in which the computer works on that user's tasks before moving on to another user's tasks. **Response time** is the time between the user's typed computer request and the computer's reply. The system of having users take turns is called **round-robin scheduling.**

- **Parallel processing** uses multiple CPUs, a feature that permits *simultaneous* processing.

- Through the **resource allocation** process, the operating system coordinates resource availability with the requirements of the various programs. Most operating systems are able to prevent a **deadlock,** a condition in which two programs come into conflict, with neither one willing to give up the resource it is holding until it gets the resource the other is holding.

- **Memory management** is the process of allocating memory to programs and of keeping the programs in memory separate from each other. Some operating systems divide memory into separate areas of fixed size; others allow variable sizes. Large all-purpose computers often divide memory into a **foreground** area for programs with higher priority and a **background** area for programs with lower priority. Programs waiting to be run are kept on the disk in **queues.**

- In the **virtual storage** (or **virtual memory**) technique of memory management, part of the applications program is stored on disk and is brought into memory only when needed for execution. Memory is considered **real storage;** the secondary storage holding the rest of the program is considered virtual storage.

- Virtual storage can be implemented in several ways. **Paging** divides a program into equal-size pieces (**pages**) that fit exactly into corresponding memory spaces (**page frames**).

- In multiprogramming, **memory protection** is an operating system process that defines the limits of each program in memory, thus preventing programs from accidentally destroying or modifying one another.

- **Spooling** prevents printouts that are a combination of the output from concurrently processed programs. Each file to be printed is written temporarily onto a disk instead of being printed immediately. When this spooling process is complete, all the appropriate files from a particular program can be printed intact.

- **Translators** convert programs into machine language. High-level languages usually use a **compiler** (which completes the translation before the program is executed) but sometimes use an **interpreter** (which translates and executes the program one instruction at a time as it executes). A third type of translator program, the **assembler,** is used with assembly languages. All three types of translators use the applications program, or **source module,** as input.

- Compilers and assemblers can generate three types of output: (1) an **object module,** which is the machine-language version of the program; (2) **diagnostic messages,** which indicate **syntax errors** (language errors); and (3) the **source program listing,** which is a list of the program as the programmer wrote it.

- During the **link/load phase,** prewritten programs may be added to the object module by means of a link/loader. The output from the link/load step is called the **load module.**

- **Utility programs** are prewritten standard programs that perform many repetitive file-handling tasks such as file conversions and sort/merge operations.

- **UNIX,** a multiuser, time-sharing operating system developed in 1971 by researchers at Bell Labs, has become a dominant generic operating system. A **generic operating system** is one that works with more than one manufacturer's computer system.

- **Booting** the system is the process of loading the operating system into memory. A **prompt** signals the user when this process is complete and the operating system is ready for a command.

- MS-DOS programs are executed by issuing a **command,** a name that invokes the correct program. **Internal DOS commands** are placed into your computer's memory when you turn on the computer. The other DOS commands, which reside on the DOS disk, are called **external DOS commands.** The **default drive,** also called the **current drive,** is the drive that the computer is currently using.

- In general, personal computer software written to be run on one operating system will not run on another one. Therefore, most software developers maximize sales by writing programs for the most widely used operating systems, such as IBM's MS-DOS.

- Some operating systems provide pictures and/or simply worded choices instead of giving a prompt. In effect, these pictures and choices form a user-friendly "coating," or **shell,** around the operating system. They create a comfortable **operating environment** for the user, who does not have to remember or look up the appropriate commands.

Review Questions

1. What is an operating system?

2. What are the three main functions of an operating system?

3. How does an operating system improve efficiency?

4. Describe how multiprogramming works.

5. Explain how time-sharing works.

6. Describe the process of resource allocation.

7. Why is memory management necessary?

8. Why do some computer systems divide the memory into foreground and background areas?

9. Describe paging.

10. In multiprogramming, what prevents one program from destroying or changing another program?

11. Explain how spooling works and why it is useful.

12. Explain what a compiler is, and describe its three possible outputs.

13. How does an interpreter differ from a compiler?

14. What do utility programs do?

15. What is the difference between internal and external MS-DOS commands?

16. What is meant by the current drive?

Discussion Questions

1. How would programming be affected if there were no operating systems?

2. Discuss the advantages and disadvantages of having a standard operating system.

Chapter 10. Systems Analysis and Design: Change and the Computer

10

Systems Analysis and Design

Change and the Computer

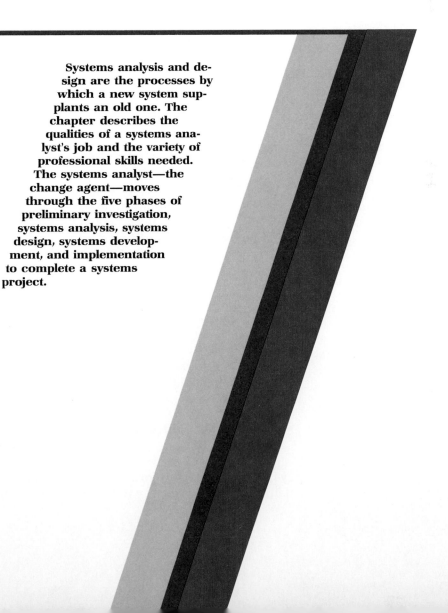

Systems analysis and design are the processes by which a new system supplants an old one. The chapter describes the qualities of a systems analyst's job and the variety of professional skills needed. The systems analyst—the change agent—moves through the five phases of preliminary investigation, systems analysis, systems design, systems development, and implementation to complete a systems project.

LEARNING OBJECTIVES
- Understanding the terms *system, analysis,* and *design.*
- Understanding the nature of change within an organization.
- Knowing the principal functions of the systems analyst.
- Knowing the phases of the systems development life cycle.
- Familiarity with data gathering and analysis tools.
- Familiarity with systems design tools.
- Understanding the concept of prototyping.
- Understanding the value of CASE tools.

TEST BANK
Mult. Choice	1-10
T/F	1-12
Matching A	2-4, 6, 9-10
Fill-in-the-Blank	1-6

LECTURE ACTIVITY
Have class discuss how they resist change, especially when forced upon them by others. Some examples of change: moving to a new home; starting college; getting a new roommate; changing family traditions. In what other situations do they resist change?

Carly Mack, operations manager of an airport car rental agency, was looking for ways to improve customer service. Surveys showed that customers put standing in line at the top of their list of annoyances. Interviews with rental clerks, however, revealed that the key to the long lines was geographic uncertainty—most of the customers were from out of town and needed time-consuming directions.

Brainstorming managers, along with a computer consultant, came up with the idea of a computer system so simple that the customers could run it themselves. The system centered on a touch screen that would display nearby locations; the customer need only touch the desired location and the computer would take it from there.

Although the idea was still in the formative stages, Carly was surprised to find resistance from the rental clerks. They did not like the idea of sharing their expertise and were uneasy about being "replaced" by a computer.

People are generally uncomfortable about change, even change in apparently minor matters. People sense the stress that comes with change and thus tend to avoid change. But sometimes change is someone else's idea, an idea forced upon you. So, not only is the change set in motion externally, but it is accompanied by fear of diminished control. This is often how the stage is set at the first mention of the word *computer*.

7 The Systems Analyst

The boss tells you someone is coming to look over the work situation and ask you a few questions, "get a fix on the work flow, maybe see if we can't streamline some things and get them on a computer system."

Your ears perk up. A computer? Suddenly you feel very nervous. They're going to take your job and give it to a computer! Congratulations. You are about to be visited by a systems analyst.

A systems analyst with any experience, however, knows that people are uneasy about having their job situations investigated, that they may be nervous about computers, and that they may react adversely by withholding their cooperation (sometimes subtly, sometimes quite aggressively). Attitudes depend somewhat on prior experience with computer systems.

7 The Analyst and the System

What is a systems analyst? Although we will describe a systems project more formally later in the chapter, let us start by defining what we mean by the words *system, analysis,* and *design.* A

MICROCOMPUTERS IN ACTION

High-Tech Dining

You are out for dinner in a lively Italian restaurant, far from the flash of the computer screen and the tippity-tap of the keyboard. But wait. What is that, *right next to the table* where you are being seated? It is a personal computer which, with a little help, is going to order your dinner for you.

The restaurant is Cucina Cucina, in Seattle, Washington. And the techie computer floor show is your waitperson as he or she taps the screen to enter your order. In fact, the entire restaurant menu is presented on the computer screen. Your waitperson's fingers skip quickly from item to item, touching the name of each food you order. Your

order is flashed on another screen in the kitchen. But this is only the part of the system you can see.

Computers have trickled down to even the smallest businesses, doing all sorts of useful work. The restaurant-management computer system at Cucina Cucina goes beyond the dining room/

kitchen interface. The system handles the restaurant's point-of-sale transactions—the cash register—and food inventory, sales, and accounting. With add-on software, the system can also keep track of employee hours and payroll and chart individual worker productivity.

system is an organized set of related components established to accomplish a certain task. There are natural systems, such as the cardiovascular system, but many systems have been planned and deliberately put into place by people. For example, the lines you stand in, stations you go to, and forms you fill out on your college's registration day constitute a system to get qualified students into the right classes. A **computer system** is a system that has a computer as one of its components.

Systems analysis is the process of studying an existing system to determine how it works and how it meets user needs. Systems analysis lays the groundwork for improvements to the system. The analysis involves an investigation, which in turn usually involves establishing a relationship with the client for whom the analysis is being done and with the users of the system. The **client** is the person or organization contracting to have the work done. The **users** are people who will have contact with the system, usually employees and customers. For instance, in a college registration system, the client is the administration, and the users are both the school employees and the students.

Systems design is the process of developing a plan for an improved system, based on the results of the systems analysis. For instance, the analysis phase may reveal that students waste time standing in lines when they register in the closing weeks of the fall semester. The new system design might involve plans for a preregistration process.

The **systems analyst** normally performs both analysis and design. (The term *systems designer* is not common, although it is used in some places.) In some computer installations a person who is mostly a programmer may also do some systems analysis and have the title **programmer/analyst.** Traditionally, most people who have become systems analysts have done so by way of programming. Starting out as a programmer helps the analyst appreciate computer-related problems that arise in analysis and design work. As we will see, programmers often depend on systems analysts for specifications from which to design programs.

A systems analysis and design project does not spring out of thin air. There must be an *impetus*—motivation—for change and related *authority* for the change. The impetus for change may be the result of an internal force, such as the organization's management deciding a computer could be useful in warehousing and inventory, or an external force, such as government reporting requirements or customer complaints about billing (Figure 10-1). Authority for the change, of course, comes from higher management.

7 The Systems Analyst as Change Agent

The systems analyst fills the role of **change agent.** That is, the analyst must be the catalyst or persuader who overcomes the natural inertia and reluctance to change within an organization. The

Figure 10-1   Impetus for change.   Internal and external sources can initiate a system change.

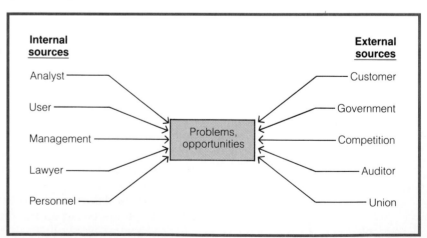

key to success is to involve the people of the client organization in the development of the new system. The common industry phrase is **user involvement,** and nothing can be more important to the success of the system. The finest system in the world will not suffice if users do not perceive it as useful. Users must be involved in the process from beginning to end. The systems analyst must monitor the user pulse regularly to make sure that the system being planned is one that will meet user needs.

7 What It Takes to Be a Systems Analyst

Not every computer professional aspires to the job of systems analyst. Before we can understand what kind of person might make a good systems analyst, we need to look at the kinds of things an analyst does. The systems analyst has three principal functions:

- **Coordination.** An analyst must coordinate schedules and system-related tasks with a number of people: the analyst's own manager; the programmers working with the system; the system's users, from clerks to top management; the vendors selling the computer equipment; and a host of others, such as postal employees handling mailings and carpenters doing installation.

- **Communication, both oral and written.** The analyst may be called upon to make oral presentations to clients, users, and others involved with the system. The analyst provides written reports—documentation—on the results of the analysis and the goals and means of the design. These documents may range from a few pages long to a few inches thick.

- **Planning and design.** The systems analyst, with the participation of members of the client organization, plans and designs the new system. This function involves all the activities from the beginning of the project until the final implementation of the system.

With these as principal functions, the kind of personal qualities that are desirable in a systems analyst must be apparent: an *analytical mind* and good *communication skills*. Perhaps not so obvious, however, are qualities such as *self-discipline* and *self-direction*—a systems analyst often works without close supervision. An analyst must have good *organizational skills* to be able to keep track of all the information about the system. An analyst also needs *creativity* to envision the new system. Finally, an analyst needs the *ability to work without tangible results*. There can be long dry spells when the analyst moves numbly from meeting to meeting, and it can seem that little is being accomplished.

Let us suppose that you are blessed with these admirable qualities and that you have become a systems analyst. You are given a job to do. How will you go about it?

7 How a Systems Analyst Works: Overview of the Systems Development Life Cycle

Whether you are investigating how to improve registration procedures at your college or any other task, you will proceed by using the **systems development life cycle** (**SDLC**), illustrated in Figure 10-2. The systems development life cycle has five phases:

1. Preliminary investigation—determining the problem
2. Analysis—understanding the existing system
3. Design—planning the new system
4. Development—doing the work to bring the new system into being
5. Implementation—converting to the new system

Table 10-1   Systems Development Life Cycle

Phase	Focus
Phase 1: Preliminary investigation	True nature of problem Problem scope Objectives

Phase 2: Systems analysis	Data gathering
	    Written documents
	    Interviews
	    Questionnaires
	    Observation
	    Sampling
	Data analysis
	    Charts
	    Tables
	System requirements

Phase 3: Systems design	Alternative candidates Output Input Files Processing Controls Backup
Phase 4: Systems development	Programming Testing
Phase 5: Implementation	Training Equipment conversion File conversion System conversion

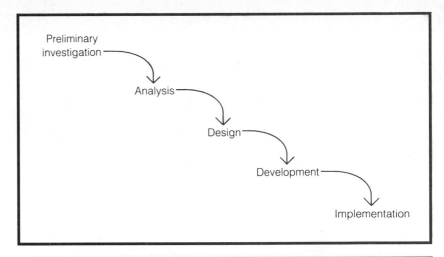

TRANSPARENCY ACETATE #10B
Figure #10-2

Figure 10-2   Systems development life cycle.

These simple explanations for each phase will be expanded to full-blown discussions in subsequent sections; each phase is summarized in Table 10-1. As you read about the phases of a systems project, follow the Swift Sport Shoes inventory case study in the adjacent boxes. Although space prohibits us from presenting a complete analysis and design project, this case study gives the flavor of the real thing. Let us begin at the beginning.

Phase 1: Preliminary Investigation

The **preliminary investigation**—often called the **feasibility study** or **system survey**—is the initial investigation, a brief study of the problem. It consists of the groundwork necessary to determine if the systems project should be pursued. You, as the systems analyst, need to determine what the problem is and what to do about it. The net result will be a rough plan for how—and if—to proceed with the project.

Essentially, this means you must be able to describe the problem. To do this, you will work with the users. One of your tools will be an **organization chart,** which is a hierarchical drawing showing management by name and title. Figure 10-3 shows an example of an organization chart. Constructing such a chart is not an idle task. If you are to work effectively within the organization, you need to understand what the lines of authority through the formal communication channels are.

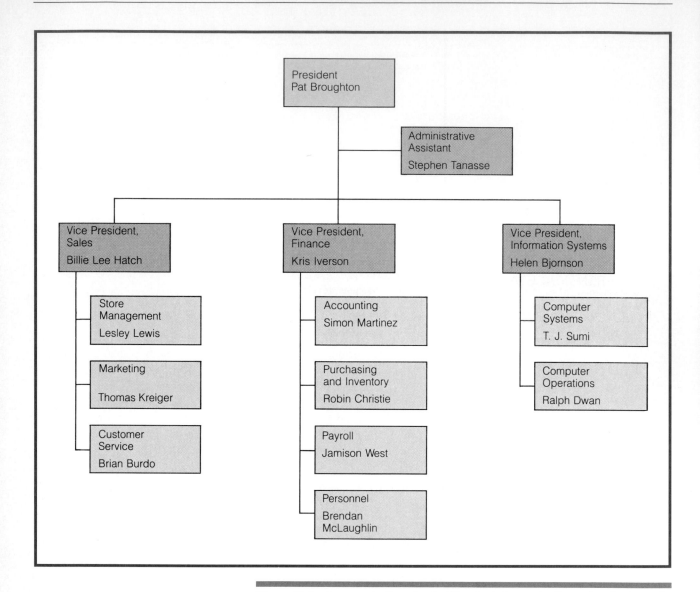

Figure 10-3   An organization chart.   The chart shows the lines of authority and formal communication channels. This example shows the organizational setup for Swift Sport Shoes, a chain of stores.

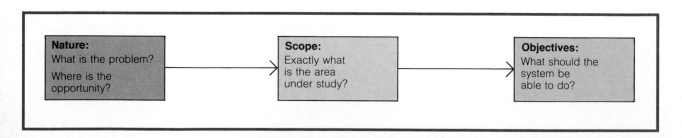

Figure 10-4   Problem definition overview.

```
SWIFT SPORT SHOES: PROBLEM DEFINITION

True Nature of the Problem

The nature of the problem is the existing manual
inventory system. In particular:

—Products are frequently out of stock

—There is little interstore communication about
 stock items

—Store managers have no information about stock
 levels on a day—to—day basis

—Ordering is done haphazardly


Scope

The scope of the project will be limited to the
development of an inventory system using appropriate
computer technology.


Objectives

The new automated inventory system should provide
the following:

—Adequate stock maintained in stores

—Automatic stock reordering

—Stock distribution among stores

—Management access to current inventory information

—Ease of use

—Reduced operating costs of the inventory function
```

Figure 10-5   Problem definition.   The nature and scope of the problem along with system objectives are shown for the Swift Sport Shoes system.

7 Problem Definition: Nature, Scope, Objectives

Your initial aim is to define the problem. You and the users must come to an agreement on these points: You must agree on the nature of the problem and then designate a limited scope. In the process you will also determine what the objectives of the project are. Figure 10-4 shows an overview of the problem definition process, and Figure 10-5 gives an example related to the Swift Sport Shoes project.

Nature of the Problem

Begin by determining the true nature of the problem. Sometimes what appears to be the problem turns out to be, on a closer look, only a symptom. For example, suppose you are examining customer complaints of late deliveries. Your brief study may reveal that the problem is not in the shipping department, as you first thought, but in the original ordering process.

CASE STUDY

SWIFT SPORT SHOES: PHASE 1

Preliminary Investigation

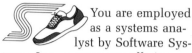 You are employed as a systems analyst by Software Systems, Inc., a company offering packaged and custom software as well as consulting services. Software Systems has received a request for a systems analyst; the client is Swift Sport Shoes, a chain of stores carrying a huge selection of footwear for every kind of sport. Your boss hands you this assignment, telling you to contact company officer Kris Iverson.

In your initial meeting with Mr. Iverson, who is Vice President of Finance, you learn that the first Swift store opened in San Francisco in 1974. The store has been profitable since the second year. Nine new stores have been added in the city and nearby shopping malls. These stores also show a net profit; Swift has been riding the crest of the fitness boom. But even though sales have been gratifying, Mr. Iverson is convinced that costs are higher than they should be.

In particular, Mr. Iverson is disturbed about inventory problems, which are causing frequent stock shortages and increasing customer dissatisfaction. The company has a superminicomputer at the headquarters office, where management offices are. Although there is a small information systems staff, their experience is mainly in batch financial systems. Mr. Iverson envisions more sophisticated technology for an inventory system and figures that outside expertise is needed to design it. He introduces you to Robin Christie, who is in charge of purchasing and inventory. Mr. Iverson also tells you that he has sent a memo to all company officers and store managers, indicating the purpose of your presence and his support of a study of the current system. Before the end of your visit with Mr. Iverson, the two of you construct the organization chart shown in Figure 10-3.

In subsequent interviews with Ms. Christie and other Swift personnel, you find that deteriorating customer service seems to be due to lack of information about inventory supplies. Together, you and Ms. Christie determine the problem definition, as shown in Figure 10-5. Mr. Iverson accepts your report, in which you outline the problem definition and suggest a full analysis.

DISCUSSION QUESTION
Why is it important to clearly establish the scope of the problem? What might be the consequences if the scope is not made clear? Example: Suppose the analyst thinks the project is for the installation of a local area network, but the user expects the work to also include a micro-to-mainframe link?

Scope

Establishing the scope of the problem is critical because problems tend to expand if no firm boundaries are established. Limitations are also necessary to stay within the eventual budget and schedule. So in the beginning the analyst and user must agree on the scope of the project: what the new or revised system is supposed to do—and not do. If the scope is too broad the project will never be finished, but if the scope is too narrow it may not meet user needs.

Objectives

You will soon come to understand what the user needs—that is, what the user thinks the system should be able to do. You will want to express these needs as objectives. Examine the objectives for the Swift inventory process. The people who run the existing inventory system already know what such a system must do. It remains for you and them to work out how this can be achieved on a computer system. In the next phase, the systems analysis phase, you will produce a more specific list of system requirements, based on these objectives.

TEST BANK
Mult. Choice	23-39
T/F	22-42
Matching A	5
Matching B	2-3, 5-10
Matching C	2, 5-6
Matching D	6
Fill-in-the-Blank	13-25

DISCUSSION QUESTION
What is wrong with the following statement? "The more written documents you have on the user's problem, the faster you will be able to determine the source of the problem and solve it."

Wrapping Up the Preliminary Investigation

The preliminary investigation, which is necessarily brief, should result in some sort of report, perhaps only a few pages long, telling management what you found and listing your recommendations. At this point management has three choices: They can (1) drop the matter; (2) fix the problem immediately, if it is simple; or (3) authorize you to go on to the next phase for a closer look.

Phase 2: Systems Analysis

Let us suppose management has decided to continue. Remember that the purpose of **systems analysis** is to understand the existing system. A related goal is to establish the system requirements. The best way to understand a system is to gather all the data you can about it; this data must then be organized and analyzed. During the systems analysis phase, then, you will be concerned with (1) data gathering and (2) data analysis. Keep in mind that the system being analyzed may or may not already be a computerized system.

Data Gathering

Data gathering is expensive and requires a lot of legwork and time. There is no standard procedure for gathering data because each system is unique. But there are certain sources that are commonly used:

- Written documents
- Interviews
- Questionnaires
- Observation
- Sampling

Sometimes you will use all these sources, but in most cases it will be appropriate to use some and not others. All references to data gathering techniques assume that you have the proper authority and the cooperation of the client organization before proceeding.

Written Documents

These include procedures manuals, reports, forms, and any other kind of material bearing on the problem that you find in the organization. You may find very few documents and no trail to

SOME TIPS FOR SUCCESSFUL INTERVIEWING

- Plan questions in advance—even if you vary from them during the interview. .
- Listen carefully to the answers and observe the respondent's voice inflection and body movements for clues to evaluate responses.
- Dress and behave in a business-like manner.
- Avoid technical jargon.
- Respect the respondent's schedule.
- Avoid office gossip and discussion of the respondent's personal problems.

DISCUSSION QUESTION
What are the advantages and disadvantages of using interviews for gathering data on problems that users are having? What tips might help make the interview more successful?

DISCUSSION QUESTION
What are the advantages and disadvantages of using questionnaires for gathering data on problems that users are having?

follow. Sometimes the opposite is true: There are so many documents that it is difficult to know how to sift through them. Thus, judgment is required, or you will spend hours reading outdated reports or manuals that no one follows. In particular, take time to get a copy of each form an organization uses.

Interviews

This method of data gathering has advantages and disadvantages. A key advantage is that interviews are flexible; as the interviewer, you can change the direction of your questions if you perceive a fertile area of investigation. Another bonus is that you can probe with open-ended questions that people would balk at answering on paper. You will find that some respondents yield more information in an interview than they would if they had to commit themselves in writing. You can also observe the respondent's voice inflection and body motions, which may tell you more than words alone. Finally, of course, there is the bonus of getting to know clients better and establishing a rapport with them—an important factor in promoting user involvement in the system from the beginning.

Interviews have certain drawbacks. They are unquestionably time-consuming and therefore expensive. You will not have the time or the money to interview large numbers of people. If you need to find out about procedures from 40 mail clerks, for example, you are better off using a questionnaire.

There are two types of interviews—structured and unstructured. A **structured interview** includes only questions that have been planned and written out in advance. The interviewer sticks to those questions and asks no others. A structured interview is useful when it is desirable—or required by law—to ask identical questions of several people. However, the **unstructured interview** is often more productive. An unstructured interview includes questions prepared in advance, but the interviewer is willing to vary from the line of questioning and pursue other subjects if they seem appropriate.

Questionnaires

Unlike interviews, questionnaires can be used to get information from large groups. They allow people to respond anonymously—the respondents just complete forms and turn them in—and presumably, they respond more truthfully. Questionnaires do have disadvantages, however. Some people will not return questionnaires because they are wary of putting anything on paper, even anonymously. And the questionnaires you do get back may contain biased answers.

There are many types of questionnaires; the ballot-box type (in which the respondent simply checks off "yes" or "no") and the qualified response (in which one rates agreement or disagreement with the question on a scale from, say, 1 to 5) are two common examples. In general, people prefer a questionnaire that is quick and simple. Analysts also prefer simple questionnaires because they are easier to tabulate. If you have long, open-ended questions, such as "Please describe your job functions," you should probably save them for an interview.

Observation

As an analyst and observer, you go into the organization and watch how data flows, who interrelates with whom, how paper moves from desk to desk, and how it comes into and leaves the organization. Normally, you make arrangements with a group supervisor, and you return on more than one occasion so that the people under observation become used to your presence. The purpose of your visits is known to the members of the organization. One form of observation is **participant observation;** in this form the analyst temporarily joins the activities of the group. This practice may be useful in studying a complicated organization.

Sampling

You may need to collect data about quantities, costs, time periods, and other factors relevant to the system. How many phone orders can be taken by an order entry clerk in an hour? If you are dealing with a major mail-order organization, such as L. L. Bean in Maine, this type of question may be best answered through a procedure called sampling: You need not gather all the data, only a certain representative subset. For example, instead of observing all 75 clerks filling orders for an hour, pick a sample of 3 or 4 clerks. Or, in the case of a high volume of paper output, such as customer bills, you could collect a random sample of a few dozen.

Data Analysis

Your data-gathering processes will probably produce an alarming amount of paper and a strong need to get organized. It is now time to turn your attention to the second activity of this phase, data analysis. What, indeed, are you going to do with all the data you have gathered? There are a variety of tools—charts and diagrams— used to analyze data, not all of them appropriate for every system. You should become familiar with the techniques, then use the tools that suit you at the time. We will consider two typical tools: data flow diagrams and decision tables.

The reasons for data analysis are related to the basic functions of the systems analysis phase: to show how the current system works and to determine the system requirements. In addition, data analysis materials will serve as the basis for documentation of the system.

CASE STUDY

SWIFT SPORT SHOES: PHASE 2

Systems Analysis

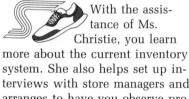 With the assistance of Ms. Christie, you learn more about the current inventory system. She also helps set up interviews with store managers and arranges to have you observe procedures in the stores and at the warehouse. As the number of stores has increased, significant expansion has taken place in all inventory-related areas: sales, scope of merchandise, and number of vendors.

Out-of-stock situations are common. The stock shortages are not uniform across all ten stores, however; frequently one store will be out of an item that the central warehouse or another store has on hand. The present system is not effective at recognizing this situation and transferring merchandise. There is a tendency for stock to be reordered only when the shelf is empty or nearly so. Inventory-related costs are significant, especially those for special orders of some stock items. Reports to management are minimal and often too late to be useful. Finally, there is no way to correlate order quantities with past sales records, future projections, or inventory situations.

During this period you also analyze the data as it is gathered. You prepare data flow diagrams of the various activities relating to inventory. Figure 10-7 shows the general flow of data to handle purchasing in the existing system. You prepare various decision tables, such as the one shown in Figure 10-8b.

Your written report to Mr. Iverson includes the list of system requirements in Figure 10-9.

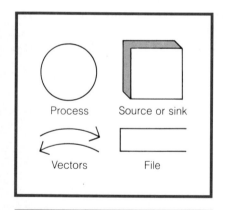

Figure 10-6   Data flow diagram symbols.

TRANSPARENCY ACETATE #10C
Figure #10-6

Data Flow Diagrams

A **data flow diagram** (**DFD**) is a sort of road map that graphically shows the flow of data through a system. It is a valuable tool for depicting present procedures and data flow. Although data flow diagrams can be used in the design process, they are particularly useful for facilitating communication between you and the users during the analysis phase. Suppose, for example, you spend a couple of hours with a McDonald's franchise manager, talking about the paperwork that keeps the burgers and the customers flowing. You would probably make copious notes on what goes where. But that is only the data gathering function—now you must somehow analyze your findings. You could come back on another day with pages of narrative for the manager to review or, instead, show an easy-to-follow picture. Like everyone else, users prefer pictures.

There are a variety of notations for data flow diagrams. The notation used here is promoted by Tom DeMarco, who wrote a book on the subject, because it is informal and easy to draw and read.

The elements of a data flow diagram are processes, files, sources and sinks, and vectors, as shown in Figure 10-6. Note also the DFD for Swift Sport Shoes (Figure 10-7) as you follow this discussion.

Processes, represented by circles, are the actions taken on the data—comparing, checking, stamping, authorizing, filing, and so forth. A **file** is a repository of data—a tape or disk file, a set of papers

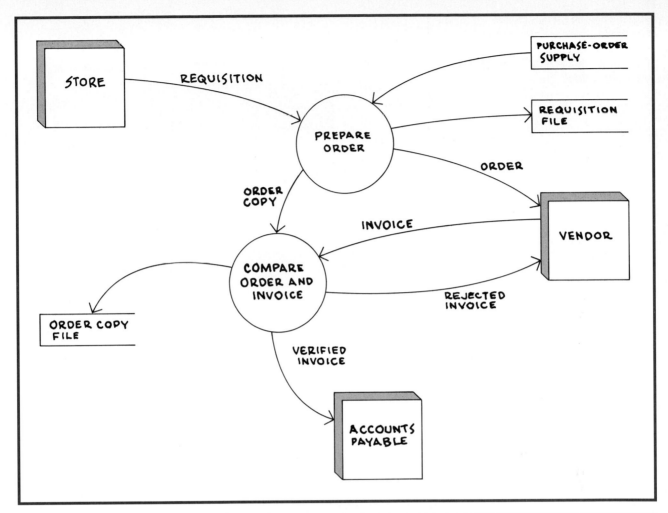

Figure 10-7   A data flow diagram.   This "map" shows the current flow of data in the purchasing department at Swift Sport Shoes. The diagram (greatly simplified) includes authorization for purchases of goods, purchase-order preparation, and verification of the vendor's invoice against the purchase order. Note that the stores, vendors, and accounts payable are in square boxes because they are outside the purchasing department.

DISCUSSION QUESTION
In Figure 10-7, why are square boxes used for the store, vendor, and accounts payable?

DISCUSSION QUESTION
In Figure 10-7, why can there be no arrow from the accounts payable box to the vendor box?

in a file cabinet, or even mail in an in-basket or blank envelopes in a supply bin. In a DFD a file is represented by an open-ended box.

A **source** is a data origin outside the organization. An example is a payment sent to a department store by a charge customer; the customer is a source of data. A **sink** is a destination for data going outside the organization; an example is the bank that is sent money from the accounts receivable organization. A source or a sink is represented by a square. **Vectors** are simply arrows, lines with directional notation. A vector must come from or go to a process bubble.

DISCUSSION QUESTION
Are there any sets of conditions
not accounted for in Figure 10-8?
If so, describe them; if not, should
we expect any?

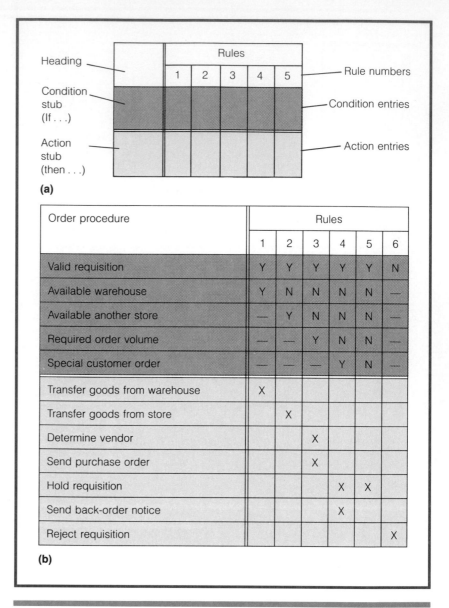

(a)

Order procedure	Rules					
	1	2	3	4	5	6
Valid requisition	Y	Y	Y	Y	Y	N
Available warehouse	Y	N	N	N	N	—
Available another store	—	Y	N	N	N	—
Required order volume	—	—	Y	N	N	—
Special customer order	—	—	—	Y	N	—
Transfer goods from warehouse	X					
Transfer goods from store		X				
Determine vendor			X			
Send purchase order			X			
Hold requisition				X	X	
Send back-order notice				X		
Reject requisition						X

(b)

TRANSPARENCY ACETATE #10D
Figure #10-8

Figure 10-8   Decision tables.   (a) Format of a decision table. The table is organized according to the logic that "If this condition exists or is met, then do this."
(b) A decision table example. This decision table, which describes the current
ordering procedure at Swift Sport Shoes, takes into consideration whether a requisition for goods from a store is valid, ascertains if the wanted goods are available
in the warehouse or some other Swift store, checks the order volume to see if it is
sufficient to place an inventory order, and checks to see if it is a special order for
a customer. Examine rule 4. The requisition is valid, so we proceed. The desired
goods are not available in either the warehouse or in another store, so they must
be ordered. However, there is not the required volume of customer demand to
place a standard inventory order now, so the requisition is put on hold until there
is. (In other words, this order will be joined with others.) And, finally, since this
is a special customer order and the order is on hold, a back-order notice is sent.

Figure 10-9   System requirements.
These are the requirements for an inventory system for Swift Sport Shoes.

```
SWIFT SPORT SHOES: REQUIREMENTS

The requirements for the Swift Sport Shoes inventory
system are as follows:
-Capture inventory data from sales transactions
-Implement automatic inventory reordering
-Implement a standardized interstore transfer system
-Provide both on-demand and scheduled management reports
-Provide security and accounting controls throughout the
 system
-Provide a user-oriented system whose on-line usage can
 be learned by a new user in one training class
-Reduce operating costs of the inventory function by 20%
```

Decision Tables

A **decision table,** also called a **decision logic table,** is a standard table of the logical decisions that must be made regarding potential conditions in a given system. Decision tables are useful in cases that involve a series of interrelated decisions; their use helps to ensure that no alternatives are overlooked. Programmers can code portions of programs right from a decision table. Figure 10-8a shows the format of a decision table; Figure 10-8b gives an example of a decision table that applies to the Swift Sport Shoes system.

These data analysis vehicles are typical, but the list presented here is by no means exhaustive.

System Requirements

As we mentioned, the purpose of gathering and analyzing data is twofold: to understand the system and, as a by-product of that understanding, to establish the system requirements. The description of the system was quite broad in the preliminary investigation phase, but now you are ready to list precise system requirements. You need to determine and document specific user needs. A system that a bank teller uses, for example, needs to be able to retrieve a customer record on the CRT screen within five seconds. The importance of accurate requirements cannot be overemphasized because the design of the new system will be based on the system requirements. Note the requirements for the Swift system, in Figure 10-9.

Report to Management

When you have finished the systems analysis phase, you present a report to management. This comprehensive report, part of the continuing process of documentation, summarizes the problems you found in the system, describes the system requirements, and makes recommendations on what course to take next. If management decides to pursue the project, you move on to phase 3.

7 Phase 3: Systems Design

The **systems design** phase is the phase in which you actually plan the new system. This phase is divided into two subphases: **preliminary design,** in which the analyst establishes the new system concept, followed by **detail design,** in which the analyst determines exact design specifications. The reason this phase is divided into two parts is that an analyst wants to make sure management approves the overall plan before spending time on details.

7 Preliminary Design

The first task of preliminary design is to review the system requirements, then consider some of the major aspects of a system. Should the system be centralized or distributed? Should the system be on-line? Should packaged software be purchased as opposed to having programmers write new software? Can the system be run on the user's microcomputers? How will input data be captured? What kind of reports will be needed?

The questions can go on and on. Eventually, together with key personnel from the user organization, you determine an overall plan. In fact, it is common to offer alternative plans, called **candidates.** Each candidate meets the user's requirements but with variations in features and costs. The chosen candidate is usually the one that best meets the user's needs and is flexible enough to meet future needs. The selected plan is expanded and described so that it can be understood by both the user and the analyst.

At this point it is wise to make a formal presentation of the plan or perhaps all the alternatives. The point is that you do not want to commit time and energy to—nor does the user want to pay for—a detailed design until you and the user agree on the basic design. Such presentations often include a drawing of the system from a user perspective, such as the one shown in Figure 10-10 for the Swift Sport Shoes system. At this point you want to emphasize system benefits—see the list in Figure 10-11.

7 Prototyping

The idea of building a prototype—a sort of guinea-pig model of the system—has taken a sharp upward turn in popularity recently. Considered from a systems viewpoint, a **prototype** is a limited working system—or subset of a system—that is developed

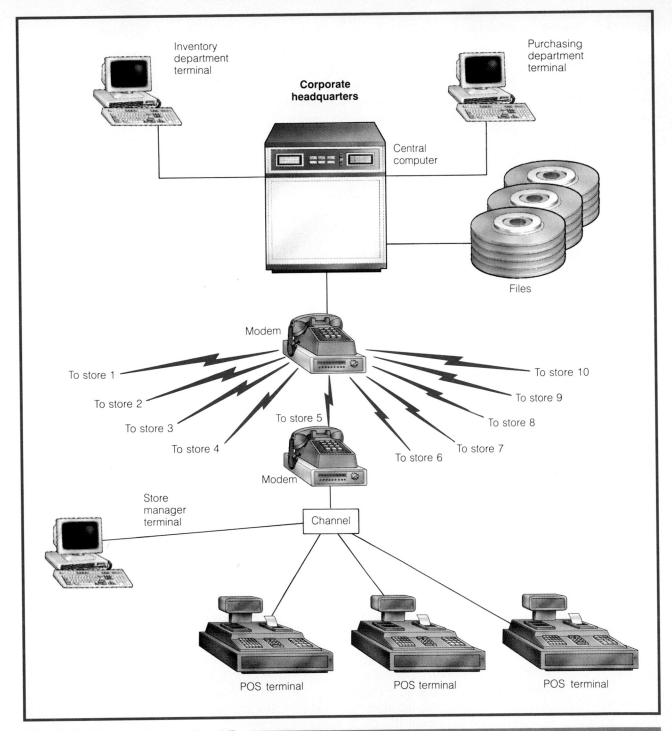

Figure 10-10   Overview of the system.   This overview shows the Swift Sport Shoes inventory system from a user's point of view. *Input* data is from POS terminals. Except for local editing, *processing* takes place on the central computer. All *storage* files are located at the central site. *Output* is in the form of screen displays and printed reports.

Figure 10-11   Benefits. Benefits are usually closely tied to the system objectives. These are the anticipated benefits of the new Swift Sport Shoes inventory system.

```
SWIFT SPORT SHOES: ANTICIPATED BENEFITS

—Better inventory control

—Improved customer service

—Improved management information

—Reduced inventory costs

—Improved employee morale
```

DISCUSSION QUESTION
What advantage is there to using a prototype before developing a whole system?

quickly, sometimes in just a few days. A prototype is a working model, one that can be tinkered with and fine-tuned. The idea is that users can get an idea of what the system might be like before it is fully developed. If they are not satisfied, they can revise their requirements before a lot has been invested in developing the new system.

Could you adopt this approach to systems development? It seems at odds with this chapter's systems development life cycle, which promotes doing steps in the proper order. And yet, some analysts in the computer industry are making good use of prototypes. We need to ask how and why. The "how" begins with prototyping tools.

Prototyping Tools

The prototype approach exploits advances in computer technology and uses powerful high-level software tools. These software packages allow analysts to build quick systems in response to user needs. In particular recall the fourth-generation languages we discussed in Chapter 8. One of their key advantages was that they could be used to produce something quickly. The systems produced can then be refined and modified as they are used, in a continuous process, until the fit between user and system is acceptable.

Why Prototyping?

Many organizations use prototyping on a limited basis. For example, an organization may prototype a certain data entry sequence, a particular screen output, or an especially complex or questionable part of a design. That is, prototyping does not necessarily have the scope of the final system. Some organizations use prototyping on a throwaway basis, using it only to get a grip on the requirements; then they begin again and go through the systems development life cycle formally. Other organizations start with a prototype and keep massaging it until it becomes the final and accepted version. In either case a prototype forces users to get actively involved.

Prototyping is a possibility if you work in an organization that has quick-build software and management support of this departure from traditional systems procedures.

CASE STUDY

SWIFT SPORT SHOES: PHASE 3

Systems Design

 The store managers, who were uneasy at the beginning of the study, are by now enthusiastic participants in the design of the new system they are counting on for better control of their inventory. As part of the preliminary design phase, you offer three alternative system candidates for consideration. The first is a centralized system, with all processing done at the headquarters computer and batch reports generated on a daily basis. The third takes the opposite approach, placing all processing in the stores on their own minicomputers. The second candidate, the one selected, includes processing at the central site; however, data will be edited locally, at the individual stores, before transmission to the central site.

The chosen alternative makes use of point-of-sale terminals at the store checkout counters, where inventory data is captured as a by-product of the sale. There will be continuous two-way data transmission between the stores and the central site. All files will be maintained at the central site. Output will be in two forms: printed reports and on-demand status reports on terminal screens available to store managers locally and to department managers in the headquarters office. Figure 10-10 shows the overall design from a user's viewpoint. The key ingredient of the proposed solution is an automatic reorder procedure: The computer generates orders for any product shown to be below the preset reorder mark.

You make a formal presentation to Mr. Iverson and other members of company management. Slides you prepared on a microcomputer (with special presentation software) accent your points visually. After a brief statement of the problem, you list anticipated benefits to the company; these are listed in Figure 10-11. You explain the design in general terms and describe the expected costs and schedules. With the money saved from the reduced inventory expenses, you project that the system development costs will be repaid in three years. Swift Sport Shoes management accepts your recommendations, and you proceed with the detail design phase.

You design printed reports and screen displays for managers; samples are shown in Figures 10-13 and 10-14. There are many other exacting and time-consuming activities associated with detail design. Although space prohibits discussing them, we list some of these tasks here to give you the flavor of the complexity: You must plan the use of wand readers to read stock codes from merchandise tags, plan to download (send) the price file daily to be stored in the POS terminals, plan all files on disk with regular backups on tape, design the records in each file and the methods to access the files, design the data communications system, draw diagrams to show the flow of the data in the system, and prepare structure charts of program modules. Figure 10-16 shows a skeleton version of a systems flowchart that represents part of the inventory processing. Some of these activities, such as data communications, require special expertise, so you may be coordinating with specialists. Several systems controls are planned, among them a unique numbering system for stock items and editing of all data input at the terminal.

You make another presentation to managers and more technical people, including representatives from information systems. You are given the go-ahead to proceed.

Prototype Results

What is the net result of a prototype system? What will it produce for users? If the whole system is being prototyped, it initially will look something like this: minimum input data, no editing checks, incomplete files, limited security checks, sketchy reports, and minimum documentation. But actual software uses real data to produce real output. Remember that prototyping is an iterative process; the system is changed again and again.

The computer industry is looking even beyond prototyping, to a future using CASE tools.

Figure 10-12 CASE tools: Excelerator in use. Notice that Excelerator uses rounded squares for data flow diagram processes.

7 CASE Tools

CASE tools turn traditional systems approaches upside down. The set of software known as **CASE**—for **Computer-Aided Software Engineering**—tools goes beyond the concept of prototyping. Although CASE tools are still an emerging technology, it is already clear that they are a significant factor in the development of systems. CASE tools provide an automated means of designing and changing systems (Figure 10-12). In fact, integrated CASE tools can automate most of the systems development life cycle.

These tools let the systems analyst generate designs right on the computer screen. Thus, a key ingredient of a package of CASE tools is a graphics interface. What is more, that screen is usually part of a personal computer. Other important CASE ingredients are a data store—often called a data dictionary or even encyclopedia—and the ability to automatically generate code right from the automated design.

CASE tools have several advantages. Foremost is the ability to note inconsistencies in the system design. CASE tools can also make global changes related to a single change; for example, a name changed in one place would be changed automatically throughout the design specifications.

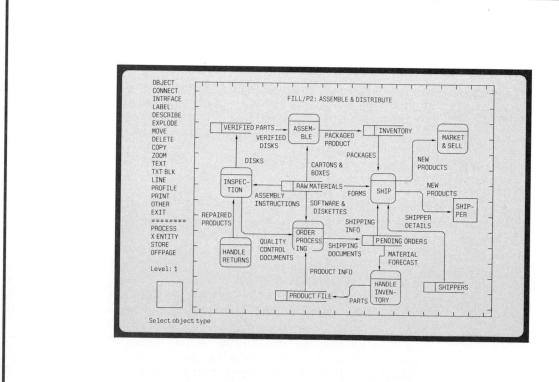

The glitter of CASE tools is unmistakable. But are they worth the hefty price tag? Users report that the products live up to the hype: CASE tools provide consistency, speed, increased productivity, and cost savings.

CASE tools are not a panacea, however. To begin with, they really have value only for new systems—an estimated 80% of computer organization time is devoted to the maintenance of existing systems. Secondly, standards have not been established, leading to a hodgepodge of methodologies from a variety of vendors. Lastly, it is the nature of evolving technology to have setbacks.

But evolve it will. Business demands faster, better ways to create new systems. CASE tools have already been accepted as a major part of the solution.

7 Detail Design

Let us say that the users have accepted your design proposal—you are on your way. You must now develop detail design specifications. This is a time-consuming part of the project, but it is relatively straightforward.

In this phase every facet of the system is considered in detail. Here is a list of some detail design activities: designing output forms and screens, planning input data forms and procedures, drawing system flowcharts, planning file access methods and record formats, planning database interfaces, planning data communications interfaces, designing system security controls, and considering human factors. Some analysts choose to plan the overall logic at this stage, preparing program structure charts, pseudocode, and the like.

This list is not comprehensive, nor will all activities on it be used for all systems. These are just some of the possibilities. Normally, in the detail design phase, parts of the systems are considered in this order:

■ Output requirements

■ Input requirements

■ Files and databases

■ Systems processing

■ Systems controls and backup

Output Requirements

Before you can do anything, you must know what the client wants the system to produce—the output. You must also consider the *medium* of the output—paper, CRT screen, microfilm, and so on. In addition, you must determine the *type* of reports needed (summary, exception, and so on) and the *contents* of the output—what data is needed for the reports. What *forms* the output will be printed on is also a consideration; they may need to be custom

DISCUSSION QUESTION
What are some of the detail design decisions that must be made before proceeding on to coding?

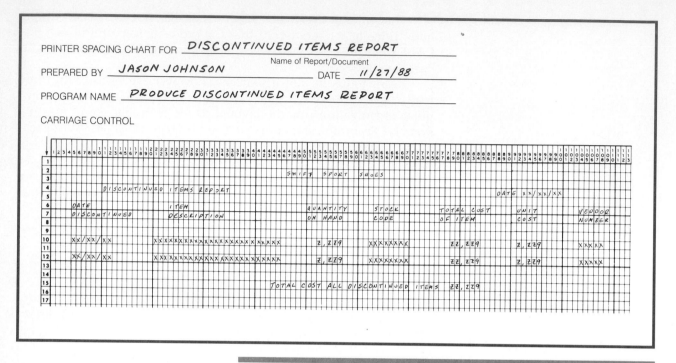

Figure 10-13   Example of a printer spacing chart. This chart shows how a systems analyst wishes the report format to look—headings, columns, and so on—when displayed on a printer. This example shows discontinued items, a report that is part of the new Swift Sport Shoes system.

printed if they go outside the organization to customers or stockholders. You may wish to determine the report format by using a **printer spacing chart,** which shows the position of headings, the spacing between columns, and the location of date and page numbers (Figure 10-13). You may also use screen reports, mock-ups on paper of how the CRT will respond to user queries. A sample screen report is shown in Figure 10-14.

DISCUSSION QUESTION
What would be the result if an analyst tried to plan input requirements before planning output requirements?

Input Requirements

Once your desired output is determined, you must consider what kind of input is required to produce it. First you must consider the input *medium:* Will you try to capture data at the source via POS terminals? Will you put it on diskettes? Next you must consider *content* again—what fields are needed, the order in which they come, and the like. This in turn may involve designing *forms* that will organize data before it is entered. You need to plan some kind of input *editing* process, a check as to whether the data is reasonable—you would not expect a six-figure salary, for example, for someone who works in the mail room. Finally, you need to consider input *volume,* particularly the volume at peak periods. Can the system handle it? A mail-order house, for instance, may have to be ready for higher sales of expensive toys at Christmastime than at other times of the year.

```
                    SWIFT SPORT SHOES              99/99/99
                    INVENTORY QUERY
            Enter stock code ===> XXXXXXX
   Item description  : XXXXXXXXXXXX
   Supplier code     : XXXXX
   Retail price      : $9,999.99
   Location      Qty on hand      Location      Qty on hand
     XXX          99999             XXX          99999
     XXX          99999             XXX          99999
     XXX          99999             XXX          99999
     XXX          99999             XXX          99999
   Total Qty on hand  : 999999
   Total Qty on order : 999999
   Print inventory report Y/N? ===> X
```

Figure 10-14 Example of the design for a screen report. This screen report has been designed as part of the Swift Sport Shoes system to give information about how much of a given stock item is in each store. The report shows an approximation of what the user will see on the CRT after entering a stock code.

Files and Databases

You need to consider how the files in your computer system will be organized: sequentially, directly, with an index, or by some other method. You also need to decide how the files should be accessed. They might be organized as indexed files but be accessed directly or sequentially, for example. You need to determine the format of records making up the data files. If the system has one or more databases, collections of interrelated data (a subject we will cover at length in Chapter 14), then you will have to coordinate your systems design efforts with the database administrator, the person responsible for controlling and updating databases.

Systems Processing

Just as you drew a flow diagram to describe the old system, now you need to show the flow of data in the new system. One method is to use standard ANSI flowchart symbols (Figure 10-15) to illustrate what will be done and what files will be used. Figure 10-16 shows an example of a resulting **systems flowchart.** Another popular way to describe processing is the structure chart we studied in Chapter 7. Note that a systems flowchart is not the same as a logic flowchart. The systems flowchart describes only the "big picture"; a logic flowchart (which you may have used to write programs) gives detailed program logic.

DISCUSSION QUESTION
How do system and logic flowcharts differ?

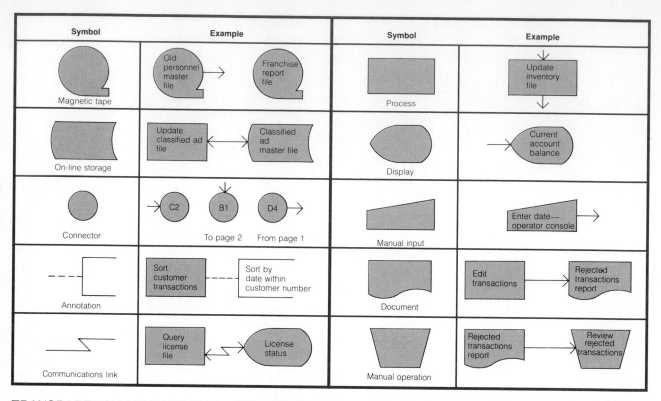

TRANSPARENCY ACETATE #10G
Figure #10-15 (left)

TRANSPARENCY ACETATE #10H
Figure #10-15 (right)

Figure 10-15   ANSI systems flowchart symbols.   These are some of the symbols recommended by the American National Standards Institute for systems flowcharts, which show the movement of data through a system.

Systems Controls and Backup

To make sure data is input, processed, and output correctly and to prevent fraud and tampering with the computer system, you will need to institute appropriate controls. Begin with the source documents, such as time cards or sales orders. Each document should be serially numbered so the system can keep track of it. Documents are time stamped when received and then grouped in batches. Each batch is labeled with the number of documents per batch; these counts are balanced against totals of the processed data. The input is controlled to make sure data is accurately converted from source documents to machine-processable form. Data input to on-line systems is backed up by **system journals,** files whose records represent the transactions made at the terminal, such as an account withdrawal through a bank teller. Processing controls include the data editing procedures we mentioned in the section on input requirements.

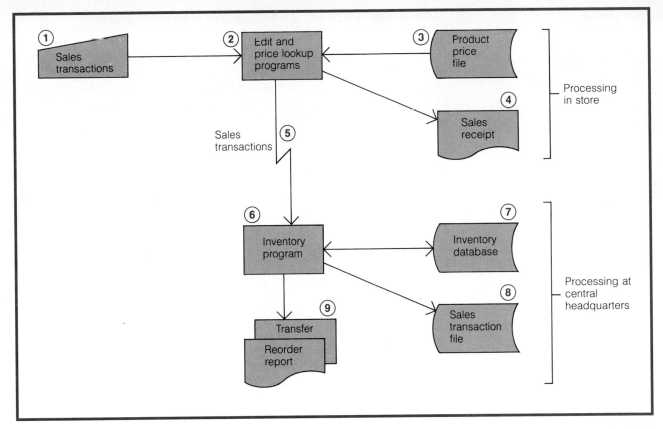

TRANSPARENCY ACETATE #10I
Figure #10-16

Figure 10-16   Systems flowchart.   This very simplified systems flowchart shows part of the processing for the new Swift Sport Shoes inventory system. Note that the top half of the drawing shows processing that takes place in the store. The processing uses a sophisticated POS terminal while the customer waits. The bottom part of the drawing shows processing that is done on the computer at the central headquarters site. The clerk (1) inputs sales transaction data, which (2) is edited by the POS terminal processor. The POS terminal also looks up the item price from the (3) files downloaded earlier in the day from the central site, then (4) prints a sales receipt. That takes care of the customer. Meanwhile, (5) the sales transaction data is sent over data communications lines to the central computer, which (6) processes it for inventory purposes by updating the (7) inventory database, placing the (8) sales transaction on its own file for later auditing and for producing (9) transfer and reorder reports as needed.

It is also important to plan for backup of system files; copies of transaction and master files should be made on a regular basis. These file copies are stored temporarily to back up the originals if they are inadvertently lost or damaged. Often the backup copies are stored off site for added security.

As before, the results of this phase are documented. This large and detailed document, usually referred to as the detail design specifications, is an outgrowth of the preliminary design document. A presentation often accompanies the completion of this stage. Unless something unexpected has happened, it is normal to proceed now with the development of the system.

TEST BANK
Mult. Choice   54-56
Matching D   3, 5, 8-9
Fill-in-the-Blank   32-34

DISCUSSION QUESTION
What do Gantt charts show us?
How are they structured?

7 Phase 4: Systems Development

Finally, the system is actually going to be developed. As a systems analyst you prepare a schedule to monitor the principal activities in **systems development**—programming and testing.

7 Scheduling

Figure 10-17 shows what is known as a **Gantt chart,** a bar chart commonly used to depict schedule deadlines and milestones. In our example the chart shows the work to be accomplished over a given period. It does not, however, show the number of work hours required. If you were the supervisor, it would be common practice for you to ask others on the development team to produce individual Gantt charts of their own activities.

7 Programming

Until this point there has been no programming. (Sometimes people jump the gun and start programming early, but the task often has to be done over if started with incomplete specifications.) Before programming begins, you need to prepare detailed design specifications. Some of this work may already have been done as part of the design phase, but usually programmers participate in refining the design at this point. Design specifications can be developed through detailed logic flowcharts and pseudocode, among other tools.

TRANSPARENCY ACETATE #10J
Figure #10-17

Figure 10-17   Gantt chart.   This bar chart shows the scheduled tasks and milestones of the Swift Sport Shoes project.

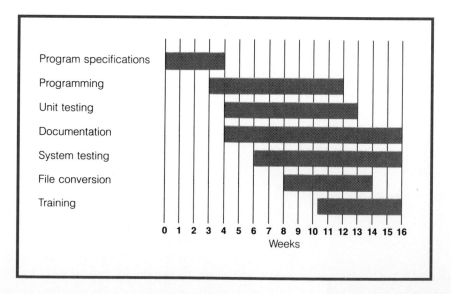

CASE STUDY

SWIFT SPORT SHOES: PHASE 4

Systems Development

 Working with Dennis Harrington of the information systems department, you prepare a Gantt chart, as shown in Figure 10-17. This chart shows the schedule for the inventory project.

Program design specifications are prepared using pseudocode, the design tool Mr. Harrington thinks will be most useful to programmers. The programs will be written in COBOL since that is the primary language of the installation, and it is suitable for this business application. Three programmers are assigned to the project.

You work with the program-

mers to develop a test plan. Some inventory data, both typical and atypical, is prepared to test the new system. You and the programmers continue to build on the documentation base by implementing the pseudocode and by preparing detailed data descriptions, logic narratives, program listings, test data results, and other related material.

---

7 Testing

Would you write a program, then simply turn it over to the client without testing it first? Of course not. Thus, the programmers perform **unit testing,** by which they individually test their own programs, using test data. This is followed by **system testing,** which determines whether all the programs work together satisfactorily. During this process the development team uses test data to test every part of the programs. Finally, **volume testing** uses real data in large amounts. Volume testing sometimes reveals errors that do not show up with test data—errors such as table overflow.

As in every phase of the project, documentation is required. Indeed, documentation is an ongoing activity (as the Gantt chart in Figure 10-17 shows). In this phase documentation describes the program logic and detailed data formats.

7 Phase 5: Implementation

Even though **implementation** is the final phase, a good deal of effort is still required, including the following activities:

- Training
- Equipment conversion
- File conversion
- System conversion

- Auditing
- Evaluation
- Maintenance

Users who resist computers usually cause a marked slump in system use or avoid contact with the computer altogether. In fact, resistance may be so intense that it entails acts of sabotage. Systems people who puzzled over the problem have put resistance into three categories, which blame either (1) the user, (2) the system itself, or (3) some interaction between them. These categories are important to the systems analyst because they guide implementation strategy, particularly in the area of training users.

The theory that blames the user assumes that the system is "good" and that people who resist it are therefore "bad." This theory assumes that resistance can be removed by educating and cajoling users.

The theory that blames the system itself also assumes that the system is good but that resistance can be removed by technical refinements to the system. Somewhere in the heart of this theory, the term *user friendly* was born.

The interaction theory assumes that resistance reflects a conflict between the goals of the system and the goals of the users. This often happens when a system is planned by one group of users but, eventually, other users must deal with the repercussions of its implementation. The message here, of course, is to look to the future when planning systems. Easier said than done.

DISCUSSION QUESTION
What is wrong with the following statement? "Most users learn how to use a new system by reading a manual on the system."

7 Training

Often systems analysts do not give training the attention it deserves because they are so concerned about the computer system itself. But a system can be no better than the people using it. A good time to start training—for at least a few of the users—is at some point during the testing, so that people can begin to learn how to use the system even as the development team is checking it out.

An important tool in training is the user manual, a document prepared to aid users not familiar with the computer system. The user manual can be an outgrowth of the other documentation. But user documentation is just the beginning. Any teacher knows that students learn best by doing. Besides, users are as likely to read a thick manual as they are to read a dictionary. The message is clear: Users must receive hands-on training to learn to use the system. The trainer must prepare exercises that simulate the tasks users will be required to do. For example, a hotel clerk learning a new on-line reservation system is given typical requests to fulfill and uses a terminal to practice. The user manual is used as a reference guide. Setting all this up is not a trivial task; the trainer must consider class space, equipment, data, and the users' schedules.

7 Equipment Conversion

Equipment considerations vary from almost none to installing a mainframe computer and all its peripheral equipment. If you are implementing a small- or medium-size system on established equipment in a major information systems department, then perhaps your equipment considerations will involve no more than negotiating scheduled run time and disk space. If you are purchasing a moderate amount of equipment, such as terminals and modems, then you will be concerned primarily with delivery schedules and compatibility. A major equipment purchase, on the other hand, demands a large amount of time and attention.

For a major equipment purchase you will need site preparation advice from vendors and other equipment experts. You may be considering having walls moved! You will need to know the exact dimensions and weight of the new equipment. There are infamous stories of the new computer being too big to get through the door; one computer, in fact, had to be hoisted by ropes through a window. You will have to consider electrical capacity and wiring hookups. You may need new flooring—probably raised artificial flooring to hide cabling and ease access for repairs to large computers and related equipment. Finally, most medium to large machines need air conditioning and humidity control.

Microcomputer systems are far less demanding, but they too require site planning in terms of the availability of space, accessibility, and cleanliness. And, as the analyst, you are probably the one who does the actual installation.

7 File Conversion

This activity may be very tricky if the existing files are handled manually. The data must be prepared in such a way that it is accessible to computer systems. All the contents of the file drawers in the personnel department, for instance, must now be keyed to disk. Some scheme must be used to input the data files and keep them updated. You may need to employ temporary help. However, many files have already been converted to some machine-accessible form—for use in a prior automated system—so you may need to write a program to convert the old files to the format needed for the new system. This is a much speedier process.

7 System Conversion

This is the stage in which you actually "pull the plug" on the old system and begin using the new one. There are four ways of handling the conversion.

Direct conversion means the user simply stops using the old system and starts using the new one—a somewhat risky method since there is no other system to fall back on if anything goes wrong. This procedure is best followed only if the old system is in unusable condition. A **phased conversion** is one in which the organization eases into the new system one step at a time so that all the users are using some of the system. In contrast, in a **pilot conversion** the entire system is used by some of the users and is extended to all users once it has proved successful. In **parallel conversion**—the most prolonged and expensive method—the old and new systems are operated simultaneously for some time, until users are satisfied that the new system performs to their standards.

System conversion is often a time of stress and confusion for all concerned. As the analyst, your credibility is on the line, for you must now come up with a usable system. During this time users are often doing double duty, trying to perform their regular jobs and simultaneously cope with a new computer system. Problems seem to appear in all areas, from input to output. Clearly, this is a period when your patience is needed.

7 Auditing

Security violations, whether deliberate or unintentional, can be difficult to detect. Once data is in the system and on media such as disks, it is possible for it to be altered without any trace in the source documents—unless the systems analyst has designed an **audit trail** to trace output back to the source data. In real-time systems security violations can be particularly elusive unless all CRT terminal transactions are recorded on disk or tape for later references by auditors. Modern auditors no longer shuffle mountains of paper;

DISCUSSION QUESTION
Which system conversion method might be appropriate in these situations?
(1) The system will be used by branches in different cities. The branch in Tulsa is supportive, others less so. (Pilot)
(2) The system will support critical life-sustaining functions at a hospital. (Parallel)
(3) The old system is in disarray and the key employees are all new. (Direct)
(4) The system is complex and management wants to ease into it. (Phase)

CASE STUDY

SWIFT SPORT SHOES: PHASE 5

Implementation

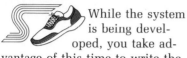 While the system is being developed, you take advantage of this time to write the user and operator manuals. This is done in conjunction with your plans for training store personnel and managers in the use of the system. The training is not a trivial task, but you do not have to do all of it yourself. Training on the new POS cash registers will be done by the vendor. You plan to hold training classes for the people who will use the local micros to run programs and to send data to the computer at headquarters. You will have separate classes to train managers on retrieving data from the system via terminal commands. In both cases training will be hands-on. Company personnel should find the training enjoyable because CRT dialogue procedures are user friendly—the user is instructed clearly every step of the way.

File conversion is painful. One evening after the stores close, the staff works overtime to take inventory in the stores. Temporary personnel are hired to key an inventory master file from this data. Transactions for the master file are accumulated as more purchases are made, up until the time the system is ready for use; then the master will be updated from the transactions generated by the POS terminals. After discussing the relative merits of the various system conversion methods, you and Ms. Christie agree that a pilot conversion would be ideal. Together you decide to bring up the original store first, then add other stores to the system one or two at a time.

Mr. Iverson puts together a local team consisting of Ms. Christie, a programmer, and an accountant to evaluate the new system. Since your documentation is comprehensive, it is relatively easy for the team to check the system completely to see if it is functioning according to specifications. The evaluation report notes several positive items, including: out-of-stock conditions have almost disappeared (only two instances in one store in one month), inventory transfer among stores is a smooth operation, and store managers feel an increased sense of control. Negative items are relatively minor and can be fixed as the system goes into a maintenance operation.

---

instead, they have computer programs of their own to monitor applications programs and data.

7 Evaluation

Is the system working? How well is it meeting the original goals, specifications, budgets, schedules, and so forth? Out of such evaluation will come adjustments that will improve the system. Approaches to evaluation vary. Sometimes the systems analyst and someone from the client organization evaluate the system against preset criteria. Some organizations prefer to bring in an independent evaluating team on the assumption that independent members will be free from bias and expectations.

7 Maintenance

Many consider maintenance to be a separate phase, one that begins only when the initial development effort is complete. In any case the maintenance process is an ongoing activity, one that lasts the lifetime of the system. Monitoring and necessary adjustments continue so that the computer produces the expected results. Maintenance tasks also include making revisions and additions to the computer system. As more computer systems are implemented, organizations will obviously have an increased number of systems to maintain. In many computer installations a very high percentage of personnel and effort is dedicated to maintenance. This necessarily limits the number of personnel available for systems development. The net result is often a backlog of development projects.

7 Putting It All Together: Is There a Formula?

The preceding discussion may leave the impression that by simply following a recipe a magical system can be developed. In fact, novice analysts sometimes have the impression that there is a formula for developing systems. It would be more correct to say that there are guidelines. Each system is unique, so there can be no one way that fits every one.

Historically, even analysts who followed the guidelines were not always successful in developing systems. Systems analysts have been embarrassed to find that they were not always good at estimating time, so schedules constantly slipped. (Budget overruns are one of the obvious results of sliding schedules.) Some observers, in fact, think that systems analysis is so ambiguous that analysts do not even know when they are finished. Sometimes it seems that the definition of project completion is the point at which analysts have run out of time on the schedule.

Another frequent problem has been imperfect communication between analysts and users. Poor communication results in poorly defined specifications, which, in turn, result in a supposedly complete system that does not do what the user expects. In addition, by-guess-and-by-gosh methods of analysis and design have often been used instead of formal tools. In the 1960s and 1970s some systems were completed according to plan and schedule, but many others were not.

Out of these experiences, however, have come some solutions. Managers have become more sophisticated—and more realistic—in planning schedules and budgets. Analysts have learned to communicate with users. In addition to the analysis and design approach described here (which is considered the traditional way of creating a system), there are other, newer approaches, which are beyond the scope of this book. If you pursue a career in systems analysis, you will no doubt encounter these approaches and find them useful.

Being a systems analyst can be important work; an analyst is in a position to help institute fundamental changes that alter business operations, work habits, and use of time. As we suggested at the

PERSPECTIVES

CAN WE ABSOLUTELY POSITIVELY GUARANTEE THE SYSTEM?

Some jobs have little room for error or second guessing—the job must be done right the first time. An air traffic controller has such a job; for example, directing a plane to the wrong altitude could have fatal consequences. Systems analysts, on the other hand, have many opportunities to ponder, to test, to re-think. Given those opportunities, it seems reasonable to hope that the completed system will have a high degree of reliability. In fact, some people think that an analyst should be able to absolutely positively guarantee that the system works as it is supposed to.

However, reliability has not historically been the hallmark of computer systems. There are several reasons for this. One is the inherent complexity of most computer systems; a related reason is the failure to understand the complexity at the outset. The

most perplexing is that, despite heroic efforts by the analyst, the nature of the desired system often changes as it is developed. Finally, we must acknowledge the possibility of incompetent computer personnel.

Although many systems are less than perfect when first implemented, computer personnel usually work out the kinks until the system becomes acceptable. Systems that are true disasters are often hidden from view; few organizations want to highlight the details of computer fumbles. However, some unreliable systems are so much in the public eye that the bad news cannot be concealed. An example is the doomed computer system for the New Jersey Division of Motor Vehicles, which left thousands of angry motorists with invalid registrations or licenses through no fault of their own.

Users stuck with unreliable systems are changing their focus from "What went wrong?" to "Who is going to pay?" That is, they want to know who is liable. Liability concerns also extend to unreliable purchased software. In the rush to be first on the market with innovative software, program bugs seem inevitable. In fact, there is probably no software publisher who could certify that a program is bug-free.

What is an analyst to do? Work harder? Be more careful? There are no simplistic answers. A competent analyst in a professional environment should produce a successful product. But the day may be coming when analysts and software vendors carry liability insurance. If this sounds far-fetched, remember that doctors thought liability insurance was a joke just a few years ago.

beginning of this chapter, however, a systems analyst must be sensitive to the possible effects of his or her work on people's lives. The real danger, it has been remarked, is not that computers will begin to think like people, but that people will begin to think like computers.

7 Getting Closer to Computers

This chapter has addressed a broad spectrum of system change, taking into account its effects on the entire organization. But an organization is composed of individuals, and individuals these days are likely to have their own personal computers. This important topic deserves special consideration, so we devote the next five chapters to personal computers and their applications in business and in the home.

Summary and Key Terms

■ A **system** is an organized set of related components established to accomplish a certain task. A **computer system** has a computer as one of its components. A **client** requests a **systems analysis,** a study of an existing system, to determine both how it works and how well it meets the needs of its **users,** who are usually employees and customers. Systems analysis can lead to **systems design,** the development of a plan for an improved system. A **systems analyst** normally does both the analysis and design. Some people do both programming and analysis and have the title **programmer/ analyst.** The success of the project requires both *impetus* and *authority* within the client organization to change the current system.

■ The systems analyst must be a **change agent** who encourages **user involvement** in the development of a new system.

■ The systems analyst has three main functions: (1) **coordinating** schedules and task assignments, (2) **communicating** analysis and design information to those involved with the system, and (3) **planning and designing** the system with the help of the client organization. A systems analyst should have a creative, analytical mind, good communication and organizational skills, self-discipline and self-direction, and the ability to work without tangible results.

■ The **systems development life cycle** (SDLC) has five phases: (1) preliminary investigation, (2) analysis, (3) design, (4) development, and (5) implementation.

■ Phase 1, which is also known as the **feasibility study,** or **system survey,** is the **preliminary investigation** of the problem to determine how—and if— an analysis and design project should proceed. Aware of the importance of establishing a smooth working relationship, the analyst refers to an **organization chart** showing the lines of authority within the client organization. After determining the nature and scope of the problem, the analyst expresses the users' needs as objectives.

■ In phase 2, **systems analysis,** the analyst gathers and analyzes data from common sources such as written documents, interviews, questionnaires, observation, and sampling.

■ The client organization determines what data sources are accessible, but the analyst must then decide which are appropriate. The analyst must evaluate the relevance of **written documents** such as procedure manuals and reports. **Interview** options include the **structured interview,** in which all questions are planned and written in advance, and the **unstructured interview,** in which the questions can vary from the plan. Although interviews can allow flexible questioning and the establishment of rapport with clients, they can also be time-consuming. **Questionnaires** can save time and expense and allow anonymous answers, but response rates are often low. Another method is simply **observing** how the organization functions, sometimes through **participant observation,** temporary participation in the organization's activities. Statistical **sampling** is also useful, especially when there is a large volume of data.

■ The systems analyst may use a variety of charts and diagrams to analyze the data. A **data flow diagram (DFD)** provides an easy-to-follow picture of the flow of data through the system. The elements of a DFD are processes, files, sources and sinks, and labeled vectors. **Processes** are the actions taken on the data. A **file** is a repository of data. A **source** is a data origin outside the organization; a **sink** is a destination for data going outside the organization. **Vectors** are arrows indicating the direction in which the data travels. Another common tool for data analysis is the **decision table,** or **decision logic table,** a standard table indicating alternative actions under particular conditions.

■ Upon completion of the systems analysis phase, the analyst submits a report summarizing the system's problems and requirements and making recommendations to the client on what course to take next.

■ In phase 3, **systems design,** the analyst submits a general preliminary design for the client's approval before proceeding to the specific detail design.

■ **Preliminary design** involves reviewing the system requirements before submitting an overall plan or, perhaps, alternative **candidates.** The analyst presents the plan in a form the users can understand. The analyst may also develop a **prototype,** a limited working system or part of a system that gives users a preview of how the new system will work. The set of software known as **CASE**—for **Computer-Aided Software Engineering**—tools goes beyond prototyping, providing an automated means of designing and changing systems.

- **Detail design** normally involves considering the parts of the system in the following order: output requirements, input requirements, files and data-bases, system processing, and system controls and backup. Output requirements include the *medium* of the output, the *type* of reports needed, the *contents* of the output, and the *forms* on which the output will be printed. The analyst might determine the report format by using a **printer spacing chart,** which shows the position of headings, columns, dates, and page numbers. Input requirements include the input *medium*, the *content* of the input, and the design of data entry *forms*. The analyst also plans an input *editing* process for checking whether the data is reasonable and makes sure that the system can handle variations in input *volume*. The organization of files and databases must be specified. The processing must also be described, perhaps by using a **systems flowchart** that illustrates the flow of data through ANSI flow-chart symbols or by using the hierarchical organization of a structure chart. The analyst must also spell out system controls and backup. Data input to on-line systems must be backed up by **system journals,** files that record transactions made at the terminal. Processing controls involve data editing procedures. Finally, copies of transaction and master files should be made regularly.

- Phase 4, **systems development,** consists of scheduling, programming, and testing. Schedule deadlines and milestones are often shown on a **Gantt chart.** The programming effort involves selecting the program language and developing the design specifications. Programmers then do **unit testing,** (individual testing of their own programs), which is followed by **system testing,** (the assessment of how the programs work together). **Volume testing** tests the entire system with real data. Documentation of phase 4 describes the program logic and the detailed data formats.

- Phase 5, **implementation,** includes these activities: training, to prepare users of the new system; equipment conversion, which involves ensuring compatibility and providing enough space and electrical capacity; file conversion, making old files accessible to the new system; system conversion;

auditing, the design of an **audit trail** to trace data from output back to the source documents; evaluation, the assessment of the system's performance; and maintenance, the monitoring and adjustment of the system.

- System conversion may be done in one of four ways: **direct conversion,** immediately replacing the old system with the new system; **phased conversion,** easing in the new system a step at a time; **pilot conversion,** testing the entire system with a few users and extending it to the rest when proved successful; and **parallel conversion,** operating the old and new systems concurrently until the new system is proved successful.

7 Review Questions

1. What is the distinction between systems analysis and systems design?

2. Describe the main duties of a systems analyst.

3. List some qualities of a good systems analyst, and discuss the importance of each one.

4. Name the five phases of the systems development life cycle.

5. Describe the preliminary investigation phase and explain why it is necessary.

6. Discuss the advantages and disadvantages of the most common sources of data about a system.

7. Describe the use of data flow diagrams.

8. Describe the prototyping approach and explain:
   a. how it differs from the traditional systems development life cycle, and
   b. why it is useful.

9. Describe the main activities involved in detail design.

10. Discuss what is involved in systems development.

11. Describe the main activities in the implementation phase.

12. Why is documentation of each phase important?

Discussion Questions

1. Which qualities of a systems analyst do you consider to be the most important? Explain your answer.

2. Does following the traditional guidelines limit the creativity of a systems analyst? Explain your answer.

3. Explain why it is so important that a systems analyst interacts well with others.

4. Should system evaluation be done by the analyst and the client organization or by an independent evaluating team? Explain your answer.

How to Buy Your Own Personal Computer

Owning a personal computer is not like owning a toaster or a television set, nor is buying one like buying a suit off the rack. There is a lot to learn about the new technology and the ways in which it might help you.

We cannot pick your new computer system for you any more than we could pick a new car for you. But we can tell you what to look for. We do not mean that we can lead you to a particular brand and model—so many new products are introduced into this area every month that doing so would be impossible. If you are just starting out, however, we can help you define your needs and ask the right questions.

Where Do You Start?

Maybe you have already done some thinking and have decided that a personal computer offers advantages. Now what?

Who Needs It?

Here are some common home applications for personal computers:

- Education for children
- Filing and retrieving records

- Word processing
- Business "homework"
- Entertainment, games
- Running a home business
- Personal finance

- Desktop publishing
- Access to remote information
- Learning programming
- Shopping and banking from home

You can start by talking to other personal computer owners about how they got started and how to avoid pitfalls. (Plan on a long conversation. Personal computer owners are notoriously talkative on this subject.) Or you can read some computer magazines, especially ones with evaluations and ratings, to get a feel for what is available. Next visit several dealers. Don't be afraid to ask questions. You are considering a major purchase, so plan to shop around.

Analyze Your Wants and Needs

You may want to narrow your computer search by determining what price range you are in. But it might make more sense to begin with a needs/wants analysis. Why do you want a computer? Be

Shopping for software and hardware. *There is a wide range of useful products available today. Many users spend more on software than they did on the original equipment.*

realistic: Will it probably wind up being used for games most of the time or for business applications? People use personal computers for a variety of applications, as noted in the box called "Who Needs It?" Prioritize your needs; don't plan to do everything at once. At some point you will have to establish a budget ceiling. After you have examined your needs, you can select the best hardware/software combinations for the money. Before we look at hardware and software in detail, pause to consider whether you want to buy now or buy later.

Buy Now or Buy Later?

People who are interested in buying a computer may delay their purchases because the price is too high or because they think more sophisticated computers are coming soon. Prices are certainly variable, and it is quite true that you may get a bargain by waiting. And it is also true that something will no doubt come along in a year or two (or even sooner) that will make present equipment seem inadequate in some way. Improvements usually take the form of (1) the same kind of equipment becoming available at a lower price; (2) new models or competing equipment offering more power (more speed, more memory), easier handling, or a wider range of better-designed software; or (3) the quality of the new models is better for a lower price.

Yet, clearly, the longer you wait to buy, the longer you miss out on acquiring experience and expertise with personal computers. And, of course, you miss out on the usefulness and fun. Certainly, if you want a machine for word processing or for business-related purposes, there is no point in waiting. If you want something that is easier to use than the equipment you see now, however, you may be advised to put it off for at least a year.

What to Look For in Hardware

The basic microcomputer system consists of a central processing unit (CPU) and memory, a monitor, a keyboard, a storage device (diskette or hard-disk drive), and a printer. Unless you know someone who can help you out with technical expertise, you are probably best advised to look for a packaged system— that is, one in which the above components (with the possible exception of the printer) are assembled and packaged by the same manufacturer. This gives you some assurance that the various components will work together.

Let us now take a quick look at the various parts of the system: CPU, memory, monitor, keyboard, secondary storage, printers, and other hardware options. Then we will consider portability and some hardware options.

Central Processing Unit

Personal computers started out with what is known as an 8-bit processor, but now most manufacturers make machines with 16-bit or 32-bit processors. More bits mean more power, faster processing, more memory, and a larger and more complex instruction set.

Memory

Memory is measured in bytes. The amount of memory you need in your computer is determined by the amount of

The complete microcomputer system. *You may not need fine oak furniture right away, but to have a complete microcomputer system you will need a central processing unit and memory, monitor, keyboard, storage device, and printer.*

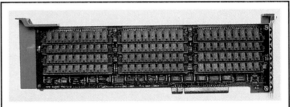

Adding memory. *This add-on memory board gives an IBM PS/2 an additional 12 million bytes of memory.*

memory required by the applications programs (like word processing or spreadsheets) that you want to use. A minimum of 640K bytes is suggested for personal computers used for business applications. You may be able to get by with less, however, if you buy a home computer primarily for games or word processing. Most machines have expandable memory, so you can add more later if you need it. If you plan to use the IBM OS/2 operating system, you will need 2MB to run the applications programs written for OS/2.

Monitor

Sometimes called a video display screen, the monitor is a very important part of your computer system—you will spend all your time looking at it. Before you buy any monitor, you should test it by attaching it to the computer you intend to purchase and running some of the applications programs you intend to use. This is the only way to be sure that you will not be disappointed when you take your computer home.

Discussion of some of the factors you should consider when selecting a monitor follows.

Monitor displays. *(Top) Color monitors let you see your graphic displays and text in a multitude of colors. (Bottom) High-resolution monochrome monitors are highly readable.*

Screen Width. Although some Macintosh computers have a 9-inch screen, most monitors have a screen display of between 12 and 14 inches. Generally, a larger screen provides a display that is easier to read, so you will probably want at least a 12-inch screen. Some monitors called Full-Page monitors can display a complete $8\frac{1}{2}$-by-11-inch page of text on the screen. These monitors are especially useful for desktop publishing applications. For most other purposes, a screen that displays 25 lines of 80 characters each is the standard.

Screen Readability. As you shop for your monitor, be sure to compare the readability of different monitors. First, make sure that the screen is bright and has minimum flicker. Next, check the shape of the characters. Some screens are difficult to read because they chop off the descenders—the tails that fall below the line—of the lowercase letters *g, p, q,* and *y.* In addition, look to see whether the characters appear crowded on the screen—that is, jammed together to a degree that makes them difficult to read. Glare is another major consideration: Nearby harsh lighting can cause glare to bounce off the screen, and some screens seem more susceptible to glare than others. Check to see whether a glare-reducing screen is available for the monitor.

A key factor affecting screen quality is resolution, a measure of the number of dots, or pixels, that can appear on the screen. The higher the resolution—that

Color or Monochrome. Monochrome (green, amber, or white on a black background) monitors are best when a computer will be heavily used for word processing applications. If you want to create graphics on your screen or if you plan to run entertainment programs on your computer, you will probably want to buy a color monitor. Color monitors are sometimes called RGB (for Red, Green, Blue) monitors. RGBI (for Red, Green, Blue with Intensity adjustability) monitors are more modern than RGB monitors. Many programs are written to be run solely on computers with color monitors. Some color monitors have a text switch on the front; pressing the switch changes a color monitor into a monochrome monitor for word processing applications.

is, the more dots—the more solid text characters appear. For graphics, more pixels means sharper images. But do not be tempted to pay a higher price for the best resolution unless your applications need it.

Graphics Adapter Boards. If you want to use an applications program that displays graphics and the computer you are considering does not come with the ability display them, you will have to buy a graphics adapter board (sometimes called a graphics card) to insert in the computer. There are several different standards for graphics adapter boards. Monitors designed for use with one type of card may not be capable of understanding the signals from a different type. Multiscan monitors, also called multimode monitors, are designed to work with a variety of graphics adapter boards. Check carefully to be sure that you have the right monitor/graphics board combination.

Ergonomic Considerations. Look to see whether the monitor can swivel and tilt, since this will remove the need to sit in one position for a long period of time. The ability to adjust the position of

the monitor becomes an important consideration if there are different users for the same computer. Another possibility is to purchase add-on equipment that will perform these functions. If you need a portable computer to haul back and forth to different places, however, a screen that is attached to the keyboard will be easier for you to handle and less likely to be damaged in transit.

Keyboard

Keyboards vary a lot in quality. The best way to know what suits you is to sit down in the store and type for a while. Consider how the keys feel; the color, slope, and layout of the keyboard; and whether it is detachable.

Keyboard Feel. You will find that there are real differences in the feel of keyboards. Find a keyboard that lets you know through your sense of touch when you have engaged a key and released it. Make sure the keys are not cramped together; you will find that your typing is error-prone if your fingers are constantly overlapping more than one key. This is especially of concern if you have large hands, chubby fingers, or long fingernails.

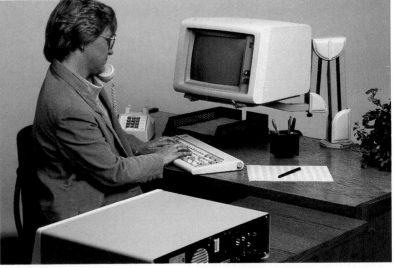

Ergonomic considerations. (Left) By placing a glare shield over your CRT monitor, you decrease glare and increase the clarity of the characters. (Right) This monitor stand tilts and swivels so that your neck does not have to.

Typewriter-style keyboard. *Many keyboards now have 12 function keys along the top of the board, a numeric keyboard on the right, plus an extra cursor movement pad.*

Secondary storage. *(Top) $3\frac{1}{2}$-inch diskette drives are the standard on IBM PS/2 and Macintosh computers. The $3\frac{1}{2}$-inch diskette is enclosed in a plastic case, which helps protect the disk. $5\frac{1}{4}$-inch floppy diskettes are widely used on the IBM personal computer line and its compatibles. (Bottom) The inside of this hard disk drive shows the access arm hovering over the disk.*

Keyboard Color. Ideally, keys should be gray with a matte finish. The dull finish reduces glare.

Keyboard Slope. If you plan to use your keyboard for many hours at a time, its slope will be very important to you. A keyboard slope should be a minimum of 7 degrees and a maximum of 15 degrees. Slopes outside this range can cause discomfort in the wrist and, consequently, high error rates. Some personal computer keyboards have adjustable slopes.

Keyboard Layout. Besides evaluating keyboard feel, look at the layout of the keyboard. Most follow the standard QWERTY layout of typewriter keyboards. However, some also have a separate numeric keypad to the right of the character keys. You may find this useful if you enter a lot of numbers. In addition, some keyboards have separate function keys. The IBM Personal System/2, for instance, has 12 function keys in a row above the regular keys. These keys are used to move things around on the screen, delete, and so on. To accomplish these tasks with computers without function keys, you must hold down a pair of keys (not labeled as to function) simultaneously. This is less convenient.

Detachable Keyboard. Although you may be used to typing on a typewriter, where the keyboard is not separate from the rest of the machine, you may find a computer with a detachable keyboard—onc that can be held on your lap, for example—desirable. You can move a detachable keyboard around to suit your comfort. This feature becomes indispensable when a computer is used by people of different sizes, such as large adults and small children.

Secondary Storage

You will need one or more disk drives to read programs into your computer and to store any programs or data that you wish to keep.

Diskettes. Most personal computer software today comes on diskettes. Floppy disks, used with many older personal computers, are $5\frac{1}{4}$ inches in diameter. New diskettes are only $3\frac{1}{2}$ inches across and have become the modern standard. Because $3\frac{1}{2}$-inch diskettes are smaller and protected inside a plastic case, they fit in convenient places, such as a purse or a pocket. Their drives take up less space in the computer, and they can hold more data.

On most systems at least one disk drive is built right into the computer. Although not always necessary, you may find it helpful to have two (dual) disk drives to facilitate copying of disks for safekeeping. If your system has only one built-in drive, you may purchase another drive as a separate component.

Hard Disks. Most hard disks (also called *fixed disks*) are 5-inch or $3\frac{1}{2}$-inch Winchester disks. Although more expensive than diskette drives, hard disks are fast and reliable and hold more data. These features have made the hard disk an increasingly attractive option for personal computer buyers. Many personal computers come with a built-in hard-disk drive with a storage capacity of at least 20 million bytes—characters—of data; greater capacities are available if you can pay for them. A hard disk can also be bought separately.

Printers

A printer is probably the most expensive piece of peripheral equipment you will buy. Although some inexpensive printers are available, most likely you will find that those costing $400 and up are the ones most useful to you.

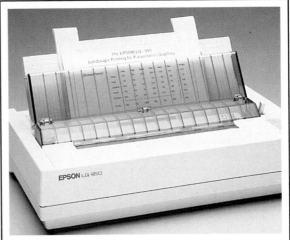

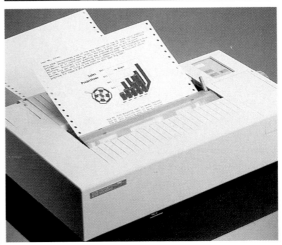

Printers. *(Top) 24-pin dot-matrix printers, such as this one, can produce results of near letter quality. (Middle) Laser printers are often used with desktop publishing software. (Bottom) Ink-jet printers can produce colorful graphic output.*

A dot-matrix printer in draft mode can print fast. However, the type is less readable than output from other printers or from a dot-matrix printer in near letter quality mode.

This is an example of near letter quality output. A dot-matrix printer prints each character twice or uses a more dense array of dots for improved quality.

Letter-quality printers with a daisy wheel are relatively slow. However, as shown here, they produce fully-formed characters that rival output from the finest typewriters. This makes them desirable for business correspondence.

Laser printers are fast and they produce high quality output, as shown here. They are useful for desktop publishing, which often combines text and graphics in one document. Generally, laser printers are more expensive than most other printers.

Examples of output from various printers.

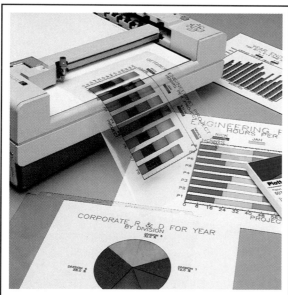

A plotter. *Plotters for personal computers can produce high-quality graphic output.*

When choosing a printer, you will want to consider speed, quality, and cost. Also verify whether a printer will work with the applications software you intend to use. For example, will it print graphs created with Lotus 1-2-3? If you plan to use your personal computer for desktop publishing, you want a printer with an established page description language such as PostScript.

Dot-Matrix Printers. For "everyday" printing, a dot-matrix printer, costing about $500, will do very nicely. A dot-matrix printer can print as many as 250 characters per second, forming each character out of a grid of pins or dots much like the lights on a bank temperature sign or stadium scoreboard. The appearance of the characters is not as good as those you would get from, say, an electric typewriter. This is why they are not considered "letter-quality" printers—that is, adequate for office correspondence. Some dot-matrix printers, however, can make a second pass at the characters or use a more dense array of dots and make the letters more fully formed; the result is called near letter quality. Dot-matrix printers can also be used for printing computer-generated graphics.

Letter-Quality Printers. A letter-quality printer produces the sharp characters that are a must for business correspondence. Most letter-quality printers use a daisy wheel, a device that can be removed, like a typewriter element, and replaced with another wheel with a different type font on it. The disadvantage of the daisy wheel printer is that it is relatively slow—it often produces only 55 characters per second or less. A letter-quality printer typically costs between $500 and $3000. Daisy wheel printers cannot print computer-generated graphics.

Ink-Jet Printers. Although relatively slow, ink-jet printers can produce text and graphics whose color range and density usually surpass the color graphics of dot-matrix printers. The price spectrum is from $300 to several thousand dollars.

Laser Printers. These printers are top of the line in print quality and speed. They are also the most expensive, starting at about $2000. Laser printers are used by desktop publishers to produce text and graphics on the same page.

Plotters. Plotters draw hard-copy graphics output in the form of maps, bar charts, engineering drawings, overhead transparencies, and even two- or three-dimensional illustrations. Plotters often come with a set of six pens in six different colors.

Printer Covers. Although quiet printers are available, most dot-matrix and letter-quality printers are noisy. An unmuffled printer generates about 80 decibels of sound, somewhere between a typewriter (70 decibels) and an outboard motor (90 decibels). If you will be working in an enclosed environment with your printer, the noise may become irritating. To reduce the problem, consider inexpensive, sound-absorbing pads to go under the printer. If the problem is extreme, plastic printer covers are available that will reduce the noise to the level of a quiet conversation.

Portability

Do you plan to let your computer grow roots after you install it, or will you be moving it around? Do you want a large video display or will the smaller versions on portable computers do? Portable computers have found a significant niche in the market, mainly because they are

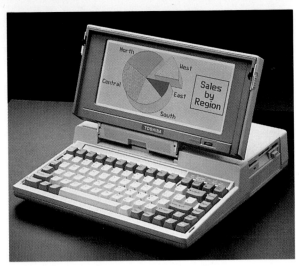

A laptop computer. *These small computers, which often include built-in software, are an attractive option for users who travel.*

packaged to travel easily. The ultimate in portability is the laptop computer, which is lightweight (often under 10 pounds) and small enough to fit in a briefcase. There are trade-offs, however, such as screen readability and the amount of internal power available. Consider all aspects carefully.

Other Hardware Options

There are a great many hardware variations; we will mention a few here.

Communications Connections. If you wish to connect your computer via telephone lines to electronic bulletin boards, mainframe computers, or information utilities such as CompuServe or The Source, you will need a modem. This device converts computer data into signals that can be transmitted over telephone lines. The Hayes Smartmodem family of products has become the industry standard; most new modems claim some degree of Hayes compatibility. A modem with a speed of 1200 or 2400 bits per second is sufficient for most uses, although modems with speeds up to 9600 bits per second are available.

Other Input Devices. If you are interested in games, you may wish to acquire a joy stick, which looks sort of like the stick shift on a car. A joy stick allows you to manipulate a cursor on the screen.

A more sophisticated device is a mouse, a gadget that you roll on a table-top to move the cursor on the screen to make menu selections. Many software packages and operating systems are designed to let you work most efficiently if your computer has a mouse attached. If you are planning to use your computer for desktop publishing, a mouse is essential.

A scanner or digitizer is very useful if you need to store pictures and typed documents in your computer. Scanners are frequently purchased by people who want to use their computers to do desktop publishing.

There are several other input devices available. Ask your dealer about the equipment that follows.

Color Slide–Producing Equipment. If you plan to use your computer primarily to produce text and graphics slides for presentations, consider purchasing one of the devices designed to produce 35mm color slides from computer images.

Surge Protectors. These devices, sometimes called power protectors, protect against the electrical ups and downs that can affect the operation of your computer. Some of the more expensive models provide up to 10 minutes of full power to your computer if the electric power in your home or office is knocked out. This gives you time to save your work to disk (so that it won't be lost as the power fails) or to print out a report you need immediately. If lightning storms or power fluctuations occur in your area, you would be well advised to purchase a surge protector if one is not supplied with your computer.

A modem. *This external modem can be used with a variety of computers and can be moved from one machine to another.*

Color slide–producing equipment. *Data from the computer screen is transferred to the screen of the Polaroid Palette, where it can be photographed and developed quickly into color prints, slides, or overheads.*

Interface Boards and Cabling. All the hardware components of your system need to be connected with the proper cables. Sometimes these cables and any of the interface boards they require are sold as separate components. Check to be sure that you have all the necessary boards and cables when you buy your system. If you ask a dealer for a printer, you will get a printer; do not forget to add that you need the proper cable and any additional hardware required to connect it to your computer.

Sound. Be sure to check out sound effects, particularly if you are interested in games. Make sure there are different tones, that they are not unpleasant, and that you have control over starting and stopping them. Many systems also have packaged software that allows you to produce computer-generated music.

What to Look For in Software

There was a time when standardization of personal computers was non-existent; each type of personal computer had its own operating system. Software that ran on one computer did not necessarily run on another. This is still true to some extent, but great strides have been made.

In a nutshell, the current standard is MS-DOS, made popular by IBM. Most personal computers today are compatible with the established IBM standard. Another new standard from IBM, called OS/2, is beginning to emerge. Applications programs that will do what you want to do are available for your use if you purchase a computer that uses one of

> **System Requirements**
> **Operating Systems:**
> PC-DOS (2.0 or higher for single user)
> **Hardware Requirements:**
> IBM PC, XT, AT and compatibles.
> Hard disk required.
> **Main Memory:**
> Minimum of 640K bytes of RAM required.
> **Printer:**
> Any IBM PC compatible printer.

Read the directions. Make sure your hardware works with the software you are buying by reading the fine print carefully.

these two operating systems. There are also many excellent programs written to run on the Apple Macintosh.

We have noted the main categories of software in the list in the box called "Who Needs It?" Now let us consider hardware requirements, brand names, demonstrations, and languages.

Hardware Requirements for Software

When you look at a software package in a store, be sure to read what kind of hardware it requires. For example, you may read "This package requires two disk drives, an 80-character display screen and printer, 256K of memory and MS-DOS." You would hate to get home with your new software package and find you need to spend more for a joy stick or a few hundred dollars for a special circuit board that goes inside the computer. Usually, the salesperson can advise you on hardware requirements for any particular software you might want to buy.

Brand Names

In general, publishers of brand-name software usually offer better support than smaller, less well-known companies. Support may be in the form of tutorials, classes by the vendor or others, and the all-important hotline assistance. Support may be crucial. In addition, brand-name publishers usually produce superior documentation and offer upgrades to new and better versions of the software.

Software Demonstrations

Wherever you can, ask to have the software demonstrated. You should not buy anything until you see that it works.

Despite this admonition, we must acknowledge that approximately half of the software purchased for personal computers is ordered through the mail from advertisements in computer magazines. In some cases, you may rely on the reputation of the software manufacturer or a recommendation from a friend. Other useful aids are the detailed software reviews found in trade publications such as *InfoWorld* or *PC Magazine*.

Languages

You may purchase languages on disk if you wish to write your own applications programs. BASIC is the most popular language for personal computers, but some personal computers can use FORTRAN, Pascal, C, and other languages.

Shopping Around: Where to Buy

Where you buy is important, and usually the trade-off is between price and service—but not necessarily.

The Dealer

The important point to remember is that you are buying a relationship with a dealer at the same time you are buying your computer. In a sense, you are also paying for your dealer's expertise. Answers to your questions, both now and in the future, may be the single most important part of your purchase. Vendors like IBM, Hewlett-Packard, and Apple have established a nationwide organization of authorized dealers. A vendor-authorized dealer is usually a well-established business with recognized expertise in the product they sell.

You can also buy a personal computer in a computer store such as Computer-Land. You can buy one from a discount house or a bookstore. You can buy one

Dealer support. *Some dealers provide software demonstrations so you can try before you buy.*

from the manufacturer's own retail outlets; Tandy-Radio Shack has its own stores.

Of course, you can buy a personal computer or peripheral by mail or from an individual. But we don't recommend this unless you have a lot of experience, because such a sale is usually without dealer support. Furthermore, you need to be absolutely certain that the software and the equipment you are buying—processing unit, monitor, printer, and any other peripherals—will work together as a unit.

If you work for a large company or educational institution, check to see whether your employer has made an employee purchase arrangement with a vendor. Substantial discounts are often available under such programs.

Questions to Ask the Salesperson at the Computer Store

- How many units of this machine do you sell in a month?

- Is the machine popular enough to have a user's group in my area?

- Is there anyone I can call about problems?

- Does the store offer classes on how to use this computer and software?

- Do you offer a maintenance contract for this machine?

- Does someone in your store fix the machines?

- Can I expand the capabilities of the machine later?

Financing

One advantage of going to a dealer is that the seller may help you finance your purchase by either carrying the loan or making arrangements with a financial institution.

Service and Support

Perhaps the biggest single argument for buying at a specialized computer store is service and support. Who is going to help you through the rough spots? Computer-store salespeople may be qualified to demonstrate different equipment and software and to make sure everything works before it leaves the store. Some computer stores will help you over the

Repair. *If your computer breaks down, you will probably need to take it to a repair center.*

phone with any glitches you encounter at home. You will have to be your own judge about how much help to expect, however. There is a great deal of turnover of computer-store personnel; equipment and software change rapidly, and you may find, in fact, that the personnel are not as knowledgeable and helpful as you had hoped.

Many stores offer training classes (free or for a price). Many will replace your computer, if there is a warranty to that effect. Some offer a loaner while your computer is being repaired.

Maintenance Contract

When buying a computer, you may wish to consider a maintenance contract, which should cover both parts and labor. Such a contract has five basic levels of comprehensiveness:

- The most comprehensive type of contract offers a repair person who will fix your system on-site within a certain number of hours. This option is usually available only for significant business customers.

- The next best is a courier pickup and delivery repair service. This usually costs 25% less than on-site repair.

- Carry-in service allows you to bring your machine in for repairs. With courier or carry-in service, the store may provide you with a loaner while they fix your hardware.

- Another type of contract provides a hot line you can call. The person at the other end will help you troubleshoot. Clearly, this service resolves only basic problems; you should not get inside the machine with tools.

- The least convenient maintenance contract requires you to mail the machine in for repair.

Used Computers

Used-car lots are common enough. Could used-computer stores become a staple in society? Probably not, because there is too little profit for dealers, and they do not want to warrant the goods. But it may be possible to pick up a bargain from an individual. Check the ads in your local newspaper.

But be careful. There is no way, for instance, for you to know what kind of workout the secondhand computer has had. Did the owner just play with it from time to time? Or was it the office workhorse every day for two years? Try out everything you can. Try each key on the keyboard and test all the disk drives.

Another angle, and this may be a psychological one, is that the seller may

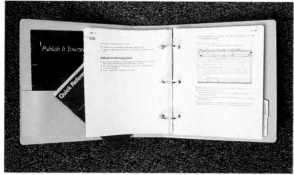

Documentation. *Clear, easy-to-follow documentation is one of the most important features of a software package.*

want to charge you a price that is related to the original price. Perhaps the seller paid $5000 for the system and thinks that $3000 is a fair price for the used equipment. But new comparable equipment may now cost less than $3000. Always compare the cost of a used computer system with today's prices.

Despite these reservations, there certainly may be some real bargains available in used equipment. Shop carefully.

Now That You Have It, Will You Be Able to Use It?

Once the proud moment has come and your computer system is at home or in the office with you, what do you do with it?

Documentation

Nothing is as important as documentation, the written manuals and instructions that accompany hardware and software. Unfortunately, some of it is inadequate. The weakest link in personal computer systems is the documentation. Ask to see the documentation when you buy. See if you can perform one of the procedures described in the documentation on a machine in the store. The instructions should be simple to understand and contain very little jargon.

Documentation should include simple instructions so you can perform basic tasks in short order. Some documentation goes on for many pages about a particular activity; it gives you all the variations for all the options, when all you really need to get started is the simplest form of the activity. The frills can come later.

Visual clarity is another characteristic of effective documentation. Sections in a manual should be separated with durable tabbed pages. There should be lots of white space, pictures, demonstrations, and examples so that you have no trouble following what is happening. The documentation should also have attractive, practical packaging, it should not be just a collection of typewritten sheets. Effective packaging alone, of course, does not guarantee good documentation.

Training

Can you teach yourself? Besides the documentation that comes with your computer and with software packages you may buy, there are numerous books on the market that can teach you about various software packages and programming. There are several books on the popular Lotus 1-2-3 package, for example, and hundreds on the BASIC language. Magazines can also help you, and several have columns to answer questions from readers.

As mentioned, some computer stores offer classes in the use of computers. Private parties do too, although the fees are often substantial. Many local colleges offer courses, although you may want to get in line early for sign-ups. It may also be possible to get private lessons. Although this may be the most expensive method, it might be very effective.

Some computer manufacturers and software vendors provide self-teaching material on diskettes that can teach you through hands-on participation right on your own computer. These lessons, called tutorials, may be the most effective teaching method of all.

Training. *Hardware and software purchases, especially in business, sometimes include classes provided by the dealer.*

that the most technologically advanced or the most powerful is automatically the best, but great power is of real importance in only a few applications. Why buy features that you will never need?

For businesspeople, what often matters most is compatibility—that is, assurance that the machine will run the software used at the office. It may be that for you, the "best" computer is one just like the one you will use at work or in school. For the uninitiated, support may be more important than any other single factor: Just who is going to answer your questions, once you bring all the boxes home?

The Very Best?

Best is a relative term. Clearly, each computer has its own strengths and weaknesses, and an expert will recommend different computers for different users and applications. Some people think

Survey for the Prospective Buyer

With this background we hope you are now in a position to answer some questions about the kind of computer you want. Take a copy of the filled-in survey with you when you shop.

Survey for the Prospective Buyer

1. Price Range. I can spend:

____ under $1000
____ up to $1500
____ up to $2500
____ up to $3500
____ up to $4500
____ more

2. Uses for Computer. Rank these uses in order of importance. I wish to use the computer for:

____ Entertainment and games
____ Adult education (e.g., foreign-language drill, learning programming)
____ Children's education (e.g., teaching math, typing, programming)
____ Word processing (writing papers, reports, memos, letters)
____ Business applications (e.g., spreadsheets, database management, accounting, scheduling)
____ Business "homework"
____ Mailing lists
____ Personal record keeping (e.g., address lists, list of insured possessions, appointment calendar, fitness progress)
____ Personal finance (e.g., taxes, budget, tracking stock market, banking from home)
____ Information retrieval (from services such as CompuServe, The Source, or more specific information sources)
____ Producing graphics

____ Desktop publishing (e.g., producing newsletters, advertising fliers)
____ Programming
____ Other

3. Hardware Features. I want the following features on my computer:

____ MS-DOS compatible
____ OS/2 compatible

____ 16-bit processor
____ 32-bit processor

____ 256K bytes of memory
____ 640K bytes of memory
____ 1MB of memory
____ 2MB of memory

____ Monochrome screen
____ Color screen
____ 80-column screen
____ Extra-large screen
____ Excellent screen readability

____ Color graphics capability
____ Multiscan monitor
____ EGA graphics standard
____ VGA graphics standard
____ Other graphics standard
____ Tilt and swivel screen
____ Glare shield

____ Numeric keypad
____ Function keys
____ Detachable keyboard

____ Single disk drive
____ Dual disk drives
____ 5-¼-inch disk drives
____ 3-½-inch disk drives
____ Hard-disk drive

____ Dot-matrix printer
____ Letter-quality printer
____ Ink-jet printer
____ Laser printer
____ Printer cover

____ Portability
____ Modem
____ Joy stick
____ Mouse
____ Scanner
____ Device to produce color slides
____ Surge protector
____ Cables and interface boards
____ Sound

____ Other

4. Software. I want the following software:

____ Games and recreation
____ Word processing
____ Spreadsheets
____ Database management
____ Graphics
____ Desktop publishing
____ Communications
____ Information services
____ Education packages
____ Home business packages
____ BASIC
____ Pascal
____ FORTRAN
____ COBOL
____ C
____ Other

5. Other Features. The following are important to me:

____ Manufacturer's reputation
____ Dealer's reputation
____ Dealer financing
____ Service and support
____ Maintenance contract
____ Documentation quality
____ Training
____ Other

PART 4

USING MICROCOMPUTERS

As we traveled through the hardware and software sections of the book, we continually made references to microcomputers. But now it is time to give them space of their own. This section begins with a chapter on the computers themselves, followed by separate chapters on applications software for microcomputers.

We begin with basic microcomputer topics and then present the burning question: But what would I use a microcomputer for? Educators and businesspeople already have some clear directions, and we suggest even more possibilities for home use of the personal computer.

These important types of applications software are described in detail: word processing, spreadsheets, graphics, database management, and desktop publishing. What would you use a microcomputer for? All of these tasks and more.

Chapter 11. Personal Computers: A Computer of Your Own

11

Personal Computers

A Computer of Your Own

Do you really need a personal computer? This chapter will help you answer that question. A description of the components of a personal computer—and the many accessories available—is followed by a discussion of possible uses in the home, school, and business. The rest of the chapter is devoted to the personal computer industry, the marketplace, and personal computer care.

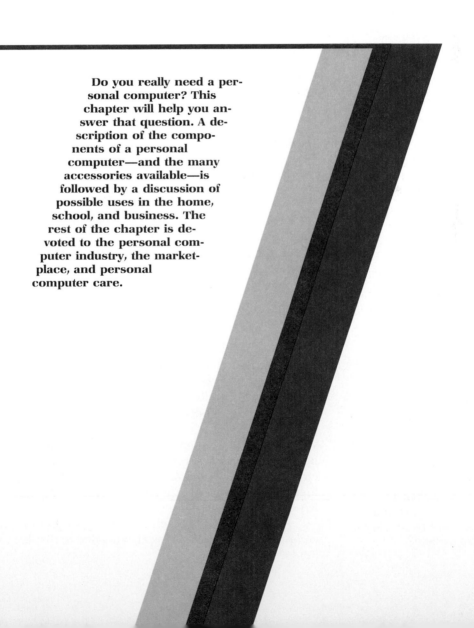

Janice Edwards, having had a little exposure to personal computers in college, wandered into her local software store one day. The store specialized in a hands-on approach—letting customers try any software package they fancy. Janice fancied several. She tried game programs with enticing names like The Hunt for Red October, The Defender of the Crown, and Life and Death (she was the surgeon!). She also noted the sports games on the shelf—especially her favorites, basketball and golf. As she examined more software, she was attracted to Tax View Planner (would that really make April 15th easier?), Address Book (goodbye dog-eared notebook), and Memory Mate (a "place" to keep notes and information scraps). But she knew that the most useful software package for her would probably be word processing. However, Janice is really only window-shopping at this point—she does not have a personal computer. Yet.

A computer of your own. A computer used for personal tasks. Will every home have a computer? Taking this a step further, will each *person* have a *personal* computer? **Personal computers,** or microcomputers, are the fastest-growing sector of the computer industry.

But, people say, do I really need a personal computer? What would I use it for? Before we begin to suggest the possibilities, let us consider what a personal computer—a microcomputer—is.

7 The Complete Personal Computer

Just how complete your personal computer will be is a matter of personal taste, interest, and budget. You can scale way down to get by with the bare minimum, or you can go first class from the start with top-of-the-line equipment and all the trimmings. Or, like most people, you can start out with a moderate investment and build on it.

7 A Review: The Basic Components

The heart of the personal computer is the microprocessor, the "computer on a chip" that we discussed in Chapter 3. In addition to the microprocessor, the microcomputer has two kinds of main storage: RAM and ROM. As you will also recall from Chapter 3, RAM stands for random-access memory. This is the computer's "scratch pad," which keeps the intermediate results of calculations. ROM stands for read-only memory; its contents are programmed into the hardware by the microcomputer manufacturer. ROM contains systems programs that are not changeable through the keyboard. See Figure 11-1 for a view inside a personal computer, including the RAM and ROM chips.

A keyboard is needed, of course, so you can interact with the computer. A video screen is also needed to display input and output.

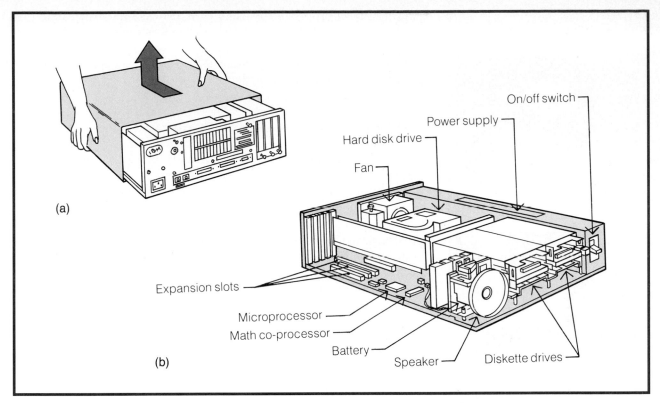

(a)

On/off switch
Power supply
Hard disk drive
Fan
Expansion slots
Microprocessor
Math co-processor
Battery
Speaker
Diskette drives

(b)

TRANSPARENCY ACETATE #11A
Figure #11-1

Figure 11-1 Inside a microcomputer. It is usually quite easy to see the inside of a microcomputer. Begin by disconnecting all cords from electrical outlets. Then, (a) as shown for this IBM PS/2, loosen a couple screws in the back, then slide the cover slightly forward and lift it. (b) The computer's innards are shown front viewpoint. The RAM and ROM chips are visible only if you lift up the structure that supports the hard disk drive.

LECTURE ACTIVITY
Some microcomputers are built in a very modular fashion, such as the DEC Rainbow or the IBM PS/2. Disassemble one in class, and put it back together, explaining what each part is and how it is used by the system.

Some microcomputers combine computer and keyboard and screen in a single unit, but most microcomputers have a separate screen monitor and a detached keyboard, so their positions can be adjusted for individual comfort.

For secondary storage purposes, a disk drive is needed to read and write on diskettes. In addition, hard disk is also available for most personal computers. Optical storage is also an option, but the relatively high price makes it practical only if you need it for a home business.

LECTURE HINT
See Appendix C for more information on the history of microcomputers.

Memory: How Much Is Enough?

Early personal computers usually came with a standard 64K RAM—that is, 64 kilobytes of memory. (Recall that K stands for 1024.) By today's standards 64K is not much; most of the popular software packages require more. Many machines today come with 640K or more memory, but it is not unusual for new machines to have millions of bytes of memory. Those interested in serious business applications often choose the high end. Larger memories are

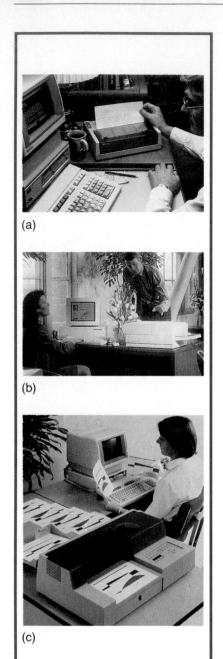

(a)

(b)

(c)

Figure 11-2   Printed output for personal computers. (a) Inexpensive dot-matrix printers are the most popular. (b) Laser printers are more expensive but are fast, quiet, and produce high-quality output. (c) Plotters for personal computers produce surprisingly good pictures.

particularly appropriate for users of **RAM-resident programs,** programs that the user loads into the computer's memory after turning the power on. A good example of a RAM-resident program is a spelling checker, a program you might want in the background, ready to spring into action when needed.

7 Special Attention to Printers

Basic microcomputer hardware consists of memory, central processing unit, monitor, keyboard, and storage device. In addition, many systems have a printer. Personal computer users often want a printer quite soon after they have purchased the basic hardware; paper is a communication medium that is hard to do without. We discussed types of printers in some detail in Chapter 4 on input and output, so you should already be familiar with the basic workings of dot-matrix, daisy-wheel, laser, and other kinds of printers. Here we want to focus on printers most often used with personal computers (Figure 11-2).

The choice for a printer has traditionally been between **dot-matrix printers** (which are fast and adequate) and **daisy-wheel character printers** (which are slow and very good). Most people with home computers will tolerate neither the high cost nor the sluggish pace of character printers and figure they can manage without the superior **letter-quality printing** that the slower printers produce. The net result has been dot-matrix printers for the masses and daisy-wheel character printers for those who need letter-quality printing for formal correspondence and documentation.

But changes are here. **Laser printers** have impressed personal computer users with their speed, their first-rate print quality, and their quiet operation. But while the top-of-the-line laser printer seizes the limelight, that old standby, the dot-matrix printer, has quietly been making some technological leaps of its own. The latest models feature high-quality text, fast printing, and a variety of graphics capabilities. The key to the versatility of the new dot-matrix printers is a 24-pin printhead, which uses many more dots to form a character, thus producing printing known as **near letter quality.**

Picking the best printer from among the hundreds available might seem a difficult task. But once you narrow down your preferences, the choices narrow as well. You can pay as little as a few hundred dollars for a serviceable printer or as much as a few thousand for a printer with all the options. But many personal computer users still settle on the versatile dot-matrix printer, somewhere in the $200 range. This type of printer produces standard copy quickly but can print correspondence by using the near-letter-quality option.

You may have special considerations for a printer, such as graphics output or color. And, as we noted in Chapter 4, excellent plotters are available for personal computers. Again, there are several choices. We also examine printer purchases in the Buyer's Guide following page 320.

Figure 11-3 Extra circuitry. This add-on circuit board is being inserted in an expansion slot of this Apple computer.

SUGGESTED ACTIVITY
Demonstrate in class how one adds or removes a board from an open architecture computer like an Apple II or IBM PC. Warn students to make sure the power is off when changing boards, lest you burn out one of the boards.

LECTURE HINT
Other add-in boards of interest: stereo processor, controller for a synthesizer, an ultra-fast co-processor and associated memory, a graphics display board, a network board to allow your computer to be inserted in a network.

DISCUSSION QUESTION
What boards might a personal computer owner want to add to a home computer?

DISCUSSION QUESTION
What supplies might a computer owner want?

LECTURE HINT
Describe vaporware (software that has been announced but not delivered).

The Goodies: Add-ons and Supplies

You have seen people buy every kind of gadget for their boat or car or camper. For computer users, the story is no different. In this discussion *add-ons* refers loosely to any semi-permanent device that attaches to the computer so that it can be directly affected by computer processing. An example is an extra disk drive. *Supplies,* on the other hand, are necessary or not-so-necessary accessories such as printer ribbons and dust covers.

Is "the box" open or closed? That is the heart of the architecture—and add-on—discussion. **Open architecture** means that the computer is designed so that users can buy additional circuit boards and insert them in **expansion slots** inside the computer to support add-ons (Figure 11-3). **Closed architecture** means that add-ons are limited to those that can be plugged into the back of the computer. If you have a machine with open architecture, there is a host of add-ons you might like to consider: more memory, a hard disk, a random-access memory (RAM) disk, a color monitor, a modem, a video camera, and input devices such as a joy stick, light pen, or mouse. See how it grows.

Supplies are readily available and often not dependent on computer brand or model. Dozens of catalogs advertise computer supplies, and most items are also sold in computer stores. Supplies for personal computers are many and diverse, from serious to silly. In addition to standard items such as print wheels, printer ribbons, diskettes, and paper, consider these sample goods: locking rolltop diskette trays, disk-drive head cleaning kits, diskette markers, complete microcomputer cleaning kits, keyboard drawers (so you can slide the keyboard under the computer when not in use), monitor stands that swivel and tilt, dust covers, anti-glare screen shields, hanging monitor racks, wrist supports (to hold your wrists over the keyboard), copyholders, lockup cables, security alarms, surge protectors (to prevent electric surges from hurting your files), printer forms in every conceivable style (letterhead, invoices, paychecks, address labels, envelopes, Rolodex cards, and so forth), ergonomic footrests, antistatic mats, "sound-barrier" printer covers, and a complete emergency power system (Figure 11-4). A most appealing item is the portable vacuum cleaner for your printer—it has a shoulder strap for convenient operation.

But you need not pick up one item at a time; in fact, you are encouraged to buy the complete computer workcenter, which includes furniture—desk, cabinets, shelves, and adjustable chair—a complete setup with a price to match.

And of Course—Software

Would you buy a fine sound system if there were no tapes or compact disks to play on it? Of course not. Unless you are determined to write all your own software—an unlikely scenario—a com-

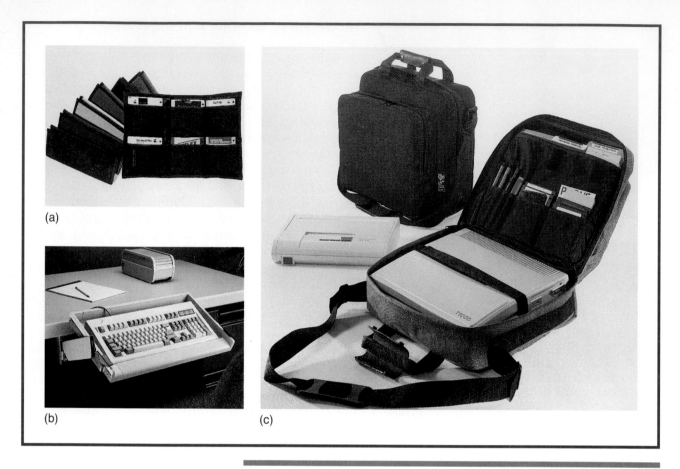

(a)

(b)

(c)

Figure 11-4　Personal computer supplies.　(a) Diskette wallets, shown here in a variety of colors, are convenient for workers who need to carry software or data diskettes with them. (b) Workers use this hidden drawer to slide the keyboard out of sight when it is not in use. (c) This convenient carrying case holds a laptop computer, as well as the usual supplies for workers who travel.

LECTURE HINT
Though there is plenty of software, beware that software might not work on your computer. It is always risky being one of the first people to buy a particular computer because it has not been tested to see if the software for it really works. Also, if the computer does not sell well, not much software will be developed for it (and therefore it will not sell well, creating a vicious circle).

TEST BANK
Mult. Choice	13-24
T/F	22-34
Matching A	4
Matching B	3, 5-7, 9, 10
Matching D	9
Fill-in-the-Blank	12-14

puter is only as good as the software available for it. But, of course, software for the personal computer is abundant. In fact, your software purchases may rapidly exceed the cost of the computer itself. Software can be very tempting: The range is dazzling, the power dizzying, and the simplicity enticing. In this chapter we will touch on the variety of packages available. But we will go further than that—the next four chapters cover the use of software in much greater detail.

7　Personal Computers in the Home

Do you really need a computer? There are opposing points of view. Advertisements would have you believe that a personal computer is all but indispensable. Perhaps you remember the dreadful television commercial in which a college-bound young man is bid farewell by his beaming parents—immediate fade to his return, shoulders slouched, parents tearful. *Voice-over:* "He didn't know computers." Until recently, messages in responsible journals have been much the same: Get a computer or be left behind.

But now strident voices can be heard on the other side of the question—voices like this: "Personal computers have been vastly oversold to the public. If you have serious business or education needs, fine. If you want to play games, fine—just buy an inexpensive computer. But all this talk about recipe files or balancing your checkbook: For heaven's sake, use a recipe box or a calculator." Well. Such a speech is persuasive, but let us look further before reaching any firm conclusions.

7 Home Sweet Computer

The first wave of computer users have been like the newest-is-best types who were always first with new audio equipment. But these people are not a sufficient base for an industry—home computers must be useful and easy to use for large numbers of consumers. The big market lies not with those who want to be computer experts but with customers who want machines to do things for them without a lot of fuss. So there it is: Let's have a machine that can do something for plain folks without making them stand on their heads.

But what would make a computer indispensable? That is like asking Thomas Edison what people are going to use electricity for. The personal computer does not yet seem indispensable. That will come. For now, we can say that it can be a convenience in a number of ways.

Communications

As already noted in Chapter 6 on data communications, home users find many reasons to connect their personal computers to the rest of the world. Some people telecommute—that is, they work at home and use their machines as a link to the office or customers. But most people have more mundane applications. A popular activity is hooking up to information services like CompuServe or The Source. These networks offer, for a fee, an astounding variety of services: stock prices, foreign-language drills, tax assistance, airline and hotel reservation services, consumer guidance, home buying and selling information, daily horoscopes, gourmet recipes, sports news, and much, much more (Figure 11-5). Other people use their networking capabilities to contact friends and colleagues through bulletin boards or use their machines as remote devices to shop or bank or pay bills. Beyond letting "your fingers do the walking," you can let your fingers do the work right at your computer—and in short order, too.

DISCUSSION QUESTION
What benefit can we get from linking a computer into an information source? What are the two most popular information services?

Figure 11-5 Computer uses through networking. This woman runs a business out of her home, communicating via computer to place orders with the headquarters office.

Figure 11-6 Education. College students in every type of major are learning to put computers to use in their studies.

DISCUSSION QUESTION
How is a microcomputer useful for youngsters? What are the advantages and disadvantages of getting children involved with computers?

DISCUSSION QUESTION
What are the advantages and disadvantages of letting a computer control many devices within the house and yard?

Education

One mistake that many parents make is thinking that placing a computer in front of a child will automatically create a whiz kid. Another is equating the playing of video games with learning. That might be like saying, "I think my little girl is going to grow up to be a television electronics expert. She watches TV all the time." But, smart remarks aside, a home computer and the right software can create an entertaining environment for learning. Educational software often includes color animation, flashing lights, sounds, and music that give positive reinforcement and can make learning a great deal of fun.

A computer is a patient and consistent tutor for preschool, elementary, and high-school students. One warning, however: When left to their own devices, most children are more likely to play zap-'em games than to learn grammar or arithmetic. At the college level, computers are used for everything from writing plays to plotting business takeovers (Figure 11-6). However, education is not just for formal students; adults can learn typing, foreign languages, and even how to play musical instruments. But perhaps you would like something a little more offbeat; there is educational software to help you study Morse code, survival skills, driving safety, stress management, resume writing, and how to predict the eruption of a volcano!

Home Controls

Most of us would welcome a little household help, especially if no salary is expected. But robots have yet to be useful around the house, so why not make the house itself a servant? That is the premise behind a class of products loosely known as **home controls.** Make your dwelling the smartest house on the block by hooking these devices up to your computer.

Rudimentary devices that control lighting, heating and cooling, smoke detectors, burglar alarms, and almost anything else have been available for years. But now there is the possibility of operating all these devices from a single control center: your computer. A computerized house is especially handy when no one is home. For example, a heat-sensitive system can be set to detect intruders.

Home controls work like this: Lamps, air conditioners, or anything else to be controlled are plugged into little boxes that are in turn plugged into wall sockets. The little boxes receive instructions over existing house wiring from a larger box that receives and remembers instructions from a personal computer (Figure 11-7).

The system can be used to schedule electrical events in a house. You could, for instance, program the heat to be turned down at night or plan a random pattern of lights and radios to go on and off during the day to make the house look occupied. This is all possible, but we must add that it is not practical for the average home user. Some systems tie up the entire computer, and many require more knowledge of electronics than most people possess. Even so, just imagine the luxury of coming home to a house that is lighted and warm, with the sound system turned on and dinner bubbling in the oven.

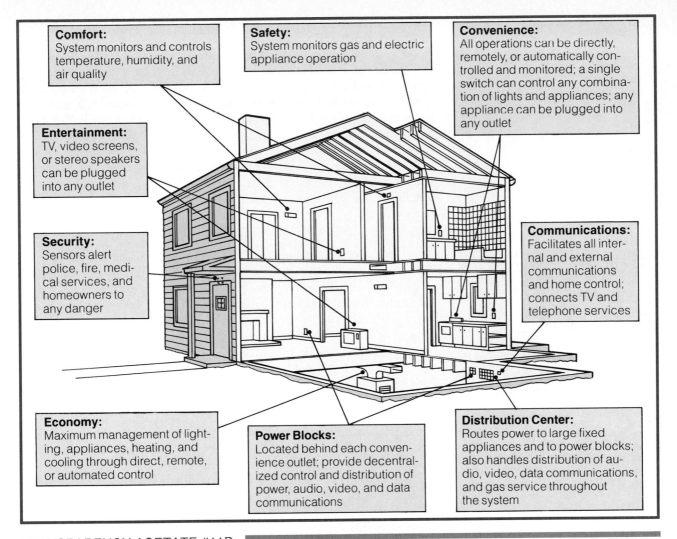

Comfort:
System monitors and controls temperature, humidity, and air quality

Safety:
System monitors gas and electric appliance operation

Convenience:
All operations can be directly, remotely, or automatically controlled and monitored; a single switch can control any combination of lights and appliances; any appliance can be plugged into any outlet

Entertainment:
TV, video screens, or stereo speakers can be plugged into any outlet

Security:
Sensors alert police, fire, medical services, and homeowners to any danger

Communications:
Facilitates all internal and external communications and home control; connects TV and telephone services

Economy:
Maximum management of lighting, appliances, heating, and cooling through direct, remote, or automated control

Power Blocks:
Located behind each convenience outlet; provide decentralized control and distribution of power, audio, video, and data communications

Distribution Center:
Routes power to large fixed appliances and to power blocks; also handles distribution of audio, video, data communications, and gas service throughout the system

TRANSPARENCY ACETATE #11B
Figure #11-7

Figure 11-7   Computers for home control.   Computer control systems are being built into new homes at the high-end price range. Computers can control temperature, air-conditioning, appliances, entertainment, and security.

The Home Office

Let us begin with word processing. Other factors being equal, which report will get the higher grade, the typed one covered with smudges and whiteout or the neatly presented paper prepared on a word processor? Let's face it: neatness counts. Even the children get in on "home office" equipment. Children as young as nine or ten are impressing their teachers with word-processed essays and reports prepared at home. And, yes, for the most part, they do it themselves. Word processing really is not much of a trick (we will look at it in more detail in the next chapter), and the rudiments can be learned easily by all family members able to dress themselves. Word processing is also a key application for adults who want to do some office work at home. Word processing is used for letters, reports, articles, mailing lists, newsletters, announcements, and even books. Many people justify a home computer for word processing alone.

There are two other primary home office uses. The first is using the computer for various calculations in the form of *spreadsheets*—rows and columns of data. People use spreadsheets for everything from home budgets to investment planning. Chapter 13 presents spreadsheets in more detail. The second home office use is *database management*—software to store and retrieve data. Any set of data that needs to be filed away but accessed quickly sometime in the future is a good candidate for database management software, the subject of Chapter 14. Unlike word processing, spreadsheets and databases are likely to be applications for adults, and only some of them at that.

Entertainment

You have seen the ads: The whole family—even the dog—is gathered merrily around the computer. The message is clear: The computer brings the family together. But family computing does not exist, at least not the way that it is usually portrayed. The home computer is not a shared commodity; it is a device used by individuals to perform specific tasks. Having said all that, however, we can note that entertainment is a possible exception because family members can take turns keying or can use two joy sticks.

Some people scoff at the idea of buying a computer for entertainment. But entertainment is a perfectly valid use. In fact, surveys consistently show that most people use their personal computers for entertainment at least some of the time. Games can range from the purely recreational, such as the famous Pac-Man and Donkey Kong, to the more subtle games of knowing trivia or psychoanalyzing your friends (Figure 11-8). There are several challenging software offerings for chess, backgammon, and bridge. Sophisticated sports-action games provide hands-on versions of pro football, baseball, and basketball. Scanning the dramatic come-ons on the computer store's game rack can keep you amused for some time.

Cautions About Keyed Input

There is indeed no place like home, but your computer may gather dust there if you buy it to keep track of home records that require a lot of keyed input. Think about it. If you want to use your computer to keep track of your budget or checkbook or business expenses or income taxes, *you must key in every single item.* Not only that, but you probably already wrote the data down once in a checkbook register or someplace else—keying means transferring the record you already have to a computer file. This gets old fast, and only the most dedicated will follow through. Many other uses—recipes, diets, stamp collections—contain the same fatal flaw: They require extensive keying to input. In short, unless you have the time and energy to support such applications, they are probably insufficient justification for a home computer.

Figure 11-8   The computer as entertainer. Even children too young to read can be entertained by the computer. In this example, the clown can be activated by voice commands.

FROM RUSSIA WITH LOVE

Before we tell you anything about Tetris, the game invented by a young Russian hacker, we must warn you that the game is addictive. Many Americans are heeding the call of the computer for just one more game—several times a day. Just what is so tantalizing?

As you can see in the center of the Tetris screen, the player is presented with a series of boxes, coming in a steady pattern from above. Points accumulate as the boxes land. The idea is to use the keyboard or a joy stick to maneuver the boxes neatly into place, with minimum wasted space. Each filled line across disappears, leaving space for more boxes. The game ends when the space is filled to the top. If your score is high enough, you are invited to type your name in on the list of "top ten comrades."

The game has several variations, including moving to higher— faster—levels of competition, each with a different Russian scene in the background. For under $30, you too can join the ranks of the addicted.

However, if you are serious about entering large quantities of data, there is an alternative to typing. As we noted in Chapter 4, a scanner can be used to transfer data from a written source to the computer. Scanners are becoming commonplace in offices and will become an important tool at home for some users.

Miscellaneous

Many software packages available for personal computers defy categorization, so we will lump them together here. (And note the box titled "But What Would I Use It For?" which describes some particular items in more detail.) If you want electronic help managing your life, there are a number of programs standing by to do just that. They will put you on a diet, plot your biorhythms, monitor your daily exercises, schedule a tooth extraction, revise your clothing style, chart your vacation route, and offer relief from rocky relationships. If you are an artist or a dabbler, there are a number of "palette and paintbrush" programs that offer a wondrous array of colors and ways to manipulate them on the screen (Figure 11-9).

There is more. Desktop manager programs offer "pop-up" clocks, calculators, and calendars that momentarily overlay your on-screen work-in-progress at the touch of a key. Want to know about Singapore? Travelogue programs display some facts—location, size, and so forth—accompanied by a graphics screen of local scenes. Musically inclined? Programs can help you do everything from "name that tune" to composing and printing your own musical scores. A new and attractive genre of software lets you participate in

Figure 11-9 The computer as artist.   The true artist is still a person, but computer software can provide powerful assistance with choices of shapes, colors, and placements.

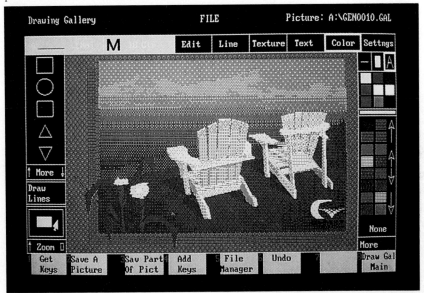

MICROCOMPUTERS IN ACTION

But What Would I Use It For?

In addition to the general categories we have mentioned in the text, there are some very specific—and idiosyncratic—software packages that find their way into home computers. See if any of the offerings in this sampler appeal to you.

- **Jigsaw.** Slide a piece into place. And then another and another. But do not plan to do anything else for a while, because it is hard to abandon this electronic jigsaw puzzle until it is complete. Several scenes, including landscapes, are included in the program. (Britannica Software)

- **VCR Companion.** Turn your home video into a major motion picture! Well, the ad may overstate the case just a bit, but you can create your own titles, credits, and graphics, then transfer them directly to videotape. (Broderbund)

- **Mastering the SAT.** The claim is straightforward: This program can dramatically improve your score on the Scholastic Aptitude Test (SAT) to get you into the college or university of your choice. In addition to teaching and testing, the program aims at improving test-taking strategies and reducing anxiety. (CBS Software)

- **Print Shop.** Design cards, posters, banners, or invitations, using a built-in art library of ready-made pictures and symbols and a dozen backgrounds and borders. Choose type style and size, all with optional outline and three-dimensional effects. You cannot produce cards that are as nice-looking as ones you buy in a store, but you can say, "Look, Mom, I made it myself." (Broderbund)

- **Flight Simulator.** Climb into the cockpit of a Cessna 182 and get ready for almost anything in a flight simulation so realistic that even licensed pilots have their hands full with it. More than a game, this approaches training and is a real challenge. (Microsoft)

- **Heart-to-Heart.** No therapists are needed—so they say—if you have this software package, aimed at mending hearts and lesser problems. Described as a "communication session for couples to help improve and expand their relationships," the program should at least wean the computer-junkie partner away from more single-minded pursuits. (Interactive Software)

writing stories, especially mysteries. And, finally, there is software for a variety of hobbies, from genealogy tracking to stamp collecting. Are all these reasons, collectively, enough to make you rush out to buy your first computer? Possibly not. So what will it take?

7 The Real Reason We Will All Buy a Computer

What will it take to saturate the market? The market is U.S. households and the product is the personal computer. How many households have a computer? Would you guess 30%? 25%?

- **HouseCall.** The advertisements for this "computerized home medical advisor," say it was written by physicians. HouseCall offers 400 diagnoses in a program that is touted as fast, easy, and fun to use. (Rocky Mountain Medical Software)

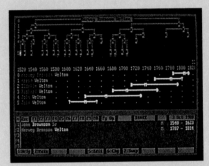

- **Roots.** If you have studied your family's history, you know how much fun—and how confusing—it can be. Roots provides an organizational framework to untangle the family data. Its searching and sorting capabilities let you note relationships among newly discovered ancestors. Family members can be looked up by name, date, location, and more. (Commsoft)

- **Business Simulator.** Tired of the games that test your reflexes? Ready to flex your mind? As the game begins, you start your own robotics company. You have $500,000 in seed money and access to robotics technology. As you play the game, you need to make all kinds of choices: prices, number of units to build, marketing, and when to offer new products. Make the wrong choices and you—just like the real world—lose. (Reality Development)

- **The Running Program.** Take just a few minutes each day to input data from your daily run so that the program can produce graphs of how you performed over different distances at different paces. It also has screens full of advice, from warm-up exercises—(including graphic demonstrations), to remedies for knee pains, to what to wear. About the only thing it does not do is get you out of bed in the morning. (MECA Software)

- **Action Planner.** Computer power for your appointment book: Organize schedule, notes, and lists automatically. Print everything on prepunched paper and enclose in a genuine leather binder (included). (Power Up!)

- **Comic Strip Factory.** Amaze your friends, as they say, with your own comic strip, featuring characters assembled from predrawn heads, arms, legs, shoes, and so forth. The backgrounds are also supplied, or you can draw your own. (Foundation Publishing)

DISCUSSION QUESTION
What other factors besides cost might limit the mass sales of microcomputers?

The answer is less than 15%, even though the home computer industry has grown 5% a year since 1983. But more of us will be buying soon.

The reason? It is becoming clearer each day: money. Cost is certainly the key limiting factor for the mass market today. Would you buy a typewriter that cost $1000? When you look at what the average person buys that costs more than a thousand dollars, you find two things: a house and a car. Those with higher salaries may buy a camper or a boat. But for an item to be a mass-market commodity like a VCR or a microwave oven, it must cost less than $500. We are getting closer. A powerful microcomputer system can now be purchased for under $1000.

Figure 11-10   Computers in education. IBM's Writing to Read software is based on the idea that children can write what they can say and can read what they can write. The Writing to Read software uses "silly" sentences to teach children vocabulary. For example, one screen says "Did you ever see a horse in a house?" The horse and the house are shown as pictures—graphics—in the sentence. The introductory Writing to Read program uses sounds, letters, graphics, and words to build reading awareness.

TEST BANK
T/F   35-37

Personal Computers in Schools

TEST BANK   Mult. Choice   25

During the last few years, most of the country's schools, often spurred on by anxious parents, have been trying desperately to work computers into their curriculums. Some have implemented exciting new programs, but, for some, computers have been an expensive distraction.

Not all schools know what to do with computers. Some, for instance, have used them exclusively for programming, almost always at the high-school level. Others rely on computers to provide extensive drills and practice exercises. Both high schools and elementary schools need to broaden their approach to computer education. Possible directions are word processing and database accessing, so that early hands-on experiences are more like what the students' parents do at work.

The picture is not uniformly bleak. Many schools have resisted introducing computers as substitute teacher devices; they recognize that computers are tools, not teachers. Few now expect the classroom of the future to look like a wired cubicle containing student and machine. The classroom, in fact, will look very much as it does today: teacher, students, blackboard, papers, books—and some computers on hand to help out (Figure 11-10).

Personal Computers in Business

The personal computer market has been enriched by the continuing flood of new uses found in business. Perhaps the most important development is that computers are no longer confined behind the castle walls of the data processing department's computer room. They appear on the desks and even in the briefcases of ordinary businesspeople. Personal computers are used in business for accounting, inventory, business planning, financial analysis, word processing, and many more functions (Figure 11-11).

There is some sentiment in the computer industry that a personal computer is just that: personal, one-on-one, even private. Are personal computers really personal? That notion is being swept aside as businesses press to the outer edges of computer usefulness. Personal computers are being hooked together in networks, personal computers are accessing mainframes, and personal computers themselves are being used as multiuser devices. So much for sentiment.

The impact of business on computers and vice versa carries major implications; we cannot mention them briefly and toss them aside. They will be examined in more detail in Chapter 16.

LECTURE HINT
Dr. Patrick Suppes of Stanford
University has taught a course in
logic for years, and has a best
selling book on the subject. He
devised a computerized course to
replace himself. Now, when
students register for his course,
they never see him; they learn
everything from the computer and
take all of their tests on the
computer. From the data bank on
the computer, Dr. Suppes
determines their grade. True,
there are not many courses like
this; but if it can be done in logic, it
could be done in other fields too.

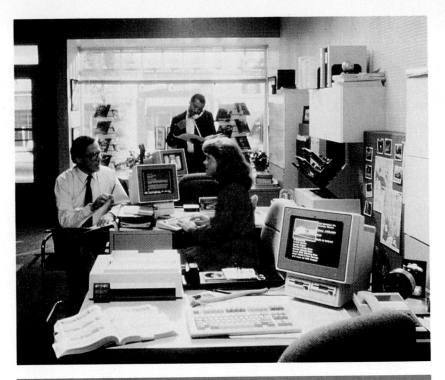

Figure 11-11   Computers in a business setting.   Applying the phrase "computers in business" to personal computers often suggests an executive image, but computers are used routinely by all workers in this realty office.

TEST BANK
Mult. Choice   26-44
T/F   38-59
Matching B   2, 4, 8
Matching C   1-10
Matching D   1-6
Fill-in-the-Blank 15-31

7 Personal Computer Manufacturers

Nothing we could possibly say here will remain true for long, since the one constant element in the personal computer industry is change.

7 The Players: How It All Began and What Is Happening Now

The microcomputer boom began in 1975 when the **MITS Altair** was offered as a kit to computer hobbyists. Building your own computer was considered an eccentric pastime. But all that has changed. Apple came along to bring a small computer, the Apple II, to the people. Tandy started selling TRS-80 computers to everyday people in Radio Shack stores. Commodore enticed school administrators to let children try their PET computer. These three—Apple, Tandy, and Commodore—led the market from about 1977 to 1982. But there was a significant entry in 1981: IBM announced its own contender, the IBM PC, and nothing has been the same since. In a mere 18 months IBM outdistanced them all.

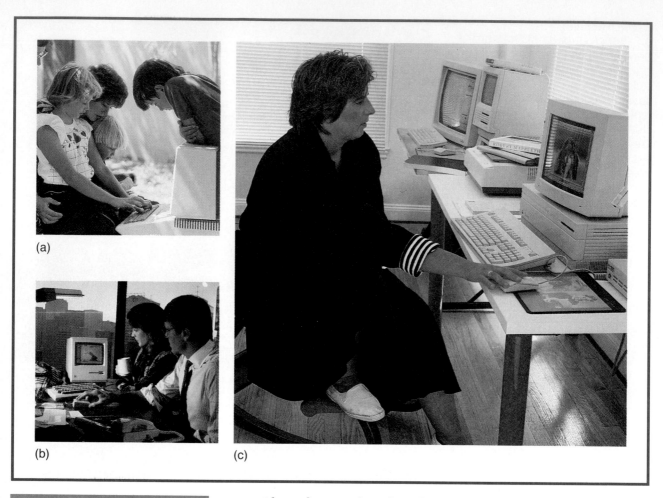

(a)

(b)

(c)

Figure 11-12   Three Apples. (a) As this scenario suggests, the Apple IIe has often been used for family entertainment and education. (b) Office workers found the Apple Macintosh easy to use. They were also attracted by its good graphics capability. The first model, shown here, was introduced in 1984. (c) The Macintosh II was the first Macintosh to offer a color screen.

Along the way there have been other manufacturers of personal computers, up to 200 at one point. Many tried and many failed. We are still in the period referred to as the Big Shakeout. At this point it is difficult to speak with confidence about any firm, but we will put our money on IBM and Apple. We will discuss them in the order of their appearance, then give some attention to other key players.

Apple: Almost First

Apple Computer was formed in 1977 by Steven Jobs and Stephen Wozniak, who were working in Silicon Valley in California. Apple computers were the first to replace complicated switches-and-lights front panels with easy-to-use typewriter keyboards. They were an immediate success. The popular Apple II, later updated to the IIe (Figure 11-12a), was followed by the bug-ridden and unsuccessful Apple III, which was discontinued. The IIc spinoff found a nice niche in the home market, but the innovative Lisa was too pricey ($10,000) for both home and business markets; Lisa was abandoned in 1984, a year after it was introduced.

Macintosh®

The Serious Macintosh

The Apple Macintosh started out as a clever toy, overpriced and underpowered. Its superb graphics interface and ease of use, however, marked it as a machine that was user friendly. The Mac won instant friends in the home market and some educational markets.

Business was another matter. Apple tried to promote the Macintosh as a serious contender in offices, but many corporations resisted the machine in favor of IBMs and compatible machines. But now the Mac is making inroads. It is used for everything from word processing to spreadsheets in such heavyweight companies as The Bank of America and the accounting firm of Peat, Marwick, Main & Co.

Why the turnaround? There are several reasons, including expanded software selection, a versatile network to hook the Macs together, desktop publishing, and—finally—the option of compatibility with IBM. Another major incentive was Macintosh price cuts. A more compelling, if less obvious, reason is that managers are now fully aware of training costs; the Mac is so easy to use that savings are substantial. In a get-it-in-the-door strategy, Apple offered Macs as loans or even corporate gifts; in most cases the result was a significant sale.

LECTURE HINT
Other reasons for the acceptance of the Macintosh: (1) The first Mac had only 128K of RAM. Now, 1M of RAM is standard, and many Macs have 4-8M of RAM. (2) The first Mac had 400K disks. Now 800K is standard, and new 1.44M disks are available. (3) The first Mac had a closed architecture. The new Macs (SE and the II) permit expansion boards. (4) The first Mac had a small, though clear, screen. The new Macs allow the use of larger screens. Also, the Mac II offers a color monitor. (5) The first Mac came with a word processor and a drawing program; nothing else was available. Now there is a version of just about any application for the Mac.

Apple used Lisa technology—graphics and pull-down menus—to create superb user interfaces for the Macintosh, which it introduced and promoted heavily in 1984. Note its all-in-one compact boxy shape (Figure 11-12b). The Macintosh has attracted a devoted following and is particularly appealing to beginners. There is now an entire family of Macintosh computers, with names such as Macintosh Plus and Macintosh SE, and varying degrees of power. Apple departed from the traditional Macintosh look with its Macintosh II, which was the first Mac to offer color and high-quality sound (Figure 11-12c).

7 IBM: Front and Center

IBM introduced its personal computer in the summer of 1981 (Figure 11-13a). The computer giant's IBM PC soon zoomed to the top in microcomputer sales. In 1983 IBM launched another version of the PC called the IBM PC XT, which featured more power, more memory, and hard disk. Other models quickly followed, and all are compatible with the original PC, which means they can all use the same software. Examples are the Portable PC, the ill-fated PCjr, the PC AT (Advanced Technology), the PC RT (RISC Technology—a topic we discussed in Chapter 3), and the laptop PC Convertible. Of these, the AT was by far the most successful. IBM's most recent entry is a family of computers called the Personal System/2—PS/2 for short (Figure 11-13b). The PS/2 comes in several different models, with power increasing with the model number.

IBM did not get there first, and many argue that IBM products are not even the best. So why has IBM dominated the personal com-

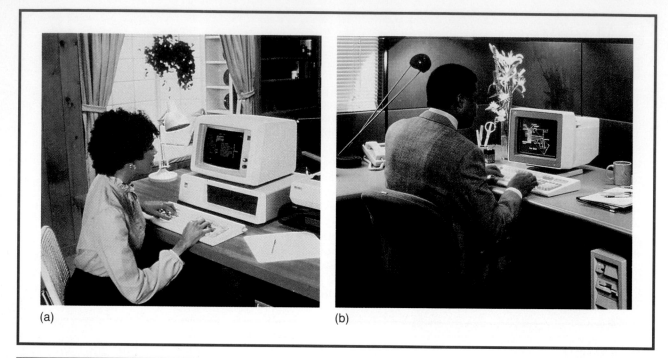

(a)   (b)

Figure 11-13 IBM personal computers. (a) From the time of its introduction in August 1981, the IBM PC took only 18 months to lead the competition. (b) The IBM PS/2 is offered in several models. The Model 80, shown here, is at the top of the power scale.

LECTURE HINT

When IBM entered the microcomputer market, many microcomputer companies were already failing. Buyers wanted to buy from a company they knew would be around for a while; IBM was the biggest, and so buyers flocked toward IBM, which soon got the market lead. IBM's success established MS-DOS as the standard 16-bit operating system.

puter market? It would be easy to say that IBM's preeminence naturally follows from their number one position in the mainframe market, but it is not that simple. There are really two sides to the story.

The first side concerns what the IBM PC provided: a processor that could address a lot of memory, an 80-column screen width, an open architecture, a keyboard with upper- and lowercase and good cursor controls, and function keys for word processing and other software. The second side of the story is the failure of other major companies to provide these same fundamental features early on. The void was there, and IBM stepped in.

The acceptance of the IBM product—and the IBM name—cultivated the ground for others to produce software and peripherals. A standard was established. IBM's standard may not be the last, but it will take a mighty force to overcome its head start.

7 And Others

We have already noted the changing nature of the personal computer market. But these significant manufacturers must be included on the list.

Tandy and Radio Shack

Headquartered in Fort Worth, Texas, the Tandy Corporation is better known to the public as the parent company of the Radio Shack electronics stores, of which there are now some 8500 world-

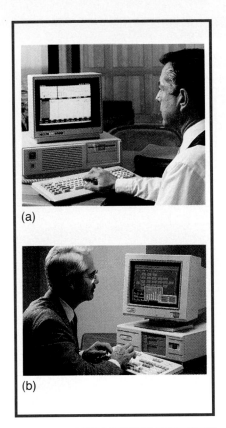

(a)

(b)

Figure 11-14 Some personal computers. (a) This businessman is using the Tandy 3000 from Radio Shack. This multiuser system is fully IBM compatible. (b) The Compaq 386 was the first personal computer to use the powerful Intel 80386 microprocessor.

LECTURE HINT
The parts on many microcomputers are almost the same. So if a company fails, another company may be able to fix your computer.

wide. Tandy exploited the advantage of having existing sales outlets by offering the TRS-80 through Radio Shacks in 1977. Radio Shack, whose computers were once thought to be no more than fancy toys, now commands respect through a wide range of products (Figure 11-14a).

Commodore

Based in Norristown, Pennsylvania, Commodore Business Machines entered the personal computer market with the PET (Personal Electronic Transactor). One of the best-selling home computers worldwide was the Commodore 64. Commodore offered the Amiga, which has outstanding graphics and sound effects, in 1985.

Compaq

Compaq played one game and played it well: piggybacking on IBM. Founded in Houston in 1982, a few months after IBM's PC went on the market, Compaq bounded onstage with a portable personal computer whose innards were as close to the IBM PC as the law allowed. Even when IBM struck back with its own portable in 1984, Compaq outsold it 5 to 1. But Compaq struck first with the Deskpro 386, which beat a comparable IBM machine—the PS/2 Model 80—to market in 1986 (Figure 11-14b). Compaq did well by hanging on to IBM's coattails; to be "IBM compatible" was everything. Read on.

7 The Compatibility Craze

How would you like to invent a new product, then be told that the best way to advertise it is to say that it is just like your competitor's product? In fact, most manufacturers of new personal computers have done just that: They proclaimed how closely their product resembled the IBM PC family. That kind of imitation was inevitable in light of the phenomenal market acceptance of the IBM PC. Some products are called **compatibles** because, in general, they can run and produce software that will also run on the IBM PC and vice versa. Such compatibility is possible by using microprocessors and operating systems that are the same as or virtually identical to those used by the IBM PC. Some personal computers are called **clones** because of their deliberate similarity to the IBM PC. IBM withdrew its own PC line in 1987, to encourage users to buy its new PS/2 line. Many users elected to buy clones instead.

Some manufacturers have taken the clone idea one step further; they have produced hybrids. A **hybrid** is a computer with its own unique design that will also simulate another computer, notably IBM. Most companies accepted the existence of the de facto ("that's the way it is") IBM standard, so they offered IBM compatibility but also found their own way to stand out in a crowd.

Figure 11-15   A supermicro.   This powerful Sun workstation is both multiuser and multitasking; these characteristics open up a higher level of personal computing.

7 Supermicros: The New Wave

They have been called the new wave of machines—the second generation of microcomputers. **Supermicros,** also called **workstations,** have a high-speed microprocessor and significantly increased memory and hard-disk storage capacity (Figure 11-15). In particular, the supermicros are **multiuser** (they can be shared by several users at the same time) and **multitasking** (they can run more than one applications package per user).

Supermicros have been called "desktop mainframes," a rather glamorous title that distances them from their more mundane microcomputer cousins. However, users do not always find supermicros glamorous to use; supermicros use the UNIX operating system, which is not noted for being user friendly. But new easy-to-use software is on the market, and more is sure to follow.

Who needs all that power? Engineers and scientists were early users. However, now that software for supermicros is turning the corner, business users are jumping aboard.

(a)

(b)

Figure 11-16   The portable worker.
(a) This worker is using a Zenith TurbosPort laptop, which features a full-size screen. (b) Compaq was the first to offer a laptop with a detachable keyboard.

MAC TO GO

In 1989 Apple Computer unveiled a lightweight Mac with graphics display as vivid as the larger models'. Featuring a transistor for each pixel, the screen is significantly sharper than most portables.

Instead of the traditional mouse, the portable Mac uses a trackball that can accommodate left- or right-handed users. The Macintosh Portable also features 1-megabyte RAM, diskette drive, optional 40-MB hard disk, built-in modem, and batteries to keep it going for 12 hours.

7 Laptops: The Incredible Shrinking Micro

A computer that fits in a briefcase? A computer that weighs less than a newborn baby? A computer you do not have to plug in? A computer to use on your lap on an airplane? A computer that is "cute"? Yes, to all questions.

It all began with the first portable computers from Osborne (later in bankruptcy), Kaypro, and Compaq. A **portable computer** looked like a sewing machine and could be carried like one. It was portable in that you could take it with you in one piece (the keyboard snapped onto the computer to form a cover), but you would not want to lug its 25 to 40 pounds through an airport. **Laptop computers** are wonderfully portable, sleek, and functional (Figure 11-16). They often weigh under 10 pounds. Many of them have built-in modems, so a traveling businessperson can send data from the hotel room to the office. Several laptops come with key software packages, such as word processing and spreadsheets, right in the computer—that is, in the ROM chips. And, almost without exception, laptops are IBM compatible. Many have small screens (16 lines), but some come with full-size screens (25 lines), and some even offer color. Some accept diskettes, so it is especially easy to move data from one machine to another. Although not commonly done, printers can be attached to laptops. Most laptops carry a price tag equivalent to a sophisticated personal computer for business.

The main laptop customers have been journalists, who prepare copy on their computers right at the site of the story. But traveling executives, sales representatives, insurance auditors, and writers are also good candidates. Lawyers frequently use portable computers in courtrooms. And there is the Internal Revenue Service, whose agents use 15,000 laptops—the better to monitor their customers.

PERSPECTIVES

FAST FORWARD

It has become fashionable, especially with the millennium just a few years away, to imagine the personal computer of the future. In fact, Apple Computer sponsored a contest in this vein. The winners, a group of college students, proposed a go-everywhere tablet-size computer that you can write on with a stylus; other features included credit-card–size file memories that can be traded as easily as baseball cards, icons to represent functions such as a telephone or calendar, and extraordinary communicating capabilities.

Other people have come up with their own lists. Voice data input is often high on the list—many people would love to get rid of all that typing. Others yearn for inexpensive super high-quality laser printers that also print in color and can even produce three-dimensional holograms. Personal computers will require no assembly or set-up time; simply take it out of the box and plug it in. Many futurists envision an entertainment center that combines video, television, and computers. Others picture a separate personal computer that comes with the purchase of a new house, much the way kitchen appliances do today; this computer will control heating, electrical systems, and security.

From the user point of view, the key item is transparent use—the ability to use a system without even being aware of an operating system, much less having to learn how to use it. And, of course, the software itself will be several orders of magnitude "smarter" than today's software. Software will be used by everyone to manage routine daily affairs.

In spite of all the advances, many people will never need or want a computer at home. But perhaps this will be balanced by people who will buy several computers, just as television buyers in the '60s began to buy more than one television.

TEST BANK
Mult. Choice   45
T/F   60
Matching D   7
Fill-in-the-Blank   32

LECTURE HINT
Anyone interested in buying or selling a used computer will be interested in looking in *The Computer Blue Book* for price comparisons. Call the Used Equipment Hotline, 1-800-346-6223

7 The Ever Changing Marketplace

The marketplace for personal computers ebbs and flows in a constantly changing scenario. Early forecasts had the general public taking to personal computers as a bear to honey. Indeed, sales rose in a gratifying way through the early 1980s. But then the industry reached a plateau—we have already alluded to the big chill the change in sales growth placed over the manufacturing industry. But other market sectors are affected as well, particularly dealers.

7 The Neighborhood Store

The number of retail outlets selling computers is in the thousands. Whether the outlet is a small independent or part of a large operation such as Sears, Macy's, or Radio Shack, it offers you the chance to examine different equipment before you buy (Figure

(a)   (b)

Figure 11-17   Retail sales.   (a) In a typical retail outlet, customers can "test drive" the hardware and peruse shelves of software. (b) The impressive Dallas Infomart, with 90 stores, is devoted to computer-related businesses.

ELECTRONIC PERKS

Standard big-shot perks—short for *perquisites*—have historically been company cars, membership in the country club, and the like. But there is a new perk in town: the opportunity to buy a computer at discount prices. And the perk recipient is not necessarily near the top of the corporate ladder; he or she can be any employee in a computer-conscious company. The most common arrangement is simply for a computer retailer to offer better prices to customers who identify themselves as the favored company's employees; the company makes up the difference.

Companies making such arrangements usually emphasize that employees are not expected to buy a computer to take work home. They feel that if employees simply become more familiar with computers, that will be of sufficient benefit to the company.

11-17a). And, speaking of large operations: Some high-tech products are now being sold in stunning buildings known as **computer marts,** buildings designed to house the dozens of stores that lure customers. The first computer mart, called the Infomart, opened in Dallas in 1985, with 90 stores devoted to computer wares (Figure 11-17b). Other centers are the World Trade Center in Boston and Techworld in Washington, D.C.

But the retail picture is changing somewhat. It was not so very long ago that consumers marveled at being able to walk right into a store that sold computers. That quaint idea is outmoded in some stores. To put it bluntly, some dealers prefer dealing with businesspeople.

For some stores the shift toward professional customers is a matter of survival. Businesspeople do not take up a lot of time with idle questions, and their buying potential for hardware, software, and service is enormous. Oh, there are still home computers for sale, but they may be upstairs or in a back room. Casual shoppers and confused first-time buyers are not likely to be heavily pursued by these stores. The consumer has not been forgotten altogether, however. At holiday time dealers still hang decorations and stay open late to serve ordinary people, especially if the key manufacturers offer special promotions.

Computer stores boomed when IBM introduced the IBM PC in 1981. But the boom ended in 1984 when IBM authorized hundreds more stores to sell its products and at the same time slashed prices. Dealers were caught with fewer customers and a narrow profit margin.

7 Vertical Markets

Some dealers saved themselves by turning to **vertical markets,** groups of similar customers such as accountants or doctors. By specializing in complete computer systems for a few vertical markets, dealers are able to give good service for good prices. But serving vertical markets really works only in large urban areas.

7 Computer Fitness and Safety

Computers are a hardy lot, primarily because they have so few moving parts. Given proper care, your computer will probably last longer than you want it—that is, you will have your eye on the latest new machine long before your current machine wears out. Still, your computer's well-being cannot be taken completely for granted. It needs proper care.

7 Proper Care

Here are some tips for keeping your printer, disk, keyboard, and screen in good working order. The printer should be vacuumed periodically and surface areas wiped clean with a light all-purpose cleaner. Do not lubricate the machine because oil will only collect dust, which practically guarantees printer failure. To keep the disk-drive read/write heads clean, use an approved head-cleaning kit occasionally (Figure 11-18). To keep the disk head properly aligned with the disk, avoid sudden jolts to the drive. Diskettes must be properly stored, since dirt is the single most common cause of disk error. A keyboard can be ruined by soda pop, coffee, or anything crumbly; keep them away from your computer. If a spill does occur, immediately take the keyboard to a service center for a good cleaning. The surface area of the keys can be cleaned with any mild cleansing agent, but the place where dirt and grime really love to gather is between and under the keys. A can of compressed air (with a narrow nozzle) effectively blows out all that residue. With the monitor turned off, wipe your screen clean with a mild cleanser occasionally. You may also wish to apply an antistatic solution.

Environmental factors can have a significant influence on computer performance. Your computer should not sit near an open window, in direct sunlight, or near a heater. Computers work best in cool temperatures—below 80° Fahrenheit (27° Celsius). Also, smoking can be hazardous to your computer's health. Smoking adds tar and particle matter to the air, where they then find their way into the computer.

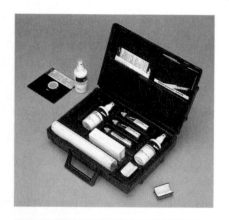

Figure 11-18   A cleaning kit. This kit contains mild solutions, a cleaning disk, swabs, and wipes for cleaning disk drives, screens, and keyboards. Follow directions carefully.

The rewards for your vigilance are largely invisible. Your computer will look a little nicer, of course, but—more important—it will run smoothly for long stretches before it needs servicing. When that time comes, however, you will be glad the computer doctor is available.

Figure 11-19   Service center. Manufacturers provide outlets where computers and peripherals can be repaired and serviced.

7 The Computer Doctor

The worst has happened. You have just witnessed your computer screen scream, flash, then go dead black. Though increasingly reliable, computers can still fizzle or fry. You need the **computer doctor,** jargon for a repairperson. Some computer doctors make house calls. They remove defective parts and replace them with good ones. Other "doctors" expect you to bring your computer to them (Figure 11-19).

The computer-repair industry is divided among computer manufacturers, retailers, and repair companies. But it is not an easy business. Stocking an inventory of spare parts takes a lot of capital. Also, it is hard to find and train good service people, and, once employed, they are expensive. And so is the service. When computer systems fail, people generally want them fixed as quickly as possible and accept premium charges.

A warning note to the sophisticated buyer who has the skills to shop around and mix and match hardware: Mixed-manufacturer systems are the most frustrating to repair because each manufacturer can claim that the problem is in the other guy's equipment.

7 Computer Security

When people talk about computer security, they are usually thinking of corporate thieves, government secrets, or teenage hackers. But for you and your personal computer, it becomes more simple: Will the machine still be there when you get home? Burglars pick items that can be easily resold. Stereos and TVs have always been favorites, but now personal computers top the list. In addition to the usual precautions, you may want to consider physical lockups for your computer.

One more note. Check your household insurance policy—there is a good chance that personal computers are specifically excluded. It is a good idea to buy separate insurance if your investment is substantial. Insurance companies now offer special packages for this purpose for a nominal annual fee. We will address the subject of security in detail in Chapter 18.

7 Moving On to the Key Software Packages

In this chapter we have referred to software in a general way, mostly in the context of what you could do with a personal computer. But many people want to know more. Indeed, if you are planning to enter a business environment, you *need* to know more. In the next four chapters we offer descriptions of how key business software packages work. Chapter 12 covers word processing, Chapter 13 covers spreadsheets and graphics, Chapter 14 covers database management systems, and Chapter 15 covers desktop publishing.

We cannot attempt to tell you exactly what key to push for what action because that varies with the brand name of the package. But our look at these important packages will be significant because we can tell you what kinds of things these packages can do for you and, in general, how they work. You may be surprised at how easy it is.

7 Summary and Key Terms

- Microcomputers are also called **personal computers.**

- The main components of a personal computer are the microprocessor, random-access memory (RAM), and read-only memory (ROM). A keyboard is used for inputting data, and a video screen displays input and output. A disk drive is used for reading and writing diskettes.

- Most of the popular software packages require more than 64K bytes of memory—especially **RAM-resident programs,** which are loaded into memory after the computer is turned on.

- Traditionally, the personal computer user has chosen either the faster **dot-matrix printer** or the slower **daisy-wheel character printer** that produces **letter-quality printing.** However, the newer **laser printers** produce fast, letter-quality printing, and the latest models of dot-matrix printers produce **near-letter-quality printing.**

- An add-on is any semi-permanent device, such as an extra disk drive, that attaches to a computer and is directly affected by computer processing. Supplies are accessories such as printer ribbons.

- **Open architecture** means that the computer design allows users to insert additional circuit boards **expansion slots** inside the computer. **Closed archi-**

tecture limits add-ons to those that can be plugged into the back of the computer. Some personal computer applications include communications, education, word processing, **home controls,** and entertainment.

- In the home, personal computers are most conveniently used for tasks that do not require extensive keying to input.

- A broadly successful integration of computers into elementary and high-school curriculums requires good software and emphasis on practical applications rather than just drills and exercises. Some business applications include accounting, inventory, planning, financial analysis, and word processing. Businesses seek to maximize the use of personal computer portability and networking.

- Personal computer manufacturing, which began in 1975 with the **MITS Altair,** was dominated by three companies—Apple, Tandy, and Commodore—until IBM entered the market in 1981. IBM came to dominate the market with its PC, which offered attractive features such as a processor that could address a lot of memory, open architecture, and function keys. Other significant manufacturers are Tandy's Radio Shack, Commodore, and Compaq.

- IBM's dominance led many manufacturers to make **compatibles,** which run the same software that runs on the IBM PC. Some personal computers are **clones** that are deliberately similar to the IBM PC;

others are **hybrids,** which have unique designs but can simulate another computer, usually the IBM PC.

- **Supermicros,** also called **workstations,** are **multi-user, multitasking** personal computers that have a high-speed microprocessor, significantly increased memory, and hard-disk storage capacity.

- The first **portable computers** weighed between 25 and 40 pounds. **Laptop computers,** which can weigh under 10 pounds, are especially convenient for journalists and traveling businesspeople.

- **Computer marts** are buildings designed to contain a large number of computer stores.

- Some personal computer dealers see more sales potential in business customers than in home computer customers.

- Some dealers turned to **vertical markets,** groups of customers with similar needs—accountants, for example.

- Proper computer care includes such precautions as vacuuming the printer, storing disks properly, keeping food and drink away, cleaning the screen, and keeping the computer away from cigarette smoke and excessive heat. Proper care lessens the chance of needing a **computer doctor,** a repairperson from a manufacturer, retailer, or repair company.

- For personal computer owners, computer security may involve specially designed security kits or cabinets and perhaps a separate insurance policy.

Review Questions

1. What are some factors that affect memory requirements?

2. Why do many personal computer owners buy dot-matrix printers?

3. Distinguish between add-ons and supplies, and give three examples of each.

4. Summarize personal computer applications in the following areas: communications, education, word processing, home controls, and entertainment.

5. Why do many consider it impractical to use a personal computer for managing a checking account?

6. How did businesses expand the usefulness of the personal computer?

7. Discuss the impact of the following companies on the personal computer market: Apple, IBM, Tandy's Radio Shack, Commodore, and Compaq.

8. Explain what compatibles, clones, and hybrids are and why they appeared on the market.

9. Explain what vertical markets are and why some dealers turned to them.

Discussion Questions

1. Do you intend to buy a personal computer? Why or why not?

2. If you were to buy a personal computer, what add-ons and supplies would you want and why?

3. Will personal computers eventually become attractive to the average buyer? Explain your answer.

Chapter 12. Word Processing: The Most Popular Use of Personal Computers

12

Word Processing

The Most Popular Use of Personal Computers

Word processing programs help people create, edit, format, store, and print text—with wonderful assistance from the computer.

Word processing software packages are the most widely used personal computer application. Many personal computer owners use their machines solely for word processing. Furthermore, there are probably more word processing packages in the marketplace than any other type of software.

LEARNING OBJECTIVES
- Appreciation of the need for word processing.
- Understanding the basic features of word processing programs.
- Familiarization with the standard programs that are related to word processing: spelling checkers, thesaurus programs, and programs for grammar and style, and form letters.

DISCUSSION QUESTION
When are perfectly typed documents required? What are some examples of cases in which perfectly typed documents are not required, but are highly desirable?

TEST BANK
Mult. Choice   1-7
T/F   1-7
Matching A   1, 3-4, 7-9
Fill-in-the-Blank   1

DISCUSSION QUESTION
What does word processing involve?

Have you ever left a sentence out of a typed term paper? And what about misspelled words or just plain typos? As a tool, the typewriter has its shortcomings. The basic problem with a typewriter is that you are producing a permanent mark whenever you press a key. Therefore, if you make a mistake, it is hard to correct without a lot of extra work.

Things get even worse if you must add or delete several sentences. At best, the whole page must be retyped. But the altered document may be longer or shorter than the original text, so the new version may not fit on one page anymore. Now you have to retype the pages that follow it, too.

Or, like many of us, you might reluctantly turn to the whiteout or to cutting and pasting, tolerating the smudged and mutilated results. You do this because you do not have the time to type it all again.

You may be able to hand in a less-than-perfect term paper, but this is not acceptable in the workplace. The appearance of a document or letter is crucial to the image of a business. And beyond image, there may be exacting legal demands. Documents submitted in a court of law, for example, must be originals (not copies) and there may be no corrections made on the document. If the same legal document needs to be sent to different people or offices, one document must be typed perfectly again and again. If an attorney notices that a required sentence or clause has been omitted, at least one page of all the documents must be redone.

For you as a student, careful typing is required when you seek employment. A poorly typed resume makes a bad impression. If you pay to have your resume typed, you may have to pay again to add more courses and experience. A customized resume for a particular position might require partial or even complete retyping of your original resume. There is a better way: word processing.

7 Word Processing as a Tool

Word processing is the creation, editing, formatting, storing, and printing of a text document. We will examine each part of the definition. First, a *text document* is anything that can be keyed in, such as a letter. *Creation* is the original composing and keying in of the document. *Editing* is making changes to the document to fix errors or improve its content—for example, deleting a sentence, correcting a misspelled name, or moving a paragraph. *Formatting* refers to adjusting the appearance of the document to make it look appropriate and attractive. For example, you might want to center a heading, make wider margins, or use double spacing. *Storing* the document means saving it on a data disk. *Printing* is producing the document on paper, using a printer connected to the computer.

MICROCOMPUTERS IN ACTION

Writers Throw Off Their Chains

Although some resist, most people who write for a living have taken the plunge into word processing. So do people who have to write reports, memos, and so forth, as a component of the job. The statements of these people tell the story.

- **Mike Royko, columnist.** The machine terrifies me but I know enough to write my column on it. When the first typewriter came out, a lot of newspaper guys said they'd never write with "that monster." They'd rather write with a pen. When my newspaper brought in its [computer] system, I was the last guy writing with a typewriter; I didn't have time to learn to use the system. Then another reporter explained enough to me in simple English so I could do my columns.

- **Esther Dyson, editor and publisher.** The first PC I ever knew was a Wang word processor I single-handedly brought into the Wall Street firm where I was working. Everyone in the office was very suspicious of the machine, but by the time I left they were all standing in line to use it.

- **Alice Kahn, author.** For me, getting a computer meant the difference between being an amateur and a pro. I used to write on yellow pads and scribble the changes into the margins before I would even go near the typewriter. Now I turn out two pieces a week, and my writing income has increased 800%.

- **Andrew Tobias, author.** The PC has changed my life in several respects. I was already an established writer, but the computer has added a whole new dimension to my career. It would be dishonest of me not to acknowledge that it has bought me a vacation house and a lot of other nice things. But more than that, I now spend half my life on this program Managing Your Money. I didn't expect it to turn out that way, but it has.

- **Chris Pray, television writer.** I have a war with machines. I don't even drive. I have a Stone Age psychology and even have a Stone Age computer: no modem, no hard disk. The first month I had my computer, I found myself thinking like a computer after I turned it off:

I'd think about deleting dumb remarks I'd made in a conversation, or inserting things, or moving things around.

- **Harvey Rosenfield, head of Ralph Nader's Access to Justice.** The special interests, with their infinitely greater resources, had access to computerized press lists and word processing. Then came the PC. Sensing vaguely what it could do for us, I took out a loan and bought a PC. It was a revolution among the revolutionaries. Suddenly, a position paper could quickly become legislative testimony; a press release, a newsletter. Most important, it helped even the odds for the consumer movement.

DISCUSSION QUESTION
In what ways are word processors superior to typewriters?

Some people think of word processing as just glorified typing. And, in a way, it is. But consider the advantages of word processing over typing. Word processing stores your typed words in the computer's memory, lets you see what you type on the screen before printing, remembers what you type and lets you change it, and prints the typed document at your request.

There are two notable differences between using a word processing program and using a typewriter. The first difference is the separation of typing from printing: When you use word processing, typing the document and printing the document do not occur at the

Figure 12-1 Entering text with word processing software. As you type in your text, the position of the cursor (the dash just to the right of the last word in the paragraph) shows you where the next character will be placed.

same time; you print the document on paper whenever you like. Perhaps you want to print an intermediate draft, just to see how it looks, and then continue making changes. Or you may choose to commit your work to paper only in the final version.

The second difference between word processing programs and typewriters is related to the first: When you use a word processing package you can make changes as you go along, or even at some later time, and print out a revised—and perfect—copy. The key here is that only the changes themselves are retyped, not the entire document.

Although word processing can be readily distinguished from typing, this is just part of the story. A word processing package is a sophisticated tool with many options. Many of the options will be covered in this chapter. We begin with an overview of how word processing works. Then we present an easy-to-follow example, where you can see how different word processing features are used.

7 An Overview: How Word Processing Works

Think of the computer's screen as a page of typing paper. On the screen the word processing program indicates the top of the page and the left and right edges (margins) of the typed material. When you type you can see the line of text you are typing on the screen—it looks just like a line of typing on paper. Remember that you are not really typing on the screen; the screen merely displays what you are entering into memory. As you type, the program displays a **cursor** (Figure 12-1) to show where the next character you

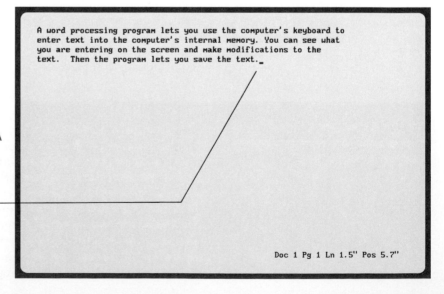

```
A word processing program lets you use the computer's keyboard to
enter text into the computer's internal memory. You can see what
you are entering on the screen and make modifications to the
text.  Then the program lets you save the text._
```

Cursor ——————————

Doc 1 Pg 1 Ln 1.5" Pos 5.7"

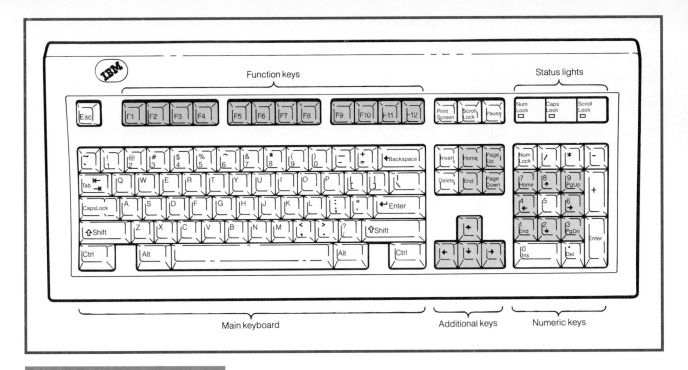

Figure 12-2 A personal computer keyboard. The cursor movement keys, highlighted in blue, let you move the cursor around on the screen.

type will appear on the screen. The cursor is usually a blinking dash or rectangle that you can easily see.

You can also move the cursor around on the screen by using special **cursor movement keys** on the right side of the keyboard (Figure 12-2). The up and down cursor movement keys move the cursor up or down one line at a time. The **PgUp** and **PgDn** keys let you move the cursor up or down a whole page—as it would be printed—at a time.

7 Scrolling

A word processing program lets you type page after page of material. Most programs show a line of dashes on the screen to mark where one printed page will end and another will begin; this line is not printed when you print your document. Most word processing programs also indicate what page the cursor is on and what line it is on.

A screen can display only about 24 lines of text. Although the screen display size is limited, your document size is not. As you continue to type new lines, the earlier lines you typed move up the screen as each new line is added at the bottom of the screen. Eventually, the first line you typed disappears off the top of the screen. But the line has not disappeared from the computer's memory.

To see a line that has disappeared from the top of the screen, use your cursor movement key to move the cursor up to the top of the screen. As you continue to press the up cursor movement key, the

LECTURE HINT
Though most displays can show 24 or 25 lines of text, some screens can show far more. For example, the Radius display on a Macintosh II can show a whole page of text at one time. But some laptop computers can display only eight to sixteen lines of text at a time.

Figure 12-3   Scrolling through a document.   Although most documents contain many lines of text, the screen can display only about 24 lines at one time. You can use the cursor movement keys to scroll up and down through the document.

TRANSPARENCY ACETATE #12B
Figure #12-3

On college campuses, computers may soon be
as common as pizza and dirty laundry. Many
colleges, including Dartmouth, Carnegie-
Mellon, Lehigh, and Drexel, require or
strongly recommend that students
purchase computers. Drexel, which requires
each entering freshman to purchase a
personal computer and software, has

thoroughly integrated computers into its
curriculum.

Drexel's ambitious development of a
computer-assisted curriculum has received
strong student and faculty support. Faculty
members developed software with the help of
student and professional programmers. For
instance, a chemistry professor designed
software that helps students understand
molecular structure by seeing the
arrangements of atoms displayed on the
computer screen. A program written by a
mathematics professor shows students how to
solve complex algebra problems. An English
professor created software that helps
students write more coherently.

Drexel's integration of computers into its
curriculum has had a positive effect on the
school's morale. A study shows that as
students and faculty become more adept
at using computers, they tend to feel more
optimistic about the future.

line that had disappeared drops back down onto the screen. The program treats the text you are typing as if it were all on a long roll of paper like a roll of paper towels or a scroll. You "roll the scroll" up or down on the screen by moving the cursor. This process, called **scrolling,** lets you see any part of the document on the screen—but only 24 or so lines at a time (Figure 12-3).

7 No Need to Worry About the Right Side

When you start to type the first line of a document, you will eventually get to the right side of the screen. The word processing program watches to see how close you are to the edge of the "paper" (the right margin). If there is not enough room at the end of a line to complete the word you are typing, the program automatically starts that word at the left margin of the next line down. You never have to worry about running out of space on a line; the word processor plans ahead for you. This feature is called **word wrap.**

DISCUSSION QUESTION
In word processing, is the return key used at the end of a line or a paragraph? What does word wrap do for the user?

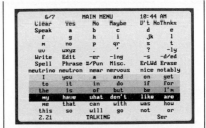

6/7		MAIN MENU		10:44 AM	
Clear	Yes	No	Maybe	D't	NoThnks
Speak	a	b	c	d	e
f	g	h	i	jk	l
m	no	p	qr	s	t
uv	wxyz	.	,	?	-ly
Write	Edit	-er	-ing	-s	-d/ed
Spell	Phrase	#/Pun	Misc.	ErLWd	Erase
neutrino	neutron	near	nervous	nice	notably
I	you	a	and	on	get
to	it	in	do	if	for
the	is	of	but	be	I'm
my	have	what	don't	like	are
me	that	can	with	was	how
this	so	will	go	not	or
2.21		TALKING			Ser

UNLOCKING HIS MIND

Imagine that you have something important to say but cannot say it. Suppose, further, that your mind is so dazzling that you could make a significant contribution to the world, if only you could express yourself. This is the situation in which Stephen Hawking, victim of Lou Gehrig's disease, found himself. But this is the age of technology, and technology solved Stephen's problem: His words are channeled from his brain to the rest of us via a computer and a very clever word processing program.

Stephen Hawking is a physicist, an unlikely candidate for making the best-seller charts. But that is exactly what he did with his book, *A Brief History of Time.* The book was written on a personal computer, using a system called *Equalizer,* which Stephen can use by wiggling a single finger on a switch. Think of a set of lines on a screen, with several words per line. When Stephen presses the switch to activate the system, the software uses a highlighting bar to scan the words on the screen. Stephen presses the switch again when the highlight bar lands on the word he wants, and the word is selected. The system is actually more powerful than this minimal description would indicate, but never is more than a flick of the switch required.

Stephen Hawking is widely regarded as the most brilliant theoretical physicist since Einstein, but he is not very interested in such descriptions of himself. Says he, "It's media hype. I'm a bit smarter than most, but not exceptional."

TEST BANK
Mult. Choice	19-32
T/F	27-39
Matching B	2-3, 5-7
Matching C	10
Matching D	1-4
Fill-in-the-Blank	8-15

You do not have to push a carriage return key at the end of each line as you would with a typewriter; in fact, you *should not* use a carriage return at the end of a line, or word wrap will not work properly. However, you can use a carriage return—that is, you can press Enter—to provide a blank line or to signal the end of a paragraph.

7 Easy Corrections

What if you make a mistake while you are typing? No problem: Move the cursor to the position of the error and make the correction. Word processing programs let you delete characters or whole words or lines that you have already typed, and they close up the resulting spaces automatically.

You can also insert new characters in the middle of a line or a word without typing over (and erasing) the characters that are already there. The program moves the existing characters to the right of the insertion as you type the new characters. However, if you wish, the word processing program also lets you *overtype* (replace) characters you typed before. We will discuss these correction techniques in more detail later.

7 Function Keys: Making It Easy

The *function keys* on a keyboard (see Figure 12-2) can save you a lot of time. Most word processing packages let you use the function keys, but the result of pressing each function key differs according to the applications program. For example, if you are using one word processing program and you want to underline a word in a report, you can press F8. But if you are using another program, you might have to press another function key or even a combination of keys to do the same task.

To help people remember which function key performs which task, software manufacturers often provide a sheet of plastic or paper that describes the use of each key. This sheet, called a **template,** fits over the function keys (Figure 12-4).

Now you are ready to see how these concepts work in a word processing package.

7 Getting Started: Using a Word Processing Package

Carl Wade has just graduated with a business degree and is looking for an entry-level job in an advertising firm. Carl already has a resume, but he wants to use a word processing package to prepare a cover letter. Carl chooses WordPerfect, the word processing package that dominates both businesses and college campuses.

WordPerfect® for IBM Personal Computers		Shell	Spell	Screen	Move	*Ctrl*	Text In/Out
Delete to End of Ln/Pg End/Pg Dn		Thesaurus	Replace	Reveal Codes	Block	*Alt*	Mark Text
Delete Word Backspace							
Go To Home		Setup	♦Search	Switch	♦Indent♦	*Shift*	Date/Outline
Hard Page Enter							
♦Margin Release Tab							
Screen Up/Down –/+ (num)		Cancel	♦Search	Help	♦Indent		List Files
Soft Hyphen –							
Word Left/Right ←/→		F1	F2	F3	F4		F5
© WordPerfect Corp. 1988 TMXXENWPIID50—6/15/88 ISBN 1-55692-200-0							

Tab Align	Footnote	Font	*Ctrl*	Merge/Sort	Macro Define		
Flush Right	Math/Columns	Style	*Alt*	Graphics	Macro		
Center	Print	Format	*Shift*	Merge Codes	Retrieve		
Bold	Exit	Underline		Merge R	Save	Reveal Codes	Block
F6	F7	F8		F9	F10	F11	F12

Figure 12-4   A function-key template. This template helps you remember which function keys perform which tasks. Without the template you would have to memorize numerous key combinations. The template is color-coded to match related keys: red for the Control (Ctrl) key, green for the Shift key, blue for the Alternate (Alt) key, and black for the function key alone. Examples: press Shift-F7 to Print, Ctrl-F2 to invoke the Spelling Checker, or just F6 for boldface. (To fit on this page the template has been split in half; normally it fits above the function keys.)

TRANSPARENCY ACETATE #12C
Figure #12-4

TRANSPARENCY ACETATE #12D
A function key template for
WordPerfect 4.2

DISCUSSION QUESTION
What is the purpose of a template, when used with the function keys?

LECTURE ACTIVITY
Illustrate with printed handouts or with a computer some of the key differences in menu systems for popular word processing programs. (Example: WordPerfect, Word Star, Microsoft Word, PC Write.)

When it is necessary to be specific in this example, we will use WordPerfect commands. In particular, we will use the latest version of WordPerfect, Version 5.0. Many people use Version 4.2; most keystrokes for WordPerfect commands are the same in both versions. However, we include keystrokes for both versions in Appendix B.

Loading the Program

As always, Carl begins by booting the computer. (This can be done by first using a Disk Operating System—DOS—disk or by using the word processing disk itself if the internal DOS files have been transferred onto it. Refer to Chapter 9, "Operating Systems," if you need help booting your computer.) After Carl boots the computer he makes sure he has his word processing disk in drive A and his formatted data disk in drive B. (Carl is using a personal computer with two disk drives.)

At this point, with the A prompt (A>) on the screen, Carl needs to type a command to get the word processing program started. The command varies with the program; examples are WS for WordStar, WORD for Microsoft Word, and WP for WordPerfect. When the appropriate command is typed, the word processing program is loaded from the disk in drive A into the computer's memory. Depending on the word processing program used, a set of choices, called a **menu,** may appear on the screen. However, WordPerfect, the program Carl is using, immediately displays an almost blank screen to represent a blank sheet of typing paper (Figure 12-5).

Figure 12-5 Getting started with WordPerfect. When Carl first loads WordPerfect, the screen is almost as blank as a fresh sheet of paper. Note the cursor in the upper left corner. The information at the bottom of the screen is called the status line. The status line includes the document number, the page number, the position of the cursor in inches from the top of the page (Ln 1"), and the position of the cursor in inches from the left edge of the paper (Pos 1").

Status line ————————

Doc 1 Pg 1 Ln 1" Pos 1"

DISCUSSION QUESTION
What steps must you apply to use WordPerfect to write and print a short letter to a friend? Describe each step, including how to fix errors, save the letter, and print the letter.

LECTURE HINT
With WordPerfect on MS-DOS, the Backspace key deletes the character to the left of the cursor, and the Del key deletes the character at the cursor position.

DISCUSSION QUESTION
What is wrong with the following statement? "As text is entered and corrected, the results are stored immediately on disk."

7 Creating the Cover Letter

The following steps describe, in a general way, how Carl creates (enters), saves, and prints his letter. Although the specific keystroke instructions refer to WordPerfect, the general approach fits any word processing package. (Note: A summary of specific keystrokes for this and other examples in this chapter can be found in Appendix B.) Once Carl has loaded the word processing program, he proceeds as follows.

Entering the Letter

Carl starts by typing the letter (Figure 12-6) on the computer's keyboard. He uses the keyboard as he would a typewriter. He can see the results of his keystrokes on the screen. If he needs to make corrections, he can use the Backspace key or the Del (delete) key. To enter his address and the date on the right side of the letter, he presses the Tab key several times. Carl knows the letter is being stored in memory as he types, so as he continues to use the word processing package, he can continue to make changes to any part of the letter.

Saving the Letter

When Carl has finished keying in the letter and has corrected his mistakes, he stores—saves—the letter in a file on his data disk. (Recall that memory keeps data only temporarily; you must save your typed documents on disk if you want to keep them.) To save the letter on disk, Carl presses the F10 function key. The words "Document to be saved:" appear at the bottom of the screen, and Carl needs to enter a file name for his document. A file name lets DOS keep track of the file's location on a disk so the file can be found when requested in the future. Carl names his file B:CLETTER—the B: tells the program which disk to store the file on, and CLETTER (an

Figure 12-6   The first draft of Carl's cover letter. Carl can enter this draft and use WordPerfect to make the changes described in the text.

```
                                              18 Leroy Street
                                              Binghamton, NY  10037
                                              July 13, 1992


        Ms. Louise Graham
        Director of Personnel
        Charnley Advertising, Inc.
        1900 Corporate Lane
        Baltimore, Maryland  21200

        Dear Ms. Graham:

        I am writing to inquire about the possibility of a position in
        Charnley's accounts department.

        I recently graduated from Pennsylvania State University with a BA
        in business.  My area of interest was marketing.

        I became acquainted with your company through my intern work at the
        Dunhill Agency in New York.  I have always hoped to combine my
        background in business and my interest in marketing.  Charnley
        Advertising seems to offer the best opportunity for doing this.

        I will be in Baltimore on July 28 and 29.  Would it be possible for
        us to meet to discuss this further?  I can be reached at 600-623-
        4667.  I look forward to hearing from you.

        Sincerely,


        Carl Wade
```

LECTURE HINT
Remember that MS-DOS retains only the first eight letters of a file name.

LECTURE HINT
Note that the option to print the whole document is choice 1; the number 1 is pressed, not the function key F1.

abbreviation for *cover letter*) is the name of the file. Carl then presses Enter. By storing the letter on his data disk, Carl has made sure that he will always have a copy of the letter if he needs it again.

Printing the Letter

Carl decides he wants to see a printed copy of what he has written so far. After turning on the printer, he holds down the Shift key and presses the F7 function key. WordPerfect then gives him a list of choices—a menu—related to printing. He can choose to print the full document (choice 1) or only one page at a time (choice 2). Because he has only a one-page letter, it really makes no difference which he chooses. He presses 1 for choice 1. This activates the printer, and his letter is printed.

Exiting the Program

Once Carl has finished using the program, he presses the F7 function key to exit the program. WordPerfect then presents a question at the bottom of the screen: "Save document?" Carl types N for *no* since the file has already been saved. WordPerfect then asks "Exit WP?" and Carl types Y for *yes*. This loads him back to the A>. If Carl wanted to start a new file without leaving the program, he could clear the screen by typing N in response to the second question.

LECTURE HINT
Another method of retrieving the file is to use the F5 key and press ENTER to see the directory of disk B: use the cursor keys to highlight the file desired. Then depress the numeric 1 key to retrieve the file. This method is longer than in text; but if you cannot remember the exact spelling of the file name, this may be the only way to proceed.

7 Editing the Letter

As we said, a significant payoff of word processing is the ease of making corrections to existing documents. Suppose Carl decides, for example, that his cover letter would be more effective if he made several changes. Consider for a moment what Carl would have to do if the letter had been prepared on a typewriter. He would, of course, have to retype the entire letter. Now follow the word processing approach to making changes.

Since Carl is not already using the word processing program, he places the word processing disk in drive A and his data disk in drive B and loads WordPerfect into memory, as before.

Retrieving the Letter

Carl presses the Shift key and the F10 function key together to retrieve the file. When WordPerfect asks for the name of the document to retrieve, he types B:CLETTER, as illustrated in Figure 12-7. When he presses Enter, the current version of his letter, just as he last saved it on his data disk, is loaded into memory and then displayed on the screen.

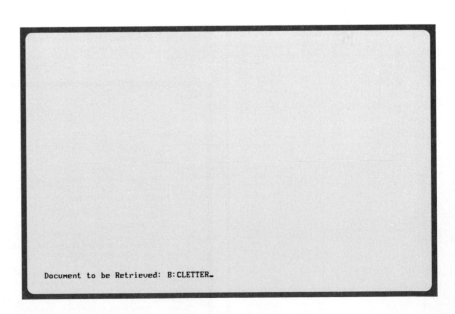

Figure 12-7   Retrieving the letter. To retrieve a document, Carl must type in the name of the file he wants. B: tells the computer the drive that holds the diskette with the file; CLETTER tells the computer the name of the file that holds the document.

Document to be Retrieved: B:CLETTER_

Making the Changes

We have already described how existing text can be moved over to allow new text to be inserted. This is called the **insert mode,** and it is the standard way of inserting corrections when you are using word processing. For example, suppose Carl wants to add the word "express" before the word "interest" in the second paragraph. All he has to do is move the cursor so it is below the "i" in "interest" and then type the word "express" and press the Spacebar. This automatically adds the word to the sentence (Figure 12-8a).

Another correction option is to type right over the existing text. This feature, called **typeover mode,** allows you to replace the existing text with the new text. If Carl wants to replace the word "ex-

Figure 12-8 Editing the letter. Carl uses the flexibility of word processing to edit his letter. (a) First he uses the insert mode to add the word "express" in the middle of a line. He positions the cursor and types in the word and a space. (b) Carl decides to use the typeover mode to change "express" to "special." As Carl keys in the word "special," he types over the word he wants to replace. In the screen shown here, he has typed "spec" so far, so we still see the "ess" of "express."

```
                                        18 Leroy Street
                                        Binghamton, NY  10037
                                        July 13, 1992


Ms. Louise Graham
Director of Personnel
Charnley Advertising, Inc.
1900 Corporate Lane
Baltimore, Maryland 21200


Dear Ms. Graham:

I am writing to inquire about the possibility of a position in
Charnley's accounts department.

I recently graduated from Pennsylvania State University with a BA
in business.  My area of express interest was marketing.

I became acquainted with your company through my intern work at the
Dunhill Agency in New York.  I have always hoped to combine my
B:\CLETTER                                  Doc 1 Pg 1 Ln 4.33" Pos 4.3"
```

(a)

```
                                        18 Leroy Street
                                        Binghamton, NY  10037
                                        July 13, 1992


Ms. Louise Graham
Director of Personnel
Charnley Advertising, Inc.
1900 Corporate Lane
Baltimore, Maryland 21200


Dear Ms. Graham:

I am writing to inquire about the possibility of a position in
Charnley's accounts department.

I recently graduated from Pennsylvania State University with a BA
in business.  My area of specess interest was marketing.

I became acquainted with your company through my intern work at the
Dunhill Agency in New York.  I have always hoped to combine my
Typeover                                    Doc 1 Pg 1 Ln 4.33" Pos 3.9"
```

(b)

press'' with the word ''special,'' he presses the Insert (Ins) key, moves the cursor under the ''e'' in ''express,'' and types ''special'' (Figure 12-8b). Then he presses Ins again to turn off the typeover mode. It may seem odd that Carl presses the Ins key to enter the typeover mode. This occurs because the program starts with the insert mode as the default mode, and the Ins key acts as a **toggle switch,** allowing you to switch between the insert mode and the typeover mode.

Carl also wants to add several sentences that explain his experience. He decides to insert the sentences between the third and fourth paragraphs. To insert the new sentences, Carl uses the cursor movement keys to position the cursor at the point where he wishes to add the new sentences. Then he types the sentences. He may, of course, make any other changes he wishes at this time. When he is finished, he presses Enter to provide the proper spacing at the end of the new paragraph. Compare the final version (Figure 12-9) with the original version (Figure 12-6).

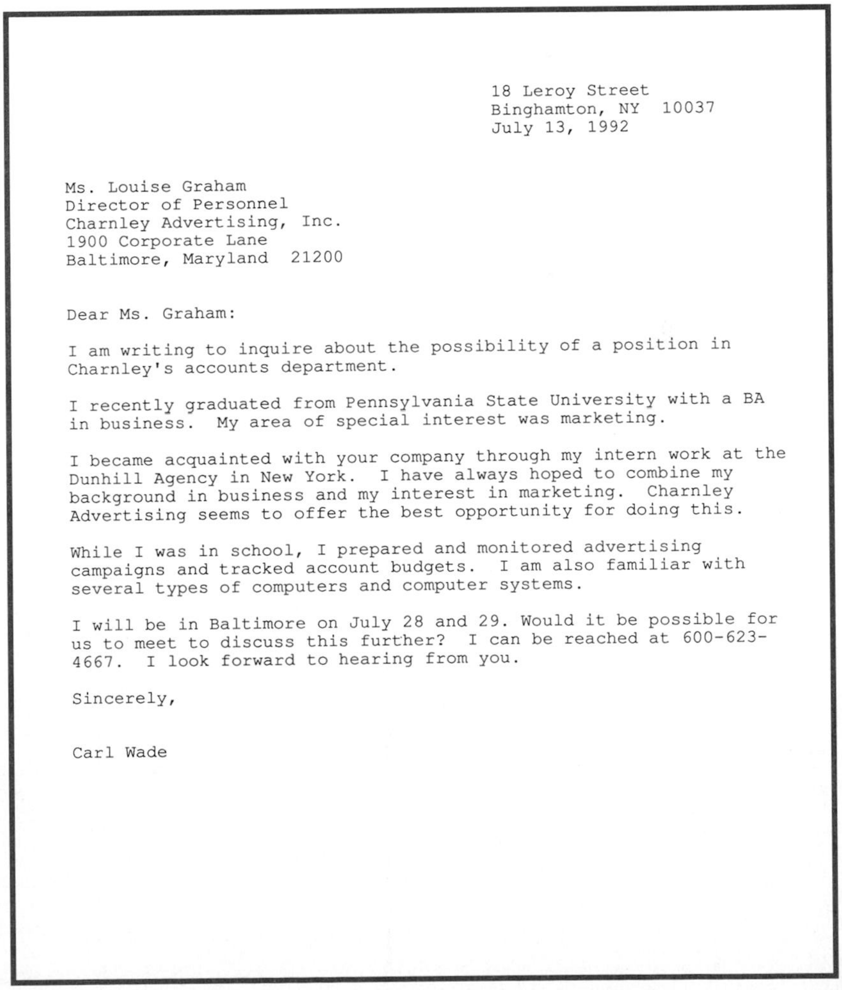

DISCUSSION QUESTION
What is a toggle switch?

Figure 12-9   The corrected letter.
Carl prints out the corrected letter, knowing he can make further changes later if he wishes.

```
                                              18 Leroy Street
                                              Binghamton, NY   10037
                                              July 13, 1992


         Ms. Louise Graham
         Director of Personnel
         Charnley Advertising, Inc.
         1900 Corporate Lane
         Baltimore, Maryland   21200

         Dear Ms. Graham:

         I am writing to inquire about the possibility of a position in
         Charnley's accounts department.

         I recently graduated from Pennsylvania State University with a BA
         in business.  My area of special interest was marketing.

         I became acquainted with your company through my intern work at the
         Dunhill Agency in New York.  I have always hoped to combine my
         background in business and my interest in marketing.  Charnley
         Advertising seems to offer the best opportunity for doing this.

         While I was in school, I prepared and monitored advertising
         campaigns and tracked account budgets.  I am also familiar with
         several types of computers and computer systems.

         I will be in Baltimore on July 28 and 29. Would it be possible for
         us to meet to discuss this further?  I can be reached at 600-623-
         4667.  I look forward to hearing from you.

         Sincerely,


         Carl Wade
```

Saving the Corrected Letter

As before, Carl presses the F10 key to save the letter on his disk. WordPerfect asks if Carl wants to replace the earlier version of the letter with the new version. Carl types Y for *yes*, and the letter is again saved in a file named B:CLETTER. If he had pressed N for *no*, WordPerfect would have asked for the name of the document to be saved, and Carl could have entered a different name.

After you have practiced a bit, you will see that making changes with word processing is swift and efficient, even for a short document such as a letter. Considering the volume of correspondence—or any kind of typing—in an office, the labor savings is significant.

TEST BANK
Mult. Choice   33-48
T/F   40-53
Matching B   1, 4, 9-10
Matching C   9
Matching D   5-9
Fill-in-the-Blank   16-25

TRANSPARENCY ACETATE #12E
Figure #12-10

7 Formatting: Making It Look Nice

Now that you know the basics of creating text with a word processing program, you can turn your attention to the appearance, or **format,** of the document. This is not a trivial matter. In fact, one of the most appealing aspects of word processing is the ability it gives you to adjust the appearance of a document. You can use this capability to present your company—or yourself—attractively on paper.

Figure 12-10   Formatting considerations. Word processing software lets you change the look of your document. For example, you can change the margins or center a page with just a few keystrokes. You can also alter the indentations, use double spacing, or make dozens of other style changes in a matter of seconds.

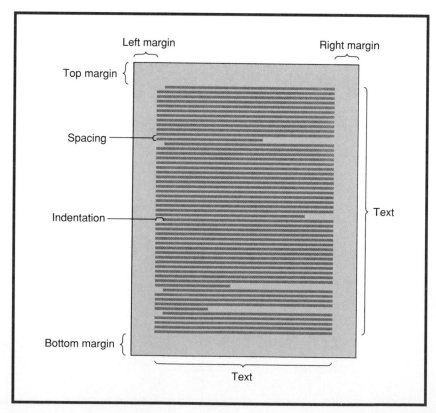

Image is important. A multimillion-dollar company that relies on public opinion certainly wants to appear at its best on paper. So do little companies that do not have money to spend on fancy typesetting and printing. All these companies, big and small, can afford word processing.

The format of a document is the way the document appears on the page. *Format* refers to the size of the margins, the organization of text, the space between the lines, and all the other factors that affect appearance. Figure 12-10 shows some format considerations. Word processing software offers many features to control and vary the format of a document.

To show you how formatting works, we return to Carl Wade.

The Resume Example

Once Carl finishes his cover letter, he takes another look at his resume (Figure 12-11). He sees at a glance that it can use some improvement: The resume is bunched up at the top of the page, giv-

Figure 12-11   The first draft of Carl's resume. This is Carl's first draft of his resume. It is a good start, but he can make it much better. If Carl had to rely on a typewriter to make the corrections described in the text, he would have to retype the entire page.

```
CARL WADE
18 LEROY STREET
BINGHAMTON, NY  10037
600-623-4667


CAREER OBJECTIVE
Challenging position with an advertising agency as an entry-level
account representative.  Seeking the experience that leads to a
career as an accounts manager.

EDUCATION
College: The Pennsylvania State University
Degree: Bachelor of Arts
Major: Business
Specialization: Marketing
GPA: 3.8

HONORS AND ACTIVITIES
Lloyd B. Trennon Honor Scholarship (2 years)
Kiwanis Achievement Scholarship (3 years)
Class Treasurer (Junior year)
President, Computer Club (Senior year)

EMPLOYMENT HISTORY
Junior Intern.  The Dunhill Agency, Binghamton, NY.  Earned one of
three student internships.  Assisted in preparing and monitoring
advertising campaigns.  Used Lotus 1-2-3 to track account budgets.
(Full time for two summers, part time senior year.)

Receptionist.  Martin Lumber Company, Binghamton, NY.
Responsibilities included greeting customers, coordinating
calendars and appointments, and taking community groups on company
tours.  (Summer job.)

REFERENCES
Available on request.
```

DISCUSSION QUESTION
What formatting options are usually available in word processors? Identify them, describe what each means, and describe how to use them in WordPerfect.

ing it a short, squatty look. Carl wonders if the name and address lines would look better if they were centered. And he sees that the text runs together, making it hard to read. As Carl ponders various ways to fix the resume, he loads the original version from the disk and studies it on the screen.

Carl decides to try several format changes to make the resume longer and more attractive. These changes are (1) adding a space after each major heading, (2) centering the name and address lines, (3) centering the text vertically on the page, (4) widening the width of the margins, (5) evening up the right-hand margin, and (6) using boldface and underlining to highlight certain words.

Adding Blank Lines

The first change is easy enough: Carl positions the cursor at the end of each major heading (for example, the heading "Career Objective") and presses Enter. This moves the cursor one line down and adds a blank line in the text.

Centering Lines

To **center** the name and address lines between the left and right sides of the page, Carl positions the cursor under the leftmost character of a line, presses the Shift key and the F6 key simultaneously, and then presses the down cursor key. This automatically centers the line of text. He repeats this process for each of the next three lines. Figure 12-12 shows the results.

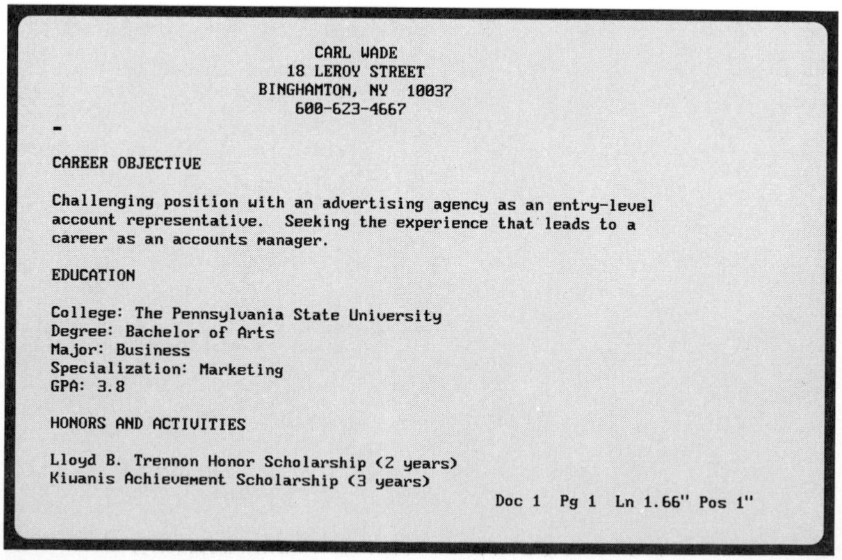

Figure 12-12 Easy centering. Carl can center the top four lines without the risk of introducing typing errors.

```
                          CARL WADE
                        18 LEROY STREET
                     BINGHAMTON, NY  10037
                        600-623-4667

    -

    CAREER OBJECTIVE

    Challenging position with an advertising agency as an entry-level
    account representative.  Seeking the experience that leads to a
    career as an accounts manager.

    EDUCATION

    College: The Pennsylvania State University
    Degree: Bachelor of Arts
    Major: Business
    Specialization: Marketing
    GPA: 3.8

    HONORS AND ACTIVITIES

    Lloyd B. Trennon Honor Scholarship (2 years)
    Kiwanis Achievement Scholarship (3 years)
                                          Doc 1  Pg 1  Ln 1.66" Pos 1"
```

7 Vertical Centering

Carl's next improvement is to center the resume on the page, a process called vertical centering. **Vertical centering** adjusts the top and bottom margins so the text is centered vertically on the printed page. This eliminates the need to calculate the exact number of lines to leave at the top and bottom of a page, a necessary process if centering vertically using a typewriter.

To center the whole page vertically, the cursor must be at the top of the page. After Carl moves the cursor, he presses the Shift key and the F8 key at the same time to access the format menu. Next he types 2 to see the page format menu, and then types 1 to choose the option for centering the page top to bottom. He finally presses Enter twice to return to the document. The document does not look any different on the screen, but when it is printed it will be centered vertically.

7 Changing Margins

When Carl first typed his resume, he left the margins—left and right, top and bottom—on their original settings. The original settings are called **default settings**—settings used by the word processing package unless these settings are deliberately changed by the user. Both the default left and right margins are usually 1 inch (ten characters) wide, leaving room for about 65 characters per line of text. The default top and bottom margins are also usually 1 inch each; these settings allow about 55 lines of text per page.

Documents are often typed using the default margin settings. However, if the document would look better with narrower or wider margins, the margin settings can be changed accordingly. Most packages even allow several different margin settings in various parts of the same document. Carl wants to widen the left and right margins for the entire resume. To do this, he must first move the cursor to the top of the document. He presses the Shift key and F8 at the same time to access the format menu, and then presses 1 to get the line format menu, and then 7 to choose the margin option. To change the left margin from the default setting of 1 inch to 1.75 inches, he types 1.75 and presses Enter. To change the right margin to 1.5 inches, he types 1.5 and presses Enter. He presses Enter twice to get back to the document. To see the results of his changes, shown in Figure 12-13, he must move the cursor past the centered lines.

When the margin settings are changed, most word processing software automatically adjusts the text to accommodate the new margins. This is called **automatic reformatting.** Figure 12-13 illustrates how WordPerfect automatically reformatted the text so that the resume now has wider margins. With some word processing packages, you may have to press special keys to initiate the reformatting.

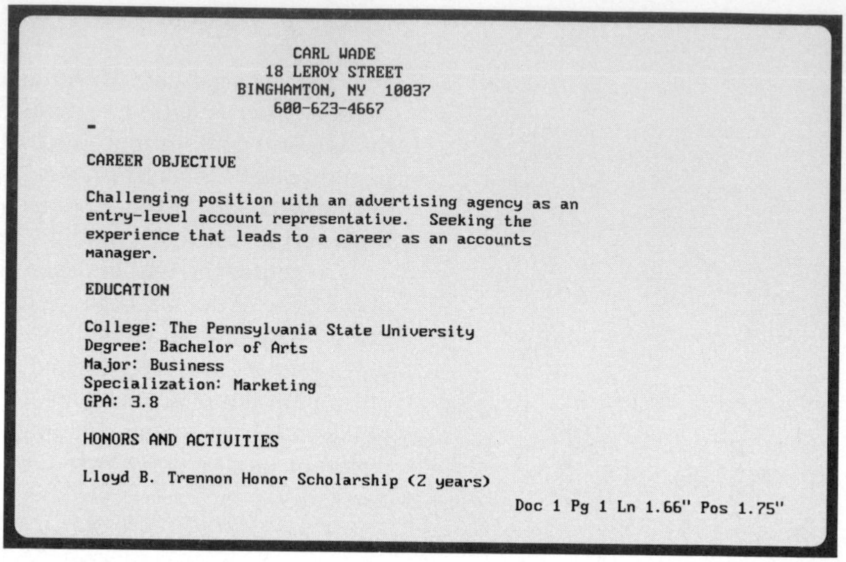

Figure 12-13   Changing the margins.
When Carl widened the margins, WordPerfect automatically shifted the text to fit into the narrower space. Notice how the CAREER OBJECTIVE paragraph now takes up four lines rather than three.

```
                      CARL WADE
                   18 LEROY STREET
                BINGHAMTON, NY  10037
                   600-623-4667
   -

   CAREER OBJECTIVE

   Challenging position with an advertising agency as an
   entry-level account representative.  Seeking the
   experience that leads to a career as an accounts
   Manager.

   EDUCATION

   College: The Pennsylvania State University
   Degree: Bachelor of Arts
   Major: Business
   Specialization: Marketing
   GPA: 3.8

   HONORS AND ACTIVITIES

   Lloyd B. Trennon Honor Scholarship (2 years)

                              Doc 1 Pg 1 Ln 1.66" Pos 1.75"
```

DISCUSSION QUESTION
What does "justified" mean in word processing?

LECTURE HINT
Types of justification: (1) Left (left margin is fixed for every non-indented line). (2) Right (right margin is fixed for every line). (3) Left-Right (neither margin is ragged; enough spaces are inserted into the line to do this).

Justifying the Right Margin

Carl now wants to make the right-hand margin even. Notice in Figure 12-11 that the left side of the resume is neatly lined up but the right side is uneven, or ragged. **Ragged right margin** means that the end of each line does not end in the same position on the right side of the document. But Carl wants his right margin to be **justified,** that is, to line up neatly on the right-hand side.

Some word processing software assumes right justification as the default setting, meaning that the right margin is automatically justified unless a user specifically requests a ragged right edge. Many word processing packages, such as WordPerfect, automatically justify the right margin when the document is printed, even though the right margin appears ragged on the screen. The advantage of this approach is that inadvertent blanks between words can be seen and removed before the document is printed. In Figure 12-14 Carl's resume has been printed. WordPerfect has justified the right margin by spreading each line of text from margin to margin, leaving some extra spaces between words.

If Carl wanted to print his resume with a ragged right margin, he would first move the cursor to the top of the page. Next, he would press the Shift and F8 keys at the same time to access the format menu, and then type 1 for the line format menu. Carl would then type 3 for "Justification" and type N for *no* (he does not want justification).

Adding Boldface and Underlining

Finally, Carl decides to add a few special touches to his resume. He wants to use darker text, or **boldface** text, for the address and name lines and the major headings, and he wants to underline his job titles to emphasize them. To boldface a group of words, he

Figure 12-14 Justified margins.
When Carl prints out his resume, WordPerfect justifies, or evens up, the right-hand margin.

```
                          CARL WADE
                        18 LEROY STREET
                    BINGHAMTON, NY  10037
                        600-623-4667


        CAREER OBJECTIVE

        Challenging position  with an  advertising agency as an
        entry-level  account  representative.       Seeking  the
        experience  that  leads  to  a  career  as  an  accounts
        manager.

        EDUCATION

        College: The Pennsylvania State University
        Degree: Bachelor of Arts
        Major: Business
        Specialization: Marketing
        GPA: 3.8

        HONORS AND ACTIVITIES

        Lloyd B. Trennon Honor Scholarship (2 years)
        Kiwanis Achievement Scholarship (3 years)
        Class Treasurer (Junior year)
        President, Computer Club (Senior year)

        EMPLOYMENT HISTORY

        Junior Intern.   The  Dunhill  Agency,  Binghamton, NY.
        Earned one  of three  student internships.  Assisted in
        preparing and  monitoring advertising  campaigns.  Used
        Lotus 1-2-3  to track  account budgets.  (Full time for
        two summers, part time senior year.)

        Receptionist.  Martin Lumber  Company, Binghamton, NY.
        Responsibilities     included     greeting    customers,
        coordinating  calendars  and  appointments,  and taking
        community groups on company tours.  (Summer job.)

        REFERENCES

        Available on request.
```

LECTURE HINT
Alt-F4 is used to define a block of text, all to be modified in the same way or moved. (See Figure 12-4.) F6 is used to convert the block to boldface. F8 for underlining works the same way.

positions the cursor at the beginning of the first word and presses the Alt key and the F4 key together. The words "Block on" flash in the lower-left corner of the screen. Then he moves the cursor to the end of the last word. This highlights the block of words (Figure 12-15a). Next Carl presses F6. The words "Block on" disappear, and the words that will be printed in boldface appear brighter, dimmer, or a different color than the surrounding words on the screen, depending on the word processing package (Figure 12-15b). When the resume is printed, the marked words will appear darker than the rest of the text. If Carl wants to enter the command to boldface text as he types in a document, he can press F6 before he starts to type the word or words he wants to be bold and then press F6 again after he has finished typing them.

Underlining is also easy. To underline his job titles, which have already been typed, Carl positions the cursor at the beginning of the words he wants to underline. Next he presses the Alt key and F4

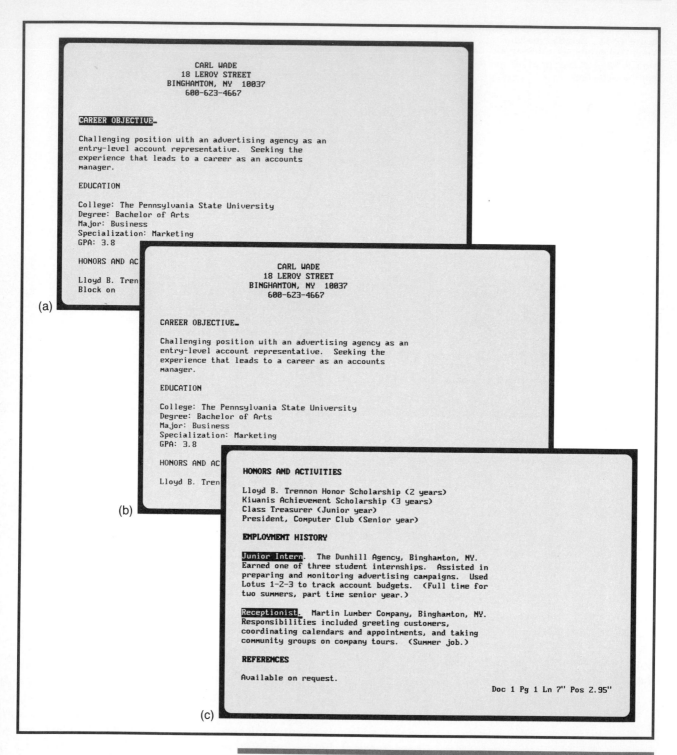

Figure 12-15 Marking text. (a) Carl marks—highlights—the text he wants in boldface. (b) When Carl presses F6 to boldface the text, the marked text appears darker than the surrounding text. (c) Carl uses the F8 key to underline key words in his resume.

Figure 12-16   The final draft.
Compare this version of Carl's resume
to his first draft in Figure 12-11.

CARL WADE
18 LEROY STREET
BINGHAMTON, NY   10037
600-623-4667

CAREER OBJECTIVE

Challenging position with an advertising agency as an
entry-level account representative.   Seeking the
experience that leads to a career as an accounts
manager.

EDUCATION

College: The Pennsylvania State University
Degree: Bachelor of Arts
Major: Business
Specialization: Marketing
GPA: 3.8

HONORS AND ACTIVITIES

Lloyd B. Trennon Honor Scholarship (2 years)
Kiwanis Achievement Scholarship (3 years)
Class Treasurer (Junior year)
President, Computer Club (Senior year)

EMPLOYMENT HISTORY

<u>Junior Intern</u>.   The Dunhill Agency, Binghamton, NY.
Earned one of three student internships. Assisted in
preparing and monitoring advertising campaigns. Used
Lotus 1-2-3 to track account budgets. (Full time for
two summers, part time senior year.)

<u>Receptionist</u>.   Martin Lumber Company, Binghamton, NY.
Responsibilities   included   greeting   customers,
coordinating calendars and appointments, and taking
community groups on company tours. (Summer job.)

REFERENCES

Available on request.

---

simultaneously. He then moves the cursor to the end of the block of words to be underlined. After he has done this, he presses F8. The text will be highlighted on the screen (Figure 12-15c), but will be underlined when it is printed (Figure 12-16). If Carl wants to underline while he is typing, he presses F8 to start the underlining command and then presses F8 again when he wants to stop the underlining.

Carl's final version of his resume is shown in Figure 12-16. As you can see, the resume is much more attractive and readable than the original version. As before, Carl saves his resume on the data disk, so he has the option of making more changes in the future. The changes can be format changes or changes to the substance of his resume; he can, for example, add job experience as he gains it.

7 Text Blocks

A **text block** is a unit of text in a document. It can consist of one or more words, phrases, sentences, paragraphs, or even pages. Text blocks can be moved, deleted, copied, saved, and inserted. You can manipulate text blocks by using just a few keystrokes. To appreciate the power of these commands, imagine trying to move a paragraph to another place in a paper if your only tool is a typewriter.

7 The Survey Example

Barbara Crim is taking her first sociology course at California College. Halfway through the term, she is asked to write a survey that evaluates people's eating and exercising habits. After class Barbara goes to the school's computer lab, checks out WordPerfect, and sits down to write the survey.

After reading the first draft of her survey (Figure 12-17), Barbara decides that it needs some changes. She wants to reverse the order of questions 4 and 5 so all of the eating-habit questions will be together. She also wants to eliminate question 9, since it deals with hobbies rather than eating or exercising. And finally, she needs to type the Never–Always scale for questions 2 through 8. Before Barbara can do any of these tasks, however, she must first define—or **mark**—the blocks she wants to manipulate.

7 Marking a Block

Marking a block of text is done in different ways with different word processing software. In general, you move the cursor to the beginning of the chunk of text that constitutes the block. Then you either press a function key or use the keys to place block markers there. You do the same thing at the end of the block. Once the block is marked, it can be subject to a variety of block commands.

Since Barbara is using WordPerfect, she positions the cursor at the beginning of question 4 (just under the "4"), and presses Alt and F4 at the same time. This turns on the Block command. WordPerfect reminds Barbara that the command is on by flashing the words "Block on" in the lower-left corner of the screen. Next Barbara moves the cursor until the entire question is highlighted. Now the block is marked (Figure 12-18).

DISCUSSION QUESTION
What is reverse video? What does it often indicate?

Notice that the marked block stands out on the screen. Many word processing programs present marked blocks in **reverse video**— the print in the marked area is the color of the normal background and the background is the color of the normal print. If, for example, the screen normally has white letters on a black background, the marked portion of the text shows black letters on a white background.

Figure 12-17   The first draft of Barbara's survey.   Barbara enters this draft of her survey.

Newspapers, magazines, and TV shows are filled with stories on health and fitness. But just how healthy are people today? An introductory sociology course at California College is conducting a survey to evaluate community attitudes and activities. We would appreciate your helping us by answering the following questions. Please circle the number that corresponds to the answer that best describes your behavior.

1.   Do you eat a variety of foods from each of the four food
     groups each day?
     Never   1   2   3   4   5   Always

2.   Do you limit the amount of fat and cholesterol you eat?

3.   Do you limit the amount of salt you eat?

4.   Do you maintain your desired weight--being neither overweight
     nor underweight?

5.   Do you limit the amount of sugar you eat?

6.   Do you exercise vigorously for 15-30 minutes at least 3 times
     a week?

7.   Do you walk to nearby locations rather than driving your car?

8.   Do you take part in leisure activities that increase your
     level of fitness?

9.   Do you participate in group activities or hobbies that you
     enjoy?

10. What is your age?
     a. under 18   b. 18-21   c. 22-35   d. 36-50   e. over 50

11. What is your sex?
     a. male   b. female

12. What is your marital status?
     a. single   b. married   c. divorced

Figure 12-18   Marking a block of text. Barbara uses the Alt and F4 keys to mark question 4.

Newspapers, magazines, and TV shows are filled with stories on health and fitness. But just how healthy are people today? An introductory sociology course at California College is conducting a survey to evaluate community attitudes and activities. We would appreciate your helping us by answering the following questions. Please circle the number that corresponds to the answer that best describes your behavior.

1.   Do you eat a variety of foods from each of the four food
     groups each day?
     Never   1   2   3   4   5   Always

2.   Do you limit the amount of fat and cholesterol you eat?

3.   Do you limit the amount of salt you eat?

4.   Do you maintain your desired weight--being neither overweight
     nor underweight?

5.   Do you limit the amount of sugar you eat?

6.   Do you exercise vigorously for 15-30 minutes at least 3 times
     a week?

Block on   Doc 1 Pg 1 Ln 4" Pos 3.1"

DISCUSSION QUESTION
How can a section of the text be
moved from its current location to
another?

DISCUSSION QUESTION
When would using the "cut and
paste" command save time?

Moving a Block

Once the block is marked, Barbara can use the Block
Move command. The **Block Move command** removes a block of text
from its original location and places it in a second location—the
block still occurs only once in the document. Moving a block from
one location to another is also called *cutting and pasting*, a reference
to what literally would have to be done if you were using a typewriter.

Different word processing packages move text blocks in different ways. Some packages require only that you move the cursor to
the new location; then, when you press a certain key or keys, the
block disappears from its old location and is inserted at the location
of the cursor. However, other word processing packages, such as
WordPerfect, have separate commands: one that means "cut"—or
delete the block from the old location—and another that means
"paste"—or insert the block in the new location.

To move question 4 under question 5, Barbara has marked question 4—the block she wants to move. Now she presses the Ctrl key
and F4 simultaneously to select the Block command options (Figure
12-19a). Next she presses 1 to indicate she is working with a block,
then 1 to move the block (that is, question 4). Question 4 disappears
from the screen (Figure 12-19b). Barbara now moves the cursor to the
position where she wants to insert question 4—under question 5.
She presses the Enter key to move the text to the current cursor
location. Figure 12-19c shows the survey after the question has been
moved. Barbara then changes the numbering so the order is correct
and adjusts the space between lines as necessary.

Deleting a Block

Barbara is not done yet; she must get rid of question 9.
One way to do this is to mark the question as a block and then use
the **Block Delete command.** In WordPerfect the Block Delete command is the first half of the Block Move command—the "cut" part of
"cut and paste." Other word processing programs may have a separate command for deleting blocks.

As before, Barbara marks the block—in this case question 9.
Then she presses Ctrl and F4 simultaneously, presses 1 to indicate
she is working with a block, and then presses 3 to delete the block.
An alternate method of deleting a block is to mark the block and then
press the Del key.

As you can see, the Block Delete command makes it easy to
remove chunks of unwanted text from a document. Although the
same thing can be accomplished with character-by-character deletions, this approach is not very efficient for a large amount of text.

Figure 12-19 Easy moves. (a) After Barbara marks the text she wants to move, she accesses the Block command options by pressing Ctrl-F4. (b) Barbara selects 1 and the text disappears from the screen. Barbara then moves the cursor to the spot where she wants to insert the question. (c) When she selects 1 from the Block command options, the text appears in its new location.

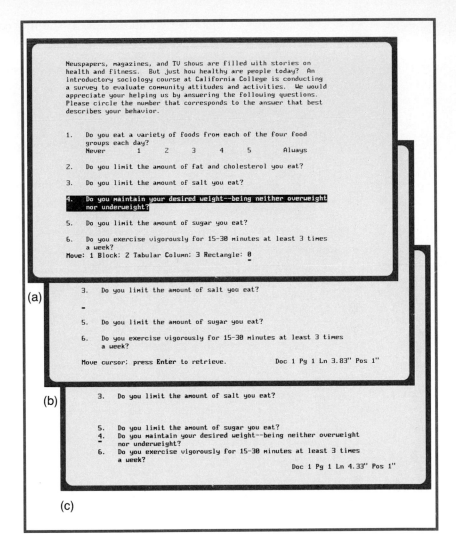

Copying a Block

Now Barbara wants to add the Never–Always scales. Since they will all be the same, she can do this easily by using the Block Copy command. The Block Copy command is similar to the Block Move command. The **Block Copy command** copies the block of text into a new location. However, the block also stays in its original location—that is, the same text appears twice (or more) in the document. The Block Copy command comes in handy when similar material is needed repeatedly in the same document, since you have only to key in the text once.

Barbara has already typed the scale once, as shown in Figure 12-17. Now she marks the block of text and presses Ctrl-F4, presses 1 to indicate she is working with a block, and then presses 2 to select the copy function. Next she moves the cursor to the position where she wants to insert the text—under question 2—and presses Enter to copy the text. She repeats these steps to copy the answer line under question 3 through question 8. The final survey is shown in Figure 12-20.

TEST BANK
Mult. Choice   59
T/F   66-67
Matching C   3, 5
Fill-in-the-Blank 29

7 Some Other Important Features

Popular word processing packages offer more features than most people use. We cannot discuss every feature here, but we want to mention two that you will find handy—spacing and searching.

Figure 12-20 The final draft. Barbara has made all the changes she wants at this time, so she prints the final draft of her survey.

Newspapers, magazines, and TV shows are filled with stories on health and fitness. But just how healthy are people today? An introductory sociology course at California College is conducting a survey to evaluate community attitudes and activities. We would appreciate your helping us by answering the following questions. Please circle the number that corresponds to the answer that best describes your behavior.

1. Do you eat a variety of foods from each of the four food groups each day?
    Never   1   2   3   4   5   Always

2. Do you limit the amount of fat and cholesterol you eat?
    Never   1   2   3   4   5   Always

3. Do you limit the amount of salt you eat?
    Never   1   2   3   4   5   Always

4. Do you limit the amount of sugar you eat?
    Never   1   2   3   4   5   Always

5. Do you maintain your desired weight--being neither overweight nor underweight?
    Never   1   2   3   4   5   Always

6. Do you exercise vigorously for 15-30 minutes at least 3 times a week?
    Never   1   2   3   4   5   Always

7. Do you walk to nearby locations rather than driving your car?
    Never   1   2   3   4   5   Always

8. Do you take part in leisure activities that increase your level of fitness?
    Never   1   2   3   4   5   Always

9. What is your age?
    a. under 18   b. 18-21   c. 22-35   d. 36-50   e. over 50

10. What is your sex?
    a. male   b. female

11. What is your marital status?
    a. single   b. married   c. divorced

PERSPECTIVES

CHOOSING A SOFTWARE PACKAGE

People use many different kinds of software. But exactly *what* are they using? What is the brand name of the product, and where did it come from? How much did it cost? Perhaps more to the point, how was the selection made? Some software brand names seem to be well established. But much software—and certainly its price—is changing too frequently to be listed anywhere but in a weekly or monthly periodical. We can, however, address the selection process.

For any given application category there are literally dozens or even hundreds of products for sale. Which way should you turn? Suppose you want to purchase a word processing package.

- **Hardware.** If you already have a computer in mind, hardware is your first limitation. That is, you can buy only software that works on your machine. If your computer is an uncommon brand, your software choices are significantly narrowed. If you have a brand for which there is a wide software selection, proceed with the search.

- **Standards.** If you will be working with others—say, sending word-processed documents for their perusal—then your choice of a word processing package is constrained by their choice. You must choose to agree. Sometimes the process is even more straightforward: If you work for an organization with established software standards, you use the package the organization has selected.

- **Recommendations.** Everyone has an opinion. Trade journals make it their business to have opinions, offering elaborate rating systems and survey results. Salespeople in retail software stores also have opinions and are usually happy to share them. And do not forget your friends and colleagues.

- **Join the crowd.** Sometimes it is worth going with the most "popular" package just because all those people must be right, and at least you will share common ground. Many entrenched software packages stay that way, even when superior technology comes along. An established base, if it works adequately, is expensive to replace.

7 Spacing

Most of the time you will want your documents—letters, memos, reports—to be single spaced. But there are occasions when it is convenient or necessary to double space or even triple space a document. Word processing lets you do this with ease. In fact, a word processing program lets you switch back and forth from one type of spacing to another, just by pressing a few keys. A writer, for example, can print one copy of a new chapter single spaced for ease of reading. Then the same document can be double spaced and printed for the editor, who will appreciate the space to make changes.

7 Search and Replace

Suppose you type a long report in which you repeatedly spell the name of a client as "Mr. Sullavan." After you submit the report to your boss, she sends it back to you with this note: "Our client's name is Sullivan, not Sullavan. Please fix this error and send me a corrected copy of the report."

DISCUSSION QUESTION
How can you fix the spelling error "recieve" to "receive" easily if it occurs many times in the text?

You could scroll through the whole report, looking for "Sullavan" and replacing it with "Sullivan." Then you could save and reprint the report. There is, however, a more efficient way—the **search and replace function.** This function can search through a document quickly, finding each instance of a certain word or phrase and replacing it with another word or phrase as desired. Note that you make the request just once, but the replacement is done over and over. Most word processing programs offer **conditional replace,** which asks you to verify each replacement. In other instances, the search function can be used by itself to find a particular item in a document.

TEST BANK
Mult. Choice   60-66
T/F   68-74
Matching C   2, 4, 6-7
Fill-in-the-Blank   30-33

7 Extra Added Attractions

The popularity of word processing programs has encouraged the development of some very helpful programs that are used in conjunction with word processing software. These programs analyze text that has already been entered. Some of the most widely used programs of this type can check spelling, provide a thesaurus, monitor grammar and style, and write form letters. If your reports are riddled with spelling errors and typos, then you might find the spelling checker especially helpful.

DISCUSSION QUESTION
What programs are often used along with the word processor? Describe what each one does.

7 Spelling Checker Programs

A **spelling checker program** will find any spelling errors you may have made when typing a document. The program compares each word in your document to the words it has in its "dictionary." A spelling checker's dictionary is a list of from 20,000 to 100,000 correctly spelled words. If, while looking through your document, the spelling checker program finds a word that is not on its list, it assumes that you have misspelled or mistyped that word. Some spelling checkers place a special mark (such as the @ symbol) next to the doubtful word. Others highlight the word by making it brighter or a different color. When the checker program is finished, you use your word processing program to look through your document for any marked words. Spelling checkers often do not recognize proper names, such as Ms. Gillen, or acronyms, such as NASA. So you must decide if the word is actually misspelled. If the word is misspelled, you can correct it easily with the word processing software. If the word is correct, then you delete the mark.

A more sophisticated type of spelling checker program highlights a word that it believes is misspelled. Then it displays all the words from its dictionary that are close in spelling or sound to the word you typed. In other words, the program tries to help you out by displaying all the words that it thinks you may be trying to spell (Figure 12-21). If you recognize the correct spelling of the word in the list you are given, you can replace the incorrect word with the correct word from the list. If the word the program thought was misspelled is correct, you just leave it unchanged and signal the spelling checker to continue searching through your document. Some spelling checkers even check your spelling as you are typing. As soon as you type a word that the checker does not recognize, it causes the computer to sound a beep to catch your attention. Then it offers suggestions in the usual way. (Some people do not like machines beeping at them. They prefer to turn this feature off and find their errors later.)

The best spelling checkers let you create your own auxiliary dictionaries. If a word in your document is not in the spelling checker's main dictionary, the program then searches through your special dictionaries. This can be very useful. Suppose, for example, that you often write to a client named Mr. Mitchell and use computer jargon such as *byte* and *mainframe*. An ordinary dictionary would flag the words "Mitchell," "byte," and "mainframe" as misspelled. If you add these terms, which are correct in your environment, to your auxiliary dictionary, they will be considered correct in the future. If you have this type of spelling checker, you should add to your auxiliary dictionary the names of your friends and business associates and words that are often used in your job or field of study.

Figure 12-21 Spelling checker. The highlighted word "conjusion" is a misspelling, so the spelling checker offers some alternatives in the area below the dashed lines. In this case, pressing A replaces the misspelled word with the correct spelling.

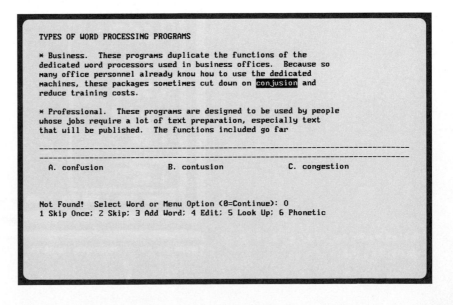

```
TYPES OF WORD PROCESSING PROGRAMS

× Business.  These programs duplicate the functions of the
dedicated word processors used in business offices.  Because so
many office personnel already know how to use the dedicated
machines, these packages sometimes cut down on conjusion and
reduce training costs.

× Professional.  These programs are designed to be used by people
whose jobs require a lot of text preparation, especially text
that will be published.  The functions included go far

------------------------------------------------------------------
------------------------------------------------------------------
    A. confusion          B. contusion          C. congestion


Not Found!  Select Word or Menu Option (0=Continue): 0
1 Skip Once; 2 Skip; 3 Add Word; 4 Edit; 5 Look Up; 6 Phonetic
```

Many word processing programs include their own spelling checkers as part of the word processing package; that is, the spelling checkers are built in. This makes the checkers very easy to use. Once you have entered your text by using the word processing software, all you have to do to check your spelling is press a key.

7 Thesaurus Programs

Have you ever chewed on the end of your pencil trying to think of just the right word—a better word than the bland one that immediately comes to mind? Perhaps you were energetic enough to get a thesaurus and look it up. A thesaurus is a book that gives synonyms (words with the same meaning) and antonyms (words with the opposite meaning) for common words. But never mind the big books. Now you can have a great vocabulary at your fingertips—electronically, of course. Your access to this word supply is via a **thesaurus program,** which may be part of your word processing program or a separate disk used in conjunction with the program.

Suppose you find a word in your document that you have used too frequently or that just does not quite seem to fit. Place the cursor on the word. Then press the appropriate key to activate the thesaurus program. The program immediately provides a list of synonyms for the word you want to replace (Figure 12-22). You can then replace the old word in your document with the synonym you prefer. It is easy, and it is even painlessly educational.

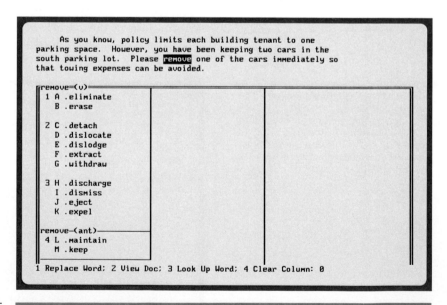

Figure 12-22 A thesaurus program. The words labeled A through K are synonyms for the highlighted word, "remove."

GETTYSBURG REVISITED

Some people are worried that the style and grammar programs will remove true originality and give all prose an unattractive sameness. Consider the ringing words of Abraham Lincoln at Gettysburg: "Fourscore and seven years ago our fathers brought forth on this continent, a new nation, conceived in liberty, and dedicated to the proposition that all men are created equal."

When rewritten by a style program, this Gettysburg line became: "Eighty-seven years ago our ancestors started a free country here, where people are equal." Not exactly inspiring. Obviously, we need not always take a computer's advice.

DISCUSSION QUESTION
Do spelling checkers pick up every spelling error?

Grammar and Style Programs

A computer program cannot offer creativity, inspiration, class, elegance, or ingenuity. In short, no program will make you the next Shakespeare or Hemingway. But there are programs that can improve your writing: They are called **grammar and style programs.** When you write using a word processing program, these extra programs can identify some of your grammatical or stylistic flaws. Let us consider some specific features.

A grammar and style program—sometimes called an editing program—can identify unnecessary words or wordy phrases that appear in your writing. To help you eliminate repetition, it can check to see if particular patterns of words appear again and again. It also can check for sentences that seem too long (run-on sentences) and indicate that you should break them up into several short sentences for clearer writing.

Grammar and style programs can also identify spelling errors that a spelling checker program cannot pick up. For example, the word "four" is a correctly spelled word and would not be flagged by a spelling checker. However, "four example" is an incorrect use of the word "four," and thus a spelling error. Editing programs identify this kind of problem. Consider another error that many spelling checkers do not notice: double-typed words correctly spelled. For example, if you inadvertently type "on the the table," some spelling checkers would pass right over the two occurrences of the word "the." Editing programs spot such errors for you. Even if you are not the next great American novelist, you can use these programs to produce correct and clear English.

Form Letter Programs

A form letter used to be rather primitive, with your name typed—often in a different typeface—as an afterthought. No more. Now **form letter programs**—sometimes called mail-merge programs—can be used to send out masses of "personalized" letters that cannot be distinguished from a letter produced on a fine typewriter. These programs have been a boon to fund-raising and political groups and a bane to the weary citizens who are tired of mounds of junk mail in their mailboxes. But, junk or not, these mailings are effective and, therefore, here to stay. In fact, you can join in and use them for your own group or organization. Here is how form letter programs work.

- First you create and store the form letter by using your word processing program. Instead of actually typing a person's name and address, you type some predefined symbols in the appropriate places in the letter.

Macintosh®

Another Way with Words

Because of its special screen technology, the Macintosh is best known for allowing people to create graphics—illustrations, charts, and diagrams. This capability also makes it a special kind of word processor. Type can be virtually any size, and instead of waiting for your document to roll off the printer, you can get a good idea of just how a page will look from viewing portions of it on the Mac screen.

With the Macintosh you can "format" your text directly using the mouse. Words that you want printed in boldface or underlined show up that way on the screen, as shown in screen (a) below. True to the Mac's visual presentation, most word processing programs on the Mac have a ruler running across the top of the screen that you can use to set tabs, center or align text, and adjust margins.

Moving text is the same on all Mac programs. Using the mouse to highlight the text you want moved, you first "cut" and then "paste" the text where you want it. The real advantage of this method is that you can copy selections from other documents and programs—spreadsheets, databases, even graphics. The Mac's "clipboard" stores the data while you change files or programs.

The Macintosh comes with several typefaces, but hundreds more are available, so that you have virtually unlimited choice in determining the look of your document. Type on the screen closely resembles what comes out on your printer. Using a laser printer, often available at copy centers and instant print shops, you can produce high-quality, professional-looking documents formatted to your liking. Most word processors for the Mac have special typographic effects like shadow and outline type, and more sophisticated programs allow you to create tables and multiple columns. With this kind of flexibility you can create newsletters as well as eye-catching memos, reports, and term papers. On the Mac, word processing becomes more like typesetting and less like typewriting.

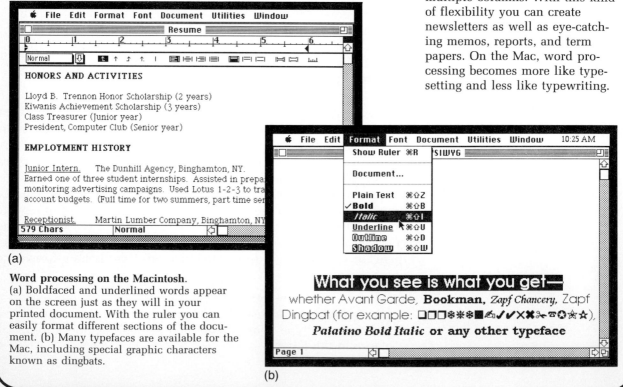

(a)
Word processing on the Macintosh.
(a) Boldfaced and underlined words appear on the screen just as they will in your printed document. With the ruler you can easily format different sections of the document. (b) Many typefaces are available for the Mac, including special graphic characters known as dingbats.

(b)

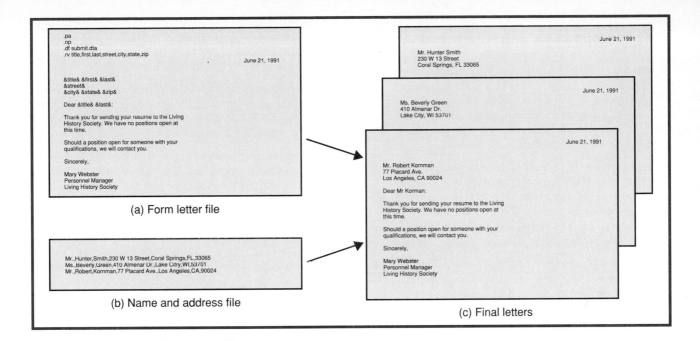

(a) Form letter file

(b) Name and address file

(c) Final letters

Figure 12-23   A form letter program.
A form letter program works in conjunction with your word processing program. With them you combine (a) text with (b) names and addresses to create (c) good-looking individualized letters.

TRANSPARENCY ACETATE #12H
Figure #12-23

LECTURE HINT
The form letter is often called boilerplate.

- Using your word processing program, you then store all the individual names and addresses in a second file.

- Your last step is to ask the form letter program to print, on your printer, a form letter for each name in your second file.

Each time the program prints a letter, it replaces the symbols with a new name and address from the second file. The form letter program automatically adjusts the form letter for differences in the length of each person's name and address. Each one of the letters looks as if it has been typed especially for the addressee (Figure 12-23). This is the "personal touch" in the electronic age.

THE MOVE TOWARDS DESKTOP PUBLISHING

Some recent versions of word processing packages, including WordPerfect 5.0, offer several desktop publishing features. Desktop publishing software and a high-quality printer allow you to design and print professional-looking documents. Desktop publishing has been rapidly growing in popularity, and we will look at this important topic more closely in Chapter 15.

7 We Hope You Are Convinced

We hope you are convinced that word processing is a great time-saver. We hope you are convinced that word processing is easy to learn. We hope you are convinced that word processing is the best software tool—well, one of the best tools—for microcomputers. And, most of all, we hope you are convinced that word processing is essential for your career, no matter what it is.

Word processing, however, is not the only important software tool. Some people, in fact, are much more interested in software that works with numbers rather than words. We are talking, of course, about spreadsheet software. This important topic is the subject of our next chapter.

/ Summary and Key Terms

- **Word processing** is the creation, editing, formatting, storing, and printing of a text document. The advantages of word processing over typing are that you can store your document, which makes it easier to incorporate changes, and you can see what you type before printing it.

- As you type, the screen displays a **cursor** to show where the next character you type will appear. You can move the cursor around on the screen by using **cursor movement keys** on the right side of the keyboard. The **PgUp** and **PgDn** keys let you move the cursor up or down a whole page at a time.

- Word processing programs treat the text you type as if it were on a long roll of paper, or scroll. You "roll the scroll" up or down on the screen by moving the cursor. This process, called **scrolling,** lets you see any part of the document on the screen.

- When a word that you type at the end of a line cannot fit on that line, the word processing program automatically starts that word on the next line. This feature is known as **word wrap.** Do not use the carriage return (that is, do not press Enter) at the end of a line unless you want to signal the end of a paragraph or provide a blank line.

- Word processing programs let you delete characters, words, or lines and close up spaces automatically; you can also insert text by typing new characters or replace old text by typing new text over the old.

- The use of each function key differs according to each applications program. A paper or plastic **template,** which fits over the function keys, briefly describes the use of each key.

- To load the word processing program, type a command at the A prompt (A>). A set of choices, called a **menu,** may appear on the screen.

- To enter text, use the keyboard as you would a typewriter. After completing the document and making corrections, save the document on a data disk.

- To edit a document, you must first retrieve it from the disk. The **insert mode** is the standard way of inserting corrections when using word processing.

Typeover mode allows you to replace the existing text with new text. The Ins key acts as a **toggle switch,** allowing you to switch between the insert mode and the typeover mode.

- The **format** of a document is the way the document appears on the page: the organization of text, margin width, line spacing, use of boldface and underlining, and so on.

- **Centering** text usually refers to centering text on a line. **Vertical centering,** however, adjusts the top and bottom margins so the text is centered vertically on the page.

- The original margin settings are called the **default settings.** Both the default left and right margins are usually one 1 inch (or ten characters) wide, leaving room for about 65 characters per line of text. The default top and bottom margins are also usually 1 inch each, allowing about 55 lines of text per page. When the margin settings are changed, most word processing software automatically adjusts the text to fit the new margins. This is called **automatic reformatting.**

- **Ragged right margin** means that the end of each line does not end in the same position on the right side of the document. **Justified** text lines up neatly on the right-hand side, creating an even margin.

- **Boldface** words appear brighter, dimmer, or a different color than the surrounding words on the screen, depending on the word processing package used. When the document is printed, the marked words will appear darker than the rest of the text. **Underlined** words are underscored when printed.

- A **text block** is a unit of text—one or more words, phrases, sentences, paragraphs, or even pages. Text blocks can be moved, deleted, copied, saved, and inserted. To manipulate a block of text, you must first define, or **mark,** the block. The marked block often stands out in **reverse video** on the screen.

- Use the **Block Move command** to move the text to a different location; this process is also known as cutting and pasting. The **Block Delete command** lets you delete a block of text. The **Block Copy command** copies the block of text into a new location, leaving the text in its original location as well.

- The **search and replace function** quickly searches through a document to find each instance of a certain word or phrase and replaces it with another word or phrase. Most programs offer **conditional replace,** which asks you to verify each replacement.

- A number of special programs work in conjunction with the word processing software, analyzing text that has been entered already. These programs include a **spelling checker program,** which includes a built-in dictionary, and a **thesaurus program,** which includes a reference that supplies synonyms and antonyms. **Grammar and style programs,** sometimes called editing programs, identify wordy phrases, repetition, run-on sentences, and spelling errors that cannot be identified by a spelling checker. **Form letter programs,** sometimes called mail-merge programs, let you create "personalized" form letters automatically.

7 Review Questions

1. What are the basic functions of word processing?

2. How is word processing different from typing?

3. What is the cursor?

4. What is meant by the term *word wrap?*

5. What is meant by the term *scrolling?* How do you use scrolling when you are viewing a long document on the screen?

6. What is the difference between the insert mode and the typeover mode when using word processing? How do you get into insert mode?

7. When should Enter be used when entering text? Why?

8. How do you move the cursor up and down a line? How do you move the cursor from left to right?

9. How do you delete a character?

10. How do you separate paragraphs when using word processing?

11. What happens to an unsaved file when you turn the computer off?

12. What is meant by the term *boldface?*

13. What is the format of a document? What is reformatting?

14. How is vertical centering different from centering?

15. What is meant by the term *text block?*

16. Name five operations that can be performed on a block of text.

17. What is the difference between a block move and a block copy operation?

18. How does a spelling checker recognize spelling errors in a document?

19. What is the function of a thesaurus program?

Chapter 13 Spreadsheets and Business Graphics: Facts and Figures

13

Spreadsheets and Business Graphics

Facts and Figures

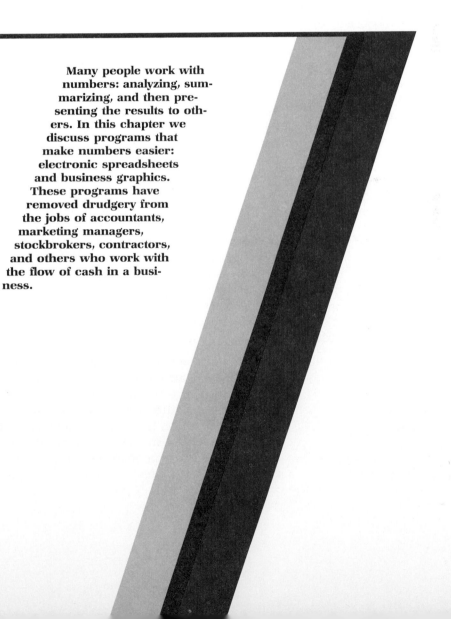

Many people work with numbers: analyzing, summarizing, and then presenting the results to others. In this chapter we discuss programs that make numbers easier: electronic spreadsheets and business graphics. These programs have removed drudgery from the jobs of accountants, marketing managers, stockbrokers, contractors, and others who work with the flow of cash in a business.

Do you remember Bob Cratchit in Charles Dickens's *A Christmas Carol?* He spent his time shivering in Scrooge's business office, copying figures into ledger books. The pages in such books, ruled into rows and columns, are called worksheets or **spreadsheets** (Figure 13-1a). The manually constructed spreadsheet has been used as a business tool for centuries. Spreadsheets can be used to organize and present business data, thus aiding managerial decisions. But spreadsheets are not limited to businesses. Personal and family budgets, for example, are often organized on spreadsheets.

Unfortunately, the work involved in manually creating a large spreadsheet is time-consuming and tedious, even when using a calculator or copying results from a computer printout. Another problem with manual spreadsheets is that it is too easy to make a mistake. You may not discover the mistakes, and this could have serious consequences for the business and possibly your job. If you do discover the mistake after the spreadsheet is finished, you must manually redo the calculations that used the wrong number.

7 Electronic Spreadsheets

An **electronic spreadsheet** is a computerized version of a manual spreadsheet (Figure 13-1b). Working with a spreadsheet on a computer eliminates much of the toil of setting up a manual spreadsheet. In general, it works like this: You enter the data you want in your spreadsheet and then key in the types of calculations you need. The electronic spreadsheet program automatically does all the calculations for you and produces the results. The program does not make any calculation errors, and if you want a printed copy of the spreadsheet, it can be done quickly. Also, you can store your electronic spreadsheet on your disk so that it can be used again. But the greatest labor-saving aspect of the electronic spreadsheet is that when you change one value or formula in your worksheet, all the rest of the values on the spreadsheet are recalculated automatically to reflect the change.

Spreadsheet programs are very versatile. Let us pause for just a moment to list some specific business applications.

- **Budget management.** You can use a spreadsheet to list anticipated expenses for your business. You can also list all the anticipated sources of income. Then use the spreadsheet to analyze your expenditures. In addition, you can analyze expenditures by categories such as labor, office rent, and loan interest. When things change, you can easily see the effect. Suppose, for example, you hire more workers or increase the price of a product. You can check quickly the effect of your move on anticipated profits.

Figure 13-1 Manual versus electronic spreadsheets. (a) This manual spreadsheet is a typical spreadsheet consisting of rows and columns. (b) The same spreadsheet created with a spreadsheet program.

TRANSPARENCY ACETATE #13A
Figure #13-1

	JAN.	FEB.	MAR.	APR.	TOTAL	MIN	MAX
SALES	1750	1501	1519	1430	6200	1430	1750
COST OF GOODS SOLD	964	980	932	943	3819	932	980
GROSS MARGIN	786	521	587	487	2381	487	786
NET EXPENSE	98	93	82	110	383	82	110
ADM EXPENSE	77	79	69	88	313	69	88
MISC EXPENSE	28	45	31	31	135	28	45
TOTAL EXPENSES	203	217	182	229	831	182	229
AVERAGE EXPENSE	68	72	61	76	227	61	76
NET BEFORE TAXES	583	304	405	258	1550	258	583
FEDERAL TAXES	303	158	211	134	806	134	303
NET AFTER TAX	280	146	194	124	744	124	280

(a)

```
                    A        B      C      D      E      F      G      H      I
                1            JAN    FEB    MAR    APR    TOTAL  MIN    MAX
                2   ==========================================================
                3   SALES            1750   1501   1519   1430   6200   1430   1750
                4   COST OF GOODS SOLD 964    980    932    943   3819    932    980
                5
                6      GROSS MARGIN   786    521    587    487   2381    487    786
                7
                8   NET EXPENSE       98     93     82    110    383     82    110
                9   ADM EXPENSE       77     79     69     88    313     69     88
               10   MISC EXPENSE      28     45     31     31    135     28     45
               11   ------------------------------------------------------------
               12      TOTAL EXPENSES 203    217    182    229    831    182    229
               13      AVERAGE EXPENSE 68     72     61     76    227     61     76
               14
               15   NET BEFORE TAX   583    304    405    258   1550    258    583
               16   FEDERAL TAXES    303    158    211    134    806    134    303
               17   ------------------------------------------------------------
               18      NET AFTER TAX 280    146    194    124    744    124    280
               19
               20
```

(b)

LECTURE HINT
Other applications of spreadsheets: (1) Solve set of linear equations. (2) Compute term grades in a course. (3) Sort expenses by category before working on personal income taxes. (4) Compute paths of planets in solar system. (5) Make advisee/advisor assignments for college students. (6) Make table of payments on loan as function of percent interest, number of months, per $1000.00.

LECTURE HINT
NASA uses a personal computer to run a spreadsheet program that considers the variables of a lunar base. The simulation can accommodate hundreds of variables, including the number of crew members needed, length of stay on the moon, crew activities, and oxygen and food required. Calculations that would have taken weeks by hand are now done in minutes.

■ **Competitive bidding.** Many industries use spreadsheet software to prepare a bid to compete for a contract. In the construction industry, for example, you can enter the spreadsheet materials and other resources needed to complete the project. Then you can explore "What if . . . ?" scenarios by changing types and costs of materials, delivery dates, equipment rentals, number and types of workers, and so forth. This is the way businesspeople determine what combination produces the best—and possibly lowest—bid.

■ **Investments.** In the finance and investments industries, spreadsheets are used to analyze the costs of borrowing money and the profits anticipated from lending money. Spreadsheets are used to analyze investment portfolios by keeping track of dividends and increases or decreases in the value of individual investments. By using spreadsheets to play out various stock-market and economic

PERSPECTIVES

CONSIDERING A SIGNIFICANT EVENT

Once in a great while an invention is considered to be the spark for an entire industry. Many people consider the electronic spreadsheet to be the linchpin of the personal computer industry. Consider how Dan Bricklin found his claim to fame.

In 1977 Dan was a student in the Harvard School of Business. He spent most of his evenings working on case studies for his classes. This work required preparing manual spreadsheets for financial models. To make decisions about the way the case study businesses should be run, Dan had to prepare separate spreadsheets analyzing each alternative available to him as a manager. He often made errors and had to spend hours redoing his calculations. He, like other students and business managers around the world, was spending

too much time doing and redoing arithmetic with a paper, pencil, and calculator. This left less time to study and understand the results of the calculations and to consider what they meant for business.

But what was the alternative? Dan toyed with the idea of doing the calculations for each case on the computer. However, each case study was so different that it would require a new computer program to analyze each case. This was just not possible. During the winter of 1978, Bricklin and Robert Frankston, a programmer friend, worked to develop a general-purpose program that could be used to solve any spreadsheet problem. This program evolved into the first electronic spreadsheet, called VisiCalc for *Visible Calculator*.

When VisiCalc was modified

to run on the inexpensive Apple II personal computer, a combination was formed that was eagerly accepted by students, businesspeople, and professionals who used numbers in their work. In fact, VisiCalc is credited with being a major factor in making the Apple computer a popular success. For several years VisiCalc was the best-selling software for a personal computer. Since the introduction of VisiCalc, other companies have produced dozens of different spreadsheet programs.

The electronic spreadsheet placed the personal computer squarely in the business community, where it has grown and flourished. There have been other significant applications, but none have had the impact that the spreadsheet has.

DISCUSSION QUESTION
When spreadsheets were adapted to computers what was the effect of sales on a specific computer and why?

scenarios, the crucial question—"Do I buy more now or do I sell now?"—is more easily answered. The spreadsheet program gives you the tools to analyze masses of complex economic data accurately and quickly.

The tasks just described would be tedious and time-consuming if done with a calculator. Electronic spreadsheet programs reduce work for accountants, marketing managers, stockbrokers, contractors, and others who work with the flow of cash in a business.

TEST BANK
Mult. Choice	5-20
T/F	7-32
Matching A	2-10
Matching B	2-8
Matching C	1
Fill-in-the-Blank	1-11

7 Spreadsheet Fundamentals

Before we can show you how to use a spreadsheet, we must first discuss some basic spreadsheet features. The characteristics and definitions that follow are common to all spreadsheet programs.

7 Cells and Cell Addresses

Figure 13-2 shows one type of spreadsheet—a teacher's grade sheet. Notice that the spreadsheet is divided into rows and columns, each labeled with a number or a letter. The rows have *numeric labels* and the columns have *alphabetic labels*. There are actually more rows and columns than you can see on the screen; some spreadsheets have 8192 rows and 256 columns—more than you may ever need to use.

The intersection of a row and column forms a **cell.** Cells are the storage areas in a spreadsheet. When referring to a cell, you use the letter and number of the intersecting column and row. For example, in Figure 13-2, Cell B7 is the intersection of column B and row 7. This reference name is known as the **cell address.**

On a spreadsheet there is always one cell known as the **active cell,** or **current cell.** When a cell is active, you can enter data or edit the cell's contents. The active cell is marked by a highlighted bar—the spreadsheet's cursor. The spreadsheet cursor is also called a **pointer.** The upper-left corner of the screen will display the active cell address. The active cell in Figure 13-2 is Cell A1.

DISCUSSION QUESTION
How is the current active cell indicated and labeled in most spreadsheet programs?

Figure 13-2   Anatomy of a spreadsheet screen.   This screen shows a typical spreadsheet—a teacher's grade sheet. It provides space for 20 rows numbered down the side and 8 columns labeled A through H. The intersection of a row and column forms a cell. When the cursor is on a cell, that cell is known as the active cell.

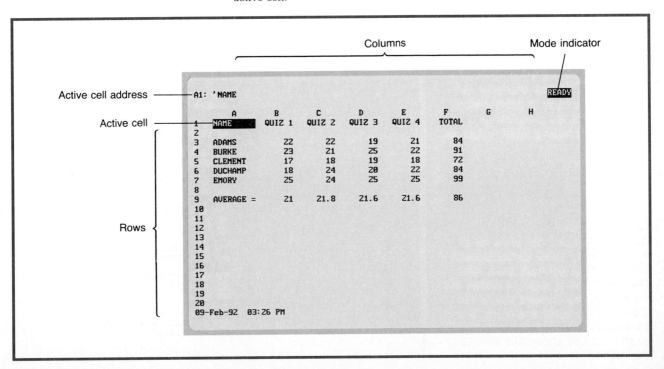

DISCUSSION QUESTION
What are the types of information that can be stored in a given cell?

LECTURE HINT
A label in a spreadsheet program does not have to be unique. Labels are similar to comments in programming languages.

DISCUSSION QUESTION
What do the symbols * and / mean in formulas?

LECTURE HINT
Some spreadsheets will also allow the user to attach comments to the cell.

Figure 13-3   Some spreadsheet formulas. Spreadsheet formulas use arithmetic operators to perform calculations.

LECTURE HINT
A cell with a formula in it usually starts with a special character (an arithmetic symbol or parenthesis). This enables the program to distinguish it from a label, value, or function.

LECTURE HINT
A cell often does not show its actual content. Most spreadsheets have a space (formula area) near the top of the screen. It shows the content of the current active cell. If the cell contains a formula, that formula is shown in the formula area. The cell shows the results of the formula.

7 Contents of Cells: Labels, Values, Formulas, and Functions

Each cell can contain one of four types of information: a label, a value, a formula, or a function. A **label** provides descriptive information about entries in the spreadsheet. A cell that contains a label cannot be used to perform mathematical calculations. For example, in Figure 13-2, Cells A1, A9, and F1 contain labels.

A **value** is a number entered into a cell to be used in calculations. Values can also be the result of a calculation. In Figure 13-2, for example, Cell B3 contains a value.

A **formula** is an instruction to the program to calculate a number. A formula generally contains cell addresses and one or more arithmetic operators: a plus sign (+) to add, a minus sign (−) to subtract, an asterisk (*) to multiply, and a slash (/) to divide. When you use a formula rather than entering the calculated result, the software can automatically recalculate the result if any of the values change. Formulas must be entered without spaces between the characters. Figure 13-3 shows some common formulas.

A **function** is a preprogrammed formula. Functions let you perform complicated calculations with a few keystrokes. Two common functions are the @SUM function, which calculates sums, and the @AVG function, which calculates averages. Most spreadsheet programs contain a number of different functions. Figure 13-4 shows some common functions.

FORMULA	MEANING
(A1+A2) or +A1+A2	The contents of cell A1 plus the contents of cell A2
(A2−A1) or +A2−A1	The contents of cell A2 minus the contents of cell A1
(A1*A2) or +A1*A2	The contents of cell A1 times the contents of cell A2
(A2/A1) or +A2/A1	The contents of cell A2 divided by the contents of cell A1
+A1+A2*2	The contents of cell A2 times the number 2 plus the contents of cell A1
(A1+A2)*2	The sum of the contents of cells A1 and A2 times 2
+A1+A2/4	The contents of cell A2 divided by the number 4 plus the contents of cell A1
(A1+A2)/4	The sum of the contents of cells A1 and A2 divided by 4
(A2−A1)*B1	The difference of the contents of cells A1 and A2 times the contents of cell B1
(A2−A1)/B1	The difference of the contents of cells A1 and A2 divided by the contents of cell B1

DISCUSSION QUESTION
What functions are often available to spreadsheet users? How are functions distinguished from values, labels, and formulas?

FUNCTION	MEANING
@SUM(range)	Calculates the sum of a group of numbers specified in an entire range. For example, the formula @SUM(A1..A10) calculates the sum of all numbers in cells A1 through A10.
@AVG(range)	Calculates the average of a group of numbers. For example, the formula @AVG(A1..A10) calculates the average of all the numbers in cells A1 through A10.
@SQRT(y)	Calculates the square root of a number. For example, @SQRT(A2) calculates the square root of the value contained in A2.
@COUNT(range)	Counts the number of *filled* cells in a range and displays the total number of cells containing a value. For example, the formula @COUNT(B1..B5) counts the number of cells in that range that contain values. If there are five of these cells in the range, the function will display the number 5.
@MIN(range)	Calculates and displays the smallest value contained in a range of values.
@MAX(range)	Calculates and displays the largest value contained in a range of values.
@PMT(principal,interest,term)	Calculates the individual payments on a loan with known principal, interest rate, and term. For example, the formula @PMT(A1,B1,C1) calculates the monthly payment by using the contents of A1 as the principal, the contents of B1 as the interest rate, and the contents of C1 as the term of the loan.
@IF(cond,x,y)	Determines whether a condition is true or false by using logical operators to compare numbers. Logical operators include equals (=), less than (<), greater than (>), less than or equal to (<=), and greater than or equal to (>=). The program then processes the data in a certain way, depending on whether the condition is true or false.
@COS(y)	Calculates the cosine of the value y.
@SIN(y)	Calculates the sine of the value y.
@TAN(y)	Calculates the tangent of the value y.

Figure 13-4   Some Lotus 1-2-3 functions. This figure shows some of the built-in functions available in Lotus 1-2-3. These functions let you perform difficult or repetitive calculations with just a few keystrokes.

Figure 13-5   Ranges.   A range is a
group of one or more cells arranged in
a rectangle. You can name a range or
refer to it by using the addresses of the
upper-left and lower-right cells in the
group.

TRANSPARENCY ACETATE #13B
Figure #13-5

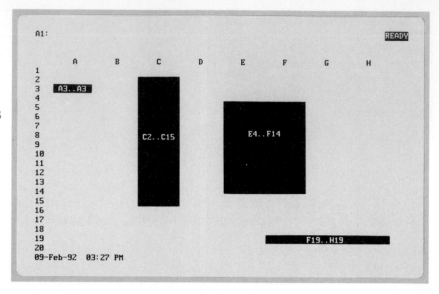

DISCUSSION QUESTION
How is a range of cells specified?
Is it possible to define a block of
cells including rows 1-4 in column
A plus rows 2-3 in column B?

7 Ranges

Sometimes it is necessary to specify a range of cells to
build a formula or perform a function. A **range** is a group of one or
more cells arranged in a block shape that the program treats as a unit
during an operation. Figure 13-5 shows some ranges. To define a
range, you must indicate the upper-left and lower-right cells of the
block. The cell addresses need to be separated by a period. For example, in Figure 13-2 the QUIZ 1 range is referenced as B3.B9 and the
ADAMS range is referenced as B3.F3.

DISCUSSION QUESTION
How can the active cell be
changed? Is there more than one
method?

7 Moving the Cursor

To place data in a cell, you must first move the cursor to
that cell. You can use the cursor movement keys to move the cursor
one row or column at a time. You can also use the cursor movement keys to scroll through the spreadsheet both vertically and
horizontally.

However, moving around a large spreadsheet via the cursor keys
can be tedious at times. Most programs let you zip around the
spreadsheet by pressing predefined keys and function keys. For example, if you press the Home key, the cursor moves "home" to Cell
A1. Or you can go directly to a cell by pressing a designated **GoTo
function key,** also known as the **Jump-To function key.** When you
press this key, the software asks you for the desired cell address. You
type in the address—for example, D7—and press Enter. The cursor
immediately moves to Cell D7. Depending on the current location of
the cursor, using the GoTo function key may be the fastest way to get
to a cell.

DISCUSSION QUESTION
What are three operating modes
commonly used in spreadsheet
programs? What are the purposes
of each mode? Is it possible to
switch modes?

Operating Modes

A **mode** is the condition, or state, in which the program is currently functioning, such as waiting for a command or allowing the selection of a menu item. Most spreadsheets have three main operating modes: the READY mode, the ENTRY mode, and the MENU mode. The Lotus 1-2-3 spreadsheet screen displays a **mode indicator**—a message that tells you the spreadsheet's current mode of operation—in the upper-right corner of the screen. In Figure 13-2 the mode indicator is labeled.

The READY Mode

Most spreadsheets are in the READY mode as soon as they are loaded into the system and the spreadsheet appears on the screen. The **READY mode** indicates that the program is ready for whatever action you want to take, such as moving the cursor, entering data, or issuing a command. As you begin entering data into a cell, you automatically leave the READY mode and enter the ENTRY mode.

The ENTRY Mode

When you are in the **ENTRY mode,** you can enter data into the cells. When a label is being entered, the word "LABEL" appears in the mode indicator; a label is recognized by a beginning alphabetic character (Figure 13-6a). The word "VALUE" appears in the mode indicator when a number or formula is being entered into a cell (Figure 13-6b). After you key in the data and press Enter, the

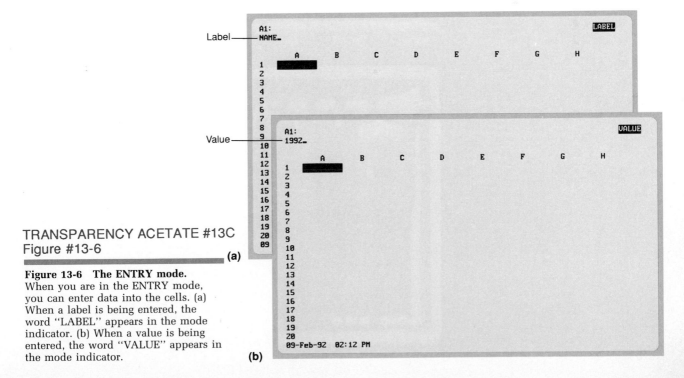

TRANSPARENCY ACETATE #13C
Figure #13-6

(a)

Figure 13-6   The ENTRY mode.
When you are in the ENTRY mode,
you can enter data into the cells. (a)
When a label is being entered, the
word "LABEL" appears in the mode
indicator. (b) When a value is being
entered, the word "VALUE" appears in
the mode indicator.

(b)

information is stored in the cell and the program returns to the READY mode.

When you are in the ENTRY mode, the program does not let you jump or scroll around the spreadsheet—you can only create new cells or make changes to filled cells. The ENTRY mode lets you work on only one cell at a time. But sooner or later you will need to work on a whole group of cells. To do this, you need to enter the MENU, or command, mode.

The MENU Mode

The **MENU mode** lets you use commands to manipulate a large number of cells at one time. Programs display commands in a **command menu,** which is shown near the top of the screen (Figure 13-7). The command menu contains a list, or menu, of different options, such as File and Move. The commands are very important, and we will discuss them in more detail later in the chapter. For now, all you need to know is that to enter the MENU mode, you press the Slash (/) key.

7 The Control Panel

Spreadsheets can get complicated. To help you keep track of what you are doing, most spreadsheet programs show a **control panel** at the top of the screen. The spreadsheet's control panel usually consists of three lines.

DISCUSSION QUESTION
Where is the control panel located on the screen? What information is typically shown in the control panel?

Figure 13-7   The MENU mode.   When you are in the MENU mode, a command menu appears near the top of the screen.

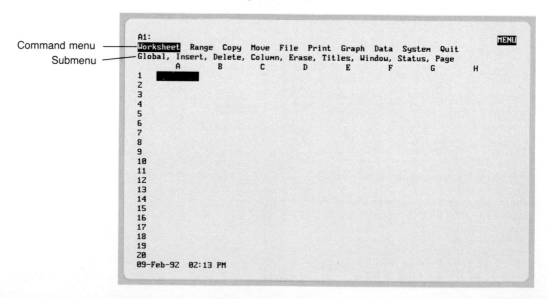

Command menu
Submenu

The First Line

The first line of the control panel is a status line. This line tells you the cursor location (the cell address) and the contents of that cell. An apostrophe at the beginning of the contents indicates that the cell contains a label. At times the status line will also show the format—appearance—of the value or label in the cell and the width of the cell. (It is possible to change the appearance of the cell contents and also the cell's width, but that is beyond the scope of this text.)

To the far right of the status line is the mode indicator. As we mentioned earlier, this indicator tells you the spreadsheet's current mode of operation.

The Second Line

LECTURE HINT
Usually, corrections are made to a cell's contents in this second line, using an editor.

The second line of the control panel is used in a variety of ways, depending on the operating mode. If you are in the ENTRY mode, the line displays the data you are typing in before it is actually entered into the cell (Figure 13-8a). This lets you make changes and corrections before entering the data. If you are in the MENU mode, the line shows the current menu options (Figure 13-8b). This line is also occasionally used for prompts—that is, questions to prompt you for further information needed by the program.

The Third Line

LECTURE HINT
In Lotus 1-2-3, the sub-menu shown in the third line corresponds to the highlighted option in the second line; if that option is a command, then the third line describes what the command does. If that is not what is wanted, the cursor keys can be used to highlight other options. To go back up the menu structure, use the ESC key.

The control panel's third line appears only when the program is in the MENU mode and you have placed the cursor over one of the options. This line shows a **submenu,** a list of options for the command you are choosing (Figure 13-8b).

Let us look at menus and submenus in more detail.

Menus and Submenus

We have already mentioned that you can select spreadsheet commands by choosing from the command menu. Sometimes selecting a command from the menu does not cause a command to be executed; instead, you will see a submenu. This is an additional set of options that refer to the command you selected from the command menu. For example, in Figure 13-8b, the second menu row shows the subcommands—Global, Insert, Delete, Column, and so forth—for the major command Worksheet. Moving the cursor to another major command in the menu causes a different set of commands to appear (Figure 13-8c).

Submenus let you pick only the options that pertain to a particular command. Some of the choices on submenus have options of their own that are displayed on yet another submenu. This layering of menus and submenus lets you first give the computer the big picture with a general command such as "Print a spreadsheet" and then select a particular option such as "Print the first page."

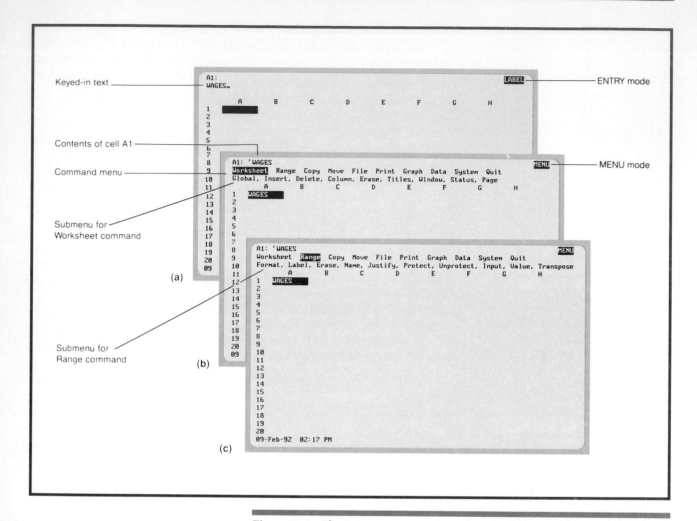

Keyed-in text

Contents of cell A1

Command menu

Submenu for
Worksheet command

(a)

Submenu for
Range command

(b)

(c)

ENTRY mode

MENU mode

Figure 13-8   The Lotus 1-2-3 control panel.   The first line of the control panel shows you the cursor location and the contents of that cell. (a) When you are in ENTRY mode, the second line of the panel displays the data you are typing in before it is entered into the cell. (b) When you are in the MENU mode, the second line of the panel shows the current menu options, and the third line shows the submenu for the command that the cursor is on. (c) When you move the cursor to another command, the submenu changes.

Now that we have covered the basics of spreadsheets, let us pull this information together and see how you can use spreadsheet software for a practical application.

7 Creating a Simple Spreadsheet

Learning to use an electronic spreadsheet program requires time. It might be a good idea to read the manual that comes with the program and spend some time experimenting with the program. Electronic spreadsheet programs have much

NEWER AND BETTER

Lotus 1-2-3, which has sold more than 5 million copies since 1984, is the most popular software ever. But Lotus Development Corporation's domination of the market was threatened by endless delays of the promised Release 3.0, which finally crossed the finish line in the summer of 1989. Worth waiting for? You bet.

When you are the market leader, all you have to be is good; Lotus 3.0 is judged by the critics to be very good. One of the key features of Release 3.0 is its ability to link as many as 256 spreadsheets. The best news is that advanced features have been integrated in such a way that current Lotus users will feel at home right away. Lotus is also offering Release 2.2 for those users who do not need all the bells and whistles of 3.0.

greater capabilities than the average user will ever need. To explain an electronic spreadsheet program completely would require an entire book. However, you can understand how such programs work by studying some examples. The examples we will present use Lotus 1-2-3. Lotus has established a standard approach to electronic spreadsheets; most popular spreadsheet programs work in a similar manner.

Lotus refers to the collection of data keyed into the program as a **worksheet.** Lotus emphasizes the worksheet terminology by saving spreadsheet files with the file name extension WK1 or WKE. We will use the terms *worksheet* and *spreadsheet* interchangeably.

The Expense Sheet Example

Lyle Mayes teaches a biology course at Wilson High School. He recently bought the Lotus 1-2-3 program and uses it to keep track of his class's grades. Now he wants to use the program to keep track of his expenses. His expense sheet for the months of January through April is shown in Figure 13-9. Notice that each type of expense appears in a separate row of the expense sheet and each column is labeled with the name of a month. The amount of money spent on each item is entered in the cell at the intersection of the appropriate row and column.

The rightmost column of the spreadsheet contains the total amount spent on each item and the total income for the four-month period. At the bottom of each month column, Lyle enters the total amount spent and the balance of his account—the total amount of income minus the total amount of the expenses. As you can see,

Figure 13-9 Lyle's expense worksheet. This is Lyle's handwritten expense sheet. Notice that if he makes any changes to one of the values—for example, the March food expense—he has to do numerous recalculations.

	JAN.	FEB.	MAR.	APR.	TOTAL
INCOME	2300	2300	2300	2300	9200
EXPENSES					
Rent	525	525	525	525	2100
Food	140	150	150	150	590
Phone	50	64	37	23	174
Heat	80	50	24	20	174
Insurance	75	75	75	75	300
Car	200	200	200	200	800
Leisure	105	120	95	125	445
TOTAL EXPENSES	1175	1184	1106	1118	4583
BALANCE	1125	1116	1194	1182	4617

creating an expense sheet can be a time-consuming chore, and if a mistake is made, a number of recalculations must be done.

Now let us follow the steps that Lyle takes to create this spreadsheet with Lotus 1-2-3. (A list of keystrokes for the discussion that follows can be found in Appendix B.)

DISCUSSION QUESTION
How can a spreadsheet be created to keep track of expenses and income over a four month period?

7 Loading the Program

To start his work, Lyle first boots the system. Then he places his formatted data disk in drive B and the Lotus 1-2-3 disk in drive A. He types the command to execute the program—either Lotus or 123, depending on his version of the program. Then he responds to the program prompts until he sees an empty spreadsheet with the cursor positioned in Cell A1 (Figure 13-10). Because a personal computer's screen can display only about 24 lines on a screen with 80 characters per line, the screen display shows only part of all the rows and columns that are available in the computer's memory. An electronic spreadsheet is like a piece of paper; you use only as much as you need. For the expense sheet, Lyle needs to use only columns A through F and rows 1 to 17.

7 Entering the Labels and Values

Since Lyle already knows what he wants to type into the spreadsheet, he starts by entering the labels—the names of the months and the types of expense. Starting with Cell A3, Lyle types the word "INCOME." As he types, the mode indicator display changes from READY to LABEL. When Lyle finishes typing, the sec-

Figure 13-10   A blank spreadsheet. The blank display indicates that Lotus 1-2-3 is loaded and ready to accept data.

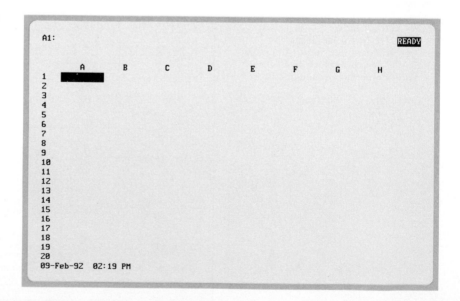

ond line of the control panel displays the text, "INCOME." Lyle then presses Enter to store his entry in the cell (Figure 13-11). When he does this, the mode indicator immediately returns to READY.

To enter the rest of the labels and numbers, Lyle follows the same procedure, moving the cursor from cell to cell by using the cursor movement keys. If he makes a mistake as he is typing, he can use the Backspace key to make the correction before moving from the cell. Remember that the cursor must be on a cell to store data in the cell. Figure 13-12 shows Lyle's spreadsheet with all the labels and numbers entered in their cells.

Figure 13-11 Entering labels. Lyle begins to set up his spreadsheet by entering the labels. When he presses Enter, the label is stored in the cell.

```
A3: 'INCOME                                                    READY

          A         B         C         D         E         F         G         H
 1
 2
 3  INCOME
 4
 5
 6
 7
 8
 9
10
11
12
13
14
15
16
17
18
19
20
09-Feb-92  02:20 PM
```

Figure 13-12 Entering values. This screen shows Lyle's spreadsheet with all the labels and numbers entered.

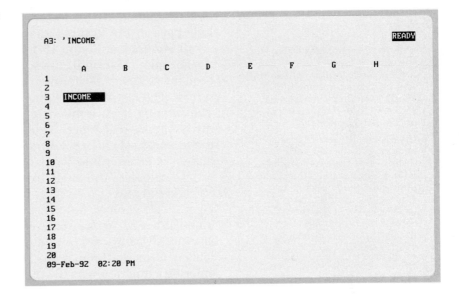

```
F3:                                                           READY

          A         B         C         D         E         F         G         H
 1                 JAN       FEB       MAR       APR      TOTAL
 2
 3  INCOME        2300      2300      2300      2300
 4
 5  EXPENSES
 6  Rent           525       525       525       525
 7  Food           140       150       150       150
 8  Phone           50        64        37        23
 9  Heat            80        50        24        20
10  Insurance       75        75        75        75
11  Car            200       200       200       200
12  Leisure        105       120        95       125
13
14  TOTAL
15  EXPENSES
16
17  BALANCE
18
19
20
09-Feb-92  02:25 PM
```

1. Determine the results you want to display on your spreadsheet.

2. Determine the data you have to input to your spreadsheet to calculate the results you want.

3. Write down the rules for converting the spreadsheet's inputs to its outputs. These are usually formulas that relate the input values to the output values.

4. Write down the names of the input and output values that you will use in your spreadsheet and the equations you will use. Record the exact form in which they will be entered in your spreadsheet. Then double-check this information to make sure that it is completely correct.

5. Create the electronic spreadsheet by typing in the necessary information. Test your spreadsheet with a range of test values. Check the results produced by the spreadsheet against your own calculations that use the test data. If the results differ, go through your spreadsheet to find your mistake.

7 Entering the Formulas and Functions

Lyle must enter the total income for the four months in Cell F3. Lyle could retype each value contained in row 3 (2300+2300+2300+2300) into Cell F3 and then press Enter—the spreadsheet would calculate the total for him and enter the result in F3. But if any of the values in the equation changed, Lyle would have to retype the entry. Instead, Lyle uses a formula that will add the contents of each of the four cells, regardless of their value. The formula he uses is (B3+C3+D3+E3). This formula tells the program to add the values that appear in the Cells B3, C3, D3, and E3. Note that all formulas must be enclosed in parentheses or begin with an operation symbol; otherwise, the program will read the formula as a label. Lyle keys in the formula and presses Enter to store it in Cell F3.

If you look at Figure 13-13, you see that Cell F3 does not show the formula—instead it shows the *result* of the formula. If the cursor is on the cell, then the formula appears in the upper-left corner of the screen. The result of the formula is the **displayed value** of the cell. The formula itself is the actual **cell content.** This is an important distinction to remember. Displayed values change if other values in the spreadsheet change. Formulas can be changed only if new information is entered into the cell.

To calculate the totals in the other rows, Lyle could enter the formula (B6+C6+D6+E6) for row 6, and so on, for each of the Cells F6 to F12. However, Lotus provides a simpler way of summing columns or across rows—the @SUM function. For example, Lyle can key in @SUM(B6..E6) in Cell F6. This tells Lotus to add up the contents of Cells B6 through E6. The @ symbol tells Lotus that you are entering a function. The (B6..E6) part of the function is a range; recall that a range is a group of one or more cells arranged in a block. Lyle

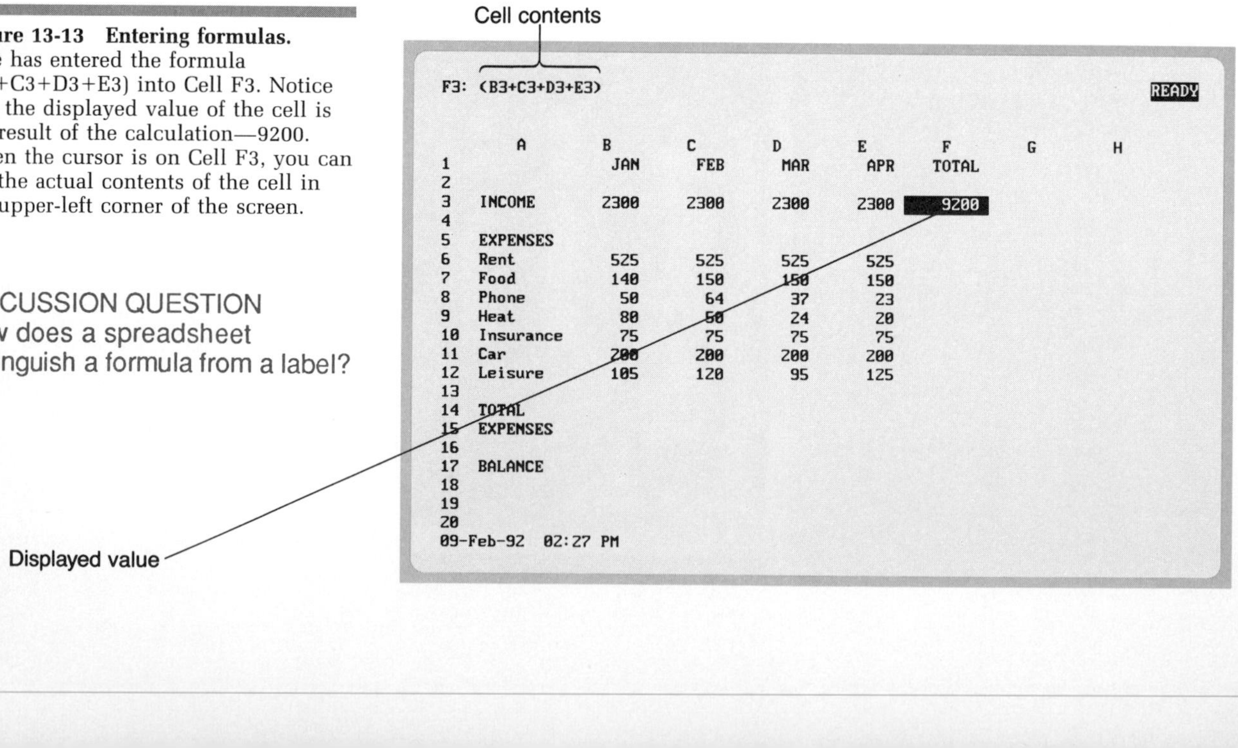

Figure 13-13   Entering formulas.
Lyle has entered the formula (B3+C3+D3+E3) into Cell F3. Notice that the displayed value of the cell is the result of the calculation—9200. When the cursor is on Cell F3, you can see the actual contents of the cell in the upper-left corner of the screen.

DISCUSSION QUESTION
How does a spreadsheet distinguish a formula from a label?

Cell contents

Displayed value

```
F3:  (B3+C3+D3+E3)                                                         READY

          A        B        C        D        E        F        G        H
                  JAN      FEB      MAR      APR     TOTAL
  1
  2
  3     INCOME    2300     2300     2300     2300     9200
  4
  5     EXPENSES
  6     Rent       525      525      525      525
  7     Food       140      150      150      150
  8     Phone       50       64       37       23
  9     Heat        80       50       24       20
 10     Insurance   75       75       75       75
 11     Car        200      200      200      200
 12     Leisure    105      120       95      125
 13
 14     TOTAL
 15     EXPENSES
 16
 17     BALANCE
 18
 19
 20
 09-Feb-92  02:27 PM
```

uses the @SUM function with the appropriate ranges for Cells F6 through F12 and Cells B15 through F15. Figure 13-14 shows the result.

Finally, Lyle needs to use a formula to compute the monthly balance. Remember, the monthly balance is the monthly income minus the monthly total expenses. So, for January, Lyle places the formula (B3−B15) in Cell B17. This tells Lotus to take the value of Cell B15 and subtract it from the value of Cell B3. Lyle then fills in the rest of the balance row. Figure 13-15 shows the completed spreadsheet.

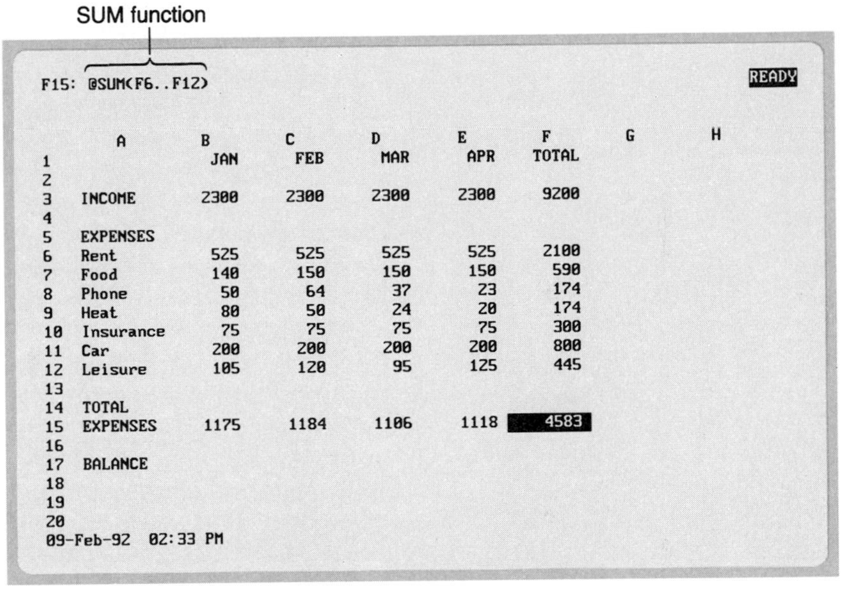

Figure 13-14   Entering functions.
Lyle has entered the Lotus 1-2-3 function @SUM(F6..F12) in Cell F15. In this function (F6..F12) is the range. As with formulas, the cell shows the result of the calculation, and the function is shown in the first line of the control panel.

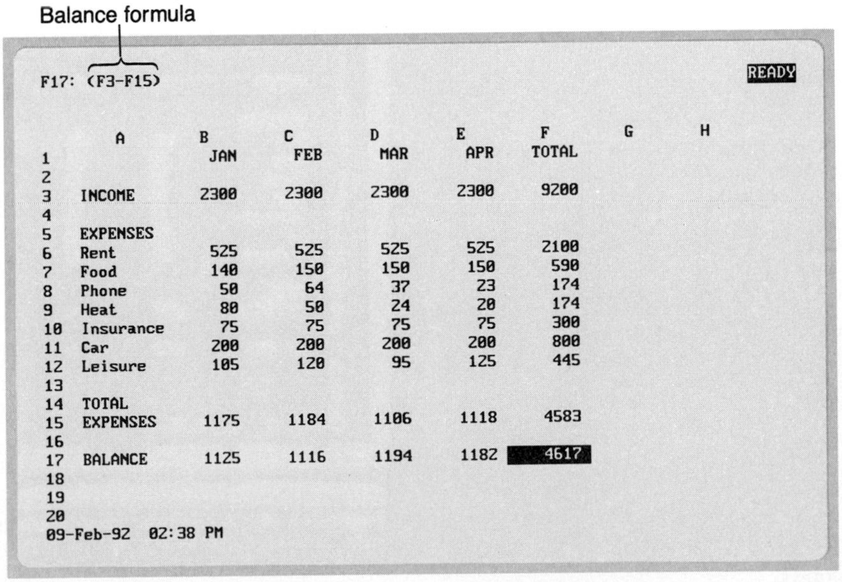

SUM function

F15: @SUM(F6..F12)   READY

	A	B	C	D	E	F	G	H
1		JAN	FEB	MAR	APR	TOTAL		
2								
3	INCOME	2300	2300	2300	2300	9200		
4								
5	EXPENSES							
6	Rent	525	525	525	525	2100		
7	Food	140	150	150	150	590		
8	Phone	50	64	37	23	174		
9	Heat	80	50	24	20	174		
10	Insurance	75	75	75	75	300		
11	Car	200	200	200	200	800		
12	Leisure	105	120	95	125	445		
13								
14	TOTAL							
15	EXPENSES	1175	1184	1106	1118	4583		
16								
17	BALANCE							
18								
19								
20								

09-Feb-92 02:33 PM

Figure 13-15   A complete spreadsheet.
This screen shows Lyle's spreadsheet with all the labels, values, formulas, and functions in place.

Balance formula

F17: (F3−F15)   READY

	A	B	C	D	E	F	G	H
1		JAN	FEB	MAR	APR	TOTAL		
2								
3	INCOME	2300	2300	2300	2300	9200		
4								
5	EXPENSES							
6	Rent	525	525	525	525	2100		
7	Food	140	150	150	150	590		
8	Phone	50	64	37	23	174		
9	Heat	80	50	24	20	174		
10	Insurance	75	75	75	75	300		
11	Car	200	200	200	200	800		
12	Leisure	105	120	95	125	445		
13								
14	TOTAL							
15	EXPENSES	1175	1184	1106	1118	4583		
16								
17	BALANCE	1125	1116	1194	1182	4617		
18								
19								
20								

09-Feb-92 02:38 PM

DISCUSSION QUESTION
How can data entered into a spreadsheet be corrected? Is it necessary to re-type the functions and formulas after such changes?

7 Making Corrections

Suppose that Lyle realizes that he made a mistake in his January food expense (the correct amount is 150). He also made a mistake in his April leisure expense (the correct amount is 123). Since the cells are already filled with incorrect data, Lyle needs to position the cursor on each filled cell and type in the new data; the keyed-in changes will appear in the second line of the control panel. When Lyle presses Enter, the old data in the cell will be replaced by the new data. Lyle begins by moving the cursor over Cell B7 and typing in 150. He presses Enter. Then he moves the cursor to Cell E12, types in 123, and presses Enter.

If the expense sheet were done manually, Lyle would also have to recalculate the totals for row 7 and row 12, and the total expenses and balances for columns B, E, and F. But since the expense sheet is now entered as an electronic spreadsheet, the spreadsheet program instantly recalculates these values. Figure 13-16 shows the result of typing only the two changed values. Nothing else had to be changed in the worksheet—it automatically adjusted all contents to reflect the changed values.

Automatic recalculation of the whole worksheet usually takes only several seconds. This ability to recalculate a spreadsheet at the touch of a button is what has revolutionized the processes of budgeting and financial modeling. Now people who work with numbers can spend their time analyzing their spreadsheets rather than doing arithmetic.

Now that Lyle has entered his worksheet, he can use the command menu to save, retrieve, and print it.

```
E12: 123                                                          READY

         A       B       C       D       E       F       G       H
                JAN     FEB     MAR     APR    TOTAL
 1
 2
 3      INCOME  2300    2300    2300    2300    9200
 4
 5      EXPENSES
 6      Rent    525     525     525     525     2100
 7      Food    150     150     150     150     600
 8      Phone   50      64      37      23      174
 9      Heat    80      50      24      20      174
10      Insurance 75    75      75      75      300
11      Car     200     200     200     200     800
12      Leisure 105     120     95      123     443
13
14      TOTAL
15      EXPENSES 1185   1184    1106    1116    4591
16
17      BALANCE 1115    1116    1194    1184    4609
18
19
20
09-Feb-92  02:39 PM
```

Figure 13-16 Automatic recalculation. Lyle enters in the changes for January's food expense and April's leisure expense. Lotus 1-2-3 automatically recalculates the affected totals and balances.

7 Using Spreadsheet Commands

Using the layered command menu can be a little tricky at first. To help make choosing the proper menus and submenus easier, you can create a command tree. A **command tree,** which looks somewhat like an upside-down tree, shows choices from the main command menu and choices from associated submenus (Figure 13-17). The main command menu line at the top forms the trunk of the tree. Making a command choice from this menu leads you down on a submenu branch. Some of the branches are short and simple, like the one for the Insert command. Others, like Worksheet and Range, have many branches. Each successive branch is reached by selecting from the chain of submenus that appears on the screen.

To take some action—execute an instruction—on your spreadsheet, you must work your way out toward the tip of a branch. The commands along the way, as you go through the layers of menus, are merely vehicles for getting you to the instruction that will take the action you want. You must choose the right options from the sub-

Figure 13-17 A command tree. This command tree shows all the submenus associated with the Worksheet command. Notice that if you follow the Worksheet-Erase path there are no additional submenus. However, if you follow the Worksheet-Global path, there are many different choices you can make.

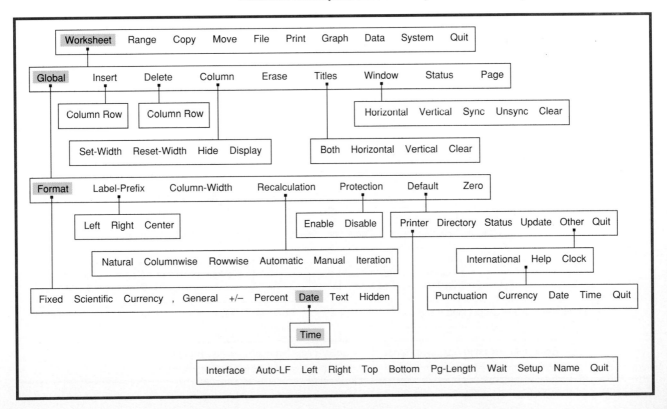

menus to get there. If you make a false step (get into the wrong sub-menu), you can get back to the next higher menu by pressing the Esc key. In fact, you can get out of the MENU mode completely by continuing to press the Esc key until you see READY in the mode indicator. Remember that you work your way down through the levels of submenus by moving the menu cursor to a selection and pressing Enter. You can undo a selection and work your way back up to a previous menu by pressing the Esc key.

Now let us show you the steps Lyle takes to use several of the important commands on the main menu. (A list of the keystrokes for the discussion that follows can be found in Appendix B.)

7 The File Command

The **File command** lets you manipulate the Lotus 1-2-3 files on your data disk. You can use the File command to perform such tasks as saving files, retrieving files, erasing files, and listing files. Figure 13-18 shows the command tree for the File command. We will look at how to use the File command to save, retrieve, and list files.

Saving a File

DISCUSSION QUESTION
Why save a spreadsheet to disk?

Since Lyle is finished with his spreadsheet, he can save it on his data disk by using the File command. To use this command, Lyle must press the / key to obtain the command menu. Next he moves the menu cursor to the word "File" (Figure 13-19a). Notice that Save is one of the choices on the File submenu. With the cursor

Figure 13-18 The File command. This figure shows the command tree for the File command.

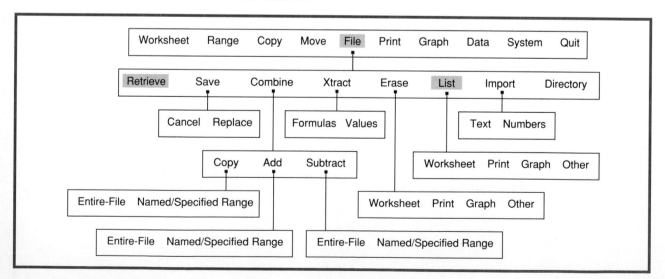

Figure 13-19 Saving a file. (a) To select the File command, Lyle moves the cursor to the word "File." Note the submenu now shows options for the File command. Then Lyle presses Enter. (b) Now the submenu becomes the active menu. Lyle moves the cursor to the word "Save" and presses Enter. (c) Lotus 1-2-3 then asks him to enter a file name.

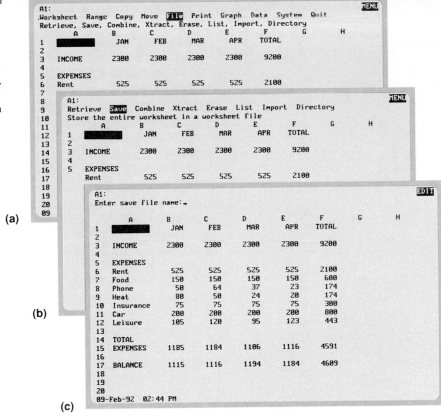

(a)

(b)

(c)

on File, Lyle presses Enter to access the File submenu. Now the submenu is the active menu. Lyle moves the cursor to Save. When he does, the bottom line of the control panel shows a description of the Save option (Figure 13-19b). Lyle presses Enter to select Save, and Lotus 1-2-3 prompts him for the file name he wishes to use (Figure 13-19c). Remember that file names can be up to eight characters long. Spreadsheet file names can contain letters, numbers, hyphens, and the underscore character. Lyle chooses the name B:EXPENSES, types it in, and presses Enter. (Lotus automatically adds an extension.) Since this is a new file, it is saved immediately.

There is another, faster, way to make these types of menu choices: Just type the first letter of the option you want to use, rather than moving the cursor. For example, Lyle can save his file more quickly by typing / (to access the MENU mode), then F (for file), S (for save), followed by the file name. So Lyle could type:

    /FSB:EXPENSES

and press Enter to save his file. The shortcut method can be used for any of the menu commands.

DISCUSSION QUESTION
What are methods of retrieving an
existing spreadsheet file on disk
or finding names of files on disk?

Retrieving a File

Like the Save command, the Retrieve command is a File subcommand. If Lyle wants to retrieve the EXPENSES file, he needs to press the / key to obtain the command menu. Then he selects the File command and the Retrieve subcommand. Selecting the Retrieve command erases the current worksheet (if there happens to be one in memory) and then loads and displays the requested worksheet.

Lotus 1-2-3 then prompts Lyle for the name of the file he wants to retrieve. The program will jog Lyle's memory by listing the names of his stored files on the bottom line of the control panel (Figure 13-20). Lyle can either type in the name of one of the listed files and press Enter, or he can move the cursor to that file name and press Enter.

After Lyle enters the name of the file, the mode indicator flashes the word "WAIT"—this indicates that Lotus is loading the worksheet. When the worksheet appears on the screen, the mode indicator displays the word "READY."

Listing Files

If Lyle wants to check to see what worksheet files he has on his data disk, he can use the List subcommand. To do this, he types / and selects the File option. Then he selects List from the first submenu and Worksheet from the second submenu. Lotus then displays a list of the worksheet files on the screen. When Lyle wants to return to the worksheet, he presses Enter.

7 The Print Command

Spreadsheet programs generally let you print a copy of the spreadsheet at any time during the session. The **Print command**

Figure 13-20 Retrieving a file. When Lyle wants to retrieve a file, Lotus 1-2-3 displays a list of the worksheet files stored on Lyle's disk.

```
A1:
Name of file to retrieve: B:\*.wk?                                    FILES
EXPENSES.WKE    GRADES1.WKE      GRADES2.WKE
          A        B        C        D        E        F        G        H
 1                JAN      FEB      MAR      APR      TOTAL
 2
 3     INCOME    2300     2300     2300     2300     9200
 4
 5     EXPENSES
 6     Rent       525      525      525      525     2100
 7     Food       150      150      150      150      600
 8     Phone       50       64       37       23      174
 9     Heat        80       50       24       20      174
10     Insurance   75       75       75       75      300
11     Car        200      200      200      200      800
12     Leisure    105      120       95      123      443
13
14     TOTAL
15     EXPENSES  1185     1184     1106     1116     4591
16
17     BALANCE   1115     1116     1194     1184     4609
18
19
20
09-Feb-92  02:46 PM
```

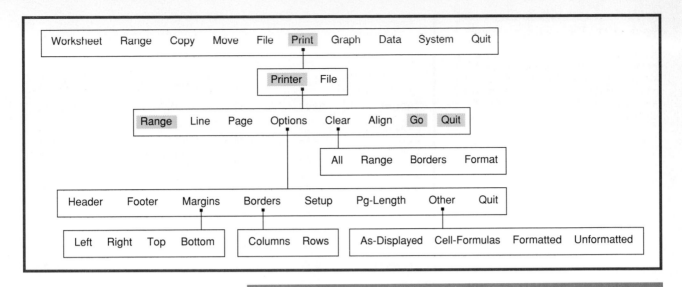

Figure 13-21   The Print command.   This figure shows the command tree for the Print command.

DISCUSSION QUESTION
What series of commands/options are invoked to print out a spreadsheet?

provides options for printing all or part of a spreadsheet on paper. Figure 13-21 shows the command tree for the Print command.

Lyle wants to print a copy of his spreadsheet. To do this, he must tell Lotus 1-2-3 what part of the spreadsheet he wants to print and whether he wants the spreadsheet printed on paper or stored on a disk.

Lyle begins by selecting the Print option from the menu. Then he selects Printer from the first submenu because he wants to have a printed copy of the spreadsheet. When Lyle selects Printer, another submenu appears (Figure 13-22).

Figure 13-22   Printing a worksheet.
After Lyle chooses the Print option from the menu and the Printer option from the first submenu, another submenu appears. This submenu lets Lyle describe the range he wishes to print, start the printing process, and leave the Print menu.

```
A1:                                                              MENU
Range  Line  Page  Options  Clear  Align  Go  Quit
Specify a range to print
        A        B        C        D        E        F        G        H
1                JAN      FEB      MAR      APR      TOTAL
2
3    INCOME      2300     2300     2300     2300     9200
4
5    EXPENSES
6    Rent        525      525      525      525      2100
7    Food        150      150      150      150      600
8    Phone       50       64       37       23       174
9    Heat        80       50       24       20       174
10   Insurance   75       75       75       75       300
11   Car         200      200      200      200      800
12   Leisure     105      120      95       123      443
13
14   TOTAL
15   EXPENSES    1185     1184     1106     1116     4591
16
17   BALANCE     1115     1116     1194     1184     4609
18
19
20
09-Feb-92  02:47 PM
```

Figure 13-23   The printed worksheet.
For Lyle, getting a printed spreadsheet that shows his revisions takes only a few keystrokes. If he had been working with a handwritten ledger, making revisions would have been tedious and the result less attractive than this printed spreadsheet.

	JAN	FEB	MAR	APR	TOTAL
INCOME	2300	2300	2300	2300	9200
EXPENSES					
Rent	525	525	525	525	2100
Food	150	150	150	150	600
Phone	50	64	37	23	174
Heat	80	50	24	20	174
Insurance	75	75	75	75	300
Car	200	200	200	200	800
Leisure	105	120	95	123	443
TOTAL					
EXPENSES	1185	1184	1106	1116	4591
BALANCE	1115	1116	1194	1184	4609

DISCUSSION QUESTION
How is a spreadsheet printed if it has too many columns to fit across an 8.5-inch wide paper?

TRY LYING ON YOUR SIDE

When you are displaying your spreadsheet on your computer's screen, you can move along a row to see all the columns of data in that row. Even if your screen can display only 80 characters on a line, you can still scroll sideways along a line by moving the cursor. However, when a wide spreadsheet is printed, the columns that will not fit across the page appear on a separate page. This means that you will have to cut and paste—literally—your printed copy of the spreadsheet.

Most printers usually print 80 characters per line. When printing in compressed mode, they can print 132 characters per line. If this is still not sufficient to print all the columns in your spreadsheet, you can purchase software that will turn your spreadsheet sideways, printing the spreadsheet along the length of the printer paper. With the output from your spreadsheet in this form, you will have all the rows running continuously on the same piece of fanfold paper. This makes the printed spreadsheet much easier to read.

Now Lyle must tell Lotus how much of the spreadsheet he wants to print. Notice that there is a Range command in the second submenu. To tell Lotus which part of the spreadsheet he wants to print, Lyle must define the range he wants to print. Notice that Lyle's work does not occupy the whole spreadsheet. Rather, it is clustered in a small block. The upper-left corner of the block is Cell A1. The lower-right corner is Cell F17. The two cell addresses define the range of the worksheet that needs to be printed.

To tell Lotus the range, Lyle selects the Range command. Then he types A1 (the cell in the upper left of his worksheet) followed by a period and F17 (the cell in the lower right of his worksheet). Lyle then presses Enter. This returns him to the menu he just left. Next Lyle makes sure that his printer is on and ready to print. Then he selects Go from the second submenu to begin the printing. Figure 13-23 shows the final printed spreadsheet.

When the printing is completed, the second submenu is still the active menu. To return to the READY mode, Lyle must select the Quit command from the submenu.

Like the other commands we have discussed, the commands involved in the printing task can be entered quickly by typing:

```
/PPRA1.F17
```

pressing Enter, and then typing G. When you want to leave the PRINT mode, type Q.

The Worksheet Erase Command

If Lyle wants to start another worksheet without leaving and reentering the Lotus 1-2-3 program, he can use the **Worksheet Erase command.** This command clears the worksheet in the computer's memory of any information that has been entered, and an empty worksheet appears on the screen. The Worksheet Erase command does not erase any worksheets saved on a disk.

To use the Worksheet Erase command, Lyle presses the / key. Then he selects Worksheet from the menu and Erase from the submenu. When Lotus asks if he really wants to erase the worksheet, Lyle types Y for *yes.* The new worksheet appears on the screen.

The Quit Command

To leave the spreadsheet program and return to DOS, you must use the **Quit command** from the command menu. Many spreadsheet programs do not automatically save your file when you use the Quit command, so always remember to save before you quit.

Since Lyle has already saved his file, he selects the Quit command. Lotus 1-2-3 asks him to confirm the command with a Y (yes, leave the program) or an N (no, do not leave the program). Lyle presses Y, and the DOS prompt appears.

Using the Help Key

The wide assortment of commands can be bewildering to the novice user. In fact, command choices can be confusing to an experienced user, too. But help is as close as your computer. When you are lost or confused, press the **Help key** (F1). Pressing the Help key places you in the HELP mode. You can press the Help key any time, even in the middle of a command.

The HELP mode is useful in two ways. First, it is **context sensitive,** that is, it offers helpful information related to the command you are using when you press the Help key. Second, you can select the **help index,** which—for all practical purposes—gives you access to a reference manual right on your screen. Use the help index to select a topic, and the spreadsheet program supplies aid on that topic. It is easy to get out of the HELP mode: Press the Esc key once.

DISCUSSION QUESTION
Where can the Quit command be found in the command tree?

TEST BANK
Mult. Choice	49-50
T/F	46-64
Matching D	1-2
Fill-in-the-Blank	17, 18

LECTURE HINT
In addition to the Help key (F1), the Edit key (F2) is useful for beginners, especially unskilled typists. This key will allow using the left-right cursor keys to move back and forth in a cell-image and correct it in either insert or type-over mode. The entire contents do not need to be retyped to correct errors.

TEST BANK
Mult. Choice   51-55
Matching D   3-4, 6
Fill-in-the-Blank   19-23

DISCUSSION QUESTION
What are some advantages of
integrated packages?

7 Integrated Packages

The concept of an **integrated package** of programs—an all-in-one set—is very appealing: Join word processing, spreadsheet, database, and graphics programs into one package. Integrated packages are especially useful when numeric data must be included in textual reports or when a graphic representation of numbers can more easily show what the numbers mean.

Furthermore, with an integrated package you do not need to learn completely different programs that use different commands. Perhaps the most difficult steps you have to take when you learn to use a new program are the first few. After that, you have oriented yourself to the "feel" of the program and can start being productive with it. Programs in an integrated package share a common methodology and command structure so that you do not have to begin anew to use a particular program in the package; there is a familiar flavor in each of the programs.

Another advantage is the fast, easy transfer of data among the programs in the package. For example, it is easy to move a table of spreadsheet numbers into a word processing report. Graphs can be prepared using the graphics program, then easily inserted into text prepared using the word processing program. However, if you are using a separate word processing program and separate spreadsheet and graphics programs, you will find that moving data from one program to another program is not simple. And even though there are certain standard file types, they cannot always store exactly what you want to pass to the second program. Ease of information transfer among programs and a common command structure has created a user demand for integrated packages.

7 The First Integrated Package: Lotus 1-2-3

Although Lotus 1-2-3 does not have word processing capability, it does integrate a very powerful spreadsheet program with a business graphics program and a limited database program. All three functions in the package are based on storing data in a spreadsheet. After you enter the data in the spreadsheet, you can view the data graphically using the graphics program. You can also use commands available through the database program to sort the data in your spreadsheet or to find rows in the spreadsheet that match certain conditions.

Each of the programs has a menu that lets you choose what task you want to perform. You can also move instantly from one program to another by making a selection from a menu. Furthermore, once your graphs and database are set up, you can stay in the spreadsheet program and see graphs of your data or select records from your database by simply pressing one key. Lotus also stores the graphs and database with the spreadsheet file on which they are based.

LECTURE HINT
Mitch Kapor founded the Lotus Development Corporation, which pioneered Lotus 1-2-3, the first integrated package, in 1981. Lotus soon became the number one software house in the world.

In 1986, Kapor announced that he was leaving Lotus to "pursue other endeavors." As Kapor put it, five years ago "we were a small band setting out on a great adventure. Now we have 1200 employees and two million customers. It's a radically different situation." It seems to make sense for entrepreneurs to move on.

7 To Integrate or Not?

The popularity of Lotus has led to the development of a number of different packages that integrate program functions. Two different approaches have been taken by software developers:

- Including word processing, spreadsheet, graphics, and database capabilities in one program package. Some of the more popular programs of this type are Framework II and Symphony for the IBM PC, and Excel for the Apple Macintosh.

- Allowing a user to purchase the individual word processing, spreadsheet, graphics, and database programs that are most appealing for that user. These **stand-alone programs** are then integrated by a **universal manager program** that coordinates the separate programs. The manager program also presents a common interface to the user and handles data transfer among the programs. An example of this approach is Microsoft's Windows program.

DISCUSSION QUESTION
Why have integrated packages not sold as well as initially anticipated?

Despite their many advantages, sales of integrated packages have not skyrocketed. There are several reasons for this. First, the individual functions—like word processing or graphics—within an all-in-one integrated package are not usually as strong as those in stand-alone packages. If you need state-of-the-art word processing and state-of-the-art database management, you would probably be better served by buying two stand-alone programs. Second, integrated packages are rather expensive, and you pay for all the functions in the package even if you really need only two or three. Third, integrated packages require more computer memory than one stand-alone program does. You may have to purchase additional memory for your computer to run the integrated package.

TEST BANK
Mult. Choice   56-59
Matching D   7-9
Matching E   1-2
Fill-in-the-Blank 24-25

7 Business Graphics

The change from numbers to pictures is a refreshing variation. But graphics used in business are not a toy. In fact, graphics can show words and numbers and data in ways that are meaningful and quickly understood. This is the key reason they are valuable. (You can see a variety of graphics in Gallery 3, which follows page 416.)

Personal computers give people the capability to store and use data about their businesses. These same users, however, sometimes find it difficult to convey this information to others—managers or clients—in a meaningful way. **Business graphics**—graphics that represent data in a visual, easily understood format—provide an answer to this problem.

Figure 13-24   Business graphics.
(a) A large amount of data can be translated into (b) one simple, clear graph.

TRANSPARENCY ACETATE #13E
Figure #13-24

| Material | Units Sold Each Month | | | |
	Jan.	Feb.	Mar.	Apr.
Copper	6	10	13	22
Bronze	18	28	36	60
Iron	9	15	19	32
Gold	32	52	64	110
Silver	20	32	40	68
Totals:	85	137	172	292

(a)

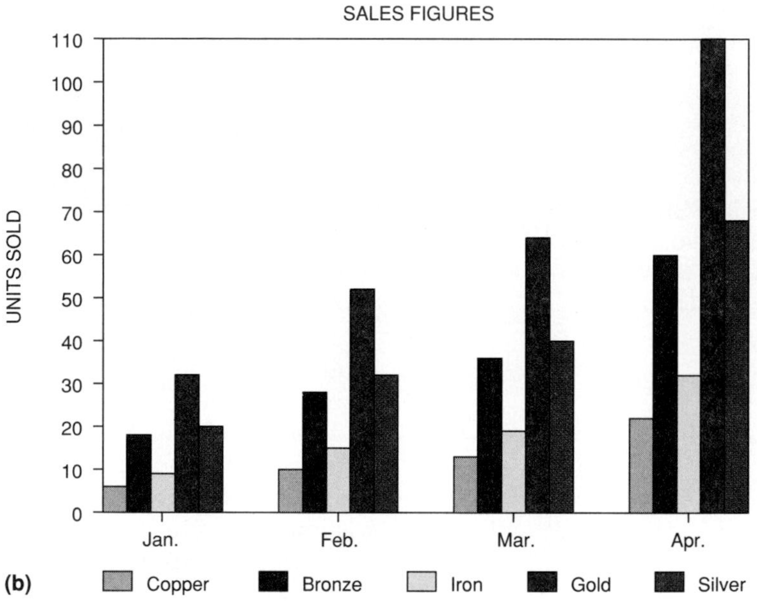

(b)

SALES FIGURES

Copper   Bronze   Iron   Gold   Silver

DISCUSSION QUESTION
In what situations would graphics applications be especially useful?

7 Why Use Graphics?

Graphics generate and sustain the interest of an audience by brightening up any lesson, report, or business document. In addition, graphics can help get a point across by presenting an overwhelming amount of data in one simple, clear graph (Figure 13-24). What is more, that simple graph can reveal a trend that could be lost if buried in long columns of numbers. To sum up, most people use business graphics software for one of two reasons: (1) to view and analyze data and (2) to make a positive impression during a presentation. To satisfy these different needs, two types of business graphics programs have been developed: analytical graphics and presentation graphics.

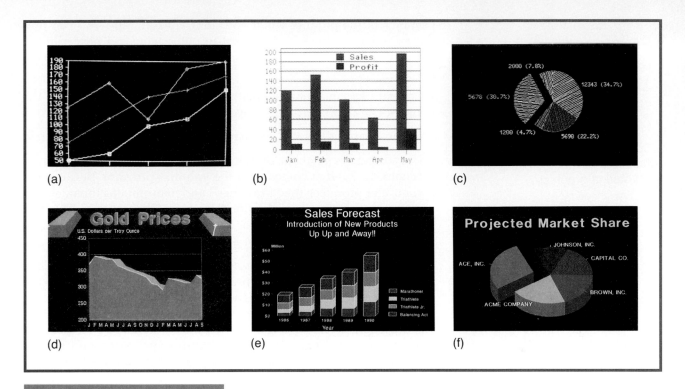

Figure 13-25   Analytical graphics compared to presentation graphics. Analytical graphics (a, b, and c) are certainly serviceable, but they lack the clarity and appeal of presentation graphics (d, e, and f). Compare the line graphs (a and d), bar graphs (b and e), and pie charts (c and f).

Analytical Graphics

Analytical graphics programs are designed to help users analyze and understand specific data. Sometimes called analysis-oriented graphics programs, these programs let you use already entered spreadsheet or database data to construct and view line, bar, and pie-chart graphs (Figure 13-25a–c).

Although analytical graphics programs do a good job of producing simple graphs, these programs are too limited and inflexible for a user who needs to prepare elaborate presentations. Lotus 1-2-3, for example, lets you choose from only a small number of graph types, and the program's formatting features—which allow different graph sizes, different color possibilities, and different types of lettering—are limited. These limitations may be of little concern to some users. But those who require sophisticated graphics will want to consider presentation graphics.

Presentation Graphics

Presentation graphics programs are also called **business-quality graphics programs** or presentation-oriented desktop graphics programs. These programs let you produce charts, graphs, and other visual aids that look as if they were prepared by a professional graphics artist (Figure 13-25d–f). However, you can control the appearance of the product when you do it yourself, and you can produce graphics faster and make last-minute changes if necessary.

Most presentation graphics programs help you do three kinds of tasks:

- Edit and enhance charts created by other programs, such as the analytical graphs produced by Lotus 1-2-3.

- Create charts, diagrams, drawings, and text slides from scratch.

- Use a library of symbols, drawings, and pictures—called **clip art**—(Figure 13-26) that comes with the graphics program. Because the computer produces the "drawings" and manipulates them, even a nonartist can create professional-looking illustrations. The box called "Presentation Graphics Everywhere" shows some presentation graphics made with clip art.

Presentation graphics increase the impact of your message. They make the information you are presenting visually appealing, meaningful, and comprehensible. High-quality graphics have been shown to increase both the amount that a listener learns in a presentation and the length of time that the information is retained by the listener. Also, an audience perceives you as more professional and knowledgeable when you include overhead graphics and slides in your presentation.

You can produce high-quality output on a variety of media: CRT screens, printers, plotters, overhead transparencies, or slides for projection. Some presentation graphics programs let you store pictures, text slides, charts, and graphs on disk. This means you can use the computer to present a series of text or graphic images, one after the other, on your display. When you make a presentation, you can run the display manually or have the screens presented by the computer automatically, in time increments ranging from four seconds to four minutes per image. A few programs let you animate your images. For example, graph bars might grow as product sales increase.

Figure 13-26 Enhancing graphics with symbols. Presentation graphics programs provide a library of symbols, which users can choose from. As shown here on the left, such symbols can add interest to columns of numbers.

Economic Growth	East	Central	West
Government	6%	3%	23%
Manufacturing	29%	-11%	23%
Construction	27%	24%	28%
Mining	9%	16%	48%
Services	40%	42%	18%
Agriculture	15%	27%	4%

Made with 35mm Express software/MAGICorp Network

1

2

Just as people look at pictures first in a book, so they turn first to graphics in a computer publication. Graphics offer variety, color, and drama. The graphics examples in this gallery were chosen for their utility and their beauty, although many fulfill both purposes. Study and enjoy.

The computer graphics artist who produced the mathematical solids shown on the opening page shows considerable skill. In particular, note the shadows and reflections on the objects.

Geography

Geographic information systems are one of the fastest-growing areas of computer graphics. By combining automated map-making with other information, such as census data, people have new tools for decision-making.

(1) A manager for the Potlatch Corporation, which owns 600,000 acres of timber in Idaho, prints a computer-generated map showing land ownership. This information helps the company plan its timber harvesting.

(2) The United Nation's Food and Agricultural Organization created a computerized atlas of Africa. This map of Tanzania shows the regions that are most suitable for irrigation in white, followed by the red, blue, and dark green regions.

(3) This computer-generated nautical chart of Greece was created for the Greek Navy. It shows topographical contours, depth soundings, and annotations.

3

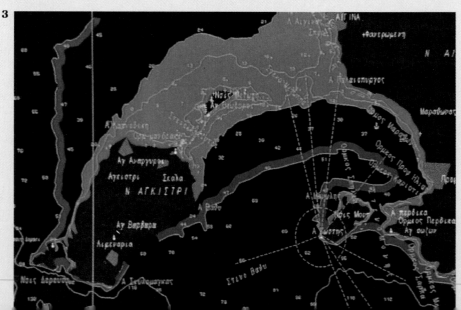

(4) This map shows the number of clerical and administrative workers in each Zip Code region of Washington, D.C. Such maps, made by linking maps and geographic databases, are useful for selling products to specific customers.

(5) This computer graphic shows response times by emergency vehicles in Salt Lake City in the event of an earthquake. Areas shown in blue could be reached within 2.5 minutes, while streets shown in white would be more than 10 minutes from help.

(6) The subdued hues in this graphic represent normal traffic in downtown Burbank, California, showing the time it takes to drive from the center of town outward. Each colored band represents 30 seconds of travel time. **(7)** Evening rush hour traffic is simulated graphically with the bright colors shown in the center of this screen. The greater travel time is represented by the greater number of colored bands. To produce an accurate simulation of driving times, the computer must first be fed data on important variables such as traffic light timing and automobile density.

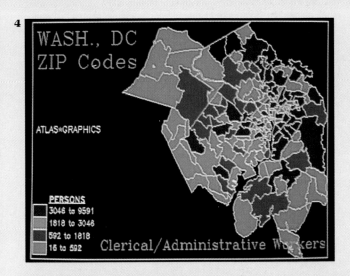

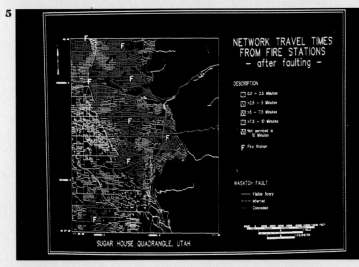

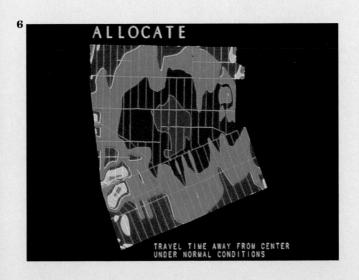

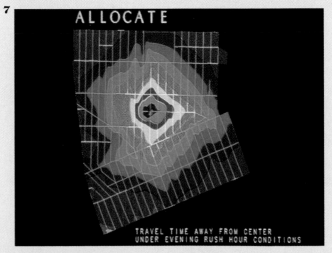

8

9

Animation

(8) The design of this screen conveys motion as an attention-getting sales pitch for a music video station. This animated sequence, called "Cakewalk," involves a shooting match between slices of cake and spinning coffee cups.

(9) The double dragon, a Korean symbol of success and good fortune, was animated in a commercial for Ssangyong, Korea's 6th largest company. A bolt of lightning flashes in the clouds as the dragons burst through the ocean waves, spiraling around each other as they rise through the mist. When the dragons reach the sky, their bodies form the double "S" of the Ssangyong logo.

(10) This screen is one in a series of screens that, together, show the pattern of the jet stream. The graphics software provides animation features, such as the alternating red/yellow squares seen here; the squares begin in the west and move east in successive screens to show the movement of the jet stream.

(11) The Evening Magazine television show announces itself with a series of moving computer images, including the one shown here.

(12) This exquisite graphic is but one from a computer-animated film called "Red's Dream." Red is a unicycle who can be observed in the very back of the picture, relegated to the "sale" section. But Red dreams of joining the circus, and when he does, he ends up saving the show. "Red's Dream" shows that computer animation can convey stories with the emotion and visual intensity of classic cartoon animation.

10

11

12

13

14

15

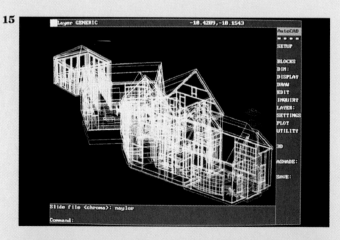

16

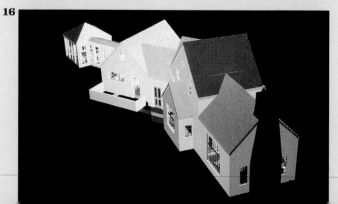

Architecture

(13) These architects use a computer system to design buildings from concept to completion. A key advantage of the computer is that drawings can be changed easily, so the architect can try out different designs, and can quickly make any alterations that the client requests. Proposed buildings can be viewed from any angle, in any light. The computer also calculates costs and energy usage for the proposed buildings. Architects use computer-aided design to minimize tedious work, thus freeing their time for the more creative aspects of the business.

(14) This computer graphic shows an architect's plan for a project called Villa Capra, located in Montreal. A three-dimensional view of the building is "floating" over the floor plan, shown in blue.

The computer is a key player as this house design progresses from **(15)** a wireframe drawing to **(16)** the shaded image of a custom home.

(17) This computer image represents the architectural drawing for the Pacific Bell Administrative Center in San Ramon, California. The entire project was handled on computer—from design through moving in all 8000 employees.

(18) Computer-aided design software can create images of the interior of buildings as well as the exterior. Users can take a computerized tour of rooms on the screen.

(19) Land planning software assists landscape architects by providing a library of symbols for showing trees, shrubs, bridges, benches, and people on computer in two-dimensional or three-dimensional drawings. To assist in selecting plants, the software includes detailed descriptions of over 850 plants. After placing plants in the drawing, the architect can watch the plants grow on the screen to see how the landscape will change over time.

17
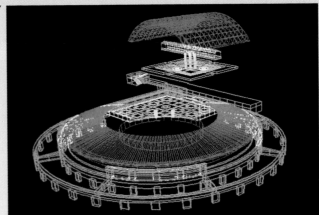

18

19

20

21

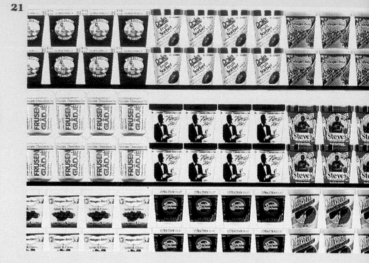

22

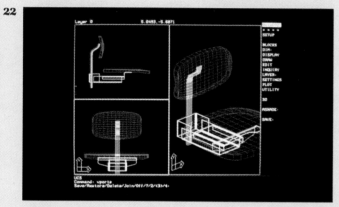

23

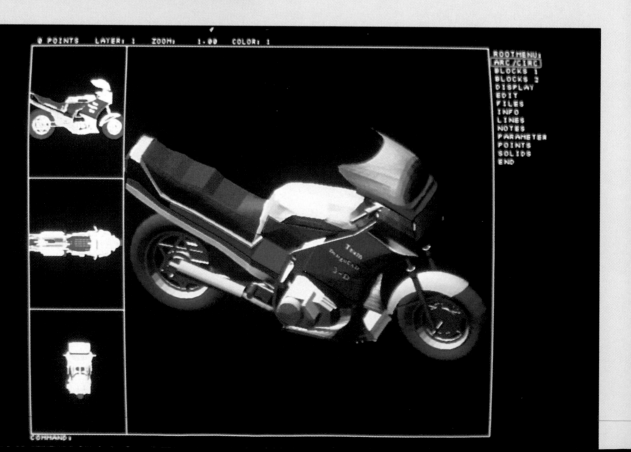

Design

(20) Clothing designers use computer graphics software to show the same style in different fabrics and colors.

(21) Designer ice cream? Marketers know that packaging can make or break sales. This screen shows a computer-generated design for "Perché No!" ice cream as it would look sitting in the store next to package designs for competing products.

(22) This office chair being designed by computer can be seen from a different angle in each window on the screen.

(23) The main view of this motorcycle design is shown in the large screen window, with other angles presented in the smaller side windows. The extensive shading helps give this image its realistic three-dimensional look.

(24) This crystal champagne goblet was designed with graphics software on a personal computer.

The design of a piano progresses through various stages on computer. **(25)** This screen shows a computer-generated three-dimensional wireframe drawing, used as a visualization tool. **(26)** The next step is more surface oriented, hiding lines that would not be seen if the object were solid. **(27)** The final screen presents a more finished solid model, showing a painted surface and shadows.

24

25

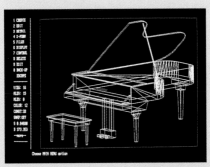

26

27

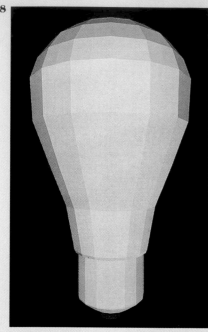

Realistic Art

These computer-generated light bulb images illustrate the evolution of realistic graphics. **(28)** In the late 1970s curved surfaces appeared as a series of flat surfaces. **(29)** By the 1980s models could be produced with smooth, curved surfaces; this quality is now possible on some personal computers. **(30)** This realistic computer-generated model, with numerous textures and transparent surfaces, can be produced by powerful workstations.

(31) This realistic bus scene was created to grace the cover of Computer Graphics World magazine. Note the snow effect on the bus and buildings.

(32) This computer-generated image of a Japanese teacup is so realistic that we must make a disclaimer—it is not a photograph.

(33) Although the brilliant, clear colors used in this computer-generated image are reminiscent of nature, the artist's hand is clearly evident.

(34–35) These images of an artist's studio show soft shadows and subtle shading on the surfaces. The image on the left took five hours to compute, but the variation on the right—showing the same scene from a different angle—required only 15 minutes.

32

33

34

35

36

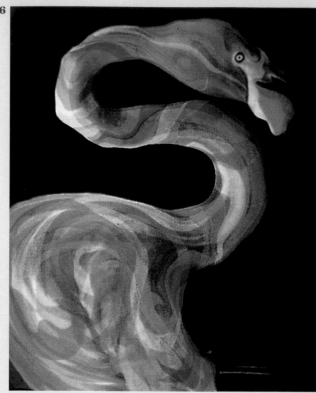

Abstract Art

(36) Abstract or not, this artwork, generated with personal computer software, still gives the appearance of a flamingo.

(37) The subject matter in abstract art, even computer-generated, is sometimes in the eye of the beholder. In this whimsical piece, we think that there is a cat in the lower right-hand corner.

(38) Computer artist Melvin Prueitt is famous for brilliant colors, stripes, and odd shapes. In this slight departure, he presents balloons with a new look.

(39–41) These three artistic renditions were all created by Steve Wilson, an art professor at California State University at Chico. Professor Wilson is a highly respected innovator in the field of computer graphic art.

37

38

42

43

44

Fractal Art

Fractals are based on the principle of "self-similarity": A large form is composed of smaller, similar shapes. This repetitive approach is particularly suited to computer art.

(42–44) These three versions of the same landscape vary from rough to smooth, depending on the size of the fractal used; a smaller fractal produces a smoother result.

(45) In this fractal image, note how the small elements of the structure resemble the larger patterns.

(46) This stunning image of fractal mountains set against a fractal moon was created by pioneer Benoit Mandelbrot and F. Kenton Musgrave of Yale University.

(47) This pattern is known as a "fish-eye" picture.

(48) Note the "blades of grass" recurrent pattern. A single fractal shape can be manipulated—enlarged, reduced, stretched in a variety of ways—to produce many variations on the same theme.

45

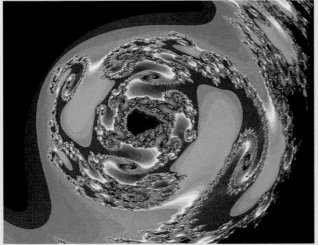

Fine Art

(49) Artist Larry Rivers drew this simulated watercolor portrait using a stylus, not a keyboard.

(50) "Best of Show" is quite a compliment for any artist. Computer artist Philip High took that honor in an art contest sponsored by a microcomputer videographics company. This is what he says about his piece, entitled "Thread": "It came to represent a recurring theme in my work: A common thread that unites apparently unrelated elements or circumstances—like art and computers."

49

50

MICROCOMPUTERS IN ACTION

Presentation Graphics Everywhere

Why are people taking the trouble to get information all gussied up with fancy graphics when the unembellished numbers would be quite acceptable? The answer is that graphics are worth the trouble. The most effective way to make a presentation is to take advantage of visual aids. Studies show that graphics—especially color graphics—increase persuasiveness by as much as 50%.

As you can see from these representative samples, colorful graphics can be given a three-dimensional look and enhanced with drawings of related objects, such as planes and bottles.

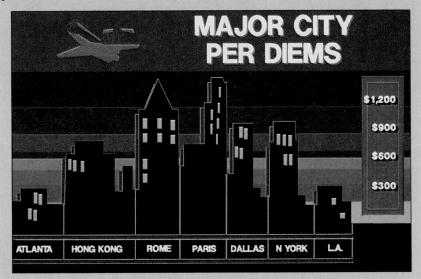

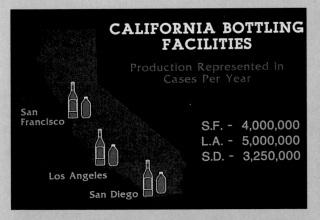

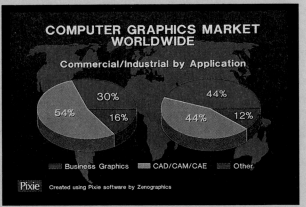

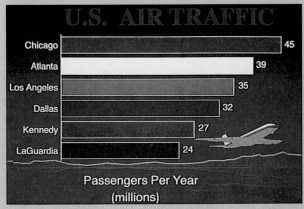

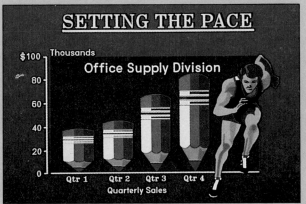

DISCUSSION QUESTION
Compare the types of graphs available in graphics programs, identifying the advantages of each.

7 Some Graphics Terminology

To use a graphics program successfully, you should know some basic concepts and design principles. Let us begin by exploring the types of graphs you can create.

7 Line Graphs

One of the most useful ways of showing trends or cycles over the same period of time is to use a **line graph.** For example, the graph in Figure 13-27 shows company costs for supplies, utilities, and travel during a four-month period. Line graphs are appropriate when there are many values or complex data. In the business section of the newspaper, line graphs are used to show complex trends in gross national product, stock prices, or employment changes over a period of time. Also, corporate profits and losses are often illustrated by line graphs.

In the line graph in Figure 13-27, notice the lines that run vertically along the left edge and horizontally along the bottom. Each line is called an **axis.** (The plural of *axis* is *axes.*) The horizontal line, called the **x-axis,** normally represents units of time, such as days, months, or years. The vertical line, called the **y-axis,** usually shows measured values or amounts, such as dollars, staffing levels, units sold, and so on. The area inside the axes is called the **plot area**—the space in which the graph is plotted, or drawn.

Graphics programs automatically scale (arrange the units or numbers on) the x-axis and y-axis so that the graph of your data is nicely proportioned and easy to read. When you become proficient with a graphics program, you can select your own scaling for the x- and y-axes.

Each dot or symbol on a line graph represents a single numeric quantity called a **data point.** You must specify the data to be plotted on the graph. This data is usually referred to as the *values.* The items that the data points describe are called **variables.** Most graphs are produced from the data stored in the rows and columns of spreadsheet files. Recall from the spreadsheet discussion that you can refer to particular rows or columns of a spreadsheet as a *range.* A graph that plots the values of only one variable is sometimes referred to as a **single-range graph** (Figure 13-28a). If more than one variable is plotted on the same graph, it is referred to as a **multiple-range graph** (Figure 13-28b).

To make the graph easier to read and understand, **labels** are used to identify the categories along the x-axis and the units along the y-axis. **Titles** summarize the information in the graph and are used to increase comprehension.

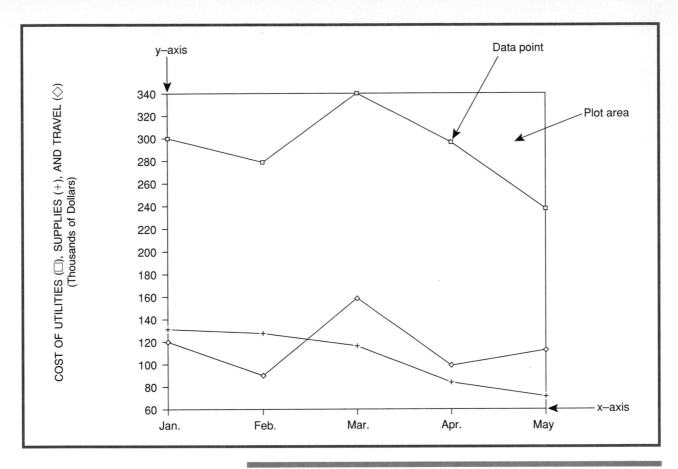

Figure 13-27   A line graph.   Line graphs are useful for showing trends over a period of time. In many analytical programs, different symbols are used to show the different types of data being plotted.

7 Bar Graphs

Bar graphs are used for graphing the same kinds of data that line graphs represent. Notice in Figure 13-29 that **bar graphs** shade an area up to the height of the point being plotted, creating a bar. These graphs can be striking and informative when they are simple. They are often used to illustrate multiple comparisons such as sales, expenses, and production activities. Bar graphs are useful for presentations, since the comparisons are easy to absorb. However, if there is a lot of data for several variables, the bars on the graph become narrow and crowded, making a confusing and busy graph; in such a case a line graph is preferable.

Figure 13-28 Types of line graphs.
(a) Single-range graphs show only one variable or line. (b) Multiple-range graphs show several different variables or lines.

TRANSPARENCY ACETATE #13F
Figure #13-28

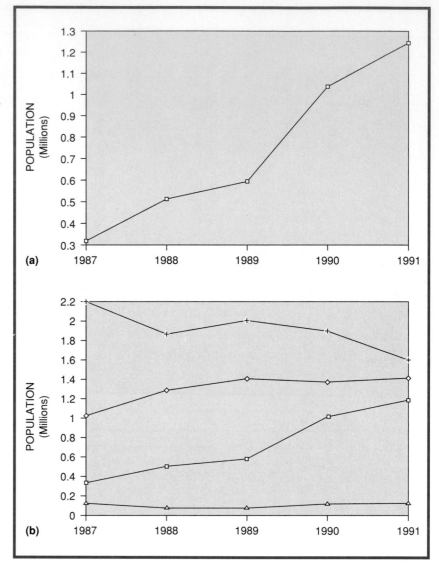

In Figure 13-29, there are three different types of bar graphs. The first is a **single-range bar graph** in which only one variable is involved; in this example the single variable is monthly expenses. The second type of bar graph is a multiple-range bar graph called a **clustered-bar graph.** In this type of graph, data values for three different variables—supplies, utilities, and travel—are plotted next to each other along the x-axis. Because clustered-bar graphs contain so much information, it is important to label each cluster clearly. You can create a **legend,** or list, that explains different colors, shadings, or symbols in the graph. A legend is used at the bottom of Figure 13-29b. The third type of bar graph, the **stacked-bar graph,** is also a multiple-range bar graph. In this graph, however, the different variables are stacked on top of one another. All the data common to a given row or column appear in one bar.

Figure 13-29 Types of bar graphs.
(a) A single-range bar graph shows only one variable—in this case, monthly expenses. Multiple-range bar graphs show several variables. The other two graphs in this figure show the two basic types of multiple-range bar graphs: (b) A clustered-bar graph shows several variables. (c) A stacked-bar graph shows the different variables stacked on top of one another.

TRANSPARENCY ACETATE #13G
Figure #13-29

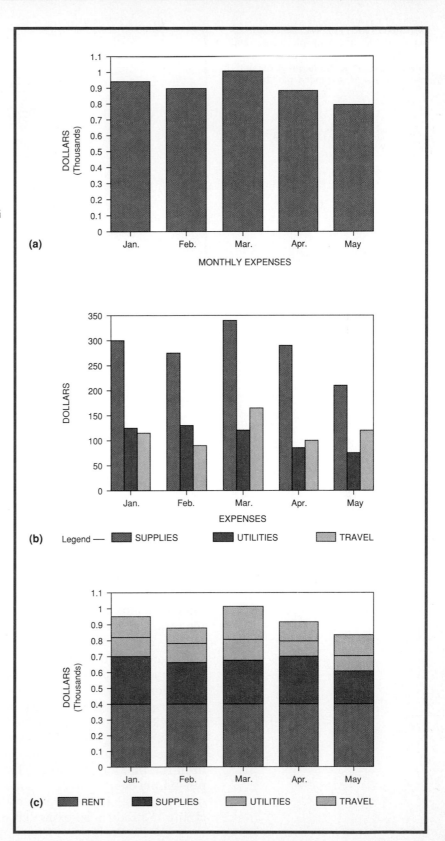

Figure 13-30   Types of pie charts. Pie charts are used to show how various values make up a whole. (a) A regular pie chart. (b) An exploded pie chart.

TRANSPARENCY ACETATE #13H
Figure #13-30

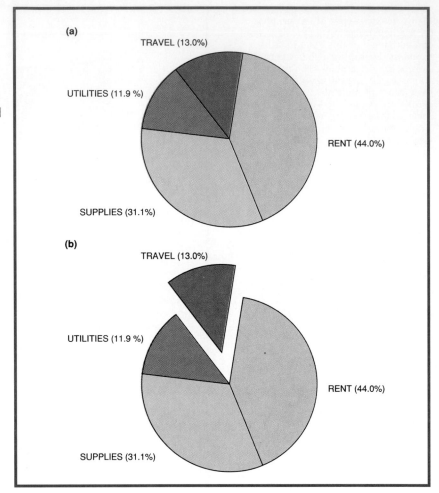

Figure 13-30   Types of pie charts. Pie charts are used to show how various values make up a whole. (a) A regular pie chart. (b) An exploded pie chart.

7 Pie Charts

Representing just a single variable, a **pie chart** shows how various values make up a whole. These charts really look like pies; the whole amount is represented by a circle, and each wedge of the pie represents a value. Figure 13-30a shows a pie chart.

Pie charts can show only the data for one variable, January in this example. However, this pie chart does the best job of showing the proportion of the "pie" dollar that goes for rent, supplies, and so forth during that one month. Notice that pie charts often have the written percentage shown by each separate wedge of the pie. It is best to keep pie charts simple; if the pie contains more than eight wedges, you might consider using a bar graph or line graph instead.

Figure 13-30b shows one of the wedges pulled slightly away from the pie, for emphasis. This type of pie chart is called an **exploded pie chart.** This technique loses its effectiveness if more than one or two "slices" are separated. Not all graphics programs have the ability to produce an exploded pie chart.

Macintosh®

Graphics at Your Fingertips

The Macintosh is justly famous for its graphics capabilities. The combination of Macintosh hardware and software gives artists and businesspeople alike an easy-to-use tool for expressing ideas visually.

The special screen technology of the Macintosh lets users create images out of "pixels"—the dots on the screen.

Macintosh graphics programs provide "palettes" of icons instead of the traditional artist's palette of paint. Screen (a) below shows a typical Macintosh paint program. With the tools palette shown on the right side of screen (a), you can easily create standard shapes—rectangles, ovals, and polygons—in any size. Or, you can draw your own shape by using the mouse to move the pencil tool around the screen. To draw with a thicker line, you can use the paintbrush tool, and you can change the shape and texture of the "brush" as you like. If you make a mistake or change your mind, just use the eraser tool. Using the "lasso," you can select part of an illustration and move it to another area of the screen. By zooming in on an area of your picture, you can change your drawing a pixel at a time, refining your image in detail.

With the pattern palette shown on the left side of screen (a), you can fill shapes with a variety of patterns, such as dots, lines, or solid black. Screen (a) shows the paint bucket tool being used to fill in patterns on a beachball image. If you want a pattern to be "splattered" over an area, you can use the spray can tool.

If you don't consider yourself an artist, you can use a device called a scanner to convert an existing drawing or photograph into pixels that can be displayed on the screen. You can also buy clip art software—useful images that are already on disk. Once you have a drawing or photograph in the computer, you can use graphics software to change it the same way you would change an image created on the Mac. Dabbling in art has never been so easy!

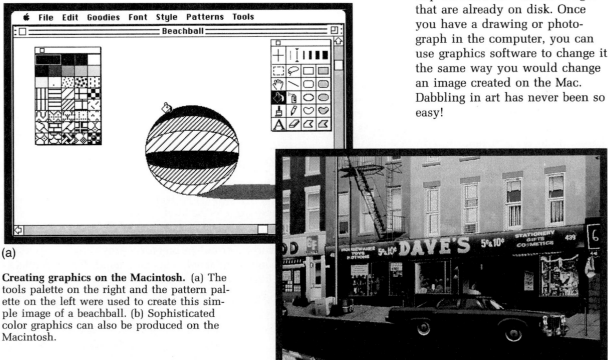

(a)

(b)

Creating graphics on the Macintosh. (a) The tools palette on the right and the pattern palette on the left were used to create this simple image of a beachball. (b) Sophisticated color graphics can also be produced on the Macintosh.

7 On to Storing Data

Thus far in the applications chapters, we have moved from words to numbers to pictures. Another powerful application is storing data so it is easily accessible in databases—the subject of our next chapter.

7 Summary and Key Terms

- Forms that are used to organize data into rows and columns are called **spreadsheets.** An **electronic spreadsheet** is a computerized version of a manual spreadsheet. The electronic spreadsheet program quickly and automatically performs calculations to reflect changes in values or formulas. In Lotus 1-2-3, an electronic spreadsheet is called a **worksheet.**

- The intersection of a row and column forms a **cell.** Cells are the storage areas in a spreadsheet. When referring to a cell, you use the letter and number of the intersecting column and row. This reference name is the **cell address.**

- There is one cell known as the **active cell,** or **current cell.** The active cell is marked by the spreadsheet's cursor, also called a **pointer.**

- Each cell can contain one of four types of information. A **label** provides descriptive information about entries in the spreadsheet. A **value** is an actual number entered into a cell. A **formula** is an instruction to the program to perform a calculation. A **function** is a preprogrammed formula. Sometimes you must specify a **range** of cells to build a formula or perform a function.

- You can use the cursor movement keys to scroll through the spreadsheet horizontally or vertically. You may also use a **GoTo function key,** also known as the **Jump-To function key.**

- A **mode** is the condition or state in which the program is currently functioning. Most spreadsheets have three main operating modes: the **READY mode,** the **ENTRY mode,** and the **MENU mode.** The spreadsheet screen displays a **mode indicator,** which tells you the current mode.

- Spreadsheet programs display commands in a **command menu** shown near the top of the screen. The command menu contains a list, or menu, of different options.

- Most spreadsheet programs display a **control panel** to help you keep track of what you input. The control panel usually consists of three lines. The first line is the status line; the second line is used in a variety of ways; and the third line shows a **submenu,** which lists options for the command you are choosing.

- To create a spreadsheet you enter labels, values, formulas, and functions into the cells. Formulas and functions do not appear in the cells; instead, the cell shows the result of the formula or function. The result is called the **displayed value** of the cell. The formula or function is the **cell content.** To make corrections to data in a cell, you must move the cursor to that cell.

- A **command tree** shows all the choices from the main command menu and all the choices from associated submenus.

- The **File command** lets you manipulate the Lotus 1-2-3 files on your data disk. You can use the File command to save, retrieve, list, and erase files.

- The **Print command** provides options for printing all or part of a spreadsheet on paper. It also lets you store a "printed" spreadsheet on disk.

- The **Worksheet Erase command** clears the current worksheet out of memory, providing you with a blank worksheet. This command does not affect already saved worksheets.

- To leave the spreadsheet program and return to DOS, you must use the main **Quit command** from the command menu. Always save your file before you quit, since many spreadsheet programs do not automatically save files.

- The **Help key** places you in the HELP mode. This mode is **context sensitive**—that is, it offers helpful information related to the command you were using when you pressed the Help key. While in HELP mode, you can select the **help index,** which gives you access to an on-screen reference manual.

- Programs in an **integrated package** share a common methodology and command structure, which make learning and data transfer easier. **Stand-alone programs** can be integrated by a **universal manager program** that presents a common interface to the user and handles data transfer among the programs.

- **Business graphics** represent business data in a visual, easily understood format. They help users analyze data, and they help make business reports more interesting.

- **Analytical graphics** programs help users analyze and understand specific data. **Presentation graphics programs,** or **business-quality programs,** produce more sophisticated graphics that are appropriate for formal presentations. Presentation graphics programs also contain a library of symbols and drawings called **clip art.**

- A **line graph** has lines that define a period of time and the units measured. Each line is called an **axis.** The horizontal line is called the **x-axis,** and the vertical line is called the **y-axis.** The area inside the x-axis and y-axis is the **plot area.** Each dot or symbol on a line graph is a **data point.** Each data point represents a value. The items that the data points describe are called **variables.**

- Graphs that plot the values of only one variable are called **single-range graphs.** A **multiple-range graph** plots more than one variable.

- **Bar graphs** show data comparisons by the lengths or heights of bars in columns or rows. In a **single-range bar graph,** only one variable is involved. A **clustered-bar graph** shows more than one variable. A **stacked-bar graph** also shows multiple variables, but the bars are stacked on top of one another. You can create a **legend** to explain the colors or symbols on a complex graph. **Labels** identify the categories along the x-axis and the units along the y-axis. **Titles** summarize the information in the graph.

- A **pie chart** represents a single variable and shows how different values make up a whole. Each wedge of the pie represents a value. On an **exploded pie chart,** a wedge is pulled slightly away from the pie for emphasis.

7 Review Questions

1. In a spreadsheet, what is the intersection of a row and column called?

2. Where are the entries in a spreadsheet stored?

3. How are individual columns and rows identified on an electronic spreadsheet?

4. What is meant by the formula @AVG(B1..B10)? Where will the result of calculating this formula be displayed on the screen?

5. What is another way to write the formula +A1+A2+A3+A4+A5?

6. What is a range?

7. Regardless of the cursor's location in the spreadsheet, what are three ways in which you can move the cursor to Cell A1?

8. What are three of the modes in which Lotus 1-2-3 operates?

9. What mode must you be in to make an entry in a cell? Can you make an entry in a cell when you see the command menu on the screen?

10. What key do you press to access the command menu?

11. What is displayed in the mode indicator when you start to enter a value in a cell? What is displayed in the mode indicator when you start to enter a label in a cell?

12. What are some of the commands available in the command menu?

13. What is a submenu? How do you access a submenu? How do you make a choice from a submenu?

14. What is automatic recalculation?

15. What command in Lotus 1-2-3 lets you store, retrieve, list, or erase your worksheet files?

16. Why are personal computer graphics used in business?

17. Explain the difference between analytical and presentation graphics.

18. Describe the similarities and differences between a single-range bar graph, a clustered-bar graph, and a stacked-bar graph.

19. What is an exploded pie chart?

Chapter 14. Database Management Systems: Getting Data Together

14

Database Management Systems

Getting Data Together

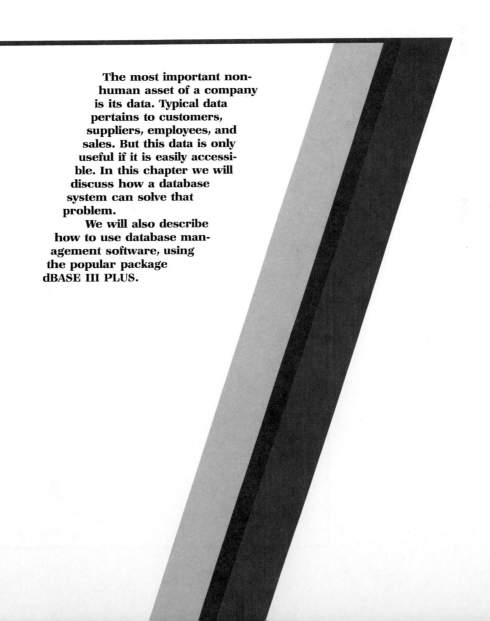

The most important non-human asset of a company is its data. Typical data pertains to customers, suppliers, employees, and sales. But this data is only useful if it is easily accessible. In this chapter we will discuss how a database system can solve that problem.

We will also describe how to use database management software, using the popular package dBASE III PLUS.

Storing and using data is absolutely vital in today's society. A **database** is an organized collection of related data. In a loose sense you are using a database when you use a phone book, look in a library's card catalog, or take a file out of a file cabinet. Unfortunately, as the amount of data increases, creating, storing, changing, sorting, and retrieving data become overwhelming tasks. For example, suppose you had a collection of names and addresses, each on a separate index card stored in a box (Figure 14-1). If you had only 25 cards, putting the cards in alphabetical order or even finding all the people who have the same zip code would be fairly easy. But what if you had 100, or 1000, or 10,000 cards? What if you had several different boxes, one organized by names, one by cities, and one by zip codes? What if you had different people adding more cards each day, not knowing if they were duplicating other cards in the file? And what if you had another set of people trying to update the data on the cards? As you can see, things might get out of hand. Enter computers and database management software.

7 Getting It Together: Database Programs

A **database management system (DBMS)** is software that helps you organize data in a way that allows fast and easy access to the data. In essence, the program acts as a very efficient and elaborate file system. With a database program you can create, mod-

Figure 14-1   An index-card database.   Each card in this index-card file contains one person's name and address. The cards are arranged alphabetically by last name.

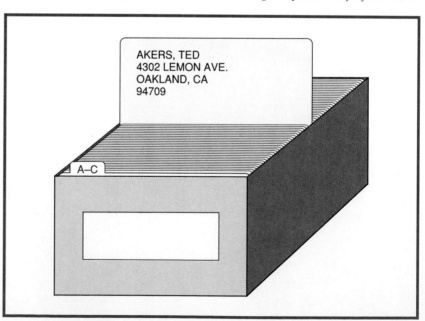

AKERS, TED
4302 LEMON AVE.
OAKLAND, CA
94709

A–C

MICROCOMPUTERS IN ACTION

When The Doctor Needs Help—Fast

The girl brought to the emergency room was bitten by a poisonous snake. The obvious treatment is an antipoison drug. But sometimes things are not simple. The "obvious" treatment is risky because the girl already has a blood disorder. Time is of the essence. Fortunately, speed and the computer are one.

The name of the computer system is MEDLINE, and it saves lives. In the snakebite case, an aid uses a hospital terminal to tap into the MEDLINE database at the National Library of Medicine in Bethesda, Maryland. In seconds, the computer searches

through millions of medical journal articles, and the doctor selects pertinent ones from the titles that appear on the terminal screen. The drug will not help, but a blood transfusion will.

MEDLINE is used in emergency rooms, operating rooms, and wherever else doctors need help in a hurry. It is especially helpful in rural areas where a doctor may not have seen a particular set of symptoms before. Medical expertise is as close as the terminal and as fast as the computer. It is also reasonably priced: An average database search costs less than $3.

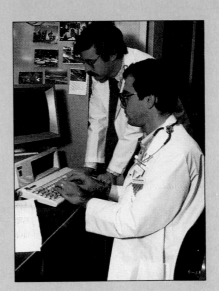

TRANSPARENCY ACETATE #14A
Multiple Uses of a File

DISCUSSION QUESTION
What are some advantages of
database management systems?

ify, store, and retrieve data in a variety of ways. Some benefits of database management system software are

- **Integrated files.** Using a database, separate files can be joined together. For example, consider two file drawers, one for customers and one for sales representatives. Suppose you needed data— perhaps the address of a sales rep who helped a particular customer. You would have to look first in the customer drawer to find the name of the sales rep and then in the sales rep drawer to find the sales rep's address. Database programs smooth the way for these types of searches by storing the relationships needed to combine data from different files stored on disk.

- **Reduced redundancy.** When businesses have many different files, the same data is often stored in several different places. In a database, data is usually stored in just one place. This reduces the amount of duplicate data in the system. In addition, updating can be done quickly and efficiently without having to track down the repeated data.

- **Shared data.** Data in files can be shared by different people. Separate files for each department or function are unnecessary. Data can be stored once and accessed by authorized people using computers.

- **Centralized security.** When data is all in one place, you have better control over access to it. Scattered files are more difficult to

The databases are out there, thousands of them, but who gets to use them? You—if you can pay the price. A whole new business has sprung up around databases and the research expertise needed to use them.

Consider this example. Suppose you are a businessperson contemplating investing in a food product that depends on tomatoes. But you are concerned about the effect of recent weather on the crop and, therefore, on the price of tomatoes. Before you invest your money, you might choose to call an information broker who has access to on-line databases. You can ask the broker as many questions as you like. Who grows tomatoes? How are they processed? What about pesticides? Which major companies buy tomatoes? Is there a coming shortage? And so forth.

Many databases can be accessed on-line—that is, from a computer using a modem. For this example, the information broker might tap these databases: Agricola (from the U.S. National Agricultural Library), the Trade and Industry Index, the American Statistical Index, and Food Science and Technology Abstracts.

But this is just one example. The approximately 3000 on-line databases cover every subject from computer dating to brain surgery.

TRANSPARENCY ACETATE #14B
Skeleton drawings of database models

TEST BANK
Mult. Choice	5-26
T/F	10-51
Matching A	4-10
Matching B	2-8
Matching C	3-10
Matching D	1-2
Fill-in-the-Blank	5-30

protect. Security is particularly important for personnel files, restricted product information, customer credit ratings, marketing plans, and similar sensitive data.

In this chapter we will show you how to create and modify a database. But first we need to discuss some of the general terms used with databases.

7 Using a Database Management System

There are a large number of DBMS programs on the market today. Covering all the operations, features, and functions of every individual package would be impossible. Therefore, throughout this chapter, we will discuss the characteristics and features of one of the most popular database programs—dBASE III PLUS, which we will call dBASE for short. This program has many features in common with other database software packages.

7 Database Organization

In a file system, data is stored in segregated files. A file system cannot store information about how data in one file is related to data in another file. A database, however, can store data relationships, so files can be integrated. Data stored in integrated files can be combined. The way the database organizes data depends on the type, or **model,** of the database.

There are three database models—hierarchical, network, and relational. Each type structures, organizes, and uses data differently. Hierarchical and network databases are usually found on mainframes and minicomputers, so we will not discuss them here. On personal computers, however, relational databases are usually used.

A **relational database** organizes data in a table format consisting of related rows and columns. Figure 14-2a shows an address list; in Figure 14-2b, this data is laid out as a table. In a relational system, data in one file can be related to data in another, allowing you to tie together data from several files.

7 Fields, Records, and Files

In a relational database a table is called a **relation.** Notice in Figure 14-2b that each box in the table contains a piece of data, known as a **data item.** Each column of the table represents a **field,** or **attribute.** The specific data items in a field may vary, but each field contains the same type of data—for example, first names or zip codes. In a given relation there is a fixed number of fields. All the

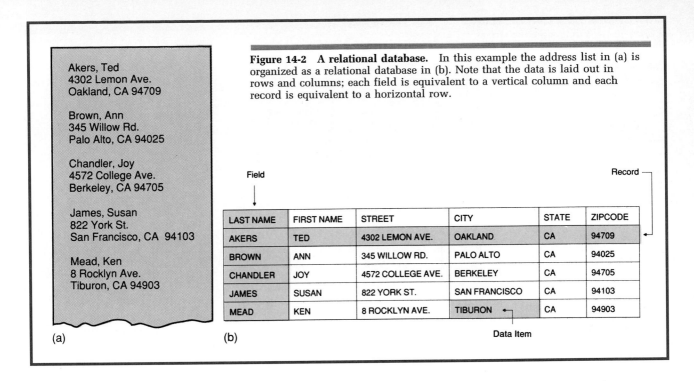

Akers, Ted
4302 Lemon Ave.
Oakland, CA 94709

Brown, Ann
345 Willow Rd.
Palo Alto, CA 94025

Chandler, Joy
4572 College Ave.
Berkeley, CA 94705

James, Susan
822 York St.
San Francisco, CA 94103

Mead, Ken
8 Rocklyn Ave.
Tiburon, CA 94903

Figure 14-2   A relational database.   In this example the address list in (a) is organized as a relational database in (b). Note that the data is laid out in rows and columns; each field is equivalent to a vertical column and each record is equivalent to a horizontal row.

Field

Record

LAST NAME	FIRST NAME	STREET	CITY	STATE	ZIPCODE
AKERS	TED	4302 LEMON AVE.	OAKLAND	CA	94709
BROWN	ANN	345 WILLOW RD.	PALO ALTO	CA	94025
CHANDLER	JOY	4572 COLLEGE AVE.	BERKELEY	CA	94705
JAMES	SUSAN	822 YORK ST.	SAN FRANCISCO	CA	94103
MEAD	KEN	8 ROCKLYN AVE.	TIBURON	CA	94903

(a)   (b)   Data Item

TRANSPARENCY ACETATE #14C
Figure #14-2

data in any given row is called a **record,** or **tuple.** Each record has a fixed number of fields, but there can be a variable number of records in a given relation. Figure 14-2b shows five records—one for each person. A relation—a table—is also called a **file.** Furthermore, a database file can be considered a collection of records. Although we have introduced the formal terms *attribute, tuple,* and *relation* in this discussion, we shall be referring to them by their more common names: *field, record,* and *file,* respectively.

File Structure

There are two steps to creating a database file: designing the structure of the file and entering the data into the file. To create the file structure, you must choose meaningful fields. The fields you choose should be based on the data you will want to retrieve from the database. For example, if you are creating a list of addresses, you might define fields for name, street address, city, state, and zip code. After you load the program and tell the software that you want to create a file structure, you see a structure input form on the screen. The form is similar to Figure 14-3. Notice that the program asks for several types of information. Let us take a look at each one.

Field Names

Names of the types of data you want to use are called **field names.** For example, a field called PHONE could be used to contain a phone number. A field name can be up to ten characters long, must

Figure 14-3　Building the file structure. When you create a file structure, you must fill in information about the field name, field type, and field width for each field in your database.

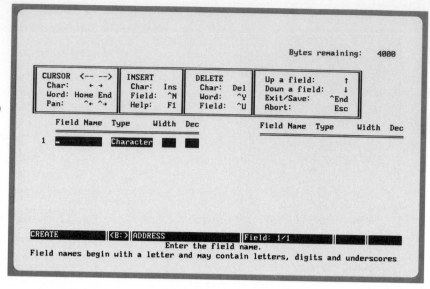

begin with a letter, and cannot contain a space or any punctuation. Letters, numbers, and underscores are permitted.

Field Types

There are four commonly used **field types:** character fields, numeric fields, date fields, and logical fields. **Character fields** contain descriptive data such as names, addresses, and telephone numbers. **Numeric fields** contain numbers used for calculations. When you enter a numeric field, you must specify the number of decimal places you wish to use. **Date fields** are automatically limited to eight characters, including the slashes used to separate the month, day, and year. **Logical fields** accept only single characters. Logical fields are used to keep track of true and false conditions. For example, if you want to keep track of whether a bill has been paid, you could use a logical field and enter Y for *yes* or N for *no.*

Field Widths

The **field width** determines the maximum number of characters or digits to be contained in the field, including decimal points. Most database programs let you enter up to 128 fields in each record, and each character type field can be up to 254 characters.

7 Telling the Program What to Do

The dBASE program gives you two options for entering commands: You can either use a menu—called the **Assistant menu**—or type in commands directly by using the **COMMAND mode.** Either method gets the job done.

Figure 14-4   Telling dBASE III PLUS what to do.   The dBASE program gives you two options for entering commands: (a) The Assistant menu offers you a series of choices. You can use the cursor movement keys and Enter to make your selections. (b) When you are in the COMMAND mode, you see a dot—called the dot prompt—near the lower left of your screen. With the limited-use version of dBASE III PLUS, the prompt is a dot followed by the word (DEMO). In this mode you simply type in the command you want to use and then press Enter.

TRANSPARENCY ACETATE #14E
Figure #14-4

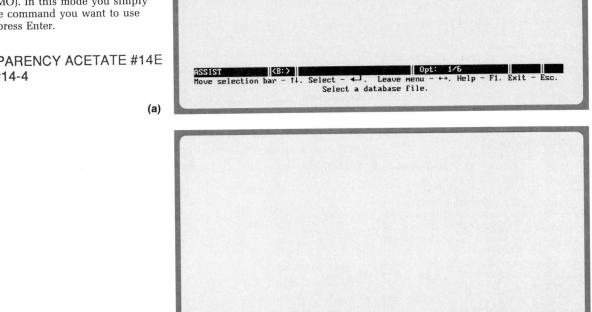

(a)

(b)

Dot prompt

DISCUSSION QUESTION
In the Assistant menu, how is the desired command selected? Which keys are used in this process?

The Assistant Menu

When you first access dBASE, the Assistant menu appears on the screen, as shown in Figure 14-4a. This menu offers a set of choices. Each selection on the top line of the menu has an associated **selection bar** that appears when the main selection is highlighted by the cursor. In Figure 14-4a, for example, the cursor rests on Set Up; the associated selection bar offers the choices "Database file," "Format for Screen," "Query," "Catalog," "View," and "Quit dBASE III PLUS." You can use the right and left cursor keys to move the cursor back and forth across the menu choices on the top line. When you wish to select an option, highlight that option with the cursor and press Enter.

MUSEUMS NEED COMPUTERS TOO

You are in charge of a large art museum and have a chance to make some money for the museum if you can put together a traveling collection of landscape oils in two weeks. Should you—your official title is curator—just wander around the museum and lift some appropriate candidates off the walls? Unfortunately, it is not that simple. Some of the landscapes are not in oil. Some are on loan from individuals or other museums. Some have been judged too fragile to be moved. And so on. All this information is in a file drawer—somewhere—but it will be impossible to get everything organized in two weeks. The computer to the rescue!

Modern museums have information about their collections stored in computer databases. Using appropriate search fields, such as subject matter (LANDSCAPE in this example), a list of appropriate candidates can be printed quickly. Other concerns, such as ownership, can be built into the search. Such databases store all sorts of information about the collection—location, donor, date, value, and so forth. All kinds of searches can be performed.

Museums use databases to store another important set of data, their donors. Once entered into the database, donors' names can be retrieved in a variety of ways. For example, if you are a major contributor (say, "amount greater than 10,000"), your record might be retrieved so that you can be invited to a special awards dinner.

The COMMAND Mode

If you want to issue commands directly to dBASE, you need to dismiss the Assistant menu and enter the COMMAND mode. To do this, press the Esc (Escape) key once. The menu screen disappears and a dot, called the **dot prompt,** appears near the lower left of your screen (Figure 14-4b). When you see the dot prompt, the program is ready for you to type a command. It is similar to the A prompt (A>) that signals you that the operating system is ready for a DOS command. After typing each command, press Enter. You can return to the Assistant menu any time by typing ASSIST after the dot prompt and then pressing Enter. In fact, you can switch back and forth between the Assistant menu and the dot prompt any time you want to; as noted, Esc takes you from the menu to the dot prompt, and ASSIST takes you from the dot prompt to the Assistant menu.

7 Relational Operators

At times, you will need to use a **relational operator** when making comparisons or when entering instructions. The following relational operators are commonly used:

Command	Explanation
<	Less than
>	Greater than
=	Equal to
<=	Less than or equal to
>=	Greater than or equal to
<>	Not equal to

These operators are particularly useful when you want to locate specific data items. For example, to instruct a program to search through an address database and find the records of all the people who live in Wisconsin, you would enter the command

```
LIST FOR STATE = "WI"
```

This tells the program to look for the characters WI in the state field.

Now that we have reviewed the basics of database programs, let us move on to the most critical part of using a DBMS—the design and creation of a database.

7 Building a Database

Rita Chung works as an intern for a public television station in the San Francisco area. One of her jobs is to keep track of the people who have pledged to donate money to the station. Currently, each person's name, city, and phone number is kept on a separate card, along with the amount pledged and the date the pledge was made. Rita wants to place this data into a computer by

Figure 14-5 Designing the file structure. Rita quickly sketches how she wants to set up her database. Note that she has seven fields—LNAME, FNAME, CITY, PHONE, AMOUNT, DATE, and PAID.

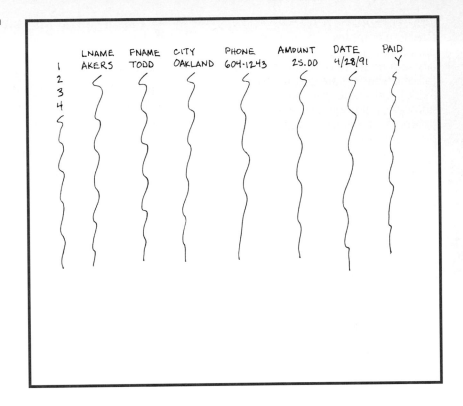

using dBASE. She also wants to add another column of data that tells whether each person has actually paid the amount he or she pledged.

First Rita sketches on paper the structure of the database—what data she wants in each row and column (Figure 14-5). Her next step is to enter this structure into the computer. (An abbreviated version—keystrokes only—of the following discussion appears in Appendix B.)

7 Loading the Program

To use dBASE, Rita must first boot the system. Once she sees the A> on the screen, she places dBASE Disk #1 in drive A and her formatted data disk in drive B. Then she types DBASE and presses Enter. When the program has been loaded, dBASE displays a copyright notice and asks Rita to press Enter to start the program. Then dBASE displays the instruction "Insert System Disk 2 and press Enter, or press Ctrl-C to abort."

Rita removes Disk #1, and places Disk #2 in drive A. Then she presses Enter again, which causes the Assistant menu to appear on the screen. Throughout the rest of this chapter we will be using the COMMAND mode, but Appendix B includes keystrokes for executing these examples using the COMMAND mode and using the Assistant menu.

TRANSPARENCY ACETATE #14F
Figure #14-6

Figure 14-6 Creating the file structure. (a) Once Rita is in the COMMAND mode, she types in CREATE after the dot prompt and presses Enter. dBASE then asks her to name the new file. (b) After Rita enters the name B:PLEDGES, a Create screen appears. The lower highlighted line on the screen tells Rita several pieces of information (from left to right): the mode she is in (CREATE), the disk drive where her file will be stored (B), the name of her file (PLEDGES), and the number of fields currently in the file (1/1). The program uses the last two lines to prompt Rita regarding her next step.

7 Creating the File Structure

As we mentioned earlier, before Rita can enter data into her database, she needs to create the file structure for her files. She starts by pressing the Esc key to leave the ASSISTANT mode. The dot prompt appears in the lower-left corner of the screen. This means that the program is ready for Rita to enter a command. To create a file structure, she types CREATE and presses Enter. dBASE responds by asking for the name of the file she wishes to create (Figure 14-6a). Because Rita wants to store the data file on her data disk in drive B, she types in B:PLEDGES and presses Enter. When she does this, a Create screen appears, and the cursor flashes under

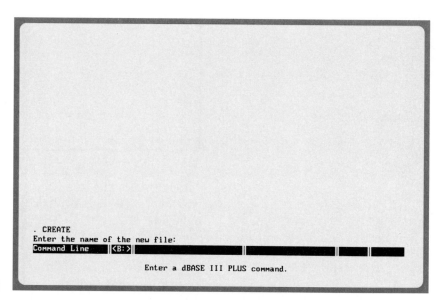

(a)

(b)

the Field Name heading (Figure 14-6b). Notice that "CREATE" appears in the lower-left corner of the screen. dBASE uses this space to tell you what command you are currently using. Under the lower highlighted bar, the program prompts Rita regarding her next step. In this case, dBASE prompts her to enter a field name and also defines the guidelines for doing so.

Now Rita fills in the blanks for each field in her database. She types in LNAME for *last name* (remember, dBASE does not accept spaces in field names) and presses Enter. The cursor moves to the Type column. In Figure 14-7a notice the word "Character" under the Type column. If Rita wanted to enter another type of field, she could press the Spacebar until the appropriate field type appeared in the

Figure 14-7   Entering fields into the file structure. (a) Rita starts to fill in the definitions for the first field in her file. When she presses Enter, the cursor moves to the next column. (b) When Rita has completed the information for one field, the cursor moves down to the next line.

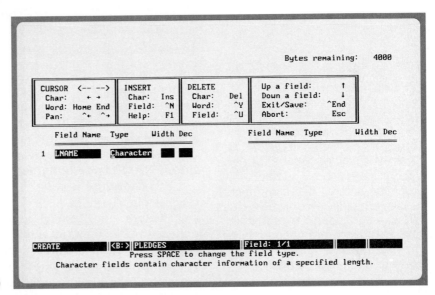

(a)

(b)

Figure 14-8 The completed file structure. Rita has filled in all the information on the file structure. To save this structure and return to the dot prompt, Rita can press Enter or Ctrl-End.

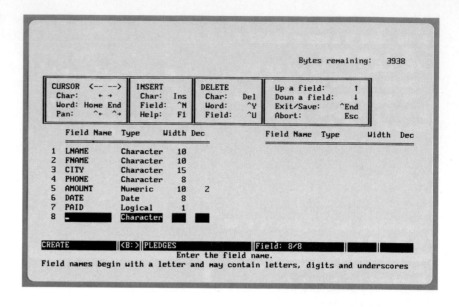

DISCUSSION QUESTION
A phone number consists of three sets of digits: area code, city code, and exchange number. How would this be coded in dBASE III files? Would it be entered as three integer fields? (The number would be entered into a character field of ten digits — or twelve digits if dashes are used. Two or three character fields are needed only if the user requires access by city code or exchange number.)

DISCUSSION QUESTION
How is the computer told that no more fields will be added to the structure?

DISCUSSION QUESTION
How can the entire structure be viewed after the structure is completed?

column. However, LNAME is a character field, so she simply presses Enter and the cursor moves on to the Width column. Rita wants the width of the LNAME field to be ten characters wide, so she types 10. After she presses Enter, the cursor moves down to the next line (Figure 14-7b). Note that the decimal place column (Dec) was ignored, since LNAME is not a numeric field.

Rita continues to enter the fields. The completed field structure is shown in Figure 14-8. Notice that she defined the PHONE field as a character field. Although a phone number contains numbers, it is not used in calculations and is, therefore, a character field. Rita did not have to define a width for the DATE field or the PAID field; the widths for date fields and logical fields are entered automatically when the field types are defined.

Once Rita has finished creating the file structure, she signals dBASE that she is done by pressing Enter without filling in any data. The program asks her to confirm her action by pressing Enter. When she does, dBASE responds with the prompt "Input Data Records Now? (Y/N)." Rita wants to double-check her file structure before she enters the data, so she types N. This returns her to the COMMAND mode.

7 Viewing the Structure

Rita can view the completed file structure by using the List Structure command. At the dot prompt she types in LIST STRUCTURE and presses Enter. dBASE responds by displaying the screen shown in Figure 14-9. Notice that the number of data records shown is 0. When Rita enters the data, this number will change to show the total number of records she has entered.

Figure 14-9 Viewing the structure.
Rita uses the List Structure command to look at the structure of her data file. Notice that the total number of characters for this file is one more than the sum of the numbers in the Width column. The reason for this is that dBASE automatically adds a one-character field at the beginning of each record to make room for special symbols.

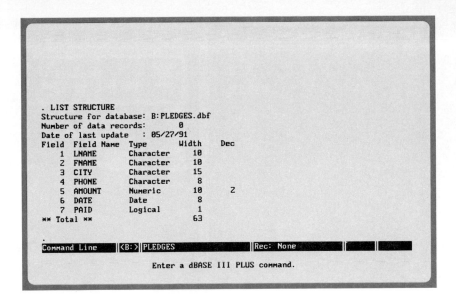

DISCUSSION QUESTION
What command do we use to enter data into the structure formed earlier?

7 Entering the Data

To enter records into the database, Rita uses the Append command. When she sees the dot prompt, she types APPEND and presses Enter. dBASE uses the database structure—the field definitions she just typed in—to provide an input form, as shown in Figure 14-10. The designated width for each field is highlighted.

Figure 14-10 The data input form.
Rita uses the Append command to access a data input form for her file. The highlighted areas show the designated field width for each field.

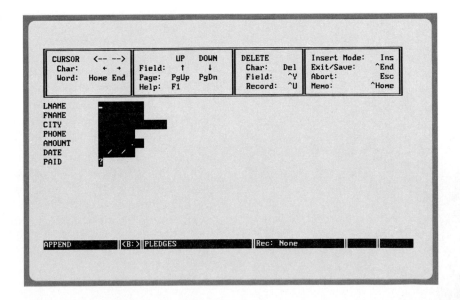

Figure 14-11 Entering the data. Rita fills in the data for the first record.

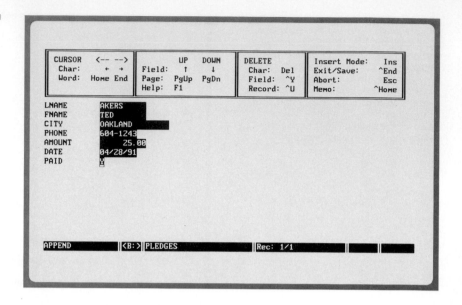

DISCUSSION QUESTION
Once a field of data is entered, how is the next field entered within the same record? What is the procedure to quit a record? How do you indicate that you are finished entering records?

Using the input form is easy—all Rita has to do is fill in the blanks. Each time Rita finishes typing in an entry, she presses Enter to move to the next field. However, if the width of the entry is exactly the size of the field, the program automatically advances to the next field. If Rita tries to enter too much data into the field, the system beeps or displays an error message. If Rita makes a mistake while she is typing, she can use the Backspace key to make corrections. Once Rita has filled in all the data for the first record (Figure 14-11), dBASE displays another blank input form, so Rita can enter the data items for the fields in the second record. She continues in this manner until all the data records are entered. Then she presses Enter or holds down the Ctrl key while pressing the End key. All the created records are stored automatically, and dBASE returns to the dot prompt.

7 Listing the Records

DISCUSSION QUESTION
Is it possible to view the records compactly (one record per line)?

The entry screens are adequate for entering data, but it is hard to go through them to look for errors—especially if the database is very large. dBASE has a handy command for viewing the contents of a file—the List command. To see a list of all the records she just typed in, Rita types LIST and presses Enter. A list of the records, as shown in Figure 14-12a, appears on the screen. Notice that under the PAID column a "T" (true) or an "F" (false) appears, although Y or N were entered. Since the PAID column is a logical field, dBASE automatically translates the Y and N into T and F, respectively. After the listing appears, dBASE returns to the dot prompt.

Figure 14-12 Listing records. (a) Rita uses the List command to look at the records she has entered into the PLEDGES file. (b) Rita can use a variation of the List command to view data in specific fields. In this case she wants to see the data contained in the LNAME, PAID, and PHONE fields.

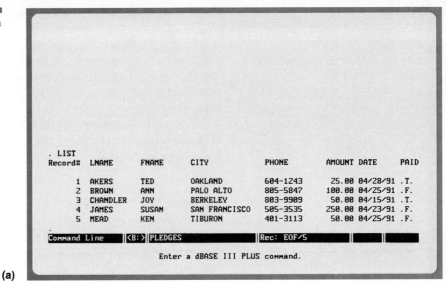

```
. LIST
Record#  LNAME      FNAME     CITY            PHONE      AMOUNT  DATE      PAID

      1  AKERS      TED       OAKLAND         604-1243    25.00  04/28/91  .T.
      2  BROWN      ANN       PALO ALTO       805-5847   100.00  04/25/91  .F.
      3  CHANDLER   JOY       BERKELEY        803-9909    50.00  04/15/91  .T.
      4  JAMES      SUSAN     SAN FRANCISCO   505-3535   250.00  04/23/91  .F.
      5  MEAD       KEN       TIBURON         401-3113    50.00  04/25/91  .F.

Command Line     <B:> PLEDGES                Rec: EOF/5

              Enter a dBASE III PLUS command.
```

(a)

```
. LIST LNAME, PAID, PHONE
Record#  LNAME      PAID  PHONE
      1  AKERS      .T.   604-1243
      2  BROWN      .F.   805-5847
      3  CHANDLER   .T.   803-9909
      4  JAMES      .F.   505-3535
      5  MEAD       .F.   401-3113
.
Command Line     <B:> PLEDGES                Rec: EOF/5

              Enter a dBASE III PLUS command.
```

(b)

DISCUSSION QUESTION
If only a few fields are to be selected, can you specify viewing several records simultaneously?

Listing Specific Fields

Suppose Rita wants to see only some of the fields in the database. She can use a variation of the List command to do this. At the dot prompt, she types LIST followed by the fields she wants to see in the order she wants to see them. For example, Rita decides she wants to see a list that shows just the LNAME, PAID, and PHONE fields, in that order. To do this, she types:

```
LIST LNAME, PAID, PHONE
```

and presses Enter. dBASE then displays the list shown in Figure 14-12b.

DISCUSSION QUESTION
What is the procedure for saving
information on disk?

7 Closing the Files and Exiting the Program

To close the file without leaving dBASE, Rita types in USE at the dot prompt and presses Enter. The current file closes and the dot prompt reappears. Rita can either reopen the file by typing USE again or create another database file by using the Create command.

Now Rita wants to exit the program and return to DOS. She does this by typing QUIT. The Quit command closes all the files and returns Rita to DOS.

DISCUSSION QUESTION
How can the Help function be
accessed? (There are two ways to
access it.)

7 Getting Help

If Rita needs help when using dBASE III PLUS, she can use the F1 function key to access a help program. If she has the Assistant menu on her screen, she can get information on each choice by using the cursor movement keys to highlight a choice on the menu. Then she presses the F1 key. A help screen for that choice appears. She presses the Escape key to leave the help screen and resume her work.

When she is using dot prompt commands, she can get help by typing HELP followed by a space and then the command name. For example, if she wants help with the List command, she types:

```
HELP LIST
```

and presses Enter (Figure 14-13).

Figure 14-13   A help screen. The dBASE help feature provides an on-line user guide. In this example Rita has asked for information about the List command by typing HELP LIST at the dot prompt.

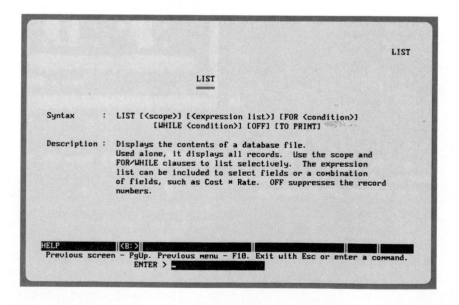

PERSPECTIVES

DO YOU WANT YOUR PICTURE IN THE COMPUTER?

Take the concept of database one step further: In addition to storing data about an object, the computer can store its picture. The idea is a natural for computers that have high-resolution screens. It is also a good fit for any application where visuals enhance knowledge. But what if the "object," whose data and picture are stored in a database, is a person?

For example, personnel records often include a photo database. Employers use such files for employee identification and a host of other reasons. Consider this scenario. Company executives gather in the boardroom to discuss promoting stellar employees to partner status. At one point the discussion focuses on Robert Smith. However, an executive from a different division cannot recall who Robert is. No problem. In moments the face of Robert Smith, along with related career information, is retrieved from the company database and flashed on the overhead screen. Ah, yes. Robert is the fellow who gave the dynamic presentation on new marketing directions at the annual meeting. Robert is in.

There certainly are advantages in having photos of employees available from the computer. This is especially true of large firms with offices in several states or even countries. Some companies have found computer retrieval

useful for the employee review process. Companies who used to rely on slide presentations were constrained by a prescribed presentation order; a database system permits any employee record to be retrieved at any time.

However, photo identification presents a new set of problems. First on the list is privacy. Think of all the computer files that contain your name and address, and then consider how that information is shared and sold, with very little control. The net result is in your mailbox. Although many of us have resigned ourselves to losing control over our addresses, having our pictures passed from computer to computer is another matter.

Photo identification also makes all kinds of discrimination possible. Discrimination by race, sex, or age is illegal in the United States, but a photo increases the opportunity for such discrimination. In addition, an employee could be discriminated against for being overweight, bald, or poorly dressed. In fact, just about any subjective reason will do if a viewer is inclined to discriminate.

You may be required to smile for the corporate camera. Companies thus far have been responsible about protecting employee photos. Be cautious, however, about letting your picture be part of just any computer file.

DISCUSSION QUESTION
Can problems occur when
pictures are stored in databases?

BIRDS OF THE COMPUTER

Photo researchers specialize in finding just the right pictures for books and articles. Working from a list of photo requests, they contact their sources, which range from agencies that keep thousands of pictures on hand to an individual photographer who has taken a single exquisite picture. The job is time-consuming and the pressure is always on to make deadlines. But photo researchers now have a new tool: a visual archive, by way of computer photo databases.

A photo researcher can use a data communications system to retrieve the flamingo shown above from a distant photo database and view it on a computer screen.

TEST BANK

Mult. Choice	34-44
T/F	62-76
Matching D	5-10
Fill-in-the-Blank	36-43

DISCUSSION QUESTION
How is an existing database file in dBASE III PLUS opened?

DISCUSSION QUESTION
What are some methods for modifying existing records in a dBASE III PLUS database file?

7 Changing the Database

Once a database file exists, it is unlikely to stay the same for very long. Over a period of time, new records are added, and others are changed or even deleted. Changes can be made to every record in the database, selected records, or one specific record. Most database programs provide a variety of commands that let you maintain data. The main editing commands in dBASE are Edit, Browse, Append, and Delete. Let us return to Rita Chung to see how these different commands work.

7 Opening Files

To add, edit, or delete data in a file, it is necessary to tell dBASE which file it needs to use. The Use command, followed by a file name, opens the desired file. Rita presses the Esc key to access the dot prompt mode. Then she types USE B:PLEDGES, which tells dBASE to open the file called PLEDGES—that is, to make PLEDGES available for use. Then Rita presses Enter. When a database file is open, the name of the file will be displayed at the bottom of the screen.

7 Modifying Existing Records

When one of Rita's coworkers hands her a list of pledge activity, she notices that one of her existing records, Record 1, needs to be updated—Ted Akers has a new phone number. She also notices that Ann Brown has paid, so Rita needs to record the payment in Record 2. To modify these records, Rita can use one of two commands: the Edit command or the Browse command. We will use the Edit command to change one record and then use Browse to change the other.

Using the Edit Command
The Edit command allows editing of data in an individual record. Therefore, to use it, Rita must tell dBASE which record she wants to see. To edit Record 1, Rita types EDIT 1 and then presses Enter. Record 1 appears on the screen (Figure 14-14a). Rita moves the cursor to the PHONE field, then types in the new phone number. (If necessary, she can also use the Ins and Del keys to make additional changes to the data.) Notice in Figure 14-14b that the new data is written over the old data. To store the changed record in the database and return to the dot prompt, Rita presses Ctrl-End.

Once Rita has used the Edit command to access a particular record, she can edit previous or succeeding records in the file by pressing the PgUp or PgDn key. The PgUp key moves her to a previous record; the PgDn key moves her to the next record.

Figure 14-14 Modifying records with the Edit command. (a) Rita uses the Edit command to make changes to Record 1. (b) As she types in the changes, the new data is written over the old.

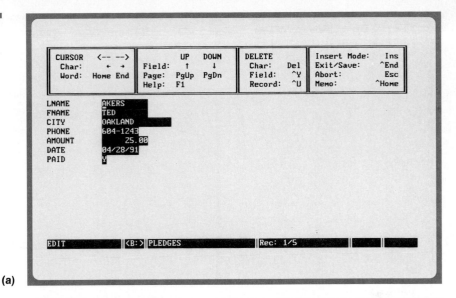

(a)

(b)

DISCUSSION QUESTION
How do the Edit and Browse commands differ?

Using the Browse Command

The Browse command provides the same editing capabilities as the Edit command. However, Browse displays all the records in the database. The program displays only as much data as will fit on the screen—usually about 12 records. To see records not shown on the screen, you can scroll up and down by using the PgUp and PgDn keys. If there are a number of fields in a record, you may have to **pan**—move horizontally across the screen—to the left or right by using the Ctrl key and the left or right cursor key.

To use the Browse command, Rita types in BROWSE and then presses Enter. Since there are currently only five records in her file,

Figure 14-15   The Browse screen.
Rita can use the Browse command to view and modify the records in her database.

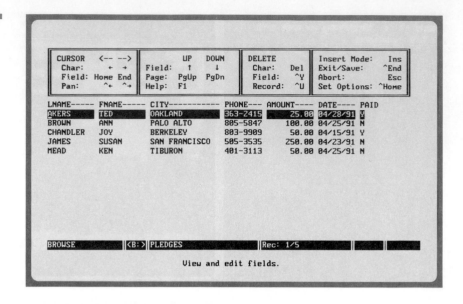

CURSOR	<-- -->		UP	DOWN	DELETE		Insert Mode:	Ins
Char:	← →	Field:	↑	↓	Char:	Del	Exit/Save:	^End
Field:	Home End	Page:	PgUp	PgDn	Field:	^Y	Abort:	Esc
Pan:	^← ^→	Help:	F1		Record:	^U	Set Options:	^Home

```
LNAME----- FNAME----- CITY---------- PHONE--- AMOUNT---- DATE---- PAID
AKERS      TED        OAKLAND        363-2415    25.00 04/28/91 Y
BROWN      ANN        PALO ALTO      805-5847   100.00 04/25/91 N
CHANDLER   JOY        BERKELEY       883-9909    50.00 04/15/91 Y
JAMES      SUSAN      SAN FRANCISCO  505-3535   250.00 04/23/91 N
MEAD       KEN        TIBURON        401-3113    50.00 04/25/91 N
```

```
BROWSE            <B:> PLEDGES              Rec: 1/5
                    View and edit fields.
```

the screen displays all the records (Figure 14-15). To update Record 2, Rita moves the cursor down to Record 2 and over to the PAID field. Then she types Y. After she has made the change, she presses Ctrl-End to save the data and return to the dot prompt.

7 Adding Records

When Rita wants to add new records to her database, she can use either the Append command or the Browse command. Suppose Rita receives data on two new subscribers—Mary Schwartz and Ted Greenlee—to add to the database. Let us examine how she would use each command.

Adding Records with Append

To add the first new record—Mary Schwartz—Rita types APPEND and presses Enter. A blank data entry form for the PLEDGES file, just like the one used to add the original records, appears on the screen. Rita types in the data on Mary Schwartz, pressing Enter after typing data into each field. The completed screen is shown in Figure 14-16.

Before Rita stores the data in the database, she wants to check to make sure everything is correct. Since the program automatically moved to the next record when Rita filled in the PAID field, she has to use the PgUp key to return to Mary's record. After Rita has checked over the data, she presses Enter, and a blank input screen appears. Rita can continue adding records to the database in this manner. When she is finished, she presses Ctrl-End. The dot prompt reappears.

Figure 14-16   Adding records with Append. Rita uses the Append command to add Mary Schwartz's record.

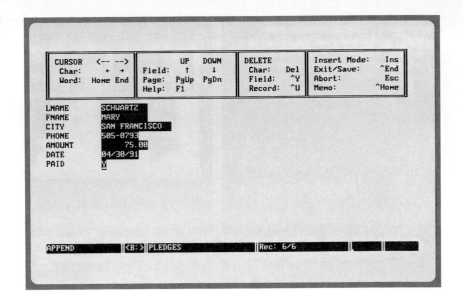

Adding Records with Browse

As we mentioned before, the Browse command displays a number of records at one time. To use this command to add records, Rita types BROWSE and presses Enter. Then she moves the cursor to the last record in the file. Next Rita presses the down cursor key to move beyond the last record (Figure 14-17a). dBASE asks her if she wants to add records. When she types Y for *yes*, a new blank record appears. Rita types in the data on Ted Greenlee (Figure 14-17b). When she is done, she once again presses Ctrl-End to store the data.

7 Deleting Records

Sometimes a record must be removed—deleted—from a database file. Deleting records from a file is a two-step process. First, the specific records must be marked for deletion by using the Delete command or the Browse command. Second, the record must be permanently removed from the file by using the Pack command. Note that once you remove a record by using the Pack command, the record cannot be recovered.

Deleting with the Browse Command

Suppose Rita receives a note indicating that Joy Chandler has moved and no longer wishes to donate to the station; the Chandler record needs to be deleted from the PLEDGES file. Rita types BROWSE and presses Enter. Then she moves the cursor to Chandler's record and presses Ctrl-U. The word "Del" appears in the

DISCUSSION QUESTION
How can a record be marked for deletion? How can it be completely removed? What keyboard keys are used to perform these tasks?

Figure 14-17   Adding records with Browse.   (a) To add a record by using the Browse command, Rita must move beyond the last record in the file. (b) Then she can type in the new information.

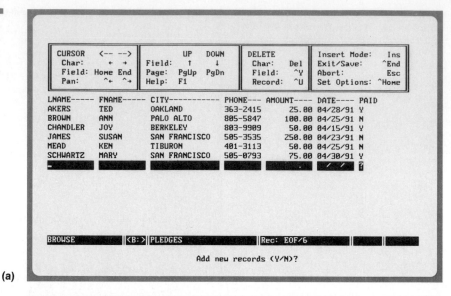

(a)

(b)

lower-right corner of her screen (Figure 14-18a). The Chandler record is now marked for deletion. If Rita accidentally marks the wrong record, she can press Ctrl-U again, and the deletion mark will be removed.

Since Rita wants to delete the Chandler record, she checks to see that the record is properly marked. First she exits the BROWSE mode by pressing Ctrl-End. Then she uses the List command. When the list of records is displayed, dBASE indicates a record marked for deletion by placing an asterisk in front of the record (Figure 14-18b).

To actually delete the record, Rita uses the Pack command. At the dot prompt, she types in PACK and presses Enter. dBASE displays the message "6 records copied." This tells Rita that there are now only six records in the PLEDGES file—the Chandler record is not one of them. Rita can verify this by using the List command again (Figure 14-18c).

Figure 14-18   Deleting records with Browse. (a) To delete a record, Rita moves the cursor to the record she wants to remove and presses Ctrl-U. Note that the word "Del" appears in the lower highlighted area of the screen. (b) When Rita lists the records, the asterisk next to the Chandler record tells her that the record is marked for deletion. (c) After Rita uses the Pack command to remove the record, the record is no longer listed.

LECTURE HINT
Note that control/U is the key-combination used to mark a record for deletion, as shown in the figure on this page.

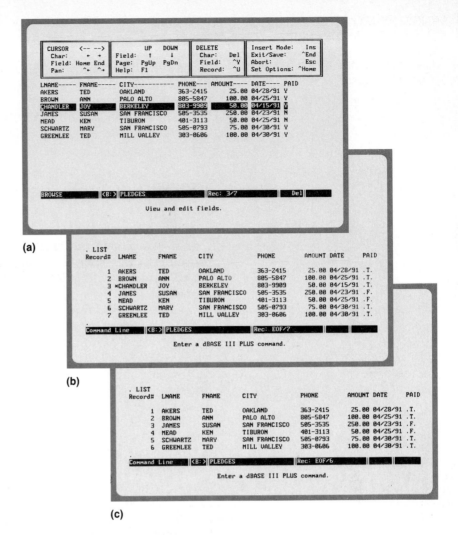

(a)

(b)

(c)

Deleting with the Delete Command

The Delete command is useful for deleting a specific record from a file when the record number is unknown. As with the Browse command, Rita must first mark the record for deletion. To mark Ken Mead's record, for example, Rita types:

```
DELETE FOR LNAME = "MEAD"
```

Then she presses Enter. Notice the use of the relational operator in this command. This tells dBASE to search for the record in which the last name field contains the name MEAD. The quotation marks around MEAD indicate that MEAD is a character field. The program indicates the number of records marked for deletion—in this case, one record. As before, Rita uses the List command to check that the proper record has been marked for deletion.

If Rita makes a mistake, she can use the Recall command to unmark the record she has marked. She would type:

```
RECALL FOR LNAME = "MEAD"
```

DISCUSSION QUESTION
Will the Delete command
completely remove a record from a
file? What is the function of the
Pack command?

and press Enter. When she uses the List command, the asterisk
would no longer be next to the record. Recall is a useful command,
but only if used *before* the Pack command is issued.

Now Rita is ready to delete the record. As before, she types
PACK and presses Enter. And as before, the program responds with
the number of records copied.

When Rita has finished with her editing, she types QUIT to
close the file and exit the program.

7 New and Improved: dBASE IV

As users have explored the capabilities of database management programs, they have seen the need for some improvements. In response to user requests, Ashton-Tate created a new
DBMS program—dBASE IV. dBASE IV has over 200 new or improved features and works much faster than dBASE III PLUS. dBASE
IV was designed so that users of dBASE III PLUS could immediately
use the new program without a lot of training. All of the commands
that you learned and used in this chapter work in exactly the same
way in dBASE IV. And dBASE III PLUS data files can be used by
dBASE IV without any modification. dBASE IV also includes an
improved help function that is like the help screen available in
dBASE III PLUS—but better.

In dBASE IV the dBASE III PLUS Assistant menu has been replaced by a superior system of menus called **work surfaces.** These
menus let you edit, display, and manage your data. The most important new menu is called the **Control Center.** This is the first menu
you see after loading dBASE IV. Unlike the Assistant in dBASE III
PLUS, the Control Center provides access to nearly all of the features
of dBASE IV and is much simpler to use. As shown in Figure 14-19,
the Control Center menu consists of six panels, which display various options. Users will do most of their work by using the Control
Center. This menu system uses the same selection technique (called
point and shoot) that was used with the dBASE III PLUS menus.
First you move a pointer to a menu item by using your cursor movement keys. Then you select the item by pressing Enter.

TRANSPARENCY ACETATE #14H
Figure #14-19

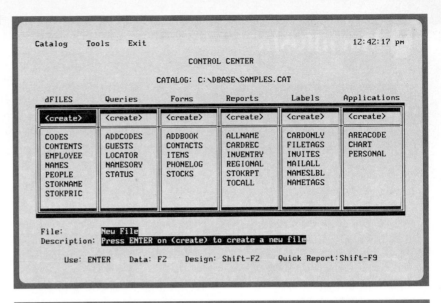

Figure 14-19   dBASE IV Control Center screen.   The dBASE IV Control Center screen lets you access nearly all of the features included in dBASE IV.

7 Just a Start

Although we have only scratched the surface of database management, this chapter shows how simple yet powerful a database can be. However, there are many options beyond the basic steps of setting up and changing a database. Those options are beyond the scope of this book, but we encourage you to learn all the bells and whistles of whatever database management package you may use in the future; the payoff in time-saving convenience will make the learning curve worthwhile.

Macintosh®

HyperCard: Linking Information Electronically

When Apple Computer introduced its HyperCard program for the Macintosh in 1987, a lot of people thought it was just a database manager with a big ego. But HyperCard, distributed free with every Mac sold, deliberately does not compete with the many database management programs available for the Mac.

HyperCard can be used as a personal information organizer. It comes with an electronic appointment calendar and an address file, as shown in (a).

The real power of HyperCard is its ability to let you link information. You place information on screen-sized "cards," just as you would put information on index cards. Related cards are organized into "stacks." Information on cards is linked to other cards or stacks by "buttons" on the screen. The left side of screen (a) shows six buttons that take you from the address card stack to other stacks. HyperCard automatically transfers you to a new stack or a related card when you "click" on a button (that is, when you move the screen arrow to the button and then press the button on the mouse).

HyperCard is an ideal educational tool. Using ready-made stacks, students can follow their own curiosity in pursuing a topic. For example, in the bird anatomy card shown in screen (b), clicking on any part of the bird brings up another card with detailed information about that part of the bird.

People have found some very creative uses for HyperCard:

- The Voyager Company created a stack that runs a videodisk tour of 1500 images from the National Gallery of Art. You can take notes in HyperCard and you can use the built-in index to search for a particular artist or period.
- Because HyperCard stacks can easily incorporate digitized speech, sounds, and music as well as illustrations, many teachers have designed stacks to teach language— foreign language pronunciation for Americans, English for non-native speakers, and ABCs for preschoolers.

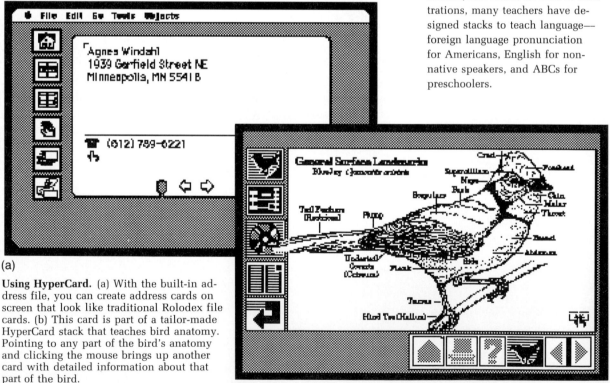

(a)

(b)

Using HyperCard. (a) With the built-in address file, you can create address cards on screen that look like traditional Rolodex file cards. (b) This card is part of a tailor-made HyperCard stack that teaches bird anatomy. Pointing to any part of the bird's anatomy and clicking the mouse brings up another card with detailed information about that part of the bird.

Summary and Key Terms

- A **database** is an organized collection of related data. A **database management system (DBMS)** is software that creates, manages, protects, and provides access to a database.

- A database can store data relationships so that files can be integrated. The way the database organizes data depends on the type, or **model,** of database. There are three database models—hierarchical, network, and relational.

- In a **relational database,** data that is organized logically in a table is called a **relation,** or **file.** Each "box" in the table contains a piece of data known as a **data item.** Each column of the table represents an **attribute,** or **field.** All the data in any given row is called a **tuple** or **record.**

- There are two steps to creating a file: designing the structure of the file and entering the data. When a file structure is defined, many database programs require the user to identify the **field names,** the **field types,** and the **field widths.** There are four commonly used types of fields: **character fields, numeric fields, date fields,** and **logical fields.** The field width determines the maximum number of letters, digits, or symbols to be contained in the field.

- dBASE III PLUS gives you two means of entering commands: the Assistant menu and the COMMAND mode. The **Assistant menu** has a number of options on the top line of the menu. Each option has an associated **selection bar,** which appears when the main selection is highlighted by the cursor. When you are in the **COMMAND mode,** the menu screen disappears and a **dot prompt** appears.

- At times, a **relational operator** is needed when making comparisons or when entering instructions. Some commands generally used as operators include =, <, and >.

- Like most database programs, dBASE III PLUS has a number of commands that let you create a file structure, enter records, update records, delete records, edit records, and list records. These commands include the Create command, the List Structure command, the Append command, the List command, the Edit command, the Browse command, the Delete Command, the Use command, and the Pack command.

- If you need help when using the database program, you can press F1 to access a help screen.

- At times you may have to **pan**—move sideways across the screen—to view all the fields in a database.

- Deleting records from a file is a two-step process. The specific records must be marked for deletion by using one command. Then the record is removed from the file by using another command.

- dBASE IV uses a system of menus called **work surfaces.** The most important menu is the **Control Center,** which provides access to nearly all of the features of dBASE IV.

Review Questions

1. What is a database?

2. What is a database management system?

3. Explain how a database management system benefits users.

4. Explain how a relational database organizes data.

5. Define the following database terms: *field, record, file.*

6. Describe the difference between the Assistant menu and the COMMAND mode.

7. What is the database prompt that tells you that you are in COMMAND mode?

8. What does the Create command let you do?

9. List the four types of information that the database program needs to have to create a file structure.

10. List the four most common types of fields.

11. What command(s) could you use to edit data in a database record?

12. What command(s) could you use to add a record to a database file?

13. What steps are needed to delete a record from a file by using the Browse command? By using the Delete command?

Chapter 15.   Desktop Publishing: Publishing with Your Computer

15

Desktop Publishing

Publishing with Your Computer

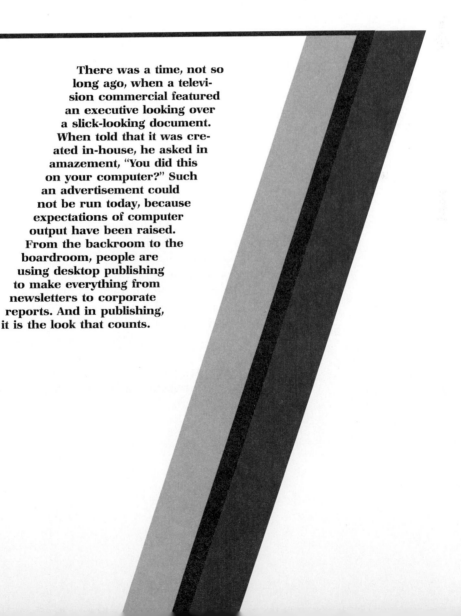

There was a time, not so long ago, when a television commercial featured an executive looking over a slick-looking document. When told that it was created in-house, he asked in amazement, "You did this on your computer?" Such an advertisement could not be run today, because expectations of computer output have been raised. From the backroom to the boardroom, people are using desktop publishing to make everything from newsletters to corporate reports. And in publishing, it is the look that counts.

LEARNING OBJECTIVES
- Appreciating the advantages of desktop publishing.
- Understanding desktop publishing terminology.
- Understanding hardware and software requirements for desktop publishing.

TEST BANK
Mult. Choice	1-3
T/F	1-6
Matching A	1-2
Fill-in-the-Blank	1-4

DISCUSSION QUESTION
What issues impact small companies using conventional means of publishing?

LECTURE ACTIVITY
Before class, create text concerning your course, department, or school. In class, create a design related to your course, department, school, or an activity on campus. If you have access to desktop publishing software, combine these to produce a one or two page newsletter.

Would you like to be able to produce well-designed pages that combine elaborate charts and graphics with text and headlines in a variety of typefaces? Would you like to be able to do all this at your desk, without a ruler, pen, or paste? The technology that lets you do all this is here today, and it is called **desktop publishing,** or, sometimes, **electronic publishing.** You can use desktop publishing software to design sophisticated pages and, with a high-quality printer, print a professional-looking final document (Figure 15-1).

7 Desktop Publishing: An Overview

Until recently, people who wanted to publish had just two alternatives—the traditional publishing process or word processing. Both processes have significant disadvantages. In the mid-1980s, the development of desktop publishing offered a solution to the publishing problems of both large companies and individuals.

Consider the case of Andy Clark. Andy is an investment counselor who wants to send a newsletter to his clients. He wants to use the newsletter to outline conditions in investment markets, make investment recommendations, and describe some client success stories. In the past Andy tried to publish a newsletter by hiring conventional publishing services. But timing was a problem: By the time the newsletter was printed, the investment advice was out of date. Furthermore, using outside help to produce the newsletter was expensive. Andy also tried to produce the newsletter himself, using word processing software; but the result was an unprofessional-looking flyer.

With desktop publishing Andy can produce a newsletter by himself that looks professional, without the cost and delay of going to outside services. Unlike word processing, desktop publishing gives the personal computer user the ability to do **page composition.** That is, Andy can decide where he wants text and pictures on a page, what typefaces he wants to use, and what other design elements he wants to include. He can also insert graphics into the text. Desktop publishing fills the gap between word processing and professional typesetting.

In this chapter we will present some publishing terminology and then discuss desktop publishing software and the hardware needed to support it.

The Massachusetts Horticultural Society

Leaflet

March/April 1988
Volume IX, Number 2

Highlights
Flower Show reminders, page 3
Spring/Summer courses, page 5
Associates of the Library, page 7
Community gardening, page 9
Orchids, page 11

Protea cynaroides

From the director

The Hidden Flower Show

As splendid and overwhelming as the Spring Show is, most people see only a fraction of the Show. The Hidden Show consists of all the levels on which the Show can be enjoyed and, of course, all the behind the scenes activity that makes it happen. One of the reasons that the Show is so successful year after year is that as each individual's interest and expertise develops and changes so does what the Show offers.

The Show is a horticultural extravaganza, and most people appreciate on some level the horticultural excellence of the Show. But beyond the obvious color spectacle, and not at all to demean enjoying the Show just on that level, there are other Shows of great educational value. There are ideas for both novices and experts to learn from on landscaping and floral design. Some people study the plant labels which we work so hard to produce so that they can add to their own gardens or windowsills. We provide printed material such as the program which explains each exhibit and what the creators are trying to accomplish.

For those who visit during the day, we offer continuous live educational programs on topics ranging from attracting wildlife to your yard to floral design. We provide special educational tours for school children and their teachers. What we strive for is to provide a wide enough array of ways to learn about the plant world that everyone who visits the Show is touched in some way. We know they will be inspired.

There is another hidden aspect of the Show. That is the people. The staff of the Society led by Rick Chamberlain, Show manager; the volunteers led by Susan Dumaine; the amateur and professional exhibitors; the retail merchants; the security guards; the electricians and carpenters. This year more than 100,000 hours of time will go into the Show - all volunteered to the Society. To all of those behind the scenes, I give my heartfelt thanks. To all the others, I urge you to become part of the Show next year!

– R.H.D.

L. Hunkel
ary, Clerk

ldwin
oger J. Bullock
s T. Cefalo Jr.
Crossman
R. Godine
nd W. Heimlich
e J. Hill III
Hunnewell
ewell III
a Jones
e Lewis
cKey
ert Mill
aniel Pierce
organ H. Plummer Jr.
lfred G. Rindler
Schumacher Jr
enry S. Streeter
nthony Thacher
Thomson
athleen Warren

d H. Daley
tive Director

llustration from *Cyclopedia of
n Horticulture* (1901), by L. H.
Other illustrations in this issue of
from *The Illustrated Dictionary of
ng* (1885), edited by George
on. MHS Library.

Calendar

March 3, 4 & 5
The first annual *Maine Flower and Garden Show* will be held at the Maine Mall in South Portland. For more information, call Martha Sharp at (207) 829-3211

March 25 & 26
Landscape Preservation Seminar at the University of Massachusetts, Amherst. For registration information contact Alice Szlosek, Program Coordinator, Division of Continuing Education, 608 Goodell Building, University of Massachusetts, Amherst, MA. 01003. (413) 545-2484

April 9 - May 8
Annual Spring Bulb Display at Blithwold Gardens and Arboretum, Ferry Road, Bristol, RI. 02809. For more information, call (401) 253-2707.

prunus sp.

Figure 15-1 Desktop publishing. With desktop publishing software and a high-quality laser printer, you can create professional-looking newsletters and documents.

Figure 15-2   High-end desktop publishing. This professional-looking magazine cover was produced entirely with computer software. The totem-pole art was created with graphics software. The type and layout were produced with desktop publishing software, which was also used to combine the text and art. In a separate step, the magazine cover was printed by a professional color printer.

TEST BANK
Mult. Choice	4-19
T/F	7-38
Matching A	3-6
Matching B	1-5, 10
Fill-in-the-Blank	5-23

DISCUSSION QUESTION
What important decisions must be made when designing the layout of a page?

7 The Publishing Process

Sometimes we take the quality appearance of the publications we read for granted. A great deal of activity goes on behind the scenes to prepare a document for publication. Writers, editors, artists, designers, typesetters, and printers all contribute their knowledge and experience to complete a finished document (Figure 15-2). When you begin to plan your own publications, you will play several roles.

Figure 15-3 shows the main steps involved in publishing a newsletter. Desktop publishing makes it possible for the user to complete the editing, design, and production cycles by using a personal computer. Desktop publishing also eliminates the time-consuming measuring and cutting and pasting involved in traditional production techniques.

7 The Art of Design

Word processors can generate lines of text that look like a typed page, but if you are producing a brochure or newsletter, a more sophisticated design is expected. One part of the design is **page layout**—how the text and pictures are arranged on the page. For example, magazine publishers have found that text organized in columns and separated by a solid vertical line is an effective page layout. If pictures are used, they must be inserted into the text. Their size might need to be adjusted so they will fit the page properly. In addition to page layout, designers must take into account such factors as headings, type size, and typefaces. Are general headings used? Do separate sections or articles need their own subheadings? Does the size of the type need to be increased or decreased to fit a story into a predetermined space? What is the best typeface to use? Should there be more than one kind of typeface used on a page?

To help you understand how some of the decisions are made, we need to discuss some of the publishing terminology involved.

7 Typefaces: Sizes and Styles

The type that a printer uses is described by its size, typeface, weight, and style. **Type size** is measured by a standard system that uses points. A **point** equals about $1/72$ inch. Point size is measured from the part of the letter that rises the highest above the "baseline" (in letters such as h and l) and from the baseline to the part of the letter that descends the lowest (in letters such as g and y). The text you are now reading has been typeset in 10-point type;

PRINCIPLES OF GOOD DESIGN

Desktop publishing programs put many different fonts and images at your disposal, but you can overwhelm a document if you crowd all these onto a page. The guidelines that follow will help get favorable reviews for you and your document.

- Do not use more than two or three typefaces in a document.
- Be conservative: Limit the use of decorative or unusual typefaces.
- Use different sizes and styles of one typeface to distinguish between different heading levels, rather than several different typefaces.
- Avoid cluttering a document with fancy borders and symbols.
- Do not use type that is too small to read easily, just to fit everything on one page.

DISCUSSION QUESTION
What guidelines are appropriate for designing an attractive easy-to-read document?

LECTURE HINT
Some cautions about desktop publishing. Consider avoiding:
- Underlining text.
- Setting headings in all capital letters.
- Putting long stretches of copy in italic or boldface.
- Making column width wider than 40 characters.
- Crowding out all white space.
- Getting "boxitis" (use boxes only to set off type that logically should be isolated).
- Using more than three typefaces on a page (if you need more variety, use different styles of the same typeface).

WRITING CYCLE

1. Write manuscript
2. Make preliminary illustration suggestions

EDITING CYCLE

1. Edit manuscript
2. Suggest illustrations
3. Copyedit manuscript
4. Prepare manuscript for production and design

DESIGN CYCLE

1. Estimate total length of manuscript
2. Design pages
3. Choose type
4. Design other page elements
5. Choose colors
6. Produce sample pages
7. Generate illustrations

PRODUCTION CYCLE

1. Typeset text
2. Proofread text
3. Place text on pages
4. Place illustrations on pages
5. Add finishing touches to prepare for printing

PRINTING CYCLE

1. Strip in halftones and four-color separations
2. Make plates
3. Print documents
4. Bind document if necessary

Figure 15-3   The publishing process.   Desktop publishing users can complete the editing, design, and production cycles with the help of their personal computers.

Helvetica (12 pt)
Helvetica (18 pt)
Helvetica (24 pt)
Helvetica (36 pt)
Helvetica (48 pt)

Figure 15-4 Different point sizes. This figure shows a variety of different point sizes in the typeface called Helvetica.

LECTURE HINT
Serif fonts, such as the Melior used in the body of the text, have tiny tails on the edges of the font to enhance readability by guiding the eye from letter to letter. Sans serif fonts, such as Helvetica, are cleaner but slow down the eye so the reader must pay closer attention. Sans serif fonts are especially appropriate for headings.

margin notes, however, have been set in 8-point type. Figure 15-4 shows type in different sizes.

The shape of the letters and numbers in a published document is determined by the typeface selected. A **typeface** is a set of characters—letters, symbols, and numbers—of same design. The typeface for the text you are now reading is called Melior. Some common typefaces are shown in Figure 15-5. Notice that a typeface can be printed in a specific **weight**—such as boldface, which is extra dark—or in a specific **style**—such as italic. These changes in typeface provide emphasis and variety. A **font** is a complete set of characters in a particular size, typeface, weight, and style.

As shown in Figure 15-6a, varying the size and style of the type used in a publication can improve the appearance of a page and

Figure 15-5 Samples of typefaces. Shown here are different weights and styles of typefaces. Notice that changing the weight or the style of a typeface can change its appearance.

Helvetica:
ABCDEFGHIJKLMNOPQRSTUVWXYZ
abcdefghijklmnopqrstuvwxyz
abcdefghijklmnopqrstuvwxyz
abcdefghijklmnopqrstuvwxyz

Bodoni:
ABCDEFGHIJKLMNOPQRSTUVWXYZ
abcdefghijklmnopqrstuvwxyz
abcdefghijklmnopqrstuvwxyz
abcdefghijklmnopqrstuvwxyz

ITC Korinna:
ABCDEFGHIJKLMNOPQRSTUVWXYZ
abcdefghijklmnopqrstuvwxyz
abcdefghijklmnopqrstuvwxyz
abcdefghijklmnopqrstuvwxyz

Garamond:
ABCDEFGHIJKLMNOPQRSTUVWXYZ
abcdefghijklmnopqrstuvwxyz
abcdefghijklmnopqrstuvwxyz
abcdefghijklmnopqrstuvwxyz

Zapf Chancery Light:
ABCDEFGHIJKLMNOPQRSTUVWXYZ
abcdefghijklmnopqrstuvwxyz
abcdefghijklmnopqrstuvwxyz
abcdefghijklmnopqrstuvwxyz

Euro-stile:
ABCDEFGHIJKLMNOPQRSTUVWXYZ
abcdefghijklmnopqrstuvwxyz
abcdefghijklmnopqrstuvwxyz
abcdefghijklmnopqrstuvwxyz

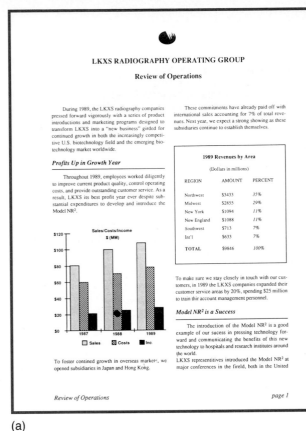

(a)

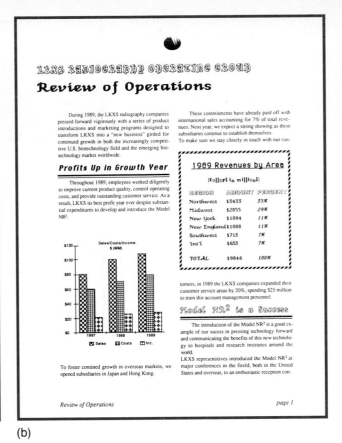

(b)

TRANSPARENCY ACETATE #15B
Figure #15-6

DISCUSSION QUESTION
What are some issues to be
considered when selecting a
typeface?

Figure 15-6   Sample designs. (a) This example uses complementary typefaces to produce a professional-looking document. (b) The same page created with clashing typefaces.

draw attention to the most important sections. However, using too many different fonts or using clashing fonts can create a page that is unattractive and hard to read (Figure 15-6b). You should use different fonts with discretion.

Most printers used in desktop publishing store a selection of fonts in a ROM chip in the printer. These are called the printer's **internal fonts.** Also, most desktop publishing programs provide a **font library** on disk. A font library contains a wide selection of type fonts called **soft fonts.** A soft font can be sent—downloaded—from the library disk in the computer's disk drive to the printer. Then the printer can print type in the new font.

7 Leading and Kerning

Two terms you will encounter when you begin desktop publishing are *leading* and *kerning*. **Leading** (pronounced "ledding") refers to the spacing between the lines of type on a page. Leading is measured vertically from the base of one line of type to

Figure 15-7   Leading.   Increasing the amount of leading between lines of type increases the amount of white space between lines.

Solid leading (9/9)

When I wrote the following pages, or rather the bulk of them, I lived alone, in the woods, a mile from any neighbor, in a house which I had built myself, on the shore of Walden Pond, in Concord, Massachusetts, and earned my living by the labor of my hands only.
—Henry David Thoreau

+1-point leading (9/10)

When I wrote the following pages, or rather the bulk of them, I lived alone, in the woods, a mile from any neighbor, in a house which I had built myself, on the shore of Walden Pond, in Concord, Massachusetts, and earned my living by the labor of my hands only.
—Henry David Thoreau

+2-point leading (9/11)

When I wrote the following pages, or rather the bulk of them, I lived alone, in the woods, a mile from any neighbor, in a house which I had built myself, on the shore of Walden Pond, in Concord, Massachusetts, and earned my living by the labor of my hands only.
—Henry David Thoreau

Figure 15-8   Kerning.   (a) In this example, the space between the characters is not altered. (b) Kerning, or adjusting the space between the characters, can improve the overall appearance of the characters.

(a) Unkerned:

WAVE

(b) Kerned:

WAVE

the base of the line above it (Figure 15-7). Leading—just like type size—is measured in points. **Kerning** refers to adjusting the space between the characters in a line. In desktop software each font has a default kerning. Occasionally, you might want to change the kerning to improve the appearance of the final typeset work. An example of kerning is shown in Figure 15-8.

7 Halftones

Halftones, which resemble photographs, appear in newspapers, magazines, books, and desktop publishing documents. Halftones are representations made up of black dots printed on white paper. Different numbers and sizes of dots in a given space produce shades of gray. As you can see in Figure 15-9, the smaller the dot pattern used, the clearer the halftone. Most printers used in desktop publishing produce halftones that meet professional standards.

Now let us put this publishing background to work by examining desktop publishing in more detail.

Figure 15-9   Halftones. Halftones consist of a series of dots. Reducing the size of the dots makes the resulting halftone clearer.

TEST BANK
Mult. Choice	20-25
T/F	39-48
Matching A	7
Matching B	6-7
Fill-in-the-Blank	24-27

IT USED TO BE SO EASY TO TELL THEM APART

Perhaps you have seen proposals or newsletters or contracts done with desktop publishing. They look so good. You want your stuff to look good too—crisp, professional, as if it just came from the typesetter. You want desktop publishing.

Or do you?

Many people who think they want desktop publishing are actually attracted to the quality printing—the output from a laser printer. Those same people may want a few of the tricks of the trade—putting the word "memo" in inch-high letters across the top of the page or perhaps putting a nice heavy line across the bottom of the page and then the page number. However, users who want such features may not want to switch to desktop publishing—it is not worth their time. Word processing vendors, recognizing a need, are upgrading their products to include some desktop publishing features.

First there was word processing and then there was desktop publishing. What will the hybrid be called? High-end word processing? Super-processing? Word publishing?

7 Desktop Publishing Software

Desktop publishing systems let users create text and images, design the layout for a publication, move the text and images into the layout, and print the result. You have already studied how to create text with a word processing program, and you have seen images produced with graphics programs. Moving text and images and printing are straightforward once you become familiar with the desktop publishing software. It is the design of the pages, however, that is the heart of desktop publishing.

Imagine planning headlines not just in terms of what they say, but in terms of the size of the typeface and the spacing between the letters. Now try to decide just where a certain drawing should go, and how large it should be. Should the text be in columns? If so, how many columns and how wide? These are only some of the design issues to consider. But addressing these issues is easy with desktop publishing software; it lets you plan and change the page—right on your computer screen.

The software requirements for desktop publishing are

- A word processing program to create the text to be used in the publication

- A graphics program to create and use graphics for the publication

- A page composition program

Page composition programs, also called **page makeup programs** or **desktop publishing programs,** make it possible for you to design the layout of each page of a publication on the computer screen. Using these programs you can determine the number and the width of the columns of text to be printed on the page. You can also indicate where pictures, charts, graphs, and headlines should be placed.

MICROCOMPUTERS IN ACTION

Sampler of Desktop Publishing Projects

These brief portraits show the variety of ways people use microcomputers for desktop publishing.

Annual reports. Colorful charts and diagrams for the annual report of Great Northern Nekoosa Corporation, a paper manufacturer, are designed with PageMaker software on the Macintosh computer.

Civic newsletters. The Orange County Trust newsletter is produced with PageWriter software. One issue of the four-page newsletter takes the designer just four hours to create.

Economic newsletters. Metlife Capital Credit's *ECONOMIC Quarterly* is produced by using a combination of Excel, a spreadsheet package, and the desktop publishing software QuarkXPress.

Industry newspapers. The American Electronics Association's trade association newspaper, *Update*, is produced with PageMaker.

Consumer guidebooks. The *Complete Car Cost Guide* is a guidebook exploring costs for new and used cars. The designer uses PageMaker to lay out the text and Adobe Illustrator to create icons. The graphs that make up the guide are created separately and then imported into the design.

Corporate magazines. The inside pages of *IN Magazine*, a publica-

tion for a design and marketing communications firm, are designed with a desktop publishing package called QuarkXPress. This particular package was chosen for its ability to print around picture images: The expected image area is blocked out, and the text runs around the edges of the area.

Literary magazines. Published in New York City, the magazine *Contemporaries* is created using the software package called Ventura Publisher. The magazine's publishers chose Ventura because it supports PostScript, a page description language that lets them produce fonts of various sizes.

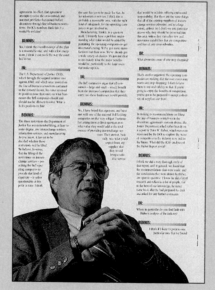

Viewer's updates. The "Insider" section of *TV Guide* is produced with Superpage. This colorful section displays text, photographs, and illustrations.

Video tape catalogs. The *Captain Video Catalog*, which lists 14,000 movies available from Captain Video, is produced with Ventura Publisher.

Consumer pamphlets. D.I.N. Publications creates an assortment of brochures, flyers, and posters on health-linked topics using PageMaker software. Various font styles and headline sizes are included in each brochure, along with eye-catching boldface and underlining techniques.

Figure 15-10 A desktop publishing menu. Most desktop publishing software lets you choose typefaces, type styles, and type sizes from a menu.

TRANSPARENCY ACETATE #15C
Figure #15-10

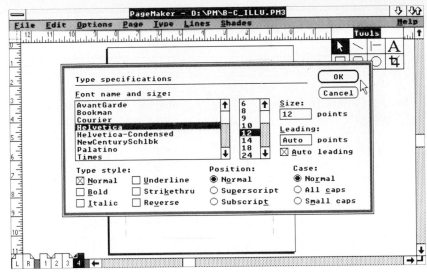

Page composition programs provide menus, as shown in Figure 15-10, that let you specify the fonts you want to use in your publication. These programs also let you adjust the default leading, if necessary, to fit a block of text that is a little too long or too short into a column of your page layout.

Once you have created the design for each page, the page composition program takes the text files created by your word processing program and the graphics you produced with your graphics program and inserts them into the page design that you have laid out. Page composition programs also let you move blocks of text and pictures around on your page. If you are not satisfied with the way the page looks, you can change the size of the type or the pictures or edit them.

Once the document is filled with words and graphics and in final design form, printing can be done in a variety of ways.

- If only a few copies of the finished work are needed, they can be printed on the computer's attached printer.

- To create several copies, a high-speed copier can be used to reproduce the original hard copy from the computer's printer.

- If the highest-quality copies are required, the file created by the desktop system can be stored on disk and taken to a sophisticated typesetting system to produce typeset copy. This can then be professionally printed if a large number of copies is needed.

Some page composition programs offer **desktop publishing templates,** which are prepared page layouts stored on disk. Templates provide predesigned outlines that are then filled in with text and graphics. Designed by experienced professional designers to guide the novice desktop publisher, templates suggest page design elements such as headline placement, the number and width of text columns, the best fonts to use, and image placement.

Macintosh®

So You Want to Be a Publisher

If there is one application that sets the Macintosh apart from other computers, it is desktop publishing. Combining a page-layout program with a laser printer allows people to create attractive publications—from posters and newsletters to full-sized books.

Because you can move text and graphics around on the screen, Mac page-layout programs simulate what graphic artists do when they cut and paste type and art on a drafting table.

But buying a desktop publishing program does not turn a person into a graphic designer. In fact, it is much easier to use page composition programs than it is to create a page that looks attractive. Although most of us pick up a little something about perspective drawing and mixing colors during our school days, design literacy definitely has not made it to the national educational agenda. As a result, most people do not know where to begin in laying out a publication.

Fortunately, you do not have to start designing pages from scratch. To help desktop publishers who lack design experience, some companies produce *templates,* page layouts by professional designers that can be used with your own text and graphics. For example, PageMaker from Aldus Corporation comes with a set of designs for a brochure, newsletter, calendar, and directory. Aldus also markets collections of templates, such as a portfolio of 21 newsletter designs and a package for businesses that features designs for proposals, reports, memos, overhead transparencies, and so on.

Designing pages electronically takes time getting used to, even for professional graphic artists. Although the process can be frustrating at times, the results can be ultimately gratifying. When your final version rolls off the laser printer, you can show it off with justifiable pride.

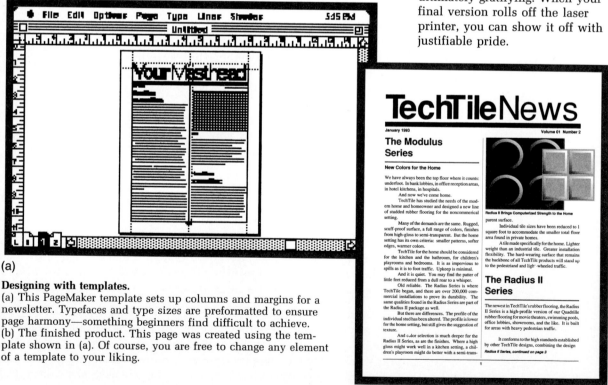

(a)

Designing with templates.
(a) This PageMaker template sets up columns and margins for a newsletter. Typefaces and type sizes are preformatted to ensure page harmony—something beginners find difficult to achieve.
(b) The finished product. This page was created using the template shown in (a). Of course, you are free to change any element of a template to your liking.

(b)

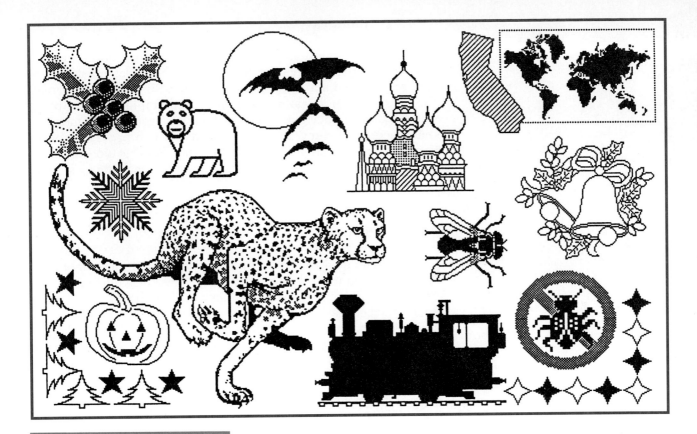

Figure 15-11   Clip art. A variety of clip art software can be purchased and used to improve the appearance of a document. Typical clip art is quite mundane—standard sketches of everyday items such as cars, flags, food, and household implements. The items pictured here offer a little more visual enhancement than the usual clip art software.

TEST BANK
Mult. Choice   36-35
T/F   49-73
Matching A   8-10
Matching B   8-9
Fill-in-the-Blank   28-38

DISCUSSION QUESTION
What is the minimum hardware needed to produce a desktop-published document?

Page composition programs can also integrate **clip art**—images already produced by professional artists for public use—into your publication to enliven your text. You can purchase disks that contain various kinds of clip art. Figure 15-11 shows examples of the kinds of illustrations included in a clip art library.

7 Hardware for Desktop Publishing

Computer hardware in general was described in detail in prior chapters. The discussion that follows focuses on the special needs of desktop publishing.

Input Devices

The input devices used in desktop publishing are the keyboard and the mouse. A scanner may also be used for inputting. Text is entered by using the keyboard. A mouse is often used to make menu selections and to manipulate blocks of text and graphics on the screen. Existing text and graphics can be entered in the desktop publishing system by using a scanner.

7 Monitors

For desktop publishing, the quality of the monitor is particularly important. The pages displayed on the screen must be very clear, so you need a high-resolution monitor. Since images are usually included in publications, you also need graphics capability. If you use color in your publications, then you need a color monitor. Some documents show an illustration across two pages; magazine advertisements are often laid out in this way. For this type of work a special monitor is needed so both pages can be seen side by side on the screen.

7 Printers

The quality of the printer is one of the most important aspects of desktop publishing. Although most desktop publishing systems include either a laser printer or a high-quality dot-matrix printer, the best desktop publishing printers must be capable of producing text that closely resembles the quality of professional typesetting. If you need clearer, sharper text, an alternative is to send the disk file produced by a page composition program to a typesetter equipped with a special interface so it can print your file. In either case, you can get a printout that is **camera-ready**—that is, it is ready to be photographed to make a plate for printing.

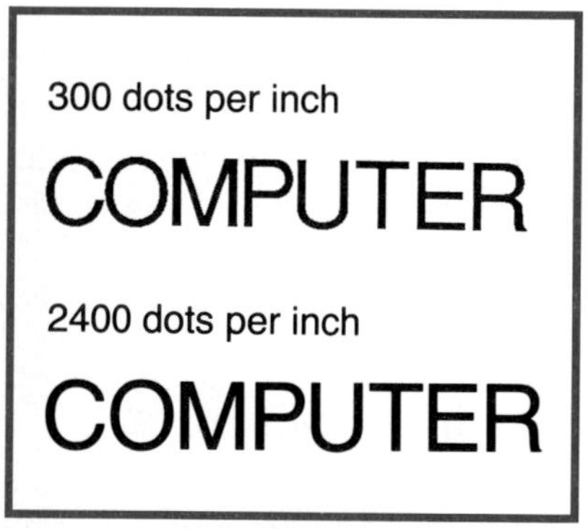

Printer Resolution

The characters and pictures that you are reading in this book (which was typeset) and other publications are actually made up of thousands of tiny dots. The smaller the dots that a device can print, the higher the **resolution.** The size and density of the dots is measured in dots per inch (dpi). The more dots per inch, the clearer and sharper the characters and graphics produced by the printer (Figure 15-12).

Typesetters can produce camera-ready originals at resolutions of 1200 to 2540 dots per inch; the dots are so small that they cannot be seen even under a magnifying glass. This level of resolution is called **typeset quality.** To approximate typeset quality, printers used in desktop publishing must be able to print text and graphics at resolutions of at least 300 dots per inch. Some laser printers can print at resolutions of 1200 dots per inch. The quality of resolution is a factor to consider, since research has shown that text printed at a higher resolution is more readable and understandable than text printed at a lower resolution.

Page Description Languages

Printers used for desktop publishing must have a **page description language** (**PDL**) embedded in a ROM chip. PDLs let a page composition program tell the printer exactly how to use fonts, type sizes, text, and graphics. That is, after you compose a page on

300 dots per inch

COMPUTER

2400 dots per inch

COMPUTER

Figure 15-12   Comparing dots per inch.   The higher the number of dots per inch (dpi), the greater the resolution of the text. Most laser printers produce output between 300 and 1200 dpi.

the computer, the page composition program sends the correct instructions to the printer's PDL. Since your page composition program is what gives the PDL its instructions, you do not need to worry about learning the PDL yourself.

Printer Speeds and Duty Cycles

In addition to the resolution of a printer and the PDL, the speed of the printer and its duty cycle are important for desktop publishing. For business use, desktop printers should have a print speed of at least eight pages a minute. The **duty cycle** is a measurement of ruggedness. To designate the recommended level of use for a printer, duty cycle is usually expressed in pages printed per month. A printer used for desktop publishing in most businesses should have a duty cycle of at least 4000 pages per month.

Desktop Publishing: The Payoff

The design, typesetting, and printing costs incurred by company publications are a major business expense. In fact, in American businesses, the cost of publications is second only to personnel costs. Many companies spend hundreds of thousands of dollars annually on publishing. Publications are a major expense for nonprofit organizations as well.

Most newsletters, advertising leaflets, technical manuals, and in-house business publications do not have to be of the finest quality. They can be designed, produced, and printed with desktop publishing. Even in cases where a large quantity of copies is needed and it is more practical to employ a professional printer, desktop publishing can still be used to design and produce the publication.

Because of their speed, flexibility, and output quality, desktop publishing systems can rapidly produce not only newsletters, forms, and technical documents but also letterheads with company logos and manuals with magazine-style layouts. Users value the time and money savings, but what they value even more is the control—the ability to see exactly how a change in the type size or layout looks by observing the results immediately on a computer screen and to decide if the change is appropriate. No more company newsletters filled with crooked lines and amateurish drawings—most offices are moving to the greener pastures of desktop publishing.

Coming Up: The Workplace

We have devoted the last five chapters to the important subject of microcomputers and the software most often used on them. Now we are going to take a broad look at the uses of computers in business.

PERSPECTIVES

WHAT NEXT?

What will desktop publishing do for us—and to us? What's next in desktop publishing?

In the immediate future, we can expect some desktop publishing users to be unable to resist touching up graphics in their documents; next they will want to make them fancier. That is, ordinary personal computer users may perform work formerly in the realm of professional artists and designers. But page composition and design is a complicated business; expect specialists to evolve or be appointed. Can Chief Publishing Officer be far behind?

Looking a little further down the road, consider these possibilities:

- Graphics and text design courses offered in high schools, much as typing and word processing are offered now

- Any group organization, whether the bowling league or the volunteer group or the investment club, produces its own professional-looking news-letters and brochures

- Something beyond the current "junk mail": the evolution of thousands of on-my-soapbox narrow-interest publications

And one final prediction: Any book you want from a store is available—have it printed while you wait.

7 Summary and Key terms

- **Desktop publishing,** or **electronic publishing,** helps people produce professional-looking high-quality documents containing both text and graphics. Desktop publishing can save time and money and can give people better control over the final product.

- The publishing process includes editing, designing, producing, and printing.

- One part of the overall design of a document is **page layout**—how the text and pictures are arranged on the page. Adding type to a layout is called **page composition.**

- Printers offer a variety of type. Type is described by **type size, typeface, weight,** and **style.** Type size is measured by a standard system based on the **point.** A **font** is a complete set of characters in a particular size, typeface, weight, and style.

- Most printers used in desktop publishing contain **internal fonts** stored in a ROM chip. Most desktop publishing programs provide a **font library** on disk, containing a selection of type fonts called **soft fonts.**

- **Leading** refers to the spacing between the lines of type on a page. **Kerning** refers to adjusting the space between the characters in a line.

- A **halftone**—a representation made up of dots—can be produced by desktop publishing printers.

- The software requirements for desktop publishing include a word processing program, a graphics program, and a page composition program. **Page composition programs,** also called **page makeup programs** or **desktop publishing programs,** enable the user to design the page layout.

- Some page composition programs offer **desktop publishing templates**—prepared page layouts stored on disk. Page composition programs may also let a user integrate **clip art**—prepared drawings stored on disk.

- Input devices used in desktop publishing are the keyboard and the mouse. Scanners can also be used to input text and graphics.

- For the highest-quality publications, high-resolution monitors and printers should be used. Printer quality is particularly important if the user wishes to produce **camera-ready** printout.

- Printed characters and pictures are actually made up of tiny dots. The smaller the dots printed, the higher the **resolution.** The size and density of the dots is measured in dots per inch (dpi). Resolutions of 1200 to 2540 dpi are called **typeset quality.**

- Printers used for desktop publishing must have a **page description language** (**PDL**) embedded in a ROM chip.

- In addition to the resolution of a printer and the PDL, the speed of the printer and its duty cycle are important. **Duty cycle** is expressed in pages printed per month.

Review Questions

1. What is desktop publishing?

2. What advantages does desktop publishing have over word processing?

3. What advantages does desktop publishing have over traditional publishing methods?

4. How is the size of type specified?

5. What is a typeface?

6. What is a font?

7. What are a printer's internal fonts? What are soft fonts?

8. What is meant by the term *leading*?

9. What is meant by the term *kerning*?

10. What are halftones?

11. What is a page composition program?

12. What are desktop publishing templates?

13. What is clip art?

14. What input and output hardware are needed for desktop publishing?

15. What is meant by the resolution of a printer?

16. What is the function of a page description language?

Discussion Questions

1. Check your local software store for desktop publishing software. Consider asking these questions: What is the best-selling desktop publishing software? Which printers are in most common use for desktop publishing? How many hours, approximately, does it take to learn how to use a particular desktop publishing software package? Are there classes available? Try to get samples of desktop publishing output.

2. Suppose you were familiar with a particular word processing package that is offered in a new version that includes some desktop publishing features. Would you be inclined to switch to the new version or to buy a separate desktop publishing package? There are many considerations. Take one position or the other and justify it.

PART 5

COMPUTERS IN THE WORKPLACE

The story of computers in the workplace is an all-encompassing one. Most of us know that computers are found in offices and factories, but computers are also found in stores, parks, repair shops, boats, restaurants, and just about any place else your work may take you. As we note in Chapter 16, large organizations have large computers. Most workplaces —large or small—have personal computers and the business software that runs on them.

Someone must manage all these computer resources, from the Management Information Systems Department to far-flung microcomputers, and that is the focus of Chapter 17.

And, finally, company resources must be applied to keep computers and their data secure and private—the subject of Chapter 18.

Chapter 16. Computers on the Job: How Workers Use Computers

16

Computers on the Job

How Workers Use Computers

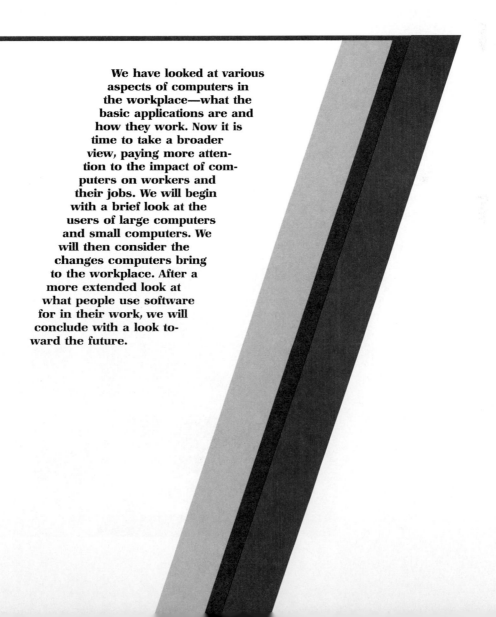

We have looked at various aspects of computers in the workplace—what the basic applications are and how they work. Now it is time to take a broader view, paying more attention to the impact of computers on workers and their jobs. We will begin with a brief look at the users of large computers and small computers. We will then consider the changes computers bring to the workplace. After a more extended look at what people use software for in their work, we will conclude with a look toward the future.

When Autry Bishop accepted a job as an accountant at The Boeing Company, he expected to have access to a personal computer. He also knew that the company had larger computers, and he anticipated working with accounting systems that run on them. But he was somewhat startled to discover the company's commitment to a full range of computers. The computers themselves run the gamut from supercomputers through mainframes and minicomputers, to—literally—thousands of personal computers. The uses of computers are as varied as the company activities: research, management, engineering, programming, finance, personnel, manufacturing, and much more. Boeing is a sophisticated computer user. There are few limits to the uses of computers in a complex business enterprise.

7 The Big Guys: Users of Mainframe Computers

The companies that use mainframe computers today are mostly the same companies that were using large computers 30 or 40 years ago: large corporations that have large budgets. These organizations, typically banks, insurance firms, and aerospace companies, were the pioneers (Figure 16-1). The computers they used were potent by then-current standards, even though today's personal computers are more powerful. In the 1950s and early 1960s, many companies obtained big computers because they somehow envisioned that computers would provide a competitive edge. This turned out to be true, but it was a long time before managers really understood the true promise of the computer.

Figure 16-1   Mainframe computer.

Early users were somewhat uncertain about how to use the new tool. In fact, their idea of the range of functions appropriate for a computer was extremely limited: from clerical to clerical. Pioneering applications for many companies were payroll and accounting systems. The idea was to save labor costs by having the computer do some of the work. Some users, including the government, used computers as "number crunchers," grinding away at variations on formulas. When computers began to be used interactively, businesspeople saw that the computer could be used as a service tool, giving instant reservations or bank balances. Now the computer is used in every conceivable way, from research to manufacturing.

Mid-range computers made number crunching and computerized service available to medium-size companies. But it was the highly affordable personal computer that really opened up computing for the worker.

7 Personal Computers in the Workplace: Where Are They?

Rather than ask where computers are in the workplace, it would be easier to ask where personal computers are *excluded* from the workplace. The list of where computers are, however, is instructive: retail, finance, insurance, real estate, health care, education, government, legal services, sports, politics, publishing, transportation, manufacturing, agriculture, construction, and on and on (Figure 16-2).

Figure 16-2 Personal computer users.   Personal computers support businesspeople in a variety of ways. (a) Architects use the computer's graphic abilities to render and revise their drawings. (b) This scuba gear vendor uses a computerized database to check inventory.

(a)   (b)

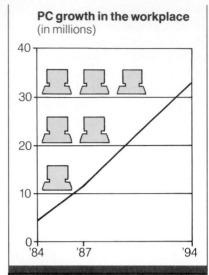

PC growth in the workplace
(in millions)

**PERSONAL COMPUTERS
TO COME**

The number of PCs in the business marketplace is skyrocketing. In 1987, the year PCs took off, there were about 11 million personal computers in use in business, enough for about 25% of anticipated use. The number of units is expected to climb to over 30 million by 1994—a virtual saturation of the market. Politicians in the past have sought to reassure us with talk of "a chicken in every pot" or "a car in every garage." Perhaps they should now talk about "a computer on every desk."

DISCUSSION QUESTION
What are the three phases of personal computer usage? Who can benefit from learning to use a computer?

Asked how her company used personal computers, a staffer replied, "You might as well ask how we use telephones. The computers are everywhere. We use them for everything." It was not always that way.

Evolution of Personal Computer Use

Personal computer use seems to evolve in three phases. Personal computers were first used in business by individual users to transform tasks. The much erased manual spreadsheet, for example, becomes the automatically recalculated electronic spreadsheet. This individual productivity boost can be considered the first phase of the personal computer evolution. Many organizations are still in phase one.

Many more organizations have entered the second phase. That is, they have gone beyond the individual, using personal computers to transform a working group or department. This department-oriented phase probably embraces a network and may also include personal computer access to the mainframe computers. This phase requires planning and structure.

The third phase of personal computer evolution is the most dramatic, calling for the transformation of the entire business. Practically speaking, however, phase three is really just an extension of the earlier phases: Each individual and each department uses computers to enhance the company as a whole. Few companies have come close to this idyllic state. This three-stage transformation—individual, department, and business—broadly describes a company's progress at blending its computer and business goals.

The Impact of Personal Computers

In the decades to come, personal computers will continue to radically alter the business world, much as the automobile did. For more than 50 years, the automobile fueled the economy, spawning dozens of industries, from oil companies to supermarkets. Other businesses, like real estate and restaurants, were transformed by the mobility provided by the car. Personal computers will have a similar effect, for two reasons: (1) they have brought the cost of computing down to the level of a mass-produced consumer product and (2) they have worked their way into most business organizations.

Now that they are there, let us consider who really needs to use them in business.

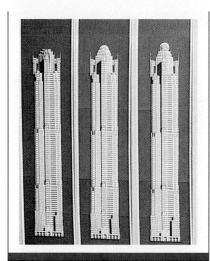

SKYSCRAPERS BY COMPUTER

Planning a skyscraper is a complicated business. Part of that complication comes from the need for many architects, with various specialties, to communicate with each other. At the Chicago architectural firm of Skidmore, Owings & Merrill, long known as a designer of high-tech skyscrapers, the communication problem has been solved: Each architect has a personal computer and the computers are hooked together in networks.

Skidmore has local area networks on several floors of a downtown office building; the networks are linked together by yards and yards of fiber optics cable. Project managers can divide a job of designing a building into several manageable pieces, and individual architects can pick up their slice of the job via the network. Architects working on the same job can exchange files and even complex drawings over the network. The network allows them to do multiple activities without getting in each others' way.

In addition, since the firm is working on about 100 buildings at a given time, one architect may be working on several jobs at once. Once a portion of a job is done, that segment can be sent electronically to the centralized printing facility.

Skidmore, the high-tech architect, just went one high-tech step further.

Where PCs Are Almost a Job Requirement

Who absolutely positively must know how to use a personal computer to perform some part of a job? As we have already implied, the answer may soon be "everyone." But we are not close to that landmark yet. Even if you can see that your intended job is in the must-know category, it is likely that you can receive some on-the-job training. Let us browse through some probable could-need-a-PC jobs. Notice that many of the jobs mentioned would probably fit in more than one category.

- Anyone who needs to search for information in a variety of ways: real estate broker, attorney, doctor, auto mechanic.

- Anyone who needs to analyze data: accountant, tax planner, medical researcher, farmer, psychologist, budget manager, financial planner, stockbroker.

- Anyone who needs to write and change documents: advertising copy writer, secretary, author, teacher, legislator.

- Anyone who needs to share data with other workers: designer, editor, nurse, members of the military, retail sales manager.

- Anyone who must keep track of schedules: project leader, construction manager, reservations agent, trucker, factory supervisor.

- Anyone giving a compare-the-results sales pitch: insurance salesperson, fitness consultant, political candidate, sports manager.

This list may make you pause; perhaps it is a bit futuristic in spots. But there is no question that computers are changing the way we work.

How Computers Change the Way We Work

TEST BANK
Mult. Choice   9-15
T/F   20-30
Fill-in-the-Blank 10-13

Computers are changing the way we work for both individuals and for organizations.

The Name of the Game Is Speed

Not the computer game—the *business* game. From California to Maine, a principal topic among management consultants and business school professors is pure speed. Why? Who cares? And, if there really is a good reason, how is it gained?

The *why* question has the most straightforward answer: Speed kills the competition. If your product gets to market first, you have a sale. Lag behind and get left out.

Who cares? Managers, of course, and—perhaps surprisingly—

PERSPECTIVES

THE ELECTRONIC SUPERVISOR

Did you work hard at the office today? Most people, when surveyed, report a full day's work. But managers have long suspected that this is not so. In fact, many employees spend more time at the coffee machine or in personal conversations than they realize. Others may be daydreaming while giving the appearance of working at their desks. Those days are over for employees monitored by software right inside their computers.

The computer is a see-all, tell-all supervisor. Surveillance software can count the number of keystrokes (and number of typos), keep track of how much time you actually spend working on the computer, monitor your telephone calls, and compare your keying speed with other employees.

Those who work directly with computers most of the day, such as data entry operators or word processors, are the most vulnerable to such a system. But others who work at machines are exposed too. Check sorters and mailroom employees, for example, work with machines that can be outfitted with computers to keep track of the amount of work processed in a given time period, such as an eight-hour shift. Workers such as telemarketers, who make outgoing phone calls as part of their jobs, are often monitored by computers.

Already, about 5 million workers are so monitored. Some experts have predicted that, as the number of computer-monitored workers increases, so will related personnel problems, such as increased stress and lowered morale. In fact, critics predict an "electronic sweatshop," where employees must do boring, fast-paced work that requires constant alertness and attention to detail. And worst of all, the supervisor is not even human.

DISCUSSION QUESTION
Why is obtaining results quickly more important in some professions than in others?

employees. Employee satisfaction improves when employees are working for a responsive, successful company. Also, speeding up operations with computers gives employees more responsibility and flexibility.

So, how is speed achieved? Do we just put out an order to step on the gas? Probably not—that would just speed up the mess and burn out machines and workers. There are many ways to speed up operations, including worker incentives, reducing the number of approvals needed for action, and—of course—putting the computer to work whenever possible.

The recent example of General Electric is instructive. GE reduced the time from order to delivery of its custom-made circuit breaker box from three weeks to three *days*. To do this, GE moved all circuit breaker operations to one location, reduced the parts inventory, moved most of the engineering work to the computer, and used a computerized ordering system.

The computer is not the only answer, but it is a major factor in shaping business.

More Time to Get Things Done

By providing timely access to data, computers let us spend less time checking and rechecking data—and more time getting things done. This inspires informed decision making and improves overall productivity. Today's computer systems speed memos, documents, and graphs to workers throughout the organization. This kind of direct people-to-people communication enriches every aspect of a business.

The Portable Worker

Many workers attribute their success to plain hard work—and they want the potential to take their work with them wherever they go. These days, taking work along means taking the computer along.

The Tools of Portability

This is the ideal set of machines a worker needs for portability: personal computers, a laptop computer, a laser printer, and a facsimile machine. Keep in mind that it is the worker who is "portable," not all these machines. Most of these machines are in the office and, for some workers—especially managers—they are also in the home. (One executive goes so far as to have a PC, phone, and fax machine in his "office" van.) The computers all have modems. They also have appropriate software for anything a worker might want to do, from answering electronic mail to writing reports to comparing financial options for a possible merger. Some workers keep computers at work and at home and also carry a laptop when traveling (Figure 16-3). Workers can use technology to send electronic and voice mail messages that can be picked up at the recipient's convenience. A report prepared at home or on the road can be sent via communications devices to the office, where it is printed on a laser printer, and then sent by fax to other interested parties. These electronic tools are catching on rapidly, and they are spreading beyond the traditional office.

LECTURE HINT
Portable users who want a FAX machine should consider the expenses. Most people will find a $1000.00 model adequate. Users will need to install an extra phone line, at a cost of about $100.00, and then pay a monthly line fee. (Phone bills can be lowered by transmitting at night.) The paper cost is a few cents per page.

Figure 16-3   Computers on the go. This engineer uses a personal computer at his desk but carries a laptop to the construction site to support his discussions with the foreman.

The New Convenience

Some say the new technology goes beyond convenience, and that a better word is *liberation*. Liberation from the confines of the office. Liberation from the 9-to-5 day with a commute on each end. Liberation from telephone tag. Liberation from time zone barriers. Telecommuting, as we have mentioned before, is ideal for some workers. But the liberation being described here is not a pattern of being at home—it is the lack of a pattern. Workers can, for all practical purposes, stay in touch with the office and the action 24 hours a day, seven days a week—from any location.

7 Personal Information Managers

No, this is not about managers whose job is to look after personal information. A **personal information manager** (**PIM**) is software that can help any office worker, but especially a manager, cope with information overload. The basic idea behind PIMs is that most people live in a world overloaded with assorted bits of information, such as telephone messages, Post-it notes, newspaper clippings, expense tabs, appointment cards, and other scraps of paper. Typical types of information that a PIM can handle are appointments, travel plans, phone numbers, and various lists and memos. PIMs use windows, so that several features can be on-screen at the same time (Figure 16-4).

Figure 16-4   A personal information manager. This sample from a product called Info-XL shows several windows on a single screen. The manager window gives the "big picture" for the project or person. The records window can show records, one at a time, in a format that suits the user. As a user moves the cursor through the calendar days, the daily schedule for each day appears in the adjoining window. The comments window is for free-form text. The search window shows a sample of words and phrases used to search for related information.

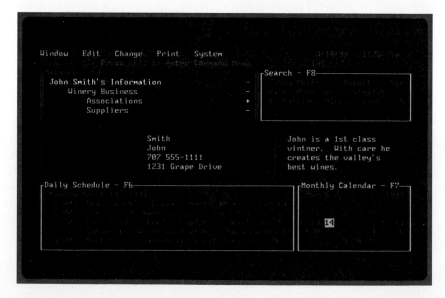

LECTURE ACTIVITY
Challenge the class to identify areas where software packages could be developed. Examples could include household chores, leisure activities, or family gatherings.

TEST BANK
Mult. Choice   16-19
T/F   31-41
Matching A   1, 3, 6-7, 9-10
Fill-in-the-Blank   14-16

LECTURE HINT
Passwords, specific commands and other security safeguards impede access to computers. Without these safeguards, Sabre could be accessed. The airline reservations system could be made useless by fictitious reservations that would fill flights or alter passenger data, cancelling booked flights.

Some PIMs offer quite sophisticated features, organizing diverse text-based information for project management or business analysis. A PIM is sometimes referred to generically as a productivity tool, because it makes order out of chaos. As one office worker put it, "It allows me to keep all these balls in the air without getting hit on the head."

7 Software at Work

Consider some specific business applications for the software tools in the marketplace.

7 Communications Software

If you have a computer, a modem, and some communications software, you have the capability to access any other computer system similarly configured. Businesses are the major users of communications software. There are as many applications as there are entrepreneurs to devise them and users to buy them. Here are some on-line services that workers value.

On-Line Reservations

Need a reservation? Don't call your travel agent—reach for your computer. The American Airlines reservation system, called Sabre, is one of the major reservation systems used by travel agents and airlines around the world. Now, for a fee, any business can have direct access to the Sabre system through its own computer. Individuals can have access to Sabre too. Users have immediate access to air fares at any hour of any day. Sabre reports an airline's on-time performance, uses a personalized profile to sort through flights and seating arrangements, spells out applicable restrictions, and summarizes your travel arrangements. Of course, you can get all this free from an airline or your travel agent, but some people prefer the convenience of making their own arrangements.

Weather Forecasting

We have long relied on the media, both television and print, to keep us informed about the weather. This service is adequate for most of us. Some businesses, however, are so dependent on the weather that they need constantly updated information. On-line services offer analysis of live weather data, including air pressure, fog, rain, and wind direction and speed. Businesses that depend on the weather include agriculture, amusement parks, ski areas, and transportation companies, all of which make business decisions based on weather forecasts. (This software, by the way, is not intended for large airports, which have their own trained meteorologists on staff.)

On-Line to the Stock Exchange

Stock portfolios can be managed by software that takes quotes on-line directly from established market monitors such as Dow Jones. The software keeps records and offers quick and accurate investment decisions. And, of course, the stock exchange itself is a veritable beehive of computers.

We must computer-communicate, but, increasingly, we must also use computer output in the forms of pictures.

7 Graphics Software

DISCUSSION QUESTION
How would a presentation prepared for a sales group differ from a presentation prepared by an advertising firm to a potential client? (Sales history and projections versus representations of advertising campaigns.)

Computer graphics are sometimes an appendage that can delight and entertain and inform. Businesspeople like to make a point by using graphics to express numbers in an easily understood form. But sometimes graphics are the chief function of a computer system. That is, some workers use graphics as an integral part of their jobs. We begin our list of examples with researchers.

Researchers

Some of us worry a little about earthquakes, but others get paid to worry about them. In particular, they care about underground formations, which can be shown effectively in graphic form (Figure 16-5a). Another research example did not originate as a computer-generated graphic; satellite photographs were digitized, reassembled in the computer, and produced in graphic form. These two examples are of government research, but private firms do an enormous amount of research to strengthen their product lines.

Artists and Designers

As a tool of their craft, artists can use sophisticated software to produce stunning computer art or produce a series of drawings that can be used in rapid sequence for animation. A clear business application of graphics is design. Everyone from architects to engineers to fashion designers can use the computer to design and simulate products (Figure 16-5b).

Musicians

Remember the old movies, the musicals that showed inspired composers hanging over the piano in the middle of the night? First we would see a few fingers dabbling at the keys, then a pause, a cocked ear, another bit of key tinkling and—finally—a pencil writing the notes on paper. Many composers work that way today. But some do not. Instead, they *play* the notes, and the computer—equipped with listening software—captures the notes and reproduces them as graphics on the screen (Figure 16-5c). The process can seem magical to people who are unaware of such computer prowess.

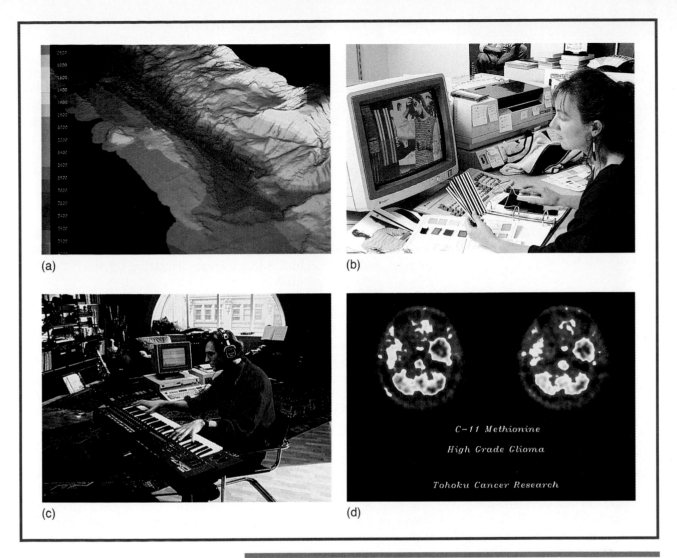

(a)

(b)

(c)

(d)

Figure 16-5   Graphics software at work.   (a) Off the coast of Chile, three rocky plates that make up the ocean floor come together. Varying growth rates are causing one of the plates to slide under another, disappearing the way the steps at the bottom of an escalator seem to vanish. (b) A designer at Levi Strauss creates fashions with the click of a mouse. (c) This musician is using a computer system that translates sounds into musical notation, bridging the gap between the inspiration that creates new music and the laborious task of writing the notes down. (d) Computer-generated PET scans give physicians and researchers information about the brain's activity. The uses of PET scans vary from diagnosing mental illnesses to identifying the parts of the brain involved in speech.

Doctors

How do you look inside the body to take its picture? The question is a little silly, but it illustrates the frustrations of doctors who have to work from fuzzy X rays. But medical imaging exploits computer power to make sharp snapshots of internal organs (Figure 16-5d).

SOFTWARE FOR YOUR CAREER

Paralyzed at the thought of finding your first job? Bored with the job you have and not sure how to look for a new one? You are a good candidate for career software, which will help you conduct a thorough and organized job search. A typical package takes you by the hand and teaches you how to assess your skills, develop career objectives, and write your resume and cover letters.

DISCUSSION QUESTION
How would decision-making software be implemented by an attorney, an office administrator or an engineer?

7 Decision-Making Software

You recall the columns of rows and numbers called spreadsheets. A key advantage of spreadsheets is swift automatic recalculation when variables are changed. The monthly payment on a loan, for example, is automatically recalculated when interest rates and time periods are varied. Once buyer and lender find an agreeable monthly payment, they can decide on the interest rate and time period of the loan. Beginning with loan amortization, let us consider some of the significant ways that businesses use decision-making software.

Loan Amortization

Software for loan amortization determines due dates, payment number, payment amount, principal, interest, accumulated interest, and loan balance. Most loan amortization software also produces yearly and monthly reports.

Break-Even Analysis

Can we afford the new equipment? Should we buy or lease? Should we try to compete in that market? Is the cost worth it? What is the payoff? At what point do we break even? Break-even software answers these questions and more—analyzing the relationships among variable costs, fixed costs, and income—and produces alternatives to consider. It sure beats hunches scribbled on the back of an envelope.

Property Management

Sometimes referred to as "the landlord," software can be used to manage any income property, whether marina, apartment complex, or shopping mall. The software can record charges and payments for each renter and produce a variety of reports, such as a lease expiration list and tax analysis lists for each property.

To make their business decisions, workers must often rely on stored information, our next topic.

7 Storage and Retrieval Software

Office workers and salespeople and manufacturers all use computers as tools in their businesses; most of these workers rely on access to stored information. In some cases, however, the computer service offered *becomes* the business. Some of these systems, such as the legal services described below, are major businesses, and others come from entrepreneurs working on computers in their homes. We begin with the standard type of information retrieval.

Crime Detection

A lot of crime detection involves a process of elimination, which is often tedious work. A tedious task, however, is often the kind the computer does best. Once data is entered into databases, then searching by computer becomes possible. Examples: Which criminals use this particular mode of operation? Which known criminals are on record as associates of this suspect? Is license number AXB221 a stolen car? And so on. A productive crime detection computer system is the fingerprint-matching system, which can match crime-scene fingerprints against computer-stored fingerprints (Figure 16-6a).

Sports Statistics

Here is the situation. Tied game, bases loaded, two outs, left-handed batter, bottom of the ninth. If you are coaching the team in the field, do you leave in the right-handed pitcher or pull him for a lefty? The seat-of-the-pants hunch is less common these days. Coaches and managers in professional sports want any help they can get. A wonderful source of help, one that can be carried right to the edge of the field, is the computer. All kinds of statistics can be stored in a database and retrieved on the spot (Figure 16-6b). For our bases-loaded example above, the manager can check statistics from the batter's past performance against each available pitcher.

Figure 16-6 Storage and retrieval software at work. (a) The Automated Fingerprint Identification System (AFIS) matches crime-scene fingerprints with fingerprints in computer files—in minutes instead of the days it takes human workers. (b) Coaches, managers, and commentators in professional sports have instant access to statistics about any player from any team.

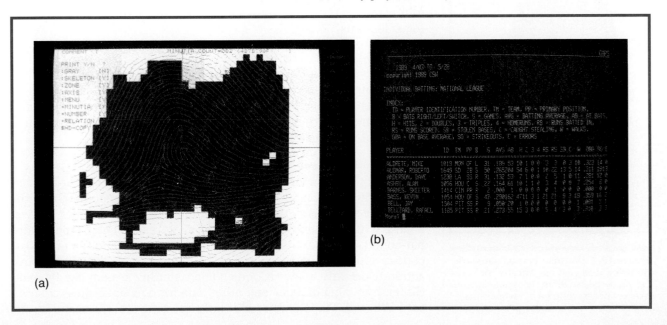

(a)

(b)

Performing Arts

People in the performing arts use computers as a standard business tool. They find databases particularly useful. Database software, for example, can search for the names of needed items, say all 20-minute violin pieces by German composers. The American Ballet Theatre takes their computers on tour: One database is used to plot rehearsal schedules, and another to keep track of sets, lighting, and costumes. Some sophisticated organizations use databases to coordinate ticket sales with fundraising; as a patron, this probably means that you will receive your tickets with great efficiency but also be solicited for a donation.

Legal Services

You have seen the formal photograph of the judge, the attorney, the politician—each with a solid wall of law books in the background. Those books are not just decoration, however. Any law office needs to be able to research legal precedents and other matters relating to the law. But why not take the information in those books and just "drop it" into the computer? That is, in essence, what has been done, converting the information in the books into computer-accessible databases, and cutting legal research time significantly. Two common computerized legal research systems are LEXIS and WESTLAW, available in most law libraries and law firms.

7 Vertical Market Software

Recall that a **vertical market** is a group of similar customers such as accountants or doctors. Some software makers specialize in computer systems for such markets (Figure 16-7). This user-oriented software usually presents options with a series of easy-to-follow menus that minimize training needed. Here are some interesting selections.

Auto Repair Shop

Designed in conjunction with people who understand the auto repair business, this all-in-one software can prepare work orders, process sales transactions, produce invoices, evaluate sales and profits, track parts inventory automatically, print reorder reports, and update the customer mailing list.

Videotape Rental

The primary goal is fast service. The concept for fast service is simple enough: Let the computer match customers and the tapes they rent. Here is how it works. Each regular customer is given a card with an identifying bar code on it; each rental tape is also bar-coded. At rental time, the customer's bar code and the tape's bar codes are scanned, causing an invoice to be printed. The entire transaction takes only a few seconds. (The scanning system can be overridden by typing in name and other data for new or cardless customers.) When the tape is returned, only the tape label is scanned; the

Figure 16-7   Vertical market software. Software designed specifically for vertical markets—such as accountants, engineers, lawyers, and real estate agents—is becoming increasingly popular.

MICROCOMPUTERS IN ACTION

Business Software Sampler

Going past the standard business software—spreadsheets, general ledger, payroll, desktop publishing, and so on—there are many interesting offerings. Brand names change, so we will describe software categories. Some serious and some less so, here are some samples:

- **Name Tag Kit.** Prepare professional-looking tags inexpensively, and still have the flexibility to include last-minute attendees. Complete kit includes software, blank name tags, and plastic holders. Several fonts available.
- **Client Tracker.** This package is for any business that has a customer sales component. A typical package keeps a complete, up-to-date record of all business contacts, available at a moment's notice. Software tracks clients, sets up daily call lists, prepares sales reports, and prints mailing labels.
- **Employee Training Tutorials.** Some managers think that the computer can be an effective and relatively inexpensive way to train employees. Software is available, by product brand name, to train people at their own pace in word processing, spreadsheets, database management, and other commonly used applications. The teaching packages use interactive instruction methods—trainees follow instructions on the screen and then note feedback on their performance as they go along.

- **Banner Maker.** Get employee attention by announcing events in a big way. Banner software can produce quality output on a simple dot-matrix printer. Mix styles and letter sizes on the same banner. Great for office parties, too.
- **Disk Labeler.** This handy program reads the files on a diskette in a given drive and then prints a label listing all the files. The label can then be attached to the exterior of the disk, for easy identification. This is particularly useful for a user who must keep track of many diskettes.
- **Certificate Maker.** This type of software lets users create awards and certificates for employees. A typical package offers several hundred options. A user picks borders, enters a specific message, and leaves room for a gold foil seal, included in the package.

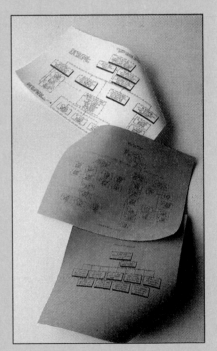

- **Organization Charts.** Here is the fastest way to create professional-looking organization charts. Just type in names, titles, projects, and so on and let the software do the rest. The charts can be changed easily when personnel change.

MIRROR, MIRROR ON THE WALL

Never mind the mirror—let's check the computer. Computers are used for many applications, most of them more serious than this one. However, it will probably become routine to check out a new hair style on the computer before making a mistake that will take six months to grow out.

Begin by selecting a hairdo from a catalog. The computer preview system compares a computer image of the "real you" with one that adds a new style or color from the computer's repertoire. Too fluffy? Too short? Too dark? No problem: Simply select another style and repeat the process until you are satisfied.

STUDENT PROJECT
Challenge students to determine how a video rental store would need to be equipped to handle tape rental and return by computer. What hardware and software would be needed?

system automatically credits the proper customer with the return. The software can produce a variety of reports, such as reports of overdue rentals and mailing lists.

Beauty Salon

Does your hairdresser really remember exactly how to do your hair and that you like yard work and movies? Maybe. But it is more likely that a card is on file somewhere, listing your preferences. In some shops, that "card" is stored in the computer. Before you arrive, this information can be pulled up on a screen. After you leave, the salon immediately updates your customer history. In addition, the computer credits your stylist for providing the service and uses this data to calculate the stylist's commission. Reports include sales summary by period, product inventories, appointment reminder cards, thank you cards, and promotional letters.

Mailing Lists

Traditionally ignored as a "nickel and dime" expense, managers are now viewing their company mailing list as a target for cost reduction. There are many software packages to generate mailing lists; cost savings can result from trimming and focusing them. "Hunter-killer" software roots out incomplete addresses and duplicates, even if they are not quite identical in appearance. This kind of software can use addresses intelligently. For example, if the mailing is to be a lawn care circular, it can eliminate addresses that include "Apt."

7 What Could Possibly Be Next?

What indeed! The future is already in sight. In just a few years, workers of all kinds will wonder how today's mute, passive boxes were ever called computers. Say it again—*in just a few years*—personal computers, or terminals hooked up to bigger machines, will talk and listen and display full-color life-like images. No computer will be an island: They will seamlessly talk to one another, taking calls and writing memos. Computers will provide easy guidance through vast "storehouses" of information—encyclopedias, huge databases, newspapers, films, stockholder reports, and much more. People who cannot leave their computers at home will take them along—but the newer, smaller models will be appropriately called pocket computers.

Other computers may disappear altogether, disappearing into the furniture to become part of the desk, the cabinet, the blackboard. For it is the fate of the computer to move into the background—and to be everywhere.

Summary and Key Terms

- The companies that use mainframe computers today are mostly the same companies that were computer pioneers, large corporations that have large budgets. Early users used computers for clerical tasks. When computers began to be used interactively, businesspeople saw that the computer could be used as a service tool.

- Mid-range computers made "number crunching" and computerized service available to medium-size companies. But it was the highly affordable personal computer that really opened up computing for the worker.

- A partial list of where computers are used: retail, finance, insurance, real estate, health care, education, government, legal services, sports, politics, publishing, transportation, manufacturing, agriculture, and construction.

- Personal computer use seems to evolve in three phases: transformation of an individual's productivity, transformation of a department, and transformation of a business.

- Personal computers will radically alter the business world for two reasons: (1) They have brought the cost of computing down to the level of a mass-produced consumer product and (2) they have worked their way into most business organizations.

- Many workers must know how to use a personal computer to perform some part of a job. If a job requires the use of a personal computer, it is likely that the worker will receive some on-the-job training.

- Computers are changing the way individuals and organizations work.

- There are many ways to speed up business operations, including putting the computer to work whenever possible.

- By providing timely access to data, computers let us spend less time checking data and more time getting things done.

- The ideal set of machines for achieving worker portability consists of personal computers, a laptop computer, a laser printer, and a facsimile machine. The computers have modems and appropriate software.

- A **personal information manager** (**PIM**) is software that helps any worker cope with assorted information in different formats, such as telephone messages, Post-it notes, newspaper clippings, expense tabs, appointment cards, and other scraps of paper. PIMs use windows so that several features can be on-screen at the same time. Some PIMs offer quite sophisticated features, organizing diverse text-based information for project management or business analysis.

- Businesses use software for communications, graphics, decision-making, and storage and retrieval of information.

- **Vertical market software** is software for a group of similar customers such as accountants or doctors.

- In just a few years, personal computers, or terminals hooked up to bigger machines, will talk, listen, and display full-color life-like images. Computers will talk to one another, taking calls and writing memos. Computers will provide easy guidance through vast amounts of information. Computers will move into the background and be everywhere.

Discussion Questions

1. Consider these five firms. What uses would each have for computers? Mention as many possibilities as you can.

   Security Southwestern Bank, a major regional bank with several branches

   Azure Design, a small graphic-design company that produces posters, covers, and other artwork

   Checkerboard Taxi Service, whose central office manages a fleet of 160 cabs that operate in an urban area

   Gillick College, a private college that has automated all student services, such as registration, financial aid, testing, and more.

   Duffin Realty, a realty firm with multiple listings and 27 agents.

2. What careers are you considering? Discuss how you might use computers in a future career.

17

Management Information Systems

Managing Computer Resources

Who is going to manage the computer sprawl—the corporate mainframes, the personal computers, the computer-controlled factory, and all the networks that tie them together? In this chapter we will discuss how management is aided by information systems and look at the Management Information Systems (MIS) Department, which has the responsibility for computer systems. We will also consider how managers themselves benefit from personal computers.

LEARNING OBJECTIVES
* Understanding the main functions of managers — planning, organizing, staffing, controlling, and directing.
* Knowledge of the purpose and components of a management information system (MIS).
* Understanding the functions of the microcomputer manager.
* Understanding the need for decision support systems.
* Familiarization with the use of expert systems in business.

Mark Dalton pursued a business degree with the goal of a career in management. He was uncertain, however, about his career ambitions. He thought that someday he would like to be at the very top of an organization, with—perhaps—an office with a stunning view. He thought it was more likely, however, that he would end up somewhere in the middle, reporting to the top bosses but with responsibilities for major activities below him. He assumed that his entry to management would be at the lowest rung on the ladder, in direct contact with the workers, supervising their operations and making sure they had what they needed to do the job.

As it happened, Mark did all these things, but not in the way he expected. While he was in college, he began a computer word processing service, typing up his classmates' term papers and resumes. He used part of his profits to buy a laser printer and desktop publishing software, and thus was able to produce professional-looking documents, a service he offered to local small businesses. Mark's business-on-the-side grew beyond his expectations; he decided to go into business for himself full-time after graduation. Mark was his own boss and managed a group of employees. As the company grew, he managed at all levels, and eventually had an office that overlooked the cityscape.

But whether managing your own company or someone else's, whether at the top, middle, or bottom level, the challenge is the same: to use available resources to get the job done on time, within budget, and to the satisfaction of all concerned. Let us begin with a discussion of how managers do this, then see how computer systems can help them.

7 Classic Management Functions

Managers have five main functions:

* **Planning.** Managers devise both short-range and long-range plans for the organization and set goals to help achieve the plans.

* **Organizing.** Managers decide how to use resources such as people and materials.

* **Staffing.** Managers hire and train workers.

* **Directing.** Managers guide employees to perform their work in a way that supports the organization's goals.

* **Controlling.** Managers monitor the organization's progress toward reaching its goals.

All managers perform these functions as part of their jobs. The level of responsibility associated with these functions, however, varies with the level of the manager.

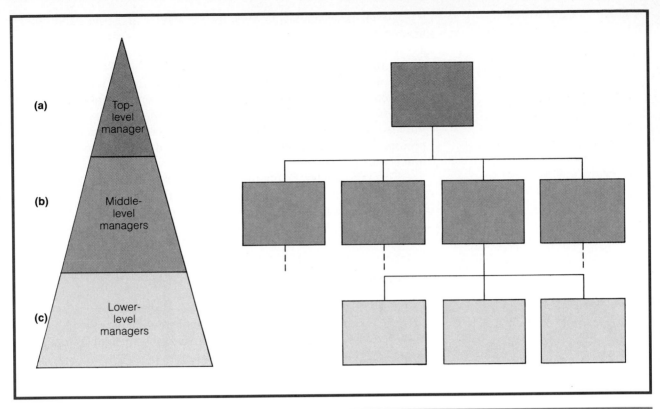

TRANSPARENCY ACETATE #17A
The Organization of an Organization

Figure 17-1 The three levels of management. (a) Top managers handle long-range planning; (b) middle managers are more concerned with the organizational and personnel issues involved in carrying out plans. (c) Lower-level managers direct and control day-to-day operations.

Whether they are the head of General Electric or an electrical appliance store or of a large company or a small one, top-level managers have to be concerned with the long-range view—with **planning** (Figure 17-1a). Consider a survey showing that Americans want family vacations and want the flexibility and economy of a motor vehicle; however, they also want more space than the family car provides. To the president of a major auto company, this information may suggest further opportunities for expansion of their recreational vehicle line.

Middle-level managers must be able to take a somewhat different view because their main concern is **organizing** (Figure 17-1b). The middle manager will prepare to carry out the visions of the top-level managers, assembling the material and personnel resources to do the job. Note that these tasks include the **staffing** function. Suppose the public is inclined to buy more recreational vehicles. To a production vice president, this may mean organizing production lines using people with the right skills at the right wage and perhaps farming out portions of the assembly that can be done by cheaper, less-skilled labor.

Lower-level managers, usually known as first-line supervisors, are primarily concerned with **directing** and **controlling** (Figure 17-1c). Personnel must be directed to perform the planned activities. These managers must also monitor progress closely. In the process the supervisor—an assembly-line supervisor in our recreational vehicle example—is involved in a number of issues: making sure that workers have the parts needed when they need them, checking employee attendance, maintaining quality control, handling complaints, keeping a close watch on the schedule, tracking costs, and much more.

To make decisions about planning, organizing, staffing, directing, and controlling, managers need data that is organized into information that is useful for them. An effective management information system can provide it.

7 MIS for Managers

A **management information system** (**MIS**) may be defined as a set of formal business systems designed to provide information for an organization. (Incidentally, you may hear the term *MIS system,* even though the *S* in the abbreviation stands for *system;* this is an accepted redundancy.) Whether or not such a system is called an MIS, every company has one. Even managers who make hunch-based decisions are operating with some sort of information system—one based on their experience. The kind of MIS we are concerned with here includes a computer as one of its components. Information serves no purpose until it gets to its users. Timeliness is important, and the computer can act quickly to produce information.

The extent of a computerized MIS varies from company to company, but the most effective kinds are those that are integrated. An integrated MIS incorporates all five managerial functions—planning, organizing, staffing, directing, and controlling—throughout the company, from typing to top-executive forecasting. An integrated management computer system uses the computer to solve problems for an entire organization, instead of attacking them piecemeal. Although in many companies the complete integrated system is still only an idea, the scope of MIS is expanding rapidly in many organizations.

The **MIS manager** runs the MIS department. This position has been called Information Resource Manager, Director of Information Services, Chief Information Officer, and a variety of other titles. In any case, the person who serves in this capacity should be comfortable with both computer technology and the organization's business.

7 MIS Reports for Managers

A computer system can produce different kinds of reports, which can be described as summary, exception, or detail reports. Reports can also be categorized as periodic or on-demand. **Periodic reports** are produced on a regular schedule, such as daily or monthly, and are preplanned to produce detail, summary, or exception data. These reports are printed. **On-demand reports** reflect their name, giving information in response to an unscheduled demand—a request—from a user. On-demand reports are often produced directly on a terminal or microcomputer screen, although the report can be printed as well. Let us look more closely at these reports in the context of their value to managers.

- **Top-level managers.** For strategic planning, high-level managers need to be able to see historical information—an analysis of data trends—not for just some parts of their business but for the total business. Moreover, such managers must be able to make decisions about things that happen unpredictably. The MIS, therefore, must be able to produce on-demand reports that integrate information and show how factors affecting various departments are related to each other. An on-demand report might show the impact of strikes or energy shortages on all parts of the company.

- **Middle-level managers.** To do their tactical planning and organizing functions, middle-level managers need to be aware of trends; to know what the business is doing and where it is going. Thus, these managers are most in need of summary reports and exception reports. **Summary reports** are limited to totals or trends. Examples of summary reports showing trends are those showing past and present interest rates or sales data (Figure 17-2a). **Exception reports** show only data that reflects unusual circumstances. Examples of exception reports are those showing depleted budgets, payments being made to temporary employees, and books temporarily out of stock or not yet published (Figure 17-2b).

- **Low-level managers.** Concerned mainly with day-to-day operations, low-level managers need **detail reports,** which give complete, specific information on routine operations; these reports help keep offices and plants running. Examples are overtime information from this week's payroll, spare parts that need to be ordered, quality-control results of yesterday's inspections at Dock B, and books to be shipped (Figure 17-2c). Many computer-based MISs are self-determining—that is, they can take some preplanned actions on their own. An MIS can, for example, automatically reorder depleted stock as directed by an inventory management program or automatically issue bonuses for salespeople when incoming orders reach a certain level.

It should be clear that an MIS must be capable of delivering both detailed and general information not only on a regular schedule but also to fill unpredictable requests.

(a) Summary report:

```
FOUR-YEAR SALES TITLE REPORT AS OF 1/31/91
MATHEMATICS-AUTHOR & TITLE

50239 LYON TRIGONOMETRY
1990 QTY        1989 QTY        1988 QTY        1987 QTY
 15,813          16,239          20,871          23,918

50240 SMITH LINEAR MATH
1990 QTY        1989 QTY        1988 QTY        1987 QTY
 25,031          25,502          29,193          22,108

50241 ANDREWS COLLEGE MATH
1990 QTY        1989 QTY        1988 QTY        1987 QTY
 20,013          18,925          19,931          23,206
```

(b) Exception report:

```
AVAILABILITY DATE LISTING-
TITLES TEMP OUT OF STOCK OR NOT YET PUBLISHED 1/31/91

CODE AUTHOR & TITLE                        AVAILABLE

00089 BYRNE ELEM STATISTICS               APR  2, 91
00093 BLUESTONE ANTHROPOLOGY              MAR  3, 91
00156 ALBRIGHT INFECTIOUS DISEASES        APR 28, 91
```

(c) Detail report:

```
DAILY SALES REGISTER BY TYPE OF SALE   1/31/91   PAGE 1

SHIP-TO ADDRESS          CODE AUTHOR&  LIST    QTY  TOTAL
                         TITLE         PRICE        AMOUNT

THE SOUTH MAIN           36980 WILSON  22.95   100  2295.00
BOOKSTORE                ANATOMY &
209 SOUTH MAIN           PHYSIOLOGY
CHICAGO, IL 60625

UNIVERSITY BOOKSTORE     50239 LYON    17.95   300  5385.00
OLD STATE COLLEGE        TRIGONOMETRY
800 W VICTORIA ST
STAMFORD, CT 06903

EASTERN ARCATA UNIV      34102 SPENCE  17.95   400  7180.00
BOOKSTORE                GENETICS
PO BOX 8769
ARCATA, CA 95521
```

Figure 17-2 Three kinds of reports. These are examples of the kinds of reports a book publisher might use. (a) This report summarizes the sales of math books over the previous four years. (b) This exception report lists titles temporarily out of stock or not yet published. (c) This report provides the details on books to be shipped.

7 The Scope of Responsibility: Turf Wars

Is the MIS manager responsible for the whole company? Not really, but sometimes it seems that way. If computers are everywhere—and they are—can the MIS department be far behind? For a long time—through the 1960s and 1970s—anyone who needed computer services made a formal request to the computer professionals. That is, employees had to present their needs to the official keepers of automated power, where information was dispensed. A great deal of power, both computer and political, was concentrated in one place. Distribution of power has come in a variety of ways. As we noted in Chapter 6, for example, placing smaller computers in remote locations, such as branch offices, gave computer users better access and, consequently, more control. But the biggest change was made by placing personal computers directly in the hands of users.

In many ways, however, this distribution of power is an illusion. Users are constrained by their needs for the corporate data, and the data is still firmly in the hands of the MIS department. Many personal computers are plugged into networks that the MIS department must control and monitor. Users also rely heavily on MIS-run information centers, which help them with computer-related problems. It certainly seems that a lot of power still rests with the MIS manager.

And recently, manufacturing has become an area of focus for the MIS department. The demand from top management to increase productivity in the manufacturing arena is escalating, and computer technology is considered the answer. So, there is one more set of technologies for the MIS manager to contend with. What this will probably mean, however, is a battle over territory. Manufacturing managers would prefer to keep the MIS department out of the production process but, as more technologies are introduced, they have no choice but to include MIS—that is, if they want to meet their end goal of increasing productivity.

The MIS manager is gaining authority over an empire that is getting more and more unruly, with computers and computer users spread all over the company. The role of the MIS department is changing from the caretaker of large computers to the supporter of computers and their networks right in the user's environment. And there is a more subtle change: MIS managers can no longer hide behind the protective cloak of technical mystery because their users have become more sophisticated. In effect, even the interpersonal style of the MIS manager is changing.

There are two issues here: control of power and the nature of the MIS manager's job. Although it is clear that the MIS department dominates the company's use of computers, ultimate control lies with the users themselves, who pay the bills for computer services. As for the MIS manager, that job will be in flux for the foreseeable future. As technology changes, so will the focus and scope of the job.

DISCUSSION QUESTION
Who controls the use of computers and data within a company?

DISCUSSION QUESTION
What is the role of the MIS department in large companies? How is it changing?

7 Managing Microcomputers

Microcomputers—personal computers—burst on the business scene in the early 1980s with little warning and less planning. The experience of the Rayer International Paper Company is typical. One day a personal computer appeared on the desk of engineer Mike Burton—he had brought his in from home. Then accountants Sandy Dean and Mike Molyneaux got a pair of machines—they had squeezed the money for them out of the overhead budget. Keith Wong, the personnel manager, got personal computers for himself and his three assistants in the company's far-flung branch offices. And so it went, with personal computers popping up all over the company. Managers realized that the reason for runaway purchases was that personal computers were so affordable: Most departments could pay for them out of existing budgets, so the purchasers did not have to ask anyone's permission.

Managers, at first, were tolerant. There were no provisions for managing the purchase or use of personal computers, and there certainly was no rule *against* them. And it was soon apparent that these were more than toys. Pioneer users had no trouble justifying their purchases with increased productivity. In addition to mastering software for word processing, spreadsheets, and database access, they declared their independence from the MIS department.

Managers, however, soon were faced with several problems. The first was incompatibility—the new computers came in an assortment of brands and models and did not mesh well. Software that worked on one machine did not necessarily work on another. Secondly, users were not as independent of the MIS department as they had thought—they needed assistance in a variety of ways. In particular, they needed data that was in the hands of the MIS department. And, finally, no one person was in charge of the headlong plunge into personal computers. Many organizations solved these management problems in these ways:

- They addressed the compatibility problem by establishing acquisition policies.

- They solved the assistance problem by creating information centers.

- They corrected the management problem by creating a new position called the microcomputer manager.

Let us examine each of these solutions.

7 Microcomputer Acquisition

In an office environment managers know they must control the acquisition and use of micros, but they are not always sure how to do it. As we noted, workers initially purchased personal computers before any companywide or even officewide policies had

MICROCOMPUTERS IN ACTION

Microcomputers in Business

Microcomputers are in businesses big and small. Here is a cross section of some computer applications.

- **Hotel management.** The Hilton Hotel chain uses a micro-to-mainframe link to connect its hotels to the main headquarters system. The system gives hotels two-way communication; the reservation system, for example, can both send and receive information.
- **Newspaper reporting.** The *Dallas Morning News* has over 100 laptop computers assigned to reporters, who take them everywhere from ballparks to inaugurations. In the office, computers are used for the extensive graphics imagery the paper uses on each page.
- **In-store shopping.** Bloomingdale's, the New York department store, offers a touchscreen computer system that lets customers select a category and then see pictures, prices, and other information about items

for sale. However, the customer still needs to find a salesperson to make a purchase.

- **Shelf stocking.** Frito-Lay employees use hand-held computers to monitor the movement of its snack food products. The data gathered helps the company justify ever scarcer shelf space to grocers.
- **Baseball records.** The Baseball Hall of Fame in Cooperstown, New York—yes, it is a business—features a user-interactive computer. Visitors can spend hours comparing the baseball statistics of their heroes.

- **Stock trading.** Shearson Lehman Hutton, the brokerage house, lets customers use their own computers to call up instant information. To gain access to these services, a customer needs only a personal computer and a modem. Software is provided by the brokerage firm.
- **Door-to-door selling.** Amway distributors, who sell cosmetics, detergents, and other household products nationwide, now have personal computers that they can use to place orders directly to the headquarters office in Michigan.
- **Restaurant management.** Las Casuelas Terraza, a restaurant in Palm Springs that seats 200 people, uses microcomputers to automate the cashier system, keep track of food inventory, design and print the menus, monitor employee comings and goings, and keep track of employee tips.

DISCUSSION QUESTION
What is the value of the MIS department initiating policies to control the acquisition of microcomputers?

been set. The resulting compatibility problems meant that they could not easily communicate or share data. Consider this example: A user's budget process may call for certain data that resides in the files of another worker's micro or perhaps output incorporating the figures produced by still a third person. If the software and machines these people use do not mesh, compatibility becomes a major problem.

In many companies MIS departments have now taken control of microcomputer acquisition. The methods vary, but often include the following:

- **Standards.** Most companies now have established standards for personal computers, for the software that will run on them, and for data communications. Commonly, users must stay within established standards so they can tie into corporate resources. For example, if IBM PS/2 architecture is the standard, then a compatible machine is acceptable.

- **Limited vendors.** Some companies limit the number of vendors—sellers of hardware and software—from whom they allow purchases. MIS managers have discovered they can prevent most user complaints about incompatibility by allowing products from just a handful of vendors.

- **Limited support.** MIS departments generally control a company's purchases by specifying which hardware and software products will be supported by the MIS department.

As you can see, these methods overlap. But all of them, in one form or another, give the MIS department control. In other words, users are being told, "If you want to do it some other way, then you're on your own."

DISCUSSION QUESTION
Which of the potential services provided by a company's information center would have the most value for different departments, such as accounting, human resources, marketing, sales or research and development?

Figure 17-3   The information center. Classes are held at the information center to teach managers and other employees how to use the company's computers.

7 The Information Center

If personal computer users compared notes, they would probably find that their experiences are similar. The experience of budget analyst Gwen Price is typical. She convinced her boss to let her have her own personal computer so she could analyze financial data. She purchased a popular spreadsheet program and, with some help from her colleagues, learned to use it. She soon thought about branching out in other areas. She wanted a statistics software package but was not sure which one was appropriate. She thought it would be useful to have a modem but did not feel she was equipped to make a hardware decision. And, most of all, she felt her productivity would increase significantly if she could get her hands on the data in the corporate data files.

The company **information center** is the MIS solution to these kinds of needs. Although no two are alike, a typical information center gives users support for the user's own equipment. The information center is devoted exclusively to giving users service. And, best of all, user assistance is immediate, with little or no red tape.

Information center services often include the following:

- **Software selection.** Information center staff helps users determine which software packages suit their needs.

- **Data access.** If appropriate, the staff helps users get data from the large corporate computer systems for use on the users' own computers.

- **Training.** Education is a principal reason for an information center's existence. Classes are usually small, frequent, and on a variety of topics (Figure 17-3).

- **Technical assistance.** Information center staff members stand ready to assist in any way possible, short of actually doing the users' work for them. That help includes advising on hardware purchases, aiding in the selection and use of software, finding errors, helping submit formal requests to the MIS department, and so forth.

DISCUSSION QUESTION
What are the attributes that make information centers within companies successful?

To be successful, the information center must be placed in an easily accessible location. The center should be equipped with microcomputers and terminals, a stockpile of software packages, and perhaps a library. It should be staffed with people who have a technical background but whose explanations feature plain English. Their mandate is "The user comes first."

7 The Microcomputer Manager

And who is going to manage the revolution? The users-get-computers revolution, that is. The benefits of personal computers for the individual user have been clear almost from the beginning: increased productivity, worker enthusiasm, and easier access to information. But once personal computers move beyond entry status, standard corporate accountability becomes a factor; large companies are spending millions of dollars on personal computers and top-level managers want to know where all this money is going. Company auditors begin worrying about data security. The company legal department begins to worry about workers illegally copying software. Before long, everyone is involved, and it is clear that someone must be placed in charge of personal computer use. That person is the **microcomputer manager.**

There are four key areas that need the attention of the micro manager:

- **Technology overload.** The micro manager must maintain a clear vision of company goals so that users are not overwhelmed by the massive and conflicting claims of aggressive vendors plying their wares. Users engulfed by phrases like *network topologies* and *file gateways* or a jumble of acronyms can turn to the micro manager for guidance with their purchases.

- **Cost control.** Many people who work with personal computers believe the initial costs are paid back rapidly, and they think that should satisfy managers who hound them about expenses. But the real costs entail training, support, hardware and software extras, and communications networks—much more than just the computer itself. The micro manager's role includes monitoring *all* the expenses.

- **Data security and integrity.** Access to corporate data is a touchy issue. Many personal computer users find they want to **download** data from the corporate mainframe to their own machines, and this presents an array of problems. Are they entitled to the data? Will they manipulate the data in new ways, then present it as the official version? Will they expect MIS to take the data back after

PERSPECTIVES

GROWING PAINS

When it comes to placing personal computers in the office, it is clear that the good outweighs the bad. Computerization is not without growing pains, however. Now that the excitement of computerization has subsided, it is possible to view the process objectively. Consider these common problems.

Hidden Costs

Placing computers in the office may involve hidden costs. The obvious costs are hardware, software, and supplies. Additional costs may include connection to a local area network, shared long-distance communications, shared database management systems, shared mainframe access—and the cost of troubleshooting all these activities. There may also be a need for changes in the office environment, such as improving lighting, rewiring the site for additional electric power, increasing the amount of air-conditioning, and providing improved acoustics to reduce the noise generated by the new equipment. Startup costs for training are obvious, but hidden startup costs may include inefficiencies in serving customers by new and unfamiliar means, time spent converting existing files to computer-readable form, job interruptions due to unfamiliar procedures, and time spent in meetings to negotiate changes in handling the work.

Personnel Problems

Fear tops the list: fear of looking stupid, fear of diminished power, fear of job loss. All these fears have some basis; or at least all are possibilities. But a manager should anticipate these problems and alleviate them with thorough training. There is also some worry about health problems, especially eyestrain and backstrain.

Mixing and Matching

Equipment for personal computers in the office is rarely acquired in one gigantic purchase. Although making purchases over time offers some advantages for cash flow, it produces an Excedrin headache in terms of problems—separately purchased machines often cannot communicate or exchange data.

Security

Personal computers in the office present a new variety of security problems. Office systems and home systems have much in common, and well-intentioned users and system abusers both find that this compatibility leads to migration of software to home computer systems. Another costly problem is that office workers are finding it easy to steal keyboards, modems, software, diskettes, and supplies. Creative fixes are on the market. One, for example, sounds a piercing alarm if a component is disconnected. This does not do much, however, about the software-laden diskettes going out the door in briefcases.

Office systems are particularly vulnerable to security lapses because they use data that is in more "finished" form. Rather than the masses of detail data being manipulated on mainframes, office systems accumulate correspondence and summary information.

DISCUSSION QUESTION
What are some of the hidden costs in buying and using microcomputers?

DISCUSSION QUESTION
How are computer junkies and hackers different? What problems can they cause?

they have done who-knows-what with it? The answers to these perplexing questions are not always clear-cut, but at least the micro manager will be tuned in to the issues.

- **Computer junkies.** And what about employees who are feverish with the new power and freedom of the computer? When they are in school, these user-abusers are called hackers, but on the job they are often called junkies because their fascination with the computer seems like an addiction. Unable to resist the allure of the machine, they overuse it and neglect their other work. Micro managers usually respond to this problem by setting down guidelines for computer use.

Figure 17-4   The boss gets a computer.

TEST BANK
Mult. Choice	26-32
T/F	50-80
Matching A	1-3, 6-7
Matching B	3, 7-8
Matching C	9-10
Fill-in-the-Blank	24-30

The person selected to be the micro manager is usually from the MIS area. Ideally, this person has a broad technical background, understands both the potential and limitations of personal computers, and is well known to a diverse group of users.

One way that the micro manager can keep the support of top-level managers is to make sure those managers have their own computers.

When the Boss Gets a Computer

All over this land business executives, frustrated by the backlog of unfinished work in their corporate MIS departments, have opted for do-it-yourself, buying their own personal computers and packaged software. Sometimes these executives are even the heads of companies (Figure 17-4).

One chief executive officer of a pharmaceutical company, for instance, wanted direct access to company finance and sales data. With some assistance from a computer specialist within the company, he purchased microcomputers for himself and his staff. They took classes in software applications, particularly spreadsheet software. This software let them examine issues of business strategy such as the level of sales discounts and advertising support needed to reach his company's sales targets. Earlier strategic planning was fairly informal: "We just eyeballed the numbers and made our best guesses." Now all that has changed. In fact, computers make a very significant difference in how managers do their jobs.

How Computers Impact Managers

People who dismiss the impact of the personal computer sometimes say, "It's just another tool." Some tool. The personal computer is making profound changes in the work lives of businesspeople who use it, though some seem unaware of what is going on.

Regional business manager Augusta Green, for example, stoutly insists, "The computer hasn't changed *my* life." But listen to the changes. When asked how she uses her machine, she begins by describing her early microcomputer projects. One was drawing up a budget and the other was designing a compensation package for the 80 people under her supervision. Later, she added hardware and software to send electronic messages to people in the office, dispatch electronic mail to other parts of the country, and call up articles from the business press. She also uses her computer to write memos and reports—"a piece of cake," she says.

Augusta eventually succumbed to a second personal computer at home, which she uses to do office work in the evening. She finds it easier to carry diskettes to and fro than to lug a briefcase full of paper. Most mornings, in fact, Augusta tosses her diskettes into her

DISCUSSION QUESTION
Why are models useful in making important business decisions?

Figure 17-5 **Making decisions with the help of a computer.** Businesspeople use computers to "try out" different scenarios, without investing a great deal of time and money.

out-box, knowing the secretary will take it from there. Finally, Augusta reflects on all this activity. "Everything I do on the computer," she says, "I do ten times faster than I used to do it."

For many managers, the machine that is "just a tool" speeds analysis to a breakneck pace, answers all sorts of "What if . . . ?" questions, sends and receives mail, and lets executives stay home more. In earlier chapters we discussed some of the key software packages—word processing, spreadsheets, graphics, database management, and desktop publishing—that help make these things possible. Now we want to take a closer look at software of special significance to managers: decision support systems and expert systems.

7 Decision Support Systems

Imagine yourself as a top-level manager trying to deal with a constantly changing environment, having to consider changes in competition, in technology, in consumer habits, in government regulations, in union demands, and so on. How are you going to make decisions about those matters for which there are no precedents? In fact, making one-of-a-kind decisions—decisions that no one has had to make before—is the real test of a manager's mettle. In such a situation, you would probably wish you could turn to someone and ask a few "What if . . . ?" questions (Figure 17-5).

"What if . . . ?" That is the question businesspeople want answered, at least for those important decisions that have no precedent. A **decision support system** (**DSS**) is a computer system that supports managers in nonroutine decision-making tasks. The key ingredient of a decision support system is a modeling process. A **model** is a mathematical representation of a real-life system. A mathematical model can be computerized. Like any computer program, the model can use inputs to produce outputs. The inputs to a model are called **independent variables** because they can change; the out-

GROWN-UP GAMES

Want to make it big in business? Test your mettle with this software game. You have to be tough to play—it's not for kids. Written by people from the prestigious Wharton School of Business at the University of Pennsylvania, the game teaches you to be a survivor in the world of business. The name of the game is—take a deep breath—the Individual Learning Edition of The Strategic Management Game.

The point of the game is to run a profitable business while the computer changes economic and political conditions. The program is set up to provide increasing levels of difficulty as you prove that you can cope with increasingly complicated conditions.

The game was originally designed to train managers at some of America's largest corporations—AT&T, IBM, and General Foods. Perhaps, when you have successfully navigated level 5, you could compete with the managers of these firms. Interested? Call SMG Inc. at (215) 387-4000. Oh, the price is $350.

DISCUSSION QUESTION
Can "computer games" fulfill training functions in the business environment?

LECTURE ACTIVITY
Demonstrate an adult computer game by obtaining a software training or assessment package from the school placement office. Many computer stores also have versions of flight simulator programs that could be demonstrated in class.

puts are called **dependent variables** because they depend on the inputs.

Consider this example. Suppose, as a manager, you have the task of deciding which property to purchase for one of your manufacturing processes. You have many factors to consider: the asking price, interest rate, down payment required, and so on. These are all independent variables—the data that will be fed into the computer model of the purchase. The dependent variables, computed on the basis of the inputs, are the effect on your cash resources, long-term debt, and ability to make other investments. To increase complexity, we could add that the availability of workers and nearness to markets are also input factors. Increasing the complexity factor, in fact, is appropriate because decision support systems often work with problems that are more complex than any one individual can handle.

Using a computer model to reach a decision about a real-life situation is called **simulation.** It is a game of "let's pretend." You plan the independent variables—the inputs—and you examine how the model behaves based on the dependent variables—the outputs—it produces. If you wish you may change the inputs and continue experimenting. This is a relatively inexpensive way to simulate life situations, and it is considerably faster than the real thing.

A decision support system does not replace MIS; instead DSS supplements MIS. There are distinct differences between them. MIS emphasizes planned reports on a variety of subjects; DSS focuses on decision making. MIS is standard, scheduled, structured, routine; DSS is quite unstructured and available on request. MIS is constrained by the organizational system; DSS is immediate and friendly.

The decision-making process must be fast, so the DSS is interactive: The user is in direct communication with the computer system and can affect its activities. In addition, most DSSs cross departmental lines so that information can be pulled from the databases of a variety of sources such as marketing and sales, accounting and finance, production, and research and development. A manager trying to make a decision about developing a new product needs information from all these sources.

Several commercial software packages are available for specific modeling purposes. The purpose might be marketing, sales, or advertising. There are also more general packages available that provide rudimentary modeling but let you customize the model for different purposes such as budgeting, planning, or risk analysis.

There is another possibility. Suppose that a full-scale decision support system is not needed. In fact, let us say that the key decisions that need support involve exploring a number of alternatives by varying assumptions about market size, market share, selling prices, manufacturing costs, and expenses. Sound familiar? Right, we are talking about a perfect application for a spreadsheet program. Today's most widely used decision support system is spreadsheet software. So, although a DSS can be very formal and complicated

DISCUSSION QUESTION
Why were expert systems
developed? How do these
programs differ from
decision-support systems?

and suited to the needs of a sophisticated user, there are several
common high-quality packages that serve the needs of everyday people who make decisions.

7 Expert Systems in Business

An **expert system** is a software package used with an extensive set of organized data that presents the computer as an expert
on some topic. The user is the knowledge seeker, usually asking
questions in a natural—English-like—language format. An expert
system can respond to an inquiry about a problem—"What will happen if the bill of particulars is not received before the adjourned
deadline?"—with both an answer and an explanation of the answer.
(This is a legal question using a lawyer's "natural language," and the
answer is probably: "Prepare a motion to dismiss the case.") The
expert system works by figuring out what the question means, then
matching it against the facts and rules that it "knows." These facts
and rules, which reside on disk, originally come from a human expert (Figure 17-6).

For years, expert systems were no more than a bold experiment,
the exclusive property of the medical and scientific community.
Special programs could offer medical diagnoses or search for mineral deposits or examine chemical compounds. But in the early
1980s, expert systems began to make their way into commercial applications. Expert systems are slowly finding a place in big business.
Consider the examples on the following page.

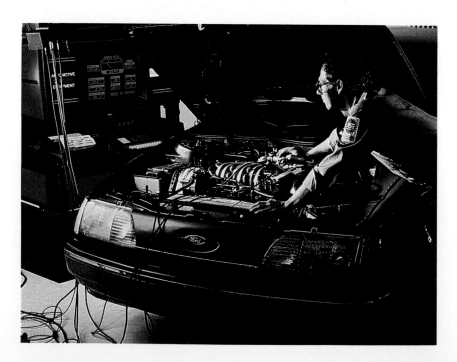

**Figure 17-6   An expert system on the
job.** This expert system helps Ford
mechanics track down and fix
problems.

- The Campbell Soup Company has an expert system nicknamed Aldo, for Aldo Cimino, a human expert who knows how to fix cooking machines. Aldo was getting on in years and being run ragged, flying from plant to plant whenever a cooker went on the blink. How would the company manage when he retired? Now Aldo's knowledge has been distilled into an expert system, which can be used by workers in any location.

- Nordstrom, a chain of stores selling high-quality clothing, uses an expert system to extend customer credit limits. Suppose that a customer wants to charge a coat whose cost pushes the total debt beyond the current credit limit. In the past, the salesperson phoned a human expert who reviewed credit records and made a decision. Meanwhile, the customer waited. Now the decision is made by an expert system, which is faster and less expensive.

- Factory workers at The Boeing Company use an expert system to assemble electrical connectors for airplanes. In the old days, workers had to hunt through 20,000 pages of cross-referenced specifications to find the right parts, tools, and techniques for the job. Each search took approximately 42 minutes. The expert system lets them do the same thing in 5 minutes.

- Employees at Coopers and Lybrand, a "Big Eight" accounting firm, use an expert system called ExperTax to help clients with tax planning. The knowledge of tax-planning experts is available to inexperienced accountants and is as close as their computers.

The cost of an expert system can usually be justified in situations where there are few experts but great demand for knowledge. It is also worthwhile to have a system that is not subject to human failings such as fatigue. Some organizations choose to build their own expert systems to perform well-focused tasks that can easily be crystallized into rules. A simple example is a set of rules for a banker to use when making decisions about whether to extend credit. But very few organizations are capable of building an expert system from scratch. The sensible alternative is to buy an **expert shell,** which consists of the basic structure to find answers to questions. It is up to the buyer to fill in the actual knowledge on the chosen subject. You could think of the expert shell as an empty cup which becomes a new entity once it is filled—a cup of coffee or a cup of apple juice.

DISCUSSION QUESTION
Do current expert systems have artificial intelligence?

We noted that expert systems are often in a natural-language format. Some industry analysts feel that expert systems are beginning to mimic the analytic processes of humans and that, as a result, these programs border on artificial intelligence. To make a computer have **artificial intelligence,** a program must be able to understand the facts it knows, come up with new thoughts, and engage in a wide-ranging coherent conversation. By these standards, expert systems today are rather dim-witted. In particular, they have intelligence on only a given topic. The subject of artificial intelligence is a fascinating one and the source of many debates (see the Perspectives box in Chapter 8 on page 234).

Expert systems will infiltrate companies department by department, much as personal computers did before them. Some expert systems are now available on personal computers. The main limitation of an expert system on a personal computer is that it requires a substantial amount of internal memory. A large amount of data in terms of rules, facts, and source code must be stored, dictating the use of hard disk. Even so, it seems likely that more expert systems for personal computers will appear in the near future.

STUDENT PROJECT
Using the "Buyer's Guide", set up a list of criteria for purchasing a microcomputer. A student might develop one set of criteria, a small business owner another, while an office manager might have a third set. Students could develop criteria for different types of purchasers and compare results.

7 Hire a Computer Person for the Top Job?

Someone once remarked, somewhat facetiously, that all top management—presidents, chief executive officers (CEOs), and so forth—should be drawn from the MIS ranks. After all, the argument goes, computers pervade the entire company, and people who work with computer systems can bring broad experience to the job. Today, most presidents and CEOs still come from legal, financial, or marketing backgrounds. But as the computer industry and its professionals mature, that pattern could change.

7 Summary and Key Terms

- All managers have five main functions: planning, organizing, staffing, directing, and controlling. Top-level managers primarily do long-range **planning;** middle-level managers focus more on the **organizing** and **staffing** required to implement plans; and lower-level managers are mainly concerned with **controlling** schedules, costs, and quality as well as **directing** the personnel.

- A **management information system** (**MIS**) is a set of business systems designed to provide information for decision making. A computerized MIS is most effective if it is integrated.

- The **MIS manager,** a person familiar with both computer technology and the organization's business, runs the MIS department.

- An MIS can produce detail, summary, and exception reports, either on a regular schedule (**periodic reports**) or in response to unscheduled requests from users (**on-demand reports**). **Detail reports** provide complete, specific information; **summary reports** are limited to totals or trends. **Exception**

reports show only data that reflects unusual circumstances.

- Top-level managers frequently require information that aids strategic planning. They often request on-demand reports on the impact of unpredictable occurrences. Middle-level managers usually need summary reports showing expenses and sales trends and exception reports on unexpected expenses and projects behind schedule. Low-level managers typically require detail reports on factors affecting routine operations.

- When microcomputers first became popular in the business world, most businesses did not have general policies regarding them, which led to several problems. Many businesses developed acquisition policies to solve the compatibility problem, established information centers to provide assistance to users, and created the position of microcomputer manager to ensure coordination of microcomputer use.

- Microcomputer acquisition policies may include establishing standards for hardware and software, limiting the number of vendors, and limiting the hardware and software that the MIS department will support.

- An **information center** typically offers employees classes on a variety of computer topics, advice on selecting software, help in getting data from corporate computer systems, and technical assistance on such matters as hardware purchases and requests to the MIS department.

- The main concerns of a **microcomputer manager** are (1) avoiding technology overload, (2) monitoring all the expenses connected with microcomputers, (3) being aware of potential data security problems when users **download** data from the corporate mainframe to their own microcomputers, and (4) setting guidelines for microcomputer use to combat user-abusers.

- An increasing number of business executives use their own microcomputers to assist them in strategic planning (mainly through spreadsheets, database access, and graphics) and communication (mainly through electronic mail and word processing).

- A **decision support system** (**DSS**) is a computer system that supports managers in nonroutine decision-making tasks. A DSS involves a **model,** a mathematical representation of a real-life situation. A computerized model allows a manager to try various "What if . . . ?" options by varying the inputs (**independent variables**) to see how they affect the outputs (**dependent variables**). The use of a computer model to reach a decision about a real-life situation is called **simulation.** Since the decision-making process must be fast, the DSS is interactive, allowing the user to communicate directly with the computer system and affect its activities.

- An **expert system** is a software package, used with an extensive set of organized data, that presents the computer as an expert on some topic. A user can ask questions, often in a natural language (English-like) format, and the system can respond with an answer and an explanation of the answer. An organization that wants an expert system can purchase an existing one, develop its own, or add the appropriate knowledge to an **expert shell** that already contains the basic structure to find answers to questions.

- One debate among computer industry analysts concerns whether expert systems are approaching **artificial intelligence,** the ability of a program to understand facts, come up with new thoughts, and engage in coherent conversation.

Review Questions

1. Describe the five main functions of managers, explaining how the emphasis varies with the level of management.

2. What is an MIS? Why is an integrated MIS the most effective type?

3. Define the following: detail report, summary report, exception report, periodic report, and on-demand report.

4. Explain how the various types of MIS reports are related to the different management levels and functions.

5. Explain why the MIS manager can be regarded as a powerful person within a company.

6. Name the three main microcomputer management problems and explain how they arose.

7. Describe three common methods through which MIS departments control microcomputer acquisition.

8. Describe the functions of an information center.

9. Describe four ways in which a microcomputer manager can help a company.

10. Discuss why an executive might buy a microcomputer.

Discussion Questions

1. Describe a problem situation that could be simulated through a decision support system. Specify the input factors and the types of output.

2. If you were seeking information on a complex topic, which source would you prefer—an expert system or a human expert? Explain your answer.

Chapter 18. Security, Privacy, and Ethics: Protecting Hardware, Software and Data

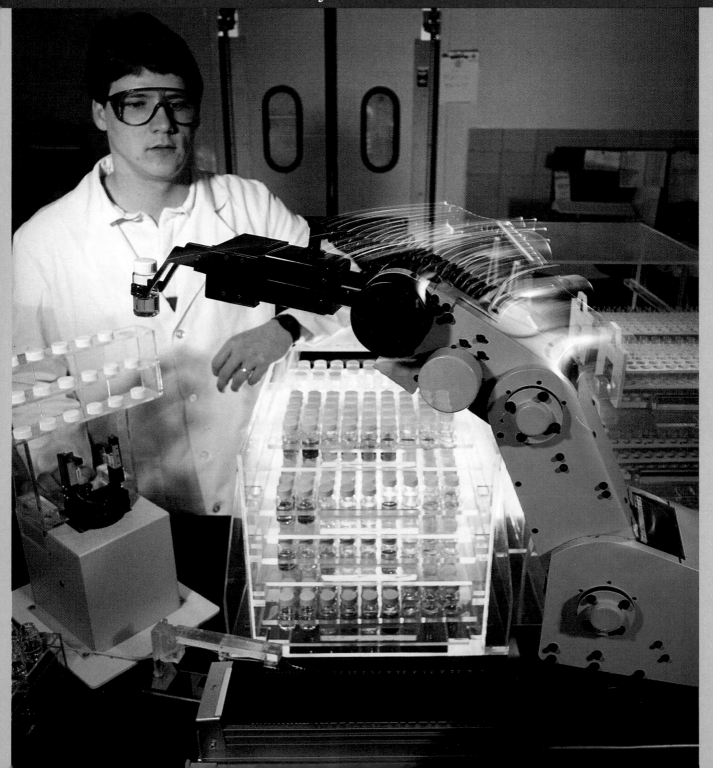

1

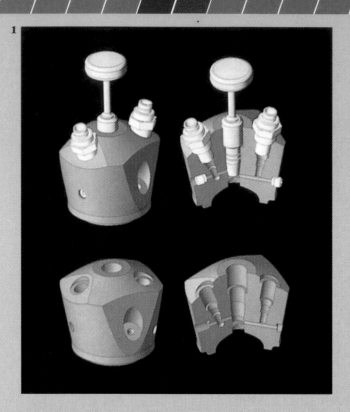

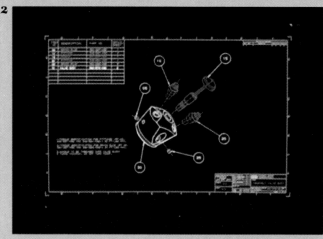

As a society, we have been comfortable with the idea of machines in factories since the Industrial Revolution. Most people think that all factories must be totally automated by now, but this is not the case. However, significant progress has been made. In this gallery we will examine the factory-by-computer and, in particular, that "affectionate" machine, the robot. The photo on the opening page shows a robot at work in the pharmaceutical industry.

CAD/CAE/CAM

This string of letters represents the ideal factory of the future: New products are devised and drawn on a computer-aided design (CAD) system. The CAD data is then transmitted electronically to a computer-aided engineering (CAE) system, where an engineer tests and finalizes the design. The modified data is then sent electronically to a computer-aided manufacturing (CAM) system, which uses the data to direct machine tools, robots, and other automated factory equipment. The final product then enters an automated warehouse. Computers coordinate every step of the process, making them the ultimate factory tool.

The photos on these two pages show the computer-aided design, engineering, and manufacturing of a plexiglass valve housing for an aircraft fuel system. The entire process uses Control Data's Integrated Computer-Aided Engineering and Manufacturing (ICEM) system. All graphic data and documentation remain on the computer system throughout the project, eliminating time-consuming drawings and reports.

2

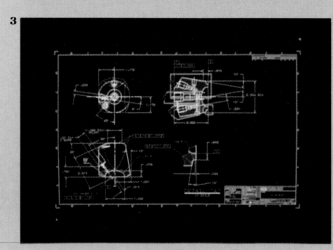

3

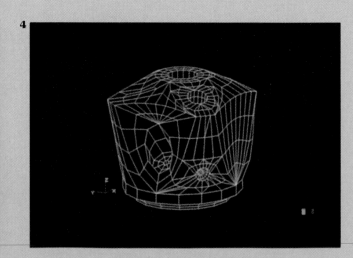

4

(1) The engineer-designer begins by creating a solid geometric model of the valve housing, which is then "exploded" on screen into component parts. (2) The engineer also creates a wireframe model that produces data for (3) drafting layouts on computer.

The design is now ready for testing. (4) A mesh model, generated from the original solid model, can be subjected to stress analysis on the computer. (5) A cross section of the valve housing shows the internal stresses generated by fuel pressures; the color scale on the right indicates the color-coded stress levels. The design is revised on screen until performance is satisfactory.

Once the design is finalized, manufacturing is ready to begin. (6) The computer system automatically generates the setup data for the machine tool that makes the valves. (7) These two views show the valve housing (yellow) displayed as it would appear when being machined from a solid plexiglass rod held in a fixture (solid white lines). (8) Finally, the actual valve housing is produced automatically on a machine tool.

5

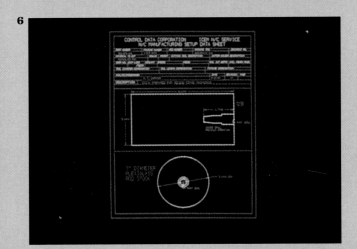

6

7

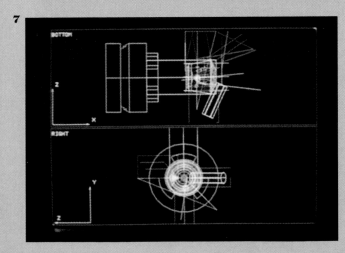

8

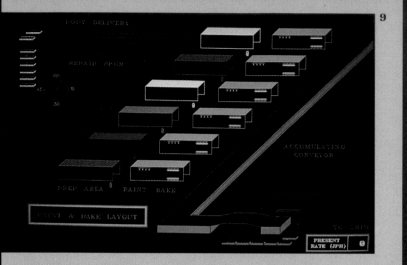

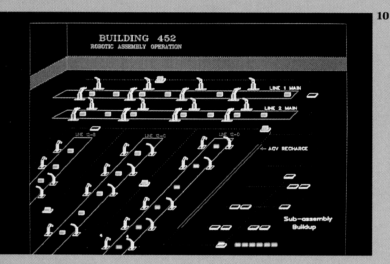

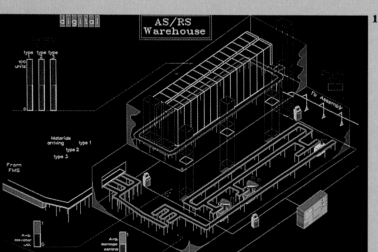

Robots at Work

Before we examine individual robots at work, consider the overall factory process. The traditional view of mass production is to buy raw materials in high volume, then propel identical products down an assembly line to get efficient labor, maximum control, low cost, and a massive product supply to be distributed to buyers. This describes many factories in the United States today. However, a more modern—and more cost-efficient—approach is to delay making parts until there is a request for them downstream in the factory process—that is, until they are needed. The name for this concept is just-in-time (JIT), meaning that there are just enough parts to do the job, and they arrive just in time.

The difference between these two approaches, in the most general sense, is that traditional factories have stacks of parts sitting around while just-in-time does not. As a result, just-in-time costs less.

(9–11) The just-in-time factory begins with planning, and that planning is done on a computer. Factory designers can build a model of a manufacturing system on screen and, using animation, see the system in action. The designer can see how parts flow, where bottlenecks occur, and how workers should be used. The result of this computer simulation is a more efficient factory.

(12) This robotic arm assists in the manufacture of television tubes.

(13) This robot retrieves printed advertisements from a press assembly line and loads them onto a pallet in an orderly fashion. The pallet can then be fork-lifted to a truck for distribution.

(14) Can a robot really fly? Yes. Flying robots have both military and civilian uses. This Sentinel robot can soar up to 10,000 feet to spy on an enemy or to inspect high-voltage wires or spot forest fires.

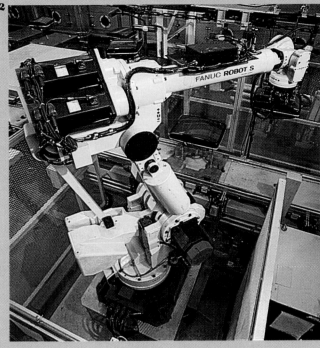

12

13

14

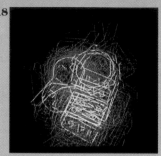

15

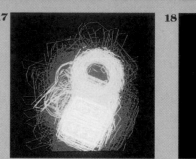

16

17

18

19 .

20

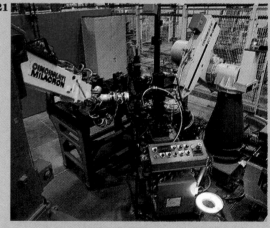

21

Robots can see. That is, they can cast light beams on objects and identify them by matching their shapes to objects already "known," objects whose shapes are computer-accessible to the robot. In this machine vision sequence, **(15)** the object is seen by the robot, **(16)** the object is matched to known shapes, **(17)** inappropriate shapes are eliminated, and **(18)** the object is recognized.

(19) This sophisticated six-axis robot uses a laser tracking system and a welding torch to simultaneously track and weld along irregular surfaces.

General Motors is putting a lot of money into future people-free factories. At this test site in GM's plant in Saginaw, Michigan, **(20)** workers monitor the robots as they **(21)** put parts together.

(22) A test system designed by Hewlett-Packard checks the onboard computers and wiring of the Buick Reatta at each assembly step at this General Motors plant. As you can see here, the system includes robots to lift and transport the cars.

(23) Robots used to be limited to the sidelines, administering from a safe distance. Now they can poke right inside the product; this robot arm reaches inside an auto body to apply sealant—glue—that bonds surfaces. As sold to the auto maker, the complete package includes the dispensing robot arm, a 3-position arm mount, and software that monitors and controls the flow of sealant.

(24) The orange platform is a computerized Automated Guided Vehicle (AGV) that is used to move car bodies from one workstation to another. AGVs receive directional commands that are electronically transmitted through wires buried in the factory floor.

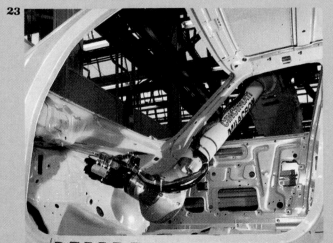

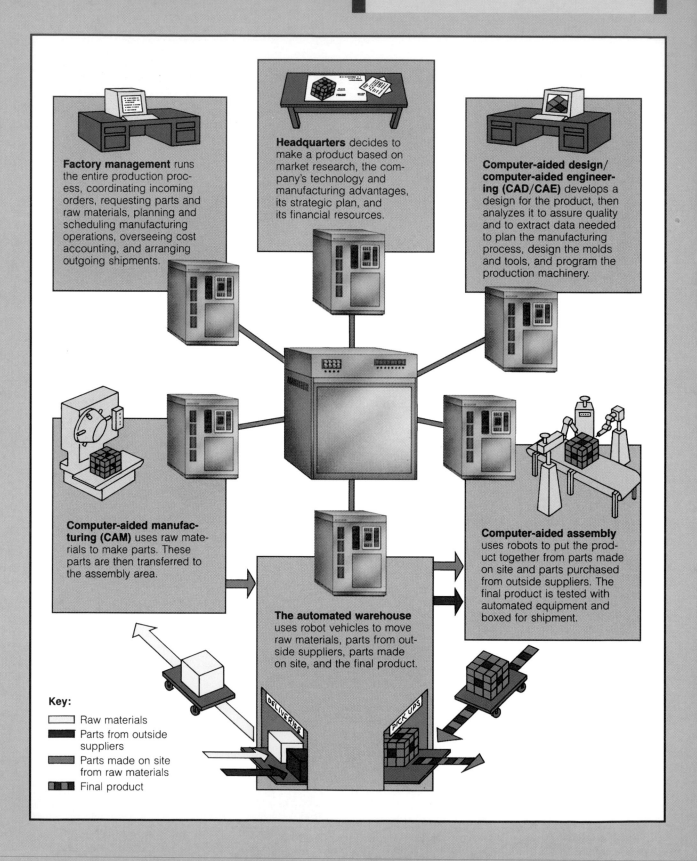

Factory management runs the entire production process, coordinating incoming orders, requesting parts and raw materials, planning and scheduling manufacturing operations, overseeing cost accounting, and arranging outgoing shipments.

Headquarters decides to make a product based on market research, the company's technology and manufacturing advantages, its strategic plan, and its financial resources.

Computer-aided design/computer-aided engineering (CAD/CAE) develops a design for the product, then analyzes it to assure quality and to extract data needed to plan the manufacturing process, design the molds and tools, and program the production machinery.

Computer-aided manufacturing (CAM) uses raw materials to make parts. These parts are then transferred to the assembly area.

Computer-aided assembly uses robots to put the product together from parts made on site and parts purchased from outside suppliers. The final product is tested with automated equipment and boxed for shipment.

The automated warehouse uses robot vehicles to move raw materials, parts from outside suppliers, parts made on site, and the final product.

DELIVERIES

PICK UPS

Key:
- Raw materials
- Parts from outside suppliers
- Parts made on site from raw materials
- Final product

18

Security, Privacy, and Ethics

Protecting Hardware, Software, and Data

Computer security has not kept up with the rapid growth of the computer industry. With more people and more computers, the security problem becomes complex. In this chapter we will examine the most manifest security breach—computer crime. Then we will explore security needs for hardware, software, and data. We will also consider privacy and the safeguarding of personal information and the issue of computer ethics.

LEARNING OBJECTIVES

- Awareness of the problem of computer crime, including criminal profiles, types of crimes, and the difficulties of discovery and prosecution.
- Awareness of the need for security, including disaster recovery plans, software and data security, and security legislation.
- Understanding the importance of privacy and how it is affected by the computer age.
- Understanding the importance of ethics as related to a computer environment.

TEST BANK

Mult. Choice	1-9
T/F	1-14
Matching A	1-2
Fill-in-the-Blank	1-4

It was 5:00 in the morning and 14-year-old Randy Miller was startled to see a man climbing in his bedroom window. "FBI," he growled, "and that computer is mine." So ended the computer caper in San Diego, where 23 teenagers, aged 13 to 17, had used their home computers to invade systems as far away as Massachusetts. The teenagers are **hackers,** people who gain access to computer systems illegally, usually from a personal computer via a telecommunications network.

In this case the hackers did not use the system to steal money. But they did change system passwords, preventing legitimate access to the computer accounts. They also created fictitious accounts and destroyed or changed some data files. And, in the crassest move of all, they threatened to destroy all the records unless they were given free access to the system. The FBI's entry through the window was calculated—they figured that, given even a moment's warning, the kids were clever enough to warn each other via computer.

This story—except for the names—is true. It could happen again tomorrow because few computer systems are totally secure. Hacker stories make fascinating reading, but hackers are only a small fraction of the security problem. Computer systems are vulnerable in a variety of ways (Figure 18-1). The security of computers and computer-related information is a large, critical issue. Let us begin by examining the most fascinating of security breaches: computer crime.

Computer Crime

Although teenage hackers are a real annoyance, the most serious losses are caused by electronic pickpockets who are a good deal older and not half so harmless. Consider these examples.

- A Denver brokerage clerk sat at his terminal and, with a few taps of the keys, transformed 1700 shares of his own stock worth $1.50 each to the same number of shares in another company worth ten times that much.

- As a "joke," a Seattle bank employee used her electronic fund transfer code to move money to the account held by her boyfriend; both the money and the boyfriend disappeared.

- In an Oakland department store, a keyboard operator changed some delivery addresses to divert several thousand dollars worth of store goods into the hands of accomplices.

- A ticket clerk at the Arizona Veteran's Memorial Coliseum issued full-price basketball tickets, then used her computer to record the sales as half-price tickets and pocketed the difference.

Figure 18-1   Is your computer secure?
The computer industry, which is vulnerable to both natural and man-made disasters has been slow to protect itself.

TRANSPARENCY ACETATE #18A
Figure #18-1

LECTURE HINT
Tiger teams, made up of computer security experts, conduct commando-style raids on computer centers to expose security weaknesses. Most of the companies in the Fortune 100 use tiger teams. One team found that the guard had "stepped out" for a moment; he and his security company were replaced in less than an hour.

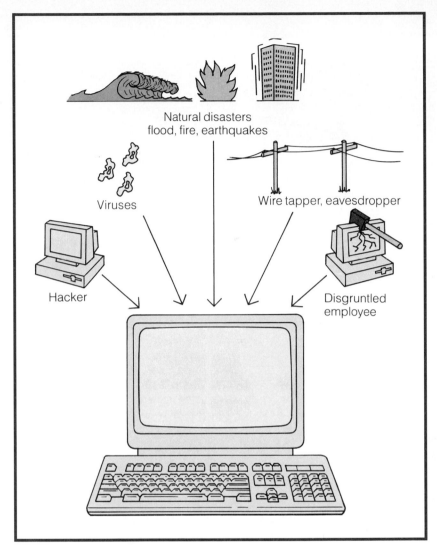

Natural disasters
flood, fire, earthquakes

Viruses

Wire tapper, eavesdropper

Hacker

Disgruntled employee

DISCUSSION QUESTION
How can various individuals, with access to computers, steal or destroy data or files, or alter programs for their own benefit?

These stories point out that computer crime is not necessarily a romantic activity done by geniuses and involving millions of dollars.

Stories about computer crime continue to fascinate the general public. They are "clean" white-collar crimes; no one gets physically hurt. They often feature people beating the system—that is, beating an anonymous, faceless, presumably wealthy organization. Sometimes the perpetrators even fancy themselves as modern-day Robin Hoods, taking from the rich to give to the poor—themselves and their friends. One electronic thief, in fact, described himself as a "one-man welfare agency."

The problems of computer crime have been aggravated in recent years by increased access to computers (Figure 18-2). More employ-

Disgruntled or militant employee could

- Sabotage equipment or programs
- Hold data or programs hostage

Competitor could

- Sabotage operations
- Engage in espionage
- Steal data or programs
- Photograph records, documentation, or CRT screen displays

Data control worker could

- Insert data
- Delete data
- Bypass controls
- Sell information

Clerk/supervisor could

- Forge or falsify data
- Embezzle funds
- Engage in collusion with people inside or outside the company

System user could

- Sell data to competitors
- Obtain unauthorized information

Operator could

- Copy files
- Destroy files

User requesting reports could

- Sell information to competitors
- Receive unauthorized information

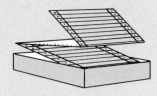

Engineer could

- Install "bugs"
- Sabotage system
- Access security information

Data conversion worker could

- Change codes
- Insert data
- Delete data

Programmer could

- Steal programs or data
- Embezzle via programming
- Bypass controls

Report distribution worker could

- Examine confidential reports
- Keep carbon copies of reports

Trash collector could

- Sell reports or carbon copies to competitors

TRANSPARENCY ACETATE #18B
Figure #18-2

Figure 18-2　The perils of increased access.　By letting your imagination run wild, you can visualize numerous ways in which people can compromise computer security. Computer-related crime would be far more rampant if all the people in these positions took advantage of their access to computers.

ees now have access to computers on their jobs. Many more people are using home computers. And more students are taking computer training. Computer crime is serious business and deserves to be taken seriously by everyone.

7 The Computer Criminal: Who and Why?

Here is what a computer criminal is apt to be like. He (we will use *he* here, but of course *he* could be *she*) is usually someone occupying a position of trust in an organization. Indeed, he is likely to be regarded as the ideal employee. He has had no previous law-breaking experience and, in fact, will not see himself as a thief but as a "borrower." He is apt to be young and to be fascinated with the challenge of beating the system. Contrary to expectations, he is not necessarily a loner; he may well operate in conjunction with other employees to take advantage of the system's weaknesses.

What motivates the computer criminal? The causes are as varied as the offenders. However, a few frequent motives have been identified. A computer criminal is often the disgruntled employee, possibly a longtime loyal worker out for revenge after being passed over for a raise or promotion. In another scenario an otherwise model employee may commit a crime while suffering from personal or family problems. Not all motives are emotionally based. Some people simply are attracted to the challenge of the crime. In contrast, it is the ease of the crime that tempts others. An experienced security consultant noted that computer crime is nothing but white-collar crime with a new medium; each employee who is trained to use a computer is also trained—potentially—to use the computer to rob the company.

In many cases the criminal activity is unobtrusive; it fits right in with regular job duties. One offender noted that his colleagues would never ask what he was doing; instead, they would make comments like, "That turkey, that technician, all he ever does is talk his buzzwords, can't talk to him," and walk away. So the risk of detection is often quite low. Computer criminals think they can get away with it. And they do—some of the time.

7 Computer Crime Types and Methods

Computer crime falls into three basic categories:

- Theft of computer time for development of software, either for personal use or with the intention of selling it.

- Theft, destruction, or manipulation of programs or data.

- Alteration of data stored in a computer file.

DIAMONDS ARE A BANK'S BEST FRIEND

Stanley Mark Rifkin had been a computer consultant for a Los Angeles bank, so his face was familiar to the guards. That is how he was able to slip by one day—with a friendly wave—into the bank's wire transfer room, where he obtained the electronic fund transfer code for the day. Later, posing as a bank manager, he called and used the code to transfer over $10 million to his own account in a New York bank. Stanley was on the next plane to New York, where he removed the funds and flew to Switzerland to deposit them in a Swiss bank account. He then drew from that account to invest in diamonds.

This story has an interesting twist. Stanley flew back to the United States and stopped off in New York to visit an old friend. He could not resist bragging about his feat. The friend was horrified and immediately notified the authorities. Stanley was arrested and convicted. The bank, ironically, came out ahead: The recovered diamonds were worth more than the original stolen funds.

A GLOSSARY FOR COMPUTER CROOKS

Although the emphasis in this chapter is on preventing rather than committing crime, it is worthwhile being familiar with computer criminal terms and methods. Many of these words or phrases have made their way into the general vocabulary.

Data diddling: Changing data before or as it enters the system.

Data leakage: Removing copies of data from the system without a trace.

Logic bomb: Sabotaging a program to trigger damage based on certain conditions and usually set for a later date—perhaps after the perpetrator has left the company.

Piggybacking: Using another person's identification code or using that person's files before he or she has logged off.

Salami technique: Using a large financial system to squirrel away small "slices" of money that may never be missed.

Scavenging: Searching trash cans for printouts and carbons containing not-for-distribution information.

Trapdoor: Leaving an illicit program within a completed program that allows unauthorized—and unknown—entry.

Trojan horse: Placing covert illegal instructions in the middle of a legitimate program.

Zapping: Bypassing all security systems with an illicitly acquired software package.

DISCUSSION QUESTION
What are some common methods used by computer criminals?

DISCUSSION QUESTION
How effective is the government in prosecuting computer criminals?

Although it is not our purpose to write a how-to book on computer crime, the margin note called "A Glossary for Computer Crooks" mentions some criminal methods as examples.

7 Discovery and Prosecution

Prosecuting the computer criminal is difficult because discovery is often difficult. Many times the crime simply goes undetected. In addition, crimes that are detected are—an estimated 85% of the time—never reported to the authorities. By law, banks have to make a report when their computer systems have been compromised, but other businesses do not. Often they choose not to report because they are worried about their reputations and credibility in the community.

Most discoveries of computer crimes happen by accident. For example, a bank employee changed a program to add 10¢ to every customer service charge under $10 and $1 to every charge over $10. He then placed this overage into the last account, a bank account he opened himself in the name of Zzwicke. The system worked fairly well, generating several hundred dollars each month, until the bank initiated a new marketing campaign in which they singled out for special honors the very first depositor—and the very last. In another instance some employees of a city welfare department created a fictitious work force, complete with Social Security numbers, and programmed the computer to issue paychecks, which the employees would then intercept and cash. They were discovered when a police officer found an illegally parked overdue rental car—and found 7100 fraudulent checks inside.

Even if a computer crime is detected, a prosecution is by no means assured. There are a number of reasons for this. First, some law enforcement agencies do not fully understand the complexities of computer-related fraud. Second, few attorneys are qualified to handle computer crime cases. Third, judges and juries are not educated in the ways of computers and may not consider data valuable.

In short, the chances of committing computer crimes and having them go undetected are, unfortunately, good. And the chances that, if detected, there will be no ramifications are also good: A computer criminal may not go to jail, may not be found guilty if prosecuted, and may not even be prosecuted.

But this situation is changing. In 1984 Congress passed the **Computer Fraud and Abuse Act,** which was a first step toward fighting the problem on the national level. Prosecutors complain, however, that the law is loose, ill-defined, and an easy target for sharp defense attorneys. This law, however, is supplemented by state statutes. Most states have passed some form of computer crime law. The number of safe places for computer desperados is dwindling fast.

Security: Keeping Everything Safe

As you can see from the previous section, the computer industry has been extremely vulnerable in the matter of security. Computer security once meant the physical security of the computer itself—guarded and locked doors. But locking up the computer by no means prevents access, as we have seen. Management interest in security has been heightened, and managers are now rushing to purchase more sophisticated security products.

What is security? We may define it as follows: **Security** is a system of safeguards designed to protect a computer system and data from deliberate or accidental damage or access by unauthorized persons. That means safeguarding the system against such threats as burglary, vandalism, fire, natural disasters, theft of data for ransom, industrial espionage, and various forms of white-collar crime.

Who Goes There? Identification and Access

How does a computer system detect whether you are the person who should be allowed access to it? Various means have been devised to give access to authorized people without compromising the system. They fall into four broad categories: what you have, what you know, what you do, and who you are.

- **What you have.** You may have a key or a badge or a plastic card to give you physical access to the computer room or a locked-up terminal. A card with a magnetized strip, for example, can give you access to your bank account via a remote cash machine.

- **What you know.** Standard what-you-know items are a system password or an identification number for your bank cash machine. Cipher locks on doors require that you know the correct combination of numbers.

- **What you do.** Your signature is difficult but not impossible to copy. Signatures lend themselves to human interaction better than machine interaction.

- **What you are.** Now it gets interesting. Some security systems use **biometrics,** the science of measuring individual body characteristics. Fingerprinting is old news, but voice recognition is relatively new. Even newer is the concept of identification by the retina of the eye (Figure 18-3), which is less easy to duplicate than a voice print. These techniques enable a machine to recognize a properly authorized human.

Some systems use a combination of the preceding four categories. For example, access to an automated teller machine requires both something you have—a plastic card—and something you know—a personal identification number.

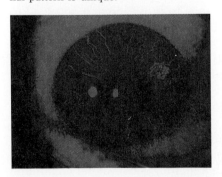

Figure 18-3   Identification by retina. The eye will soon be a means of personal identification. Each person's retinal pattern is unique.

DISCUSSION QUESTION
What disasters could hit a computer center? How would it impair the business of the company using the computer center?

7 When Disaster Strikes: What Do You Have to Lose?

In Italy armed terrorists singled out corporate and state computer centers as targets for attack, and during a ten-month period bombed ten such centers throughout the country. In California a poem, a pansy, a bag of Mrs. Field's cookies, and a message, "Please have a cookie and a nice day," were left at the Vandenberg Air Force Base computer installation—along with five demolished mainframe computers. Computer installations of any kind can be struck by natural or man-made disasters that can lead to security violations. What kinds of problems might this cause an organization?

Your first thoughts might be of the hardware, the computer and its related equipment. But loss of hardware is not a major problem in itself; the loss will be covered by insurance, and hardware can be replaced. The true problem with hardware loss is the diminished processing ability that exists while managers find a substitute facility and return the installation to its former state. The ability to continue processing data is critical. Some information industries, such as banking, could literally go out of business in a matter of days if their computer operations were suspended.

Loss of software should not be a problem if the organization has heeded industry warnings—and used common sense—to make backup copies.

A more important problem is the loss of data. Imagine trying to reassemble lost or destroyed master files of customer records, accounts receivable, or design data for a new airplane. The costs would be staggering. We will consider software and data security in more detail later in this chapter. First, however, let us present an overview of disaster recovery, the steps to restoring processing ability.

7 Disaster Recovery Plan

DISCUSSION QUESTION
Would a local consortium disaster recovery plan be effective in a region of the country affected by an earthquake?

A **disaster recovery plan** is a method of restoring data processing operations if those operations are halted by major damage or destruction. There are various approaches. Some organizations revert temporarily to manual services, but life without the computer can be difficult indeed. Others arrange to buy time at a service bureau, but this is inconvenient for companies in remote or rural areas. If a single act, such as a fire, destroys your computing facility, it is possible that a mutual aid pact will help you get back on your feet. In such a plan, two or more companies agree to lend each other computing power if one of them has a problem. This would be of little help, however, if there were a regional disaster and many companies needed assistance.

DISCUSSION QUESTION
What type of company might prefer a hot site over a cold site?

Banks and other organizations with survival dependence on computers sometimes form a **consortium,** a joint venture to support a complete computer facility. Such a facility is completely available and routinely tested but used only in the event of a disaster. Among

NO DISASTER AT DENNY'S

Remember the fire drills when you were in grammar school? They may have been a bit of a lark for you and your friends, but the school officials knew how important they were. A little practice can make all the difference if a true emergency strikes. The same is true for computer installations. Denny's, a chain of 1200 restaurants, simulated the total destruction of its data center. They wanted to see if the employees could actually put the disaster recovery plan to work.

The drill tests the contents of a 400-page disaster recovery manual. Of particular importance are the systems that support the point-of-sale network and order food supplies. This test is not an isolated incident at Denny's. Since 1983, Denny's has conducted two such drills per year. Each time the drill gets a little tougher and a little more realistic. The early drills, for example, were announced in advance so that employees had plenty of warning.

There was no warning this time, however. It began with a series of phone calls to unsuspecting employees, reporting the facility "destroyed" by an imaginary fire. Those involved in the recovery effort were hustled out of their beds at 3:00 A.M.

Within 20 hours of the first report, eight specialists had flown from the Los Angeles headquarters office to the backup site in Dallas and had reactivated the crucial systems. Fewer than 5% of all data centers test their disaster recovery plans; it is comforting to know that, no matter what happens, we can always eat at Denny's.

these facilities, a **hot site** is a fully equipped computer center, with hardware, environmental controls, security, and communications facilities. A **cold site** is an environmentally suitable empty shell in which a company can install its own computer system.

The use of such a facility or any type of recovery at all depends on advance planning—specifically, the disaster recovery plan. The idea of such a plan is that everything except the hardware has been stored in a safe place somewhere else. The storage location should be several miles away, so it will not be affected by local physical forces such as a hurricane. Typical items stored there are program and data files, program listings, program and operating systems documentation, hardware inventory list, output forms, and a copy of the disaster plan manual.

The disaster recovery plan should include these items:

- **Priorities.** This list identifies the programs that must be up and running first. A bank, for example, would give greater weight to account inquiries than to employee vacation planning.

- **Personnel requirements.** Procedures must be established to notify employees of changes in locations and procedures.

- **Equipment requirements.** Planners list needed equipment and where it can be obtained.

- **Facilities.** Most organizations cannot afford consortiums, so an alternative computing facility must be located.

- **Capture and distribution.** This part of the plan outlines how input and output data will be handled in a different environment.

Computer installations actually practice emergency drills. At some unexpected moment a notice is given that "disaster has struck," and the computer professionals must run the critical systems at some other site.

7 Software Security

Software security has been an industry concern for years. It was first posed as a question: Who owns a program? Is the owner the person who writes a program or the company for whom the author wrote the program? What is to prevent a programmer from taking copies of programs from one job to another? Or, even simpler, what is to prevent any user from copying microcomputer software onto another diskette?

These perplexing questions do, however, have answers. If a programmer is in the employ of the organization, the program belongs to the organization, not the programmer. If the programmer is a consultant, however, the ownership of the software produced should be spelled out specifically in the contract—otherwise, the parties enter extremely murky legal waters.

PERSPECTIVES

VIRUS DISEASE, VACCINE CURE

A computer with a disease? No, not really. It is actually a computer program that has a "virus," so called because it is contagious. That is, a virus, by definition, passes itself on to other programs in which it comes in contact.

Transmitting the Virus

Consider this typical example. A programmer secretly inserts a few unauthorized instructions in a personal computer operating system program. The illicit instructions lie dormant until these events occur together: (1) the disk with the infected operating system is in use, (2) a disk in another drive contains another copy of the operating system and some data files, (3) a command, such as COPY or DIR, from the infected operating system references a data file. Under these circumstances the virus instructions are now inserted into the other operating system. Thus, the virus

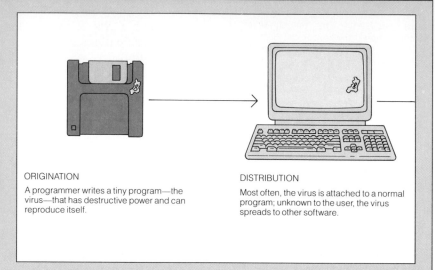

ORIGINATION

A programmer writes a tiny program—the virus—that has destructive power and can reproduce itself.

DISTRIBUTION

Most often, the virus is attached to a normal program; unknown to the user, the virus spreads to other software.

has spread to another disk, and the process can be repeated again and again. In fact, each newly infected disk become a virus carrier.

One newsworthy virus, which was originated by a student at

Cornell University, traveled the length and breadth of the land through an electronic mail network, shutting down thousands of computers. The virus was injected into the network and multiplied uncontrollably, clogging

TRANSPARENCY ACETATE #18C
How a Computer Virus Operates

According to a U.S. Supreme Court decision, software can be patented. Unfortunately, however, the answers to our questions about unlawful software duplication seem out of synch with the decision: Very little can be done to prevent the stealing of microcomputer software. Although it is specifically prohibited by law, software continues to be copied as blatantly as music from tape to tape. We will examine this issue more closely when we consider ethics later in the chapter.

7 Data Security

We have discussed the security of hardware and software. Now let us consider the security of data, which, as we said, is one of an organization's most important assets. Here too there must be planning for security. Usually, this is done by security officers who are

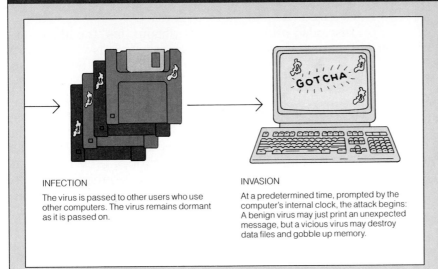

INFECTION

The virus is passed to other users who use other computers. The virus remains dormant as it is passed on.

INVASION

At a predetermined time, prompted by the computer's internal clock, the attack begins: A benign virus may just print an unexpected message, but a vicious virus may destroy data files and gobble up memory.

the memories of infected computers until they could no longer function.

Damage from Viruses

We have explained how the virus is transmitted; now we come to the interesting part—the conse-quences. In the typical example the virus instructions increment a counter each time the virus is copied to another disk. When the counter reaches 4, the virus erases all data files. But this is not the end of the destruction, of course; three other disks have already been infected. Although viruses can be destructive, some are quite benign; one displayed a peace message on the screen on a given date.

Prevention

A word of prevention is in order. Although there are programs, called vaccines, which can prevent virus activity, protecting yourself from viruses depends more on common sense than on building a "fortress" around the computer. Viruses tend to show up on free software acquired through bulletin board systems. Test all such gifts by putting write protection on other disks; if an attempt is made to write on the protected disk a warning message appears on the screen. In fact, put write protection on all files that do not need to have data written on them.

DISCUSSION QUESTION
How can files be protected from computer viruses? How can the viruses be detected before damage occurs?

part of top management. There are five critical planning areas for data security:

- Determination of appropriate policies and standards. A typical statement of policy might read: "All computer data and related information will be protected against unauthorized disclosure and against alteration or destruction."

- Development and implementation of security safeguards such as passwords.

- Inclusion of new security precautions at the development stage of new automated systems, rather than after the fact.

- Review of state and federal laws related to security. This is particularly significant in banking.

- Maintenance of historical records associated with computer abuse.

THE PARTY SEASON: SECURITY ON THE BRINK

'Tis the season to lose output, divulge passwords, and—especially—allow unauthorized persons into the computer room. Although these and other computer-related breaches do not occur exclusively during the holiday season, well-intentioned security tends to sag as spirits soar. Lax security and parties sometimes mix in such a way that a computer organization becomes vulnerable. Security managers must strike a balance between acting like Scrooge and Santa Claus to maintain a secure shop during the festive season. Although it is not usually necessary to install extra measures, it probably is necessary to be particularly alert to mistakes.

LECTURE HINT
Many companies destroy critical privileged printouts by using modern paper shredders. If the shredded paper is stolen, it is impossible to put the paper back together again on a timely basis.

LECTURE HINT
A good password is one that is easy to remember, but hard to guess. Avoid names or nicknames of associates. One method is to select a common item and intentionally misspell it. For example, sugar becomes shuger; cabbage becomes kabaj.

LECTURE HINT
It is possible to capture data sent across telephone lines by tapping the phone lines. Scrambling the data prevents the data capture.

What steps can be taken to prevent theft or alteration of data? There are several data protection techniques; these will not individually (or even collectively) guarantee security, but at least they make a good start.

Secured Waste
Discarded printouts, printer ribbons, and the like can be sources of information to unauthorized persons. This kind of waste can be made secure by the use of shredders or locked trash barrels.

Passwords
Passwords are the secret words or numbers that must be typed on the keyboard to gain access to the system. In some installations, however, the passwords are changed so seldom that they become known to many people. And some groups even tape paper with the password written on it right on the terminal. (In a case prosecuted by the federal government, the defendant admitted that he got a secret code by strolling into the programmer area and yelling, to no one in particular, "Hey, what's the password today?" He got an answer.) Good data protection systems change passwords often and also compartmentalize information by passwords, so that only authorized persons can have access to certain data.

Internal Controls
Internal controls are controls that are planned as part of the computer system. One example is a transaction log. This is a file of all accesses or attempted accesses to certain data.

Auditor Checks
Most companies have auditors go over the financial books. In the course of their duties, auditors frequently review computer programs and data. From a data security standpoint, auditors might also check to see who has accessed data during periods when that data is not usually used and who has received unusually high overtime payments. They can also be on the lookout for unusual numbers of correction entries of data, usually a trouble sign. What is more, the availability of off-the-shelf audit software—programs that assess the validity and accuracy of the system's operations and output—promotes tighter security because it allows auditors to work independently of the programming staff.

Cryptography
Data being sent over communications lines may be protected by scrambling the messages—that is, putting them in code that can be broken only by the person receiving the message. The process of scrambling messages is called **encryption.** The American National Standards Institute has endorsed a process called **Data Encryption Standard** (**DES**), a standardized public key by which senders and receivers can scramble and unscramble their messages. Although the DES has been broken, companies still use it because the

SOME GENTLE ADVICE ON SECURITY

Being a security expert is an unusual job because, once the planning is done, there is not a lot to do except wait for something bad to happen. Security experts are often consultants who move from company to company. They sometimes write books and articles for the trade press, in which they usually include long and detailed checklists. Do this, do that, and you will be OK. We cannot attempt such a set of lists, but here is a mild subset that includes some of the most effective approaches.

- **Beware of disgruntled employees.** Ed Street was angry. Seething. How could they pass over him for a promotion again? Well, if they were not going to give him what he deserved, he would take it himself. . . . Ah, the tale is too common. Be forewarned.

- **Sensitize employees to security issues.** Most people are eager to help others. They must be taught that some kinds of help, such as assisting unauthorized users with passwords, are inappropriate. Most security breaches are possible because people are ignorant, careless, or too helpful.

- **Call back all remote-access terminals.** Don't call us, we'll call you. If you arrange a computer-kept list of valid phone numbers for access to your system, you eliminate most hackers. With such a system the computer has to call the caller back for the user to gain remote access, and it will do so only if the user's number is valid. The fact that the hacker has the computer's phone number is irrelevant. What matters is does the computer have the hacker's?

- **Keep personnel privileges up to date.** And, we might add, make sure they are enforced properly. "Hi, Bill, how ya doin'?" "Pretty good, Frank, good to see you." Bill, the guard, has just swept unauthorized Frank into the computer area. Some of the biggest heists have been pulled by people who *formerly* had legitimate access to secured areas. Often, they can still get in because the guard has known them by sight for years.

method makes it quite expensive to intercept coded messages, forcing interlopers to use other methods of gathering data that carry greater risk of detection. Encryption software is available for personal computers. A typical package, for example, offers a variety of security features: file encryption, keyboard lock, and password protection.

Applicant Screening

The weakest link in any computer security system is the people in it. At the very least, employers should verify the facts that job applicants list on their resumes to help weed out dishonest applicants before they are hired.

Separation of Employee Functions

Should a programmer also be a computer operator? That would put him or her in the position of being able not only to write unauthorized programs but also to run them. By limiting employee functions so that crossovers are not permitted, a computer organization can restrict the amount of unauthorized access. That is, in an installation where the computers, mainframes or minis, are behind locked doors, only operators have physical access to them. Unfortunately, separation of functions is not practical in a small shop; usually one or more employees perform multiple functions. And, of course, separation of functions does not apply in a personal computer environment.

Built-In Software Protection

Software can be built into operating systems in ways that restrict access to the computer system. One form of software protection system matches a user number against a number assigned to the data being accessed. If a person does not get access, it is recorded that he or she tried to tap into some area to which they were not authorized. Another form of software protection is a user profile: Information is stored about each user, including the files to which the user has legitimate access. The profile also includes each person's job function, budget number, skills, areas of knowledge, access privileges, supervisor, and loss-causing potential. These profiles are available for checking by managers if there is any problem.

Security Considerations for Personal Computers

One summer evening two men in coveralls with company logos backed a truck up to the building that housed a university computer lab. They showed the lab assistant, a part-time student, authorization to move 23 personal computers to another lab on campus. The assistant was surprised but not shocked, since lab use was light in the summer quarter. The computers were moved, all right, but not to another lab. There is an active market for stolen personal

MICROCOMPUTERS IN ACTION

Your Own Security Checklist

With the subject of security fresh on your mind, now is a good time to consider a checklist for your own personal computer and its software. We will confine this list to a computer presumed to be in the home.

- No eating, drinking, or smoking near the computer.
- Do not place the computer near open windows or doors.
- Do not subject the computer to extreme temperatures.
- Clean equipment regularly.
- Place a cable lock on the computer.
- Use a surge protector.
- Store diskettes properly in a locked container.
- Maintain backup copies of all files.
- Store copies of critical files off site.

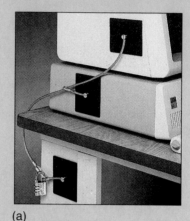

Security devices. (a) Locking up your computer can help minimize theft. (b) A surge protector can protect your computer system and files from unpredictable electrical problems.

(a)

(b)

computers and their internal components. As this unfortunate tale indicates, personal computer security breaches can be pretty basic. One simple, though not foolproof, remedy is to lock micro hardware in place.

In addition to theft, personal computer users need to be concerned about the computer's environment. Personal computers in business are not coddled the way bigger computers are. They are designed, in fact, to withstand the wear and tear of the office environment, including temperatures set for the comfort of people. Most manufacturers discourage eating and smoking near computers and recommend some specific cleaning techniques, such as vacuuming the keyboard and cleaning the disk drive heads with a mild solution. The enforcement of these rules is directly related to the awareness level of the users.

Most personal computer data is stored on diskettes, which are vulnerable to sunlight, heaters, cigarettes, scratching, magnets, theft, and dirty fingers. The data is vulnerable as well. Hard disk used with personal computers is subject to special problems too. If a computer with a hard disk is used by more than one person, your files on the hard disk may be available for anyone to browse through.

There are several precautions that can be taken to protect disk data. One is to use a **surge protector,** a device that prevents electrical problems from affecting data files. The computer is plugged into the surge protector, which is plugged into the outlet. Another precaution is to back up all files. Hard-disk files should be backed up onto diskettes or tape. Diskettes should be under lock and key.

Awareness of personal computer security needs is gradually rising. However, security measures and the money to implement them are directly related to the amount of the expected loss. Since the dollar value of personal computer losses is often relatively low, personal computer security may be less than vigorous.

7 Privacy: Keeping Personal Information Personal

Think about the forms you have willingly filled out: paperwork for loans or charge accounts, orders for merchandise through the mail, magazine subscription orders, applications for schools and jobs and clubs, and on and on. There may be some forms you filled out with less delight—for taxes, military draft registration, court petitions, insurance claims, or a stay in the hospital. And remember all the people who got your name and address from your check—fund-raisers, advertisers, and petitioners. We have only skimmed over the possibilities, but we can say with certainty where all this information went: straight to a computer file.

Where is that data now? Is it passed around? Who sees it? Will it ever be expunged? In some cases we can only guess at the answers. It is difficult to say where the data is now, and bureaucracies often are not anxious to enlighten us. It may have been moved to other files without our knowledge. In fact, much of the data is most definitely passed around, as anyone with a mailbox can attest. As for who sees your personal data, the answers are not comforting. Government agencies, for example, regularly share data that was originally filed for some other purpose. IRS records, for example, are compared with draft registration records to catch dodgers, and also with student loan records to intercept refunds to former students who defaulted on their loans. More recently, the IRS created a storm of controversy by announcing a plan to use commercial direct-mail lists to locate tax evaders. Many people are worried about the consequences of this kind of sharing (Figure 18-4). And finally, few of us can be certain that data about us, good or bad, is deleted when it has served its legitimate purpose.

There are matters you want to keep private. You have the right to do so. Let us see what kind of protection is available to preserve privacy.

Significant legislation relating to privacy began with the **Fair Credit Reporting Act** in 1970. This law allows you to have access to and gives you the right to challenge your credit records. In fact, this

IT'S ALL RIGHT TO BE JUST A LITTLE PARANOID

Once you understand the relationship between computers and your name, it seems reasonable to be concerned. There is no place to hide in a computer society. Consider:

- Computers perform 100,000 calculations each second for every man, woman, and child in the United States.

- Your name pops up in some computer approximately 40 times a day.

- The National Security Administration eavesdrops 24 hours a day, seven days a week, on all overseas phone calls.

- Much of the data stored about you by banks and retailers is vulnerable to unauthorized access.

- Private companies and government agencies increasingly use powerful systems to link and compare different databases, including IRS files, credit ratings, criminal records, bank records, telephone calls, medical records, and records of drugs purchased at pharmacies.

- There are more than 2000 retrieval services in the United States, each of which sells data gathered from various sources—often right off government computers.

DISCUSSION QUESTION
What laws exist to protect individuals from an invasion of privacy?

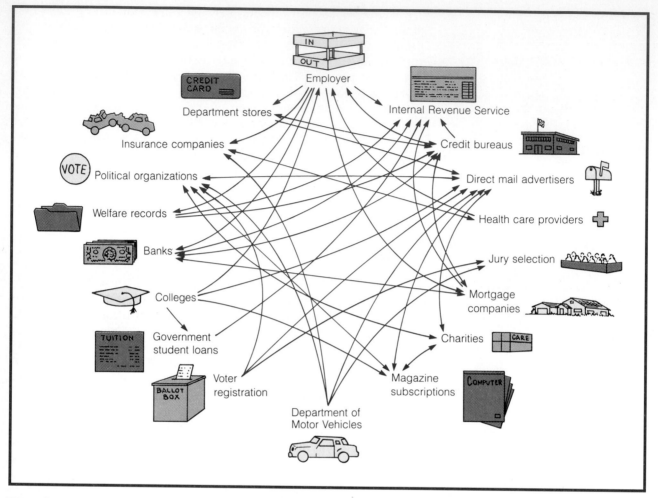

Figure 18-4   Potential paths of data.   When an organization acquires information about you, it is often shared with—or sold to—other organizations.

access must be given to you free of charge if you have been denied credit.

Businesses usually contribute financial information about their customers to a community credit bureau, which gives them the right to review a person's prior credit record with other companies. Before the Fair Credit Reporting Act, many people were turned down for credit without explanation because of inaccurate financial records about them. Because of the act, people may now check their records to make sure they are accurate. The **Freedom of Information Act** was also passed in 1970. This landmark legislation allows ordinary citizens to have access to data about them that was gathered by federal agencies (although sometimes a lawsuit has been necessary to pry data loose).

The most significant legislation protecting the privacy of individuals is the **Federal Privacy Act** of 1974. Born out of post-Water-

ACRES OF COMPUTERS

It is true—literally. Acres of computers, 5½ acres. And many of them underground, too. They could belong to none other than the federal government, specifically, the National Security Agency, which keeps a low profile with much behind-the-scenes activity. Experts say it has the largest computer complex in the world.

This profusion of crime-fighting and spying computers, some of them secret, has privacy advocates worried. These critics say that the incredible power of today's computer systems offers an immense potential for abuse.

TEST BANK
T/F   49
Fill-in-the-Blank   22

gate fears, the Federal Privacy Act stipulates that there can be no secret personal files, that individuals must be allowed to know what is stored in files about them and how it is used, and be able to correct it. The law applies not only to government agencies but also to private contractors dealing with government agencies. These organizations cannot obtain data willy-nilly, for no specific purpose; they must justify obtaining it.

The Privacy Act is not as effective as originally planned. Critics note that it still permits agencies to exchange information, virtually without restriction. The act is also outdated, because its authors did not anticipate microcomputers, which came a few years later, or the extensive use of modems.

7 A Matter of Ethics

There has always been the problem of professional computer personnel having access to files. In theory, they could do something as simple as snooping into a friend's salary on a payroll file or as complex as selling military secrets to foreign countries. But the problem has become more tangled as everyday people—not just computer professionals—have daily contact with computers. They have access to files, too. Many of those files are on diskettes and may be handled in a careless manner. As we noted earlier, data is the resource most difficult to replace, so increased access is the subject of much concern among security officers.

Where do you come in? As a student you could easily face ethical problems involving access and much more. Try some of these. A nonstudent friend wants to borrow your password to get access to the school computer. Or you know of a student who has bypassed computer security and changed grades for himself and some friends. Perhaps a "computer freak" pal collects software and wants you to copy a software disk used in one of your classes. And so on.

The problems are not so different in the business world. You will recognize that, whether you are a computer professional or a user, you have a clear responsibility to your own organization and its customers to protect the security and privacy of their information. Any compromise of data, in particular, is considered a serious breach of ethics. Many corporations have formal statements saying as much and present them to employees individually for their signatures.

If you plan to be a computer professional, you will be bombarded by articles on ethics in the trade press. Professional ethics for the computer industry is also a key topic at conferences and a lament in the halls of lawmakers. Any theme that gets this much attention usually results in action.

Most experts talk of self-regulation via the professional computer organizations. Several organizations, such as the Data Processing Management Association (DPMA) and the Association for Com-

TEST BANK
Mult. Choice   30-32
T/F   50-54
Matching B   3-4
Fill-in-the-Blank   23-26

LECTURE ACTIVITY
Introduce students to the concept of shareware by demonstrating some shareware programs. Shareware can be exchanged through bulletin boards. Caution students that some shareware may contain a virus.

DISCUSSION QUESTION
Why has software piracy occurred?

puting Machinery (ACM), already have a code of ethics. Handling this "among ourselves" is considered preferable to regulation imposed by a federal agency.

7 Copying Software

Let us move from general principles of ethics to a very individual problem—copying software. Have you ever copied a friend's music tape onto your own blank tape? Many people do so without much thought. It is also possible to photocopy a book. Both acts are clearly illegal, but there is much more fuss over illegal software copying than over copying music or books. Why is this? Well, to begin with, few of us are likely to undertake the laborious task of reproducing *War and Peace* on a copy machine. The other part of the issue is money. A pirated copy of a top-20 tape will set the recording company—and the artist—back about $10. But pirated software may be valued at hundreds of dollars. The problem of stolen software has grown right along with the microcomputer industry. Before we discuss industry solutions, we must distinguish among various kinds of software, based on its availability to the public.

7 OK if I Copy That Software?

Some software is considered to be in the **public domain** because its generous maker, probably an individual at home or an educator, chooses to make it free to all. Software called **shareware** is also given away free, but the maker hopes for voluntary monetary compensation—that is, he or she hopes that you like it well enough to send a contribution. Both public domain software and shareware may be copied freely and given to other people. But the software that people use most often, such as WordPerfect or Lotus 1-2-3, is **copyrighted software,** software that costs money and must not be copied without permission from the manufacturer. Making illegal copies of copyrighted software is called **software piracy.**

Consider this incident. Bill Huston got his computer education at a local community college. One of his courses taught him how to use software on microcomputers. He had access to a great variety of copyrighted software in the college computer lab. After graduating, he got a job at a local museum, where he used database software on a microcomputer to help them catalog museum wares. He also had his own computer at home.

One day Bill stopped back at the college and ran into a former instructor. After greetings were exchanged, she asked him why he happened to drop by. "Oh," he said, "I just came by to make some copies of software." He wasn't kidding. Neither was the instructor who, after she caught her breath, replied, "You can't do that. It's illegal." Bill was miffed, saying "But I can't afford it" and, finally, "I'm sorry I mentioned it!" But the instructor was not sorry at all. She immediately alerted the computer lab. As a result of this encounter, the staff strengthened policies on software use and increased the vigilance of lab personnel. In effect, schools must protect themselves from people who lack ethics or are unaware of the law.

There are many people like Bill. He did not think in terms of stealing anything; he just wanted to make copies for himself. But, as the software industry is quick to point out, it *is* stealing because the software makers do not get the revenues to which they are entitled. Furthermore, if software developers are not properly compensated, they may not find it worthwhile to develop new software for our use. Unfortunately, some corporations also have questionable ethics, and their attitude magnifies the software protection problem many times.

Why Those Extra Copies?

Copying software is not always a dirty trick—there are lots of legitimate reasons for copying. To begin with, after paying several hundred dollars for a piece of software, you will definitely want to make a backup copy in case of disk failure or accident. You might want to copy the program onto a hard disk and use it—more conveniently—from there. Or you might want to have one copy at the office and another to use at home. Software publishers have no trouble with any of these types of copying. But thousands of computer users copy software for another reason: to get the program without paying for it. And therein lies the problem.

Software publishers first tried to solve the problem by placing **copy protection** on their software—a software or hardware roadblock to make it difficult or impossible to make pirated copies. In effect, copy protection punishes the innocent with the guilty. There was vigorous opposition from software users, who argued that it was unfair to restrict paying customers just to outsmart a few thieves. Most software vendors have now dropped copy protection from their software, but they are still vigilant about illegal copies. For example, Lotus Development Corporation, a leading purveyor of software, has brought million-dollar lawsuits against some companies, charging them with making illegal copies of Lotus 1-2-3. But the most widespread solution seems to be vendor permission to copy software *legally*, an approach called site licensing.

Site Licensing

Although there is no clear definition industrywide, in general a **site license** permits a customer to make multiple copies of a given piece of software. The customer needing all these copies is usually a corporation, which can probably obtain a significant price discount for volume buying. The exact nature of the arrangement

DISCUSSION QUESTION
What are the advantages of site
licenses?

between the user and the software maker can vary considerably. Typically, however, a customer obtains the right to make an unlimited number of copies of a product, agrees to keep track of who uses it, and takes responsibility for copying and distributing manuals to its own personnel.

The advantages seem to be all on the user's side:

- A big price break, sometimes as high as 50%.

- The availability of as many copies as needed.

- Freedom from potential lawsuits from the software vendor.

But why does the software maker subscribe to this? The main reason is pressure from corporate customers with enormous clout. Who can ignore General Electric or Chevron?

7 Paying Attention Because We Must

The issues raised in this chapter are often the ones we think of after the fact—that is, when it is too late. The security and privacy factors are somewhat like insurance that we wish we did not have to buy. But we do buy insurance for our homes and cars and lives because we know we cannot risk being without it. The computer industry also knows that it cannot risk being without safeguards for security and privacy. As a computer professional, you will share responsibility for addressing these issues. As a computer user, in whatever capacity, you can take comfort in the fact that the computer industry recognizes their importance.

7 Summary and Key Terms

- A **hacker** is a person who gains access to computer systems illegally.

- Computer criminals are likely to be trusted employees with no previous law-breaking experience. Many are motivated by resentment toward an employer, by personal or family problems, by the challenge of beating the system, or the tempting ease with which the crime can be committed.

- Three basic categories of computer crime are (1) theft of computer time for development of software; (2) theft, destruction, or manipulation of programs or data; and (3) alteration of data stored in a computer file.

- Prosecution of computer crime is often difficult because law enforcement officers, attorneys, and judges are usually unfamiliar with the issues involved. However, in 1984 Congress passed the **Computer Fraud and Abuse Act,** which is supplemented by local laws in most of the states.

- **Security** is a system of safeguards designed to protect a computer system and data from deliberate or accidental damage or access by unauthorized persons. Common threats include burglary, vandalism, fire, natural disasters, theft of data for ransom, industrial espionage, and various forms of white-collar crime.

- The means of giving access to authorized people are divided into four general categories: (1) what you have (a key, badge, or plastic card), (2) what you know (a system password or identification number), (3) what you do (such as signing your name), and (4) what you are (by making use of **biometrics,** the science of measuring individual body characteristics such as fingerprints, voice, or retina).

- Loss of hardware and software is generally less of a problem than loss of data. Loss of hardware should not be a major problem, provided that the equipment is insured and a substitute processing facility is found quickly. Loss of software should not be critical, provided that the owner has taken the practical step of making backup copies. However, replacing lost data can be quite expensive.

- A **disaster recovery plan** is a method of restoring data processing operations if they are halted by major damage or destruction. Common approaches to disaster recovery include relying temporarily on manual services, buying time at a computer service bureau, making mutual assistance agreements with other companies, or forming a **consortium,** a joint venture with other organizations to support a complete computer facility.

- A **hot site** is a fully equipped computer facility with hardware, environmental controls, security, and communications equipment. A **cold site** is an environmentally suitable empty shell in which a company can install its own computer system.

- A disaster recovery plan should include (1) priorities indicating which programs must be running first, (2) personnel requirements specifying where employees should be and what they should do, (3) equipment requirements, (4) an alternative computing facility, and (5) specifications for how input and output data will be handled in a different environment.

- Software can be patented. If a programmer is employed by an organization, any program written for the organization belongs to the employer. If the programmer is a consultant, however, the contract must clearly state whether it is the organization or the programmer that owns the software.

- There are five critical planning areas for data security: (1) determination of appropriate policies and standards, (2) development and implementation of security safeguards, (3) inclusion of security precautions during development of new automated systems, (4) review of state and federal laws related to security, and (5) maintenance of historical records associated with computer abuse.

- Common means of protecting data are securing waste; separating employee functions; and implementing passwords, internal controls, auditor checks, cryptography, applicant screening, and **copy protection** (a software or hardware roadblock to piracy).

- Data sent over communications lines can be protected by **encryption,** the process of scrambling messages. The National Standards Institute has endorsed a process called **Data Encryption Standard** (**DES**).

- Personal computer security includes such measures as locking hardware in place, providing an appropriate physical environment, and using a **surge protector,** a device that prevents electrical problems from affecting data files.

- The security issue also extends to the use of information about individuals that is stored in the computer files of credit bureaus and government agencies. The **Fair Credit Reporting Act** allows individuals to check the accuracy of credit information about them. The **Freedom of Information Act** allows people access to data that federal agencies have gathered about them. The **Federal Privacy Act** allows individuals access to information about them that is held not only by government agencies but also by private contractors working for the government. Individuals are also entitled to know how that information is being used.

- Some software is considered to be in the **public domain** because it is free. **Shareware** software is also free, but the maker hopes for voluntary monetary compensation.

- **Copyrighted software** costs money and must not be copied without permission from the manufacturer. Making illegal copies of copyrighted software is called **software piracy.** Many software publishers offer a **site license,** which permits a customer to make multiple copies of a given piece of software.

Review Questions

1. What are some common motivations for computer crime?

2. What are the three main categories of computer crime?

3. Why is it often difficult to find and prosecute a computer criminal?

4. Name and describe the four general techniques for identifying authorized users.

5. Why is loss of data a more serious problem than loss of software or hardware?

6. What should a disaster recovery plan include and why?

7. Name five critical planning areas for data security.

8. Describe the security considerations for personal computers.

9. Name three privacy laws and explain why each one was enacted.

10. What is site licensing?

7 Discussion Questions

1. Before accepting a particular patient, a doctor might like access to a computer file listing patients who have been involved in malpractice suits. Before accepting a tenant, the owner of an apartment building might want to check a file that lists people who have previously sued landlords. Should computer files be available for such purposes? Explain your answer.

2. Discuss your reaction to the following statement: "Some software is just too expensive for the average personal computer owner to buy. Besides, I am only copying my friend's disk for personal use."

Appendix A
A Course in BASIC

Part 1: Introducing BASIC

As a language, BASIC has come a long way in a relatively short time. We examine its origins and then turn immediately to an example to give an overview of how BASIC works.

Roots

This text explains how to design and run some simple programs in BASIC, the computer language whose name is an acronym for Beginners' All-purpose Symbolic Instruction Code. BASIC was invented in 1965 by John Kemeny and Thomas Kurtz for use at Dartmouth College as a simple language for beginners in programming.

With the explosive growth of personal computers, the language has become widely popular, and more sophisticated BASIC versions have emerged. As a result, there is no one standard version of BASIC. The discussion here conforms to Microsoft BASIC, the BASIC commonly used on IBM personal computers and compatibles.

TEST BANK
Mult. Ch.   1-12
T/F   1-14
Match A   1-3
Fill-ins   1-11

Getting Started

Following is a simple BASIC program that will be used to illustrate some elementary BASIC concepts. At this point you will not completely understand how the program works, but if you read through it you will see that even without a knowledge of the language, you can understand much of what the program is instructing the computer to do.

A brief word of explanation is needed. The numerals 100 to 999 number individual lines in the BASIC program. The word RUN is an instruction to the computer; RUN tells it to execute the program. The program is followed by the output generated by the program as it executes.

Example 1

```
100 REM THIS PROGRAM PRODUCES A CHART OF MONTHS
110 REM AND THE NUMBER OF DAYS FOR EACH MONTH.
120 REM
130 REM          MONTH$ - MONTH NAME
140 REM          DAYS -   NUMBER OF DAYS PER MONTH
150 REM          COUNTER - LOOP COUNTER
160 REM
170 PRINT "MONTH", "NAME", "DAYS"
180 PRINT
190 FOR COUNTER = 1 TO 12
200     READ MONTH$, DAYS
210     PRINT COUNTER, MONTH$, DAYS
220 NEXT COUNTER
230 REM          DATA
240 DATA JANUARY,31,FEBRUARY,28,MARCH,31,APRIL,30
250 DATA MAY,31,JUNE,30,JULY,31,AUGUST,31
260 DATA SEPTEMBER,30,OCTOBER,31,NOVEMBER,30,DECEMBER,31
999 END

RUN

MONTH           NAME            DAYS

1               JANUARY         31
2               FEBRUARY        28
3               MARCH           31
4               APRIL           30
5               MAY             31
6               JUNE            30
7               JULY            31
8               AUGUST          31
9               SEPTEMBER       30
10              OCTOBER         31
11              NOVEMBER        30
12              DECEMBER        31
```

The program begins with comments, lines that explain the program but are not executed. Lines 170 and 180 print the headings and a blank line, respectively. Lines 190 through 220 form a loop—that is, they are executed repeatedly, 12 times in this case. Line 200 picks up data from line 240, JANUARY for MONTH$ and 31 for DAYS, and line 210 prints that information. This process is repeated until the last month is read and printed, at which time the program stops. This minimal explanation is just to give you a handle; these BASIC statements and all the others will be explained in detail in the sections that follow.

A **program** is a series of instructions telling the computer how to solve a problem. In BASIC programming each statement is composed of a line number, a BASIC command or instruction, and various **parameters,** which are elements that complete the skeleton structure whose functions are to change a general format into a specific format. Example 2 shows the format for a BASIC statement.

Example 2

Statement Format:
Line number INSTRUCTION Parameters

Sample Statement:
```
200 READ MONTH$, DAYS
```

7 Line Numbers

Every BASIC statement appears on a separate line and has its own **line number.** The line number can be any whole number between 1 and 9999. Although programmers can number the statements 1, 2, 3, . . . , it is common programming practice to number the lines by tens rather than by ones. This numbering system allows the programmer to insert a statement between two existing statements without having to renumber the entire program. The computer will perform statements in numeric order unless specifically instructed otherwise. Each line number can be used only once. If the programmer uses a number that has been used previously, the last statement with that number will replace any previous one. This is a technique that programmers often use to correct lines containing errors. Example 3 illustrates what takes place.

Example 3

```
190 FOR COUNTRE = 1 TO 12     This statement contains an error.
190 FOR COUNTER = 1 TO 12     This correct statement replaces the previous
                              statement.
```

Likewise, if you want to delete a line from a program, enter the number of the line to be deleted and press Enter. The line will be deleted from the program.

Sometimes, programmers use one line number for more than one instruction by separating each instruction with a colon. For example:

```
170 PRINT "MONTH", "NAME", "DAYS": PRINT
```

Although this saves time by reducing keying, it produces a program listing that is not as easy to read and understand.

7 The REM Statement

A BASIC instruction called a **REMARK instruction,** abbreviated **REM,** allows a program to include lines in the program that the computer will not execute. There are many instances when the programmer wants to include such **documentation,** or information concerning the program, to make it easier for a future reader to understand. The REM statement provides the capability to document internally.

If a REM statement requires more than one line, each line must have a unique line number and a REM instruction. Because the REM statements are helpful to future readers, they should be used throughout the program. Since the computer will ignore all REM statements during translation, the program will execute the same way whether or not there are any REM statements in it.

Suggested uses for the REM statement include:

- Explaining the program or segments of the program

- Defining variable names—that is, programmer-assigned names of locations in memory

- Adding blank lines within the program to increase readability

The statements in Example 4 tell the reader what the program is about, but BASIC will ignore these statements. Therefore, they will not be executed.

Example 4

```
100 REM THIS PROGRAM PRODUCES A CHART OF MONTHS
110 REM AND THE NUMBER OF DAYS FOR EACH MONTH.
```

7 The END Statement

The **END** statement tells the computer that the last program statement in the program has been reached. The END statement also terminates execution. There is only one END statement, and it has the highest line number in the program. Frequently, programmers assign line number 9999 to the END statement to make certain that it will be the last one. See Example 5.

Example 5

Statement Format:
Line number END

Sample Statement:
9999 END

7 The STOP Statement

The **STOP** statement terminates program execution. In fact, a program can contain more than one STOP statement, thus creating the possibility of stopping the program in different places. Where the program stops depends on the circumstances of a particular program run. For example, it is possible that certain input data may cause the program to stop, but another program run using different data may run to a normal completion. Both the END statement and the STOP statement, when encountered, cause program execution to terminate. The difference between the two statements is that there is only one END statement, and it must be the last program statement.

Example 6

Statement Format:
Line number STOP

Sample Statement:
320 STOP

7 Variables

The purpose of writing programs is to process data to produce a predetermined, desired output such as a phone bill or an inventory report. The data that will be processed must be placed into memory locations during the execution of the program, and the values of the data in these storage locations may change as the processing occurs. With BASIC we do not know which memory locations are used to store the data, but we must have a method for identifying each of our elements of data so that the computer can store and retrieve them as needed. We accomplish this by naming each of our data elements, then referring to them by this assigned name. The programmer-assigned name for the memory location where the data is kept is called a **variable.** The computer finds locations in memory and associates them with the given variable names, then it is able to reference the desired data. Example 7 illustrates this.

Example 7

Data   Memory Location
JANUARY   Variable name is MONTH$

When the programmer uses the variable name MONTH$, the computer retrieves the data JANUARY from its memory location.

The variables that we use consist of:

- Numeric characters (**numeric fields**)

- Alphabetic characters or a combination of alphabetic and numeric characters (**alphanumeric fields**)

These two types of variables are handled slightly differently.

Numeric Variables

A **numeric variable** is a name for a memory location that will contain only numbers as data. All variable names must start with a letter, and they can consist of up to 40 letters and numbers. The name cannot contain a blank. Sample numeric variable names are COST, T1, and A.

Alphanumeric Variables

An **alphanumeric variable,** also called a **string variable,** is the name for a memory location for data that is composed of either alphabetic characters or a combination of alphabetic, numeric, and/or special characters such as # and %. To name these variables, use the same naming rules that apply to the numeric variables but follow the name with $. Sample variable names are NAMES$, ADDRESS$, and DESCRIPTION$.

It is the programmer's responsibility to name the variables. It is good programming practice to assign names that make sense or coincide with the type of data being identified. For example, if we were naming a storage location that was to contain the names of employees, we might name it NAMES$. An appropriate name for a field to contain the number of books read might be BOOKS or NUMBER. This method of assigning the variable a name that reflects the contents of the storage location helps the programmer remember the variable name used and also makes it easier for someone else to read and understand the program.

We have already discussed the use of a REM statement for documenting the name given to a particular variable. Example 8 illustrates this use.

Example 8

```
130 REM        MONTH$ = MONTH NAME
150 REM        COUNTER = LOOP COUNTER
```

7 Constants

A **constant** is a fixed value. Much of the processing we do involves manipulation of constants. We are able to put constants into the computer in several ways, and we receive constants as output. (The methods of input and output will be described later.) There are two types of constants: **numeric constants** and **alphanumeric constants.**

Numeric Constants

There are three types of numeric constants allowed in BASIC:

- Integers
- Decimals
- Exponential forms of numbers

When expressing any numeric constant, do not include commas or dollar signs because these symbols are reserved for other purposes.

Integers are numbers without decimal points. Integers, including zero, can be either positive or negative. If you input a number without a decimal point, the system assumes the decimal point belongs to the right of all given digits. If the number is a negative number, it should be preceded by a minus sign. If there is no minus sign, the system will assume it is a positive number. The following are examples of integers:

```
12    -3    0
```

Decimals are numbers that include a decimal point. These decimal numbers can be either positive or negative. Examples of decimals are:

```
18.    -15.03    21.8    0.0506
```

The **exponential form of numbers** is used to express either very large or very small numbers. This form is also called **scientific notation,** and the numbers are sometimes referred to as floating-point constants. Scientific notation involves raising a number to a power. The following are examples of the exponential form of numbers:

```
2.53E-04    54.23E02
```

These numbers are in a shorthand style. The number 2.53E−04 means that 2.53 is multiplied by 10 to the power—the exponent—of minus 4, or .0001. Multiplying 2.53 by .0001 gives .000253, the equivalent of 2.53E−04. Similarly, 54.23E02 means that 54.23 is multiplied by 10 to the power of 2, or 100, so 54.23E02 is the same as 5423.

Alphanumeric Constants

BASIC programming allows for alphanumeric constants as well as numeric constants. These alphanumeric data are referred to as **character strings,** or **literals.** A character string consists of one or more letters, numbers, or special characters and must be enclosed within quotation marks. The only character that cannot be included in a character string is a quotation mark. If you need a quotation mark within the string, use the single quotation (apostrophe). When character strings are used within the program, they are enclosed within quotation marks, but when they are output, the quotation marks are not displayed. Example 9 illustrates this concept.

Example 9

```
100 REM THIS PROGRAM ILLUSTRATES THE USE OF QUOTATION
110 REM MARKS WITH ALPHANUMERIC CHARACTER STRINGS
120 PRINT "THIS IS A CHARACTER STRING"
999 END

RUN

THIS IS A CHARACTER STRING
```

Alphanumeric data cannot be used for calculations. This is because alphanumeric data can include alphabetic, numeric, and special characters, and you cannot calculate with a letter of the alphabet or with a special character, such as &.

The following are examples of character strings:

```
"C"    "DATA"    "PROGRAMMING IN BASIC"    "CALCULUS 205"
```

Before we can proceed with the discussion of BASIC, we need to pause for a few necessary preliminary steps.

Booting the Operating System

Before you use the computer for BASIC or any other purpose, you must first load the operating system, called **Disk Operating System** (**DOS**) into the computer's memory. Loading the operating system is commonly known as **booting** the system. If you are not using a hard-disk drive, use these steps to load DOS:

1. Place the DOS disk in drive A and close the drive latch.
2. Turn on the computer and (if color) the monitor.
3. Type in the date and time when they are requested. If you do not wish to change the date and time, press the Enter key twice.

Now the A> prompt appears on the screen, indicating that you are using the A disk drive. The prompt shows that the operating system is loaded and awaits further instruction.

If you are using a hard-drive system, then you need follow only steps 2 and 3 above. The prompt that appears on the screen is C> because you are using the C disk drive.

Whether you are using the A drive or the C drive, you are ready to load BASIC.

Loading BASIC

Before you can enter, change, or execute a BASIC program, you must load the BASIC interpreter program into your computer's memory. When you have booted the system and see A> or C> on the screen, type:

```
BASICA
```

and press the Enter key. When BASIC has been loaded into memory, you will see a screen that is almost blank and the letters "Ok" in the upper-left corner. "Ok" is the signal that BASIC is ready to accept BASIC statements or system commands from the keyboard. We have already seen some BASIC statements, the numbered lines in a program. System commands are different from BASIC statements; system commands are used to perform some operation on the program itself. Let us consider some of the important system commands.

7 System Commands

While you are entering a program into the computer or after you have completed entering it, you need to communicate with the operating system of your computer to tell it what to do with the program. These instructions to the operating system are called **system commands.**

There are a number of different system commands. These instruct the computer to perform activities such as displaying a program on the screen or printer, executing a program, or starting a new program. Only the most common commands will be presented here.

A very simple BASIC program is presented here to let you try some of the system commands and see what results from each. At this point you may not understand all the program statements. If you make an error as you enter a statement of the program, the computer displays an error message, or **diagnostic,** on the screen. If that happens, re-enter the complete, correct statement.

```
100 REM THIS PROGRAM WILL BE USED TO TRY
110 REM SOME SYSTEM COMMANDS.
120 LET X = 2 + 2
130 PRINT X
999 END
```

Now you are ready to try a system command. The operating system has allocated an area in memory for you to use, an area called **work space.** When you keyed in your program, it was placed in this work space. Any intermediate or final results of program execution will also be placed there.

7 LIST and LLIST

The first command to try is **LIST.** LIST instructs the computer to display on the screen each line of the program that is in the work space.

Simply key in, on a line by itself (without a line number), the word LIST, press Enter, and see what happens. You should see the five lines you keyed in previously appear on the screen. Always use LIST to see your program, then verify that it is correct before executing it.

LLIST instructs the computer to print the contents of the work space on the printer rather than on the screen.

Let us manipulate the program a little to demonstrate some of the programming concepts already presented. Do you remember that we numbered our lines by increments of ten so we could add lines without retyping the complete program? Try it. After your existing program key in, one after the other:

```
125 LET Y = 4 + 4
135 PRINT Y
```

These lines are added to the existing program. Now use LIST to see your program. Your program should look like Example 10.

Example 10

```
100 REM THIS PROGRAM WILL BE USED TO TRY
110 REM SOME SYSTEM COMMANDS.
120 LET X = 2 + 2
125 LET Y = 4 + 4
130 PRINT X
135 PRINT Y
999 END
```

Notice that the new lines have been added into the program according to numeric order. Placing them in order helps you read and understand the program, but even if you had not used LIST to see the program, the computer would have performed the instructions in numeric order.

Now turn on your printer and key in LLIST. The program listing should direct your printer to produce a hard copy of the program.

7 RUN

Shall we see if the program works? When you have finished your program or a portion of your program and you want the computer to execute your instructions, key in the system command RUN and press Enter. (Note that system commands are not preceded by line numbers.) **RUN** instructs the operating system to actually perform the statements of the program that are in the work space. Try it. Based on our preceding program, what you should see on the screen is shown in Example 11.

Example 11

```
4
8
```

If you did not get the correct output, you probably made an error as you entered the program. In that case your computer may have given you a message such as "SYNTAX ERROR IN LINE 120."

One method you can use at this point to correct an error is to retype the line number, then type the correct instruction and parameters. Recall that you can use this procedure to replace the previous incorrect line with a new line that has the same number. Try it. Key in:

```
120 LET X = 5 + 5
```

Notice that, by using line number 120, the original line numbered 120 is replaced. LIST your program to verify that this is true. Now use RUN to execute the program. Your output should look like Example 12.

Example 12

```
10
8
```

A line can be deleted by keying only the line number of the line to be removed. Let us delete two lines from the program. Key in:

```
120
130
```

Now enter LIST again, and you can see that lines 120 and 130 are indeed gone. If you RUN the program again, the result is a single 8 on the screen.

7 EDIT

The **EDIT** command can also be used to change a line in a program. For example, to change a program line numbered 120, type:

```
EDIT 120
```

and press Enter. BASIC displays the current line 120. You can use the Ins and Del keys and the cursor movement keys to edit the line. When you have made all the changes to the line, press Enter. You can use the list command to make sure you have edited the line correctly.

7 CLS

CLS, short for *clear screen,* clears the screen and places the letters "Ok" in the upper left of the screen. CLS does not clear the work space in memory; your program is still there. CLS, preceded by a line number, can also be used as a BASIC statement in a program.

7 NEW

If you want to start your program over or begin another program, key in the system command **NEW.** This command erases the work space and your program. Key in NEW and press Enter. Now use LIST to see your program. Nothing! The program is gone.

If you neglect to key in the word NEW before starting another program, the first program remains in the work space; as you enter the second program, it becomes part of the first program. When you key in line 100 of the second program, for example, it replaces line 100 of the first program. If there are line numbers in the first program that are not used in the second program—that is, the lines are not replaced—those old lines will show up in a listing of your combined first and second program.

7 SAVE

There will be numerous occasions when you will write a program and want to keep it to use at some future time. Because the size of your memory is limited and because memory is volatile (that is, what is not saved on disk disappears when the computer is turned off), you will want to store the program on disk by using the system command **SAVE.** If you want to call your program PROGX, for example, type:

```
SAVE "PROGX"
```

This command places PROGX.BAS on the disk for future use.

7 LOAD

You saved your program on disk to have it available for use at a future time. When you are ready to use the file, you need to copy it back into memory by using the system command **LOAD.** Notice that the file is *copied* to memory; therefore, it also remains on disk. To load a program you saved as PROGX, type:

```
LOAD "PROGX"
```

and press Enter. Now PROGX is in memory and on the disk.

You will probably make some changes to PROGX as you work with it. It is important to remember to save the program again on disk after you have made changes. It is usual to save the program under the same name. If you use the same name, PROGX, when you save it again, the new version of PROGX overlays the old version on the disk. However, if you make changes to PROGX but neglect to save it on disk, the unaltered version (and presumably the version you no longer want) is what you end up with on disk.

7 RENUM

As you work with a program, adding and deleting lines, you may not care for the pattern of line numbering that has occurred. If you wish to renumber the program lines, use the system command **RENUM.** Type:

```
RENUM
```

and press Enter. The first line of the program is given the number 10, and subsequent lines numbers are incremented by 10. All statements in the program are automatically updated to reflect the new line numbers.

7 SYSTEM

Use the command **SYSTEM** to leave BASIC and return to DOS. SYSTEM erases your program from memory when you leave BASIC, so remember to save it on disk first. Type:

```
SYSTEM
```

and press Enter.

7 Exercises

Load BASIC and then key in the following program:

```
100 REM THIS PROGRAM WILL PROVIDE ADDITIONAL PRACTICE.
110 LET A = 5
```

```
120 LET B = 8
130 LET C - 13
140 PRINT A + B + C
999 END
```

1. Use LIST to see the program. What is displayed?

2. Use RUN to execute the program. What are the results?

3. Key in the following lines:

   ```
   150 LET D = (A + B + C) / 2
   160 PRINT D
   ```

   Use LIST to see the program. What is displayed?

4. Use RUN to execute the program. What are the results?

5. Delete line number 140. Use RUN to execute the program. What is the result?

6. Use the EDIT command to remove one of the parentheses in line number 150. Use RUN to execute the program. What happens? Now fix line 150.

7. Save the program as MYPROG. Use LIST to see the program. Is it still there?

8. Use the NEW command, followed by LIST. What happens?

9. Now leave BASIC and return to DOS. What command will you use?

/ Answers to Exercises

1. The original program should be displayed.

2. 26

3.
   ```
   100 REM THIS PROGRAM WILL PROVIDE ADDITIONAL PRACTICE
   110 LET A = 5
   120 LET B = 8
   130 LET C = 13
   140 PRINT A + B + C
   150 LET D = (A + B + C) / 2
   160 PRINT D
   999 END
   ```

4. 26
   13

5. 13

6. A message will indicate a syntax error in line 150.

7. Yes, the program is still there.

8. The program is deleted from work space; there is no program to list.

9. SYSTEM

TEST BANK
Mult. Ch.   19-26
T/F   21-32
Match A   6
Fill-ins   21-23

7 OUTPUT

Computer applications involve some form of input, processing, and output. Building on the concepts just presented, various methods for inputting information from the computer will be explained later. At this point we will focus on output.

Providing information in an appropriate format is one of the primary goals of programming. Output, then, is of tremendous importance, and techniques that provide it need to be thoroughly understood.

7 The PRINT Statement

The BASIC instruction used to output information from the computer onto the screen is **PRINT.** This is illustrated in Example 13. Notice that the statement format has the instruction name—PRINT, in this case—in capital letters.

Example 13

Statement Format:
Line number `PRINT` Parameters

Sample Statement:
`280 PRINT "CUSTOMER NO", NUMBER`

The PRINT instruction is used to print parameters that are numeric constants, character strings, or the value of variables at the time the PRINT statement is executed. We will examine each of these in the next three sections. Output using the PRINT statement might be a heading in a report, a detail data line, or a total line, incorporating the variables and constants as needed. Let us take a closer look at how printing works.

Printing Numeric Constants

To print a numeric constant, simply follow the instruction PRINT with the desired numeric constant, as shown in Example 14.

Example 14

Sample Statement:
`160 PRINT -13`

Output:
`-13`

We are now able to write a simple program. Notice the output when we use RUN to execute the program in Example 15.

Example 15

```
100 REM ILLUSTRATION PRINTING NUMERIC CONSTANTS.
110 PRINT 1
120 PRINT 2
130 PRINT 3
999 END

RUN

    1
    2
    3
```

Since the REM statement was only for internal documentation, it did not result in any output. The three PRINT statements instructed the computer to print the numeric constants 1, 2, and 3 on separate lines.

Printing Character Strings

To print a character string, follow the PRINT instruction with the desired literal output. Do not forget to enclose the character string in quotation marks. Whatever is within the quotation marks is printed. Example 16 illustrates this procedure.

Example 16

Sample Statement:
```
130 PRINT "YEARLY SALES REPORT"
```

Output:
```
YEARLY SALES REPORT
```

Example 17 illustrates the use of the PRINT command to output character strings.

Example 17
```
100 REM THIS PROGRAM USES CHARACTER STRINGS AS OUTPUT
110 REM TO PROVIDE INSTRUCTIONS TO THE USER.
120 PRINT "ENTER YOUR NAME, SOCIAL SECURITY NUMBER AND"
130 PRINT "ADDRESS."
140 PRINT "SEPARATE EACH BY COMMAS."
999 END

RUN

ENTER YOUR NAME, SOCIAL SECURITY NUMBER AND
ADDRESS.
SEPARATE EACH BY COMMAS.
```

Again, the REM statements did not result in any output. The three PRINT statements instructed the computer to output the three character strings on separate lines, one line per PRINT statement.

Printing Variables

A variable value can also be part of the output. To incorporate a variable value, follow the PRINT instruction with an appropriate variable name. Upon execution the computer will print the current value of the variable on the screen. See Example 18, in which STEPHEN RYAN has been assigned to the variable NAMES$. That is, STEPHEN RYAN is the actual data in the memory location called NAMES$.

Example 18

Sample Statement:
```
280 PRINT NAMES$
```

Output:
```
STEPHEN RYAN
```

The program in Example 19 uses the PRINT command for character strings, numeric constants, and variables. At this point we must assume that the computer has established the value of the variable. (Caution: This program is incomplete. If you key and run it, it will not give the output shown here. This is because we have assumed that there is already a data value in the variable NAMES$.)

Example 19

```
100 REM THIS PROGRAM USES THE PRINT COMMAND TO OUTPUT
110 REM CHARACTER STRINGS, NUMERIC CONSTANTS, AND
120 REM VARIABLES.
130 PRINT NAMES$;" WILL BE YOUR INSTRUCTOR."
140 PRINT "THERE WILL BE";30;"STUDENTS IN THAT CLASS."
150 PRINT "PLEASE BE ON TIME TO YOUR CLASS."
999 END

RUN

ANN ROGER WILL BE YOUR INSTRUCTOR.
THERE WILL BE 30 STUDENTS IN THAT CLASS.
PLEASE BE ON TIME TO YOUR CLASS.
```

The first PRINT statement instructs the computer to print a variable value—ANN ROGER—followed by a character string. The second PRINT statement instructs it to print character strings and a numeric constant—30. The third PRINT statement instructs the computer to print a character string. The spacing of the output lines will be discussed in the next section.

7 Output Format

When the computer executes a PRINT instruction, the output is displayed at the left side of the screen. This placement is usually appropriate if there is only one item in the output. Frequently, however, you want the output to include multiple variable values, constants, or combinations of both. In that case you may follow the PRINT instruction with a list of parameters, each separated by a comma or semicolon, as in Example 20. The following sections describe the differences in using commas and semicolons.

Example 20

Sample Statement:
```
360 PRINT "CUSTOMER NAME",NAMES$
```

Sample Statement:
```
360 PRINT "CUSTOMER NAME";NAMES$
```

With BASIC programming the computer divides the output area (for example, the screen) into **zones.** Example 21 shows the zones used by BASIC.

Example 21

Columns 1–14 Zone 1	Columns 15–28 Zone 2	Columns 29–42 Zone 3	Columns 43–56 Zone 4	Columns 57–80 Zone 5

The placement of the output on the screen depends on whether you use a comma or a semicolon to separate the output parameters.

Formatting Output with Commas
Separating the parameters in a PRINT statement with commas causes the information contained in each parameter to begin to print at the next available zone. In Example 22 you can see the column number directly above each character string. The column numbers are used here as examples; they do not show on the screen.

Example 22   **Sample Statement:**
```
100 PRINT "SALESMAN","AMOUNT","DEPARTMENT"
```

Output:
```
1               15              29 ←——————— Column numbers
SALESMAN        AMOUNT          DEPARTMENT
```

Notice that the commas between the character strings place AMOUNT beginning at column 15 and DEPARTMENT beginning at column 29. Each of these columns is the beginning of the next print zone.

The commas now between the parameters have the same result if they are placed between two variables or between a character string and a variable. Assuming that WENDY DOUGLAS is in variable NAMES$, notice the output in Example 23.

Example 23   **Sample Statement:**
```
560 PRINT "WELCOME",NAMES$
```

Output:
```
1               15 ←——————— Column number
WELCOME         WENDY DOUGLAS
```

If an output parameter is longer than the zone size, the output continues into the next zone, and the following parameter starts at the beginning of the next available zone. This is illustrated in Example 24.

Example 24   **Sample Statement:**
```
180 PRINT "SALESPERSON OF THE YEAR",NAMES$
```

Output:
```
1               15              29 ←——————— Column number
SALESPERSON OF THE YEAR         ERIN
```

The ability to use commas to separate parameters in PRINT statements is important when producing tabular reports—that is, reports with columns of data. The zones function like tab stops on a typewriter, and the columns can be positioned easily.

Formatting Output with Semicolons

There will be many applications where you will not want the output results to be spaced so far apart. Look at the output in Example 25. Variable COST has been assigned the value 4000, and variable ITEM$ has been assigned the value "TERMINAL". The commas caused each item to begin printing at the next print zone, leaving unattractive gaps. This is not the way you want the sentence to appear. (On the output, the column numbers are correct, although this page width prohibits accurate placement.)

Example 25   **Sample Statement:**
```
180 PRINT "THE COST WOULD BE",COST,"FOR A NEW",ITEM$
```

Output:
```
1               15      29      43              57 ←——————— Column Number
THE COST WOULD BE       4000    FOR A NEW       TERMINAL
```

Placing semicolons between parameters in a PRINT statement instructs the computer to print out the information blocks in the parameters so they are immediately next to each other, as shown in Example 26.

Example 26

Sample Statement:
```
150 PRINT "THE COST WOULD BE";COST;"FOR A NEW";ITEM$
```

Output:
```
THE COST WOULD BE 4000 FOR A NEWTERMINAL
```

But there is still a problem. Notice that in this example the semicolons between parameters did exactly what they were supposed to do—they caused the information in the parameters to print right next to each other. Although we do not want our line spread out the way it was when we used commas to separate parameters, we also do not want it to be printed with no spaces between words.

To correct this situation, it is necessary to force desired spacing by enclosing spaces within the quotation marks. Remember, the computer is going to print character strings exactly as they are contained within the quotation marks, and this includes any spaces. To correct the output in Example 26, we need to insert a space at the end of the character string, ''FOR A NEW''. For example:

Sample Statement:
```
150 PRINT "THE COST WOULD BE";COST;"FOR A NEW ";ITEM$
```

Output:
```
THE COST WOULD BE 4000 FOR A NEW TERMINAL
```

You might have noticed that we did not force a space before or after the numeric variable in Example 26. When a numeric value is printed, a space is reserved for the sign preceding the value. If the value is a positive value, no sign is printed, and a space is printed out. A space will automatically be printed following a numeric value. In Example 27, you can see illustrations of this concept.

Example 27

Sample Statement: Positive Value
```
420 PRINT "TOTAL DUE";AMOUNT
```

Output:
```
TOTAL DUE 546
```

Sample Statement: Negative Value
```
PRINT "TOTAL DUE ";AMOUNT
```

Output:
```
TOTAL DUE -592
```

Note the space included in the quotes after TOTAL DUE. Of course, to space output you can combine commas and semicolons, as illustrated in Example 28.

Example 28

Sample Statement:
```
160 PRINT "MEGAN IS";AGE1,"BRIAN IS";AGE2
```

Output:
```
MEGAN IS 9     BRIAN IS 12
```

If you end a PRINT statement with a semicolon or a comma, it instructs the computer to print the information from the next PRINT statement on the same line, as illustrated in Example 29.

Example 29

Sample Statement:
```
280 PRINT "THREE BLIND MICE,"
290 PRINT "THREE BLIND MICE"
```

Output:
```
THREE BLIND MICE,
THREE BLIND MICE
```

Sample Statement:
```
280 PRINT "THREE BLIND MICE, ";
290 PRINT "THREE BLIND MICE"
```

Output:
```
THREE BLIND MICE, THREE BLIND MICE
```

At this point you should recognize that there are various methods for controlling the spacing in a PRINT statement. One very common use of the PRINT statement is to print headings on a report.

Example 30
```
100 PRINT "            MONTHLY REPORT"
110 PRINT
120 PRINT "SALES","PROFIT","LOSS"
130 PRINT
```

Output:
```
        MONTHLY REPORT

SALES           PROFIT          LOSS
```

In Example 30, spaces inserted in the character string in line 100 move the first heading line over to the right. Line 110 causes a blank line to be placed between the first and second heading lines. Commas between character strings in line 120 cause each to print starting at the next print zone. Line 130 causes a blank line to be printed after the second heading line.

TAB Function
There will be times when formatting your output by using commas or semicolons to separate the parameters does not provide enough flexibility. For these instances BASIC provides a **TAB function,** which is used with the PRINT statement to improve control over the spacing in output. The TAB function operates like a tab on a typewriter and is very convenient for formatting columnar reports.

Example 31

Statement Format:
Line number PRINT TAB(N) Parameters ← N is a column number

Sample Statement:
```
150 PRINT TAB(20) COST;TAB(40) ITEM$
```

The sample statement in Example 31 instructs the computer to have the value of COST printed out beginning at column 20 and the value of ITEM$ printed out beginning at column 40. The value of N in the statement format expresses the distance in columns from the left margin that the value should be printed and not how many columns from the previous printing position. The value of N must be a positive number that can be expressed with a numeric constant, a numeric variable, or an arithmetic expression.

Numeric variables, alphanumeric variables, and character strings can all be included in PRINT statements using the TAB function. See Example 32.

Example 32

Sample Statement:
```
230 PRINT TAB(2) "CITY";TAB(19) CITY$;TAB(39) DIST
```

Output:
```
2                      19                     39
  CITY                   SAN ANTONIO            456
```

Notice that the TAB function can be used more than once in a statement. Each use of the TAB function may be separated from the rest of the statement by semicolons.

7 PRINT USING

Although the PRINT statement with the TAB function permits increased flexibility for formatting output, there will still be times when your formatting ability is limited. BASIC provides a means for programmers to designate an exact picture of the desired output format. This feature uses the **PRINT USING** statement.

Some of the things you may want to do with a PRINT USING statement are

- Placing a dollar sign to the left of a value

- Inserting commas in a long number

- Controlling the placement of a decimal point

- Lining up numbers in columns

- Inserting plus or minus signs before or after numbers

- Placing asterisks in unused positions to the left of numbers

Example 33 provides the statement format and a sample statement for the PRINT USING statement.

Example 33

Statement Format:
Line number PRINT USING "Literals and/or format";Variables and/or literals

Sample Statement:
```
130 PRINT USING "$##.##";TOTAL
```

The sample statement in Example 33 instructs the computer to output the current value of TOTAL according to the format provided between the quotation marks.

The PRINT USING statement can be used to format lines consisting of constants and/or variables. The constants and the variables may be either alphanumeric or numeric.

PRINT USING Numeric Formats

The examples that follow illustrate some of the format notations used to produce specified numeric output.

Sample Format: ###

The number sign (#) reserves space for one numeric character. Any digit 0 through 9 may be output for each number sign. Any unused positions to the left of the first significant digit will be filled with spaces. If you do not reserve enough space for the number, the number will be output with the % character in front to signal the error.

Sample Format: $$###

Two dollar signs placed at the left of a format produce a floating dollar sign. The floating dollar sign causes a dollar sign to print out in the position immediately to the left of the first significant digit. One of the two dollar signs also reserves a space for a digit.

Sample Format: ###.##

A decimal point inserted within a format causes a decimal point to print out in that position.

Sample Format: ##,###

A comma inserted within a format causes a comma to print out in that position when the number is large enough to warrant it.

Example 34 illustrates output that will result from the use of various format notations.

Example 34

Data in Memory	Format	Output
684.23	#,###.##	684.23
57.23	$$###.##	$57.23
2634.53	$$##,###.#	$2,634.5

PRINT USING String Formats

The PRINT USING statement can be used to output a line that includes string data—either constants or variables. The following examples illustrate the use of the PRINT USING statement to output string data.

Example 35

Sample Format:
\   \

Sample Statement:
```
400 PRINT USING "\              \";NAMES$
```

Backslashes reserve spaces for string data. The number of positions reserved is equal to the number of spaces between the two backslashes plus one for each of the backslashes. If the value of NAMES$ is "PEARL LEE", when the sample statement in Example 35 is executed, the output will be:

```
PEARL LEE
```

If the number of characters in the string is greater than the number of positions reserved by the backslashes, the rightmost characters will be truncated. If the number of characters in the string is less than the number of spaces reserved by the backslashes, spaces will be printed in the rightmost positions.

Example 36

Sample Format:
!

Sample Statement:
```
440 PRINT USING "!";LAST$
```

An exclamation mark instructs the computer to print the first character of a string. The sample statement in Example 36 instructs the computer to print the first character in the string LAST$. If the value of LAST$ is JEFFRIES, the output for this statement is:

J

The various numeric and string formats can be combined in one PRINT USING statement by inserting appropriate horizontal spacing as illustrated in Example 37.

Example 37

```
300 PRINT USING "\                \      ###.##";CUSTOMER$,DUE
```

Output:
```
ROGER STEWART     543.33
```

```
350 PRINT USING "!       !      !       ##";A$,B$,C$,V
```

Output:
```
J             A           T               45
```

```
350 PRINT USING "THE TOTAL IS $$###.## FOR \          \";T,I$
```

Output:
```
THE TOTAL IS $13.98 FOR ENVELOPES
```

```
450 PRINT USING "\       \      $$#.##";"TOTAL",3.99
```

Output:
```
TOTAL              $3.99
```

TEST BANK
Mult. Ch. 27-31
T/F   33-43
Match B   4-5
Match C   8
Fill-ins   24-26

7 INPUT

One technique for inputting data into the computer uses an INPUT statement; the other technique uses READ/DATA statements. The INPUT statement is used to input data into the computer as the program is executing, but the READ/DATA statements are used to provide data for the program prior to processing. Let us look at each in detail.

The INPUT Statement

The **INPUT** statement is used when the program needs data supplied by a user in an interactive mode. This means that the user and computer are communicating as the program is executing; there is input from the user and output from the computer.

Example 38

Sample Format:
Line number INPUT Parameters

Sample Statement:
150 INPUT NAMES$

    The INPUT command instructs the computer to obtain data that has just been keyed in and to place this data into memory locations. The sample statement in Example 38 tells the computer to obtain the data keyed in by the user, place it in memory, and assign the variable name NAMES$ to that memory location. From this point on, when the programmer uses the variable name NAMES$, whatever data is in that storage location will be retrieved.

    An INPUT statement may have more than one alphanumeric or numeric variable as parameters. When there are more than one, separate each with a comma. For example:

260 INPUT NAMES$,ADDRESS$,CITY$,STATE$

    When the computer executes an INPUT statement, a question mark appears on the screen to inform the user that the computer is waiting for a response. The user must key in a response and press Enter to make the data available to the computer. To help the user supply the desired data, the programmer uses a PRINT statement to **prompt** the user for data. For example, if the program needs the name and address of a person to process a credit application, the programmer may prompt for the correct data with the PRINT statement shown in Example 39. The highlighted rectangle indicates the information entered by the user. Notice that the INPUT statement causes a question mark to appear on the screen.

Example 39

280 PRINT "ENTER THE APPLICANT'S NAME AND ADDRESS"
290 PRINT "SEPARATED BY A COMMA."
300 INPUT NAMES$,ADDRESS$
999 END

RUN

ENTER THE APPLICANT'S NAME AND ADDRESS
SEPARATED BY A COMMA.
?RHONDA TRAINOR, 2008 DEER COVE LANE

    If the variable named in the parameter is a numeric variable, the computer does not accept a user response that is not strictly numeric. If nonnumeric data is entered, the user receives a prompt from the computer to resubmit the data. The prompt is the statement "?REDO FROM START". The computer does not execute the next statement until the INPUT statement has been satisfied, so the programmer needs to anticipate user responses when designing PRINT statements to be used as prompts.

    As an alternative, it is possible to include the instructions from the PRINT statement right in the INPUT statement; simply place the instructions in quotation marks before the variable name or names. (See exercise 3 after this section.)

7 The READ and DATA Statements

When data is available before the program executes and when there is a large amount of data to input, the programmer may enter it into the computer through the use of **READ** and **DATA** statements. The READ statement instructs the computer to find values within the DATA statements and assign these values to the variables in the READ statement. See Example 40.

Example 40

Statement Formats:
Line number READ Parameters
Line number DATA Parameters

Sample Statements:
```
140 READ PRICE,DESCRIPTION$
350 DATA 250,END TABLES
```

The DATA statement provides the values to be assigned to the variables listed in the READ statement. In Example 40 value 250 is placed in the memory location whose variable name is PRICE. Similarly, END TABLES goes to the memory location whose variable name is DESCRIPTION$. A DATA statement may contain multiple constants (numeric or string) as parameters. If more than one constant is used, separate each with a comma. Enclose string constants that include commas or semicolons with quotation marks.

If you indicate a numeric variable in a READ statement, be sure the corresponding DATA element is a numeric constant. If you have a numeric variable in the READ statement that is paired with an alphanumeric constant, a syntax error occurs. That is, the DATA statement cannot offer nonnumeric data when numeric data is expected.

A program may contain multiple DATA statements, and, although it is permissible to place the DATA statements anywhere within the program, it is common practice to place them in a group just preceding the END statement. The programmer may place READ statements throughout the program, wherever logic dictates.

The computer accesses the data elements in the order in which they are found in the statements. It is not necessary to pair each READ statement with a DATA statement having the same number of elements. The only requirement is that the total number of elements within all DATA statements be sufficient to supply a data element for every parameter in all READ statements.

Each READ statement may contain multiple numeric or alphanumeric variables, each separated by a comma as shown in Example 41.

Example 41

```
160 READ POINTS,AVERAGE,TEAM$
300 DATA 89,76,SPARTANS
```

Upon executing statement 160, the computer establishes memory locations for the variables POINTS, AVERAGE, and TEAM$ and places the values 89, 76, and SPARTANS, respectively, into those locations. Any future reference to those three variables will enable the computer to retrieve or use the values now associated with them.

When reading several data items with a single READ statement, as in this example, the set of data items is often referred to as a **record.** The record concept will be more important in Part 2.

Exercises

1. Give an appropriate PRINT statement to produce the following output. (The underlined words are values of variables.)
    a. YOUR CHANGE WILL BE 2.53
    b. YOUR DATSUN 280ZX WILL GET 28 MILES PER GALLON.
    c. YOUR NEW BOSS WILL BE CLAYTON LONG.

2. Write a PRINT USING statement to produce the following output. (The items underlined are variable values.)
    GROSS SALARY $1,215.26   NET SALARY $1,042.99

3. Write a simple program that asks a person to key in his or her name at the keyboard. The program should place that name in memory, then display it on the screen within a message.

4. Use the following statements to determine what values the listed variables have.

    ```
    100 READ A,B,C,D$
    160 READ T,Y$,S

    300 DATA 152,-13,43.6,WILLIAM
    310 DATA -10,TRIBUNE,194
    ```

    a. B
    b. D$
    c. Y$
    d. S

5. Give appropriate DATA statements to accompany the following READ statements.
    a. 230 READ N$,P,T
    b. 240 READ I$,A

Answers to Exercises

1. a. 200 PRINT "YOUR CHANGE WILL BE";CHANGE
    b. 200 PRINT "YOUR ";AUTO$;" WILL GET";GALLON;" MILES PER GALLON
    c. 200 PRINT "YOUR NEW BOSS WILL BE ";BOSS$;"."

2. a. 200 PRINT USING "GROSS SALARY $$#,###.##";GROSS,
       210 PRINT USING "NET SALARY $$#,###.##";NET

3.  ```
    100 REM THIS IS A SIMPLE PROGRAM TO USE THE PRINT AND INPUT
    110 REM STATEMENTS.
    120 PRINT "WHAT IS YOUR NAME?"
    130 INPUT NAMES$
    140 PRINT "HELLO, "NAMES$;" IT'S NICE TO MEET YOU."
    ```

    An alternative solution includes the character string to be printed in the INPUT statement. If you run both versions, you will see that the question mark prompt appears on the next line in version one but right after the question in version two.
    ```

```
100 REM THIS IS A SIMPLE PROGRAM TO USE THE PRINT AND INPUT
110 REM STATEMENTS.
120 INPUT "WHAT IS YOUR NAME?";NAMES$
130 PRINT "HELLO, "NAMES$;" IT'S NICE TO MEET YOU."
```

4. a. -13
    b. WILLIAM
    c. TRIBUNE
    d. 194

5. The following are only a sample of the many possibilities. Just be sure that you show alphanumeric data for an alphanumeric field and numeric data for a numeric field.

```
550 DATA BILL,100,123
560 DATA TRICYCLE,38.99
```

TEST BANK
Mult. Ch.	32-39
T/F	44-58
Match B	6
Match D	1-10
Fill ins	27-31

7 Calculations

We have examined ways to get data in and out of the computer. Now it is time to consider how to use data for calculations. We begin with the LET statement, which has several uses.

7 The LET Statement

The INPUT and READ/DATA statements provide a means to enter data into your program. The **LET** statement provides a third method; the LET statement enables you to assign a value to a variable.

Example 42

Statement Format:
Line number LET Variable name = Arithmetic expression or constant

Sample Statement:
200 LET NET = GROSS - DEDUCTIONS

The LET statement is called an **assignment statement** because the variable to the left of the equals sign is assigned the value of the expression or constant to the right of the equals sign. In Example 42 numeric variable NET is assigned the value of the difference between the values GROSS and DEDUCTIONS. The value of NET is placed in memory to be used later, and it remains there until it is changed. The word LET is optional.

7 Arithmetic Operations

There are five common arithmetic operations: (1) exponentiation, (2) addition, (3) subtraction, (4) multiplication, and (5) division. These are illustrated in Example 43.

Example 43

Addition	200 LET A = B + C
Subtraction	200 LET A = B - C
Multiplication	200 LET A = B * C
Division	200 LET A = B / C
Exponentiation	200 LET A = B ^ C

Notice the symbols used for exponentiation, multiplication, and division.

7 Hierarchy of Operations

Combinations of mathematical operators and numeric variables and constants make up arithmetic expressions. The computer performs the mathematical operations according to a hierarchy. Hierarchy means the order from the top down; as applied to computer math, it means the order in which operations are performed. Since the computer works according to a hierarchy, so must you. Operations are performed in the following order: exponentiation, division and multiplication, then addition and subtraction. The computer evaluates an arithmetic expression moving from left to right, performing mathematical operations according to the hierarchy. First, all exponentiation; then moving again from left to right, all multiplication and division; then, moving again from left to right, all addition and subtraction. Example 44 illustrates this concept. The circled numbers indicate the order of operation.

Example 44

```
                  ①    ③    ②
240 LET B = 5  *  4  +  2 / 2
            20     +  2 / 2
            20     +  1
               21
```

Example 44 demonstrates the order in which the computer solves the problem. Realize, of course, that the programmer enters only the LET statement, and the computer does not print intermediate results. The value of B that is calculated can be printed by using a PRINT statement, or it can be used in subsequent calculations.

7 Using Parentheses

Often a programmer wants the computer to perform addition or subtraction before multiplication or division. Correct placement of parentheses within the arithmetic expression allows the programmer to do this.

The parentheses override the rules of the hierarchy. The computer performs the operations within parentheses first, then reverts to the rules of the hierarchy— division and multiplication first, followed by addition and subtraction. See Example 45.

Example 45

```
                  ①        ③        ②
150 LET E = (2 + 5)  *  (6 - 4)
               7     *     2
                    14
```

In statement 150 the computer performs the calculations of $2 + 5$ and $6 - 4$ first because each is within parentheses. After evaluating the expressions within the parentheses, the computer calculates the remainder of the expression which, in this case, is the multiplication of the interim values 7 and 2.

7 Assigning a Value to a Variable by Using LET

You can assign a value to a variable by using a LET statement. This assignment is illustrated in Example 46.

Example 46

```
150 LET TOTAL = 0
160 LET COURSE$ = "BEGINNING BASIC"
```

Notice the quotation marks around the character string. These quotation marks are required.

7 Writing Programs Using LET

Using the READ/DATA, INPUT, END, and PRINT statements, a programmer can incorporate the LET statement. The following programs illustrate principles covered to this point. The REM statements in each program tell which principle the program applies.

In the program in Example 47, the values for variables A, B, and C are assigned using the LET statement, then the values are used to calculate the value of variable D. (Note that multiplication is done before addition.)

Example 47

```
100 REM PRINTING A CALCULATION OF NUMERIC VARIABLES1
110 LET A = 39
120 LET B = 20
130 LET C = 2
140 LET D = A + B * C
150 PRINT D
999 END

RUN

 79
```

The PRINT statement is used in Example 48 to print a character string and the sum of two numbers.

Example 48

```
100 REM PRINTING A CHARACTER STRING
110 REM AND THE RESULT OF A CALCULATION
120 LET A = 5 + 4
130 PRINT "THE SUM OF 5 + 4 =";A
999 END

RUN

THE SUM OF 5 + 4 = 9
```

READ/DATA statements are used in Example 49 to supply variable values for the calculations to be performed in the program.

Example 49
```
100 REM PRINT A CHARACTER STRING AND THE RESULT OF A
110 REM CALCULATION USING READ/DATA STATEMENTS
120 PRINT "CALCULATION OF NUMERIC VARIABLES"
130 READ B,C
140 LET A = B * C
150 PRINT A
160 READ D,E
170 LET F = D + E
180 PRINT F
190 READ X,Y
200 LET Z = X / Y
210 PRINT Z
220 DATA 3,3
230 DATA 5,3
240 DATA 4,4
999 END

RUN

CALCULATION OF NUMERIC VARIABLES
 9
 8
 1
```

The program in Example 50 illustrates the use of the INPUT statement to supply the numeric values for the calculation in the LET statement. The highlighted rectangle indicates the numbers input by the user.

Example 50
```
100 REM CALCULATIONS USING THE INPUT STATEMENT
110 PRINT "ENTER 2 NUMBERS SEPARATED BY COMMAS"
120 INPUT X,Y
130 LET Z = X + Y
140 PRINT "THE SUM OF";X;"AND";Y;"IS";Z
999 END

RUN

ENTER 2 NUMBERS SEPARATED BY COMMAS
?4,10
THE SUM OF 4 AND 10 IS 14
```

Example 51 illustrates the use of the LET statement to set constant values and the use of the PRINT statement to print the values.

Example 51
```
100 REM PRINTING NUMERIC CONSTANTS
110 LET D = 10
120 LET A = 30
130 LET C = 50
140 PRINT D,A,C
999 END

RUN

 10              30              50
```

Exercises

1. Determine the values for the variables in the following LET statements.
   a. LET D = 10 / 2 * 3 + 5
   b. LET A = 4 + 5 * 3 / 3
   c. LET T = 5 * 8 * (8 - 2) * (4 - 1)
   d. LET N = 6 / 2 + (4 + 4)

2. Correct any errors in the following statements:
   a. LET N = 3 - 2 X 1
   b. LET Z = TOTAL AMOUNT
   c. LET 4 = A
   d. LET A AND B = 0

3. What is the value of N in the following program?

```
100 LET A = 4
110 LET C = 10
120 LET T = A * C
130 LET N = C + T
140 PRINT N
999 END
```

4. Write a program to calculate the product of 6 and 4 and print the following output:

```
6 MULTIPLIED BY 4 = 24
```

Answers to Exercises

1. a. 20
   b. 9
   c. 720
   d. 11

2. a. LET N = 3 - 2 * 1
   b. LET Z$ = "TOTAL AMOUNT"
   c. LET A = 4
   d. LET A = 0:LET B = 0

3. 50

4.
```
100 REM THIS PROGRAM CALCULATES THE VALUE OF 6
110 REM MULTIPLIED BY 4.
120 LET M = 6 * 4
130 PRINT "6 MULTIPLIED BY 4 =";M
999 END
```

Sample Program: Floor Covering

The sample program in Example 52 illustrates concepts that have been presented thus far. This program calculates the cost of floor covering. Data used in the calculations, such as length and width, is input by the user.

Example 52

```
100 REM COST OF FLOOR COVERING PROGRAM
110 REM
120 REM THIS PROGRAM CALCULATES COST OF FLOOR COVERING BASED
130 REM ON THE INPUT OF LENGTH AND WIDTH OF THE AREA TO
140 REM BE COVERED AND THE PRICE PER YARD ENTERED.
150 REM
160 REM     VARIABLE NAMES:
170 REM      LENGTH - LENGTH OF AREA
180 REM      WIDTH - WIDTH OF AREA
190 REM      YARD - PRICE PER YARD
200 REM      COST - TOTAL COST
210 REM      AREA - AREA TO BE COVERED
220 REM
230 PRINT "THIS PROGRAM CALCULATES THE COST OF FLOOR COVERING,"
240 PRINT "GIVING YOU AT THE END THE TOTAL SQUARE YARDS YOU NEED"
250 PRINT "AND THE TOTAL COST. YOU WILL BE ASKED TO ENTER THE"
260 PRINT "LENGTH AND WIDTH OF YOUR ROOM, SEPARATED BY A COMMA,"
270 PRINT "AND ALSO THE COST PER SQUARE YARD."
280 PRINT
290 PRINT "ENTER ROOM DIMENSIONS: LENGTH, WIDTH"
300 INPUT LENGTH, WIDTH
310 PRINT "ENTER PRICE PER SQUARE YARD"
320 INPUT YARD
330 LET AREA = LENGTH * WIDTH / 9
340 LET COST = AREA * YARD
350 PRINT USING "YOU NEED ##.## SQUARE YARDS AT $$##.##";AREA,YARD
360 PRINT USING "PER YARD FOR A TOTAL OF $$#,###.##";COST
999 END

RUN

THIS PROGRAM CALCULATES THE COST OF FLOOR COVERING,
GIVING YOU AT THE END THE TOTAL SQUARE YARDS YOU NEED
AND THE TOTAL COST. YOU WILL BE ASKED TO ENTER THE
LENGTH AND WIDTH OF YOUR ROOM, SEPARATED BY A COMMA,
AND ALSO THE COST PER SQUARE YARD.

ENTER ROOM DIMENSIONS: LENGTH, WIDTH
?20,40
ENTER PRICE PER SQUARE YARD
?5.99
YOU NEED 88.88 SQUARE YARDS AT $5.99
PER YARD FOR A TOTAL OF $532.39
```

The sample program in Example 52 begins with line 100. Lines 100 through 220 are REM statements that serve as internal documentation. Notice that this documentation consists of an explanation of the program and a definition of variables used in the program.

Lines 230 through 270 are the PRINT statements that provide general instructions to the user. Although it may seem repetitious to state the purpose of the program again (we already did in the REM statements), remember that as the program runs, only PRINT statements cause output to be displayed on the screen. Notice how the PRINT statements are written. The literals are enclosed in quotation marks, and the absence of any punctuation at the end of the lines ensures that each line will be printed on separate lines as shown in the output of the program. The single PRINT statement on line 280 leaves a blank line between the general instructions and the first prompt for data. This increases the readability of the program.

Lines 290 and 310 issue the input instructions by using the PRINT statement. Lines 300 and 320 cause question marks to appear on the screen, prompting the user to key in length and width and price per square yard. The values keyed in by the user are then placed in memory locations.

Lines 330 and 340 perform the necessary calculations. Data given by the user is used in the calculations to determine the area and the total cost.

Lines 350 and 360 write the output of the program by using PRINT USING statements. This is a message to the user; it gives the number of square yards needed, the price per square yard, and the total cost. Notice the $$ in the formats to float the dollar sign to the left of the first significant digit.

The program ends with line number 999, which signals the end of the program by using the END statement.

7 Control Structures

Control structures let the programmer exercise control in the program by changing the sequence in which program statements are executed. All the programs we have written thus far have been executed line by line, beginning with the lowest line number and ending with the highest number. A programmer often wants to reroute the logic to statements other than the line of code immediately following the one the computer is currently executing. We will now use the GOTO, the IF-THEN, and the IF-THEN-ELSE statements to control the logic of the program and allow the programmer much greater programming versatility.

7 The GOTO Statement

The **GOTO** statement is called an **unconditional transfer** statement. If you consider the meaning of the word *unconditional,* you may be able to understand more easily the use of this statement. An unconditional situation is one in which the action is taken regardless of the conditions. This is in sharp contrast to the IF-THEN statement, for which a specific condition must be met before the statement is executed. Look at the unconditional nature of the GOTO statement in Example 53.

Example 53

Statement Format:
Line number GOTO Line number

Sample Statement:
200 GOTO 180

The unconditional nature of the transfer, or branch, occurs in the sample statement in line 200. When the computer executes line 200, it will go back automatically to line 180 rather than on to the next line of code following line 200.

Example 54 uses this sample statement in a program to further illustrate the use of the GOTO statement.

Example 54

```
160 REM THIS PROGRAM CONTAINS AN ERROR
170 LET A = 0
180 LET A = A + 1
190 PRINT A
200 GOTO 180
999 END
```

The computer moves through the program statements in Example 54 in this order: 170, 180, 190, 200; 180, 190, 200; 190, 190, 200; and so on. In the sequencing of program statements, the repetition of statements is called a **loop.** The loop involves the repetition of lines 180, 190, and 200 over and over again. When will the program end? You may conclude that the program will end when the computer reads statement 999, which is the END statement. However, the computer will never get to line 999 because every time it gets to line 200, it is unconditionally directed to line 180. This is an **endless loop,** or **infinite loop;** the computer repeats the same statements over and over again, never coming to an END statement. Make certain that you always provide a means to exit a loop. We will discuss this further in Part 2.

7 The IF-THEN Statement

The **IF-THEN** statement is called a **conditional transfer** because a particular condition must exist before the computer will transfer to the line number or statement specified, instead of automatically executing the line immediately following the IF-THEN statement. Example 55 provides the statement format and sample statements.

Example 55

Statement Format:
Line number IF Condition exists THEN Line number or statement

Sample Statements:
```
310 IF NAMES$="END OF FILE" THEN 440

420 IF C > B THEN PRINT "OVER"
```

In the first sample statement, if the alphanumeric variable, NAMES$, equals the alphanumeric constant, "END OF FILE", then the computer is directed to immediately execute line 440. If NAMES$ does not equal "END OF FILE", the computer executes the next line of code following the IF-THEN statement. That is, the transfer to line 440 takes place only on the *condition* that NAMES$="END OF FILE". (Note: Some programmers prefer to write ...THEN GOTO 440, which is the equivalent of ...THEN 440.)

In the second sample statement, if variable C is greater than variable B, the computer prints OVER. After performing the PRINT statement, the computer executes the line immediately following the line that contains the IF-THEN statement.

The = and > conditions are tested in the sample statements. A variety of conditions can be tested using the IF-THEN statement. Let us first consider the six conditions called **relational operators.**

Relational Operators
The relational operators that make comparisons possible within an IF-THEN statement are shown in Example 56.

Example 56

	Operator Symbol	Meaning	Example
①	=	Equal to	220 IF A = 6 THEN 410
②	<	Less than	220 IF A < B THEN 410
③	>	Greater than	220 IF A$ > B$ THEN 410
④	<= or =<	Less than or equal to	220 IF A <= (B + C) THEN 410
⑤	>= or =>	Greater than or equal to	220 IF A >= B THEN 410
⑥	<> or ><	Not equal to	220 IF A$ <> "DATE" THEN 410

Within the IF-THEN statement format in Example 55, the "Condition exists" portion is made up of comparisons of numeric and alphanumeric variables and numeric and alphanumeric constants made possible by the relational operators in Example 56. Notice the variety of comparisons that can be made. ① uses the relational operator = to compare numeric variable A with numeric constant 6. ③ compares the alphanumeric variable A$ with the alphanumeric variable B$ by using > (greater than). ④ compares the numeric variable A with the arithmetic expression (B + C) by using the <= (less than or equal to). ⑥ uses < > (not equal to) to compare the alphanumeric variable A$ with the alphanumeric constant "DATE".

The partial program in Example 57 illustrates the use of relational operators.

Example 57

```
100 REM THIS PARTIAL PROGRAM PRINTS THE EMPLOYEE'S NAME
110 REM IF THE EMPLOYEE IS FEMALE AND UNDER 40 YEARS OLD
120 REM WITH AT LEAST 4 YEARS OF EMPLOYMENT.
130 REM
140 READ EMPLOYEE$,SEX$,AGE,YEARS
150 IF SEX$ = "M" GOTO 999
160 IF AGE >= 40 GOTO 999
170 IF YEARS < 4 GOTO 999
180 PRINT EMPLOYEE$
190 DATA MARION SCHORR,F,29,6
999 END

RUN

MARION SCHORR
```

Logical Operators

The IF-THEN statement is a logical expression because the comparison within the condition tested is either true or false. In addition to the six relational operators that were introduced, three **logical operators—AND, NOT,** and **OR**—can also be used to form logical expressions. Example 58 illustrates the use of the logical operator AND.

Example 58

```
300 IF NAMES$ = "STEVE" AND AGE > 30 THEN 530
```

When using the logical operator AND in an IF-THEN statement, *both* comparisons joined by AND must be true for the instruction or line number of the statement following THEN to be executed.

Example 59 illustrates the use of the logical operator OR.

Example 59

```
400 IF A < 1 OR A > 50 THEN 500
```

The logical operator OR requires that only one of the comparisons joined by OR be true for the compound expression to be true. In Example 59 either A must be less than 1 or A must be greater than 50 for line 500 to be executed.

Example 60 illustrates the use of the logical operator NOT.

Example 60

```
420 IF NOT X > Y THEN 600
```

In Example 60 if it is not true that X > Y, the condition following IF is true, and line 600 is executed. If it is true that X > Y, then the condition following IF is false, and the line after line 420 is executed.

It is possible to use more than one logical operator in a logical expression. Just as there is a hierarchy of mathematical operations, there is a hierarchy of logical operators. Parentheses affect the order in which the steps in a logical expression are performed just as they do with mathematical operations. The computer performs comparisons in logical expressions containing more than one logical operator in the following order: The logical operator NOT is performed first, the logical operator AND is performed second, the logical operator OR is performed last. Example 61 illustrates the priority of operations in a compound logical expression.

Example 61

Hierarchy of Operations

Operation	Symbol
Parentheses	( )
Arithmetic operators	+, -, *, /
Relational operators	=, <, >, <=, =<, >=, =>, < >, > <
Logical operators	NOT, AND, OR

Example 62 demonstrates the order in which the computer solves a compound logical expression.

Example 62

```
300 LET A = 1
310 LET B = 5
320 LET C = 2
330 LET D = 3
340 LET E = 4
350 IF A > B OR C = D AND (C < D + E) THEN 490
```

1. The expression within parentheses is evaluated.

```
(C < D + E)
(2 < 3 + 4)
    TRUE
```

2. The relational operators are considered next.

```
A > B
1 > 5
FALSE

C = D
2 = 3
FALSE
```

3. The computer considers the logical operators last.

```
C = D and C < (D + E)
2 = 3       2 < (3 + 4)
FALSE AND        TRUE
     FALSE


A > B OR C = D AND C < (D + E)
1 > 5     2 = 3      2 < (3 + 4)
FALSE OR FALSE AND     TRUE
FALSE OR         FALSE
     FALSE
```

4. The complete IF expression is false, so control passes to line 360, the statement following the IF statement, rather than to line 490.

7 The IF-THEN-ELSE Statement

The IF-THEN statement has its limitations: It performs an operation, such as a transfer, only when the condition following IF is true. The IF-THEN-ELSE statement transfers program logic when the condition is either true or false. If the condition is true, logic transfers to the statement or line number following THEN; if the condition is false, logic transfers to the statement or line number following ELSE.

Example 63

Statement Format:
Line number IF Condition THEN Statement(s) or line number
            ELSE Statement(s) or line number

Sample Statement:
```
400 IF A = B THEN LET C = C + 1
    ELSE 600
410 . . .
```

The statement format in Example 63 illustrates that more than one BASIC statement or a line number can follow THEN and ELSE. In the sample statement if it is true that A equals B, then the LET statement is executed. Because there is not a line number following THEN, after the LET statement is executed, control passes to line 410. If A does not equal B, the program logic transfers to line 600, the line number following ELSE.

An advantage of the IF-THEN-ELSE statement is that fewer programming statements are required. Although the IF-THEN statement could be used to accomplish the same tasks as the sample statement, an IF-THEN would require more than one statement.

Consider a situation in which a discount varies: All customers get at least a 10% discount, but senior citizens get a 20% discount. In the partial program in Example 64, assume the variable SENIOR$ contains either Y or N.

Example 64

```
         .
         .
         .
210 IF SENIOR$ = "Y" THEN DISCOUNT = .20
    ELSE DISCOUNT = .10
```

Exercises

1. What would be the output of the program below? (Hint: In line 180 the T on the left is assigned the current value of T, plus 3.)

```
170 LET T = 2
180      LET T = T + 3
190      PRINT T;
200 GOTO 170
999 END
```

2. What would be the output in the program in question 1 if line 200 were changed to:

```
200 GOTO 180
```

3. Write a program to count by twos and produce the following output. Note that the output is all on one line, each output value in a new zone.

```
2           4           6           8           10
```

4. True or false: If A is greater than B in the statement that follows, the line following line 200 is executed.

```
200 IF A > B THEN 340
```

5. True or false: Numeric value A is being compared with numeric value B in the statement that follows.

```
410 IF A$ = B$ THEN 500
```

6. Look at the IF-THEN-ELSE statement that follows. What is executed if the condition is true? What is executed if the condition is false?

```
460 IF T > S THEN 500 ELSE PRINT T
```

7. What does this program print?

```
370 A = 1
380 B = 6
390 C = 7
400 IF (A + B) < 8 OR C < B AND A = 2 THEN PRINT "TRUE"
    ELSE PRINT "FALSE"
```

Answers to Exercises

1. 5 5 5 5 5 5 . . .   (endless loop)

2. 5 8 11 14 17 . . .   (endless loop)

3.
```
100 LET N = 0
110 IF N > 10 THEN 999
120      LET N = N + 2
130      PRINT N,
140 GOTO 110
999 END
```

4. False—statement 340 is executed.

5. False—A$ and B$ are alphanumeric variables.

6. If it is true that T > S, program logic transfers to line 500. If it is false that T > S, the PRINT statement following the ELSE is executed and program logic transfers to the line after the IF-THEN-ELSE statement.

7. TRUE
(If you think the answer should be FALSE, remember to evaluate AND before OR.)

Part 2: More Examples

This section will not introduce any new BASIC statements. Instead, some programming concepts will be introduced to support programs that are more complex. If you have studied Chapter 7, "Beginning Programming," some of these concepts will already be familiar to you.

7 Flowcharting

Before we continue our discussion of BASIC, we pause to consider the use of flowcharts, one method of representing a solution to a problem. A BASIC program can be written from the guidelines in a flowchart. A **flowchart** is essentially a picture that consists of arrows that represent the direction the program takes and of boxes and other symbols that represent actions. Some standard flowchart symbols have been established and are accepted by most programmers. The most common symbols, shown in Example 65, represent process, decision, connector, start/stop, input/output, and direction of flow.

Example 65   **Flowchart Symbols:**

- The rectangular **process** box indicates action to be taken.

- The diamond-shaped box is a **decision** box. The decision box asks a question that requires a yes-or-no answer. It has two paths or branches—one path represents the response *yes*, the other, *no*.

- The circle is called a **connector** because it connects the paths. (This symbol can also be used as an on-page connector when transferring to another location on the same sheet of paper.)

- A flowchart begins and ends with the oval **start/stop** symbol.

- A parallelogram-shaped symbol is used for **input** or **output**, such as reading or printing.

Now let us move on to the more complex examples.

7 More Programming Concepts

Earlier we mentioned looping, the process of repeating a sequence of statements. Looping is a powerful tool because it reduces drudgery. Suppose, for example, that you worked for a manufacturer and were assigned the task of summing up the purchases of each customer. If you could tell the computer how to go about summing up the purchases for one customer and then use that same set of instructions for all customers, it certainly would be easier than starting from scratch for each customer.

Many business activities involve repetitive tasks, for which the computer is well suited. Consider the task of printing all employee names from a computer file. Although the idea is simple, this job introduces further programming concepts. We present the solution first in a flowchart in Example 66 and then as a matching program in Example 67.

Example 66
Flowchart for
Example 67

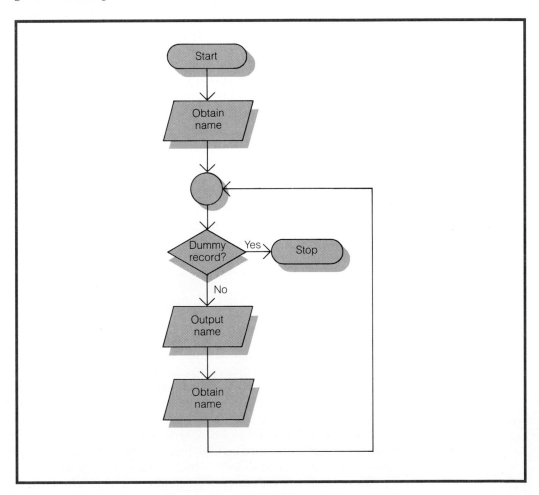

Note the use of different flowchart boxes in Example 66. The oval is used for start and stop. The parallelogram is used for both input ("Obtain name") and output. The diamond shape is used for the decision ("Dummy record?") to get out of the loop. The presence of dummy data, also called an end-of-file indicator, means that all the real data has been read and processed, so the program can stop. The circle is used as a connector, in this case as the place to return to when looping.

Now consider the matching program in Example 67. At this point we need to pause to mention structured programming and then see how it applies to programs like the one in Example 67. Although the details of structured programming are beyond the scope of this discussion of BASIC, we need to present a brief overview.

7 Structured Programming

In a program, **control structures** control how the program executes. **Structured programming** is a technique that, among other things, uses a limited number of control structures to minimize the complexity of programs. There are three basic control structures in structured programming: sequence, selection, and iteration.

The **sequence control structure** is the most straightforward: One statement simply follows another in sequence. In BASIC, this could be any two statements following in order, such as those in lines 190 and 200 in Example 67. The **selection control structure** is used to make logic decisions. You have already seen this control structure in BASIC as IF-THEN and IF-THEN-ELSE. The **iteration control structure** is a looping mechanism. There is more than one approach to looping in BASIC; Example 67 uses a combination of GOTO (line 210) to loop and IF-THEN (line 180) to get out of the loop.

Another consideration related to structured programming is the priming read. Notice that there are two READ statements in Example 67, lines 170 and 200. The first READ statement, called the **priming read,** makes the first set of data available to be processed. You may wonder about the second READ, in statement 200. Why not, instead, loop back to the READ in line 170? This is not permitted in structured programming, where an exit from a loop must be made at the beginning or end of the loop. In this example and in future program examples that use noncounting loops, we will conform to this standard by using the second READ at the end of the loop. Now we need to continue on with Example 67, observing how the loop is exited.

7 Checking the End-of-File Condition

The IF-THEN statement in line 180 of Example 67 directs the computer to check for the end-of-file indicator, "END OF FILE". The END OF FILE on line 230 sometimes is called a trailer record because it trails, or is the last record, following the data records that are to be processed by the program. As we have noted, it is also referred to as a dummy record. If a record is received that is not END OF FILE, the processing of the loop continues. The instructions within the loop will be executed until the condition of the end-of-file indicator is checked and found to be true. When true, the computer executes the line number following the THEN portion of the statement format, or line 999, which ends the program.

The end-of-file indicator is particularly useful when the number of data values to be read varies from one program execution to the next. The logic is not planned to loop a certain number of times; instead, it loops through whatever data values are present until it reaches a trailer value—that is, some end-of-file indicator. In this case, for example, we have used just 4 employee names, but the program would work just as well if there were 400 names; in each case the end of file would be indicated in the same way.

As we will see in subsequent examples, however, some loops are controlled by counters instead, meaning that the loops will execute a predetermined number of times.

Example 67

```
100 REM THIS PROGRAM COMPARES AN ALPHANUMERIC VARIABLE TO AN
110 REM ALPHANUMERIC CONSTANT TO CHECK FOR THE END-OF-FILE
120 REM CONDITION IN THE DATA STATEMENT.
130 REM
140 REM     VARIABLE NAMES:
150 REM         NAMES$ - NAMES OF EMPLOYEES
160 REM
170 READ NAMES$
180 IF NAMES$ = "END OF FILE" THEN 999
190     PRINT NAMES$
200     READ NAMES$
210 GOTO 180
220 DATA MEREDYTH CHAMP,TOM MYERS,RICHARD ALLAN,DAVID BYARD
230 DATA END OF FILE
999 END

RUN

MEREDYTH CHAMP
TOM MYERS
RICHARD ALLAN
DAVID BYARD
```

Example 67 includes two important programming techniques: internal documentation using REM statements and indentation of statements with the loop. Both these techniques make the source program easier to read.

A numeric value could also be used as an end-of-file indicator. When choosing the value, whether alphanumeric or numeric, be sure to use a value that would not occur in the actual data elements. Remember, each READ instruction must be fulfilled. If your READ statement contains more than one variable, your trailer record must contain sufficient data elements. That is, two READ variables, two trailer values; three READ variables, three trailer values; and so on. Also be sure to match string variables with string data and numeric variables with numeric data. Example 68 illustrates these concepts. Assume that there are other data statements, although only the trailer record, line 500, is shown here. Notice that there are exactly two trailer values, which match the two variables in the READ statement. Also note that the type of trailer values matches the type of variable: XXX for NAMES$ (both alphanumeric) and 00 for AGE (both numeric).

Example 68

```
200 READ NAMES$,AGE
500 DATA XXX,00
```

7 More Looping Examples

Example 69 uses the LET statement to count the number of records being processed and prints an item count and item list as output. See if you can draw the flowchart to match the program. Be sure to include both READ statements.

Example 69

```
100 REM THIS PROGRAM PRINTS AN INVENTORY LISTING INCLUDING
110 REM AN ITEM COUNT.
120 REM
130 REM     VARIABLE NAMES:
140 REM        ITEM$ - INVENTORY ITEMS
150 REM        C - COUNTER
160 REM
170 LET C = 0
180 READ ITEM$
190 IF ITEM$ = "END OF FILE" THEN 999
200     LET C = C + 1
210     PRINT C,ITEM$
220     READ ITEM$
230 GOTO 190
240 REM     DATA
250 DATA SHOES,TIES,SOCKS,SLACKS,SHIRTS
260 DATA END OF FILE
999 END

RUN

1           SHOES
2           TIES
3           SOCKS
4           SLACKS
5           SHIRTS
```

The counter (C) in line 170 was initialized to 0 prior to accumulating. Numeric variables are automatically initialized to 0 at the beginning of a program, but this step was taken for the purpose of internal documentation.

The program in Example 70 also uses a counter, but, rather than an item counter as in Example 69, the next program prints a single total for all items processed.

Example 70

```
100 REM THIS PROGRAM PRINTS THE TOTAL NUMBER OF ITEMS
110 REM IN AN INVENTORY LISTING.
120 REM
130 REM    VARIABLE LIST:
140 REM
150 REM        NUMBER - NUMBER OF ITEMS SOLD
160 REM        ITEM$ - NAME OF ITEM
170 REM        PRICE - PRICE OF ITEM
180 REM        TOTAL - TOTAL NUMBER OF ITEMS PROCESSED
190 REM
200 LET TOTAL = 0
210 READ NUMBER,ITEM$,PRICE
220 IF NUMBER = 000 THEN 270
230     LET TOTAL = TOTAL + NUMBER
240     PRINT NUMBER,ITEM$,PRICE
250     READ NUMBER,ITEM$,PRICE
260 GOTO 220
270 PRINT
280 PRINT "TOTAL NUMBER OF ITEMS PROCESSED";TOTAL
290 REM     DATA
300 DATA 13,CANDLES,1.19,23,VASE 7 INCH,3.99
310 DATA 3,PLATE HANGER,1.19,45,COASTER,1.29
320 DATA 8,PLACEMAT OVAL,4.98,000,X,0
999 END

RUN

13           CANDLES           1.19
23           VASE 7 INCH       3.99
```

Example 70 continues

Example 70, continued	3	PLATE HANGER	1.19
	45	COASTER	1.29
	8	PLACEMAT OVAL	4.98

TOTAL NUMBER OF ITEMS PROCESSED 92

Notice that the end-of-file processing, which prints the total number of items processed, does not occur until the trailer record (000,X,0) at the end of the file is read and equals the IF condition in line 220 (NUMBER = 000). Also note that the number of trailer values—three—is the same as the number of variables in the READ statement.

The program in Example 71 illustrates the use of an INPUT statement to provide the end-of-file indicator. Report titles are printed as part of the output.

Example 71

```
110 REM THIS PROGRAM ALLOWS THE USER TO ENTER INVENTORY
120 REM AND SALES INFORMATION AND, AT THE END OF
130 REM PROCESSING, PRINTS TOTALS FOR NUMBER OF ITEMS
140 REM PROCESSED AND THE SALES FOR THE SESSION.
150 REM
160 REM     VARIABLE NAMES:
170 REM
180 REM          ITEM$ - NAME OF ITEM
190 REM          NUMBER - NUMBER OF ITEM
200 REM          PRICE - PRICE OF ITEM
210 REM          QUANTITY - QUANTITY SOLD
220 REM          TOTAL - TOTAL ITEMS SOLD
230 REM          SALES - SALES PRICE
240 REM          VOLUME - TOTAL SALES VOLUME
250 REM          MORE$ - YES OR NO ANSWER
260 REM
270 LET TOTAL = 0
280 LET VOLUME = 0
290 PRINT "THIS PROGRAM PRINTS A LISTING OF THE TOTAL NUMBER"
300 PRINT "OF ITEMS PROCESSED AND THE SALE VALUE OF ITEMS"
310 PRINT "PROCESSED. YOU WILL BE ASKED TO ENTER THE"
320 PRINT "ITEM NAME, ITEM NUMBER, PRICE, AND QUANTITY SOLD."
330 PRINT "SEPARATE EACH WITH A COMMA."
340 PRINT "YOU WILL BE ABLE TO END PROCESSING BY ENTERING"
350 PRINT "YES OR NO TO THE QUESTION, 'MORE ITEMS TO BE"
360 PRINT "PROCESSED?'"
370 PRINT
380 PRINT "ENTER NAME, ITEM NUMBER, PRICE, QUANTITY"
390 INPUT ITEM$,NUMBER,PRICE,QUANTITY
400      LET TOTAL = TOTAL + QUANTITY
410      LET SALES = PRICE * QUANTITY
420      LET VOLUME = VOLUME + SALES
430      PRINT "MORE ITEMS TO BE PROCESSED?"
440      INPUT MORE$
450      IF MORE$ = "NO" THEN 470
460 GOTO 370
470 PRINT
480 PRINT "TOTAL ITEMS PROCESSED";TOTAL
490 PRINT "TOTAL SALES          ";VOLUME
999 END

RUN

THIS PROGRAM PRINTS A LISTING OF THE TOTAL NUMBER
OF ITEMS PROCESSED AND THE SALE VALUE OF ITEMS
PROCESSED. YOU WILL BE ASKED TO ENTER THE
ITEM NAME, ITEM NUMBER, PRICE, AND QUANTITY SOLD.
```

Example 71 continues

Example 71, continued

```
SEPARATE EACH WITH A COMMA.
YOU WILL BE ABLE TO END PROCESSING BY ENTERING
YES OR NO TO THE QUESTION, 'MORE ITEMS TO BE
PROCESSED?'

ENTER NAME, ITEM NUMBER, PRICE, QUANTITY
?TABLES,2321,15.00,2
MORE ITEMS TO BE PROCESSED?
?YES

ENTER NAME, ITEM NUMBER, PRICE, QUANTITY
?LAMP,104,13.98,3
MORE ITEMS TO BE PROCESSED?
?YES

ENTER NAME, ITEM NUMBER, PRICE, QUANTITY
?CHAIR,4576,39.95,4
MORE ITEMS TO BE PROCESSED?
?NO

TOTAL ITEMS PROCESSED 9
TOTAL SALES              231.74
```

Part 3: Advanced BASIC Topics

Although you can certainly write programs without using the FOR/NEXT statement combination, most programmers consider it an essential component in the BASIC language. We will devote a significant amount of attention to FOR/NEXT and then consider some other important statements.

TEST BANK
Mult. Ch.	45-47
T/F	64-66
Match C	3, 10
Fill-ins	36-37

7 The FOR/NEXT Statement

Another looping structure, the **FOR/NEXT** statement, has wide application in BASIC programming and offers some distinct advantages. The statement format for the FOR/NEXT looping structure is shown in Example 72.

Example 72

Statement Format:
Line number FOR Variable = Initial value TO Test value [STEP Variable increment]
Line number NEXT Variable

Sample Statement:
```
150 FOR X = 1 TO 20 STEP 5
  .
  .
  .
200 NEXT X
```

In Example 72 the initial value in the sample statement is the numeric constant 1. The test value is the numeric constant 20. The value of the initial value or the test value can be a constant, a variable, or an arithmetic expression. The loop performed by the FOR/NEXT statements will be terminated when the value of the FOR variable is greater than the test value. The STEP parameter of the statement format is an optional parameter. If no STEP increment is specified in the program statement, an increment value of 1 is implied.

It is important to understand that when using the FOR/NEXT statements, the words FOR and NEXT must be used together.

An application of the sample statement in Example 72 is shown in Example 73. Any BASIC statements can be used within the body of a FOR/NEXT loop. Statements between the FOR and NEXT statements are indented. In this program the PRINT statement is used in the body of the loop. Note the matching flowchart.

Flowchart for
Example 73

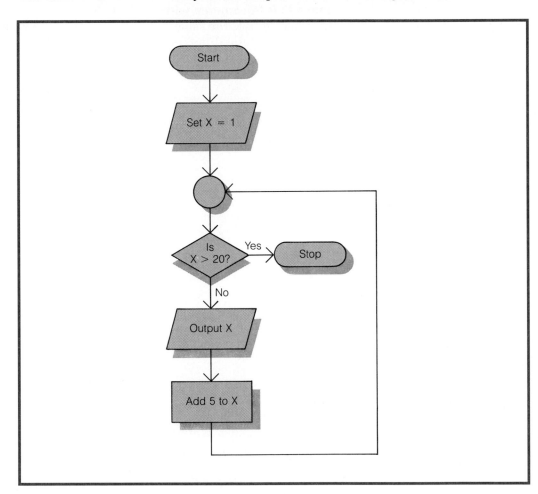

Example 73

```
100 REM THIS PROGRAM CALCULATES THE VALUE OF VARIABLE X.
110 REM
120 FOR X = 1 TO 20 STEP 5
130     PRINT X;
140 NEXT X
999 END

RUN

  1   6   11   16
```

Variable X is assigned the initial value of 1 by the FOR statement in line 120.

The value 20 is the test value following the word TO, and the STEP increment 5 indicates that 5 is to be added to the value of X with each pass through the loop. The semicolon after the PRINT statement in line 130 causes the output to be printed across the page. If 5 is added to the last value, 16, one more time, the final value would exceed the test value of 20. The loop, therefore, executes four times and terminates when the value of X is 21. After the loop is terminated, the line number following the NEXT statement, which in this case is line 999, is executed.

The STEP Parameter with FOR/NEXT

Example 74 uses the same values as Example 73 but does not include the STEP parameter. Notice the difference in the output.

Example 74

```
100 REM THIS PROGRAM CALCULATES THE VALUE OF VARIABLE X.
110 REM
120 FOR X = 1 TO 10
130     PRINT X;
140 NEXT X
999 END

RUN

    1   2   3   4   5   6   7   8   9   10
```

A negative value is used as the STEP increment of the FOR statement in the program shown in Example 75.

Example 75

```
100 REM THIS PROGRAM CALCULATES THE VALUE OF VARIABLE T
110 REM USING A NEGATIVE VALUE IN THE STEP PARAMETER.
120 REM
130 FOR T = 15 TO 5 STEP -5
140     PRINT T,
150 NEXT T
999 END

RUN

    15              10              5
```

When using a negative increment, the initial value must be greater than the test value. It is not possible to descend to a number from a lower number. For example, the statement

```
200 FOR T = 1 TO 15 STEP -5
```

would not be executed by the computer.

It is also possible to use a decimal value for the STEP increment. Example 76 illustrates a STEP increment of 0.5.

Example 76

```
100 REM THIS PROGRAM CALCULATES THE VALUE OF VARIABLE C IN
110 REM STEP INCREMENTS OF .5
120 REM
130 FOR C = 1 TO 3 STEP .5
140     PRINT C,
150 NEXT C
999 END
```

Example 76 continues

Example 81
Flowchart for
Example 80

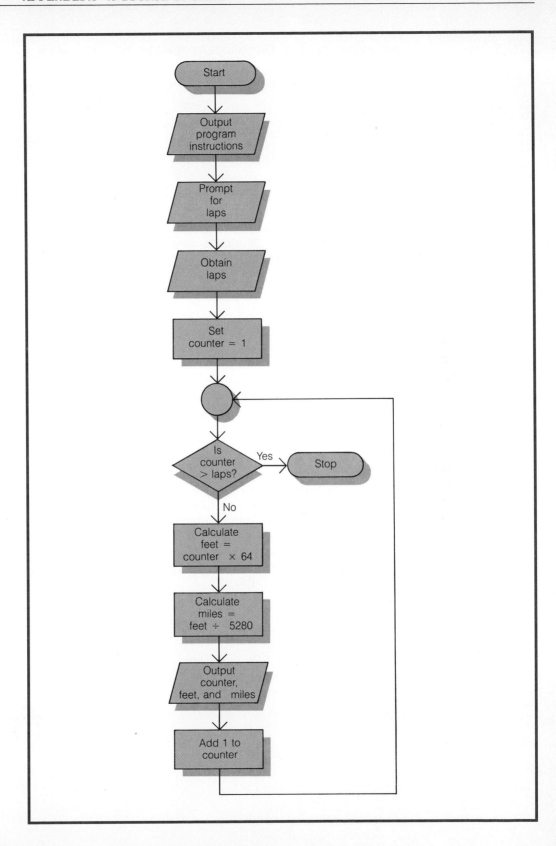

Example 80, continued

```
270 PRINT
280 PRINT "ENTER THE HIGHEST NUMBER OF LAPS SWUM."
290 INPUT N
300 PRINT
310 PRINT "LAPS","FEET","MILES"
320 PRINT
330 FOR C = 1 TO N
340     LET FEET = C * 64
350     LET MILES = FEET/5280
360     PRINT C,FEET,
370     PRINT USING "##.##";MILES
380 NEXT C
999 END

RUN

THIS PROGRAM WILL PRINT A LISTING OF EACH LAP
SWUM, THE DISTANCE IN FEET, AND DISTANCE TO
HUNDREDTHS OF A MILE. YOU WILL BE ASKED TO
ENTER THE HIGHEST NUMBER OF LAPS SWUM.

ENTER HIGHEST NUMBER OF LAPS SWUM.
?6

LAPS    FEET    MILES

1        64      0.01
2       128      0.02
3       192      0.04
4       256      0.05
5       320      0.06
6       384      0.07
```

The advantage of using an INPUT statement to set the test value is that the user can enter any number to be processed.

Arithmetic Expressions in the FOR Statement

As noted earlier, arithmetic expressions can be used for the initial value or test value in the FOR statement. The program in Example 82 uses an arithmetic expression as the test value.

Example 82

```
100 REM THIS PROGRAM USES AN ARITHMETIC EXPRESSION
110 REM AS THE TEST VALUE.
120 REM
130 LET A = 2
140 LET B = 3
150 FOR I = 1 TO A * B
160     PRINT I
170 NEXT I
180 PRINT
190 PRINT "TOTAL NUMBERS PRINTED =";I - 1
999 END

RUN

1
2
3
4
5
6

TOTAL NUMBERS PRINTED = 6
```

The value of I represents the value that, after the final loop, is equal to 7. When the value 7 is compared with the test value of $\Lambda * B$, or 2×3, it is found to exceed the test value; therefore, the FOR/NEXT loop terminates and the statement following the NEXT I, line 180, is executed. Line 190 causes the total line to print. The total of numbers printed is one less than the final value of variable I. The subtraction of 1 is necessary to remove the last addition of 1 from the variable I—this last addition is the one that causes the value to exceed the test condition.

The READ/DATA Statements with FOR/NEXT

The use of the INPUT statement to enter a variable amount in the FOR statement has already been demonstrated. The program in Example 83 illustrates the use of the READ/DATA statements to set the test value in the FOR statement.

Example 83

```
100 REM THIS PROGRAM USES THE READ/DATA STATEMENTS TO
110 REM PROVIDE THE TEST VALUE IN THE FOR STATEMENT.
120 REM
130 REM      VARIABLE NAMES:
140 REM
150 REM      TOTAL - TOTAL NUMBER PROCESSED
160 REM      N - TEST VALUE
170 REM      A - FIRST VALUE TO BE READ
180 REM      B - SECOND VALUE TO BE READ
190 REM      C - LOOP COUNTER
200 REM
210 LET TOTAL = 0
220 READ N
230 FOR C = 1 TO N
240     READ A,B
250     PRINT A,B
260     LET TOTAL = TOTAL + 2
270 NEXT C
280 PRINT
290 PRINT "TOTAL NUMBERS PROCESSED";TOTAL
300 REM      DATA
310 DATA 8
320 DATA 1,2,3,4,5,6,7,8
330 DATA 9,10,11,12,13,14,15,16
999 END

RUN

1              2
3              4
5              6
7              8
9              10
11             12
13             14
15             16

TOTAL NUMBERS PROCESSED 16
```

The READ statement in line 220 obtains the value of 8 from the DATA statement in line 310, thus providing the value for the test value in the FOR statement in line 230. The READ statement in line 240 provides the data to be processed as variables A and B within the FOR/NEXT loop. The value 8 in line 310 could have been included as part of the DATA statement on line 320, but when it is set apart as it is here, it is easily seen by the reader.

Example 84

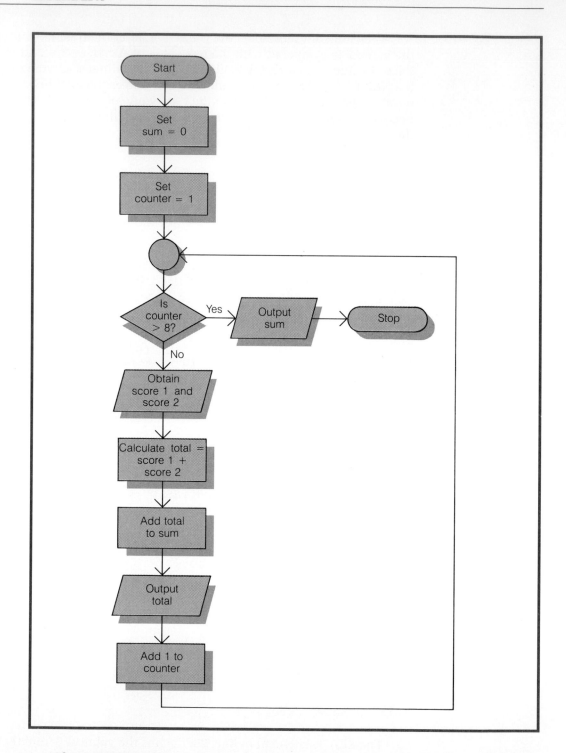

The FOR/NEXT loop is repeated eight times, the value of N. There are, however, a total of 16 numbers processed, as shown in the output. This is because the READ statement in line 240 directs the reading of two variables at a time, not one; therefore, the eight loops read a total of 16 numbers. The total of numbers processed, variable TOTAL, is incremented by 2 in line 260. Each time a loop is performed, 2 is added to the value of TOTAL because two variables, A and B, are read by the READ statement in line 240.

The program in Example 85, accompanied by the flowchart in Example 84, uses READ/DATA statements to supply values for scores that are added, then it prints the sum.

Example 85

```
100 REM USE READ/DATA STATEMENTS TO SUPPLY VALUES FOR
110 REM VARIABLES WITHIN THE FOR/NEXT LOOP AND PRINT THE SUM.
120 REM
130 REM          VARIABLE NAMES:
140 REM          C - COUNTER FOR FOR/NEXT LOOP
150 REM          SUM - SUM OF NUMBERS
160 REM          TOTAL - TOTAL OF TWO NUMBERS READ
170 REM          SCORE1 - FIRST SCORE READ
180 REM          SCORE2 - SECOND SCORE READ
190 REM
200 LET SUM = 0
210 REM
220 FOR C = 1 TO 8
230     READ SCORE1,SCORE2
240     LET TOTAL = SCORE1 + SCORE2
250     LET SUM = SUM + TOTAL
260     PRINT TOTAL
270 NEXT C
280 PRINT
290 PRINT "SUM OF NUMBERS IS";SUM
300 REM     DATA
310 DATA 85,43,23,33,22,99,78
320 DATA 67,45,32,76,51,22,89
330 DATA 28,71
999 END

RUN

  128
  56
  121
  145
  77
  127
  111
  99

SUM OF NUMBERS IS 864
```

Control Within a FOR/NEXT Loop

It is possible to transfer control within a FOR/NEXT loop by using an IF-THEN statement. The program in Example 86 demonstrates this technique. This program prints a listing of names and total scores. A row of asterisks is printed for those people with scores over 250.

Example 86

```
100 REM THIS PROGRAM TRANSFERS CONTROL WITHIN THE FOR/NEXT
110 REM LOOP USING THE IF-THEN STATEMENT.  OUTPUT CONSISTS
120 REM OF A LIST OF NAMES AND TOTAL SCORES, THOSE TOTAL
130 REM SCORES OVER 250 WILL HAVE A ROW OF ASTERISKS AFTER
140 REM THE SCORE.
150 REM
160 REM          VARIABLE NAMES:
170 REM          NAMES$ - NAMES
```

Example 86 continues

Example 86, continued

```
180 REM           SCORE1 - FIRST SCORE READ
190 REM           SCORE2 - SECOND SCORE READ
200 REM           SUM - SUM OF TWO SCORES
210 REM           C - FOR/NEXT LOOP COUNTER
220 REM
230 FOR C = 1 TO 4
240      READ NAMES$,SCORE1,SCORE2
250      LET SUM = SCORE1 + SCORE2
260      IF SUM > 250 THEN 290
270      PRINT NAMES$,SUM
280      GOTO 300
290      PRINT NAMES$,SUM;" *****"
300 NEXT C
310 REM      DATA
320 DATA TED,190,231,LEE,189,90
330 DATA JACK,110,130,MICKEY,200,110
999 END

RUN

TED          421 *****
LEE          279 *****
JACK         240
MICKEY       310 *****
```

Example 86 illustrates an appropriate transfer of control with the FOR/NEXT loop using the IF-THEN statement. Some transfer techniques, however, are not correct. Example 87 illustrates a similar program but shows an incorrect transfer.

Example 87

```
250 FOR C = 1 TO 4
260      READ NAMES$,SCORE1,SCORE2
270      LET SUM = SCORE1 + SCORE2
280      IF SUM > 250 THEN 300
290      PRINT NAMES$,SUM
300      GOTO 250
310 NEXT C
```

The GOTO statement in line 300 bypasses the NEXT statement in line 310. This is incorrect programming procedure. The NEXT C statement causes variable C to be incremented. The program would be correctly written if the IF-THEN statement directed the program to the NEXT statement in line 310.

Likewise, it is incorrect to transfer into a FOR/NEXT loop. Example 88 is an outline of a program that illustrates an incorrect programming procedure using a GOTO statement to transfer into a FOR/NEXT loop.

Example 88

```
220 GOTO 300
230 -------
240 -------
250 -------
260 FOR C = 1 TO 10
270      ----------
280      ----------
290      ----------
300      PRINT NAMES$
310      ----------
320 NEXT C
```

The program statements in Example 89 illustrate transferring out of a loop with an IF-THEN statement. Although this program will run, it does not represent good programming technique.

Example 89

```
230 FOR C = 1 TO 30
240      LET T = A + B
250      IF T > 100 THEN 290
260      PRINT T
270 NEXT C
280 ----------
290 ----------
```

Examples 87 through 89 illustrate this general rule: Do not transfer into or out of FOR/NEXT loops except through the FOR and NEXT statements.

Nested FOR/NEXT Loops

It is possible to place a FOR/NEXT loop within another FOR/NEXT loop. Multiple FOR/NEXT loops are called nested loops and are referred to as inner and outer loops. The flowchart and program in Examples 90 and 91, respectively, illustrate nested FOR/NEXT loops.

Example 90
Flowchart for
Example 91

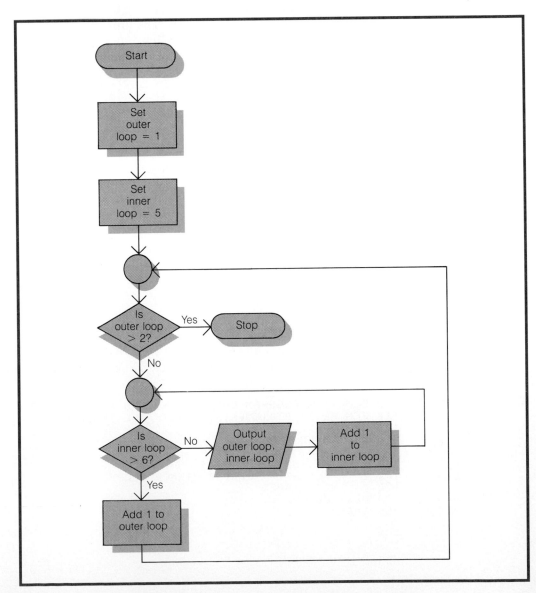

Example 91

```
100 REM THIS PROGRAM DEMONSTRATES A NESTED FOR/NEXT LOOP.
110 REM
120 FOR OUTER = 1 TO 2
130     FOR INNER = 5 TO 6
140          PRINT OUTER,INNER
150     NEXT INNER
160 NEXT OUTER
999 END

RUN

1                  5
1                  6
2                  5
2                  6
```

Notice the spacing of the FOR/NEXT loops in the program. The inner loop, lines 130 through 150, is contained and executed within the outer loop, lines 120 through 160. Initially, variable Outer in the outer loop is given a value of 1, and variable Inner in the inner loop is given a value of 5. The inner loop is performed repeatedly until the condition of the FOR statement in line 130 is satisfied, which means that the test value of 6 is reached. Then the NEXT statement in line 160 is executed, giving variable Outer the value of 2. The inner loop is repeated again with the values of 5 and 6 for the values of variable Inner.

The large brackets in Example 92 indicate an important point: The inner loop cannot intersect the outer loop; completion of the inner loop must be totally within the outer loop structure. It is possible to have more than one nested loop, but the loops cannot intersect each other. Notice that the structures are labeled "Correct" and "Incorrect." The incorrect structure contains intersecting loops.

Example 92

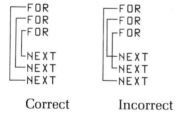

    Correct   Incorrect

The PRINT Statement with FOR/NEXT

The program in Example 93 uses PRINT statements within both the inner and outer loops to illustrate the logical progression of nested FOR/NEXT loops.

Example 93

```
100 REM THIS PROGRAM CONTAINS NESTED FOR/NEXT LOOPS INCLUDING
110 REM PRINT STATEMENTS IN BOTH THE INNER AND OUTER LOOPS.
120 REM
130 FOR OUTER = 1 TO 3
140     PRINT "OUTER LOOP"
150     FOR INNER = 1 TO 3
160          PRINT TAB(5);"INNER LOOP"
170     NEXT INNER
180 NEXT OUTER
999 END

RUN
```

Example 93 continues

Example 93, continued
```
OUTER LOOP
      INNER LOOP
      INNER LOOP
      INNER LOOP
OUTER LOOP
      INNER LOOP
      INNER LOOP
      INNER LOOP
OUTER LOOP
      INNER LOOP
      INNER LOOP
      INNER LOOP
```

Calculations with FOR/NEXT

As mentioned, calculations can be made within FOR/NEXT loops. This is true for both inner loops and outer loops. The program in Example 94 illustrates this concept by calculating variable N within the inner loop.

Example 94
```
100 REM THIS PROGRAM USES THE VALUES OF VARIABLES IN BOTH
110 REM FOR STATEMENTS FOR CALCULATIONS WITHIN THE INNER LOOP.
120 REM
130 FOR O = 1 TO 4
140     FOR I = 2 TO 5
150           LET N = O * I
160           PRINT N;
170     NEXT I
180 NEXT O
999 END

RUN

 2   3   4   5   4   6   8   10   6   9   12   15   8   12   16   20
```

The use of the IF-THEN statement to transfer control within a FOR/NEXT loop has already been discussed. The program in Example 95 uses the IF-THEN statement to transfer control within an inner FOR/NEXT loop.

Example 95
```
100 REM THIS PROGRAM USES THE INPUT STATEMENT TO INPUT TWO
110 REM VARIABLE VALUES AND USES THE IF-THEN STATEMENT TO
120 REM TRANSFER CONTROL WITHIN THE INNER FOR/NEXT LOOP TO
130 REM PRINT NO RESULTING NUMBERS LARGER THAN 10.
140 REM
150 PRINT "ENTER FIRST VALUE"
160 INPUT VALUE1
170 PRINT "ENTER SECOND VALUE"
180 INPUT VALUE2
190 REM
200 FOR O = 1 TO VALUE1
210     PRINT "LOOP";O
220     FOR I = 1 TO VALUE2
230           LET S = (O + I) * 2
240           IF S > 10 THEN 260
250           PRINT S
260     NEXT I
270 NEXT O
999 END

RUN

ENTER FIRST VALUE
```

Example 95 continues

Example 95, continued

```
?3
ENTER SECOND VALUE
?4
LOOP 1
 4
 6
 8
 10
LOOP 2
 6
 8
 10
LOOP 3
 8
 10
```

The value of S is calculated on line 230. Line 240 checks the value of S to determine if, after calculations, it has exceeded 10. If so, control within the inner FOR/NEXT passes to line 260, NEXT I, without the value of variable S being printed. Therefore, no numbers greater than 10 are printed in the output.

7 Exercises

1. Look at the following statements. How many times would the loop be performed?
```
450 FOR M = 1 TO 5 STEP 2
460     PRINT M
470 NEXT M
```

2. What would be the output from the following statements?
```
330 FOR N = 10 TO 5 STEP -1
340     PRINT N;
350 NEXT N
```

3. What would be the output from the following statements?
```
220 PRINT "T MULTIPLIED BY 3 AND 4"
230 FOR T = 2 TO 8
240     PRINT T * 3,T * 4
250 NEXT T
```

4. What would be the output from the following statements?
```
350 FOR B = 5 TO 10 STEP -1
360    PRINT B
370 NEXT B
```

5. What would be the output from the following statements?
```
220 LET T = 5
230 LET N = 10
240 LET S = 1
250 FOR C = T TO N STEP S
260     PRINT C
270 NEXT C
```

Answers to Exercises

1. The loop would be performed three times, with M = 1, 3, and 5.

2.   10   9   8   7   6   5

3. T MULTIPLIED BY 3 AND 4

```
     6            8
     9           12
    12           16
    15           20
    18           24
    21           28
    24           32
```

4. The statements would not execute because you cannot go from a lesser number to a greater number with a negative STEP increment.

5.
```
    5
    6
    7
    8
    9
   10
```

Sample Program: Price Markups

The sample program that follows illustrates concepts presented thus far. The program uses nested FOR/NEXT loops to calculate markup percentages on prices. The flowchart in Example 96 is labeled to highlight three major steps. It corresponds to the BASIC program in Example 97.

① Step 1 in the flowchart uses an input/output symbol to indicate that headings must be printed first.

② Step 2 uses a decision symbol to check the value of the price to determine if it exceeds 10.00. If it does, the program terminates as indicated with the "Stop" in the oval symbol. If the computer determines that the price does not exceed the test value of 10.00, the outer loop is performed. This loop begins with an input/output symbol that prints the current value of the variable assigned to price.

③ Step 3 involves another decision symbol; this one checks the value of the markup to determine if the amount exceeds 25%. If the value does not exceed 25%, the inner loop is performed. A total is calculated and printed as indicated in the processing and input/output symbols in the flowchart. When the value of the markup exceeds the test value of 25%, the loop is completed and control passes to the decision symbol in step 2.

Example 96
Flowchart for
Example 97

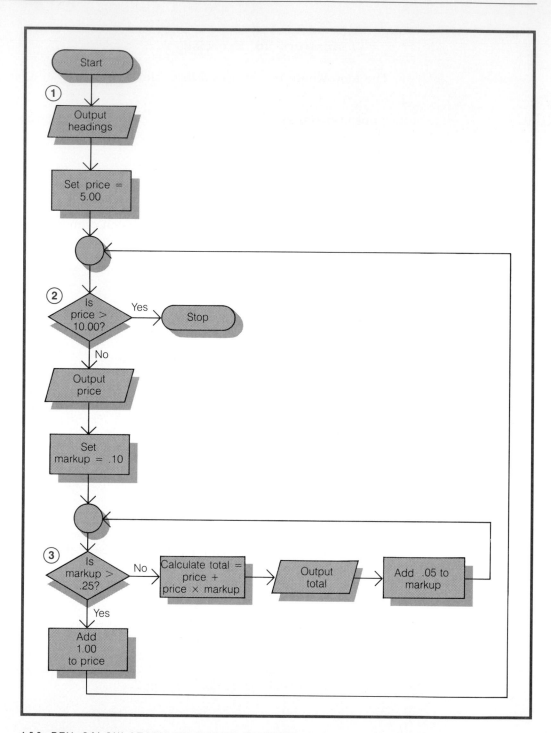

Example 97

```
100  REM CALCULATION OF PRICE MARKUPS
110  REM
120  REM THIS PROGRAM CALCULATES MARKUP PERCENTAGES ON PRICES
130  REM FROM $5.00 TO $10.00 IN INCREMENTS OF 10%, 15%, 20%,
140  REM AND 25%.  OUTPUT CONSISTS OF A LISTING OF THE PRICES
150  REM AND THE PRICES WITH THE MARKUP INCLUDED.
160  REM
170  REM          VARIABLE NAMES:
```

Example 97 continues

Example 97, continued

```
180 REM          PRICE - PRICE OF ITEM
190 REM          MARKUP - MARKUP AMOUNT
200 REM          TOTAL - PRICE + MARKUP
210 REM
220 PRINT "PRICE","10%","15%","20%","25%"
230 PRINT
240 FOR PRICE = 5.00 TO 10.00
250     PRINT USING "###.##";PRICE,
260     FOR MARKUP = .10 TO .25 STEP .05
270         LET TOTAL = PRICE + (PRICE * MARKUP)
280         PRINT USING "###.##";TOTAL,
290     NEXT MARKUP
300 NEXT PRICE
999 END

RUN
```

PRICE	10%	15%	20%	25%
5.00	5.50	5.75	6.00	6.25
6.00	6.60	6.90	7.20	7.50
7.00	7.70	8.05	8.40	8.75
8.00	8.80	9.20	9.60	10.00
9.00	9.90	10.35	10.80	11.15
10.00	11.00	11.50	12.00	12.50

As in previous programs, this program begins with the important REM section in lines 100 through 210, which includes the description of the program, definitions of variable names, and spacing to make the program easier to read.

Lines 220 and 230 accomplish the printing of the headings, allowing for a blank line between the heading line and the first detail line of the report. Line 220, ① on the flowchart, carries out the processing for printing the report headings, as indicated in the input/output symbol.

Lines 240 through 300 form the outer FOR/NEXT loop. The beginning of this loop corresponds with the decision symbol in the flowchart, ②. This loop processes the prices in the range of prices from 5.00 to 10.00. If it is determined, when the value is checked, that the value does not exceed 10.00, then line 250 is executed. Line 250 codes the printing of the line by using the PRINT USING statement.

The inner FOR/NEXT loop is coded in lines 260 through 290. On the flowchart the beginning of the inner FOR/NEXT loop is depicted by the decision symbol ③. The inner loop processes the markup percentage that is to be added to the price. Calculation of the total of the price plus the markup is coded on line 270. This corresponds to the first processing symbol within the inner loop on the flowchart. Line 280 prints the value of the total by using the PRINT USING statement. This statement precedes the NEXT statement on line 290, which transfers processing of the loop to line 260, the FOR statement.

The NEXT statement on line 300 continues the processing of the outer loop, directing control to the FOR statement in line 240. Once the test value of 10.00 has been exceeded, the computer executes the line following the NEXT statement, which is line 999, the END statement.

This program illustrates a distinct advantage of FOR/NEXT statements: The values contained within the FOR/NEXT statements can be adjusted easily. If a different range of prices is to be computed using the same markup percentages, changes can easily be made in the outer FOR statement. Likewise, if a different set of percentages is to be used within the inner FOR/NEXT loop, it is simple to insert those values in the inner FOR statement.

TEST BANK
Mult. Ch.   48-53
T/F   67-68
MatchB   10
Fill-ins   38-41

7 Arrays

So far, in dealing with variable names, we have understood that the computer establishes a storage location in memory and gives the location the variable name. The computer is able to retrieve the data from that location when it encounters the variable name. This method has been sufficient for all the programs we have written thus far, but occasionally, we will find that it limits the techniques we can use to manipulate the data.

In particular, we may want to manipulate data in groups such as all the grades for a class, or all the days in a calendar month, or all the completion times of a marathon. In each group there are too many data values to juggle individually; at the very least it would be inconvenient to give each item a separate variable name. But like data can be processed as a group. As you will see, the FOR/NEXT statement is especially suited to this purpose. We begin with single-dimensional arrays—lists of data—then move to two-dimensional arrays.

7 Single-Dimensional Arrays

To provide manipulation capabilities to process arrays, you will use **subscripted variables.**

Let us look at the difference between a variable and a subscripted variable. As mentioned, a variable name designates one location in memory. A subscripted variable, however, references multiple locations used to store similar items. Example 98 illustrates this concept.

Example 98   ①

A

② Array A(X)

A(1)	A(2)	A(3)	A(4)	A(5)

In ① the variable name A references one storage location, represented by the single block. In ② each of the blocks represents one storage location. Each of these storage locations is referenced by a variable of the form A(X), where the value of X determines the specific block being referenced. Values can be placed into and retrieved from these storage locations. You may wonder how one variable name can be used to reference multiple locations. This is made possible by subscripts.

The group of similar items referenced by a subscripted variable is called an **array.** Each item within an array is called an **element** of the array. To reference one particular element within an array, the variable name should be followed by a value in parentheses. This variable followed by a value in parentheses is called a **subscripted variable,** and the value within the parentheses is a **subscript.** In ② of Example 98, the subscript is the value X. A subscript can be a numeric constant, a numeric variable, or an arithmetic expression. The value of the subscript cannot be negative, and it should not be larger than the size of the array. The subscripted variable may be either alphanumeric or numeric. Example 99 demonstrates various forms of subscripted variables.

Example 99   A(1)   NAME$(X)   A(T + 4)

To demonstrate the use of a subscripted variable, let us consider the ages of five children: 5, 14, 7, 12, and 2. Perhaps we want the ages of all the children to be available at the same time to determine the age of the oldest child. We could give each of these ages its own variable name—such as AGE1, AGE2, AGE3, AGE4, and AGE5—as illustrated in Example 100.

Example 100

AGE1	AGE2	AGE3	AGE4	AGE5
5	14	7	12	2

This method limits the manipulation capabilities we have. On the other hand, we could give the array of ages one variable name by subscripting that variable name, as shown in Example 101. We will return to this data in Example 103.

Example 101

A(X)

5	14	7	12	2

The DIM Statement

If you use a subscripted variable, most versions of BASIC automatically set up an array with ten elements. If, however, you want a larger number of storage locations for any particular list in your program, you have to instruct the computer to reserve those locations. For this purpose you use a DIM statement. DIM stands for *dimension*, and Example 102 illustrates the format of the dimension statement.

Example 102

Statement Format:
Line number DIM Variable name (Number of locations needed for this variable)

Sample Statement:
220 DIM NET(15)

The sample statement tells the computer to reserve 15 storage locations for the array named NET. When determining the size of the array, make sure you reserve enough locations to meet your needs. If you attempt to use an array with an inadequate number of storage locations reserved, you will receive an error message like "SUBSCRIPT OUT OF RANGE." Do not, however, arbitrarily reserve an unreasonably large number of locations because you will use up too much memory needlessly.

The DIM statement may be placed anywhere within the program as long as it precedes any statement that uses the subscripted variable. Quite often, programmers place the DIM statements toward the beginning of the program. Although it is necessary to give a dimension to any list that has more than ten elements, many programmers automatically dimension all arrays, even those with less than ten elements. The use of DIM statements for all arrays, regardless of size, provides additional internal documentation. This documentation increases the ease of debugging by demonstrating which variables are subscripted and how many elements the array contains.

A single-dimensional array is known as a **list.** You have already seen how a DIM statement is used to reserve memory locations for the elements in a list. You have also seen how a variable is subscripted to reference an element within that list. We now need to see how we can actually place data into those storage locations and how we can manipulate and retrieve data from them.

Data can be placed into the storage locations reserved for an array by using LET, READ, or INPUT statements.

Using LET Statements to Load an Array

Remember, the purpose of the subscript following a variable is to identify which element of the array is being referenced. A(1) references the first element in the list named A, A(2) references the second element in the list named A, and so on. To place values in the storage locations—that is, to load the array—we can use the LET statement as shown in Example 103. The LET statement in this example gives the subscripted variable A(1) the value of 7.

Example 103

```
30 LET A(1) = 7
```

Consider our example of an array with children's ages in Example 101. To place the ages 5, 14, 7, 12, and 2 into the appropriate storage locations, we could use the following LET statements:

```
200 LET A(1) = 5
210 LET A(2) = 14
220 LET A(3) = 7
230 LET A(4) = 12
240 LET A(5) = 2
```

After executing these statements, the array is loaded and the values can be referenced by using the subscripted variable names.

Using READ Statements to Load an Array

Just as we can use READ/DATA statements to assign values to variables, we can also use them to assign values to subscripted variables. We could load the age array with the following statements:

```
200 READ A(1),A(2),A(3),A(4),A(5)
500 DATA 5,14,7,12,2
```

Using INPUT Statements to Load an Array

The INPUT statement may also be used to assign values to variables. The following statements would load the age array with the ages of the children.

```
250 PRINT "ENTER THE AGES OF THE CHILDREN, EACH SEPARATED"
260 PRINT "BY A COMMA."
270 INPUT A(1),A(2),A(3),A(4),A(5)
```

Variables as Subscripts

Remember, a subscript can be a numeric constant, a numeric variable, or an arithmetic expression. Using subscripted variables increases the ability to manipulate data in an array. But the key to this advantage is to make the subscripts themselves variables.

Look again at the example of using READ/DATA statements to load an array.

```
200 READ A(1),A(2),A(3),A(4),A(5)
500 DATA 5,14,7,12,2
```

The subscripts in this example—1, 2, 3, 4, and 5—are constants, not variables. But notice that each subscript value is increased by 1 to reference the next element in the age array. By using a variable as the subscript, we can use a FOR/NEXT loop to increment the subscript value and, therefore, perform the identical process of referencing each element. The FOR/NEXT loop instructions are as follows:

```
200 FOR I = 1 TO 5
210     READ A(I)
220 NEXT I
230 DATA 5,14,7,12,2
```

Statements 200 and 220 instruct the computer to perform statement 210 five times, each time increasing the value of I by 1. The following READ statements are executed in this loop.

```
READ A(1)
READ A(2)
READ A(3)
READ A(4)
READ A(5)
```

These instructions perform the same process as the original READ statement:

```
200 READ A(1),A(2),A(3),A(4),A(5)
```

Although these examples demonstrate how a variable subscript can be used to load arrays, you may not yet see the advantages inherent in using the variable subscript over using the numeric constant subscript. However, if we had been processing the ages of a large number of children instead of only five, the advantages would be much more apparent. For example, you can write a FOR/NEXT loop with the READ statement to obtain the ages of 100 children using variables as subscripts:

```
200 FOR I = 1 TO 100
210     READ A(I)
220 NEXT I
```

These statements demonstrate that the ability to use a variable subscript can save a great deal of time and effort. Later we will see additional examples of the advantages of variable subscripts.

Variable subscripts can also be used to print information. Using the FOR/NEXT loop, the ages of the five children can be printed as shown in Example 104.

Example 104

```
250 FOR I = 1 TO 5
260     READ A(I)
270 NEXT I
280 FOR I = 1 TO 5
290     PRINT A(I)
300 NEXT I
310 DATA 5,14,7,12,2
999 END

RUN

 5
 14
 7
 12
 2
```

These two FOR/NEXT loops can be combined into one FOR/NEXT loop that accomplishes the same result, as shown on the following page.

```
250 FOR I = 1 TO 5
260     READ A(I)
270     PRINT A(I)
280 NEXT I
290 DATA 5,14,7,12,2
```

How do you think the output would appear if you replaced the PRINT instruction with the following statement?

```
270 PRINT A(I);
```

The output would look like that shown in Example 105.

Example 105   5   14   7   12   2

7 Two-Dimensional Arrays

So far, our discussion concerning subscripted variables has dealt with single-dimensional arrays, or lists. But we are also able to store information in two-dimensional arrays, which are frequently referred to as **tables**. Example 106 illustrates the difference between a single-dimensional array and a two-dimensional array.

Example 106   Array A(X)

A(1)	A(2)	A(3)	A(4)	A(5)	. . .

Array A(X,Y)

A(1,1)	A(1,2)	A(1,3)	A(1,4)	A(1,5)	A(1,6)
A(2,1)	A(2,2)	A(2,3)	A(2,4)	A(2,5)	A(2,6)
A(3,1)	A(3,2)	A(3,3)	A(3,4)	A(3,5)	A(3,6)

                                                              . . .

The single-dimensional array, or list, is arranged with one element next to the other. The two-dimensional array is arranged in a rectangle composed of rows and columns. The variable names for single-dimensional arrays are subscripted with one subscript, which references a particular element within the list. The variable names for two-dimensional arrays are subscripted with two subscripts to reference a particular element within the table. Example 107 illustrates the difference between subscripts for single-dimensional arrays and subscripts for two-dimensional arrays.

Example 107   **Single-Dimensional Array Variable Names**:

N(1)   N(Y)   N(Y+4)

Two-Dimensional Array Variable Names:

N(1,4)   N(Y,D)   N(Y+3,4)

The first subscript for the two-dimensional array is the number of the element's row, and the second subscript is the number of the element's column. Therefore, NAME$(1,4) refers to an element named NAME$ in the first row of the fourth column of the table. This concept is illustrated in Example 108.

Example 108

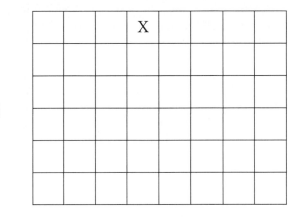

NAME$(1,4)

Dimensioning a Two-Dimensional Array

With a two-dimensional array most versions of BASIC automatically reserve ten row locations and ten column locations for each row—hence, 100 locations. If more locations are needed, it is necessary to dimension the table according to the statement format illustrated in Example 109.

Example 109

Statement Format:
Line number DIM Array name(X,Y) where X is the row element and Y is the column element

Sample Statement:
200 DIM P(12,26)

As with the single-dimensional arrays, good programming practices dictate dimensioning all two-dimensional arrays, regardless of size.

Multiple single-dimensional and/or two-dimensional arrays may be dimensioned with one DIM statement as illustrated in Example 110.

Example 110

230 DIM X(5,20),Y(6),R(3),T(4,16)

Using FOR/NEXT to Load a Two-Dimensional Array

To place values into tables, process the values, and print them, it is necessary to use nested FOR/NEXT loops. The following statements are used to load a two-dimensional array of three rows and five columns:

```
300 FOR ROW = 1 TO 3
310     FOR COLUMN = 1 TO 5
```

Example 110 continues

Example 110, continued

```
320              READ A(ROW,COLUMN)
330      NEXT COLUMN
340 NEXT ROW
350 REM    DATA
360 DATA 2,4,6,8,10
370 DATA 3,5,7,9,11
380 DATA 16,15,14,13,12
999 END
```

Line 300 instructs the computer to repeat the instructions from line 300 through line 340 three times. Another FOR/NEXT loop is located within these statements. When one FOR/NEXT loop is nested within another FOR/NEXT loop, the computer increments the value of the outer loop one time, then the inner FOR/NEXT loop is repeated until the test value, in this case 5, is reached. As the computer performs the inner FOR/NEXT loop, the variable COLUMN is incremented once for each pass through the loop. Therefore, the first time the computer reads a DATA statement, the subscript values are 1 for the row (variable ROW) and 1 for the column (variable COLUMN). This is because the outer FOR/NEXT loop set the row subscript to 1 and the inner FOR/NEXT loop set the column subscript to 1.

When the computer reads the first DATA element, it is given the variable name A(1,1). The second time the computer reads a DATA element, the element is given the variable name A(1,2) because the subscript COLUMN has increased in value by 1. The third time the computer reads a DATA element, the element is given the variable name A(1,3) because the subscript COLUMN has again increased in value by 1. When the computer has completed the inner FOR/NEXT loop, the value of the subscript referenced by the outer FOR/NEXT loop increases by 1; thus, the variable name becomes A(2,1). This process continues, with the value of COLUMN increasing by 1 for every pass through the inner loop (as indicated by the FOR statement in line 310), and the value of ROW increasing by 1. Upon completion of the nested FOR/NEXT loops, the following variables have values as shown:

A(1,1) = 2	A(1,2) = 4	A(1,3) = 6	A(1,4) = 8	A(1,5) = 10
A(2,1) = 3	A(2,2) = 5	A(2,3) = 7	A(2,4) = 9	A(2,5) = 11
A(3,1) = 16	A(3,2) = 15	A(3,3) = 14	A(3,4) = 13	A(3,5) = 12

Processing Variables in a Two-Dimensional Array

Variables in a two-dimensional array are processed using the same nested FOR/NEXT loop techniques just presented. Let us say we want to add all the elements that have already been placed in a table for a final total value. Examine the following statements:

```
190 LET TOTAL = 0
200 FOR ROW = 1 TO 3
210      FOR COLUMN = 1 TO 5
220              LET TOTAL = TOTAL + A(ROW,COLUMN)
230      NEXT COLUMN
240 NEXT ROW
250 PRINT TOTAL
```

The computer performs line 220, changing the value of COLUMN 5 times before it changes the value of ROW. Thus, the LET statement is performed 15 times, and each time the value of the next element in the table is added to the already accumulating total.

Printing Two-Dimensional Arrays

Printing two-dimensional arrays also requires nested FOR/NEXT loops. When run, the statements in Example 111 produce the table shown.

Example 111

```
200 FOR ROW = 1 TO 3
210     FOR COLUMN = 1 TO 5
220          READ AMOUNT(ROW,COLUMN)
230          PRINT AMOUNT(ROW,COLUMN),
240     NEXT COLUMN
250     PRINT
260 NEXT ROW
270 DATA 1,15,2,44,51,43,12,74,5,123,4,9,1,2,6
999 END

RUN

1              15             2              44             51
43             12             74             5              123
4              9              1              2              6
```

/ Exercises

Answer exercises 1 through 5, using the following program.

```
200 FOR X = 1 TO 10
210     READ N(X)
220     PRINT N(X)
230     LET A = N(X) + X
240     PRINT A
250 NEXT X
260 DATA 20,83,6,14.2,18,92.4,3,1,100,813
999 END
```

1. What output will result from the first pass through the FOR/NEXT loop?

2. How many times will the computer execute the READ statement?

3. What output will result from the last pass through the FOR/NEXT loop?

4. Is a DIM statement required for the program?

5. Write a DIM statement for the program.

6. Write a single DIM statement to reserve storage locations for an array named T with five rows and six columns and an array named C with seven elements.

7. Write a nested FOR/NEXT loop to place values into a table as shown.

   ```
   6              7              13
   2              5              9
   ```

8. Add two statements to your program in exercise 7 that will add all the values and one statement that will print the total.

7 Answers to Exercises

1. 20
   21

2. Ten times

3. 813
   823

4. A DIM statement is not required because the computer automatically reserves ten storage locations for an array.

5. 150 DIM N(10)

6. 200 DIM T(5,6),C(7)

7. 180 FOR O = 1 TO 2
   190   FOR I = 1 TO 3
   200   READ S(O,I)
   210   PRINT S(O,I),
   220   NEXT I
   230   PRINT
   240 NEXT O
   250 REM DATA
   260 DATA 6,7,13,2,5,9

8. 170 LET T = 0
   201 LET T = T + S(O,I)
   241 PRINT T

TEST BANK
Mult. Ch.   54-59
T/F   69-71
Match B   9
Match C   4-5
Fill-ins   42-44

7 Menus and Subroutines

A **menu** is not a list of food dishes and prices, but it is like a restaurant menu in the sense that it is a list of choices. A menu offers an easy way for users to interact with the computer, particularly users who are only minimally trained to use existing software. For instance, a menu for a word processing program might appear on the CRT screen as follows:

```
MENU

1 CREATE A DOCUMENT
2 UPDATE A DOCUMENT
3 PRINT A DOCUMENT

ENTER YOUR CHOICE:
```

To make a selection for, say, printing a document, you would type in the number 3. The computer system would then give you other options related to printing the document.

Now let us see how menu choices are used within the program.

7 ON GOTO

Let us now look at menus used with the **ON GOTO** statement. Instead of having an IF statement, where there are two choices (yes and no), the ON GOTO statement gives you several choices—a format that fits very nicely into a menu. The format of the ON GOTO statement is as follows:

Example 112   **Statement Format:**
Line number ON N GOTO Line number, Line number, Line number, . . .

Sample Statement:
200 ON N GOTO 330, 340, 350

The value in location N—a BASIC variable—will be whatever the user places in it by typing in the menu choice. The program in turn will place that menu choice in location N by using an input statement: INPUT N. For instance, if the value in location N is 1, then the program transfers to the first line number—330—in the list of line numbers that we separated with commas. If it has a value of 2, it goes to 340. If 3, it goes to 350. If the value is none of these numbers, then the next statement in the series of BASIC statements is executed.

This ON GOTO concept can appear complicated in the abstract; after the subroutine discussion, which follows, read on to the hot tub example (Example 114) to see how it really works.

7 GOSUB and RETURN

A **subroutine** in BASIC is a sequence of statements grouped as a unit within the program. The transfer to the subroutine is made from the **GOSUB** statement. The GOSUB statement specifies the line number of the statement that starts the subroutine. At the end of the subroutine, the **RETURN** statement transfers control back to the statement after the GOSUB. Note how these work in the following program segment:

Example 113

```
                    .
                    .
                    .
   ┌─200 GOSUB 900
  ┌─→210  .
  │        .
  │        .
  │ └─→900 REM SUBROUTINE PROFIT COMPUTATION
  │        .
  │        .
  └───970 RETURN
```

The GOSUB statement causes transfer to line 900, where the subroutine is located in the program. Line 970 is the last line of the subroutine; the RETURN statement causes a transfer to line 210.

Subroutines are particularly useful when program coding is executed more than once. Instead of repeating the code, it can be written in a subroutine; the subroutine is invoked (GOSUB) each time it is needed. After each use, the computer carries on from the line following the GOSUB.

7 Menus and Subroutines: The Hot Tub Example

Which hot tub salesperson has the hottest sales? As the remarks section (lines 120 through 130) of Example 114 indicates, we are demonstrating a program that uses a menu selection to call subroutines to produce information—such as top salesperson—related to hot tub sales data.

Example 114

```
100 REM   HOT TUB SALES MENU                    J. HARRIS
110 REM
120 REM THIS PROGRAM USES A MENU SELECTION TO CALL SUBROUTINES
130 REM TO PRODUCE OUTPUT RELATED TO HOT TUB SALES DATA.
140 REM
150 REM           VARIABLE NAMES
160 REM           NAMES$   - SALESPERSON NAME ARRAY
170 REM           UNITS    - UNITS SOLD ARRAY
180 REM           NUMBER   - NUMBER OF ITEMS IN ARRAY
190 REM           MENU     - MENU SELECTION
200 REM           HIGH     - HIGH SALES HOLD AREA
210 REM           HIGHSP$  - HIGH SALESPERSON HOLD AREA
220 REM           TOTAL    - TOTAL SALES
230 REM           AVG      - AVERAGE SALES
240 REM
250 DIM NAMES$(100),UNITS(100)
260 REM READ IN ARRAYS
270 READ NUMBER
280 FOR S = 1 TO NUMBER
290     READ NAMES$(S),UNITS(S)
300 NEXT S
310 REM PRINT MENU
320 PRINT
330 PRINT "HOT TUB SALES MENU"
340 PRINT
350 PRINT " CODE    FUNCTION"
360 PRINT
370 PRINT "1 - TOP SALESPERSON"
380 PRINT "2 - AVERAGE SALES"
390 PRINT "3 - TOTAL SALES"
400 PRINT "4 - STOP"
410 PRINT
420 PRINT "ENTER A NUMBER, 1 THROUGH 4: ";
425 INPUT MENU
430 REM USE MENU SELECTION TO GO TO CORRECT SUBROUTINE
440 ON MENU GOTO 450, 470, 490, 510
450 GOSUB 540
460 GOTO 320
470 GOSUB 650
480 GOTO 320
490 GOSUB 740
500 GOTO 320
510 PRINT "END OF PROGRAM"
520 STOP
530 REM TOP SALESPERSON ROUTINE
540 LET HIGH = 0
550 FOR S = 1 TO NUMBER
560     IF UNITS(S) > HIGH THEN 580
570     GOTO 600
580     LET HIGH = UNITS(S)
590     LET HIGHSP$ = NAMES$(S)
600 NEXT S
610 PRINT
620 PRINT "TOP SALESPERSON IS ";HIGHSP$
630 RETURN
```

Example 114 continues

Example 114, continued

```
640 REM AVERAGE SALES SUBROUTINE
650 LET TOTAL = 0
660 FOR S = 1 TO NUMBER
670     LET TOTAL = TOTAL + UNITS(S)
680 NEXT S
690 LET AVG = TOTAL^QNUMBER
700 PRINT
710 PRINT "AVERAGE SALES: ";AVG
720 RETURN
730 REM TOTAL SALES SUBROUTINE
740 LET TOTAL = 0
750 FOR S = 1 TO NUMBER
760     LET TOTAL = TOTAL + UNITS(S)
770 NEXT S
780 PRINT
790 PRINT "TOTAL SALES: ";TOTAL
800 RETURN
810 REM    DATA
820 DATA 6
830 DATA BOORD,176,DREY,185,FITZPATRICK,150
840 DATA GERAMI,152,MCGAHEY,120,METZGER,166
850 END
```

Each record of data (see lines 830 through 840) consists of the name of a salesperson followed by the number of hot tubs sold by that person in this fiscal year. The program (see lines 260 through 300) reads that data into two arrays: one for salespeople's names and one for the corresponding number of hot tubs sold. As lines 160 and 170 show, NAMES$ is the variable name for the salesperson name array and UNITS is the variable name for the units sold array. The program is flexible because it first reads in (on line 270) the number of salespeople (six in this example, as indicated by the data on line 820), then (on line 280) establishes a READ loop to read exactly that many salespeople.

Now that the data is available, we can print a menu, starting on line 320, to give users choices of what to do with the data. The menu gives four choices: 1 - TOP SALESPERSON, 2 - AVERAGE SALES, 3 - TOTAL SALES, 4 - STOP. The user looking at the menu can type in one of the codes, 1 through 4, which is placed in the variable MENU. Then, as line 440 shows, it is used with an ON GOTO statement. The ON GOTO causes the program to transfer to a line that calls the appropriate subroutine.

For instance, if the user types in 1, then the value of MENU is 1, and on line 440 the program transfers to line 450 because 450 is the first line number in the list of statement numbers. At line 450 the program transfers to the subroutine that begins on line 540, which determines who the top salesperson is. When that routine is complete, the RETURN statement at line 630 causes the program to transfer back to the place where it was called.

The output for the menu is shown in Example 115. (The top salesperson is Drey, with 185 hot tubs.)

Example 115

```
HOT TUB SALES MENU

CODE    FUNCTION

1 - TOP SALESPERSON
2 - AVERAGE SALES
3 - TOTAL SALES
```

Example 115 continues

Example 115, continued

```
4 - STOP

ENTER A NUMBER, 1 THROUGH 4:?1

TOP SALESPERSON IS DREY
```

The program will keep looping back to allow the user to make a selection from the menu. To stop the program, the user must type in 4, which indicates STOP.

TEST BANK
Match C   6-7
Fill-ins   45

7 Functions

Functions are precoded portions of programs. Some standard functions are available with BASIC; these are listed in Table A-1. The X in parentheses next to each function name is the argument of the function. The argument is the place holder for the data sent to the function. Functions are used either in arithmetic expressions or alone on the right side of an assignment statement. Let us look at some examples of functions to see how they work.

Table A-1

Some Standard BASIC Functions

Function	Meaning
SQR(X)	Square root of X
RND(X)	A random number between 0 and 1
INT(X)	The integer less than number X
ABS(X)	The absolute value of X
SGN(X)	The sign of X
LOG(X)	The natural logarithm (base E) of X
EXP(X)	E raised to the X power
SIN(X)	Trigonometric sine of X
COS(X)	Trigonometric cosine of X
TAN(X)	Trigonometric tangent of X
COT(X)	Trigonometric cotangent of X
ATN(X)	Trigonometric arctangent of X

7 SQR

Consider the first function shown in the table, SQR(X), which stands for "the square root of X" (X can represent any nonnegative number).

For example, the hypotenuse C of a right triangle, as related to sides A and B, is

$$C = \sqrt{A \char`^ 2 + B \char`^ 2}$$

In BASIC this is expressed as

```
200 LET C = SQR(A ^ 2 + B ^ 2)
```

7 RND

Suppose you want to find a random integer between 1 and 13 (to represent the dealing of a card in a deck):

```
200 LET C = INT(RND(X) * 13) + 1
```

In this example the **RND** function returns a value between 0 and 1. Multiplying that value by 13, then taking only the integer part of it by using INT yields a number between 0 and 12. The added 1 makes the number between 1 and 13, as desired.

7 INT

INT gives you the value of the largest integer less than or equal to the argument. When the argument is 6.41, INT(6.41) = 6. However, for negative numbers it is not so obvious. For instance, INT(-2.44) = -3.

7 Die Toss Example

This example uses two functions—the INT and the RND functions—which are combined to test the randomizing formula to see if the results really are equally distributed. We will simulate the tossing of a six-sided die. If we have a good randomizing program, the chances should be about equal that any one of the six sides (1, 2, 3, 4, 5, or 6) could appear when we toss the die. If, as the flowchart in Example 116 indicates, we are going to toss the die 1000 times, then the number of times we get any of the six numbers should be about equal. We will test this proposition with our program.

Notice in Example 117 that we have set up a FOR/NEXT loop to toss the die. In simulating the toss of the die, we will follow the formula shown on line 330 of the program in Example 117: INT(RND(X)*6) + 1. The RND function returns a number between 0 and 1; when we multiply this by 6, the result is between 0 and 5.999. When we take the INT function, that makes the number an integer between 0 and 5. When we add 1 to it, then it is an integer between 1 and 6. These two functions together deliver some integer between 1 and 6, and that integer is placed in location DIE.

To illustrate how this works, suppose the RND function yields .61. Multiply this number by 6 to get 3.66. The INT function reduces it to 3. Add 1, and the final result in DIE is 4.

Or: If RND returns .981, then 6 times .981 is 5.886, INT(5.886) is 5, 5 + 1 is 6, and the result is placed in DIE.

In either case we get a number between 1 and 6. Try other examples yourself, but be sure your original value from the RND function is between 0 and 1.

Note that on line 340 DIE is used as a subscript to add to the proper counter. For example, if 2 appeared on a particular turn, 1 would be added to the counter for 2s. The idea is that when we are done we will have six counters with six numbers corresponding to the number of times the numbers 1 through 6 were thrown by the toss of the die.

Example 116
Flowchart for
Example 117

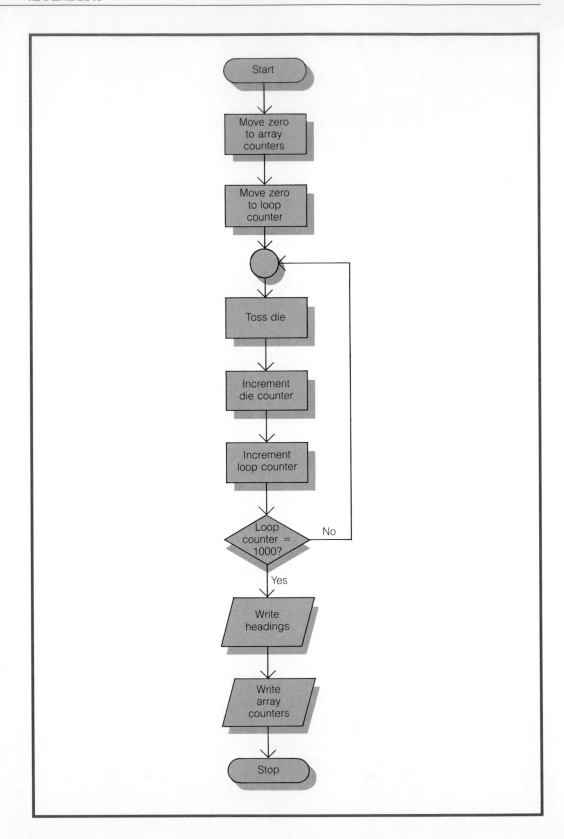

Example 117

```
100 REM USING RND TO TOSS DIE                P. L. CLARK
110 REM
120 REM USE THE RND FUNCTION TO SIMULATE TOSSING A DIE
130 REM 1000 TIMES. FOR EACH DIE TOSS, A NUMBER BETWEEN
140 REM 1 AND 6 WILL BE GENERATED. THE PROGRAM WILL COUNT
150 REM THE NUMBER OF TIMES EACH RESULT (1 THROUGH 6)
160 REM APPEARS AND PRINT THE FINAL COUNTS.
170 REM
180 REM      VARIABLE NAMES
190 REM          COUNT - COUNTER ARRAY
200 REM          DIE   - DIE TOSS
210 REM
220 DIM COUNT(6)
230 REM INITIALIZE COUNT ARRAY
240 FOR S = 1 TO 6
250     COUNT(S) = 0
260 NEXT S
270 REM DIE TOSS LOOP
280 PRINT
290 PRINT "BEGINNING DIE TOSSES...PLEASE WAIT"
300 PRINT
310 X = 1
320 FOR S = 1 TO 1000
330     DIE = INT(RND(X)*6) + 1
340     COUNT(DIE) = COUNT(DIE) + 1
350 NEXT S
360 REM PRINT RESULTS
370 PRINT "DIE","COUNT"
380 PRINT
390 FOR S = 1 TO 6
400     PRINT S,COUNT(S)
410 NEXT S
420 PRINT
430 END
```

Example 118 shows the output for this program. If you run this program, you will find the results probably vary from the results shown here. The only thing that will be the same is that the numbers will probably not vary much from each other and that they should add up to 1000.

Example 118

```
BEGINNING DIE TOSSES...PLEASE WAIT

DIE            COUNT

1              155
2              159
3              160
4              198
5              162
6              166
```

7 Programming Exercises

The following are programming exercises in the BASIC language, arranged in order of increasing difficulty and complexity. Notice that in some of the problems we provide both the input and the expected output. In others we leave it to you to determine the output.

1. Write a program to figure the difference between 33 and 13 and print the following output.

```
THE DIFFERENCE BETWEEN 33 AND 13 IS 20
```

2. Write a program using the INPUT statement to give the following output.

```
ENTER 3 NUMBERS
?
THE SUM OF THESE THREE NUMBERS IS
```

3. Write a program using the INPUT statement to give the following edited output.

```
ENTER ITEM
?SHOELACES
ENTER PRICE
?1.98
THE PRICE FOR SHOELACES IS $1.98
```

4. Use PRINT TAB to print your initials with a selected character such as X. For example:

```
XXXXX      X         X    X
   X       X         XX  XX
   X       X         X  X  X
   X       X         X     X
   X       XXXXX     X     X
```

5. Write a program to prepare a student honor roll. There are five sets of students' grades to be averaged. Any student with an average of 92 or higher is eligible for the honor roll. Input consists of the following names and grades:

Name	Grades
CATHY CARY	92,99,94,98,94
PAULETTE RACKOW	81,80,72,92,90
KITTIE STEWART	95,96,97,96,96
NORMAN LEE	71,85,88,90,89
DELORIS PUSINS	85,85,89,90,89
BRENDA WOODARD	95,94,99,96,95

6. The following inventory items are to be sold at a 15% discount. Read the item name and current price. Display the item name and discounted price. Use the following input data:

Item Name	Current Price
BRUSH	2.98
CURLERS	4.00
PINS	1.89
SHAMPOO	1.35
CONDITIONER	1.60

Expected output:

```
BRUSH        2.53
CURLERS      3.40
PINS         1.61
SHAMPOO      1.15
CONDITIONER  1.36
```

7. Write a program to list several activities and the number of calories they expend in time intervals of 15, 30, 45, and 60 minutes. Input should consist of:

Activity	Calories Burned per Minute
Sitting	.7
Driving	1.5
Swimming	13.2
Jogging	26.9

8. Read data for instructor name and three class sizes for each instructor. Display the name of any instructor with an average class size larger than 30 students. Also display the total number of students in all classes. Use the following input data:

Instructor	Class 1	Class 2	Class 3
CLAYTON LONG	30	30	25
JACK MUNYAN	35	31	30
TED BAHN	40	41	30
JOYCE FOY	25	30	35
MICKEY PERLOW	30	31	26

Show how the expected output should appear.

9. Using single-dimensional arrays, write an interactive program to input names of contributors for the local charity drive and the amount of their contributions. The program should also print a list of the names and the amounts. Include a report title, column headings, and lines that give the total number of contributors and the total contributions.

10. Write a program to read a three-by-five array (three rows, five columns) and display it by column.
Input is as follows:

```
14        6        11       3        10
1         5        8        16       20
7         4        2        18       9
```

Output is as follows:

```
14        1        7
6         5        4
11        8        2
3         16       18
10        20       9
```

NOTE: This appendix is designed to be used in conjunction with Chapter 9 (operating systems), Chapter 12 (word processing), Chapter 13 (spreadsheets), and Chapter 14 (database management systems). After studying each chapter, students can use this appendix in the computer lab to gain hands-on experience in using DOS, WordPerfect (commercial version 4.2 or 5.0 or educational version 4.2), Lotus 1-2-3 (commercial version 2.01 or student edition version 2.01), and dBASE III PLUS (commercial version or student edition version). To allow your students to spend more of their lab time on computer skills and less time on key entry, you may order the Instructor's Files Diskette, which includes the initial documents for the examples, the initial documents for the exercises, and the answers to the exercises. The answers to the exercises are also provided as hard copy in the Instructor's Guide.

Appendix B

A Guide to Using DOS, WordPerfect, Lotus 1-2-3, and dBASE III PLUS

This appendix provides an opportunity to use a microcomputer with some applications software packages. The appendix includes four sections, one each for DOS, WordPerfect (versions 4.2 and 5.0), Lotus 1-2-3, and dBASE III PLUS. The material here matches the discussions in the main body of the text. DOS is described in Chapter 9, WordPerfect in Chapter 12, Lotus 1-2-3 in Chapter 13, and dBASE III PLUS in Chapter 14.

Each section of this appendix includes a description of how to load the software, a reference guide to commands, and a set of exercises. In addition, the WordPerfect, Lotus 1-2-3, and dBASE III PLUS sections include a list of the keystrokes needed to match the examples described in Chapters 12 through 14. These keystrokes can also be used to create your own documents. To learn the fundamentals of how to use one of these applications packages, the following sequence of events is suggested:

1. Read the examples in the chapter, noting the computer screens and printed output.

2. Using the appropriate applications software, key the commands listed in the keystrokes tutorial section of this appendix.

3. Compare your results with the results in the chapter.

4. For further practice or class assignments, do the exercises in this appendix.

5. Refer to the reference guides as necessary.

This appendix will not make you an expert in any of these software applications packages, but it will show you the basics. You can then decide if you want to learn more about any of the packages. Additional instructions and exercises can be found in *Microcomputer Exercises* by M. A. Webster and *Hands-On: MS-DOS, WordPerfect 5.0, Lotus 1-2-3, and dBASE III PLUS, Second Edition*, by L. Metzelaar and M. Fox. (See the preface for more information.)

Using DOS

Loading DOS

If you are using a computer that has a hard disk, then the operating system resides on the hard disk and is automatically loaded when you turn the computer on. You may be asked for the date and time, as described in the next section. C> will appear on the screen, indicating that the computer is ready for your commands.

If the computer has only diskette drives, then follow these steps to load the operating system:

1. Insert the DOS disk in the left-hand disk drive (drive A) and shut the disk-drive door.

2. Turn the computer on. The red light in

drive A goes on, and the drive whirs for a few seconds. Then the red light goes off.

3. When the screen requests the date, you can either type the new date (month-day-year; for example, 10-13-90) and press Enter or simply press Enter without typing the new date.

4. When the screen requests the time, you can either type the new time (military time; for example, 14:30) and press Enter or simply press Enter without entering the new time.

5. When the A> appears on the screen, DOS is loaded in drive A. (If you are going to insert an applications program in drive A, you may now remove the DOS disk.)

7 Reference Guide to DOS

This reference guide assumes that your system has two diskette drives. If you have a one-drive system, you can still use the commands, but you can only refer to drive A. Also, when you use the COPY command with only one drive, you must supply a new name for the new file, since two files with the same name and extension cannot exist on the same disk. If you have a hard disk in your computer, you will probably refer to the single diskette drive as drive A and the hard-disk drive as drive C.

Make these assumptions when using this appendix:

- A is the default (current) drive, and A> is the prompt on your screen, except as noted. (If you are going to work in drive B, you can change the default drive to B and type DOS commands at the B> without typing B: every time.)

- FN stands for a file name. EX stands for an extension, which is a label used to identify a category of files. For example, you could identify all files related to customer Glennie Lee Smith with the extension GLS.

- Wherever a command appears here on two lines because of spatial limitations, type the command all on one line.

- After typing any DOS command, you must press Enter.

Internal DOS Commands

IF YOU WANT TO	THEN AT THE PROMPT, TYPE
Change the default drive to B	B:
Change the default drive to A when the prompt is B> or C>	A:
Let the computer know the date (e.g., February 2, 1991), so it is recorded on the disk with files you create or alter that day	DATE 2-2-91
Let the computer know the time so it is recorded with files you use (use military time, e.g., 14:15 to express 2:15 P.M.)	TIME 14:15
List the files on the disk in drive A	DIR
List the files on the disk in drive B	DIR B:
List drive A files in abbreviated form	DIR/W
List drive B files in abbreviated form	DIR B:/W
Print a list of drive A files	DIR >PRN
Print a list of drive B files	DIR B:>PRN
Copy a file named FN.EX from the disk in A onto the disk in B	COPY A:FN.EX B:
Copy FN1.EX1 to B with the new name FN2.EX2	COPY A:FN1.EX1 B:FN2.EX2 (Type on one line with a space before B:)
Copy all the files with extension EX from A to B	COPY A:*.EX B:
Copy all the files with file name FN from A to B	COPY A:FN.* B:

Copy all the files from A to B without over writing any files on B

`COPY A:*.* B:`

Erase (delete) the file FN.EX from A

`DEL FN.EX`

Erase (delete) the file FN.EX from B

`DEL B:FN.EX`

Erase all files with the extension EX from A

`DEL *.EX`

Erase all files with the file name FN from A

`DEL FN.*`

Erase all the files from A (Warning: You lose everything on the disk)

`DEL *.*`

Erase file FN.EX from A (produces the same effect as DEL)

`ERASE FN.EX`

Change the name of file FN1.EX1 on A to FN2.EX2

`RENAME FN1.EX1`
`FN2.EX2`
(Type on one line with a space before FN2.EX2)

Change the name of file FN1.EX1 on B to FN2.EX2

`RENAME B:FN1.EX1`
`FN2.EX2`
(Type on one line with a space before FN2.EX2)

Change the extension name of all files on A with the extension EX1 to EX2

`RENAME *.EX1 *.EX2`

External DOS Commands

IF YOU WANT TO	THEN AT THE PROMPT, TYPE
Format (prepare for use) the blank disk in drive A	`FORMAT A:`
Format the blank disk in B	`FORMAT B:`
Format the blank disk in B and transfer internal DOS to the disk	`FORMAT B:/S`
Format the blank disk in B and write a label on the disk	`FORMAT B:/V`

Format a disk in drive B to include internal DOS and a label

`FORMAT B:/S/V`

Make an exact copy of the drive A files on the disk in drive B (overwrites files on B, if any)

`DISKCOPY A: B:`

DOS for the Power User

Is it enough to know how to format a disk and to list and copy files? For some people, knowing these basics is indeed enough. But if you are serious about being in control of your personal computing, then you will want to know some of the extra DOS features.

ASSIGN Sometimes programs expect to use certain disk drives, perhaps one you do not have. For example, you may have diskette drive A and hard-disk C, but the program wants to use drive B. Use the ASSIGN command to send all files destined for drive B to drive C by typing

`ASSIGN B=C`

AUTOEXEC.BAT This special file is activated by DOS when you turn the computer on. A typical AUTOEXEC.BAT file lets you go directly to your applications software. If, for example, you usually want to set the date and then use WordPerfect, then AUTOEXEC.BAT could contain the two lines DATE and then WP.

CHKDSK If you type CHKDSK, the screen displays a disk and memory status report, which contains information such as how many bytes are free.

COPY CON You do not always have to copy from one disk file to another; you can copy a short file directly from the keyboard to the disk file XFILE by using the command COPY CON XFILE (CON stands for console). After you enter the command, type your file. Signal the end of the file by pressing the F6 key. COPY CON is often used to make AUTOEXEC.BAT files.

Directories Directory commands are especially useful if you create hard-disk files. Rather than having all your files together, you can establish a directory for each category of files.

TYPE Use the TYPE command with a file name, say TEMPO, to cause the contents of that file to appear on the screen. To execute this command, type

```
TYPE TEMPO
```

Caution: Special characters in the file may not be readable.

Wild-card characters The wild-card characters let you manipulate groups of files with a single command. A question mark is used for a single variable character and an asterisk (∗) for a file name or extension. If, for example, you want to delete files named TEMP1, TEMP2, and TEMP3, use the ? in a single command:

```
DEL TEMP?
```

If you want to list all files with the extension BAK, use

```
DIR *.BAK
```

7 Exercises for DOS

DOS-1

1. Place your DOS disk in drive A. Make sure that the drive door is closed. Turn on your computer. (If you have a color monitor, you will need to turn it on too: Turn the top dial clockwise.) If your computer is already on, press Ctrl-Alt-Del. When the internal DOS commands are read into memory, you will be asked for the time and date. Press Enter in response to both questions. You should see the A prompt (A>) in the upper-left corner of the screen. Turn the knobs on the right side of the display screen to see what they do.

   Check to see that your display is turned on. If your screen seems to be blank even though you have booted the computer—that is, loaded the operating system into memory—check to see that the brightness knob is set properly.

   If you do not get the A>, make sure that your DOS disk is inserted correctly in the A drive and that the drive door is properly closed. Then try to boot the system again.

2. After you have the A>, type DIR and press Enter. How many files are listed when you type DIR? How much storage space is left on the disk?

3. What do you see in the lower-left corner of the screen after the DIR program is finished?

4. Type B: and press Enter. Now what do you see in the lower-left corner? What happens when you type DIR and press Enter? Type A: and press Enter.

DOS-2

1. Place a DOS disk with the FORMAT.COM file in drive A. Use the DIR command to make sure that you have the proper disk in drive A.

2. Type FORMAT A: and press Enter. Then follow the directions on the screen. *Make sure you replace the DOS diskette with a blank diskette before you press the appropriate key.*

3. After the FORMAT program has finished, type N to indicate that you are finished formatting disks. You should see the A prompt (A>).

4. Now type DIR and press Enter. What message do you see?

DOS-3

1. Place the DOS disk in drive A. Place a formatted disk in drive B. The disk in drive B will be your data disk.

2. Type

   ```
   COPY A:FORMAT.COM B:
   ```

   Then press Enter.

3. When you see the A> again, type

   ```
   DIR B:
   ```

   and press Enter. What files are on the data disk now? How much storage space is left on your data disk?

4. Type

   ```
   COPY A:CHKDSK.COM B:
   ```

   Then press Enter. When you see the A> again, type DIR B: and press Enter.

5. How many files are there on your data disk now? How much storage space is available on the disk?

6. Type

   COPY A:*.EXE B:

   and press Enter. Now type

   DIR B:

   How many files were just copied onto the disk? What do these files have in common?

DOS-4

1. With the A> on your screen and your data disk in drive B, type B: and press Enter. Which drive is now the default drive?

2. Type

   RENAME CHKDSK.COM WXYZ.ABC

   then press Enter.

3. Type DIR and press Enter. What happened to the CHKDSK.COM file?

4. Type A: and press Enter to return to the A>.

DOS-5

1. With your data disk in drive B and the A> on the screen, type B: and press Enter. What prompt do you see now?

2. Type

   DEL WXYZ.ABC

   and then press Enter. Type DIR and press Enter. What has happened?

3. Type

   DEL FORMAT.COM

   and press Enter. Now type DIR. How many files are left?

4. Type

   DEL *.EXE

   and press Enter. Type DIR. Now what message do you get?

DOS-6

1. Place the DOS disk in drive A and your data disk in drive B. You will format your data disk again (there are no files there to lose

now). Then you will copy internal DOS to your data disk. Finally, you will create an internal label on your data disk to identify it.

2. Make sure that the A> is on your screen. Then type

   FORMAT B:/S/V

   and press Enter. Watch the screen for information.

3. When you are asked for a volume label, type your name (or the first 11 characters of your name). Then press Enter.

4. When you see "Format another (Y/N)?" type N and press Enter.

5. Type

   DIR B:

   What is the first line printed on the screen? Now your data disk is a system disk. Why is a system disk helpful?

6. Use the COPY command to copy the FORMAT.COM file onto your data disk. Now you have the ability to format new disks by placing your data disk in drive A and issuing the FORMAT command.

7. Remove your disks from drives A and B.

8. Turn off the computer. If you have a color monitor, turn it off as well.

9. Place both disks in their storage locations; treat the disks carefully.

7 Using WordPerfect

As in Chapter 12 on word processing, this section focuses on the latest version of WordPerfect, Version 5.0. Since many people use Version 4.2, however, keystrokes for this earlier package appear in parentheses whenever the keystrokes differ from Version 5.0. As you will see, most keystrokes for WordPerfect commands are the same in both versions.

7 Loading WordPerfect

1. Boot the computer with a DOS disk or the word processing disk if the internal DOS files have been transferred onto it.

2. Place your word processing disk in drive A and a formatted data disk in drive B.

3. At the A prompt (A>), type WP. After being loaded into the computer's memory, WordPerfect displays an almost blank screen.

Note: If you are using a computer that has a hard disk, the operating system and WordPerfect are probably already on disk drive C. In that case, you need only boot in the usual way and type WP when you see the C prompt (C>).

7 Keystrokes for the Examples in Chapter 12

The Cover Letter Example

These instructions are for creating and editing Carl Wade's cover letter, as described in the text on pages 359–364.

Entering the Letter

1. Load WordPerfect.

2. Type the letter shown in Figure 12-6 on page 360. Press the tab key several times to enter the address and date on the right side of the letter. To make corrections, use the backspace key or Del (delete) key. Press Enter only at the ends of short lines and the ends of paragraphs. Do not worry if your letter does not match Figure 12-6 exactly.

Saving the Letter

1. Press the F10 key.

2. When asked, type the document name (B:CLETTER, for example). Press Enter.

Printing the Letter

1. Turn on the printer.

2. Hold down the Shift key and press F7.

3. Press 1 to print the full document.

Exiting the Program

1. Press F7. WordPerfect asks, "Save Document? (Y/N)." Press the appropriate key. (If you have not already saved the file, press Y.)

2. WordPerfect asks "Exit WP? (Y/N)." Press Y to exit the program. Press N to remain in WordPerfect if you would like to create another document or retrieve an existing document.

Retrieving the Letter

1. If the word processing program is not already loaded, load the program.

2. Hold down the Shift key and press F10.

3. Type the complete name of the file (B:CLETTER in this example). Press Enter.

Making Changes

To use the insert mode (e.g., to add "express" before "interest" in the second paragraph):

1. Position the cursor where you wish to insert text (e.g., position cursor under "i" in "interest").

2. Type the new text (e.g., type "express" and press Spacebar).

To use the typeover mode (e.g., to replace "express" with "special"):

1. Press the Ins key to turn on the typeover mode.

2. Position the cursor under the first letter of the word (or words) you wish to type over (e.g., position cursor under "e" in "express").

3. Type the new text (e.g., "special").

4. Turn off the typeover mode by pressing the Ins key again.

To add new paragraphs:

1. Position the cursor at the insertion point (e.g., between the third and fourth paragraphs). Press Enter.

2. Type the new text (e.g., "While I was in school, I prepared and monitored advertising campaigns and tracked account budgets. I am also familiar with several types of computers and computer systems."). Press Enter. Compare your letter to Figure 12-9 on page 363.

Saving the Corrected Letter

1. Press F10. WordPerfect asks if you want to replace the earlier version of the letter. Type Y.

The Resume Example

These instructions are for editing Carl Wade's resume as described on pages 365–371. First load WordPerfect or, if you are already in WordPerfect, clear the screen by pressing F7, then Y or N, then N. Enter the resume shown in Figure 12-11 on page 365. Press "Caps Lock" to type all capital letters. To save, press F10, type B:RESUME, and press Enter.

Adding Blank Lines

1. Position the cursor at the end of the line where you want to add to a blank line (e.g., at end of each major heading). Press Enter.

Centering Lines

1. Position the cursor under the first character of the word(s) you want to center.
2. Hold down the Shift key and press F6.
3. Press the down cursor movement key.
4. Repeat for next three lines. Compare your screen to Figure 12-12 on page 366.

Vertical Centering

1. Move the cursor to the top of the document.
2. Hold down the Shift key and press F8. (Version 4.2: Hold down Alt, press F8.)
3. Press 2, then 1. Press Enter twice. (Version 4.2: Press 3, then press Enter.)

Changing Margins

1. Move the cursor to the top of the document.
2. Hold down the Shift key and press F8.
3. Press 1, then 7. (Version 4.2: Press 3.)
4. To change the left margin to 1.75 inches, type 1.75 and press Enter; to change the right margin to 1.5 inches, type 1.5 and press Enter. Press Enter twice. (Version 4.2: At "Set 10 74 to Left =," type 17 and press Enter. At "Right =," type 69 and press Enter.) To see the margins change on screen, you may need to press the down cursor key several times.

Justifying the Right Margin

1. In WordPerfect the right margin is justified when the document is printed but the text looks ragged right on the screen.
2. To print a document with a ragged right margin, move the cursor to the top of the document. Hold down Shift and press F8. Type 1, then 3, then N. (Version 4.2: Hold down Ctrl, press F8. Type 3.)

Adding Boldface and Underlining

To boldface existing text:

1. Position the cursor under the first character of the word(s) you want to boldface.
2. Hold down the Alt key and press F4.
3. Move the cursor to the end of the word(s) you want to boldface. Press F6.

To boldface as you type:

1. Press F6. Type the word(s) to be boldface.
2. Press F6 again to stop boldfacing.

To underline existing text:

1. Position the cursor under the first character of the word(s) you want to underline.
2. Hold down the Alt key and press F4.
3. Move the cursor to the end of the word(s) you want to underline. Press F8. Compare your screen to Figure 12-15 on page 370.

To underline as you type:

1. Press F8. Type the word(s) to be underlined.
2. Press F8 again to stop underlining.

The Survey Example

These instructions are for editing Barbara Crim's survey as described on pages 372–376. First load WordPerfect or, if you are already in WordPerfect, clear the screen by pressing F7, then Y or N, then N. Enter the survey shown in Figure 12-17 on page 373. To indent lines, hold down Shift and press F4 after each number. To save, press F10, type B:SURVEY, and press Enter.

Marking a Block

1. Position the cursor under the first character of the text you want to mark (e.g., under "4").

2. Hold down the Alt key and press F4. "Block on" flashes in the lower-left corner.

3. Move the cursor to the end of the block you want to mark (e.g., to the end of question 4).

Moving a Block

1. Mark the block you want to move (e.g., question 4).

2. Hold down Ctrl and press F4.

3. Press 1, then press 1 again. (Version 4.2: Press 1 once.) The block disappears.

4. Move the cursor to the location where you want to insert the text (e.g., under question 5).

5. Press Enter to retrieve the cut text. (Version 4.2: Hold down Ctrl and press F4 again. Then press 5.)

6. Change the numbering and delete or add space between lines as necessary.

Deleting a Block

1. Mark the block you want to delete (e.g., question 9).

2. Hold down Ctrl and press F4.

3. Press 1, then press 3 to delete the block. (Version 4.2: Just press 1.) Renumber.

Copying a Block

1. Mark the block you want to copy.

2. Hold down Ctrl and press F4.

3. Press 1, then 2 to select the copy function. (Version 4.2: Just press 2.)

4. Move the cursor to the location where you want to insert the copied text.

5. Press Enter. (Version 4.2: Hold down Ctrl, press F4. Type 5.)

6. To copy the text in more than one location (e.g., under questions 3–8), repeat steps 1–5.

7 Reference Guide to WordPerfect

The descriptions that follow summarize some of the most commonly used WordPerfect commands and the related keystrokes. Most of these commands are discussed in Chapter 12. Where the keystrokes for WordPerfect versions 4.2 and 5.0 differ, the keystrokes for 4.2 are given in parentheses.

The keys you should press are enclosed in brackets ([ ]). Keystrokes separated by a hyphen indicate that the first key should be held down while you press the second key. For example, for centering, [Shift-F6] means hold the Shift key down while you press the F6 function key. "Ctrl" stands for the Control key; "Alt" stands for the Alternate key.

For most of these commands, you need to use the function keys on the left side or top of the keyboard. The plastic template that fits over the function keys is a helpful reminder of what each key does.

Boldface [F6] Press the F6 key and then type the word(s) to be emphasized. After you have finished, press F6 again to signal the end of boldface. If you want to boldface words that are already typed, first mark them as a block (see "Mark Block"), then press F6.

Cancel [F1] The Cancel command cancels—or undoes—the most recent command you issued. For example, if you inadvertently delete some text, the Cancel command gives you the opportunity to restore it.

Center [Shift-F6] This command centers a line of type between the left and right margins. Press Shift-F6 before you type the line to be centered. If the line to be centered is already typed, position the cursor under the leftmost character of the line, press Shift-F6, and then press the down cursor movement key.

Copy Block After a block has been marked (see "Mark Block"), press Ctrl-F4. Then press 1, then 2 to select the copy option. (Version 4.2: Press 2.) Move the cursor to the new location. Press Enter to copy the text. (Version 4.2: Press Ctrl-F4 again, then select option 5.)

Cursor Movement The cursor movement keys move the cursor a character at a time; you can use combinations of keys to move the cursor greater distances. To move the cursor a word to the right, use Ctrl-right cursor. To move the cursor a word to the left, use Ctrl-left cursor. To return to the beginning of a document, press Home, press Home again, and press the up cursor key. To move the cursor to the end of the document, press Home, press Home again, and press the down cursor key.

Date [Shift-F5] Begin by pressing Shift-F5. If you then choose option 1, the date appears in your document at the current cursor location. (Caution: This command only *retrieves* the date. Before retrieval, the date must be set, probably by using the DATE command in DOS.)

Delete A few of the common ways to delete characters follow. Press the Del key to delete the current character. Press the Backspace key to delete the previous character. Use Ctrl-Backspace to delete the word the cursor is under. Use Ctrl-End to delete from the cursor to the end of the line.

Delete Block After a block has been marked (see "Mark Block"), press Ctrl-F4. Then press 1, then 3 to delete the block. (Version 4.2: Press 1.)

Delete File [F5 Enter] Press F5 and then press Enter. Move the cursor to highlight the file you want to delete, then select option 2.

Double Space [Shift-F8] Begin by pressing Shift-F8. Then press 1, then 6, then 2. (Version 4.2: Press 4, then 2, then Enter.) Text will be double spaced from that point forward in the document. To revert to single spacing later in the document, use the same command, but select option 1. (Version 4.2: Type 1 at "[Spacing Set].") You can also use Reveal Codes to remove the double spacing altogether.

Exit WordPerfect [F7] Press F7. When WordPerfect asks if you want to save the document, type N if you do not. You will usually type Y. After you type Y, the file name is displayed if the file already exists; simply press Enter to verify the name. If you have created a new file, you must supply a file name. (Note: If you are saving a file that already exists, you are asked if you want to replace the existing version of that file; usually, you do want to replace the existing file with a new version, so type Y.) Next, WordPerfect asks if you want to exit the program. Type Y to return to DOS, or type N to open a new WordPerfect file, or press F1 to return to the same document you have just saved.

Help [F3] If you need help with something, press F3, then press any key to see a list of functions. Choose the function you wish to learn more about. Press Enter or Spacebar to return to your document.

Indent [Shift-F4] Pressing Shift-F4 indents every line of a paragraph. To indent just the first line of a paragraph, press the Tab key.

Justification In WordPerfect, right justification is the default. However, the text does not appear justified until it is printed. To switch to ragged right, press Shift-F8, then press 1, then 3, then N to turn off justification. (Version 4.2: Press Ctrl-F8, and then select option 3.)

List Files [F5 Enter] To list the files on your data disk while you are using WordPerfect, press F5 and then press Enter.

Margin Settings [Shift-F8] Press Shift-F8. For the left margin, press 1, then 7, then type the margin width in inches. Press Enter. For the right margin, type the margin width in inches, then press Enter. (Version 4.2: Press 3 and then the left and right margin settings in characters, each followed by Enter.)

Mark Block [Alt-F4] Place the cursor at the beginning of the block you want to mark. Press Alt-F4, then move the cursor to the end of the block.

Move Block [Ctrl-F4] After a block is marked, press Ctrl-F4. Then press 1 twice. (Version 4.2: Press 1.) The block disappears. Now move the cursor to where you want to insert the block; press Enter. (Version 4.2: Press Ctrl-F4, then select option 5.) The block is inserted.

Page Numbers [Shift-F8] Press Shift-F8, then press 2, then 7. (Version 4.2: Press Alt-F8 and then select option 1.) Then choose the appropriate page-number position.

Print [Shift-F7] Press Shift-F7 and several options appear. Usually, you want to select option 1 to print the full document.

Retrieve [Shift-F10] After you press Shift-F10, WordPerfect asks for the name of the file to retrieve. This is the name you gave the file when you originally saved it.

Reveal Codes [Alt-F3] Each time you use a special feature, such as boldface or line spacing, WordPerfect places a hidden code within the text. The Reveal Codes command lets you view or delete the hidden codes (with the Backspace key). To hide the codes again, press any key that does not affect the cursor—the Spacebar is handy.

Save [F10] Press F10 and WordPerfect asks for the name of the file you want to save. If a file by that name already exists, you are asked if you want to replace the existing file with your new file. If you have just revised the existing document, you probably want to type Y. If you type N, the old file will not be replaced and WordPerfect will ask for a different file name for your new document.

Search [F2] When you press F2, the message "Srch:" appears. Type the word, phrase, or character that you want to search for, and then press F2 once more. The search progresses from the cursor to the end of the document. To search backwards from the cursor to the beginning of the document, press Shift-F2.

Search and Replace [Alt-F2] After you press Alt-F2, the message "w/Confirm?(Y/N)" appears. Type Y if you want to verify each replacement individually. Press the up cursor to search backwards or the down cursor to search forwards. (Version 4.2: Replace works only in the forward direction, so you will not be given this option.) Next, type in the word or characters you wish to replace, then press F2. The message "Replace with:" appears. Type the substitution and then press F2 again. WordPerfect asks you to confirm the replacement each time it finds the word you wish to replace.

Spelling Checker [Ctrl-F2] After pressing Ctrl-F2, select option 3 if you want to check the spelling in the entire document.

Thesaurus [Alt-F1] To use the thesaurus, place the cursor under the word you want to look up. Then press Alt-F1.

Typeover [Ins] To change from the insert mode to the typeover mode, press the Insert (Ins) key. To return to the insert mode, press the Insert key again.

Underline [F8] Press the F8 key, then type the words to be underlined. After you have finished typing, press the F8 key again to stop the underlining. If you want to underline words that are already typed, mark them as a block (see "Mark Block"), then press F8.

Vertical Centering [Alt-F8] Press Alt-F8, then select option 3 to center text vertically on a page.

7 Exercises for WordPerfect

WP-1

1. Load your word processing program and insert a formatted data disk in drive B. Then type the business letter shown in Figure B-1. The lines on your screen may not look exactly like the letter in the figure—your word processing program may allow a different number of characters per line.

2. Save the letter on your data disk. The file name should be EXWP-1.

3. Print the letter; it appears ragged right on your screen, but WordPerfect justifies the right margin when you print.

4. Exit the word processing program.

NATIONAL COMPUTER SUPPLIES COMPANY
200 WICKER DRIVE
CHICAGO, IL 60680

Ms. Jane Ejde
Wholesale Manager
Computer Supply, Inc.
1220 Oak Street
Oklahoma City, OK 40712

Dear Ms. Ejde:

Your order of May 10 for 400 boxes of 3½-inch diskettes was shipped to you on May 12 via Southwest Trucking. They have promised delivery no later than May 18.

Enclosed is our recent catalog. In addition to exciting new products, we offer competitive pricing on our standard line of computer supplies. We will continue to send you our new catalogs as they become available.

We appreciate your business. We'll do everything we can to make sure that our products and services keep you a satisfied customer.

Sincerely,

Paul Hernandez
Regional Manager

PH/rd

Enclosure: NCS Catalog

Figure B-1

WP-2

1. Load or enter the word processing program.

2. Retrieve the EXWP-1 file. Review it on the screen. Is it still the same document?

3. Make the following changes to the letter:

   Change "Ms. Jane Ejde" to "Mr. Jake Warde".

   Change "Dear Ms. Ejde" to "Dear Mr. Warde".

   Change "400 boxes" to "800 boxes".

   Add the word "most" before the word "recent" in the second paragraph.

   Add the following sentence between the first and second paragraphs:

   "Please note on the enclosed invoice that you qualify for a 5% discount because you are a new customer."

4. Save the revised letter as EXWP-2.

5. Print the revised letter.

6. Without exiting the word processing program, clear the screen. (Note for WordPerfect users: You need to press F7, then N for do not save file, then N for do not exit program.)

WP-3

1. Enter the text shown in Figure B-2, using word wrap. Note: Your margins will not be the same as those in Figure B-2. Save the file as EXWP-3.

2. Now change the margins so they are ½ inch wider.

3. Center the head "JOHN FITZGERALD KENNEDY" on the line. Then center the dates "1917-1963".

4. Boldface the two lines you centered.

5. Center the body of the text vertically on the page.

6. Underline the following lines:

   "Inaugural Address (January 1961)"

   "Address, White House dinner honoring Nobel Prize winners (April 1962)"

   "Address at the Berlin Wall (June 1963)"

JOHN FITZGERALD KENNEDY
1917–1963

And so, my fellow Americans, ask not what your country can do for you; ask what you can do for your country.
Inaugural Address (January 1961)

I think this is the most extraordinary collection of talent, of human knowledge, that has ever been gathered together at the White House, with the possible exception of when Thomas Jefferson dined alone.
Address, White House dinner honoring Nobel Prize winners (April 1962)

All free men, wherever they may live, are citizens of Berlin. And therefore, as a free man, I take pride in the words "Ich bin ein Berliner."
Address at the Berlin Wall (June 1963)

Figure B-2

7. Save the revised document as EXWP-3A.

8. Print the revised document twice; once with a justified right margin and once with a ragged right margin.

9. Use the appropriate commands to clear the screen.

WP-4

1. Write a letter to a friend by using a word processing program. The letter should have the following format:

   1½-inch margins on each side

   A blank line between each paragraph

   A right-justified margin

   At least one underlined word

   At least one boldfaced word

2. Save the letter as EXWP-4.

3. Print the letter.

ROBOTS COMING OF AGE

The robot reality of today has its roots in fantasy. For many people, that fantasy began just a few years ago when the public embraced adorable R2D2 in *Star Wars.* But robots made their debut in the 1920s, when playwright Karel Capek introduced mechanical creatures who worked as docile slaves—until a misguided scientist gave them emotions. Capek coined the word *robot,* basing it on a Czech word meaning *work.*

A recent advertisement showed a stumpy robot saying "In our day we robots did what we were told." A sleek robot, who looks as if he could handle something as delicate as a bird, responds, "But our generation is different." The point is that today's robots can be programmed—up to a point—to think for themselves.

Figure B-3

WP-5

1. Enter the document shown in Figure B-3.
2. Save the document as EXWP-5. Print the document.
3. Center the document vertically on the page. Print the document with a right-justified margin.
4. Change the margin settings so there are 2-inch margins on each side. Make sure the copy is still centered vertically and that the lines are still right-justified. Save this revised document as EXWP-5A.
5. Print EXWP-5A. How many lines longer is the printed version of EXWP-5A than EXWP-5?

WP-6

1. Type the document shown in Figure B-4(a). Format the document exactly as it is shown in the figure.
2. Save the document as EXWP-6.
3. Make the changes shown in Figure B-4(b). Realign the columns if necessary.

**AROUND-THE-WORLD TOURS
SUMMER SCHEDULE**

LOCATION	DATES
London-Paris-Rome	6/20–7/7
Rome-Athens	6/20–7/7
The Orient	6/25–7/25
Amsterdam-Berlin	6/25–7/25
Napal	6/30–7/14
Acapulco-Cozumel	7/3–7/24
Trinidad	7/3–7/24
Australia-New Zealand	7/15–8/15

(a)

**AROUND-THE-WORLD TOURS
SUMMER SCHEDULE**

LOCATION	DATES
London-Paris-Rome	6/20–7/7
Rome-Athens	6/20–7/7
Geneva – Zurich	6/25-7/15
~~The Orient~~	~~6/25–7/25~~
Hong Kong – Bangkok	
~~Amsterdam-Berlin~~	6/25–7/25
Nepal	7/1 – 7/30
	~~6/30-7/14~~
Acapulco-Cozumel	7/3–7/24
~~Trinidad~~	~~7/3–7/24~~
Australia-New Zealand	7/15–8/15
Kenya	7/30-8/20
Hawaii – Fiji	8/1 – 8/20

(b)

Figure B-4

4. Save the revised document as EXWP-6A.

5. Print EXWP-6 and EXWP-6A.

WP-7

1. Type the class information sheet shown in Figure B-5. The heading should be centered and underlined. The words on the left-hand side of the sheet (such as "OFFICE" and "OFFICE HOURS") should be boldface. Try

to line up the information exactly as it is shown.

2. Save the information sheet as EXWP-7.

3. Print the information sheet.

4. Exit the word processing program.

WP-8

1. Type the letter shown in Figure B-6, making corrections, when needed, as you type. Do not worry if the line breaks on your screen do not look exactly like those in the figure— your word processing program may allow a different number of characters per line.

2. Save the letter on your data disk. The file name should be EXWP-8.

3. Mark the second paragraph (including blank lines) as a block.

4. Use your word processing software's Block Move command to move the marked paragraph below the third paragraph.

<u>CSS 110 WINTER 1990</u>

OFFICE: 2316A

OFFICE HOURS: 10:00–10:50 AM

MATERIALS: Computers: Tools for an
                     <u>Information Age</u>, 2nd ed.
                     by H. L. Capron

                     Computer Lab Access Card

                     Two 3½-inch Disks

GRADING: 5 Quizzes   @ 6 pts = 30

                     5 Exercises   @ 3 pts = 15

                     3 Tests   @ 10 pts = 30

                     1 Final   @ 20 pts = 20

                     Participation @ 5 pts =   5

                     Total   = 100

                     92–100 = A
                     82– 91 = B
                     70– 81 = C
                     60– 69 = D
                      0– 59 = F

NOTES: 1. Class attendance is required.

                     2. Don't be late to class.

                     3. Don't miss tests or quizzes; no
                        make-ups will be given.

                     4. No incompletes will be given in
                        this class.

                     5. There are no "extra credit"
                        assignments in this class.

Figure B-5

Mr. Louis Stern
STA International
333 Homewood Avenue
Durham, NC 27702

Dear Mr. Stern:

   I am writing to inquire about any openings that STA International may have in technical writing.

   I have just graduated from the University of North Carolina, Chapel Hill, with a B.A. in writing and a minor in physics. My course work also included math, chemistry, and biology.

   As my resume shows, I have already had some experience as a free-lance editor of computer manuals. I have also been involved in other forms of editing and writing for the past two years. I have had experience in many apects of publication, including copy writing, proofreading, layout, pasteup, and typesetting.

   Would it be possible for us to meet to discuss this further? I can be reached by phone at 919-967-0000.

Sincerely,

Maria Simone

Figure B-6

5. Save the revised letter as EXWP-8A.

6. Print the letter.

WP-9

1. Retrieve the EXWP-8A file.

2. Mark the last sentence of the second paragraph as a block.

3. Use the Block Delete function to delete the block.

4. Save the new file as EXWP-9.

Using Lotus 1-2-3

Loading Lotus 1-2-3

1. Load DOS if necessary.

2. Place the program disk for Lotus 1-2-3 in drive A and place a formatted data disk in drive B.

3. At the prompt, type LOTUS or 123 and then press Enter. (Note: The command required to load Lotus varies by version. If one command does not work, try the other.)

4. Follow the instructions on the screen. Lotus has been loaded when you see a blank worksheet.

Keystrokes for the Examples in Chapter 13

The Expense Sheet Example: Creating the Spreadsheet

These instructions are for creating Lyle Mayes's expense sheet, as described in the text on pages 399–404.

Entering Labels and Values

1. Load Lotus 1-2-3.

2. To enter a label or value, move the cursor to the desired cell (e.g., Cell A3).

3. Type the label or value (e.g., "INCOME"). Your entry appears on the second line of the control panel. Use the Backspace key to make corrections.

4. Press Enter. The data appears in the cell.

5. Repeat these steps until you have entered all the labels and values for your spreadsheet. For the expense sheet example, enter the labels and values shown in Figure 13-12 on page 401.

Entering Formulas and Functions

1. To enter a formula or function, move the cursor to the desired cell (e.g., Cell F3).

2. If you are entering a formula, remember that it must be enclosed in parentheses or start with an operator [e.g., (B3+C3+D3+E3)].

3. If you are entering a function, remember that it must start with the @ symbol [e.g., @SUM(B6..E6)]. You must also define a range for the function. To do this, look for the upper-left and lower-right cells of the range you wish to use; for example, Cells B6 and E6. Then type in the starting cell address, two periods, and the ending cell address. The range for cells B6 through E6 would be typed as B6..E6. (Note: Lotus displays ranges with two periods but you may type one or two periods.)

4. Press Enter. The displayed value appears in the cell. To see the formula or function, move the cursor onto the cell and look at the first line of the control panel.

Making Corrections

1. To correct an already filled cell, move the cursor to that cell.

2. Type in the new data. If the cell should be blank, press the Spacebar.

3. Press Enter. The new data appears in the cell. Any calculations based on that cell are automatically recalculated.

The Expense Sheet Example: Using Spreadsheet Commands

These instructions summarize the basic spreadsheet commands, as described in the text on pages 405–411. To obtain the command menu, press the / key. To select a command, either move the cursor to the desired command and press Enter or type the first letter of the command. To undo a selection and back up to a previous menu, press Esc.

Saving a File

1. Press the / key to enter the MENU mode.

2. Select the File command by moving the cursor to File and pressing Enter or by typing F. A submenu appears.

3. Select the Save command by moving the cursor to Save and pressing Enter or by typing S.

4. When asked, type the file name (B:EXPENSES in this example) and press Enter. Lotus executes the command and returns you to the READY mode.

Retrieving a File

1. Press the / key to enter the MENU mode.

2. Select the File command by moving the cursor to File and pressing Enter or by typing F. A submenu appears.

3. Select the Retrieve command. (Caution: Selecting Retrieve erases your current spreadsheet—save before using this command.)

4. Lotus displays the list of files you have on disk. Either type in the name of the file (B:EXPENSES in this example) or move the cursor over the name of the file you wish to retrieve. Then press Enter.

5. The retrieved file appears on the screen, and Lotus returns you to READY mode.

Listing Files

1. Press the / key to enter the MENU mode.

2. Select the File command by moving the cursor to File and pressing Enter or by typing F. A submenu appears.

3. Select the List command. Another submenu appears.

4. Select the Worksheet command. On the screen, Lotus displays a list of your spreadsheet files.

5. To return to the current spreadsheet, press Enter.

Printing a Spreadsheet

1. Press the / key to enter the MENU mode.

2. Select the Print command by moving the cursor to Print and pressing Enter or by typing P. A submenu appears.

3. Select the Printer command. (Since the cursor is already on "Printer," you only need to press Enter or type P.) Another submenu appears.

4. Select the Range command. (Press Enter or type R.) Lotus asks you to define the range you want to print.

5. Type the range in the correct form (e.g., A1..F17). Then press Enter. Lotus returns to the second submenu.

6. Make sure your printer is turned on. Then select the Go command from the displayed submenu.

7. To return to the READY mode after the spreadsheet is printed, select Quit from the displayed submenu.

Erasing the Worksheet

1. Press the / key to enter the MENU mode.

2. Select the Worksheet command by pressing Enter or by typing W. A submenu appears.

3. Select the Erase command. Lotus asks you to confirm the command. Type Y for yes. (Caution: Remember to save your worksheet before using this command.)

Exiting the Program

1. Press the / key to enter the MENU mode.

2. To leave Lotus 1-2-3 and return to DOS, select the Quit command. (Caution: Lotus 1-2-3 does not save your files before exiting—always remember to save your file first!)

3. When Lotus asks you to confirm the command, press Y if you want to exit Lotus. The DOS prompt appears.

7 Reference Guide to Lotus 1-2-3

The descriptions that follow summarize some of the most commonly used Lotus 1-2-3 commands and the related keystrokes. Most of these commands are discussed in Chapter 13.

The keys you should press are enclosed in brackets ([ ]). When a command requires that you supply the beginning and ending cells in a group of contiguous cells (a range), the notation <range> is included with the keystrokes.

Change Cell Entry To change an already entered cell entry, move the cursor to that cell. Then type in the correct contents and press Enter.

Change Column Width of One Column [/WCS] Place the cursor in the column whose width you wish to change. Type /WCS and then type the new width (1 to 240 characters); press Enter.

Copy Cell Contents [/<FROM range> <TO range>] To create a copy of existing cell entries, type /C. When prompted for the *copy from* range, enter the range of cells you want to copy. Then press Enter. When prompted for the *copy to* range, enter the range of cells in which you want the copies to appear. Then press Enter. When you copy labels and numbers, Lotus 1-2-3 makes exact duplicates of the original entries in another location. When you copy formulas, Lotus adjusts cell addresses in the formula unless the cell addresses are absolute or mixed.

Delete Column [/WDC] Place the cursor in the column you wish to delete, type /WDC, and press Enter.

Delete Row [/WDR] Place the cursor in the row you wish to delete, type /WDR, and press Enter.

Edit Cell Entries [F2] Place the cursor on the cell whose contents you wish to edit and press the F2 key. You are placed in the EDIT mode and can use the cursor movement keys to move to the position in the current cell contents where you want to insert or delete characters. Use the Del or Backspace key to delete characters. Press Enter when you are through editing.

Erase Cell Entry [/RE] Place the cursor on the cell whose contents you want to erase. Type /RE and press Enter.

Erase Range of Cells [/RE <range>] Type /RE and the range of cells you want to erase (for example, A10.F10); then press Enter. You can point to the range of cells by moving the cursor to the first cell in the range, typing in a period, and moving the cursor to the last cell in the range. Then press Enter.

Erase Worksheet [/WEY] If you type this command, the worksheet in memory is erased and you see an empty worksheet on your screen. This command does not erase worksheets stored on disk. If you want to keep a worksheet, remember to save it on disk before you erase it.

Exit Current Menu [Esc] If you find yourself lost in the Lotus 1-2-3 menu system, you can return to familiar territory by pressing the Esc key. Each time you press the Esc key, you move up a level in the menu system. If you continue to press Esc, you eventually leave the MENU mode and return to the READY mode.

Function Keys

F1	Displays the help screen
F2	Switches to the EDIT mode
F3	Displays range names
F4	Makes or unmakes a cell address absolute
F5	GO TO key: moves cursor to a specified cell address
F6	Moves cursor between windows
F7	Repeats most recent Data Query
F8	Repeats most recent Data Table operation
F9	Recalculates formulas when using Manual recalculation
F10	Draws graph, using current graph settings

Help [F1] Display information on a topic by pressing the F1 key. The Help Index displays the major topics. Select a topic by using the cursor movement keys to place the cursor on a topic and pressing Enter. Leave the help screens by pressing the Esc key.

List Files [/FL] To display the names of all files of a particular type stored in the current directory on your disk, type /FL and choose the file type you want to list. Then press Enter.

Print Worksheet [/PPR <range>G] This command prints the contents of the cells in the range on your printer. For example, to print the worksheet in cells A1 through F20, first place your cursor in the upper-left cell of the range to print (A1, in this example). Then type /PPR and enter the range you wish to print (in this case, A1.F20). Press Enter and then type G to start the printing.

Quit Lotus 1-2-3 [/QY] To exit Lotus and return to the DOS prompt, type /Q. When prompted, type Y and press Enter.

Retrieving Worksheet Files [/FR] This command erases any worksheet in memory and replaces it with the worksheet you retrieve from disk. Type /FR and select the file you want from the menu by using the cursor movement keys and then pressing Enter.

Save Worksheet Files [/FS] Type /FS to save a worksheet in memory to your disk. If it is a new worksheet, type the name of the worksheet and press Enter. If you are modifying a worksheet that you previously retrieved from disk, Lotus displays the name of the current worksheet when it prompts you for a file name. Save the new worksheet in the existing file by pressing Enter and then typing R to replace the previous contents of the file with the new worksheet.

7 Exercises for Lotus 1-2-3

L-1

1. Place your spreadsheet program disk in drive A and your data disk in drive B. Load your spreadsheet program.

2. In which cell is the cursor? Press the right cursor key five times. In which cell is the cursor now? Press the down cursor key five times. In which cell is the cursor now? Press the up cursor key two times. In which cell is the cursor now?

3. Move the cursor to the following locations:

   A8

   F15

   B4

   AA60

   Home

4. Move the cursor to the bottom row of the spreadsheet. In which cell is the cursor now? Move the cursor to the farthest right column of the spreadsheet. In which cell is the cursor now?

5. Enter MENU mode. Exit MENU mode.

6. Exit from the spreadsheet program and return to DOS.

L-2

1. Load your spreadsheet program.

2. Enter the worksheet shown in Figure B-7.

3. Save the worksheet on your data disk as EXL-2.

4. Exit the spreadsheet program.

L-3

1. Load the spreadsheet program and retrieve EXL-2.

2. Enter the following formulas to calculate the total points for each student:

   In Cell F3:   (B3+C3+D3+E3)

   In Cell F4:   (B4+C4+D4+E4)

   In Cell F5:   (B5+C5+D5+E5)

   In Cell F6:   (18+24+25+22)

   Does the formula in F5 produce the same type of result as the formula in F3? If not, why are the results different?

3. Save the revised spreadsheet as EXL-3.

4. Increase Aldiss's grade in Cell B3 by 2 points. What happens to the total in Cell F3? Move the cursor to F3. Has the formula changed?

	A	B	C	D	E	F
1	NAME	QUIZ 1	QUIZ 2	QUIZ 3	QUIZ 4	TOTAL
2						
3	ALDISS	22	22	19	21	
4	BENKE	23	21	25	22	
5	CHANG	24	18	20	22	
6	DERRING	18	24	25	22	
7						
8						
9						
10						
11						
12						
13						
14						
15						
16						
17						
18						
19						

Figure B-7

5. Decrease Derring's grade in Cell D6 by 5 points. What happens to the total in Cell F6? Move the cursor to F6. Has the formula changed?

6. Change the formula in F6 to:

   +B6+C6+D6+E6

   Now what happens to the total in Cell F6? Increase Derring's grade in Cell D6 by 8 points. What happens to the total in Cell F6?

7. Save the revised spreadsheet as EXL-3A.

L-4

1. Retrieve EXL-3A. Enter the following functions to calculate the average for each test and the average total points:

In Cell B8:	@AVG(B3.B6)
In Cell C8:	@AVG(C3.C6)
In Cell D8:	@AVG(D3.D6)
In Cell E8:	@AVG(E3.E6)
In Cell F8:	@AVG(F3.F6)

2. Change the 18 in Cell C5 to 20. Do any changes occur in the spreadsheet? If so, what are they and where do they occur?

3. Change the 21 in Cell E3 to 25. Do any changes occur in the spreadsheet? If so, what are they and where do they occur?

4. Save the revised spreadsheet as EXL-4.

5. Print the spreadsheet.

L-5

1. Use the Worksheet Erase command to clear the spreadsheet on the screen. Then use the File List command. How many files are listed?

2. Return to the blank worksheet.

3. Enter the spreadsheet shown in Figure B-8. Use the hyphen key in Cells A4, B4, C4, and D4 to create the dashed line.

4. Use the @SUM function to calculate the total number of matches (Cell B18) and the total dollars earned (Cell C18).

5. In column D calculate the average dollars per match for each player.

6. Save the spreadsheet as EXL-5.

	A	B	C	D
1			TOTAL	AVERAGE
2			DOLLARS	DOLLARS
3	PLAYERS	MATCHES	EARNED	PER MATCH
4	---------	---------	---------	---------
5	CARVER	20	91147	
6	COLES	27	40602	
7	DANIELS	25	20026	
8	HANES	10	27000	
9	KING	22	70170	
10	LOPEZ	24	89736	
11	OKAMOTO	13	55941	
12	SEALLY	6	10200	
13	SMITH	21	91477	
14	THOMPSON	27	67403	
15	WILLS	23	75100	
16	WHITE	17	45183	
17				
18	TOTAL			
19				

Figure B-8

7. Print the spreadsheet.

8. Clear the spreadsheet to get a blank worksheet.

L-6

1. Retrieve EXL-5.

2. Enter the changes that follow. After you make each change, note changes that occur in any other cells.

In Cell B5:	25
In Cell C7:	20000
In Cell B12:	10
In Cell A15:	WILLIS
In Cell C16:	55183

3. Save the revised spreadsheet as EXL-6.

4. Print the spreadsheet.

5. Exit the program.

L-7

1. Load your spreadsheet program. Enter the spreadsheet shown in Figure B-9 and save as EXL-7.

2. Create formulas that calculate each item's total cost. [The total cost for each item equals the number of units sold multiplied by the cost of each unit. Use an asterisk (*) for "multiplied by."] Enter the formulas in the appropriate column.

ITEM	UNITS SOLD	UNIT COST	UNIT PRICE	TOTAL COST	TOTAL SALES	PROFIT
BINDER	500	4	7			
BOOKBAG	350	5	10			
CALENDAR	300	3	8			
NOTEBOOK	400	1	2			
SHIRT	800	4	8			
SCHEDULE	675	1	2			

Figure B-9

3. Create formulas that calculate each item's total sales. (The total sales for each item equals the number of units sold multiplied by the price of each unit.) Enter the formulas in the appropriate column.

4. Create formulas that calculate the profit made on each item. Enter the formulas in the appropriate cells.

5. Save the spreadsheet as EXL-7A.

6. Print the worksheet.

7. Erase the worksheet.

L-8

1. Retrieve EXL-7.

2. Make the following changes to the worksheet:

   Decrease the number of units sold of each item by 50

   Increase the unit cost of each item by 5

   Increase the unit price of each item by 10

3. Save the spreadsheet as EXL-8.

4. At the bottom of the TOTAL COST, TOTAL SALES, and PROFIT columns, place the appropriate formulas or functions to calculate the totals for each column. Enter a label that reads TOTAL in Cell A12.

5. Save the spreadsheet as EXL-8A.

6. Print the spreadsheet.

7. Exit the program.

7 Using dBASE III PLUS

Loading dBASE III PLUS

1. Load DOS.

2. Place dBASE III PLUS Disk #1 in drive A and a formatted data disk in drive B.

3. At the A>, type dBASE and then press Enter.

4. Follow the instructions on the screen. dBASE has been loaded when you see the Assistant menu (see Figure 14-4a on page 433).

7 Keystrokes for the Examples in Chapter 14

The dBASE III PLUS program allows you to enter commands by using the Assistant menu or by typing commands in the COMMAND mode. Chapter 14 gives examples in the COMMAND mode, but this appendix presents the keystrokes for both methods.

The Pledge Example: Building a Database by Using the COMMAND Mode

The instructions that follow allow you to create Rita Chung's database by using the COMMAND mode. (The text describes this method on pages 434–442.)

Creating the File Structure

1. Load dBASE III PLUS. When dBASE is loaded, the Assistant menu appears. To enter the COMMAND mode, press the Esc key. When you see the dot prompt, type CREATE and press Enter. dBASE prompts you for the name of the file.

2. Type in your file name (for example, B:PLEDGESC) and press Enter. A Create screen appears.

3. Enter the appropriate characteristics for each field (see Figure 14-8 on page 438). After you have entered the data for one field in one column, press Enter to move the cursor

to the next column. When entering data, you can use the Backspace key and Del key to make corrections. For the Type column, simply press the Spacebar until the appropriate field type appears; then press Enter.

4. Once all the fields have been defined, press Enter or Ctrl-End to save the file structure. Then press Enter to confirm the action. When dBASE displays the message "Input Data Records Now? (Y/N)," type Y if you are ready to enter records. If you would like to return to the COMMAND mode, type N. This returns you to the dot prompt. (We suggest that you return to the COMMAND mode so that you can view your file structure as described in the next section; double-check it before entering data.)

Viewing the Structure

1. To view your file structure, type LIST STRUCTURE at the dot prompt and press Enter.

2. The display automatically appears. Compare your screen to Figure 14-9 on page 439.

Entering the Data

1. At the dot prompt, type APPEND and press Enter. An input form appears on the screen.

2. Enter the data for the first record field (see Figure 14-11 on page 440). Each time you press Enter, the cursor moves to a new field in the current record. If you have filled in the last field in the record, pressing Enter displays a new record. Continue to add new records and data as needed. (See Figure 4-12a on page 441 for data in the pledge example. For Paid, you can type Y for yes and N for no, or T for true and F for false. Since Paid is a logical field, Y is translated into T and N into F.)

3. When you have finished entering all the data, press Enter or Ctrl-End. dBASE automatically stores the records and returns you to the dot prompt.

Listing the Records

1. At the dot prompt, type LIST and press Enter.

2. A list of the records appears on the screen.

Listing Specific Fields

1. Type LIST followed by the field names you wish to list, in the order in which you wish to list them. (For example, typing LIST LNAME, PAID, PHONE lists only the LNAME, PAID, and PHONE fields, in that order.)

2. Press Enter. The listing appears on the screen; compare to Figure 14-12b on page 441.

Getting Help

1. At the dot prompt, type HELP followed by a space. Then type the command name you would like information about. Press Enter.

2. A help screen for that command appears. (See Figure 14-13 on page 442 for an example.)

3. Press the Esc key to leave the help screen and return to the dot prompt.

Closing the Files and Exiting the Database Program

1. To close the file, type USE at the dot prompt and press Enter. The dot prompt reappears.

2. To reopen the file, type USE and press Enter.

3. To create another database file, type CREATE and press Enter.

4. To exit dBASE III PLUS and return to the A>, type QUIT and press Enter.

The Pledge Example: Building a Database by Using the Assistant Menu

The instructions that follow allow you to create Rita Chung's database by using the Assistant menu instead of the COMMAND mode. To select a menu option, move the cursor to that option and press Enter.

Creating the File Structure

1. When dBASE is loaded, the Assistant menu appears (see Figure 14-4a on page 433). If you are in COMMAND mode, enter ASSISTANT mode by typing ASSIST at the dot prompt and pressing Enter. The Assistant menu appears on the screen.

2. Move the cursor to the Create option at the top of the screen. Then select the Database file option from the Create menu by pressing Enter.

3. Select the disk drive you want to use to store your files (move the cursor, if necessary, and press Enter). Then, in response to the prompt "Enter the name of the file," type in the file name you wish to use (for example, PLEDGESA); press Enter. A Create screen appears.

4. Enter the appropriate characteristics for each field (see Figure 14-8 on page 438). After you have entered the data for one field in one column, press Enter to move the cursor to the next column. When entering data, you can use the Backspace key and the Del key to make corrections. To define the field type, place the cursor in the Type column and press the Spacebar until the name of the appropriate field type appears. Press Enter.

5. Once all the fields have been defined, press Enter or Ctrl-End to save the file structure. Then press Enter to confirm the action. When dBASE displays the message "Input Data Records Now? (Y/N)," type Y if you are ready to enter data records. Typing N returns you to the Assistant menu. (We suggest that you return to the Assistant menu so that you can view your file structure as described in the next section; double-check it before entering data.)

Viewing the Structure

1. To view the file structure, select Tools from the top of the Assistant menu and then select the List Structure option from the Tools menu (move the cursor to List Structure and press Enter).

2. Type N when you see the message "Direct the output to the printer? (Y/N)." The display appears on the screen.

3. Press any key to return to the Assistant menu.

Entering the Data

1. Select Update from the top of the Assistant menu, and then select the Append option from the Update menu. An input form appears on the screen.

2. Enter the data for the first record field (see Figure 14-11 on page 440). Each time you press Enter, the cursor moves to a new field in the current record. If you have filled in the last field in the record, pressing Enter displays a new record. Continue to add new records and data as needed. (See Figure 4-12a on page 441 for data in the pledge example. For Paid, type Y and N or T and F.)

3. When you have finished entering all the data, press Enter or Ctrl-End. dBASE automatically stores the records and returns you to the Assistant menu.

Listing the Records

1. Select Retrieve from the top of the Assistant menu, and then select the List option from the Retrieve menu.

2. Select Execute the Command. Type N when you see the message "Direct output to printer? (Y/N)." A list of the records appears on the screen.

3. Press any key to return to the Assistant menu.

Listing Specific Fields

1. Select Retrieve from the top of the Assistant menu, and then select the Display option from the Retrieve menu.

2. Select Construct a Field List. A submenu appears on the left, listing all the fields of the record.

3. Select the fields you wish to view, in the order you wish to view them (e.g., LNAME, PAID, PHONE). Then press either the left or right cursor movement key to return to the Display submenu.

4. Select Specify Scope. To define scope, select ALL. dBASE returns to the Display submenu.

5. Select Execute the Command. The listing appears on the screen.

6. Press any key to return to the Assistant menu.

Getting Help

1. Select the option you would like information about.
2. Press F1.
3. A help screen for that choice appears.
4. Press the Esc key to leave the help screen and return to the Assistant menu.

Closing the Files and Exiting the Database Program

1. Select Set Up from the top of the Assistant menu.
2. Select Quit dBASE III PLUS from the Set Up menu. This automatically closes all open files and returns you to DOS.

The Pledge Example: Changing a Database by Using the COMMAND Mode

The instructions that follow allow you to change Rita Chung's pledge database by using the COMMAND mode, as described in the text on pages 444–450.

Opening Files

1. If necessary, press the Esc key to access the dot prompt.
2. At the dot prompt, type USE, space, and the name of the file you wish to open (for example, B:PLEDGESC).
3. Press Enter. The file is now open and ready for use.

Modifying Existing Records by Using the Edit Command

1. At the dot prompt, type EDIT followed by a space and the number of the record you wish to edit. (For the Rita Chung example, type EDIT 1.) Then press Enter. The record appears on the screen.
2. Move the cursor to the field you wish to change; type in the new data. (For the Rita Chung example, move the cursor to the PHONE field and type in the new phone number, 363-2415. See Figure 14-14 on page

445.) You can also use the Ins and Del keys to make changes.
3. To store the changed record in the database and return to the dot prompt, press Ctrl-End.

Modifying Existing Records by Using the Edit Command

1. At the dot prompt, type BROWSE; then press Enter. The records in the file appear on the screen. Compare your screen to Figure 14-15 on page 446.
2. Move the cursor to the field you wish to change and type in the new data. (For the Rita Chung example, move the cursor to Record 2 and over to the PAID field; type Y.) You can also use the Ins and Del keys to make changes.
3. To store the changed record in the database and return to the dot prompt, press Ctrl-End.

Adding Records by Using the Append Command

1. At the dot prompt, type APPEND and press Enter. A blank entry form appears on the screen.
2. Enter the data. (For the Rita Chung example, see Figure 14-16 on page 447.)
3. Press Ctrl-End to store the data and return to the dot prompt.

Adding Records by Using the Browse Command

1. At the dot prompt, type BROWSE and press Enter. Press the up cursor key if necessary to see the records.
2. Move the cursor to the last record in the file. Then press the down cursor key to move beyond that record.
3. When dBASE asks if you want to add new records, type Y. A blank record appears on the screen.
4. Enter the data. (For the Rita Chung example, see Figure 14-17 on page 448.)
5. Press Ctrl-End to store the data and return to the dot prompt.

Deleting Records by Using the Browse Command

1. At the dot prompt, type BROWSE and press Enter. Press the up cursor key if necessary to see the records.

2. Move the cursor to the record you wish to delete. (In the Rita Chung example, move the cursor to Joy Chandler's record. See Figure 14-18 on page 449.)

3. Press Ctrl-U. The word "Del" appears in the lower-right corner of the screen. (If you wanted to remove the deletion mark, you could press Ctrl-U again.) If you want to delete more than one record, repeat steps 2 and 3 until all the records you want to remove are marked for deletion.

4. Exit the Browse mode by pressing Ctrl-End.

5. Use the List command to make sure the correct records are marked. An asterisk appears next to records marked for deletion.

6. At the dot prompt, type PACK and press Enter. The marked records are now deleted from the file. Type LIST to see the revised list of records.

Deleting Records by Using the Delete Command

1. At the dot prompt, type DELETE FOR followed by the field name, an equals sign, and a value in the field that identifies the record you want to delete. Values in character fields must be contained in quotation marks. For example, to delete a record that contains the name MEAD in the LNAME field, type

   `DELETE FOR LNAME="MEAD"`

   If you want to delete more than one record, repeat this step until all the records you want to remove are marked for deletion.

2. Press Enter. The message "records deleted" appears; it is preceded by a numeral. This numeral tells the number of records marked for deletion.

3. Use the List command to make sure the correct records are marked. An asterisk appears next to records marked for deletion.

4. To remove a deletion mark, use the Recall command. For example, to recall the record

marked in step 1, type

`RECALL FOR LNAME="MEAD"`

Press Enter. Note: You can use the Recall command only before you use the Pack command.

5. Mark the Mead record for deletion again. At the dot prompt, type PACK and press Enter. The marked records are now deleted from the file.

The Pledge Example: Changing a Database by Using the Assistant Menu

The instructions that follow describe how to change Rita Chung's pledge database by using the Assistant menu instead of the COMMAND mode.

Opening Files

1. If you are in the COMMAND mode, type ASSIST at the dot prompt. The Assistant menu appears on the screen.

2. Select Set Up from the Assistant menu. Then select the "Database file" option from the Set Up menu.

3. Select the disk drive in which your file is stored. A list of the files on the disk in that disk drive appears on the screen.

4. Select the name of the file you wish to open. (For the Rita Chung example, select PLEDGESA.) When dBASE prompts, "Is the file indexed? (Y/N)," type N. The file is now open and ready for use.

Modifying Existing Records by Using the Edit Command

1. Select Position from the Assistant menu, then select the Goto Record option from the Position menu, and then select the Record option from the Goto Record menu.

2. Type the number of the record you wish to edit. (For the Rita Chung example, type 1.) Press Enter.

3. Next select Update from the Assistant menu and then select the Edit option from the Update menu. The record appears on the screen.

4. Move the cursor to the field you wish to change and type the new data. (For the Rita Chung example, move the cursor to the PHONE field and type the new phone number, 363-2415. See Figure 14-14 on page 445.) You can also use the Ins and Del keys to make changes.

5. To store the changed record in the database and return to the Assistant menu, press Ctrl-End.

Modifying Existing Records by Using the Browse Command

1. Select Update from the Assistant menu and then select the Browse option from the Update menu. The records in the file appear on the screen. Compare your screen to Figure 14-15 on page 446.

2. Move the cursor to the field you wish to change and type the new data. (For the Rita Chung example, move the cursor to Record 2 and over to the PAID field; type Y or T.) You can also use Ins and Del keys to make changes.

3. To store the changed record in the database and return to the Assistant menu, press Ctrl-End.

Adding Records by Using the Append Command

1. Select Update from the Assistant menu and then select the Append option from the Update menu. A blank entry form appears on the screen.

2. Enter the data. (For the Rita Chung example, see Figure 14-16 on page 447.)

3. Press Ctrl-End to store the data and return to the Assistant menu.

Adding Records by Using the Browse Command

1. Select Update from the Assistant menu and then select the Browse option from the Update menu. Press the up cursor key if necessary to see the records.

2. Move the cursor to the last record in the file. Then press the down cursor key to move beyond that record.

3. When dBASE asks if you want to add new records, type Y. A blank record appears on the screen.

4. Enter the data. (For the Rita Chung example, see Figure 14-17 on page 448.)

5. Press Ctrl-End to store the data and return to the Assistant menu.

Deleting Records by Using the Browse Command

1. Select Update from the Assistant Menu and then select Browse. Press the up key if necessary to see the records.

2. Move the cursor to the record you wish to delete. (In the Rita Chung example, move the cursor to Joy Chandler's record. See Figure 14-18 on page 449.)

3. Press Ctrl-U. The word "Del" appears in the lower-right corner of the screen. (If you wanted to remove the deletion mark, you could press Ctrl-U again.) If you want to delete more than one record, repeat steps 2 and 3 until all the records you want to remove are marked for deletion.

4. Exit the Browse mode by pressing Ctrl-End.

5. Use the List command to be sure the correct records are marked. (Select Retrieve, List, then Execute the Command.) An asterisk appears next to records marked for deletion. Press any key to return to the Assistant menu.

6. Select Update from the Assistant menu and then select Pack. The marked records are now deleted from the file. Press any key to return to the Assistant menu.

Deleting Records by Using the Delete Command

1. Select the Update menu from the Assistant menu and then select Delete.

2. Select Build a Search Condition. Select a field name from the list that appears on the left. Then select the = Equal To option. Next, type the name of the field whose value identifies the record you want to delete; press Enter. For example, to delete a record that contains the name MEAD in the LNAME field, select LNAME and = Equal To, then type MEAD and press Enter. To delete more

than one record, press the Esc key and repeat step 3 until the appropriate records are marked for deletion.

3. Select No More Conditions. Then select Execute the Command. dBASE responds with a message that tells the number of records now marked for deletion.

4. Press any key to return to the Assistant menu.

5. Use the List command to make sure the correct records are marked. (Select Retrieve, then List, then Execute the Command.) An asterisk appears next to records marked for deletion. Press any key to return to the Assistant menu.

6. To remove a deletion mark, select the Recall option from the Update menu. Select Build a Search Condition. Select the appropriate conditions to identify the record you wish to recall (e.g., select LNAME, select = Equal To, type MEAD, and select No More Conditions). Select Execute the Command. Note: You can only use the Recall command before you use the Pack command.

7. Mark the Mead record for deletion again. Select Pack from the Update menu. The marked records are now deleted from the file. Press any key to return to the Assistant menu.

7 Reference Guide to dBASE III PLUS

The descriptions that follow summarize the most commonly used dBASE commands and the related keystrokes. Most of these commands are discussed in Chapter 14.

The commands you should enter are enclosed in brackets ([ ]). These commands are entered at the dot prompt. You must press Enter at the end of each command. Most commands require that a database file be active (in USE) and that the commands refer to that active database file. When a command requires that you supply a specific element, such as a file name, what you need to enter is enclosed in angle brackets (<>).

Add Records [APPEND] or [BROWSE] APPEND displays the data entry form for one record.

Data is entered into a new blank record at the end of the database file that is in use. The Browse command displays up to 17 records on a screen. With Browse you must move to the last record in the file, then press the down cursor key to move beyond the last record. When dBASE asks if you wish to add records, type Y. A blank record appears. With both Append and Browse, press Ctrl-End to save your entries and changes.

Close Active File [USE] If you are currently using a database file, typing USE and pressing Enter closes the file.

Close Multiple Files [CLEAR ALL] If you are using several files at once or a single file with indexes, entering CLEAR ALL closes all currently open files and their respective indexes.

Create File Structure [CREATE] After you enter the Create command, dBASE prompts you to type in the name of the database file you wish to create. Type the name and press Enter. The file structure form appears on the screen. Type the necessary information for each field. Press Enter to move to the next field. When you have completed the structure, press Ctrl-End and then Enter to save the structure.

Create Report Form [Create] After you enter the Create Report command, dBASE prompts you to type the name of the report file you wish to create. Type the name and press Enter. The report structure form appears on the screen. Use the cursor and the menu to select options you wish to use. Type the necessary information for each field, and select the features you want on your report—title, margin size, and so on. When you complete the structure, select Exit, then Save to save the structure and return to the dot prompt. Note: To create a report, the database file that provides the data for the report must be open.

Delete Records Deleting records is a two-step process. First mark the records for deletion by using the Delete command or the Browse command and Ctrl-U. Then delete the marked records by using the Pack command. When listed, records marked for deletion are preceded by an asterisk. To restore records marked for deletion, use the Recall command. Note: Once Pack has been used, you can no longer recall a record.

Always double-check that the correct records are marked before using the Pack command.

Edit Records [Edit<record number>] or [BROWSE] Use the Edit command to modify records in an open database file. Type Edit followed by the number of the record you want to modify. For example, to edit record 5, type Edit 5 and press Enter. The requested record appears on the screen, and you can make your changes. Press PgUp or PgDn to move to other records in the file. After making the necessary changes, press Ctrl-End to save them. The Browse command allows access to all the records in a database file. Use the cursor movement keys to move to the field(s) you wish to change. Make the necessary changes, then press Ctrl-End to save the changes.

Exit dBASE [QUIT] The Quit command closes all currently open files and returns you to the DOS prompt.

Function Keys

F1	Displays the dBASE help screen
F2	Activates the Assist menu facility
F3	Lists the records in the active database file
F4	Lists the names of all database files (DBF) on the default disk
F5	Displays the structure of the active database file
F6	Displays the current status (names of all open files, work areas, and settings) of dBASE
F7	Displays information on memory variables, which are used in the dBASE programming language
F8	Displays the current record in the active database file
F9	Signals dBASE that you wish to edit records in the active database file

Index Files [INDEX ON <key field>TO<index file name>] The Index command creates a new index file with the extension NDX. Index files order database files in a logical sequence (alphabetical, numeric, and so on) based on a character, numeric, or date field.

Join Multiple Files [JOIN WITH<file name 2> TO <new file name> FOR <link field> = B -> <link field>] The Join command creates a new database file by combining two open database files that have a common field. The database files must have previously been opened in two separate work areas (see "Open Multiple Files").

Link Multiple Files [SET RELATION TO <link field> INTO <file name of file in Work Area 2>] The Set Relation To command links two open database files by using a field that is common to both. The database files must have previously been opened in two separate work areas (see "Open Multiple Files"), and the file open in area 2 must be indexed on the link field. In addition, the index must be active (open). Note: The Set Relation To command links the two files only temporarily; it does not create a new database file.

List File Structure [LIST STRUCTURE] or [DISPLAY STRUCTURE] Use the List Structure command or the Display Structure command to display the structure of the active database file.

List Records [LIST] The List command is used to show the contents of the active database file. All records are displayed unless a selection condition is specified.

List Specific Fields [LIST <field name 1>, <field name 2>, <etc.>] To list specific fields, enter LIST followed by the fields you wish to view, in the order you wish to view them. The requested fields for all the records in the file are displayed.

List Using One Condition [LIST FOR <field name 1> = <selection condition>] To find a record or records containing a specific piece of information, enter the List For command. The equals sign in the command may be replaced with other relational operators: >, <, >=, or <=. Character values must be contained in quotation marks. The record(s) are displayed on your screen.

List Using Two Conditions [LIST FOR <field name 1> = <selection condition one> .AND. <field name 2> = <selection condition two>] The equals sign in either part of the command may be replaced with another relational operator: $<$, $>$, $>-$, or $<-$. The logical operator .AND. narrows the range of the search. If you wish to widen the range, replace .AND. with .OR. Character values must be contained in quotation marks. The record(s) are displayed on your screen.

Modify File Structure [MODIFY STRUCTURE] To change the structure of a file, enter the Modify Structure command. The file structure is displayed on the screen. Enter your changes, then press Ctrl-End to save them.

Open Multiple Files To open several files at one time, you must use the Select command in conjunction with the Use command. For example, to open two files concurrently—one in Work Area 1 and one in Work Area 2—type the following commands, pressing Enter at the end of each command line.

```
SELECT 2
USE <file name 2>
SELECT 1
USE <file name 1>
```

Unless otherwise specified, database files are always opened in Area 1. You may also use the Select command to switch back and forth between open files. For example, if you type SELECT 2 and press Enter, the file in Work Area 2 becomes the active file.

Print Report [REPORT FORM <report file name> TO PRINT] Make sure your printer is on and the database file on which the report is based is open. Then enter the Report Form command.

Seek Records [SEEK <data to be found>] The Seek command can be used only with open, indexed database files. The associated Index file must also be open. The command searches for the first record in the file that matches the criteria you enter. Character values must be contained in quotation marks. To display a record found by the Seek command, type DISPLAY and press Enter.

Sort Files [SORT ON <key fields> TO <sorted file name>] The Sort command creates and saves a new sorted database file that contains all the data in the original file. Sorted files can be ordered in a logical sequence (alphabetical,

numeric, and so on) based on character, numeric, or date fields.

Use File [USE <file name>] To open, or use, a database file, enter the Use command; the name of the open database file appears in the highlighted bar near the bottom of the screen. If the database file has been indexed, list the names of the index files after the name of the database file. For example: _USE PHONE INDEX LNAMEI.

7 Exercises for dBASE III PLUS

DB-1

1. Load your database program and insert a formatted disk in drive B.

2. Using the appropriate commands, create the file structure shown in Figure B-10a. The name of the file should be EXDB-1. The NAME field should have a width of 30 characters and the NUMBER field should have a width of 12 characters. Make corrections, as needed, as you type.

3. Use your program to view the structure of the file. How many records are in the database file at this point?

Field	Field Name	Type	Width	Dec
1	NAME	Character	30	
2	NUMBER	Character	12	

(a)

Record#	NAME	NUMBER
1	SUSAN MILLER	411-234-1900
2	FREDERICK ASTER	555-311-1234
3	JORGE AMADO	611-114-1923
4	VICTORIA COWEN	411-555-9087
5	ISAAC ADLER	611-465-0089

(b)

Figure B-10

4. Using the appropriate commands, enter the records shown in Figure B-10b into the EXDB-1 file.

5. Use your program to list the records in the file. Are all the records you entered shown on the screen?

6. Close the database file and exit the program.

DB-2

1. Reload the database program and place your data disk in drive B.

2. Using the appropriate commands, create the file structure shown in Figure B-11a. The name of the file should be EXDB-2.

3. Enter the data shown in Figure B-11b into the database file.

4. List the data on your screen.

5. Close the file.

DB-3

1. Use the database program to create a personal address file. Include the following fields:

LNAME

FNAME

STREET

CITY

STATE

ZIPCODE

PHONE

Name the file EXDB-3.

2. Enter data about at least five of your friends.

3. Close the file. Then list the contents of your database. What is displayed on your screen?

4. Retrieve the EXDB-3 file. Now list the contents of your database. What determines the order in which the database records are displayed?

5. Use the appropriate command to list only

Field	Field Name	Type	Width	Dec
1	PNUMBER	Character	3	
2	NAME	Character	10	
3	COST	Numeric	5	2
4	QUANTITY	Numeric	8	
5	ORDERED	Date	8	

(a)

Record#	PNUMBER	NAME	COST	QUANTITY	ORDERED
1	238	RAM CHIP	1.50	10	02/14/90
2	117	PROBE	15.00	5	03/17/90
3	874	L.E. PIN	2.00	7	04/02/90
4	692	RIBBON	0.89	1	02/13/90
5	799	CABLE	5.00	14	04/20/90

(b)

Figure B-11

the LNAME, FNAME, and PHONE fields, in that order.

6. Use the appropriate command to list only the FNAME, PHONE, and CITY fields, in that order.

7. Close the file.

DB-4

Assume that you are going to use your database program to maintain a record of the books you have loaned to your friends.

1. Create the file structure shown in Figure B-12a. Name the file EXDB-4.

2. Enter the records shown in Figure B-12b.

3. Use the appropriate command to add the following record to the database:

   ```
   WELLINGTON 08/09/90
   NORM YARROW 09/15/90
   ```

4. List the records in the database. Where is the new record placed in the database file?

5. Add the following two records to the file:

```
THE TAO OF PHYSICS 08/10/90
KATHLYN DUGAN       09/30/90
THE STRANGER 08/15/90
GELAREH ASAYESH 09/30/90
```

6. List the records to check your entries.

7. Use the appropriate command to list only the titles of the books borrowed and the date on which they should be returned.

8. Close the file.

DB-5

1. Retrieve EXDB-4. List all the records in the file. Are all the records there?

2. Use your program's editing feature to make the following changes:

   Change the name of the book in Record 4 to BRED IN THE BONE.

   Change Louisa Potter's RETURN_ON date to 08/25/90.

   Change the name of the book in Record 2 to LEAVEN OF MALICE.

Field	Field Name	Type	Width	Dec
1	BOOK	Character	25	
2	DATE_OUT	Date	8	
3	LOANED_TO	Character	15	
4	RETURN_ON	Date	8	

(a)

Record#	BOOK	DATE_OUT	LOANED_TO	RETURN_ON
1	HEART OF DARKNESS	07/10/90	ED GRAYSON	08/10/90
2	LEAVEN OF MIRTH	07/12/90	NORM YARROW	07/30/90
3	TIME CAPSULE	07/20/90	LOUISA POTTER	08/20/90
4	ROBERTSON DAVIES	07/25/90	KATHLYN DUGAN	09/15/90
5	THE MESSAGE MERCHANTS	07/30/90	MAURICE SAATCHI	08/05/90
6	THE GILMAN TRAIL	08/07/90	JOHN ANDRILLA	08/30/90

(b)

Figure B-12

Change the name in the LOANED_TO field of Record 2 to MICHAEL CHABON.

3. If your program has a Browse feature, use it to view the records. If not, use the appropriate command to list the records. Check to make sure the changes have been made correctly. Make any additional changes you need to make.

4. Close the file.

DB-6

1. Retrieve EXDB-4. List the contents of the file. Does the file reflect the changes you made in Exercise DB-5?

2. Delete Record 1 and Record 6. List the file to make sure the records have been deleted. How many records are now in the database file?

3. Delete the record that contains the title TIME CAPSULE.

4. Mark Kathlyn Dugan's records for deletion. View the records to verify that the records have been marked. Then use your program's Recall feature to remove the deletion mark. (Note: Some database programs use a one-step deletion process. If this is the case with your program, simply skip this step.)

5. If your program has a Browse feature, use it to make the changes that follow. If not, use the appropriate commands to make the changes.

Add the following record to the file:

```
GROWING ROSES
 08/15/90
LIA ILLGEN  09/01/90
```

Change Saatchi to Maurice Satchi.

For Record 3, change the date in the DATE field to 07/31/90.

6. View the records to make sure your changes are correct.

7. Close the file.

DB-7

Assume you are working for a employment service that provides temporary employees. You are asked to create the database shown in Figure B-13. Each employee has listed the office position(s) that he or she wishes to obtain on a temporary basis. These positions are listed in the fields SKILL1 and SKILL2. Notice that some employees will accept temporary employment in only one field. If the employee is currently seeking work, the contents of the ACTIVE field is .T. If the employee has been listed previously but is not available now, an .F. appears in the ACTIVE field.

1. Create a database that contains the data shown in Figure B-13. Name the file EXDB-7.

2. Check to see that the contents of all the fields are correct. Because each record in the databases has more fields than will fit on the screen at one time, you need to use the cursor movement keys to move to the fields that do not appear on your screen. Use the appropriate command to make any changes you need to make.

LNAME	FNAME	ACTIVE	SSN	RATE	CITY	PHONE	SKILL1	SKILL2
SMITH	ELIZABETH	.T.	001-34-7661	10.00	REDWOOD	789-8303	WORD PROCESSING	BOOKKEEPING
HOPPT	LAWRENCE	.F.	231-56-0823	15.00	CLARION	211-0963	ACCOUNTING	
REMBRANT	VERONICA	.T.	318-00-5223	20.00	MARKHAM	634-1967	PROOFREADING	EDITING
RIDLEY	HOWARD	.T.	954-87-1234	10.00	CLARION	692-2231	MAINTENANCE	LANDSCAPING
BRIDGETO	SOLOMON	.F.	562-34-9758	12.00	MARKHAM	112-3529	RECEPTION	FILING
GREEN	JANE	.T.	911-00-4286	15.00	SALTERTON	311-7398	EDITING	
FAIRMONT	ELDON	.T.	673-56-4401	15.00	STATE COLLEGE	567-0408	WINDOW WASHING	MAINTENANCE
SHILLITO	ASHLEY	.F.	088-34-3624	10.00	CLARION	566-0075	PROOFREADING	
BELL	DINAH	.T.	455-28-4582	10.00	VESTAL	864-0098	RECEPTION	WORD PROCESSING
MUNSON	MATTHEW	.F.	633-98-1185	15.00	SALTERTON	411-2323	FILING	

Figure B-13

3. Use the appropriate command to list only the FNAME, LNAME, ACTIVE, SSN, and RATE fields, in that order.

4. Use the appropriate command to list only the LNAME, CITY, and PHONE fields, in that order.

5. Use the appropriate command to list only the LNAME, ACTIVE, SKILL1, and SKILL2 fields, in that order.

6. Use the appropriate commands to update the file as follows:

   Solomon Bridgeto wishes to be listed as active.

   Ashley Shillito will also accept a temporary position as an editor.

   Dinah Bell has married. Her last name is now Ritter.

   Lawrence Hoppt has moved to Europe. His record should be deleted from the file.

   Elizabeth Smith is changing her rate of pay to $12.75.

   The firm has accepted a new employee who is currently seeking work. Add the following information to the file: Last name: Elliot; First name: Susan; Social Security number: 551-88-1071; Desired rate of pay: $20.00; no address yet; Phone: 624-1867. Susan desires employment as an editor or a proofreader.

7. List the records to check your changes.

8. Close the file and exit the program.

Appendix C

History and Industry: The Continuing Story of the Computer Age

The principles are old, but the first computer was born only about four decades ago. Before long, the first generation of vacuum tube computers was replaced by second-generation computers using transistors and then by third-generation machines using integrated circuits. The fourth generation of general-purpose microprocessors is yielding to even more high-powered machines of the fifth generation in the 1990s. This is not ancient history. It is now and it moves fast.

LEARNING OBJECTIVES
- Understanding the story of how computer technology unfolded with particular emphasis on the "generations."
- Understanding how people and events affected the development of computers.
- Familiarity with the story of microcomputer development.
- Acquaintance with the development of software.

LECTURE HINT
The first microcomputer, the Mark-8, was designed by Jonathan Titus. It appeared in the July 1974 issue of Radio Electronics Magazine, preceding Ed Robert's work by 6 months. Anyone building the Mark-8 (also called the Micro-8) had to buy parts at high prices since no kit was offered. No one knows how many were built.

Figure C-1   The Altair. The term *microcomputer* had not even been invented yet, so Ed Roberts's small computer was called a "minicomputer" when it was featured on the cover of *Popular Electronics*.

Although the story of computers has diverse roots, the most fascinating part—the history of microcomputers—is quite recent. The beginning of this history turns on the personality of Ed Roberts the way a watch turns on a jewel. It began when his foundering company took a surprising turn.

Like other entrepreneurs before him, Ed Roberts had taken a big risk. He had already been burned once, and now he feared being burned again. The first time, in the early 1970s, he had borrowed heavily to produce microprocessor-based calculators, only to have the chip producers decide to build their own product—and sell them for half the price of Ed's calculator.

But now, this new product, this was different. It was based on a microprocessor too—the Intel 8080—but it was a *computer*. A little computer. The "big boys" at the established computer firms considered their machines to be an industrial product and everyone knew that big business needed big computers. Besides, who would want a small computer? Who, indeed!

Ed was not sure that anyone would want one either, but he found the idea so compelling that he decided to make the computer anyway. Besides, he was so far in debt from the calculator fiasco that it did not seem to matter which project propelled him into bankruptcy. Ed's small computer was given a sharp boost by Les Solomon, who promised to feature the new machine on the cover of *Popular Electronics*. Ed worked frantically to meet the publication deadline, and he even tried to make the machine pretty, so it would look attractive on the cover (Figure C-1).

Making a good-looking small computer was not easy. This machine, named the Altair (after a heavenly "Star Trek" destination), looked like a flat box. In fact, it met the definition of a computer in only a minimal way: a central processing unit (on the chip), 256 characters (a paragraph!) of memory, and switches and lights on a front panel for input/output. No screen, no keyboard, no storage.

But it was done on time for the January 1975 issue and Roberts made plans to fly to New York to demonstrate the machine to Solomon. He sent the computer on ahead by railroad express. Ed got to New York but the computer did not—the very first microcomputer was lost! There was no time to build a new computer before the publishing deadline, so Roberts cooked up a phony version for the cover picture: an empty box with switches and lights on the front panel. He also placed an inch-high ad in the back of the magazine: your own Altair kit for $397.

Ed was hoping for perhaps 200 orders. But the machine—that is, the box—fired imaginations across the country. Two thousand customers sent checks for $397 to an unknown Albuquerque, New Mexico, company. Overnight, the MITS Altair microcomputer kit was a runaway success.

Ed Roberts was an important player in the history of microcomputers. Unfortunately, he never made it in the big time; most observers agree that his business insight did not match his technical skills.

But other entrepreneurs did make it. In this chapter, we will glance briefly at the early years of computers and then examine more recent history. But first, consider where you fit into the picture.

7 Placing Yourself on the Computer Timeline

As a novice in the computer field, you view the computer industry from a fresh perspective. You may see computers as a bold new thrust, representing the crest of the wave of technological developments. Microcomputers, in particular, may be your main connection to that technology. Microcomputers—personal computers—are always in the forefront of the news, generating endless headlines as they are born and changed and—in some cases—die.

But microcomputers did not spring out of thin air. They have, in fact, a set of illustrious ancestors and a noble history. It is important that you be able to place yourself on the historical computer timeline. We will trace that timeline from its fumbling beginnings to its current sophistication.

It is appropriate to discuss the history of the computer in terms of its hardware because the touchstone of the computer revolution has been its rapidly changing technology—its hardware. However, the history of the computer is by no means just a history of the machine; it is also a history of software and people.

The first person who was able to advance significantly the cause of mechanical computation was Charles Babbage, called "the father of the computer." We begin with him.

7 Babbage and the Countess

Born in England in 1791, Charles Babbage was an inventor and mathematician. When solving certain equations, he found the hand-done mathematical tables he used filled with errors. He decided a machine could be built that would solve the equations better by calculating the differences between them. He set about making a demonstration model of what he called a **difference engine** (Figure C-2). The model was so well received that in about 1830 he enthusiastically began to build a full-scale working version, using a grant from the British government.

However, Babbage found that the smallest imperfections were enough to throw the machine out of whack. Babbage was viewed by his own colleagues as a man who was trying to manufacture a machine that was utterly ridiculous. Finally, after spending its money to no avail, the government withdrew its financial support.

TEST BANK
Mult. Choice   1-2
T/F   1-2, 4
Matching A   1-2
Fill-in-the-Blank 1-2

LECTURE HINT
The success of the MITS Altair contributed to the downfall of MITS. The employees focused on kits, not on making improvements. Other companies built boards to insert inside the Altair. When these companies designed their own computers and sold them already assembled at competitive prices, MITS could no longer compete.

TEST BANK
Mult. Choice   3-4, 7
T/F   3, 5-8
Matching B   1
Matching C   1
Matching D   1
Fill-in-the-Blank 3-4

LECTURE HINT
The difference engine did computations which had to be read by a user, and those results had to be fed back into the machine at a later time. The analytical engine (described on the next page) was capable of storing intermediate computations, avoiding the error-prone human interaction.

Figure C-2　Charles Babbage's difference engine. This shows a prototype model. Babbage attempted to build a working model, which was to have been several times larger and steam-driven, but he was unsuccessful.

DISCUSSION QUESTION
What five features in the analytical engine are key features of modern computers?

Figure C-3　The Countess of Lovelace. Augusta Ada Byron, as she was known before she became a countess, was Charles Babbage's colleague in his work on the analytical engine and has been called the world's first computer programmer. A programming language sponsored by the Pentagon has been dubbed Ada in her honor.

Despite this setback, Babbage was not discouraged. He conceived another machine, christened the **analytical engine,** which he hoped would perform many kinds of calculations. This, too, was never built, at least by Babbage (a model was later put together by his son), but it embodied five key features of modern computers:

- an input device

- a storage place to hold the number waiting to be processed

- a processor, or number calculator

- a control unit to direct the task to be performed and the sequence of calculations

- an output device

If Babbage was the father of the computer, then Ada, the Countess of Lovelace, was the first computer programmer (Figure C-3). The daughter of English poet Lord Byron and of a mother who was a gifted mathematician, Ada helped develop the instructions for doing computations on the analytical engine. Lady Lovelace's contribu-

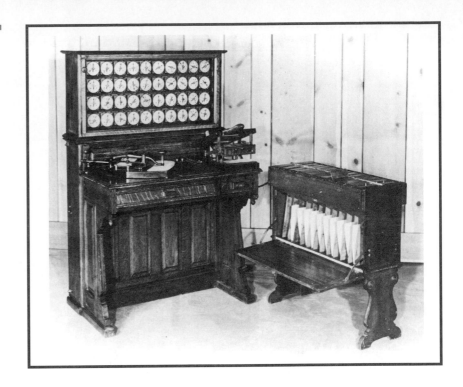

Figure C-4   Herman Hollerith's tabulating machine. This electrical tabulator and sorter was used to tabulate 1890 census data.

tions cannot be overvalued. She was able to see that his theoretical approach was workable, and her interest gave Babbage encouragement. In addition, she published a series of notes that eventually led others to accomplish what Babbage himself had been unable to do.

7 Herman Hollerith: The Census Has Never Been the Same

The hand-done tabulation of the 1880 United States census took seven and a half years. A competition was held to find some way to speed the counting process of the 1890 United States census. Herman Hollerith's tabulating machine won the contest. As a result of his system's adoption, an unofficial count of the 1890 population (62,622,250) was announced only six weeks after the census was taken.

The principal difference between Hollerith's and Babbage's machines was that Hollerith's machine used electrical rather than mechanical power (Figure C-4). Hollerith realized that his machine had considerable commercial potential. In 1896 he founded the successful Tabulating Machine Company, which, in 1924, merged with two other companies to form the International Business Machines Corporation—IBM.

Figure C-5   The original IBM building.

WATSON SMART? YOU BET!

Just as computers were getting off the ground, Thomas Watson, Sr., saw the best and brightest called to arms in World War II. But he did not just bid his employees a sad adieu. He paid them. Each and every one received one quarter of his or her annual salary, in twelve monthly installments. The checks continued to arrive throughout the duration of the war. Every month those former employees thought about IBM and the generosity of its founder.

The result? A very high percentage of those employees returned to IBM after the war. Watson got his brain trust back, virtually intact. The rest is history.

7 Watson of IBM: Ornery but Rather Successful

For over 30 years, from 1924 to 1956, Thomas J. Watson, Sr., ruled IBM with an iron grip. Cantankerous and autocratic, supersalesman Watson made IBM a dominant force in the business machines market, first as a supplier of calculators, then as a developer of computers. The original IBM building is shown in Figure C-5.

IBM's entry into computers was sparked by a young Harvard professor of mathematics, Howard Aiken. In 1936, after reading Lady Lovelace's notes, Aiken began to think that a modern equivalent of the analytical engine could be constructed. Because IBM was already such a power in the business machines market, with ample money and resources, Aiken worked out a careful proposal and approached Thomas Watson. In one of those make-or-break decisions for which he was famous, Watson gave him $1 million. As a result, the Harvard Mark I was born.

TEST BANK
Mult. Choice 8-9;   T/F 10;   Matching A   4-5;
Matching B   10;   Fill-in-the-Blank   7

Figure C-6   The ABC. John Atanasoff and his assistant, Clifford Berry, developed the first digital electronic computer, nicknamed the "ABC" for *Atanasoff–Berry computer.*

TEST BANK
Mult. Choice	10-11
T/F	11-18
Matching A	6-8
Matching B	2-3, 8-9
Fill-in-the-Blank	8-12

LECTURE HINT
The ENIAC occupied 1,500 square feet, stood two stories high, and weighed 30 tons. It could handle 300 numbers per second. The ENIAC cost $486,840 in 1946 dollars; today a $2,000 laptop computer can handle numbers about 20 times faster.

LECTURE HINT
Each time a program was changed in the ENIAC, the computer had to be laboriously rewired. Dr. John von Neumann developed the stored program concept, allowing program instructions to be stored inside the computer. Computers could switch to a different program by "reading" instructions from storage in less than a second, revolutionizing computer technology.

TEST BANK
Mult. Choice	12-30
T/F	19-42
Matching A	8
Matching C	2-10
Matching D	2-10
Fill-in-the-Blank	13-32

The Start of the Modern Era

Nothing like the **Mark I** had ever been built before. It was 8 feet high and 55 feet long, made of streamlined steel and glass, and it emitted a sound during processing that one person said was "like listening to a roomful of old ladies knitting away with steel needles." Unveiled in 1944, the Mark I was never very efficient. But the enormous publicity strengthened IBM's commitment to computer development. Meanwhile, technology had been proceeding elsewhere on separate tracks.

American military officials approached Dr. John Mauchly at the University of Pennsylvania and asked him to build a machine that would rapidly calculate trajectories for artillery and missiles. Mauchly and his student J. Presper Eckert relied on the work of Dr. John V. Atanasoff, a professor of physics at Iowa State University. During the late 1930s Atanasoff had spent time trying to build an electronic calculating device to help his students solve mathematical problems. He and an assistant, Clifford Berry, succeeded in building the first digital computer that worked electronically; they called it the **ABC,** for **Atanasoff–Berry computer** (Figure C-6).

After Mauchly met with Atanasoff and Berry in 1941, he used the ABC as the basis for the next step in computer development. From this association ultimately came a lawsuit, based on attempts to get patents for a commercial version of the machine Mauchly built. The suit was finally decided in 1974, when a federal court determined that Atanasoff had been the true originator of the ideas required to make an electronic digital computer actually work. (Some computer historians dispute this court decision.) But Mauchly and Eckert were able to use the ABC principles to create the **ENIAC,** for **Electronic Numerical Integrator and Calculator.** The main significance of the ENIAC is that, as the first general-purpose computer, it was the forerunner of the UNIVAC I, the first computer sold on a commercial basis.

The Computer Age Begins

The remarkable thing about the computer age is that so much has happened in so short a time. We have leapfrogged through four generations of technology in about 40 years—a span of time whose events are within the memories of many people today. The first three "generations" are pinned to three technological developments—the vacuum tube, the transistor, and the integrated circuit—each of which has drastically changed the nature of computers. We define the timing of each generation according to the beginning of commercial delivery of the hardware technology. Defining subsequent generations has become more complicated because the entire industry has become more complicated.

Figure C-7 The UNIVAC. The familiar but younger figure of Walter Cronkite (right) is shown here with J. Presper Eckert and an unidentified operator of UNIVAC during vote counting for the 1952 presidential election. UNIVAC surprised CBS executives by predicting—after analyzing about 5% of the vote counted—that Eisenhower would defeat Stevenson. CBS withheld announcement until it could be confirmed by the complete vote. Thus began the use of computers in predicting election outcomes—a practice that has evoked criticism when networks forecast the winner with only a small percentage of the vote counted.

DISCUSSION QUESTION
What was unique about the first UNIVAC computer? Who built it?

7 The First Generation, 1951–1958: The Vacuum Tube

The beginning of the commercial computer age may be dated June 14, 1951. This was the date the first **UNIVAC**—short for ***Univ**ersal **A**utomatic **C**omputer*—was delivered to a client, the U.S. Bureau of the Census, for use in tabulating the previous year's census. It also marked the first time that a computer had been built for business applications rather than for military, scientific, or engineering use. The UNIVAC (Figure C-7) was really the ENIAC in disguise and was, in fact, built by Mauchly and Eckert, who in 1947 had formed their own corporation.

In the first generation, **vacuum tubes**—electronic tubes about the size of light bulbs—were used as the internal computer components (Figure C-8). However, because thousands of such tubes were required, they generated a great deal of heat, causing many problems in temperature regulation and climate control. In addition, although all the tubes had to be working simultaneously, they were subject to frequent burnout—and the people operating the computer often did not know whether the problem was in the programming or in the machine.

Another drawback was that the language used in programming was machine language, which uses numbers, rather than the present-day higher-level languages, which are more like English. Using numbers alone made programming the computer difficult and time-consuming.

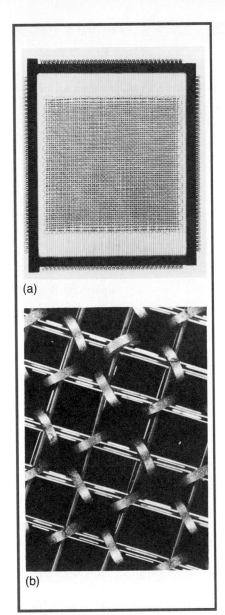

(a)

(b)

Figure C-9   Magnetic cores. (a) A 6-inch by 11-inch magnetic core memory. (b) Close-up of a magnetic core memory. A few hundredths of an inch in diameter, each magnetic core was mounted on a wire. When electricity passed through the wire on which a core was strung, the core could be magnetized as either "off" or "on." These states represented a 0 (off) or a 1 (on). Combinations of 0s and 1s could be used to represent data. Magnetic cores were originally developed by IBM, which adapted pill-making machinery to produce them by the millions.

Figure C-8   Vacuum tubes. Vacuum tubes were used in the first generation of computers. Vacuum tube systems could multiply two ten-digit numbers together in one-fortieth of a second.

The UNIVAC used **magnetic core** to provide memory. This consisted of small, doughnut-shaped rings about the size of a pinhead, which were strung like beads on intersecting thin wires (Figure C-9). To supplement primary storage, first-generation computers stored data on punched cards. In 1957 magnetic tape was introduced as a faster, more compact method of storing data.

The early generation of computers was used primarily for scientific and engineering calculations rather than for business data processing applications. Because of the enormous size, unreliability, and high cost of these computers, many people assumed they would remain very expensive, specialized tools, not destined for general use.

But at Bell Laboratories there had already been a new technological development—the transistor.

The Second Generation, 1959–1964: The Transistor

Three Bell Lab scientists—J. Bardeen, H. W. Brattain, and W. Shockley—developed the **transistor,** a small device that transfers electric signals across a resistor. (The name *transistor* began as a trademark concocted from *transfer* plus *resistor.*) The scientists later received the Nobel prize for their invention. The transistor revolutionized electronics in general and computers in particular. Transistors were much smaller than vacuum tubes, and they had numerous other advantages: They needed no warm-up time, consumed less energy, and were faster and more reliable.

PERSPECTIVES

Interesting Moments in Computer History

Item: The National Health Institute Clinic in Maryland was first to use a computer to monitor a patient. 1961.

Item: Lead me to Las Vegas. Ed Thorpe wrote *Beat the Dealer*, the first book on using a computer to win at blackjack. 1962.

Item: "Tell me more about your family." At MIT, Joseph Weizenbaum invented Doctor, a program that simulates a psychiatric session by having the computer respond to the patient's typed statements. 1963.

Item: In the first prosecuted computer crime, Texas v. Hancock, a programmer was convicted of stealing $5 million worth of his employer's software and sentenced to five years in prison. 1964.

Item: The first computer dating service, Operation Match, opened in Cambridge, Massachusetts. 1966.

Item: The mutinous computer HAL was introduced in *2001: A Space Odyssey*. 1968.

Item: Computerized music hit the charts with *Switched-On Bach* in 1968.

Item: "Is the pain sharp or dull?" The first computerized medical diagnostic program, called Dendral, was created by Stanford computer scientists. 1968.

Item: The first robot supermarket opened in San Diego. The store closed because it could not handle the volume of phone calls to the robots. 1970.

Item: First Federal Savings and Loan, in Nebraska, offered the first automated teller machine on its outside wall. 1974.

Item: "Factory Robot Kills Worker," screamed the headline.

A self-propelled factory robot ran over the worker who was trying to repair it. 1981.

Item: The first computer wedding was performed on an Apple II. The text of the ceremony was printed on the screen; the bride and groom each signaled assent by pressing the Y key. 1981.

Item: Jimmy Carter was the first president to use a computer to write his memoirs. 1982.

Item: *Time* magazine named the computer as its "Man of the Year." 1982.

Item: A robot was arrested and placed in a California prison cell while the baffled police filed a disorderly conduct charge. The robot had been calling insults to people on the street and, in fact, cried "Robot abuse!" as it was being taken away. 1985.

AN EARLY NONBELIEVER

Many rushed to embrace computer technology, but not everyone. Listen to this voice of hesitation: "Like all other automatic gadgets, computers unfortunately also have a numbing influence on the human mind. Just as the car has made walking most unpopular among some members of the new generation, computers have made research people lazy. Such people often prefer to give the calculations to the computer at once rather than to spend a little time and effort in attempting to discover whether human ingenuity can so simplify them as to make a computer unnecessary."

—Mario G. Salvadori
Mathematics, the Language of Science, 1960

During this generation, another important development was the move from machine language to **assembly languages**—also called **symbolic languages.** Assembly languages use abbreviations for instructions (for example, L for LOAD) rather than numbers. This made programming less cumbersome.

After the development of symbolic languages came **higher-level languages,** such as **FORTRAN** (1954) and **COBOL** (1959). Both languages, still widely used today (in more updated forms), are more English-like than assembly language. Higher-level languages allowed programmers to give more attention to solving problems. Also, in 1962 the first removable disk pack was marketed. Disk storage supplemented magnetic tape systems and enabled users to have fast access to desired data.

All these new developments made the second generation of computers less costly to operate—and thus began a surge of growth in computer systems. Throughout this period computers were being used principally by business, university, and government organizations. They had not filtered down to the general public. The real part of the revolution was about to begin.

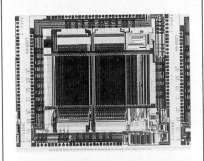

THE GREATEST INVENTION EVER

There was a time when an engineer who was also an inventor could look forward to fame as well as fortune. Thomas Edison, for example, was one of the best-known people in the world before he was 35. Today's famous people tend to come from the entertainment industry. So it is that we have lost the names of Jack Kilby and Robert Noyce, who invented the device that operates your watch, oven, calculator, and computer: the integrated circuit. Some have called it the greatest invention ever. Let us make Kilby and Noyce just a little bit famous.

Kilby and Noyce come from America's heartland, Kansas and Iowa, respectively. Both were interested in electronics. But there the differences end. Jack Kilby flunked the entrance exam at MIT and received only a single job offer when he graduated with an engineering degree from the University of Illinois. Robert Noyce, on the other hand, did get into MIT and stayed around to get a Ph.D.

Kilby and Noyce worked independently, each coming out with the integrated circuit on a chip in 1959—Kilby at Texas Instruments, Inc. and Noyce at Fairchild Semiconductor. Kilby went on to develop the first hand-held calculator and Noyce founded Intel Corporation to pursue the daring idea of putting the computer's memory on chips.

We can point with pride to Kilby and Noyce, the engineers who thought of the ingenious integrated circuit, the foundation of microcomputers and many machines that make our lives easier.

7 The Third Generation, 1965–1970: The Integrated Circuit

One of the most abundant elements in the earth's crust is silicon, a nonmetallic substance found in common beach sand as well as in practically all rocks and clay. The use of this element has given rise to the name "Silicon Valley" for Santa Clara County, which is about 30 miles south of San Francisco. In 1965 Silicon Valley became the principal site of the electronics industry making the so-called silicon chip: the integrated circuit.

An **integrated circuit** (abbreviated **IC**) is a complete electronic circuit on a small chip of silicon. The chip may be less than $\frac{1}{8}$ inch square and contain thousands or millions of electronic components. Beginning in 1965 the integrated circuit began to replace the transistor in machines now called third-generation computers. An integrated circuit was able to replace an entire circuit board of transistors with one chip of silicon much smaller than one transistor (Figure C-10).

Integrated circuits are made of silicon because it is a **semiconductor.** That is, it is a crystalline substance that will conduct electric current when it has been "doped" with chemical impurities implanted in its lattice-like structure. A cylinder of silicon is sliced into wafers, each about 6 inches in diameter, and the wafer is etched repeatedly with a pattern of electrical circuitry. Several layers may be etched on a single wafer. The wafer is then divided into several

Figure C-10   One chip, many transistors. Hundreds of thousands, or even millions, of transistors (right) can now be placed on one tiny chip (left).

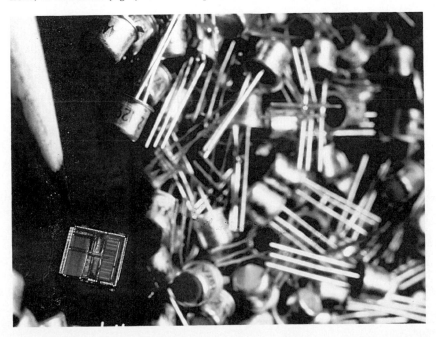

SEMICONDUCTOR DRIVE

This street sign is in Silicon Valley, an area south of San Francisco. As its name indicates, Silicon Valley is noted for silicon chips, also known as semiconductors, and other related computer industries.

DISCUSSION QUESTION
What are the advantages of integrated circuits?

LECTURE HINT
Other advantages of integrated circuits: faster execution, low production of heat.

DISCUSSION QUESTION
What was so revolutionary about the IBM 360 computer system?

hundred small chips, each with a complete circuit so tiny it is half the size of a human fingernail—yet under a microscope it looks as complex as a railroad yard. The making of a chip is examined in more detail in Gallery 1.

The chips were hailed as a generational breakthrough because they had four desirable characteristics:

- **Reliability.** They could be used over and over again without failure. This reliability is due not only to the fact that they have no moving parts but also to the fact that semiconductor firms give them a rigid work/not-work test.

- **Compactness.** Circuitry packed into a small space reduces the equipment size. The machine speed is increased because circuits are closer together, thereby reducing the travel time for the electricity.

- **Low cost.** Mass-production techniques have made possible the manufacture of inexpensive integrated circuits.

- **Low power use.** Miniaturization of integrated circuits has meant that elements can be packed more tightly and that less power is required for computer use than was required in previous generations. In an energy-conscious time, this is important.

The small-is-beautiful revolution moved from the integrated circuits of 1965 to **large-scale integration (LSI)** in 1970. Thousands of integrated circuits were crammed onto a single $\frac{1}{4}$-inch square of silicon.

The beginning of the third generation was trumpeted by the IBM 360 (named for 360 degrees—a full circle of service) series, first announced April 7, 1964. The System/360 family of computers, designed for both business and scientific use, came in several models and sizes. The equipment housing was blue, leading to IBM's nickname, "Big Blue."

The 360 series was launched with an all-out, massive marketing effort to make computers a business tool—to get them into medium-size and smaller business and government operations where they had not been used before. The result went beyond IBM's wildest dreams. The reported $5 billion the company invested in the development of the System/360 quickly repaid itself, and the system rendered many existing computer systems obsolete. Big Blue was on its way.

Software became more sophisticated during this third generation, permitting several programs to run in the same time frame, sharing the computer resources. This approach improved the efficiency of the computer system. Software systems were developed to support interactive processing, which put the user in direct contact with the computer through a terminal. This kind of access caused the customer service industry to flourish, especially in areas such as reservations and credit checks.

Large third-generation computers began to be supplemented by minicomputers, which are functionally equivalent to a full-size system but are somewhat slower, smaller, and less expensive. These computers have become a huge success with medium-size and smaller businesses.

Although the beginning of the third generation can be pinpointed by the introduction of the integrated circuit, actually there was extensive overlapping of the second and third generations. Yet the distinctions between the two seem crystal clear compared with the distinctions between the third and the fourth generations.

7 The Fourth Generation, 1971–Present: The Microprocessor

Through the 1970s computers gained dramatically in speed, reliability, and storage capacity, but entry into the fourth generation was evolutionary rather than revolutionary. The fourth generation was, in fact, an extension of third-generation technology. That is, in the early part of the third generation, specialized chips were developed for computer memory and logic. Thus, all the ingredients were in place for the next technological development, the general-purpose processor-on-a-chip, otherwise known as the **microprocessor** (Figure C-11), which became commercially available in 1971.

Nowhere is the pervasiveness of computer power more apparent than in the explosive use of the microprocessor. In addition to the common applications of digital watches, pocket calculators, and microcomputers, microprocessors can be anticipated in virtually every machine in the home or business—microwave ovens, cars, copy machines, television sets, and so on. In 1975, **very large scale**

DISCUSSION QUESTION
What is the chief characteristic of the 4th generation?

DISCUSSION QUESTION
Where are microprocessors used?

Figure C-11   A microprocessor. It is common to show a microprocessor chip near a dime or a paper clip to illustrate its small size. We have coaxed a bug onto this chip. Yes, that's an ant.

THE COMPUTER MUSEUM

The Computer Museum in downtown Boston, Massachusetts, is the world's first and only museum devoted solely to computers and computing. The museum illustrates how computers have affected all aspects of life: science, business, education, art, and entertainment. Over half an acre of hands-on and historical exhibits chronicle the enormous changes in the size, capability, applications, and cost of computers over the past 40 years. Two mini-theaters show computer classics as well as award-winning computer-animated films.

The Computer Museum Store offers a large selection of such unique items as state-of-the-art silicon chip jewelry and chocolate "chips" as well as books, posters, cassettes, and more.

LECTURE ACTIVITY
Walk students through Gallery 4, "Computers in the Factory: Robots and Beyond," which follows page 512. Robotics and vision systems are highlighted.

integration (VLSI) was achieved. As a result, computers today are 100 times smaller than those of the first generation, and a single chip is far more powerful than ENIAC.

Countries around the world have been active in the computer industry, but few are as renowned for their technology as Japan, which has proceeded in a new direction.

7 The Fifth Generation: Japan's Challenge

An interesting thing happened on the way to the fifth generation: The fourth generation got lost. The industry (and leading books) had long acknowledged the existence of the first, second, and third generations, and was quite definitive about their content. The beginning and end dates for the first and second generations were well established, but the third generation was rarely given an end date, and was said by some to be "continuing." Then Japan made a startling announcement. In 1980, signaling a bold move to take the lead in computer technology, the Japanese revealed a ten-year project to develop a so-called "fifth generation," leaving the industry scrambling to define what the fourth generation was—and is. As you have already read, the fourth generation has been tied primarily to the microprocessor.

The term *fifth generation* was coined by Japan to describe its goal of creating powerful, intelligent computers by the mid-1990s. Since then, however, it has become an umbrella term encompassing many research fields in the computer industry. Key areas of ongoing research are artificial intelligence, expert systems, and natural language. Let us briefly examine these three topics.

Artificial intelligence is a field of study that explores how computers can be used for tasks requiring the human characteristics of intelligence, imagination, and intuition. In other words, we would like to be able to interact with computers in ways that assume that they have a more human and less "machine" nature. To do this, the computer would, at the very least, need to have (1) a knowledge base equivalent to that of the average person and (2) the ability to communicate in natural human language. Both of these are tall orders. An **expert system** is software that allows the computer to be an expert on some particular subject and be available for consulting. Expert systems already exist in disciplines like geology, chemistry, and medicine. **Natural language** refers to an everyday language—in our case, English. Imagine the convenience of being able to communicate with a computer by using plain English. Other elements listed as part of the fifth-generation push are robotics, vision systems (whereby a computer takes actions based on what it "sees"), and even new types of hardware that promise greater computer speed and power.

Japan's original announcement of the fifth generation captivated the computer industry. Some view the fifth generation as a race between Japan and the United States, with nothing less than world computer supremacy as the prize. However, the Japanese budget has been cut significantly in recent years, and enthusiasm over the project has waned somewhat.

7 The Special Story of Microcomputers

Microcomputers are the machines you can "get closest to," whether you are an amateur or a professional. There is nothing quite like having your very own personal computer. Its history is very personal too, full of stories of success and failure and of individuals with whom we can readily identify (Figure C-12).

(a)

APPLE-1
OPERATION
MANUAL

APPLE COMPUTER COMPANY
770 Welch Road
Palo Alto,   Calif. 94304

(b)

(c)

Figure C-12   The making of Apple Computer, Inc. (a) Steve Jobs (left) and Steve Wozniak, cofounders of Apple, examining parts of their home-built Apple I computer. (b) Shown here is a collector's item—the very first manual for operation of an Apple computer. Unfortunately, the early manuals were a hodgepodge of circuit diagrams, software listings, and handwritten notes. They were hard to read and understand and almost guaranteed to frighten away all but the most hardy souls. (c) The Apple II microcomputer became the foundation of the company.

MICROCOMPUTERS IN ACTION

The Microcomputer Entrepreneurs

Ever thought you'd like to run your own show? Make your own product? Be in business for yourself? Entreprenuers are a special breed. They are achievement-oriented, like to take responsibility for decisions, and dislike repetitive, routine work. They also have high levels of energy and a great deal of imagination. But perhaps the key is that they are willing to take risks. Entrepreneurs often have still another quality—a more elusive quality—that is something close to charisma. This charisma is based on enthusiasm, and it allows them to lead people, form an organization, and give it momentum. Study these real-life entrepreneurs, noting their paths to glory and—sometimes—their falls.

Steve Jobs

Of the two Steves who formed Apple Computer, Steve Jobs was the true entrepreneur. Although they both were interested in electronics, Steve Wozniak was the technical genius, and he would have been happy to have been left alone to tinker. But Steve Jobs would not let him alone for a minute—he was always push-ing and crusading. In fact, Wozniak had hooked up with an evangelist, and they made quite a pair.

When Apple was getting off the ground, Jobs wanted Wozniak to quit his job so he could work full-time on the new venture. Wozniak refused. Jobs begged, Jobs cried. Wozniak gave in. While Wozniak built Apple computers, Jobs was out hustling, finding the best marketing man, the best venture capitalist, and the best company president. This entrepreneurial spirit paid off in a spectacular way, as Apple rose to the top of the list of micro-computer companies.

Bill Gates

When Bill Gates was a teenager, he swore off computers for a year and, in his words, "tried to act normal." His parents, who wanted him to be a lawyer, must have been relieved when Bill gave up the computer foolishness and went off to Harvard in 1974. But Bill started spending weekends with his friend Paul Allen, dreaming about microcomputers, which did not exist yet. When the MITS Altair splashed on the market in January 1975, both Bill and Paul moved to Albuquerque to be near the action at MITS. But they showed a desire even then to chart their own course.

7 I Built It in My Garage

As we noted in the beginning of the chapter, the very first microcomputer was the MITS Altair, produced in 1975. But it was a gee-whiz machine, loaded with switches and dials—and no keyboard or screen. It took two teenagers, Steve Jobs and Steve Wozniak, to capture the imagination of the public with the first Apple computer. They built it in that time-honored place of inventors, a garage, using the $1,300 proceeds from the sale of an old Volkswagen. Designed for home use, the Apple was the first to offer an easy-to-use keyboard and screen. The company they founded in 1977 was imme-

Although they wrote software for MITS—and Paul was actually employed there—they kept the rights to their work and formed their own company. Their company was called Microsoft.

When MITS failed, Gates and Allen moved their software company to their native Bellevue, Washington. They employed 32 people in 1980 when IBM came to call. Gates recognized the big league when he saw it and put on a suit for the occasion. Gates was offered a plum: the operating system (a crucial set of software) for IBM's soon-to-be microcomputer. Although he knew he was betting the whole company, Gates never hesitated to take the risk. He and his crew worked feverishly for many months to produce MS-DOS—Microsoft Disk Operating System. It was this product that sent Microsoft on its meteoric rise.

Mitch Kapor

Kapor did not start out on a direct path to computer fame and riches. In fact, he wandered extensively, from disk jockey to piano teacher to counselor. Along the way he picked up and then

abandoned transcendental meditation. He had done some programming, too, but did not like it much. But, around 1978, he found he did like fooling around with microcomputers. In fact, he had found his niche.

In 1983 Kapor introduced a software package called Lotus 1-2-3 and there had never been anything like it before. Lotus added the words *integrated package* to the vocabulary; the phrase described the software's identity as a combination spreadsheet, graphics, and database program. Kapor's product catapulted his company to the top of the list of independent software makers in just two years.

Bill Millard

Bill Millard believed that nothing was impossible. It was his habit, for example, to give employees of his IMSAI company impossible assignments and then exhort them to "make a miracle." IMSAI made one of the early microcomputers. IMSAI employees were inspired and they did work hard, but nobody worked harder than Bill. Sales were phenomenal. The computer, unfortunately, was not. Quality control caught up with Bill and the company eventually failed.

But not Bill. He just struck out in a new direction. He realized that people would buy microcomputers in stores, and he founded the Computerland chain in 1976. His net worth now is in the *billions* and he describes himself as "the biggest winner of all in the microcomputer industry."

Champions of Change

Entrepreneurs thrive on change. Jobs, Wozniak, and Kapor all left their original companies to start new companies. Stay tuned for future breakthroughs from these and other microcomputer entrepreneurs.

diately and wildly successful. When its stock was offered to the public in December 1980, it started a stampede among investors eager to buy in. Apple has introduced an increasingly powerful line of computers, including the Macintosh, which continues to sell well.

The other major player in those early years was Tandy Incorporated, whose worldwide chain of Radio Shack stores provided a handy sales outlet for the TRS-80 microcomputer. Other manufacturers who enjoyed more than moderate success in the late 1970s were Atari and Commodore. Their number was to grow.

Figure C-13   The IBM PC. Launched in 1981, the IBM PC took just 18 months to rise to the top of the best-seller list.

DISCUSSION QUESTION
IBM changed its strategy in what way when it produced the IBM PC? How was this strategy similar to that used by Apple for the Apple II computer? How did Apple change its strategy when it produced the Macintosh computer? (This is the open architecture issue.)

DISCUSSION QUESTION
What is a clone computer?

7 The IBM PC Phenomenon

When IBM announced its first microcomputer in the summer of 1981, Apple placed full-page advertisements in the trade press as follows:

WELCOME, IBM!

SERIOUSLY.

This was a sincere but not entirely altruistic gesture by Apple. Confident about its industry position and head start, Apple felt that IBM's entry into the market would give microcomputers a more serious image, and thus help Apple. Apple's vision was correct, but not complete: IBM captured the top market share in just 18 months, and even more important, became the industry standard (Figure C-13). This was indeed a phenomenal success.

IBM did a lot of things right, such as including the possibility of adding memory, but one key decision made the significant difference: open architecture. That is, IBM provided internal expansion slots, so that peripheral equipment manufacturers could build accessories for the IBM PC. In addition, IBM provided hardware schematics and software listings to companies who wanted to build products in conjunction with the new PC. Many of the new products accelerated demand for the IBM PC.

There is an interesting irony here. Apple pioneered the open architecture concept. IBM had always had closed architecture for its larger machines, but it went to open architecture for the PC. Apple, however, having observed success for both themselves and IBM, then turned around and produced its new Macintosh microcomputer as a *closed* architecture machine! This made it difficult for peripheral manufacturers to design add-ons for the Mac. Heavy advertising and fast scrambling saved the Macintosh, but nothing could save Steve Jobs's job. The closed architecture decision was his, and he—a founding father—was removed from all operational responsibilities in 1985.

Other microcomputer manufacturers have hurried to emulate IBM, producing "PC clones," copycat computers that can run software designed for the IBM PC. Meanwhile, IBM has offered both upscale and downscale versions of its personal computer: PC XT, PC Portable, PC AT, and various models of the PS/2 (Personal System/2). A notable failure, however, was the ill-fated PCjr. Despite a heavy advertising budget and Charlie Chaplin wheeling the PCjr in a baby carriage, IBM could not recover from initial design flaws such as a flimsy keyboard and insufficient memory. This failure left several surprised customers with orphan computers, but it caused hardly a ripple in IBM's financial picture, which continued rosy. Not everyone, however, was so fortunate.

7 The Big Shakeout

The personal computer industry grew to about 150 manufacturers in the early 1980s. What is more, an enormous industry developed around the personal computer: peripheral equipment manufacturers, software producers, computer dealers, and even computer magazines. Despite optimistic predictions, the personal computer industry began to experience a period of slowed growth in 1983. The companies that raised venture capital to jump into the fray now had to scramble to survive in the ensuing competition. Some did not survive.

Least affected is the software industry, because almost 20 million personal computers are already in use. This established customer base continues to hunger for more sophisticated software. You can compare this to the home music industry where, even if sales of tape decks slowed, there would still be customers for more tapes.

There is really nothing very wrong with the personal computer industry. The problem was that too many people tried to partake and the market was not bottomless after all. Competition, as in other businesses, weeded out the weakest. History shows that many industries go through an exuberant expansion phase followed by a shake-out.

The story of microcomputer history is ongoing, with daily fluctuations reflected in the trade press. The effects of microcomputers are far-reaching, and they remain a key topic in the computer industry.

7 Software Comes of Age

It is tempting to talk of computer history in terms of the machines, because the changes have been so dramatic and so visually obvious. But hardware is nothing without software, and software has its own history.

7 The Early Years: 1950–1964

Few people realized the potential of software during its early years. In those days, computers were used as fast, stupid clerks. They performed clerical tasks such as keeping track of payrolls and airplane seats. Some people fantasized about a giant "brain," but most people continued to see computers in clerical roles. Computers belonged only to large organizations that could afford their own programmers to produce software. In addition, each program was unique. There was no software industry.

DISCUSSION QUESTION
What was the Big Shakeout in the computer field?

7 Growing Pains: 1965–1980

Something really new happened in the world of software: interactive systems. These systems showed they could respond to input so fast that they could do better work than humans, even though the work was still clerical. Typical applications were air traffic control and banking. By 1980, interactive software such as word processing was popular on the personal computer.

During this period people began to realize that many programs, such as payroll, could be generic. That is, the same program could be used by many different users. This meant that software could be packaged and sold, leading to a new industry, the software industry.

7 Adolescence: 1981–1995

Software moved into a new era, showing the promise of much more versatility. Software was written to mimic human behavior, acting as keeper of a knowledge base. Rather than being limited only to clerical tasks, software can respond to imprecise, unpredictable, human types of problems, acting the way a human would with a certain set of information. An example is medical diagnosis. This brings us close to the field of artificial intelligence. Notice that the dates for this section slip past the present date, so we have gone beyond history. Let us take one step further into the future.

7 Maturity: 1996 and Beyond

Using computer software, we will be able to do just about anything. We will be able to point to the computer or speak to it and, with minimum effort on our part, give the computer enough data so it can produce the results we want.

7 From the Whole to the Parts

History is still being made in the computer industry, of course, and it is being made incredibly rapidly. A book cannot possibly pretend to describe all the very latest developments. Nevertheless, as we indicated earlier, the four areas of input, processing, output, and storage describe the basic components of a computer system—whatever its date.

/ Summary and Key Terms

- Charles Babbage, a nineteenth-century mathematician, is called "the father of the computer" because of his invention of two computation machines. His **difference engine,** which could solve equations, led to another calculating machine, the **analytical engine,** which embodied the key parts of a computer system—an input device, a processor, a control unit, a storage place, and an output device. Countess Ada Lovelace helped develop instructions for carrying out computations on Babbage's device.

- The first computer to use electrical power instead of mechanical power was Herman Hollerith's tabulating machine, which was used in the 1890 census in the United States. Hollerith founded a company that became the forerunner of International Business Machines Corporation (IBM).

- Thomas J. Watson, Sr., built IBM into a dominant force in the business machines market. He also gave Harvard professor Howard Aiken research funds with which to build an electromechanical computer, the **Mark I,** unveiled in 1944.

- John V. Atanasoff, with assistant Clifford Berry, devised the first digital computer to work by electronic means, the **Atanasoff–Berry Computer (ABC).**

- The **ENIAC (Electronic Numerical Integrator and Calculator),** developed by John Mauchly and J. Presper Eckert at the University of Pennsylvania in 1946, was the world's first general-purpose electronic computer.

- So far, the computer age consists of four generations, primarily attached to four technological developments: the vacuum tube (1951–1958), the transistor (1959–1964), the integrated circuit (1965–1970), and the microprocessor (1971–present).

- The first generation began June 14, 1951, with the delivery of the **UNIVAC (UNIVersal Automatic Computer)** to the U.S. Bureau of the Census. First-generation computers required thousands of **vacuum tubes,** electronic tubes about the size of light bulbs. First-generation computers had slow input/output, were programmed only in machine language, and were unreliable. The main form of memory was **magnetic core.** Magnetic tape was introduced in 1957 to store data compactly.

- Second-generation computers used **transistors,** developed at Bell Laboratories. Compared to vacuum tubes, transistors were small, needed no warm-up, consumed less energy, and were faster and more reliable. During the second generation, **assembly languages,** or **symbolic languages,** were developed. They used abbreviations for instructions, rather than numbers. Later, **higher-level languages,** such as **FORTRAN** and **COBOL,** which are more English-like than machine language, were also developed. In 1962 the first removable disk pack was marketed.

- The third generation emerged with the introduction of the **integrated circuit, (IC)**—a complete electronic circuit on a small chip of silicon. Silicon is a **semiconductor,** a substance that will conduct electric current when it has been "doped" with chemical impurities. A cylinder of silicon is sliced into wafers, which are then etched with a pattern of electrical circuitry and cut up into several hundred individual chips. The integrated circuits of 1965 progressed in 1970 to **large-scale integration (LSI),** with thousands of ICs on a single chip.

- With the third generation IBM announced the System/360 family of computers, comprising several models and sizes. The system was accepted overwhelmingly in large- and medium-size business and government operations. During this period more sophisticated software was introduced that allowed several programs to run in the same time frame and supported interactive processing, in which the user has direct contact with the computer through a terminal.

- The fourth-generation **microprocessor**—a general-purpose processor-on-a-chip—grew out of the specialized memory and logic chips of the third generation. In 1975 **very large scale integration (VLSI)** was achieved. Microprocessors led to the development of microcomputers, expanding computer markets to smaller businesses and to personal use.

- In 1980 the Japanese announced a ten-year project to develop a fifth generation, radically new forms of computer systems involving artificial intelligence, expert systems, and natural language. **Artificial intelligence** is a field of study that explores computer involvement in tasks requiring intelligence, imagination, and intuition. The development of **expert systems** (software allowing computers to be experts on particular subjects) would enable computers to serve as consultants. Research on computer use of **natural language** (everyday human language) would lead to easier interaction between people and computer systems.

■ The first microcomputer, the MITS Altair, was produced in 1975. However, the first successful computer to include an easy-to-use keyboard and screen was offered by Apple computer, founded by Steve Jobs and Steve Wozniak in 1977. Soon other companies, such as Tandy Incorporated and Commodore, entered the microcomputer market. IBM entered the microcomputer market in 1981 and captured the top market share in just 18 months.

■ From 1950 to 1964 software was used mainly by large organizations to enable computers to perform clerical tasks. The period from 1965 to 1980 saw the development of interactive software, which enabled computers to respond to input data more efficiently than people could. Generic software, programs that could be used by different user organizations, led to the development of the software industry. Since 1981, software applications have continued to increase, with promise of even greater versatility in the future.

Review Questions

1. Explain the contributions of the following people to the development of computers in the pre-electronic era: Charles Babbage, Ada Lovelace, Herman Hollerith, Thomas J. Watson, Sr.

2. Explain the contributions of: Howard Aiken, John V. Atanasoff and Clifford Berry, John Mauchly and J. Presper Eckert.

3. Explain the significance of the following computers: Mark I, ABC, ENIAC, UNIVAC.

4. Name and define the main technological development associated with the first generation of computers.

5. Name at least three disadvantages of the first-generation computers.

6. What was the memory medium in first-generation computers? What replaced this storage medium and why?

7. What main technological development is associated with the second generation of computers? How did this development revolutionize computers?

8. Explain how machine language, assembly language, and higher-level language differ.

9. Name and define the main technological development associated with the third generation of computers.

10. What are the four desirable characteristics of integrated circuits?

11. What do LSI and VLSI mean in relation to a silicon chip?

12. Name and define the main technological development associated with the fourth generation of computers.

13. Name and describe three areas of research associated with the fifth generation.

14. Describe the history of the microcomputer industry.

15. Describe the four stages in the history of software.

Discussion Questions

1. How would our world be different if the computer age had never begun? Give specific examples.

2. How do you feel about the possibility of computers that can "think" and speak? Explain.

3. What do you think will be the future of the personal computer industry? Explain.

Glossary

Access arm   A mechanical device that can access all the tracks of one cylinder in a disk storage unit.

Accumulator   A register that collects the results of computations.

Acoustic coupler   A modem that connects to a telephone receiver rather than directly to a telephone line.

Active cell   The cell available for current use on a spreadsheet. Also called the current cell.

Ada   A structured programming language, named for Countess Ada Lovelace, that encourages modular program design.

Address   A number used to designate a location in memory.

Address register   Locates where instructions and data are stored in memory.

ALGOL (ALGOrithmic Language)   A language, developed primarily for scientific programming, that has limited file-processing capabilities.

ALU   Arithmetic logic unit.

Amplitude   The height of the carrier wave in analog transmission; it indicates the strength of the signal.

Amplitude modulation   A change of the amplitude of the carrier wave in analog data transmission to represent either the 0 bit or the 1 bit.

Analog transmission   The transmission of computer data as a continuous electric signal in the form of a wave.

Analytical engine   A mechanical device of cogs and wheels, designed by Charles Babbage, that embodied the key characteristics of modern computers.

Analytical graphics   Traditional line graphs, bar charts, and pie charts used to illustrate and analyze data.

ANS-COBOL   A version of COBOL standardized in 1974 by the American National Standards Institute (ANSI).

ANSI   American National Standards Institute.

APL (A Programming Language)   A powerful, interactive, easily learned language introduced by IBM.

Applications software   Programs designed to perform specific tasks and functions.

Arithmetic/logic unit (ALU)   The electronic circuitry in a computer that executes all arithmetic and logical operations.

Arithmetic operations   Mathematical calculations performed on data by the ALU.

Artificial intelligence   The field of study that explores computer involvement in tasks requiring intelligence, imagination, and intuition.

ASCII (American Standard Code for Information Interchange)   A coding scheme using 7-bit characters to represent data characters.

Assembler program   A translator program used to convert assembly language programs to machine language.

Assembly language   A second-generation language that uses abbreviations for instructions. Also called symbolic language.

Assistant menu   The first menu that appears when accessing dBASE.

Asynchronous transmission   Data transmission in which each group of message bits is preceded by a start signal and ended with a stop signal.

Atanasoff–Berry Computer (ABC)   The first electronic digital computer, designed by John V. Atanasoff and Clifford Berry in the late 1930s.

ATM   Automated teller machine.

Attribute   Column of a relation in a relational database. Also called a field.

Audio-response unit   A device that converts data in main storage to vocalized sounds understandable to humans. Also called a voice synthesizer or a voice output device.

Audit trail   A method of tracing data from the output back to the source documents.

Auto-answer   Automatic answering by a modem of incoming calls from another modem.

Auto-dial   Automatic calling of one modem by another modem.

Auto-disconnect   Automatic disconnecting by one modem when it receives a disconnect message or when the other party hangs up.

Automated teller machine (ATM)   Input/output device connected to a computer used by bank customers for financial transactions.

Automatic redial   Automatic redialing by a modem when it receives a busy signal.

Automatic reformatting   In word processing, automatic adjustment of text to accommodate changes.

Auxiliary storage   Storage, often disk, for data and programs that is separate from the CPU and memory. Also called secondary storage.

Axis   A reference line of a graph. The horizontal axis is the x-axis. The vertical axis is the y-axis.

Background   In large computers, the memory area for programs with low priorities.

Backup system   A way of protecting data by copying it and storing it in more than one place.

Band printer   An impact printer using a horizontally rotating band containing characters that are struck by hammers through paper and ribbon.

Bar code reader   A stationary photoelectric scanner that reads bar codes by means of reflected light.

Bar codes   Standardized patterns (Universal Product Code) of vertical marks that identify products.

Bar graph   A graph made up of filled-in columns or rows that represent the change of data over time.

BASIC (Beginners' All-purpose Symbolic Instruction Code)   A high-level programming language that is easy to learn and use.

Batch processing   A data processing technique in which transactions are collected into groups, or batches, for processing.

BBS   Bulletin board system.

Binary system   A system in which data is represented by combinations of 0s and 1s, which correspond to the two states off and on.

Biometrics   The science of measuring individual body characteristics; used in some security systems.

Bit   A binary digit.

Bit-mapped display   See *Dot-addressable display*.

Block   A collection of logical records. Also called a physical record.

Block copy command   The command used to copy a block of text into a new location.

Block delete command   The command used to erase a block of text.

Blocking   The process of grouping logical records into one physical record, or block.

Block move command   The command used to remove a block of text from one location in a document and place it elsewhere.

Blocking factor   The number of logical records in one physical record.

Boldface   Printed characters in darker type than the surrounding characters.

Booting   Loading the operating system into memory.

bpi   Bytes per inch.

Branch   In a flowchart, the connection leading from the decision box to one of two possible responses. Also called a path.

Bridge   A device that connects networks of the same type, allowing equipment on one LAN to communicate with devices on another. Also called a router.

Bulletin board system (BBS)   Telephone-linked personal computers that provide public-access message systems.

Bursting   The separation of continuous-form computer paper into individual sheets.

Bus lines   Collections of wires connecting the parts of a computer.

Business graphics   Graphics that represent data in a visual, easy-to-understand format.

Business-quality graphics program   Program that allows a user to create professional-looking business graphics. Also called a presentation graphics program.

Bus network   A network that assigns a portion of network management to each computer but preserves the system if one component fails.

Byte   Strings of bits (usually 8) used to represent one data character—a letter, digit, or special character.

Bytes per inch (bpi)   An expression of the amount (density) of data stored on magnetic tape.

C   A sophisticated programming language invented by Bell Labs in 1974.

Cable interface unit   Electronic components in a box outside a computer; it sends and receives signals on the network cable.

CAD/CAM   Computer-aided design/computer-aided manufacturing.

Camera-ready   In publishing, final copy that is photographed to create printing plates.

Candidates   Alternative plans offered in the preliminary design phase of a project.

Carrier wave   An analog signal used in the transmission of electric signals.

Carterfone decision   The Federal Communications Commission decision allowing competitors in the formerly regulated domain of AT&T.

CASE   Computer-aided software engineering.

Cathode ray tube (CRT)   The most common type of computer screen.

CCITT   Consultative Committee on International Telegraphy and Telephony.

CD-ROM   Compact disk read-only memory.

Cell   The intersection of a row and a column in a spreadsheet. Entries in a spreadsheet are stored in individual cells.

Cell address   In a spreadsheet, the column and row coordinates of a cell.

Cell contents   The label, value, formula, or function contained in a spreadsheet cell.

Centering Word processing feature that places a line of text midway between the left and right margins.

Centralized computer system System that does all processing at one location.

Centralized data processing Keeping hardware, software, storage, and computer access in one location.

Central processing unit (CPU) Electronic circuitry that executes stored program instructions. It consists of two parts: the control unit and the arithmetic/logic unit.

Chain printer An impact printer consisting of characters on a chain that rotate past all print positions.

Change agent The role of the systems analyst in overcoming resistance to change within an organization.

Channel On magnetic tape, a row of bits that runs the length of the tape. Also called a track.

Character A letter, number, or special character (such as $).

Character printer Impact printer, similar to a typewriter, that prints character by character.

Characters per inch (cpi) An expression of the amount (density) of data stored on magnetic tape.

Check bit A bit added to each byte to alert the computer to an error in data transmission. Also called a parity bit.

Chief Information Officer (CIO) Manager of an MIS department.

Classify To categorize data according to characteristics that make it useful.

Client An individual or organization contracting for systems analysis.

Clip art Illustrations stored on disk that are used to enhance a graph or document.

Clock A component of the CPU that produces pulses at a fixed rate to synchronize all computer operations.

Clone A personal computer that closely imitates the operation and architecture of the IBM Personal Computer.

Closed architecture Personal computer design that limits add-ons to those that can be plugged into the back of the machine.

Clustered-bar graph Bar graph comparing several different but related sets of data.

Coaxial cable Bundles of insulated wires within a shielded enclosure that can be laid underground or undersea.

COBOL (COmmon Business-Oriented Language) An English-like programming language used primarily for business applications.

CODASYL (COnference of DAta SYstem Languages) The organization of government and industrial representatives that introduced COBOL.

Cohesion A measure of the inner strength of a program module.

Cold site An environmentally suitable empty shell in which a company can install its own computer system.

Collision The problem that occurs when two records have the same disk address.

COM Computer output microfilm.

Command A name that invokes the correct program or program segment.

Command menu The list of commands in an applications software program such as Lotus 1-2-3.

COMMAND mode One of two options for entering commands in dBASE; commands are typed in at the dot prompt.

Command tree A hierarchical diagram that shows all the choices from a main command menu and the associated submenus.

Common carrier An organization approved by the FCC to offer communications services to the public.

Communicating The continuous feedback from the systems analyst to the client organization by way of oral presentations and written documentation.

Compact disk read-only memory (CD-ROM) Optical data storage technology using disk formats identical to audio compact disks.

Compare operation An operation in which the computer compares two data items and performs alternative operations based on the comparison.

Compatible Personal computer that can run software designed for the IBM Personal Computer.

Compiler A translator that converts the symbolic statements of a high-level language into computer-executable machine language.

CompuServe A major information utility that offers program packages, text editors, encyclopedia references, games, and a software exchange, as well as services such as banking, travel reservations, and legal advice.

Computer A machine that accepts data (input) and processes it into useful information (output).

Computer-aided design/computer-aided manufacturing (CAD/CAM) The use of computers to create two- and three-dimensional pictures of manufactured products.

Computer-aided software engineering (CASE) Software that provides an automated means of designing systems.

Computer anxiety Fear of computers.

Computer conferencing A method of sending, receiving, and storing typed messages within a network of users.

Computer doctor Jargon for a computer repairperson.

Computer Fraud and Abuse Act A law passed by Congress in 1984 to fight computer crime.

Computer literacy Awareness, knowledge of, and interaction with computers.

Computer mart Large building designed to house dozens of high-tech vendors.

Computer operator A person who monitors the console screen, reviews procedures, and keeps peripheral equipment running.

Computer output microfilm (COM) Computer output produced as very small images on sheets or rolls of film.

Computer phobia See *Computer anxiety.*

Computer programmer A person who designs, writes, tests, and implements programs.

Computer system A system that has a computer as one of its components.

Computing Performing arithmetic operations.

Computing Services A department that manages computer resources for an organization. Also called Information Services or Management Information Systems.

Conditional replace A word processing function that asks the user whether to replace copy each time the program finds a particular item.

Connector A symbol used in flowcharting to connect paths.

Console The front panel of a computer system; it alerts the operator when something needs to be done.

Consortium A joint venture to support a complete computer facility to be used in an emergency.

Consultative Committee on International Telegraphy and Telephony (CCITT) An agency of the United Nations; it is involved in development of communications standards.

Context sensitivity Software feature that allows a user to access information about the application or command the user is currently using.

Continuous form paper Sheets of paper attached end-to-end to form a continuous folded sheet, with sprocket holes along the sides that help feed the paper evenly through the printer.

Continuous word system A speech recognition system that can understand sustained speech, so users can speak normally.

Controlling Monitoring the organization's progress toward reaching its goals.

Control panel The upper portion of a spreadsheet screen; it consists of status, entry, and prompt lines.

Control structure Pattern for controlling the flow of logic in a program. The three basic control structures are sequence, selection, and iteration.

Control unit The circuitry that directs and coordinates the entire computer system in executing stored program instructions.

Coordinating Orchestrating the process of analyzing and planning a new system by pulling together the various individuals, schedules, and tasks that contribute to the analysis.

Copy protection A software or hardware block that makes it difficult or impossible to make unauthorized copies of software.

Copyrighted software Software that costs money and must not be copied without permission from the manufacturer.

Coupling A measure of the strength of the relationship between program modules.

cpi Characters per inch.

CPU Central processing unit.

CRT Cathode ray tube.

Current cell The cell currently available for use on a spreadsheet. Also called the active cell.

Current drive The disk drive currently being used by the computer system. Also called the default drive.

Cursor A flashing indicator on the screen; it indicates where the next character will be inserted. Also called a pointer.

Cursor movement keys Keys on the computer keyboard that allow the user to move the cursor on the screen.

Cyberphobia See *Computer anxiety.*

Cylinder A set of tracks on a magnetic disk that can be accessed by one positioning of the access arm.

Cylinder method A method of organizing data on a magnetic disk. Data organization is vertical, which minimizes seek time.

Daisy-wheel printer A letter-quality character printer that has a removable wheel with a set of spokes, each containing a raised character.

DASD Direct-access storage device.

Data Raw material to be processed by a computer.

Database A collection of interrelated files stored together with minimum redundancy.

Database management system (DBMS) A set of programs that create, manage, protect, and provide access to the database.

Data buses See *Bus lines.*

Data collection device A device that allows direct data entry in such places as factories and warehouses.

Data communications The process of exchanging data over communications facilities.

Data communications systems Computer systems that transmit data over communications lines, such as public telephone lines or private network cables.

Data Encryption Standard (DES) The standardized public key by which senders and receivers can scramble and unscramble their messages.

Data entry operator A person who prepares data for computer processing.

Data flow diagram (DFD) A diagram that shows the flow of data through an organization.

Data item Data in a relational database table.

Data transfer The transfer of data between memory and secondary storage.

Data point A single value represented by a bar or symbol in a graph.

Date field A field used for dates and automatically limited to eight characters, including slashes used to separate the month, day, and year.

DBMS Database management system.

Deadlock The condition in which each of two programs needs resources held captive by the other, and neither is willing to release the resource it is holding until it gets the one the other is holding.

DDP Distributed data processing.

Debugging The process of detecting, locating, and correcting mistakes in a program.

Decentralized computer system System in which the computer and some storage devices are in one location, but the devices that access the computer are elsewhere.

Decision box The standard diamond-shaped box used in flowcharting to indicate a decision.

Decision logic table A standard table of the logical decisions that must be made regarding potential conditions in a given system. Also called a decision table.

Decision support system (DSS) A computer system that supports managers in nonroutine decision-making tasks.

Decision table A standard table of the logical decisions that must be made regarding potential conditions in a given system. Also called a decision logic table.

Decollating The process of removing carbon paper from between the layered copies of multiple-copy computer paper.

Default drive The disk drive to which commands refer in the absence of any specified drive. Unless instructed otherwise, an applications program stores files on the memory device in the default drive.

Default settings Settings automatically used by a program unless the user specifies otherwise.

Demodulation Reconstruction of the original digital message after analog transmission.

Density The amount of data stored on magnetic tape expressed in number of characters per inch (cpi) or bytes per inch (bpi).

Dependent variable Output of a model, so called because it depends on the inputs.

DES Data Encryption Standard.

Desk-checking A programming phase in which the logic of the program is mentally checked, to ensure that it is error-free and workable.

Desktop publishing Use of a personal computer, special software, and a laser printer to produce very high-quality documents that combine text and graphics. Also called electronic publishing.

Desktop publishing program Software package for designing and producing professional-looking documents. Also called a page composition program or a page makeup program.

Desktop publishing template Already prepared page layouts stored on disk.

Detail design A systems design subphase in which the system is planned in detail.

Detail report A report that provides complete, specific information on routine operations.

DFD Data flow diagram.

Diagnostic message A message that informs the user of programming language syntax errors.

Diagnostics Error messages provided by the compiler as it translates a program.

Difference engine A machine designed by Charles Babbage to solve polynomial equations by calculating the successive differences between them.

Digital transmission The transmission of data as distinct pulses.

Digitizer A graphics input device that converts images into digital data that the computer can accept.

Digitizing tablet A graphics input device that allows the user to create images. It has a special stylus that can be used to draw or trace images, which are then converted to digital data that can be processed by the computer.

Direct access Immediate access to a record on secondary storage, usually disk. Also called random access.

Direct-access storage device (DASD) A storage device in which a record can be accessed directly.

Direct-connect modem A modem connected directly to the telephone line.

Direct conversion A system conversion in which the user simply stops using the old system and starts using the new one.

Direct file organization Organization of records so each is individually accessible.

Direct file processing Processing that allows the user to access a record directly by using a record key.

Directing Guiding employees to perform their work in a way that supports the organization's goals.

Disaster recovery plan   A method of restoring data processing operations if those operations are halted by major damage or destruction.

Discrete word system   A speech recognition system limited to understanding isolated words.

Disk drive   A device that allows data to be read from a disk and written on a disk.

Diskette   A single magnetic disk on which data is recorded as magnetic spots. Available in both 5¼-inch format and 3½-inch format.

Disk pack   A stack of magnetic disks assembled together.

Displayed value   The calculated result of a formula or function in a spreadsheet cell. The number in a cell displayed according to a user-specified format.

Distributed data processing (DDP)   A data processing system in which processing is decentralized, with the computers and storage devices in dispersed locations.

Documentation   A detailed written description of the programming cycle and specific facts about the program. Also refers to the instruction manual for packaged software.

Dot-addressable display   A graphics display screen that is divided into dots, each of which can be illuminated individually.

Dot-matrix printer   A printer that constructs a character by activating a matrix of pins to produce the shape of a character on paper.

Dot prompt   In dBASE, the prompt that tells the user that the program is ready for a command.

Download   The transfer of data from a mainframe or large computer to a smaller computer.

Drum plotter   A graphics output device in which paper is rolled on a drum with a computer-controlled pen poised over it.

Drum printer   A printer consisting of a cylinder with embossed rows of characters on its surface. Each print position has a complete set of characters around the circumference of the drum.

DSS   Decision support system.

Dumb terminal   A terminal that does not process data. It is merely a means of entering data into a computer and receiving output from it.

Duty cycle   The number of pages printed by a printer each month. The higher the duty cycle, the more rugged the printer.

EBCDIC   (Extended Binary Coded Decimal Interchange Code) Established by IBM and used in IBM mainframe computers.

EFT   Electronic fund transfer.

Electronic disk   A chip that lets the computer regard part of its memory as a third disk drive. Also called a RAM disk or phantom disk.

Electronic fund transfer (EFT)   Payment for goods and services using funds transferred from accounts electronically.

Electronic mail (e-mail)   The process of sending messages directly from one terminal or computer to another. The messages may be sent and stored for later retrieval.

Electronic publishing   Use of a personal computer, special software, and a laser printer to produce very high-quality documents that combine text and graphics. Also called desktop publishing.

Electronic spreadsheet   An electronic worksheet used to organize data into rows and columns for analysis.

Encryption   The process of encoding communications data.

End of file   The point in a program or module where all files have been read.

End-user   Person who buys and uses computer software or who has contact with computers.

End-user revolution   Trend of computer users becoming more knowledgeable about computers and less reliant on computer professionals.

ENIAC   (Electronic Numerical Integrator And Computer) The first general-purpose electronic computer, which was built by Dr. John Mauchly and J. Presper Eckert, Jr., and was first operational in 1946.

ENTRY mode   Spreadsheet mode that lets the user enter data.

Entry point   The point in a module where control is transferred. Each module has only one entry point.

Equal to (=) condition   A logical operation in which the computer compares two numbers to determine equality.

Erasable optical disk   An optical disk on which data can be stored, moved, changed, and erased, just as on magnetic media.

Erase head   The head in a magnetic tape unit that erases any previously recorded data on the tape.

Ergonomics   The study of human factors related to computers.

E-mail   Electronic mail.

Ethernet   A popular local area network; this system accesses the network by listening for a free carrier signal.

E-time   The execution portion of the machine cycle.

Event-driven   Refers to multiprogramming; programs share resources based on events that take place in the programs.

Exception report   A report that shows only data reflecting unusual circumstances.

Exit point   The point in a module from which control is transferred. Each module has only one exit point.

Expansion slots The slots inside a computer that allow a user to insert additional circuit boards.

Expert shell Software having the basic structure to find answers to questions; the questions themselves can be added by the user.

Expert system A software package that presents the computer as an expert on some topic.

Exploded pie chart A pie chart with a "slice" that is separated from the rest of the chart.

External direct-connect modem A modem that is separate from the computer, allowing it to be used with a variety of computers.

External DOS commands Commands that access DOS programs residing on the DOS disk as program files. The programs must be read from the disk before they can be executed. These program files are not automatically loaded into the computer when it is booted. See *internal DOS commands.*

Facsimile technology (fax) The use of computer technology to send digitized graphics, charts, and text from one facsimile machine to another.

Fair Credit Reporting Act Legislation passed in 1970 allowing individuals access to and the right to challenge credit records.

Fax board A circuit board that fits inside a personal computer and allows the user to transmit computer-generated text and graphics without interrupting other applications programs.

FCC Federal Communications Commission.

Feasibility study The first phase of systems analysis, in which it is determined if and how a project should proceed. Also called a system survey or a preliminary investigation.

Federal Communications Commission (FCC) The federal agency that regulates communications facilities.

Federal Privacy Act Legislation passed in 1974 stipulating that no secret personal files can be kept by government agencies and that individuals can have access to all information concerning them stored in government files.

Fiber optics Technology that uses light instead of electricity to send data.

Field A set of related characters. In a database, also called an attribute.

Field name In a database, the unique name describing the data in a field.

Field type A category describing a field, determined by the kind of data the field will accept. Common field types are character, numeric, date, and logical.

Field width In a database, the maximum number of characters that can be contained in a field.

File A repository of data or a collection of related records. In word processing, a document created on a computer.

File command A command selection on the main menu of Lotus 1-2-3 that allows file manipulation: saving, retrieving, and erasing.

Fifth generation A term coined by the Japanese referring to new forms of computer systems involving artificial intelligence, natural language, and expert systems.

File transfer software Data communications software that lets the user transfer files between connected computers.

Firmware Read-only memory used to store programs that will not be altered.

Flatbed plotter A graphics output device that resembles a table with a sheet of paper on it and a mechanical pen suspended over it. The pen moves around on the paper under control of the computer program.

Floppy disk A flexible magnetic diskette on which data is recorded as magnetic spots.

Flowchart The pictorial representation of an orderly step-by-step solution to a problem.

Font A complete set of characters in a particular size, typeface, weight, and style.

Font library A variety of type fonts stored on disk.

Foreground An area in memory for programs that have a high priority.

Format The specifications that determine the way a document or worksheet is displayed on the screen or printer.

Form letter program A program that can be designed to send out "personalized" letters that look like letters produced on a typewriter.

Formula In a spreadsheet, an instruction to calculate a value.

FORTH A language released by Charles Moore in 1975 that was designed for real-time control tasks, as well as business and graphics applications.

FORTRAN (FORmula TRANslator) The first high-level language, introduced in 1954 by IBM; it is scientifically oriented.

Fourth-generation language A nonprocedural language. Also called a 4GL or a very high-level language.

Freedom of Information Act Legislation passed in 1970 that allows citizens access to personal data gathered by federal agencies.

Frequency The number of times an analog signal repeats during a specific time interval.

Frequency modulation The alteration of the carrier wave frequency to represent 0s and 1s.

Front-end processor A communications control unit

designed to relieve the central computer of some communications tasks.

Full-duplex transmission   Data transmission in both directions at once.

Function   A built-in spreadsheet formula.

Function keys   Special keys programmed to execute commonly-used commands.

Gallium arsenide   Material used as a substitute for silicon in chip making.

Gantt chart   A bar chart commonly used to depict schedule deadlines and milestones.

Gateway   Device that connects two dissimilar networks, allowing machines in one network to communicate with those in the other.

GB   Gigabyte.

General-purpose register   A register used for several functions, such as arithmetic and addressing purposes.

Generic operating system   An operating system that works with different computer systems.

Gigabyte (GB)   One billion bytes.

GIGO   Garbage in, garbage out: The quality of the output is directly dependent on the quality of the input.

GoTo function key   In a spreadsheet, used to get to another cell. Also called the Jump-To function key.

Grammar and style program   A word processing program that identifies unnecessary words and wordy phrases in a document.

Graphics   Pictures or graphs.

Graphics adapter board   A circuit board that enables an IBM Personal Computer to display pictures or graphs as well as text.

Graphics card   See *Graphics adapter board*.

Greater than (>) condition   A comparison operation that determines if one value is greater than another.

Green-bar paper   Computer paper with green bands.

Hacker   A person who gains access to computer systems illegally, usually from a personal computer.

Half-duplex transmission   Data transmission in either direction, but only one way at a time.

Halftone   Reproduction of a black-and-white photograph; it is made up of tiny dots.

Hardcard   20 or 40 megabytes of hard disk on a board that fits into an expansion slot inside a personal computer.

Hard copy   Printed paper output.

Hard disk   Inflexible disk, usually in a pack, often in a sealed module.

Hard magnetic disk   A metal platter coated with magnetic oxide and used for magnetic disk storage.

Hard-sectored disk   A disk with a hole in front of each sector, near the center of the disk.

Hardware   The computer and its associated equipment.

Hashing   The process of applying a formula to a record key to yield a number that represents a disk address. Also called randomizing.

Head switching   Activation of a particular read/write head over a particular track.

Help index   On-screen reference material providing assistance with the program.

Help key   Key that, when pressed, activates the HELP mode.

Hierarchy chart   See *Structure chart*.

High-level languages   English-like programming languages that are easier to use than older symbolic languages.

Home controls   Personal computer–controlled devices that receive their instructions over existing household wiring and perform some household tasks.

Host computer   The central computer in a network.

Hot site   A fully equipped computer center with hardware, communications facilities, environmental controls, and security, for use in an emergency.

Hybrid   A computer with its own unique design that will also simulate that of another computer manufacturer, notably IBM.

IBG   Interblock gap.

Icon   A small picture on a computer screen; it represents a computer activity.

Impact printer   A printer that forms characters by physically striking the paper.

Implementation   The phase of systems analysis that includes training, equipment conversion, file conversion, system conversion, auditing, evaluation, and maintenance.

Independent variable   Input to a model, so called because it can change.

Indexed file organization   Combination of sequential and direct file organization.

Indexed file processing   A method of file organization representing a compromise between sequential and direct methods.

Indexed processing   See *Indexed file processing*.

Information   Processed data; data that is organized, meaningful, and useful.

Information center   A company unit that offers employees computer and software training, help in getting data from other computer systems, and technical assistance.

Information Services   A department that manages computer resources for an organization. Also called

Computing Services or Management Information Systems.

Information utilities Commercial consumer-oriented communications systems, such as The Source and CompuServe.

Initializing Setting the starting values of certain storage locations before running a program.

Ink-jet printer A printer that sprays ink from jet nozzles onto the paper.

Input Raw data that is put in to the computer system for processing.

Input device A device that puts data in machine-readable form and sends it to the processing unit.

Inquire To ask questions about data in a mainframe computer through a computer terminal.

Inquiry A request for information.

Insert mode In word processing, a text input mode in which text is inserted at the current cursor position without overwriting any text already in the document.

Integrated circuit A complete electronic circuit on a small chip of silicon.

Integrated package A set of software that typically includes related word processing, spreadsheet, database, and graphics programs.

Intelligent terminal A terminal that can be programmed to perform a variety of processing tasks.

Interactive Data processing in which the user communicates directly with the computer, maintaining a dialogue.

Interblock gap (IBG) The blank space on magnetic tape that separates records. Also called an interrecord gap.

Internal DOS commands Commands that access DOS programs that are loaded into the computer when the system is booted.

Internal font Font built into the read-only memory of a printer.

Internal modem A modem on a circuit board that can be installed in a computer by the user.

Internal storage The electronic circuitry that temporarily holds data and program instructions needed by the CPU. Also called memory, main memory, primary memory, primary storage, and main storage.

Interpreter A program that translates and executes high-level languages one instruction at a time.

Interrecord gap (IRG) The blank space on magnetic tape that separates records. Also called an interblock gap.

Interrupt Condition that causes normal program processing to be suspended temporarily.

Interview The data gathering operation in systems analysis.

IRG Interrecord gap.

Iteration Repetition of program instructions under certain conditions. Also called a loop.

Iteration control structure A looping mechanism.

I-time The instruction portion of the machine cycle.

Joy stick A graphics input device that allows fingertip control of figures on a CRT screen.

Jump-To function key Used to get to a distant part of a file. Also called the GoTo function key.

Justification Aligning text along left and/or right margins.

KB Kilobyte.

Kerning Adjusting the space between characters to create wider or tighter spacing.

Key Unique identifier for a record.

Keyboard A common input device similar to the keyboard of a typewriter.

Kilobyte (KB) 1024 bytes.

Knowledge-based system A collection of information stored in a computer accessed by natural language.

Label In a spreadsheet, data consisting of a string of text characters.

LAN Local area network.

Laptop computer A small portable computer that can weigh less than 10 pounds.

Large-scale integration (LSI) A chip containing a large number of integrated circuits.

Laser printer A printer that uses a light beam to transfer images to paper.

LCD Liquid crystal display.

Leading The vertical spacing between lines of type.

Leading decision The loop-ending decision that occurs at the beginning of a DOWHILE loop.

Leased line A communications line dedicated to one customer. Also called a private line.

Legend Text beneath a graph; it explains the colors, shading, or symbols used to label the data points.

Less than (<) condition A logical operation in which the computer compares values to determine if one is less than another.

Letter-quality printing High-quality output produced by some printers, such as the daisy wheel.

Librarian A person who catalogs processed disks and tapes and keeps them secure.

Light pen A graphics input device that allows the user to interact directly with the computer screen.

Line graph Graph made by connecting data points with a line.

Line printer   A printer that assembles all characters on a line at one time and prints them out practically simultaneously.

Link   Physical data communications medium.

Link/load phase   The phase during which prewritten programs may be added to the object module by means of a link/loader.

Liquid crystal display (LCD)   The flat display screen found on some laptop computers.

LISP (LISt Processing)   A language designed to process nonnumeric data; popular for writing artificial-intelligence programs.

Load module   Output from the link/load step.

Local area network (LAN)   A network designed to share data and resources among several computers.

Logical field   A field used to keep track of true and false conditions.

Logical operations   Comparing operations. The ALU is able to compare numbers, letters, or special characters and take alternative courses of action.

Logical record   A record written by an applications program.

Logic chip   A general-purpose processor on a chip, developed in 1969 by an Intel Corporation design team headed by Ted Hoff. Also called a microprocessor.

Logic error   Logic flaw in a program.

Logic flowchart   A flowchart that represents the flow of logic in a program.

Logo   A language developed at MIT by Seymour Papert that features commands that move a "turtle" on the CRT screen.

Loop   Repetition of program instructions under certain conditions. Also called iteration.

LSI   Large-scale integration.

Machine cycle   Combination of I-time and E-time.

Machine language   The lowest level of language; it represents information as 1s and 0s.

Magnetic core   Flat doughnut-shaped metal used as an early memory device.

Magnetic disk   An oxide-coated disk on which data is recorded as magnetic spots.

Magnetic-ink character recognition   A method of machine-reading characters made of magnetized particles.

Magnetic tape   A magnetic medium with an iron oxide coating that can be magnetized. Data is stored on the tape as extremely small magnetized spots.

Magnetic tape unit   A data storage unit used to record data on and retrieve data from magnetic tape.

Mainframe   A large computer that has access to billions of characters of data and is capable of processing data very quickly.

Main memory   The electronic circuitry that temporarily holds data and program instructions needed by the CPU. Also called memory, primary memory, primary storage, main storage, and internal storage.

Main storage   The electronic circuitry that temporarily holds data and program instructions needed by the CPU. Also called memory, main memory, primary memory, primary storage, and internal storage.

Management Information System (MIS)   A set of formal business systems designed to provide information for an organization.

Mark   The process of defining a block of text before performing block commands.

Mark I   Early computer built in 1944 by Harvard professor Howard Aiken.

Master file   A semipermanent set of records.

MB   Megabyte.

Megabyte (MB)   One million bytes.

Memory   The electronic circuitry that temporarily holds data and program instructions needed by the CPU. Also called main memory, primary memory, primary storage, main storage, and internal storage.

Memory management   The process of allocating memory and keeping the programs in memory separate from one another.

Memory protection   The process of keeping a program from straying into other programs and vice versa.

Menu   An on-screen list of command choices.

MENU mode   Spreadsheet mode that allows the user access to command menus.

MICR   Magnetic-ink character recognition.

MICR inscriber   A device that adds magnetic characters to a document.

Microcode   Permanent instructions inside the control unit that are executed directly by the machine's electronic circuits.

Microcomputer   The smallest and least expensive class of computer.

Microcomputer manager   The manager in charge of personal computer use.

Microdisk   A 3½-inch diskette.

Microfiche   4- by 6-inch sheets of film that can be used to store computer output.

Microfloppy   See *Microdisk*.

Microprocessor   A general-purpose processor on a chip, developed in 1969 by an Intel Corporation design team headed by Ted Hoff. Also called a logic chip.

Microsecond   One-millionth of a second.

Micro-to-mainframe link   Connection between microcomputers and mainframe computers.

Microwave transmission   Line-of-sight transmission

of data signals through the atmosphere from relay station to relay station.

MICR reader/sorter A machine that reads and sorts documents imprinted with magnetic characters.

Millisecond One-thousandth of a second.

Minicomputer A computer with storage capacity and power less than a mainframe's but greater than a personal computer's.

Minifloppy A 5¼-inch floppy disk.

MIS Management Information System.

MIS manager The manager of the MIS Department.

MITS Altair The first microcomputer kit, offered to computer hobbyists in 1975.

Mode The state in which a program is currently functioning. In a spreadsheet program, there are usually three modes: READY mode, ENTRY mode, and MENU mode.

Mode indicator Message displayed on the screen by a spreadsheet program; it tells the user the program's current mode of operation.

Model 1. A type of database, each type representing a particular way of organizing data. The three database models are hierarchical, network, and relational. 2. In a DSS, an image of something that actually exists or a mathematical representation of a real-life system.

Modem Short for modulate/demodulate. A device that converts a digital signal to an analog signal or vice versa. Used to transfer data between computers over analog communication lines.

Modula-2 A Pascal-like language designed to write systems software.

Modulation The process of converting a signal from digital to analog.

Module A set of logically related statements that perform a specific function.

Monochrome A computer screen that displays information in only one color.

Monolithic Refers to the inseparable nature of memory chip circuitry.

Mouse A hand-held computer input device whose rolling movement on a flat surface causes corresponding movement of the cursor on the screen.

Multiple-range graph A graph that plots the values of more than one variable.

Multipoint line A line configuration in which several terminals are connected on the same line to one computer.

Multiprogramming Concurrent execution of two or more programs on a computer and the sharing of the computer's resources.

Multiuser, multitasking personal computer A supermicro with a high-speed microprocessor and

significantly increased memory and hard-disk capacity.

Nanosecond One-billionth of a second.

Natural language Programming language that resembles human language.

NCR paper Multiple-copy computer paper that produces copies without using carbon paper.

Near letter quality Printing produced by dot-matrix printers with 24-pin printheads.

Network A computer system that uses communications equipment to connect two or more computers and their resources.

Network cable For some LANs, the cable used to connect nodes to the LAN.

Node A device—such as a personal computer, hard disk, printer, or another peripheral—that is connected to a network.

Noise Electrical interference that causes distortion when a signal is being transmitted.

Nonimpact printer A printer that prints without striking the paper.

Nonprocedural language Language that states what task is to be accomplished but does not state the steps needed to accomplish it.

Numeric field A field that contains numbers used for calculations.

Object module Machine-language version of a program; it is produced by a compiler or assembler.

Observation A technique of systems analysis in which the subject organization is observed.

OCR Optical character recognition.

OCR-A Standard typeface for optical characters.

Office automation The use of technology to help achieve the goals of the office.

OMR Optical mark recognition.

On-demand report Report providing information in response to an unscheduled demand from a user.

On-line Refers to processing in which terminals are directly connected to the computer.

Open architecture Personal computer design that allows additional circuit boards to be inserted in expansion slots inside the computer to support add-ons.

Open Systems Interconnection (OSI) A set of communications protocols defined by the International Standards Organization (ISO).

Operating environment An operating system environment in which the user does not have to memorize or look up commands.

Operating system A set of programs through which a computer manages its own resources.

Optical-character recognition (OCR) devices Input devices that use a light source to read special characters and convert them to electrical signals to be sent to the CPU.

Optical disk Storage technology that uses a laser beam to store large amounts of data at relatively low cost.

Optical mark recognition (OMR) devices Input devices that use a light beam to recognize marks on paper.

Optical read-only memory (OROM) Optical storage media that cannot be written on but can be used to supply software or data.

Optical-recognition system A system that converts optical marks, optical characters, handwritten characters, and bar codes into electrical signals to be sent to the CPU.

Organization chart A hierarchical diagram depicting management by name and title.

Organizing Determining resource allocation for an organization.

OROM Optical read-only memory.

Orphans Personal computers that have been discontinued and are no longer supported by their manufacturers.

OSI Open Systems Interconnection.

Output Raw data that has been processed into usable information.

Output device Device, such as a printer, that makes processed information available for use.

Packaged software Software that is packaged and sold in stores.

Page composition Adding type to a layout.

Page composition program Software package for designing and producing professional-looking documents. Also called a page makeup program or a desktop publishing program.

Page description language (PDL) A language built into printers used in desktop publishing. Used by a desktop publishing program to control the way a printer prints a page.

Page frame Space in main memory in which to place a page.

Page layout In publishing, the process of arranging text and graphics on a page.

Page makeup program Software package for designing and producing professional-looking documents. Also called a page composition program or a desktop publishing program.

Pages Equal-size blocks into which a program is divided for storage.

Paging The process of keeping program pages on disk and calling them into memory as needed.

Pan To move the cursor across a spreadsheet.

Parallel conversion A method of systems conversion in which the old and new systems are operated simultaneously until the users are satisfied that the new system performs to their standards.

Parallel processing Refers to the use of many processors, each with its own memory unit, working at the same time to process data.

Parity bit A bit added to each byte to alert the computer to an error in data transmission. Also called a check bit.

Participant observation A form of observation in which the systems analyst temporarily joins the activities of the group.

Pascal A structured, high-level programming language named for Blaise Pascal, the seventeenth-century French mathematician.

Path In a flowchart, the connection leading from the decision box to one of two possible responses. Also called a branch.

PDL Page description language.

Periodic report A report produced on a regular schedule and preplanned to produce detail, summary, or exception data.

Peripheral equipment Hardware devices attached to a computer.

Personal computer The smallest and least expensive class of computer. Also called a microcomputer.

Personal information manager (PIM) Productivity software that can help office workers, especially managers, cope with information overload.

PgDn key Used to advance the document one full screen.

PgUp key Used to back up to the previous screen.

Phantom disk A chip that lets the computer regard part of its memory as another disk drive. Also called a RAM disk or an electronic disk.

Phase The relative position in time of one complete cycle of a wave.

Phased conversion A systems conversion method in which the new system is phased in gradually.

Physical record A collection of logical records. Also called a block.

Picosecond One-trillionth of a second.

Pie chart Pie-shaped graph used to compare values that represent parts of a whole.

PILOT A programming language invented in 1973; used most often to write computer-aided instruction in various subjects.

Pilot conversion Systems conversion method in which a designated group of users try the system first.

PIM Personal information manager.

Pixel Picture element on a computer display screen.

PL/I (Programming Language One) A free-form and flexible programming language designed as a compromise between scientific and business programs.

Planning and designing Creating a new system after analyzing the client organization's needs and constraints.

Plot area Area in which a graph is drawn.

Point Typographic measurement equaling approximately $\frac{1}{72}$ inch.

Pointer A flashing indicator on a screen that shows where the next user-computer interaction will be. Also called a cursor.

Point-of-sale terminal A terminal used as a cash register in a retail setting. It may be programmable or connected to a central computer.

Point-to-point line A direct connection between each terminal and the computer or between computers.

Portable computer A self-contained computer that can be easily carried and moved.

POS Point of sale.

Preliminary design The subphase of systems design in which the new system concept is developed.

Preliminary investigation The first phase of a systems analysis project in which it is determined if and how a project should proceed. Also called a feasibility study or a system survey.

Presentation graphics program Program that allows a user to create professional-looking business graphics.

Primary memory The electronic circuitry that temporarily holds data and program instructions needed by the CPU. Also called memory, primary storage, main storage, internal storage, and main memory.

Primary storage The electronic circuitry that temporarily holds data and program instructions needed by the CPU. Also called memory, primary memory, main storage, internal storage, and main memory.

Priming read The first read statement in a program.

Print command A command that provides options for printing a spreadsheet.

Printer A device for generating output on paper.

Printer spacing chart A chart used to determine and show a report format.

Private line A communications line dedicated to one customer. Also called a leased line.

Procedural language A language used to present a step-by-step process for solving a problem.

Process An element in a data flow diagram that represents actions taken on data: comparing, checking, stamping, authorizing, filing, and so forth.

Process box In flowcharting, a rectangular box that indicates an action to be taken.

Processor The central processing unit (CPU) of a computer.

Program A set of step-by-step instructions that directs a computer to perform specific tasks and produce certain results.

Programmable read-only memory (PROM) Chips that can be programmed with specialized tools called ROM burners.

Programmer/analyst A person who performs systems analysis functions in addition to programming.

Programming language A set of rules that can be used to tell a computer what operations to do.

PROLOG (PROgramming in LOGic) An artificial-intelligence programming language invented in 1972 by Alan Colmerauer at the University of Marseilles.

PROM Programmable read-only memory.

Prompt A signal that the computer or operating system is waiting for data or a command from the user.

Protocol A set of rules for the exchange of data between a terminal and a computer or between two computers.

Prototype A limited working system or subset of a system that is developed to test design concepts.

Pseudocode An English-like way of representing structured programming control structures.

Public domain software Software that is free.

Questionnaire A source of information in the data-gathering phase of systems analysis.

Queues Areas on disk in which programs waiting to be run are kept.

Ragged right margin Nonalignment of text at the right edge of a document.

RAM Random-access Memory.

RAM disk A chip that lets the computer regard part of its memory as a third disk drive. Also called an electronic disk or a phantom disk.

RAM-resident program A program that stays in memory background, ready to be activated when needed.

Random access Immediate access to a record on secondary storage, probably disk. Also called direct access.

Random-access memory (RAM) Memory that provides temporary storage for data and program instructions.

Randomizing The process of applying a formula to a key to yield a number that represents a disk address. Also called hashing.

Range A group of one or more cells, arranged in a rectangle, that a spreadsheet program treats as a unit.

Raster-scan technology Video display technology in

which electronic beams cause the CRT screen to emit light to produce a screen image.

Read   To bring data outside the computer into memory.

Read-only media   Media recorded on by the manufacturer that can be read from but not written to by the user.

Read-only memory (ROM)   Memory that can be read only and remains after the power is turned off. Also called firmware.

Read/write head   An electromagnet that reads the magnetized areas on magnetic media and converts them into the electrical impulses that are sent to the processor.

READY mode   Spreadsheet mode indicating that the program is ready for whatever action the user indicates.

Real storage   That part of memory that temporarily holds part of a program pulled from virtual storage.

Real-time processing   Processing in which the results are available in time to affect the activity at hand.

Record   1. A collection of related fields. 2. In data base management, also called a tuple.

Reduced instruction set computer (RISC)   A computer that offers only a small subset of instructions.

Reformatted   Readjustment of paragraphs that have been altered during word processing.

Refreshed   Refers to the maintenance of the image on a CRT screen.

Register   A temporary storage area for instructions or data.

Relation   A table in a relational database model.

Relational database   A database in which the data is organized in a table format consisting of columns and rows.

Relational model   A database model that organizes data logically in tables.

Relational operator   An operator (such as <, >, or =) that allows a user to make comparisons and selections.

Resolution   Clarity of a video display screen or printer output.

Resource allocation   The process of assigning resources to certain programs for their use.

Response time   The time between a typed computer request and the response of the computer.

Retrieval   Recovery of data stored in a computer system.

Reverse video   The feature that highlights on-screen text by switching the usual text and background colors.

Ring network   A circle of point-to-point connections

of computers at local sites, with no central host computer.

RISC   Reduced instruction set computer.

Robot   A computer-controlled device that can physically manipulate its surroundings.

ROM   Read-only memory.

ROM burner   A specialized device used to program read-only memory chips.

Rotational delay   For disk units, the time it takes for a record on a track to revolve under the read/write head.

Round-robin scheduling   System of having users take turns using the processor.

Router   A device that connects networks of the same type, allowing equipment on one LAN to communicate with devices on another. Also called a bridge.

RPG (Report Program Generator)   A problem-oriented language designed to produce business reports.

Sampling   Collecting a subset of data relevant to a system.

Satellite transmission   Data transmission from earth station to earth station via communications satellites.

Scan rate   The number of times a CRT screen is refreshed in a given time period.

Scanner   A device that reads text and images directly into the computer.

Screen   A television-like output device that can display information.

Scrolling   A word processing feature that allows the user to move to and view any part of a document on the screen in 24-line chunks.

SDLC   Systems development life cycle.

Sealed module   A disk drive containing the disks, access arms, and read/write heads sealed together. Also called a Winchester disk.

Search-and-replace function   A word processing function that finds and changes each instance of a repeated item.

Secondary storage   Additional storage, often disk, for data and programs that is separate from the CPU and memory. Also called auxiliary storage.

Sector method   A method of organizing data on a disk in which each track is divided into sectors that hold a specific number of characters.

Security   A system of safeguards designed to protect a computer system and data from deliberate or accidental damage or access by unauthorized persons.

Seek time   The time required for an access arm to position over a particular track on a disk.

Selection bar   The submenu that appears when a command is chosen in the Assistant Menu of dBASE.

Selection control structure   A control structure used to make logic decisions.

Semiconductor   A crystalline substance that conducts electricity when it is "doped" with chemical impurities.

Semiconductor storage   Data storage on a silicon chip.

Sequence control structure   A control structure in which one statement follows another in sequence.

Sequential file organization   Organization of records in ascending or descending order by key.

Sequential file processing   Processing in which records are usually in order according to a key field.

Server   The central computer in a network; it is responsible for managing the LAN.

Shareware   Software that is given away free, although the maker hopes that satisfied users will voluntarily pay for it.

Shell   An operating environment layer that separates the operating system from the user.

Simplex transmission   Transmission of data in one direction only.

Simulation   The use of computer modeling to reach decisions about real-life situations.

Simultaneous processing   Execution of more than one program at the same time, each program using a separate CPU.

Single entry   The unique point where execution of a program module begins.

Single exit   The unique point where termination of a program module occurs.

Single-range bar graph   A graph that plots the values of only one variable.

Single-range graph   A graph that plots the values of only one variable.

Sink   In a data flow diagram, a destination for data going outside an organization.

Site license   A license permitting a customer to make multiple copies of a piece of software.

Smalltalk   An object-oriented language in which text is entered into the computer by using the keyboard, but all other tasks are performed using a mouse.

Smart terminal   A terminal that can do some processing, usually to edit data it receives.

SNA   Systems Network Architecture.

Soft font   Font that can be downloaded from a personal computer into a printer from files stored on disk.

Soft-sectored disk   A disk whose sectors are determined by the software.

Software   Instructions that tell a computer what to do.

Software piracy   Unauthorized copying of computer software.

Sort   An operation that arranges data into a particular sequence.

Source   In a data flow diagram, an origin outside the organization.

The Source   A major information utility offering access to a broad range of services, including electronic games and a variety of news and business databases.

Source data automation   The use of special equipment to collect data and send it directly to the computer.

Source document   Paper containing data to be prepared as input to the computer.

Source module   A program as originally coded, before being translated into machine language.

Source program listing   Printed version of a program as the programmer wrote it.

Speech recognition   The process of presenting input data to the computer through the spoken word.

Speech recognition device   A device that accepts the spoken word through a microphone and converts it into digital code that can be understood by a computer.

Speech synthesis   The process of enabling machines to talk to people.

Spelling checker program   A word processing program that checks the spelling in a document.

Spooling   A process in which files to be printed are placed temporarily on disk.

Spreadsheet   An electronic worksheet divided into rows and columns that can be used to analyze and present business data.

Stacked-bar graph   Bar graph in which all data common to a given row or column appear stacked in one bar.

Staffing   Hiring and training workers.

Stand-alone programs   Individual programs, such as word processing and spreadsheet programs.

Star network   A network consisting of one or more smaller computers connected to a central host computer.

Start/stop symbol   An oval symbol used to indicate the beginning and end of a flowchart.

Start/stop transmission   Asynchronous data transmission.

Stock tab   Printer paper that is like newsprint.

Storage register   A register that temporarily holds data taken from or about to be sent to memory.

Storing   Retaining data that has been processed.

Structure chart   A chart that illustrates the top-down design of a program and is often used to either supplement or replace a logic flowchart.

Structured interview   An interview in which only planned questions are used.

Structured programming   A set of programming techniques that includes a limited number of control structures, top-down design, and module independence.

Style   The way a typeface is printed, for example, in *italic*.

Submenu   An additional set of options related to a prior menu selection.

Summarize   To reduce data to a more concise, usable form.

Summary report   A management information system report limited to totals or trends.

Supercomputer   The largest and most powerful category of computers.

Supermicro   A multiuser, multitasking microcomputer that has a high-speed microprocessor, increased memory, and hard-disk storage.

Supermini   A minicomputer at the top end of capacity and price.

Supervisor program   An operating system program that controls the entire operating system and calls in other operating system programs from disk storage as needed.

Supply reel   A reel that has tape with data on it or on which data will be recorded.

Surge protector   A device that prevents electrical problems from affecting data files.

Switched line   A communications line that connects through a switching center to a variety of destinations.

Symbolic language   A second-generation language that uses abbreviations for instructions. Also called assembly language.

Synchronous transmission   Data transmission in which characters are transmitted together in a continuous stream.

Synonyms   Records with duplicate disk addresses.

Syntax   The rules of a programming language.

Syntax errors   Errors in use of programming language.

Synthesis by analysis   Speech synthesis in which the device analyzes the input of an actual human voice, stores and processes the spoken sounds, and reproduces them as needed.

Synthesis by rule   Speech synthesis in which the device applies linguistic rules to create an artificial spoken language.

System   An organized set of related components established to perform a certain task.

System journal   A file whose records represent real time transactions.

Systems analysis   The process of studying an existing system to determine how it works and how it meets user needs.

Systems analyst   A person who plans and designs individual programs and entire computer systems.

Systems design   The process of developing a plan for a system, based on the results of the systems analysis.

Systems development   The process of programming and testing to bring a new system into being.

Systems development life cycle (SDLC)   The multiphase process required for creating a new computer system.

Systems flowchart   A drawing that depicts the flow of data through a computer system.

Systems Network Architecture (SNA)   A set of communications protocols made commercially available by IBM.

System survey   The first phase of systems analysis, in which it is determined if and how a project should proceed. Also called a feasibility study or a preliminary investigation.

System testing   A testing process in which the development team uses test data to test programs to determine whether they work together satisfactorily.

Take-up reel   A reel that always stays with the magnetic tape unit.

Tape backup system   A tape cartridge or cassette capable of holding at least 20MB of data. Used to duplicate data from a hard disk to ensure data preservation in the event of hard-disk failure.

Tape drive   Drive on which reels of magnetic tape are mounted when their data is ready to be read by the computer system.

Tariff   A list of services and rates to be charged for data communications services.

Telecommunications   Merger of communications and computers.

Telecommuting   Refers to the home use of telecommunications and computers as a substitute for working outside the home.

Teleconferencing   A system of holding conferences by linking geographically disbursed people together through computer terminals or personal computers.

Teleprocessing   A system in which terminals are connected to the central computer via communications lines.

Template   1. Plastic sheet placed over the function keys to help the user remember tasks performed by each key. 2. In a spreadsheet program, a worksheet that has already been designed for the solution of a specific type of problem.

Terminal   A device that consists of an input device, an output device, and a communications link to the main terminal.

Terminal emulation software   Data communications software that makes a personal computer act like a terminal that communicates with a larger computer.

Text block   A continuous section of text in a document.

Thesaurus program   With a word processing program, this program provides a list of synonyms and antonyms for a word in a document.

Time-delay   A modem feature that allows a computer to call another computer and transfer a file at a future time.

Time-driven   Refers to the round-robin system of scheduling multiprogramming.

Time-sharing   Concurrent use of one machine by several people, who are given time slices by turns.

Time slice   In time-sharing, a period of time—usually a few milliseconds or microseconds—during which the computer works on a user's tasks.

Title   The caption on a graph that summarizes the information in the graph.

Toggle switch   A keystroke that turns a function of a program on or off.

Token passing   The protocol for controlling access to a Token Ring Network. A special signal, or token, circulates from node to node, allowing the node that "captures" the token to transmit data.

Token Ring Network   An IBM network that uses token passing to access the shared network cable.

Top-down design   A design technique that identifies basic program functions before dividing them into subfunctions called modules.

Topology   The physical layout of a local area network.

Touch screen   A computer screen that accepts input data by letting the user point at the screen to select a choice.

Track   1. On magnetic tape, a row of bits that runs the length of the tape. 2. On magnetic disk, one of many data-holding concentric circles.

Trailing decision   The loop-ending decision that occurs at the end of a DOUNTIL loop.

Transaction file   A file that contains all changes to be made to the master file: additions, deletions, and revisions.

Transaction processing   The technique of processing transactions one at a time in the order in which they occur.

Transistor   A small device that transfers electrical signals across a resistor.

Translator   A program that translates programming language into machine language.

Transponder   A device in a communications satellite that receives a transmission from earth, amplifies the signal, changes the frequency, and retransmits the data to a receiving earth station.

Tuple   A row in a relational database model. Also called a record.

Twisted pairs   Wires twisted together in an insulated cable that are frequently used to transmit information over short distances. Also called wire pairs.

Typeface   A set of characters—letters, symbols, and numbers—of the same design.

Typeover mode   A text-entry mode in which each character typed overwrites the character at the cursor position.

Typeset quality   Printer resolution of 1200 to 2540 dots per inch.

Type size   The size, in points, of a typeface.

ULSI   Ultra large-scale integration.

Ultra large-scale integration (ULSI)   A 10-megabit chip.

Underlining   Underscoring text.

Unit testing   The individual testing of a program using test data.

UNIVAC I   (Universal Automatic Computer) The first computer built for business purposes.

Universal manager program   A program that uses a common interface to coordinate separate stand-alone programs.

Universal Product Code (UPC)   A code number unique to a product that is represented on the product's label in the form of a bar code.

UNIX   A generic multiuser, time-sharing operating system developed in 1971 at Bell Labs.

Unstructured interview   An interview in which questions are planned in advance, but the systems analyst can deviate from the plan.

Update   Keeping files current by changing data as appropriate.

Uploading   Sending a file from one computer to a larger computer.

User friendly   Refers to software that is easy for a novice to use.

User involvement   Involvement of users in the systems development life cycle process.

User   A person who uses computer software or has contact with computer systems.

Utility program A program that performs routine file conversions and sort/merge operations.

Vacuum tube An electronic tube used as a basic component in the first generation of computers.

Value In a spreadsheet, data consisting of a number representing an amount, a formula, or a function.

Value-added network (VAN) A communications system in which a value-added carrier leases lines from a common carrier. The lines are then enhanced by adding error detection and faster response time.

Variable On a graph, the items that the data points describe.

VDT Video display terminal.

Vectors The arrows—lines with directional notation—used in data flow diagrams.

Vertical centering A word processing feature that adjusts the top and bottom margins so that text is midway between the top and the bottom of the page.

Vertical market Market consisting of a group of similar customers.

Vertical market software Software for a group of similar customers such as accountants or doctors.

Very high-level language Fourth-generation language.

Very large-scale integration (VLSI) A 1-megabit chip.

Videoconferencing Computer conferencing combined with cameras and wall-size screens.

Video display terminal (VDT) A terminal with a screen.

Video graphics Computer-produced animated pictures.

Videotex Data communications merchandising.

Virtual memory See *Virtual storage.*

Virtual storage A condition in which part of the program is stored on disk and is brought into memory only as needed.

VLSI Very large-scale integration.

Voice input The process of presenting input data to the computer through the spoken word. Also called speech recognition.

Voice mail A system in which the user can dictate a message into the voice mail system, where it is digitized and stored in the recipient's voice mailbox. Later the recipient can dial the mailbox, and the system delivers the message in audio form.

Voice-output device See *Voice synthesizer.*

Voice synthesizer A device that converts data in main storage to vocalized sounds understandable to humans.

Volatile Refers to the loss of data in semiconductor storage when the current is interrupted or turned off.

Volume testing Testing of a program by using real data in large amounts.

WAN Wide Area Network.

Wand reader An input device that scans the special letters and numbers on price tags in retail stores.

Winchester disk A disk drive in which the disks, access arms, and read/write heads are combined in a sealed module.

Weight The variation in the heaviness of a typeface; for example, type is much heavier when printed in **boldface.**

Wide Area Network A network of geographically distant computers and terminals.

Winnie Winchester disk.

Wire pairs Wires twisted together in an insulated cable that is frequently used to transmit information over short distances. Also called twisted pairs.

Word The number of bits that constitute a common unit of data, as defined by the computer system.

Word processing Computer-based creation, editing, formatting, storing, and printing of text.

Word wrap A word processing feature that automatically starts a word at the left margin of the next line if there is not enough room for it on the line.

Worksheet Erase command Command that clears the current spreadsheet from memory, leaving a blank worksheet.

Workstation 1. A supermicro. 2. A personal computer attached to a LAN.

WORM Write-once, read-many media.

Write-once, read-many media (WORM) Media that can be written on only once; then it becomes read-only media.

Written documents Procedures manuals, reports, forms, and other material used in the data gathering phase of systems analysis.

x-axis The horizontal reference line of a graph, often representing units of time.

y-axis The vertical reference line of a graph, usually representing values or amounts, such as dollars, staffing levels, or units sold.

Credits

We are indebted to the many people and organizations who contributed excerpts, illustrations, and pictures to this book. The page numbers and contributors are listed below.

Text Credits

163   Margin note entitled "USA Today: Newspaper in Space" based on "USA Today: Satellite Network Delivers Daily," *Computerworld*, 10/14/85, p. 1.

Text Photo Credits

ii   Courtesy of Evans & Sutherland
iii   Courtesy of International Business Machines Corp.
vi   Wayland Lee, Photographer
viii   Top, Courtesy of International Business Machines Corp.
        Middle, © 1982 Nicholas De Sciose/ANCODYNE, Inc.
        Bottom, Tom Tracy
ix   Top, Courtesy of Zenith Data Systems
        Bottom, Courtesy of International Business Machines Corp.
x   Top left, Bell Atlantic/ R. Greenburg Assoc.
        Bottom right, Art Gallery of Ontario, Toronto, Canada
xi   Courtesy of Apple Computer Inc.
xii   Left, Photo courtesy Hewlett-Packard Co.
        Right, Courtesy of International Business Machines Corp.
xiii   Top right, Courtesy of 3M Corp.
        Bottom left, Courtesy AT&T/Bell Laboratories
xiv   Courtesy AT&T/Bell Laboratories
xv   Left, Photo courtesy of Hewlett-Packard Co.
        Right, Courtesy of Compaq Computer Corporation
xvi   Courtesy of International Business Machines Corp.
xvii   Top, Courtesy of International Business Machines Corp.
        Bottom, Jerry Spagnoli/Egghead Discount Software
xviii   Courtesy of International Business Machines Corp.
xix   Top, Courtesy of Software Publishing Company
        Bottom, Melvin R. Prueitt, © Los Alamos National Laboratory
xx   Left top, Courtesy of Apple Computer Inc.
        Bottom right, Courtesy of *Publish!* magazine
xxi   Courtesy of International Business Machines Corp.
xxii   Photo courtesy of Hewlett-Packard Company
xxiii   Wayland Lee
xxiv   Left, Courtesy of Princeton University Communications
        Right, Advanced Micro Devices
xxv   Top left, Courtesy of International Business Machines Corp.
        Bottom left, Jerry Spagnoli/ Egghead Discount Software
        Top right, Cinemaware Corp.
        Bottom right, Compaq Computer Corp.

Chapter 1

5   © Giansanti/Sygma
6   F1-1, Top left, Courtesy of International Business Machines Corporation
      F1-1, Top right, Robert Holmgren
      F1-1, Bottom left, Courtesy of Apple Computer Inc.
      F1-1, Bottom right, Courtesy of International Business Machines Corporation
8   Courtesy of International Business Machines Corporation
9   Courtesy of International Business Machines Corporation
10   F1-2 Photo courtesy of Unisys Corporation
11   F1-3 Wright, Runsted and Company/James F. Housel
12   F1-4 Courtesy of Los Alamos National Laboratory Box; Courtesy of Information Resources, Inc.
13   Courtesy of Etak Incorporated
14   F1-5 National Centre for Atmospheric Research/National Science Foundation
      F1-6 Photo by Bill Boyle/Purdue University
15   F1-7 © Nubar Alexanian/Woodfin Camp
16   F1-8 Courtesy of Boeing Computer Services
17   F1-9 Tom McCarthy/© 1988 Discover Publications
18   Courtesy Conrac Division

Chapter 2

23   Courtesy of Puget Sound Power and Light Company
25   F2-2 Top, middle, bottom left, bottom right, Courtesy of International Business Machines Corporation
      Bottom middle, Courtesy of Intel Corporation
26   F2-3(a) Photo courtesy of Unisys Corporation
      F2-3(b) Recognition Equipment Incorporated
      F2-3(c) Photo courtesy NCR Corporation
27   F2-4(a,b) Photos courtesy of Unisys Corporation
29   F2-5(a) © Dan McCoy/Rainbow
      F2-5(b) Photo courtesy of Unisys Corporation
      F2-5(c) BASF Systems Corporation
      F2-5(d) Courtesy of 3M

251   Photo courtesy of Apple Computer Inc.

Chapter 9

271   Courtesy of Microsoft
278   Microsoft® Windows/screen images copyright Microsoft Corporation, 1985–1988. Reprinted with permission from Microsoft Corporation.

Chapter 10

285   Both, Courtesy of Squirrel Companies Inc., Atlanta, Georgia

Chapter 11

326   F11-2(a,c) Photo courtesy of Hewlett-Packard Company
       F11-2(b) Photo courtesy of Apple Computer Inc.
327   F11-3 Photo courtesy of Apple Computer Inc.
328   F11-4(a,c) Courtesy of West Ridge Designs, Portland, Oregon
       F11-4(b) Courtesy of MicroComputer Accessories, Inc.
329   F11-5 Courtesy of Zenith Data Systems
330   F11-6 Photo courtesy International Business Machines Corporation
332   F11-8 Photo courtesy International Business Machines Corporation
333   F11-9 Photo courtesy of Hewlett-Packard Company; Margin note, Courtesy of Spectrum Holobyte
334   Left, Courtesy of Britannica Software
       Right, Microsoft Corporation
335   Left, Courtesy of Commsoft, Inc.
       Right, The Comic Strip Factory. Courtesy of Foundation Publishing Inc.
336   F11-10 Photo courtesy International Business Machines Corporation
337   F11-11 Photo courtesy International Business Machines Corporation
338   F11-12(a,b) Photo courtesy Apple Computers Inc.
       F11-12(c) © Robert Cardin
340   F11-13(a,b) Photo courtesy International Business Machines Corporation
341   F11-14(a) Courtesy of Radio Shack, a division of Tandy Corporation
       F11-14(b) Courtesy of Compaq Computer Corporation

342   F11-15 Courtesy of Sun Microsystems, Inc.
343   F11-16(a) Courtesy of Zenith Data Systems
       F11-16(b) Courtesy of Compaq Computer Corporation
345   F11-17(a) Jerry Spagnoli
       F11-17(b) INFOMART
346   F11-18 Inmac
347   F11-19 Courtesy of Radio Shack, a division of Tandy Corporation

Chapter 12

353   Courtesy of MECA Ventures
377   Jerry Spagnoli

Chapter 13

415   F13-25(a,c) Lotus Development Corporation. Used with permission.
       F13-25(b) Mouse Systems
       F13-25(d) Polaroid Corporation
       F13-25(e,f) Produced with 35mm Express ™ from BPS
417   Top, Courtesy of Software Publishing Company
       Middle left, Courtesy of Computer Support Corporation, Dallas, Texas
       Middle right, Created with Zenographics Software
       Bottom left, Copyright © 1981–1986, Ashton-Tate Corporation. All rights reserved. Reprinted with permission.
       Bottom right, Courtesy of Software Publishing Company

Chapter 14

429   Courtesy of the National Library of Medicine
443   Picture Power is a PC base image database from Picture Ware, Inc.
444   Picture Power is a PC base image database from Picture Ware, Inc.

Chapter 15

457   F15-1 Brochures courtesy of Xerox Corporation
458   F15-2 Courtesy of Quark, Inc.
464   Left, *IN* ™ *The Magazine for the Information Age,* published by MCI Corporation. Designed and produced by Frankfurt Gips Balkind.
       Right, Reprinted with permission from *TV Guide* magazine, Copyright 1987 by Triangle Publications Inc., Radnor, PA

467   Clip art courtesy of Dubl-Click Software, Inc.

Chapter 16

476   F16-1 Photo courtesy of Unisys Corporation
477   F16-2 (both) Courtesy of Zenith Data Systems
479   © Ralf-Finn Hestoft/Picture Group
480   Photo courtesy of Unisys Corporation
481   F16-3 Photo courtesy International Business Machines Corporation
485   F16-5 Upper left, Courtesy of Stephen C. Cande, Stephen Lewis/Lamont-Doherty Geological Observatory; Joyce Miller, Scott Fergusson/URI
       Upper right, © James Wilson/ Woodfin Camp
       Lower left, Cardiff University/ Australian Information Service
       Lower right, Courtesy of Siemens Gammasonics, Inc.
487   F16-6(a) IEEE/NEC Info Systems Inc.
       F16-6(b) Photo courtesy of Computer Sports World, Inc.
488   F16-7 Jerry Spagnoli
489   (both) Courtesy of PowerUp Software Corporation
490   © Dennis Geaney

Chapter 17

501   Courtesy of Frito-Lay Inc.
502   F17-3 Photo courtesy International Business Machines Corporation
505   F17-4 Photo courtesy International Business Machines Corporation
506   F17-5 Photo courtesy International Business Machines Corporation
508   F17-6 Courtesy of Ford Motor Company

Chapter 18

519   F18-3 © Alexander Tsiaras/ Science Source, Photo Researcher
526   (both) Misco, Inc.

Appendix C

650   FC-2 IBM Archives
       FC-3 Culver Pictures
651   FC-4 IBM Archives
652   Both, IBM Archives

653 FC-6 Iowa State University of Science and Technology
654 FC-7 Photo courtesy of Unisys Corporation
655 Both, IBM Archives
657 FC-10 Photo courtesy of Hewlett-Packard Company
658 Margin Note, Rob Alvelais, photographer
659 FC-11 Wide World Photos
660 Margin Note, Computer Museum, Boston
661 FC-12 (a,b) Margaret and Jerry Wozniak
     FC-12 (c) Photo courtesy of Apple Computer Inc.
662 Left NeXT, Inc.
     Right Microsoft Corporation
663 Lotus Development Corporation
664 FC-13 Inmac

Gallery Photo Credits

Gallery 1

Opener: Rockwell International
1. Art: George Samuelson
2. Courtesy of International Business Machines Corp.
3. Photo Courtesy of Mentor Graphics
4. TRW
5. Courtesy of Motorola, Inc.
6. Courtesy of AT&T
7. Courtesy of International Business Machines Corp.
8. Sperry Corporation
9. TRW
10. Courtesy of Motorola, Inc.
11. Courtesy of International Business Machines Corp.
12. Courtesy of Advanced Micro Devices, Inc., Sunnyvale, CA
13. Courtesy of AT&T
14–16. Photo courtesy of Hewlett-Packard
17. Courtesy of Motorola, Inc.
18. Courtesy of Advanced Micro Devices, Inc., Sunnyvale, CA
19. National Semiconductor
20. Allison Thomas Assoc.
21. Courtesy of Advanced Micro Devices, Inc., Sunnyvale, CA
22. Photo © Peter Poulides
23. Courtesy of Apple Computers, Inc.
24. Courtesy of AT&T

Gallery 2

Opener: Courtesy of International Business Machines Corp.
1. © William Taufic
2. © William Taufic
3. of Texaco
4. © Michael Freeman
5. Computer Graphics Laboratory, University of California, San Francisco
6. Computer Graphics Laboratory, University of California, San Francisco
7. Courtesy of David and Gregory Chudnovsky, Columbia University
8. Courtesy of Hewlett-Packard Co.
9. Courtesy Intel Corp.
10. © C. H. Morgan/Science Source, Photo Researchers
11. Courtesy of Spectagraphics Corp.
12. © Dan McCoy/Rainbow
13. © Dan McCoy/Rainbow
14. © Frederick Cantor/Onyx
15–18. Courtesy of Virgin Mastertronic International, Inc.
19. Courtesy of Marks Communications. Designer/Director Dale Herigstad
20–23. © Howard Sochurek
24. © 1989 Peter Menzel
25. © Alexander Tsiaras/Science Source, Photo Researchers
26–27. David Umberger, Purdue News Service
28. Cadam, Inc.
29. © Chuck O'Rear/West Light
30. © Alan Levenson
31. © Peter Poulides
32. © Ed Kashi
33. Courtesy Intel Corp.
34. © Hank Morgan/Rainbow
35. © James Wilson/Woodfin Camp
36. Courtesy of Minnesota Educational Computing Corp. (MECC)
37. © Ed Kashi
38. Courtesy of International Business Machines Corp.
39. Courtesy of Electronic Arts
40. © James Wilson/Woodfin Camp
41. © John Coletti/Picture Cube
42. Courtesy of R/Greenberg Assoc.
43. Courtesy of ChromaSet. Cityscape photography by Becker Bishop. Skater photography by David Madison.
44–45. Courtesy of Image Network, Coral Gables, FL

46. Courtesy of Activision
47. Courtesy of Apple Computer, Inc.
48. © Brian Smith

Gallery 3

Opener: Courtesy of Boeing Computer Services
1. © Robert Holmgren
2–3. Courtesy of ESRI
4. Courtesy of Strategic Locations Planning, Inc.
5. © Skip Brown
6–7. Courtesy of ESRI
8. Client: Scott Miller & Associates; Designer, Director: Scott Miller; Production Company: Pacific Data Images, Sunnyvale, CA
9. Client: Ssangyong; Production Company: Pacific Data Images, Sunnyvale, CA
10. Courtesy of Brightbill Roberts
11. Courtesy of Aurora Systems
12. © 1989 Pixar. All rights reserved.
13. © Robert Holmgren
14. Architreon II Courtesy of Gimeor, Inc.
15–16. Reprinted with permission © 1989 Autodesk, Inc.
17. Skidmore, Owings & Merrill, Architects. Bob Hollingsworth photography
18. Architreon II Courtesy of Gimeor, Inc.
19. Courtesy of LANDCADD, Inc.
20. Computer Design Consultants, New York, NY, using Lumina software from Time Arts, Santa Rosa, CA
21. Claire Barry, EPICCENTRE, San Francisco, CA, using Lumina 32 from Time Arts, Santa Rosa, CA
22. Reprinted with permission © Autodesk, Inc.
23. Courtesy of American Small Business Computer
24. © Rich Frishman
25–27. Courtesy CADKEY, Inc.
28–30. © 1989 Pixar. All rights reserved.
31. Courtesy of Alias Research
32. Seeichi Tanaka © Japan Computer Graphics Laboratory
33. Courtesy of Philip High/Data Stream
34–35. SCIENCE, Vol. 244, p. 173, 14 April 1989, "Light Reflection Models for Computer Graphics." Greenberg, D.
36. Courtesy of Flamingo Graphics

37. "Untitled Blue" © 1988 Barbara Joffe
38. Melvin R. Preuitt, © Los Alamos National Laboratory
39–41. © Steve Wilson
42–44. © Dr. Richard Voss
45. © F. K. Musgrove and Benoit B. Mandelbrot
46. Images provided by Iterated Systems, Inc., Norcross, GA. From D. Michael Barnsley's book, *Fractals Everywhere*.
47. Courtesy of John Dewey Jones/ Simon Fraser University
48. Images provided by Iterated Systems, Inc., Norcross, GA. From D. Michael Barnsley's book, *Fractals Everywhere*.
49. Marlborough Gallery/Griffin Productions, London
50. Courtesy of Philip High/ DataStream Imaging System

Gallery 4

Opener: © Andy Freeberg
1–8. Courtesy of Control Data Corp.
9–11. Graphics reproduced by permission of Systems Modeling Corp.

12. © Alan Levenson
13. Courtesy of Cincinnati Milacron
14. Courtesy Canadair
15–18. Courtesy of Thinking Machines Corp.
19. GE Robotics & Visions Systems
20–21. © Peter Yates/Picture Group
22. Photo Courtesy of Hewlett-Packard Corp.
23. Courtesy of Cincinnati Milacron

Buyer's Guide

The photos in the Buyer's Guide are unnumbered; they are referenced below by page number.

BG-1 Jerry Spagnoli/Egghead Discount Software
BG-2 Jerry Spagnoli/Egghead Discount Software
BG-3 Top right, Courtesy of Misco, Inc. Bottom right, Courtesy of IDEAssociates, Inc.
BG-4 Both Courtesy of International Business Machines Corp.

BG-5 Left, Uarco, Inc. Right, Photo Courtesy of INMAC, Santa Clara, CA
BG-6 Top, Courtesy of International Business Machines Corp. Middle, Courtesy of BASF Corp./Information Systems Bottom, Microscience International Corp.
BG-7 Top, Courtesy of Epson-America Middle and Bottom, Courtesy of Hewlett-Packard Co.
BG-8 Bottom, Courtesy of INMAC, Santa Clara, CA
BG-9 Photo Courtesy of Toshiba America, Inc., Information Systems Division
BG-10 Top, Reproduced by permission of Hayes Microcomputer Products, Inc. Bottom, Polaroid
BG-11 Jerry Spagnoli
BG-12 Jerry Spagnoli/Egghead Discount Software
BG-13 Courtesy of International Business Machines, Inc.
BG-14 Jerry Spagnoli
BG-15 Courtesy Heald Colleges of California

Index

NOTE: Page numbers in italics indicate illustrations or tables.